THE
HOLOCAUST
Roots, History, and Aftermath

DAVID M. CROWE
Elon University

Westview Press

A Member of the Perseus Books Group

USHMM image credits: When an image is credited to USHMM, it is part of the collection of and used with the permission of the United States Holocaust Memorial Museum.

Maps: All maps were created by and used with the permission of Dr. Honglin Xiao.
Every effort has been made to secure required permission to use all images, maps, and other art included in this volume.

Copyright © 2008 by David M. Crowe
Published by Westview Press,
A Member of the Perseus Books Group

Westview Press books are available at special discounts for bulk purchases in the United States by corporations, institutions, and other organizations. For more information, please contact the Special Markets Department at the Perseus Books Group, 2300 Chestnut Street, Suite 200, Philadelphia, PA 19103, or call (800) 255-1514, or e-mail special.markets@perseusbooks.com.

Designed by Brent Wilcox
Text set in 10.5 point Minion

Library of Congress Cataloging-in-Publication Data
Crowe, David.
    The Holocaust : roots, history, and aftermath / David M. Crowe.
        p.   cm.
    Includes bibliographical references and index.
    ISBN 978-0-8133-4325-9 (alk. paper)
    1. Holocaust, Jewish (1939–1945).   I. Title.
    D804.3.C77   2008
    940.53'18—dc22

                                                        2007047538

10 9 8 7 6 5 4 3 2 1

TO
Dad and Mac

Take heed . . . lest you forget the things which your eyes have seen, and . . . teach them to your children and to your children's children.

DEUTERONOMY 4:9

My sorrow is continually before me.

PSALM 38:17

You are my witnesses.

ISAIAH 43:10

CONTENTS

PREFACE

I began work on this book about a decade ago but set it aside to complete my biography of Oskar Schindler. It reflects, I think, the teaching, writing, lecturing, and research that I have done on the Holocaust for the past three decades. During that period, I served as a member of the Education Committee of the United States Holocaust Memorial Museum (USHMM) and the North Carolina Council on the Holocaust (NCCH). During the past fifteen years, I have given quite a few lectures at workshops sponsored by the USHMM and the NCCH; these activities, combined with the regular semester courses I teach on the Holocaust, have helped me develop some of the approaches I have taken in this book in regards to themes, material, and depth. I have also tried to balance the centrality of the Jewish tragedy before and during the *Shoah* with a fresh look at the plight of the Roma, the handicapped, and other groups deemed racial and biological enemies of German Nazi Aryanism.

I am fully aware of the challenges faced by professors in classes on the Holocaust. I tend to require a great deal of reading in my courses, and I have opted in this book for the same depth of coverage that I use in my classes. There is no perfect textbook to answer the needs of every person teaching a Holocaust course. Since I teach Holocaust courses both on the undergraduate level and at our School of Law, I have tried to develop a text that meets the needs of undergraduates, graduate students, and law school students.

I have always begun my courses with an in-depth look not only at the roots of anti-Judaism and anti-Semitism in the Western world but also at the Jews themselves in pre-Christian times. I strongly believe that the cauldron of anti-Jewish and anti-Semitic prejudice that developed in the Christian world prior to 1933 created the environment in which the Holocaust could take place. It would take, of course, a number of other things, particularly in Germany, for the most destructive aspects of racial anti-Semitism to be brought to life under the Nazi regime.

For thirty years I have been fortunate enough to teach at an institution that strongly encourages and supports undergraduate research. I require each student in my Holocaust and German history courses to undertake a major research project; students present their projects as lectures and in written form during the last third of each semester (which I devote to student presentations). In designing this book, I thought of my students' research needs. In addition to the chronology at the beginning of each chapter, I have tried to include a reasonably thorough bibliography of readily accessible primary and secondary source material for students to use for further study and research. Whenever possible, I have used Web-based primary source material to help students develop the interpretative skills so necessary in the fields of history, international studies, and law. I have tried to make the bibliographies as comprehensive as possible, though given the vast body of literature on the Holocaust, it would be impossible to include everything on the complex, diverse topics discussed throughout the book.

I should like to thank my editor at Westview Press, Steve Catalano, for his support and encouragement. I first got to know Steve while working on the biography of Oskar Schindler, and he has proven to be that rarity in the publishing world: a writer's editor. I should also like to thank my department chair, Dr. Jim Bissett, and the dean of the College of Arts and Sciences at Elon University, Dr. Steven House, not only for their support but also for creating an intellectual environment that encourages such scholarly endeavors. I am equally indebted to Dr. Honglin Xiao, who created the maps for this book. Finally, I should like to thank my *Beshert*, Kathryn, for her kindness, patience, and very active support during the preparation of this book.

I have dedicated this book to my father, David M. Crowe, Sr., of blessed memory, and my father-in-law, Malcolm Richardson Moore. It is my small way of thanking both of them for all that they have meant to me during my life.

Introduction

Holocaust, the term chosen by Jewish commentators to describe the fate of fellow Jews at the hands of the Germans and their collaborators from 1933 to 1945, is a term derived from the Greek word *holokauston*. Jewish scholars in the ancient world used *holokauston* to translate *olah*, a Hebrew word, into Greek. But *olah*, which is often translated into English as "what is brought up," and its Greek equivalent, *holokauston*, can also mean "burnt offering," as used in 1 Samuel 7:9: "Thereupon Samuel took a suckling lamb and sacrificed it as a whole *burnt offering to the LORD*; and Samuel cried out to the *LORD* in behalf of Israel, and the *LORD* responded to him."[1]

For Jews, the term *Holocaust* has deep spiritual and historical meaning and is linked to millenia of Jewish suffering. The first recorded use was in 1895, when, in response to reports of a Turkish massacre of Armenians, the *New York Times* proclaimed: "Another Armenian Holocaust."[2] The Hebrew word for Holocaust, *sh'oah (Shoah)* was first used in 1940 to describe the horrors befalling the Jews in Europe in a booklet published by the United Aid Committee for the Jews of Poland, *Sh'oat Yehudei Polin* (The Holocaust of the Jews in Poland). Initially, Jewish commentators during this period used the Hebrew term *hurban* (destruction) to describe the horrors in Europe, a term that had historical links to the destruction of the Second Jewish Temple in Jerusalem in 70 C.E. However, in 1942, the term *Shoah* began to be used more and more frequently, particularly after the Jewish Agency (JA) in Palestine issued a communiqué in November 1942 that described the *Shoah* taking place throughout Europe.

More recently, scholars have begun to discuss other genocidal victims of the Nazis such as the Roma and the handicapped. The term *genocide* was first used by a Polish Jewish scholar, Raphael Lemkin (1901–1959), in 1943. Lemkin, who fled Warsaw at the beginning of World War II and later settled in the United States, devoted an entire chapter of his *Axis Rule in Occupied Europe, Laws of Occupation, Analysis of Government, Proposals for Redress* (1944) to a definition of genocide. At the end of World War II, Lemkin was part of the OSS (Office of Strategic Services, forerunner of the CIA) team that advised Telford Taylor (1908–1998), one of the principal American prosecutors at the various Nuremberg war crimes trials after World War II. Lemkin explained that genocide was the "coordinated and planned annihilation of a national, religious, or racial group by a variety of actions aimed at undermining the foundations essential to the survival of the group as a group."[3]

1

According to Lemkin, genocide meant not only the murder of members of such a group but also other, less deadly, forms of persecution: those designed to weaken or destroy any of the basic characteristics, practices, or institutions of the group that would weaken it or rob group members of their "liberty, dignity, and personal security." Lemkin also considered ethnocide, a post–World War II term created by the French to define efforts to destroy a group's culture, though not the group itself, as a genocidal act.[4]

After World War II, genocide was not cited as a crime in the original International Military Tribunal (IMT) Nuremburg trial charges against Nazi Germany's major leaders, though it was a charge in the subsequent Allied Nuremburg war crimes trials. In addition, the Polish government charged some of the defendants in its war crimes trials with genocide. In 1948, the United Nations adopted the Genocide Convention, which defined genocide as

> any of the following acts committed with intent to destroy, in whole or in part, a national, ethnical, racial or religious group, as such:
>
> A. Killing members of the group;
> B. Causing serious bodily or mental harm to members of the group;
> C. Deliberately inflicting on the group conditions of life calculated to bring about its physical destruction in whole or in part;
> D. Imposing measures intended to prevent births within the group;
> E. Forcibly transferring children of the group to another group.[5]

Though some specialists thought the UN's genocide declaration was flawed because it did not distinguish between nonviolent attacks on a group and violent efforts designed to wipe out a group. Moreover, they were also concerned that the Genocide Convention did not mention murderous efforts to eliminate members of political factions and social classes. Despite these reservations, most countries have come to accept the UN definition of genocide.

Israel voiced approval of the Genocide Convention's definition when it joined the Convention on the Prevention and Punishment of Genocide in 1950. Israel also integrated this definition into its Genocide Prevention and Punishment Law 5710-1950 and in its Nazis and Nazi Collaborators (Punishment) Law 5710-1950. The latter act was used to indict and try Adolf Eichmann in 1961 because it included a section on "crimes against the Jewish People." The reason for these specific Jewish sections centers around the feeling of many Holocaust scholars and survivors that the German crimes against the Jewish people were unique and went beyond the scope of genocidal actions. According to Pinhas Rosen, the Israeli minister of justice in 1950, the Nazis and Nazi Collaborators' Law was "a statement about the past" that essentially said the Jewish people would "not forget or forgive" the crimes committed against them during the Holocaust.[6]

In the end, questions of Holocaust breadth and definition are less important than those of personal losses and victimization. The Holocaust is about people: victims and perpetrators. In the search for clues to understanding this indescribable tragedy, it is important not to get so caught up in definitions and statistics that one loses sight of the terrible human losses that occurred in Europe from 1933 to 1945. Yet truly to understand the Holocaust, it is important to look at its roots, which lie in the history of its principal victims: the Jews. Such a painful journey will not only help explain how far back the prejudices that were the cauldron of the Holocaust go but will also help underscore the rich historical, cultural, religious, and ethnic heritages that were forever lost during the Holocaust. Those who died at the hands of the Germans and their collaborators during the Holocaust were mothers and sisters, aunts and fathers, sons and daughters. They cried, they laughed, they worshiped, they sang. They cared for and loved life. They were normal people who contributed to life, but they were murdered because they innocently belonged to a religious, cultural, biological, or ethnic group, or suffered physical or mental problems, that put them outside the pale of Nazi German society. Their loss was a loss to the world and to the richness and diversity of human life.

Yet, compounding the tragedy of the *Shoah,* the perpetrators of the Holocaust were just as human. The eternal pain and scarring of the Holocaust would be much easier for some to bear if the Holocaust could be explained away as an act of madmen or sadists. And although there certainly were sadists and madmen among the large numbers of Germans and others who were involved in perpetrating the crimes of the Holocaust, for the most part those directly and indirectly responsible for the mass murders were "ordinary" Germans, Ukrainians, Latvians, Romanians, and others, many of them raised in religious Roman Catholic, Protestant, and Orthodox Christian homes. The perpetrators had families, homes, and careers, and when the war ended, many returned to them. Yet for a certain time in their lives, these "ordinary" men and women put aside a civilized value system rooted in the Western world's Judaeo-Christian heritage and had a direct or indirect hand in murdering millions of fellow human beings. This is a history of the innocent victims and of the people who played a role in snuffing out their precious lives.

SOURCES FOR FURTHER STUDY AND RESEARCH

Primary Sources

"Convention on the Prevention and Punishment of the Crime of Genocide," 1–5. General Assembly [of the United Nations] Resolution 260A of December 9, 1948. Office of the High Commissioner for Human Rights, Geneva, Switzerland. http://www.unhchr.ch/html/menu3/b/p_genoci.htm.

The Tanakh: The Holy Scriptures. Philadelphia: Jewish Publication Society, 1985.

Secondary Sources

Akçam, Taner. *A Shameful Act: The Armenian Genocide and the Question of Turkish Responsibility.* Translated by Paul Bessemer. New York: Metropolitan Books, 2006.

Balakian, Peter. *The Burning Tigris: The Armenian Genocide and America's Response.* New York: HarperCollins, 2003.

Chalk, Frank, and Kurt Jonassohn. *The History and Sociology of Genocide: Analyses and Case Studies.* New Haven: Yale University Press, 1990.

Lemkin, Raphael. *Axis Rule in Europe, Laws of Occupation, Analysis of Government, Proposals for Redress.* Washington, DC: Carnegie Endowment for International Peace, 1944.

Oron, Michael. "The Mass Murder They Still Deny." *New York Review of Books* (May 10, 2007): 1–11. http://www.nybooks.com/articles/20174.

Schaller, Dominik J., and Jürgen Zimmerer, eds. "Raphael Lemkin: The 'Founder of the United Nations' Genocide Convention as a Historian of Mass Violence." *Journal of Genocide Research* 7, no. 4 (December 2005): 441–559.

Segev, Tom. *The Seventh Million: The Israelis and the Holocaust.* Translated by Haim Watzman. New York: Hill and Wang, 1993.

CHAPTER 1

Jewish History

*Ancient Beginnings and the Evolution of Christian
Anti-Judaic Prejudice Through the Reformation*

CHRONOLOGY

- **Second Millenium** B.C.E. (Before the Common Era): Abraham receives covenant from Hebrew God YHWH
- **Thirteenth Century** B.C.E.: Moses leads Hebrews on Exodus and receives Ten Commandments
- **1025–926/925** B.C.E.: Israel created by Sol, David, Solomon
- **966–926/925** B.C.E.: Solomon builds Temple in Jerusalem for Ark of Covenant
- **722–586** B.C.E.: Israel conquered by Assyrians and Chaldeans
- **586** B.C.E.: Nebuchadnezzar destroys Jerusalem and Temple; Babylonian Captivity begins
- **586–200** B.C.E.: Jewish Bible, *Tanakh*, completed
- **164–64** B.C.E.: Maccabean rebellion leads to recreation of Israeli state
- **64** B.C.E.: Pompey conquers Palestine for Rome
- **37–4** B.C.E.: Herod the Great rebuilds Jerusalem and Second Temple
- **6–4** B.C.E.: Birth of Jesus (Joshua) of Nazareth
- **66–70** C.E. (Common Era): Jewish War and the Great Revolt leads to Roman destruction of Second Temple
- **73** C.E.: Masada falls to Romans
- **70–100** C.E.: Christian Gospels written
- **132–135** C.E.: Bar Kochba rebellion
- **312–337** C.E.: Reign of Constantine the Great
- **325** C.E.: Council of Nicaea
- **354–430** C.E.: St. Augustine. Wrote *City of God* and *Tractus adversus judaeos*
- **476** C.E.: Traditional date for collapse of Western Roman Empire
- **527–565**: Reign of Byzantine (Eastern Roman) emperor Justinian I. *Corpus Iuris Civilis*
- **768–814**: Charlemagne
- **1095–1099**: First Crusade and Christian conquest of Jerusalem
- **1147–1149**: Second Crusade
- **1187–1192**: Third Crusade
- **1135–1204**: Moses Maimonides

—**1141:** Jews accused of "ritual murder" in Norwich, England
—**1198–1216:** Reign of Innocent III
—**1202–1204:** Fourth Crusade
—**1290:** Edward I expels Jews from England
—**1306:** Jews expelled from France by Philip IV
—**1347–1351:** Black Death
—**1492:** Ferdinand and Isabella expel Jews from Spain
—**1517:** Martin Luther writes his Ninety-five Theses
—**1543:** Luther writes *On the Jews and Their Lies* and *On Schem Hemphoras and the Lineage of Christ*
—**1484–1531:** Life of Protestant reformer Ulrich Zwingli
—**1508–1564:** Life of Protestant reformer John Calvin
—**1553:** Pope Julius III orders Italian Jews to live in ghettos

In the introduction to his *The Gift of the Jews,* Thomas Cahill says that the Jews were the creators of Western culture. Whether or not one agrees with this assertion, the fact remains that the Jewish people, their religion, Judaism, and Jewish culture and history have deeply affected Western civilization. For non-Jews in particular, studying the Holocaust is usually the only contact they have with Jewish history. To avoid seeing Jews only in light of their Holocaust victimization, and to understand the rich dynamics of the Jewish past before not only the Holocaust but also during the two millenia of anti-Jewish and anti-Semitic discrimination and hatred that preceded it, it is important to see the Jews in a broader historical perspective. Embedded in this history are not only the rich stories and contributions so important to Jewish and Christian history but also examples of Jewish determination to maintain and defend their beliefs no matter what the cost. The deep commitment Jews have to their faith traditions, their culture, and their history has made them unique in Western culture. During the Holocaust, the Germans and their collaborators did everything possible to mass murder the Jews of Europe and to destroy their ancient religious, cultural, and historic traditions.

Jewish Beginnings

The history of the Jews, or as they were known in ancient times, the Hebrews, began almost 4,000 years ago in Mesopotamia. As members of the Semitic subfamily of languages that included Arabic, Ethiopic (Amharic), Phoenician, and Aramaic, the Hebrews traced their historical-spiritual roots to Abraham, the father, or patriarch, of the Hebrew people. Jewish tradition says that Abraham received a covenant from the new Hebrew god, YHWH, that would give the Hebrews, in return for their worship of YHWH alone, a promised land in Canaan. This faith and covenant formed one of the cornerstones of the early Hebrew faith. In the Jewish scriptures, various names have been used for the name of God that describe God's various characteristics, including *El, Elohim,* and *Adonai.* In the Middle Ages, Christian scholars "transformed the word YHWH with the vowelization for the word 'Adonai' into Jehovah."[1]

Abraham passed on his covenant with God to his son, Isaac, and then to his grandson, Jacob or Israel, and his descendants. The twelve tribes of the ancient Hebrews or Israelites were named after Jacob's sons. The tribe of Jacob's fourth son, Judah, would come to play a dominant role among the Hebrews, and would provide the name for the Hebrew religion, Judaism. Historically, Jews, believers in the religion of Judaism, considered themselves descended from the House of Jacob and called themselves the Children of Israel.

The early Hebrews were semi-nomads who spent considerable time in Egypt. Though originally a land of opportunity and prosperity, Egypt became a place of oppression and mistreatment, particularly after Pharoah Rameses II (r. 1301/1298–1234/1232 B.C.E.) enslaved the Hebrews. Over time, the Hebrew population became so large that, to reduce it, Rameses II ordered the murder of every Jewish male child. Moses's mother set him adrift in a reed basket to save him. Rameses II's daughter found him and adopted him. Later, when Moses learned about his roots and the mistreatment of his people, he fled into the desert; there, God told him that he had been chosen to lead his people out of bondage. Soon, Moses demanded that Rameses II's son, Pharoah Merneptah (r. 1232–1224 B.C.E.), emancipate the Hebrews. After several plagues had swept through his kingdom, Merneptah agreed. What followed was the Exodus, one of the most seminal events in Jewish history.

The Exodus transformed the Hebrew people through a new covenant inscribed by YHWH on the Tablets of the Covenant (Ten Commandments). Later housed in the Ark of the Covenant, the Ten Commandments, revered by both Christians and Jews, are the cornerstone of Jewish belief and practice. Moses emerged from this dramatic exodus as the creative center of the Jewish national concept and the central figure in the Hebrews' historic faith—Judaism. Jewish ethical monotheism, anchored by the Law of Moses, emerged during Moses's time; Jewish scholars later recorded the Law of Moses in the *Torah,* the first five books of the Hebrew Bible *(Tanach),* or, to Christians, the *Old Testament.* At its core were 613 commandments, which the brilliant Jewish scholar Maimonides (1135–1204) divided into 248 positive and 365 negative commandments. At the heart of this faith system was the link between ritual and worship on the one hand and ethics on the other within the Hebrew,

and later, Jewish traditions. The basic Jewish statement of faith, the *Sh'ma,* is in Deuteronomy 6:4: "Hear, O Israel! The Lord is our God, the Lord alone."[2]

The uniqueness of Hebrew or Jewish monotheism did little to give this small group of people easy access to their promised homeland or bestow nationhood upon them. An independent Jewish state evolved under the kingships of Saul (r. 1025–1005 B.C.E.), David (r. 1005–966 B.C.E.), and Solomon (r. c. 966–926/925 B.C.E.), driven in part by the need for a centralized military command vis-à-vis outside threats to Jewish political and territorial autonomy. David captured Jerusalem from the Philistines; his son, Solomon, fulfilled David's dream of building a Temple to house the Ark of the Covenant, which contained the Ten Commandments. He also completed David's construction of Jerusalem. Because they represented Jews' special relationship with their God, the Temple and Jerusalem have been important symbols to Jews throughout history.

During this time many of the great Hebrew prophets emerged and served as intermediaries between God and His people. As the Hebrew people struggled to develop a state, the prophets reminded them of the importance of God in their lives and society. The largest section of the Hebrew bible, the *Tanakh,* is the *Nevi'im,* which contains twenty-one books of the Prophets, beginning with *Joshua* and ending with *Malachi.* The prophets counseled the Jewish people on the importance of obeying God's commandments and warned them of impending doom if they did not.

Two separate Jewish states emerged after Solomon's death: the Kingdom of Israel in the north, its capital in Samaria; and the Kingdom of Judah (Judea) in the south, Jerusalem being its political and spiritual center. This division weakened the ability of the Jews to resist new outside threats. Amos and Jeremiah, two of the era's great prophets, warned the Jews of the implications of their drift away from their

The Wailing Wall, Jerusalem. Photo courtesy of David M. Crowe.

spiritual and historic traditions. In 722 B.C.E., the Assyrians conquered the Kingdom of Israel; a century and a half later, the Chaldeans (neo-Babylonians) under Nebuchadnezzar (r. 605–562 B.C.E.) destroyed Jerusalem and the Temple in 586 B.C.E. Afterwards, he forced the Jews into a Babylonian Captivity that would forever change Jewish history.

Exile and New Traditions of Faith

A less remarkable people would have declined, and possibly disappeared, after the loss of their precious Temple and capital. Though traumatized by this tragedy, the Jews adapted to their circumstances while remaining stubbornly faithful to their religion and culture.

Since the Chaldeans did not enslave those Jews brought to Babylon, many Jews adapted to their new surroundings and found new roles in Chaldean society. More important, the Babylonian Captivity forced Jews to

reevaluate their faith: they were determined to preserve their laws and traditions, which took on new importance not only for the priestly caste but also for the average believer. Though the Persian emperor Cyrus the Great (r. 559–530 B.C.E.), who conquered Palestine in 539 B.C.E., allowed Jews to return to their homeland and ordered the construction of a new, Second Jewish Temple in Jerusalem, many Jews continued to live elsewhere in the Middle East. During this period, Jewish scholars completed the Jewish Bible, the *Tanakh,* in much the form as we know it today. They carefully recorded and divided these select Jewish writings into three major divisions: the Torah, or the Books of Moses; the *Nevi'im,* or the major and minor prophetic texts; and the *Kethuvim,* or Sacred Writings or wisdom books that included works such as the Psalms and Proverbs. The name *Tanakh* comes from the initial letters of these three scriptural divisions. Between 400 and 200 B.C.E., the *Torah* and the *Nevi'im* acquired canon or divine status, but the *Kethuvim* would not be fully recognized as part of the Jewish scriptural tradition until the end of the first century of the Common or Christian Era (C.E., or Christian A.D. [Anno Domini, "in the year of our Lord"]). Some of these books would later be included in the Christian Old Testament. This process transformed Judaism, which now became rich in historical, literary, and religious traditions unique to the ancient Mediterranean world.

The Jews, Hellenism, and the Maccabean (Hasmonean) Rebellion

The Jewish diaspora that had begun with the Babylonian Captivity forced the Jews to deal with a much broader complexity of rulers and peoples than they had heretofore encountered. This process intensified after the Macedonian-Greek Alexander the Great (r. 336–323 B.C.E.) conquered Palestine. Now the Jews had to deal with Hellenistic Greek history, culture, and religious traditions so powerful that they dramatically transformed not only the Jews and Judaism but also Western civilization.

Judaism on the eve of the campaigns of Alexander the Great was a vibrant cultural-religious force in Judea, Samaria, and beyond. The large, steady wave of Greek settlers that moved into Palestine in the fourth and third centuries B.C.E. deeply troubled some Jews. One group, the Essenes, who wrote the Dead Sea Scrolls, tried to recapture their Mosaic past in isolated desert communities. However, a far greater number of Jews embraced many linguistic and cultural aspects of Hellenism. Wealthier Jews also saw in Hellenism a way to greater status, acceptance, and influence. A

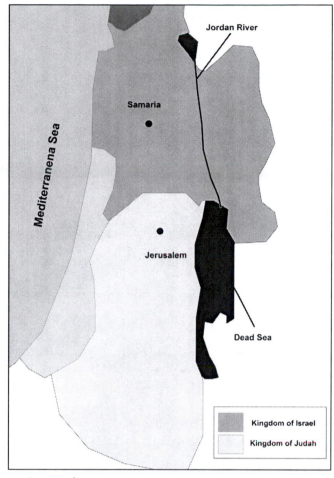

Ancient Israel.

small group of Hellenizing Jews even tried to rid contemporary Judaism of many traditional practices: They wanted to blend the ethical monotheistic essence of Judaism with a universal Greek civilization.

The growing influence of Hellenistic culture was felt most harshly after the Seleucid (the post–Alexander the Great successor state in Persia, Syria, and Asia Minor) conquest of Palestine in the late third century B.C.E. In 167 B.C.E., the Seleucid ruler Antiochus IV Epiphanes (r. 175–163 B.C.E.) replaced the Law of Moses with Seleucid Greek law and transformed the Temple into a place of worship for Greek and Hebrew gods. In response, Judas the Maccabee led a Jewish guerilla war that successfully drove the Selucids out of

Qumran. Photo courtesy of David M. Crowe.

Jerusalem and, in December 164 B.C.E., restored the Second Temple. Hanukkah ("Dedication"), the eight-day Jewish holiday, celebrates the Maccabean victory and the restoration of Jewish control over the Second Temple. During the next twenty years, the Maccabean, or Hasmonite, Jewish dynasty acquired virtual independence from Seleucid control by allying with Rome. According to Menahem Stern, the significance of the Maccabean Revolt was that "Judaism had never been in such danger of complete extinction" as it had under Antiochus IV.[3] The Maccabean Revolt was a rebellion of Jewish survival.

Hasmonean Israel and Rome

For the next seventy-nine years, Hasmonean Israel, wedged as it was between a declining Seleucid state and the growing Roman Empire, dramatically expanded its frontiers. The revolutionary spiritual zeal and rigid adherence to Mosaic Law that had neutralized the Seleucid rulers remained a driving force in the new kingdom. The principal advocates and defenders of this return to the traditions of the Mosaic codes were the Sadducees, a religious-political sect who were close allies of the Hasmonean rulers and the Jewish state's upper classes. Their main political and religious opponents, the Pharisees, sought a broader usage of biblical law and ritual.

Hasmonean Israeli independence ended in 64 B.C.E. when the Roman general and dictator, Pompey (r. 106–48 B.C.E.), conquered Judea to resolve a dynastic conflict. It took Pompey three months to take and destroy the Temple Mount; thousands of Jews died in its defense. Several decades later, Herod the Great (r. 37–4 B.C.E.), who ruled Roman Judea as King of the Jews, began a massive construction project designed to return the city and the Temple to their ancient grandeur and make Jerusalem the center of Roman Judaism. Herod, though, who owed his political fortunes to the Romans, was seen by many of his Jewish subjects as a cruel, overbearing tyrant. And although Herod gave considerable lip service to the basic tenets of Judaism, he alienated traditionalist Jews by weakening their institutions and leaders through his strong ties to the Roman state. According to some estimates, Jews made up from 8 to 10 percent of the Roman Empire's population (45 million) at this time.[4]

Roots of Anti-Jewish Sentiment: The Jewish-Greek Conflict

The Romans took direct control of Judea in 6 C.E., and, except for a brief return to Jewish rule thirty years later, directly ruled the region thereafter. The strong religious-nationalistic feelings Roman control stirred among some Jews were exacerbated by an ongoing conflict between Jews and Greeks throughout the eastern Mediterranean. The essence of Greek criticism of the Jews was that the Jews refused fully to accept the culture and values of the Greek communities. Roman writers continually used these themes to criticize Jews, whom they resented for their refusal to adopt some of the social and religious norms of the Hellenized eastern Roman Mediterranean world. Jewish commentators, who resented the Greeks' failure to respect their older culture, language, religious traditions, and literature, wrote scathing attacks against the Greeks.

Judaism, Jews, and the Coming of Christianity

In the midst of all of this, a new religion emerged from the bosom of Judaism that would forever change the course of Jewish and Western history: Christianity. The central figure in this new religion, Jesus (Hebrew, *Yehoshu'a* or Joshua; 6–4 B.C.E. to 27–29 C.E.),

the Christ (Greek, "anointed" one) or Messiah (Hebrew, *mashi'ah* or "anointed"), was born a Jew and lived and died a Jew. The concept of a Jewish Messiah evolved after the Babylonian Captivity and initially centered around belief in a strong spiritual figure who would rid Israel of its foreign rulers and restore the Kingdom of David. This new leader would rule with great wisdom and justice. The concept of a Jewish Messiah conveniently adapted itself to the various twists and turns of Jewish history over the centuries; by the time of the Hasmoneans, when the term *Messiah* was first used, the concept was increasingly linked to Jewish scriptural and other apocalyptic writings. Many Jews now believed the Messiah would be a militant figure who would drive their enemies from Israel and restore its independence. Just as the concept of the Messiah was a reflection of Jewish dissatisfaction with their plight in the Hellenistic world of Rome, the life and teachings of Jesus reflected the complexities of Judaism at this time.

Jesus taught and preached like a *rabbi* ("my master"), a teacher and interpreter of Jewish law as opposed to a priest, who wielded official spiritual power over Jews. Jesus's universalistic teachings reflected his ties to diverse Jewish groups such as the Pharisees and the Essenes, and individuals such as the ascetic John the Baptist, who preached Messianism, and Hillel the Elder (c. 70 B.C.E.–c. 10 C.E.). Hillel, a Babylonian Jew, a Pharisee, and one-time leader of the Sanhedrin, or council of Jewish elders in Jerusalem, was a contemporary of Jesus who interpreted Mosaic Law in a humane and universalistic manner. Hillel, known for his great humility and gentle spirit, tried to make Jewish teachings accessible to all Jews and converts. When asked by a non-Jew about the essence of Judaism, Hillel told him: "What is hateful to you, do not unto your neighbor: this is the entire Torah. All the rest is commentary—go and study it."[5]

Jesus's challenges of certain aspects of Jewish law and Temple worship, as well as political fears about his messianism, spelled his doom. The Sanhedrin, which tried and convicted Jesus of blasphemy, sent him to the Roman Proconsul Pontius Pilate (r. 26–36 C.E.). Pilate, hesitant to convict Jesus because of the delicate religious-political atmosphere in Jerusalem at the time—and his own doubts about his guilt—passed him on to King Herod Antipas (r. 4 B.C.E.–39 C.E.). Herod refused to involve himself further in the case and sent Jesus back to Pilate. The Roman proconsul then signed a death warrant that paved the way for Jesus's crucifixion by Roman soldiers around 27—29 C.E.

The stories of Jesus's resurrection tempered the shattering impact his execution had on his small band of followers. Slowly, his most devout adherents began to take the first steps to create a new religion—Christianity, a name taken from the Greek word, *Christos*, meaning "anointed" one or lord. Initially, the new Christians were devout Jews, particularly Pharisees, who remained faithful to Mosaic Law and Temple practices and traditions. Soon, however, the new movement began to split into Hellenistic and traditionalist Judaic factions. By 40 C.E., the Hellenistic Jewish Christians were spreading their teachings into Asia Minor and had started to call themselves Christians. They also began to convert Gentiles or non-Jews to the new religion. Serious tensions arose between Judaic and Hellenistic Jewish Christians over the status of Gentile converts under Mosaic Law and Temple ritual. The efforts of Paul (10–67 C.E.), whose missionary work and communications with the new Gentile Christian communities in Asia Minor, Greece, and Rome laid the theological foundation for the new religion, greatly enhanced the growing success of Hellenistic Jewish Christianity. Once a Pharisee (Saul of Tarsus), Paul now balanced his reverence for Jewish teachings and literature by freeing his followers from some of Judaism's more restrictive traditions. Moreover, Paul made belief in the core teachings of Christianity about life, death, and resurrection the cornerstones of this new faith. Paul's approach was much more appealing to many of the Roman Empire's non-Jews.

The Jewish War and the Great Revolt (66–70 C.E.)

Although these developments would have a profound impact on the future history of Christianity and on Jews who lived in the Christian world, at the time they were relatively minor, particularly when compared to events in Palestine and the Roman Empire. The Gospels, the first four books of the Christian New Testament, had yet to be written, and Roman and Jewish records of the time were silent on the new Jewish sect of Christians. More important to Jews at that time were violent anti-Jewish outbursts against the large Jewish community in Alexandria, Egypt, and plans by Rome's new emperor, Gaius Caligula (37–41 C.E.), who was angry about the Jewish refusal to accept his divinity, to defile the Second Temple by placing his statue there. The Jews' new king, Herod Agrippa I (r. 37–44 C.E.), a friend of Caligula's, convinced the emperor to rescind his order.

Unfortunately, Roman insensitivity to Jewish religious traditions and practices, as well as the growing persecution of some Jewish religious groups—such as the Zealots, an ultranationalist terrorist faction—inflamed Palestine. In 66 C.E., the Great Revolt began when Jewish extremists massacred the Roman garrison in Jerusalem after the region's new proconsul tried to collect Temple taxes there.[6] Rome's new emperor, Nero (r. 54–68 C.E.), sent his best general, Titus Flavius Vespasian, to deal with the Jewish crisis. Vespasian, who would become emperor in 69 C.E., secured the Palestinian countryside before turning the campaign over to his son, Titus, who brutally took Jerusalem in 70 C.E. and destroyed the Second Temple. Three years later, as the Romans moved to stamp out pockets of Jewish resistance, a band of Zealots who had fled south to Masada, a fortress built by Herod the Great near the Dead Sea, committed mass suicide to escape capture by the Romans. In his speech to the Jewish rebels at Masada, their leader, Eleazar, told them that their only alternative was to allow the Romans to abuse their wives and enslave their children.[7]

Judaism, Christianity, and the Bar Kochba Rebellion

The Jewish War devastated Palestine and decimated its Jewish population. It also stimulated a wave of anti-Jewish feeling throughout the Roman Empire, stimulated, no doubt, by Tacitus's (56/57–125 C.E.) criticism of the Jews in his monumental *Histories*. He wrote, "All we hold sacred they hold profane, and they allowed practices which we abominate." He added: "Their other customs are perverted and abominable, and owe their prevalence to their depravity." Tacitus considered the Jews a prosperous people who showed compassion to one another "but hatred and enmity for the rest of the world."[8] The Jewish War also destroyed Judaic Christianity's ties to Jerusalem; as a result, the influence of Hellenism on the new faith increased. Hellenistic Christians began to underscore their differences with the Jews, who continued to reject Jesus as the Messiah and questioned his status as both man and god. These differences also surfaced in the early books of the New Testament, the Gospels ("good tidings")—Matthew, Mark, Luke, and John—that dealt with Jesus's life, and the letters attributed to Paul (10–67 C.E.). These early Christian writings became an integral part of Christian teaching by the end of the first century C.E. Christian leaders and theologians would later

Masada. Photo courtesy of David M. Crowe.

use passages from these works to underscore Christian differences with Jews and blame them for Jesus's death.

The most important of these charges came from the first book of the New Testament (Matthew), written about 90 C.E. Considered to be the most Jewish of the four Gospels, the author described the Jewish crowd's reaction to Pontius Pilate's efforts to rid himself of responsibility for Jesus's fate at the end of Pilate's first interrogation of Jesus: "My hands are clean of this man's blood; see to that yourselves. And with one voice the people cried, 'His blood be on us, and on our children'" (Matthew 27: 24–25).[9]

In the Acts of the Apostles, one of the earliest works in the New Testament, Paul responded to the rejection of his teachings by some Antioch Jews by saying that their stance made them "unworthy of eternal life" (Acts 13:46).[10] Paul then declared that he would turn his attention to the Gentiles. Other New Testament passages underscored growing Jewish-Christian differences by demonizing the Jews. In the Gospel of John (8:44–47), which was written in 95–100 C.E. and differs greatly from the earlier "synoptic" ("similar") Gospels, for example, the author has Jesus telling a group of Jewish disbelievers, "You are of Your father the devil" and "are not of God."[11] The Epistle of Jude (10) indirectly referred to Jews as greedy and "brute beasts," and the Second Epistle of Peter (2:1,12) proclaimed that "false prophets among the people" would be "caught and destroyed, and [would] utterly perish in their own corruption."[12] Although these passages addressed Hellenistic Christian efforts to underscore their differences with Jews and strengthen Christian beliefs in Jesus's divinity, church leaders would cite them later in their efforts to institutionalize anti-Jewish prejudice in the developing Christian church.

Christianity and Judaism, despite their differences, now shared Roman disfavor. Though Rome's diverse and sometimes fractious Christian community was not large enough to draw anything more than contemptuous glances and threats from Roman officials, Christians began to be viewed, like Jews, as troublemakers because of their antagonism towards Roman imperial pretensions and refusal to participate in official Roman religious observances. These refusals, in turn, led to charges that Jews and Christians disturbed societal stability, a serious crime in Roman eyes.

Their shared outcast status did little, though, to repair growing friction between the Roman world's Jewish and Christian communities, particularly after the violent Jewish attacks against Judea's Christians during the Bar-Kochba rebellion from 132–135 C.E. Triggered by the anti-Jewish policies of

the emperor Hadrian (r. 117–138 C.E.), Jewish fighters rallied to the side of Simeon Bar-Kochba (d. 135 C.E.), whom some viewed as the Messiah. Once the Romans subdued the rebel forces, they renamed Jerusalem Aelia Capitolina. The Romans forbade Jews to enter its battered remains and referred to its provinces as Palestine (Hebrew, *Peleshet*).

The Bar Kochba rebellion underscored growing Jewish and Christian differences and convinced Christian leaders that they should do everything possible to create their own unique religious identity separate from Judaism, particularly in light of Jewish antagonism towards a new faith that seemed to discard some of the core beliefs so dear to Judaism. The inability of Roman observers to distinguish between Christians and Jews also spurred efforts by Christian leaders to separate their faith from its Jewish past. The friction grew in an atmosphere of ongoing, yet uneven, Roman persecution of Christianity, and a spreading Jewish diaspora (Greek, "dispersion"). Judaism now changed from a religion that was priestly and Temple-centered to one that followed a new leadership: rabbis or scholars who emphasized the Torah and Jewish law. Judaism now became a more portable faith that was practiced at home and in the synagogue.

The new friction between Christianity and Judaism in the second century C.E. centered more on theological differences and the threat of Judaism as a vibrant, competitive religion than on personal or group animosity. Embattled Christians, though, did occasionally accuse Jews of persecuting Christians and insulting Jesus. The dynamics of this struggle changed during the next century. For Jews, this was a time of renewed Roman toleration and prosperity, particularly after the emperor Caracalla (r. 211–217 C.E.) granted all free men, including Jews, full citizen rights in his *lex Antoniniana de civitate* (212 C.E.). These privileges remained intact throughout the rest of the century, and even Diocletian (r.

284–305 C.E.), who brutally persecuted Christians at the end of his reign because of their refusal to pay homage to the official state religion, exempted Jews from sacrificing to Roman gods in 286.

Constantine, Christianity, and the Jews

This atmosphere changed quickly after Diocletian retired from office. Seven years later, a new pretender to the Roman imperial throne, Constantine the Great (r. 312–337 C.E.), began to reunite an empire divided by Diocletian. As he gained control over the vast Roman state, Constantine showed special favor to Christians. Though he did not fully convert to Christianity until the eve of his death, his policies, which centered around the Edict of Milan (313 C.E.), gave Christians, Jews, and all other religious groups complete freedom of worship.

As Constantine became more interested in the teachings of Christianity, however, he became more critical of Judaism. In 315 C.E., for example, he issued a decree that forbade Jews from punishing anyone "who ha[d] fled this dangerous sect [Judaism]." He also made it illegal for anyone to join "their abominable sect [Judaism]."[13] Constantine criticized Judaism again during the meeting of the Council of Nicaea in 325 C.E. He had called this meeting of church leaders to resolve several disputes dividing the Christian world at the time, particularly the relationship of the Father, Son, and Holy Ghost or Spirit in Christian teachings and the date for Easter. While the council discussed the date for Easter, Constantine wrote to the council's bishops: "[I]t seems unworthy to calculate this most holy feast according to the custom of the Jews, who, having stained their hands with lawless crime [the execution of Jesus], are naturally, in their foulness, blind in soul." Constantine asked: "[W]hat right opinion can they [Jews], who, after the murder of the Lord, went out of their minds and are led, not by reason, but by uncontrolled passion?" He thought that the main objective of the council's reform efforts was to end "all communication with the perjury of the Jews."[14]

What is interesting about Constantine's sentiments concerning Jews is that they did not become part of the first draft of what would become the basic statement of faith for Roman Catholics and many Protestant Christians—the Nicene Creed. Adopted initially by the Council of Nicaea and revised by the Council of Constantinople in 381 C.E., it includes the basic tenets of the Christian faith, including the idea of the Trinity: three dimensions of one God. When it comes to the death of Jesus, which Constantine blamed on the Jews, the Nicene Creed states simply: "For our sake He [Jesus] was crucified under Pontius Pilate."[15]

Constantine's impact on the history of the early Christian church was dramatic and revolutionary. Under Constantine, the Christian espicopate [rule by bishops] emerged as "a force on a world scale."[16] Though the church still faced struggles with at least one emperor, Julian (r. 360–363 C.E.), Christianity had now "acquired the prestige and glamour of the Roman name" and was well on its way to becoming the empire's state religion.[17] Consequently, given the weight and influence of Constantine the Great on the Christian church, his attitudes and policies towards Jews are important in the development of Christian and Western thinking about Jews.

Christians lost the status and many of the privileges they had gained earlier under Julian, who sought to restore the ancient state religion. In 362 C.E., Julian issued a decree: "To All the Jews."

In former times you were made to feel the yoke of slavery, particularly by new taxes imposed upon you without warning. You were compelled to deliver untold quantities of gold to the imperial treasury. I myself have witnessed many of your misfortunes, but I learned even more when I found the tax rolls, which had been arranged for your disadvantage . . . I myself have consigned to the flames these tax rolls, which were stored in my archives, and have commanded that you shall no longer be slandered by blasphemers. Throughout my empire you will be relieved of your cares, and after the happy completion of the war against the Persians I shall once again build up the holy city of Jerusalem and have it renewed at my expense as you have long desired to have it rebuilt.[18]

Julian's sudden death in 363 saw Christianity quickly restored to its former position of prominence. Under the emperor Theodosius I (r. 379–395 C.E.), Christianity became the decaying Roman Empire's official state religion. Sadly, Julian's genuine sympathy for the Jews would later be used to perpetuate the age-old anti-Jewish stereotypes. In his late eighteenth-century *Decline and Fall of the Roman Empire* (1776–1788), Edward Gibbon, who was as hostile towards Christianity as he was towards Jews, argued that the Jews deserved Julian's patronage because of their implacable hatred of the Christian name: "The barren synagogue abhorred and envied the fecundity of the rebellious church; the power of the Jews was not equal to their malice, but their greatest rabbis approved the private murder of an apostate, and their seditious clamours had often awakened the indolence of the Pagan magistrates."[19]

Gibbon's comments, written during the Enlightenment, were taken from some of the anti-Jewish stereotypes that developed in the Roman empire.

Jews in the Last Century of the Western Roman Empire

The status of Jews during the last days of the Western Roman Empire was mixed. Theodosius I tried to protect Jews from growing at-

tacks throughout the empire, and he promised to rebuild a synagogue burned in Callinicum by order of the bishop of Edessa in 388 C.E. St. Ambrose (388–397 C.E.), the influential bishop of Milan, strongly opposed Theodosius's plan to rebuild the Callinicum synagogue. He wrote the emperor that a synagogue was a "place of irreligion and wickedness"; he added: "I myself would set fire to the synagogue, indeed, that I would have given the men the order, so that there would no longer be any place where Christ is denied."[20] Ambrose continued his criticism of this matter until Theodosius relented.

St. Gregory of Nyssa (c. 331–396 C.E.), a revered figure in the Orthodox Church, was much more virulent in his attacks on Jews. He called them

slayers of the Lord, murders of the prophets, enemies of God, haters of God, adversaries of grace, enemies of their fathers' faith, advocates of the devil, brood of vipers, slanderers, scoffers, men of darkened minds, leaven of the Pharisees, congregation of demons, sinners, wicked men, stoners, and haters of goodness.[21]

St. Gregory's contemporary, St. John Chrysostom (344–407 C.E.), the presbyter of Antioch and later the archbishop of Constantinople, delivered a series of sermons, *Adversus Judaeos* (Against the Jews), to counter strong interest in Jewish religious customs in Antioch. Chrysostom, despised by many in the church, and ultimately forced into exile by the Eastern Roman emperor Arcadius (r. 395–408 C.E.), called the synagogue "a brothel house of indecency and a theater; it is also a den of robbers and a lodging for wild beasts." He argued that God had forsaken the Jews for their murder and rejection of Christ, and that their synagogues had become nothing more than places for the "dwelling of demons."[22]

Other prominent early Christian fathers shared this dislike of Jews. St. Jerome

(348–420 C.E.), another Latin Father who translated the Old and New Testaments into Latin (the Vulgate Bible, the official Bible of the Roman Catholic Church) and worked closely with Jewish scholars in Palestine, harshly criticized Jewish pilgrims in Jerusalem. Father Edward Flannery called St. Jerome a "theological" anti-Semite, though some of St. Jerome's comments go beyond theological differences. St. Jerome said that Jews were "serpents" and "haters of all men," and claimed "their image is Judas," the disciple who betrayed Jesus to the Romans. St. Jerome felt the Jewish Holy Scriptures were like the "braying of donkeys."[23]

His contemporary, St. Augustine (354–430 C.E.), a Latin Father and the early church's most important theologian, shared St. Jerome's ambivalence towards the Jews. St. Augustine acknowledged the special role of the Jews in Christian theology; he argued in his *City of God* that the Jews, "who slew Him [Jesus] and would not believe in Him," were then "scattered throughout the world" as punishment for their disbelief. According to St. Augustine, the Jews were to "bear witness for us that we have not invented the prophecies concerning Christ."[24] St. Augustine argued that the Jews were "scattered over the whole earth" to serve as symbols of the fulfillment of scriptural prophesy.[25] According to Father Flannery, Augustine viewed the Jews as a "witness-people" whom God permitted to survive even after they had killed Jesus Christ as witnesses of "evil and Christian truth."[26] James J. O'Donnell adds that the Jews were "unique in the Christian taxonomy Augustine inherited" since they worshiped the same God as the Christians. But, O'Donnell noted, Augustine thought Jews did it "incorrectly or rather, incompletely." This, St. Augustine concluded, would result in their damnation.[27]

The Jews' continued adherence to their faith baffled St. Augustine. Yet, citing the New Testament's Letter of Paul to the Romans, chapters 9–11, Augustine considered Jews the "branches of that olive tree which was fruitful in its root of the holy patriarchs." In his sermon, *Tractatus adversus judaeos* (In Answer to the Jews), he argued that because of these roots, Christians should love "the broken branches" and say to the Jews, "'Come ye and let us walk in the light of the Lord.'" But if they refused and did not obey "he [the Jew] shall gnash with his teeth and pine away."[28]

Yet the growing intolerance towards Jews was driven by more than theological differences and the idea that the Jews had killed the founder of Christianity. The various laws at this time prohibiting contacts between Christians and Jews made it apparent that officials were worried about the vitality and attractiveness of Jews and Judaism. One statute in 357 C.E., for example, threatened Christians who converted to Judaism with loss of property; and another law in 388 C.E. forbade marriage between Christians and Jews. After 417 C.E., Jews were also forbidden to own slaves.[29] And though many codes, including the *Codex Theodosianus* (438 C.E.), a compilation of Roman laws under Christian rulers since Constantine, and the *Codex Justinianus* (529 C.E.), which included all Roman imperial laws since the second century C.E., deprived Jews of many political and civil rights, some statutes did seek to protect them from efforts by Christian communities and local governments further to limit their rights. But perhaps the most important thing to remember about these laws is their strong anti-Jewish nature. One has only to read them to realize that the body of Roman law dealing with Jews was aimed not only at their religion but at the Jews as a people.

These laws and concerns revived deep antagonisms between the Roman Empire's Jewish and Christian communities. Jewish uprisings and massacres of Christians frequently occurred in the Middle East in the fourth and fifth centuries. Christians responded with particular fury against the most prominent

Jewish religious site—the synagogue. Though officials passed laws to prevent such acts, their effectiveness was questionable.

With the death of Theodosius in 395 C.E., the Western Roman Empire declined rapidly; less than a century later, it collapsed. With its demise went many of the traditional Roman protections for the Jews. The post–Roman Christian church had a full body of theological arguments that depicted the Jews as the killers of Jesus Christ, and as such, they became the ultimate symbol of evil. These justifications, combined with a fear of Jews and their faith, created the deep hatred of Jews in the post–Roman Christian world.

Jews in Early Medieval Europe and the Byzantine Empire

The Middle Ages (600–1500), a period of growing anti-Jewish prejudice in Europe, followed the collapse of the Western Roman Empire. Perhaps nothing better symbolizes the decline of the Jewish presence in the former Roman Empire than their dramatic population decreases. At its height at the end of Augustus's reign, the Roman Empire had a Jewish population of 4.5 to 7 million out of a total population of 54 to 56 million. By the eleventh century, the Mediterranean world's scattered Jewish population had declined to 1 to 1.5 million out of a total population of 35 to 40 million. At the end of the Middle Ages, no more than 1 million Jews remained in the former Roman Empire, two-thirds of them living in the Middle East.[30]

In the early Middle Ages, which lasted from about 600 to 1000, Western and Northern Europe were increasingly controlled by the Franks of Gaul, who reached their peak under Charlemagne (r. 768–814). The Eastern Roman, or Byzantine, Empire lasted until 1453. Jews enjoyed a brief renewal of traditional rights as Roman citizens in the remnant states that arose from the ashes of the Western Roman Empire at the end of the fifth

century. This status faded quickly, particularly in the new Frankish state in Gaul. Once again, fear of Jewish influence on a developing Christianity was behind the new laws restricting Christian-Jewish ties. Though these acts had little practical impact on such relationships, their spirit would later haunt Jews. Of particular symbolic importance was the decision of the Council of Clermont in 538 to forbid Jews from mingling with Christians during the four-day Easter holiday. The council's decision to outlaw fraternization between Jews and Christians during Easter suggests considerable contact between both groups.

The status of Jews in the Byzantine Empire was much worse, particularly under its greatest ruler, Justinian I (r. 527–565). Justinian blended his strong imperial pretensions with a dynamic Christian faith that emphasized religious singularity throughout an empire that, at its peak, stretched from Italy eastward and included the Balkans, Asia Minor, the Middle East, much of North Africa, and a small portion of southern Spain. Consequently, as his jurists and scholars compiled what would become one of the Western world's most important collections of imperial Roman law, the *Corpus Iuris Civilis,* they selected laws that would weaken other religions, particularly Judaism and various pagan cults. By virtue of these selections, centuries-old anti-Jewish laws were revived in Justinian's new code. Jews and their faith, Judaism, lost some of the earlier protections they had enjoyed in earlier Roman statutes. Discrimination against Jews intensified under Justinian and his successors, and Judaism was treated as a religion inferior to that of Christianity. Pagans and wayward Christians were given the option of converting or losing their property and government positions. Justinian also placed new financial burdens on wealthy Jews, and he imposed severe religious restrictions on Jewish communities throughout his empire. These policies angered

Byzantine Jews and triggered strong Jewish reactions throughout the Eastern Empire.

In Western Europe, the Roman Catholic Church was the most important force in determining policies towards the Jews. Early medieval Europe's most important figure was Pope Gregory I (the Great) (r. 590–604), who was instrumental in formulating an official Roman Catholic policy towards Jews that would guide the church throughout the Middle Ages. The two central themes in Pope Gregory's Jewish decrees and sermons were emphasis on the law and opposition to physical violence towards Jews. Gregory the Great's ultimate goal was to create an atmosphere conducive to voluntary Jewish conversion to Christianity. He felt that the Jewish laws in Justinian's *Corpus iuris civilis* should be humanely enforced. At the same time, he expanded restrictions on Jewish-Christian professional contacts, yet spoke out strongly against infringements on remaining Jewish rights. Pope Gregory I also intervened when Jews and their communities were abused.

Such policies had little influence on most of the world's Jews, 90 percent of whom lived in the Middle East. Not long after Gregory I's death, a new force, Arabian Islam, founded by Muhammed (570–632), spread through the region. By the early eighth century, Islam was making inroads into Western Europe, particularly Spain. When the Muslims, who regarded Jews and Christians as "People of the Book," began their conquest of Visigothic Spain in the first quarter in the eighth century, Spain's Jews welcomed them. Jews in Spain had earlier suffered from harsh Spanish legislation and decrees. Under the Muslims, Jews in the Middle East regained many of their traditional privileges. Jewish life in the Arab Muslim empire flourished. The heavily urbanized Jews were found in all professions, though they were particularly prominent in trade and banking. The post-Roman chaos that had swept Western Europe and the rift between the Eastern Orthodox and Latin traditions of the Roman Catholic Church provided new opportunities for Jewish merchants. As the early medieval European world began to recover from the chaos and disorder that had plagued it for centuries, local rulers relied more and more on Jews for the conduct of business and trade. In time, Jews came to dominate the international trade of Western Europe.

In the burgeoning Carolingian empire of Charlemagne (r. 768–814), Jews also enjoyed a new era of tolerance. Jewish privileges were such under Charlemagne that Pope Stephen III (r. 768–772) wrote a complaint to one of his French bishops:

> Overcome by grief and woefully alarmed, we have received word from you that the Jewish people, who have always been rebellious toward God and hostile to our customs, live on Christian soil in full equality with Christians, calling freehold fiefs in cities and suburbs their own, and that this is done on the basis of the privileges formerly granted to them by Frankish kings. Christians till Jewish vineyards and fields; Christian men and women live under one roof with these traitors and day and night taint their souls by words of blasphemy. These unfortunates must daily and hourly humble themselves before these dogs, serving them in all their whims. . . . Justice alone demands that the promises given these traitors be declared null and void, so that the death of the crucified Saviour shall at last be avenged.[31]

In return for their extensive rights, Jews paid the Frankish emperor a 10 percent tax on their earnings. Charlemagne even encouraged new Jewish settlement in his kingdom because he respected the Jews for their hard work, intelligence, and enterprise. The status of Jews in early medieval Europe reached its pinnacle under his son, Louis I (the Pious) (r. 814–840), who valued Jewish medical skills, linguistic talents, and important trade links

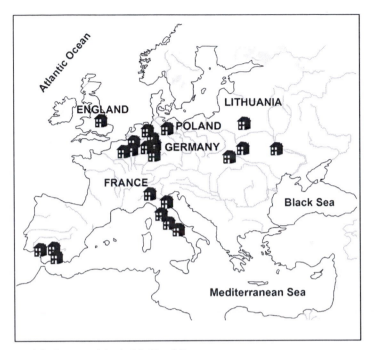

Jewish Communities in Medieval Europe.

fade when Christian armies in the eleventh century threatened the Muslim states of the Iberian Peninsula and elsewhere. The crusading atmosphere that was now enveloping the Mediterranean world would also bode ill for its Jews.

The Crusades and the Jews of the Mediterranean World

As the Roman Catholic Church entered the second Christian millenium, it found itself plagued by an irreparable split between its Latin Roman Catholic and Eastern (Greek) Orthodox branches that centered around theological differences, conflicting political ambitions between church leaders in Rome and Constantinople, and questions about papal and ecclesiastical authority. Beginning with the opening of a new Benedictine monastery in Cluny in the early tenth century, a reform movement swept the Roman Catholic Church. Perhaps nothing better reflected the church's new spirit than the Crusades, the Christian world's wars to wrest control of Palestine from the Muslims. Efforts to reform the papacy resulted in aggressive popes who sought to expand their power through involvement in affairs throughout the Mediterranean world. Beginning with the reign of Pope Leo IX (r. 1049–1054), popes became involved in an increasing number of political-religious wars against the Viking French Normans and the Muslims in Spain. In this atmosphere of aggressive papal involvement in European affairs, the crusading spirit dominated Europe. Stimulated by a request in 1095 from the Byzantine emperor, Alexios I Komenos (r. 1081–1118) for help against the Middle East's new threatening power, the Seljuk

with the Jewish communities in the Arab world. Carolingian Jews continued to enjoy these rights, even after Charlemagne's quarreling grandsons divided his kingdom in 843. Jews (known as *Ashkenazim* in this part of Europe) began to suffer from the social and economic uncertainty caused by Viking attacks along Europe's western coasts and territorial disputes among Charlemagne's descendants. In time, the term *Ashkenazim* came to refer to all Jews in Western Europe except Spain.

Jewish culture and life in Spain, whose Jews were known as the *Sephardim* (Hebrew, *Sefarad,* Spain), thrived in the ninth and tenth centuries under Spain's Muslim rulers. Spain's Arab rulers respected Jews for their diplomatic skills. Jewish culture flourished in this tolerant environment, and Jewish scholars joined their Muslim counterparts in preserving many of the great works of ancient India, Persia, Greece, and Rome. First in Cordova, and then later in Seville and Granada, the Arab-Jewish renaissance embraced science and mathematics. This brilliance would

Turks, Pope Urban II (r. 1088–1099) sought to unite Christian Europe in a religious campaign against the Turks. At a church council in Clermont, France, in November 1095, Urban II proclaimed, at least in one version of his speech,

O race of Franks! Race beloved and chosen by God! . . . From the confines of Jerusalem and from Constantinople a grievous report has gone forth that an *accursed race,* wholly alienated from God, has violently invaded the lands of these Christians, and has depopulated them by pillage and fire. They have led away a part of the captives into their own country, and a part they have killed by cruel tortures. They destroy the altars, after having defiled them with their uncleanliness. . . .

Wrest that land from a *wicked race,* and subject it to yourselves. Jerusalem is a land fruitful above all others, a paradise of delights. That royal city, situated at the center of the earth, implores you to come to her aid. Undertake this journey eagerly for the remission of your sins, and be assured of the reward of imperishable glory in the Kingdom of Heaven.[32]

As the crusading frenzy spread through Europe, Urban II's admonishments against "an accursed race, wholly alienated from God" and "a wicked race" were interpreted by some Europeans to include the Jews. As crusading armies made their way to the Middle East, bands of roving peasants, the *pauperes* (poor men), initiated horrible attacks against Jewish communities throughout Germany and France. According to one French cleric and chronicler, Guibert of Nogent, some of these camp followers thought it ridiculous to concentrate their efforts against Muslims in the far off Holy Lands when other "infidels" lived in their own midst—the Jews. Although religious zeal caused much of the anti-Jewish violence, economics also played a part because the Christian mobs often destroyed

Jewish financial records and looted Jewish property.

Despite unsuccessful efforts by Henry IV (r. 1056–1106) and Bishop Hermann III (r. 1036–1056) of Cologne to protect Jews in Germany, these groups butchered thousands of Jews. In Mainz, some Jews committed suicide to avoid humiliation and torture. Local residents initiated most of the atrocities, but they were aided by an army led by a charismatic monk, Peter the Hermit (d. 1115). According to one medieval chronicler, Albert of Aix-la-Chapelle, this group "rose in a spirit of cruelty against the Jewish people scattered throughout these cities and slaughtered them without mercy, especially in the Kingdom of Lorraine, asserting it to be the beginning of their expedition and their duty against the enemies of the Christian faith."[33] From May to July 1096, local residents and the crusaders murdered thousands of Jews and destroyed the Jewish communities in Cologne, Mainz, and Worms. Though an enraged Henry IV initiated an immediate investigation of the anti-Jewish massacres and permitted forcibly baptized Jews to return to their faith, his illegally appointed anti-Pope, Clement III (r. 1080–1100), wrote a stringent letter to one of his bishops: "We have heard that the baptized Jews have been permitted to apostatize from the church. This is something outrageous and sinful, and we require you and all Our brothers to ascertain that the Sacrament of the Church is not desecrated."[34]

Peter the Hermit's force did reach Constantinople, but the Turks later defeated it in Asia Minor. Other groups of *pauperes* were destroyed when they entered Hungary. Albert of Aix-la-Chapelle wrote that the destruction of these groups "laden with Jewish booty . . . was surely God's hand against the pilgrims who had sinned before his face with lechery and shamelessness, and who had slaughtered the homeless Jews, enemies of Christ though they are, more out of greed than fear of God."[35]

Upon returning to Europe, Peter the Hermit founded the Augustinian monastery at Neufoutier in Liège. The First Crusade's baronial armies conquered Jerusalem in 1099 and immediately began to butcher Muslims and Jews. In one instance, the Crusaders forced many of the Holy City's Jews into a synagogue and burned them alive. Robert Chazen argued that the First Crusade spawned a new threat to Judaism that centered around "the ideological negation of the legitimate place of the Jews in the Christian world."[36]

Conversion or expulsion of the Jews now became the watchword for many Christian observers. The same cycle of anti-Jewish violence repeated itself in later Crusades. On the eve of the Second Crusade (1147–1149), Abbot Peter the Venerable of Cluny (c. 1092–1156), one of the most prominent churchmen of his day, proposed that Jewish property be seized to finance the new military campaigns. His attack was driven not only by traditional Roman Catholic hatred of the Jews but also by the fact that the monastery of Cluny (the center of the early medieval church reform movement) had amassed not only great wealth but also considerable debts, some owed to local Jews. In a letter to the French monarch, Louis VII (r. 1137–1180), Abbot Peter asked:

Why should we seek the enemies of Christ in distant lands, when the blasphemous Jews, who are much worse than the Saracens, live among us and revile Christ and Christian sanctities unpunished? . . . I do not demand that these accursed people be surrendered to death, for it is written: "Thou shalt not kill!" God does not wish them to be exterminated; rather, like the fratricide Cain, they are to continue living in great torment and shame, so that life will be more bitter to them than death. They are dependent, wretched, oppressed, timid, and must remain so until they have turned to the way of salvation. You

ought not to kill them, but to punish them in a manner befitting their baseness.[37]

Once again, the issue of Jewish property was tied to the traditional hatred of the Jews as enemies of the church. To the rural peasant serf who owned little, the mere idea that the Jew was a person of substance was enough to create a new stereotype of the Jews as greedy persons of means. Since Jews played a prominent role in business, trade, and usury, the deadly stereotype about Jewish control of the economy would haunt them in the future.

Some Europeans were sympathetic to the plight of the Jews. The dissident Roman Catholic religious scholar, Peter Abélard (1079–1142), expressed such feelings through the voice of a fictitious Jew in *A Dialogue of a Philosopher with a Jew, and a Christian* (1136–1139):

There is no people which has ever been known or even believed to have suffered so much for God. Dispersed among all the nations, without a king or earthly ruler, are we not alone encumbered with such taxes that almost every day the Jews pay an intolerable ransom for our wretched lives. Indeed, we are thought by everyone to be worthy of such hatred and contempt, that whoever does them any injury believes it to be the height of justice and a supreme sacrifice offered to God. For they say that the disaster of our being made such captives would not have occurred unless God hated us enormously.

We put their lives in the hands of their enemies and are compelled to put their trust in the faith of those who are without faith. Sleep itself, which more than anything cherishes and restores human nature in relaxation, fills us with such disturbing anxiety, than even when we sleep they may think of nothing but the danger of being murdered. Nowhere but heaven may we enter safely, and even our own homes are places of danger for us. When we travel to anywhere in the neighbourhood, we must pay a high price to a guide in whom we have little trust. The very rulers who are in authority over us and whose protection we buy at much expense are all the more eager for our deaths because then they can plunder what we possess more freely. We can have no fields or vineyards or any sort of landed property, because there is no one who would protect them for us from open or covert despoilment. And so the main way which remains for us to earn an income to support our wretched lives is by lending out money at interest to those of other races; and this, indeed, makes us especially hated by those who consider that they are put under a great burden by it.[38]

Given such hatred, it should come as no surprise that anti-Jewish riots broke out in Europe during the Second (1145–1149) and Third (1187–1192) Crusades, though they were far less severe than during the First Crusade. On the eve of the Third Crusade in Europe, an officially invited delegation of prominent Jews were murdered as they tried to enter Westminster Abbey to observe the coronation of England's new monarch, Richard I (the Lionhearted) (1189–1199). Anti-Jewish riots then spread throughout London. The new king did everything possible to halt the violence: He ordered a fruitless investigation, and also decreed that Jews throughout the country were not to be harmed. Regardless, new anti-Jewish riots broke out all over England, particularly after Richard left on the Third Crusade. The worst violence took place in York, where the city's Jews fled to its royal castle for protection. Besieged by knights and townspeople, York's Jews committed mass suicide on March 17, 1190, once it became apparent that the castle would fall to its attackers. A royal investigation failed to locate any of the massacre's perpetrators.

Some church leaders and the Holy Roman Emperor Conrad III (r. 1137–1152) tried to stop the worst excesses. The Third Crusade began after Saladin (r. 1169–1193) captured Jerusalem in 1187. When anti-Jewish riots broke out in Europe, Saladin let it be known that Jews were welcome in his kingdom. Medieval Jewry's most brilliant scholar, Moses Maimonides (Rabbi Moses ben-Maimon; also Rambun, 1135–1204), not only served as Saladin's personal physician but also wrote a dozen medical books in Arabic. One of Maimonides' most important religious works was his *Mishneh Torah* (the Second Torah), his brilliant codification of all Jewish law written until that time. The Thirteen Articles of Faith he laid out in his commentary on the Mishnah became the basis of "Ani Ma'amin (I believe)," a statement of faith found today in Conservative and Reform Jewish prayer books. Other Jews were also drawn to the open atmosphere of Saladin's empire. In 1211, three hundred English and French rabbis moved to Jerusalem, where Saladin's brother, Sultan al'Adil (r. 295–1296), allowed them to build new Talmudic academies and synagogues.

Jews who received imperial protection in Europe often paid a heavy price for it. The emperors Henry IV and Conrad III (r. 1138–1152) made imperial serfs of the Jews in their realms. Though initially a device to protect Jews, imperial Jewish serfdom became a way for Holy Roman Emperors to enrich themselves by granting a town or a nobleman the right to possess the emperor's Jews. According to Haim Ben-Sasson, enserfing the Jews allowed Europe's kings and princes to assert full control over their Jewish subjects vis-à-vis the Roman Catholic Church, which claimed full authority over Jews. Their new status meant additional taxes and economic exploitation in return for a modicum of royal protection. It also signaled the loss of Jewish influence in business and trade because of the growing importance of Christian merchant guilds. To the general public, most of whom were peasants, "the legal state of [Jewish] serfdom accorded with and substantiated the ecclesiastical and popular view of the degradation and wickedness of the Jews."[39] And, as Ben-Sasson has noted, it should not be forgotten that these rulers "belonged, by education, way of thinking and religious and social complexion, to the cultural *milieu* of the masses."[40]

Rulers in England, France, and Spain soon began to enserf their Jews. They considered it such an important right that Holy Roman Emperor Albert I (r. 1298–1308) sued the French king, Philip IV (the Fair) (r. 1285–1314), when Philip expelled all French Jews in 1306, and seized their property, some of it in areas claimed by Albert I. It should come as no surprise that the Roman Catholic Church supported this practice. St. Thomas Aquinas (1224–1274) told Margaret II, Countess of Flanders (1202–1278), that he approved of Jewish enserfment but thought it should be tempered by moderation and some respect for the necessities of Jewish life.[41] But Aquinas based his call for moderation more on St. Augustine's view of the Jews as a "witness people" than any deep love for the Jews themselves. He said that Judaism "once foreshadowed the truth of the faith we now hold," and, as such, bears "witness to our faith."[42]

Pope Innocent III and the Jews

By the time of the Fourth Crusade (1202–1204), the status of Jews in Europe had changed dramatically. Under the guiding spirit of this crusade's principal sponsor, Pope Innocent III (r. 1198–1216), the Roman Catholic Church would adopt new policies towards Europe's Jews that would plague them for centuries. As pope, Innocent III had three main goals: to make the pope the most powerful figure in Europe, to reunite the Roman and Orthodox Christian churches, and to revive Europe spiritually by clearly defining Roman Catholic beliefs and prac-

tices. At first, Innocent III seemed sympathetic to the Jews. In 1199, he issued a papal bull that decreed that Jews were not to be forcibly converted, harmed, or deprived of proper legal protections. The bull also underscored the falseness of Jewish beliefs. Innocent III was not arguing against the mistreatment of Jews for humanitarian reasons; he, like St. Augustine, believed that the Jews were a "witness people," and he argued that Christians should not treat them harshly.

Over time, Innocent III began to voice darker thoughts about Europe's Jews. In a letter to one aristocrat (in 1208), he wrote:

> The Jews, like the fratricide Cain, are doomed to wander over the earth as fugitives and vagabonds and to cover their faces in shame. Christian princes are in no circumstances to show them favor, but, on the contrary, to reduce them to serfdom. Wrongly do those Christian rulers act who admit the Jews into their cities and villages and avail themselves of their usurious services to extract money from the Christian populace. It even happens that these rulers arrest Christians for neglecting payments to Jewish creditors, and, what is worst of all, tolerate it that in this way the Church loses her tithe.[43]

Embedded in Innocent III's letter were ideas drawn from the legend of the "Wandering Jew," a medieval folk myth that added to the anti-Jewish spirit of the time. According to Joseph Gaer, the Wandering Jew, who was later known as Ahasverus, was forced to wander the earth because he had rejected Jesus Christ. Gaer explained that the rejection was "the symbolic revolt against the Christian concept of redemption through Jesus, punishable by wandering in pain and sorrow until Jesus is accepted as the Messiah."[44] Thus the Wandering Jew was doomed to suffer until the final day of Christian Judgement.

This myth, which persisted well into the twentieth century, "reinforced the view of the Jew as the eternal foreigner, who would never learn to speak the national language properly or strike roots in the soil."[45]

In 1215, the church's Fourth Lateran Council (1215) issued new anti-Jewish legislation. Called by Innocent III to resolve some of the theological questions and abuses still dividing the church, the council approved laws that more clearly defined medieval Roman Catholic practices and beliefs. It also reaffirmed or created new anti-Jewish regulations that placed restrictions on usury and required Jews to pay a special church tax on their property. The council reminded converted Jews that they could not practice Jewish rites, and it forbade Jews to appear on the streets during the Easter holiday. The most humiliating decree, though, was the requirement that Jews now had to wear special clothing to distinguish them from Christians. The council thought this would help prevent sexual relations between Christians and Jews. Thomas Aquinas supported the regulations and even argued that they were "also mandated to them [Jews] by their own law, namely that they make for themselves fringes on the four corners of their cloaks," a reference to the *Tallit*, or prayer shawl, which strictly observant Jewish males wore on the way to religious services.[46] There was, of course, no way that one could equate the *Tallit* with the Jewish "badge of shame," which was usually a badge or special headpiece. Great attention was given to the design and placement of the "badge of shame" for Jews throughout Europe.

Several years earlier, Innocent III ordered King Philip II Augustus (r. 1180–1226) to begin a crusade against the Cathari (Albigensians) and Waldensian Christian dissidents in southern France. In 1233, Pope Gregory IX (r. 1227–1241) created the Inquisition to deal with the dissidents and other heretics. The Inquisition gave the church new powers to root out heresy throughout Europe. Initially, Gregory IX exempted Jews from the Inquisition unless they had attempted to convert Christians, attacked Christianity, or reconverted Christian Jews back to Judaism. He also issued a papal decree that reconfirmed Innocent III's bull on Jewish rights.

Innocent III's reign marked the high point of Roman Catholic power in medieval Europe; it also endorsed stereotypes, prejudices, and practices designed economically and socially to isolate Jews from European society. In addition to being the hated "killers of Christ" and a symbol of spiritual evil, Jews were viewed as an economic threat to the wellbeing of the average European. Stereotypically, the European Jew was slowly becoming the eternal outsider.

Medieval Usury: Christians and Jews

These images, particularly when linked to earlier church decisions on usury, had a dreadful impact of Europe's Jews. The Roman Catholic Church's policy against usury (money lending with interest) went back to pre-Christian times. By the early Middle Ages, the church had initiated regulations against usury for laymen and clergy. The Third Lateran Council of 1179 reconfirmed these strictures and said that usurers could not receive communion or be buried as Christians. European rulers had long respected Jews for their important international trade links; however, in the early Middle Ages, the average Jewish person in Europe, unlike Jews in the Muslim world, was not involved in moneylending or banking. Jews usually worked as small craftsmen, merchants, and farmers, but European laws and prejudice often drove them from these professions and forced them into more limited means of making a living. According to Benzion Netanyahu, professional choices were not always passive; sometimes "Jews shifted from profession to profession not only when the one they held appeared precarious, or became forbidden by the country's law, but because the one they adopted was more in demand, and hence more lucrative, and hence more likely to serve their needs."[47]

Yet, though the Jews helped establish and dominate Europe's banking system by the late Middle Ages with church and government support, it is often forgotten that many of Europe's most prominent bankers and moneylenders were Christians, including some Roman Catholic clergy. The monastic reformer and ascetic, St. Bernard of Clairvaux (1091–1153), who had spoken out against the mistreatment of Jews during the Second Crusade, wrote: "I will not mention those Christian moneylenders, if they can be called Christian, who, where there are no Jews, act, I grieve to say, in a manner worse than any Jew."[48]

Financial excesses, unfortunately, were the norm in medieval Europe because of the contradiction between church regulations against usury and the growing need for capital. The tenuous position of the Jews in Europe at this time forced those involved in usury to acquire as much capital as possible because they were never certain when their money or property would be seized, taxed by a local ruler, or destroyed in an anti-Jewish riot. Later, King Wladyslaw II (r. 1471–1516) of Bohemia and Hungary legally permitted Jews to charge twice the interest rates as Christian bankers for this very reason.

Yet, as Haim Ben-Sasson has pointed out, occasional abuses by Jewish moneylenders helped strengthen the negative image of the Jew as greedy and dishonest in the European collective consciousness. Moreover, such lapses also fortified the image of the Jew "as a cruel oppressor who exploited the weakness, innocence and kind-heartedness of his Christian neighbors."[49] Medieval art is full of images of crooked Jewish moneylenders. Occasionally, such depictions are blended with scenes of Jewish ritual murders or images of the Jew as a devil.

The Myth of Ritual Murder

In time, though, even the profession of moneylending was taken from the Jews through intensified persecution and, ultimately, expulsion from many countries in Europe. Although growing jealousy and resentment over Jewish moneylending practices helped create a new atmosphere of antagonism towards Jews, charges of Jewish ritual murder of Christians, particularly children, exacerbated the situation. The myth of Jewish ritual murder centered around the idea of a Jewish ritualistic sacrifice of a Christian, particularly a child, during the Easter season. In time, the charge encompassed the murder of Christians by Jews for any religious reason. The blood of the victim, so the myth went, was supposed to have special healing powers, hence the idea of the blood libel or blood accusation. Jews were first accused of ritual murder in Norwich, England, in the mid-twelfth century. During the next two hundred years, numerous unproven charges of ritual murder were made against Jews throughout England, France, and the German states; the torture and death of many innocent Jews was the result. In 1181, for example, authorities falsely accused and executed three hundred Jews for three ritual murders near Vienna. In 1235, Frederick II Hohenstaufen (r. 1212/1215–1250), who ruled the Kingdom of Sicily and the Holy Roman Empire, ordered an investigation of blood libel charges after the murder of thirty-two Jews in Fulda, Hesse (Germany). The royal commission's findings:

Neither in the Old nor in the New Testament is there any text to show that the Jews desire human blood. On the contrary, they guard themselves against being tainted by any blood at all. . . . There is little likelihood that those to whom even the blood of clean animals is forbidden would have any taste for human blood. Against this charge are its frightfulness, its unnaturalness, and the natural human feeling the Jews display toward Christians also. Moreover, it is not probable that they would risk their lives and property. We have therefore declared the Jews of Fulda . . . completely innocent of the crime with which they have been charged.[50]

Frederick II agreed with the commission's conclusions and declared it illegal for anyone to raise such charges again.

In 1247, Pope Innocent IV (r. 1243–1254) sent a letter to church leaders in Germany that underscored his concerns about the ritual murder charges against Jews. He believed the accusations were baseless and driven by a desire to use them as an excuse to persecute Jews and steal their property. Innocent IV reminded German church leaders that Jewish writings, which had strict codes against murder and the touching of a dead body during Passover, were the basis of Christianity. The pope added that the charges of blood libel against Jews had not the slightest respect for the legal protections afforded Jews by the Roman Catholic Church. Because of this mistreatment, the pope noted, some Jews not only had lost their property but had been tortured, imprisoned, impoverished, and sometimes murdered. He admonished his German clerics to insure that Jews, whom he still hoped would convert to Christianity, received the protection of the law.

Such appeals did little to temper the charges of blood libel against Jews. The "blood libel" myth became so deeply ingrained in European culture that it entered the literature of the times. Geoffrey Chaucer (c. 1340–1400) includes a story of Jewish blood libel in *The Canterbury Tales*. And though R. Po-chia Hsia says that the blood libel myth disappeared in England and France only after the expulsion of the Jews at

the end of the Middle Ages, Frank Felsenstein notes that it surfaced again in seventeenth-century England in the midst of the discussion to readmit Jews.[51] The blood libel myth persisted in the German states for centuries, and in 1900, local Jews were accused of ritual murder in Konitz (today, Chojnice, Poland). Eleven years later, Russian officials charged Mendel Beilis (1874–1934) with a similar crime in Kiev. He was later found innocent in a trial that drew worldwide attention. Julius Streicher (1885–1946), the editor of the virulently anti-Semitic Nazi newspaper *Der Stürmer* (The Stormer, or Militant), published numerous articles about blood libel cases, and Hitler thought about having a film made about the Damascus Affair, which dealt with false "blood libel" charges brought against Syrian Jews in 1840 by the city's French consul and Egyptian governor. They oversaw the murder of four Jews and the torture of nine others for the fictitious murder of a Roman Catholic monk, Father Tomas de Camangiano, in efforts to make them confess to the false charges. Like the Beilis case, the Damascus Affair drew worldwide attention to the continued evils and vitality of historic anti-Judaism; but to men such as Adolf Hitler and Julius Streicher, it only fortified their views about the basic evil of Jews and the influence of international Jewry.

The Deadly Centuries: The Jews at the End of the Middle Ages

Medieval Jews also came under increasing criticism for their most sacred religious writings. In 1230, Nicholas Donin, a French Jew who converted to Christianity and later became a Dominican priest, sent Pope Gregory IX (r. 1227–1243) a searing indictment of the *Talmud*. Donin claimed, among other things, that one of the main reasons Jews refused to convert to Christianity was that the Talmud insulted Jesus Christ and the Virgin Mary. The pope ordered the Dominican and Franciscan religious orders, recently established to root out heresy in Europe, to investigate these charges. He also ordered all *Talmud*s in England, France, and the Christian parts of Spain to be turned over to both religious orders. In France, the devout Louis IX (St. Louis) (r. 1227–1270) had all *Talmud*s burned; and in the Christian parts of Spain, the church, after seizing as many copies of the *Talmud* as it could find, removed all the offensive passages and then returned the *Talmud*s to their owners.

In the German states, violence against Jews continued, particularly during the Great Interregnum (1254–1273), when Germany was without an emperor. When this imperial crisis ended, the new Holy Roman Emperor, Rudolf of Habsburg (r. 1273–1291), asked Germany's Jewish communities to help rebuild his empire. His financial demands so impoverished German Jews that they began to leave. He responded by outlawing Jewish emigration and declared the empire's Jews crown serfs. If the Jews still chose to leave, their possessions would become royal property. German Jews also faced new, mythical charges that they had defiled special wafers used in the Eucharist, or Lord's Supper. According to the accusers, the wafers, which symbolized the body of Jesus Christ, had been robbed of their miraculous powers. In the late thirteenth century, such charges led to the massacre of entire Jewish communities throughout southern Germany and Austria. Like the charges of ritual murder, the Eucharist wafer defilement accusations would linger for centuries throughout Europe.

The Expulsion of the Jews from Western Europe

The expulsion of the Jews in Western Europe began first in England with King Edward I (r. 1272–1307), who in 1275 made it illegal for Jews to engage in usury. Twelve years later, he ordered the kidnapping and jailing of the heads of all Jewish families. After a large ransom had been paid for their release, Edward I decreed that all Jews had to leave England by All Saints Day on November 2, 1290. Jews who remained would be executed. Edward's rationale was that the country's Jews, who had once played an important part in the economy, were now no longer needed because of changing economic and social conditions.

Sixteen years later, Philip IV (the Fair) (r. 1285–1314) of France expelled his country's Jews and seized their property. His son, Louis X (r. 1314–1316), troubled by grumblings about the excesses of Christian moneylenders and worried about empty royal coffers, invited French Jews to come back. Those who returned were viciously attacked by peasant forces during the Shepard's Crusade in 1320. Pope John XXII (r. 1316–1334) ordered that the violence be halted. Pope John, who resided in Avignon, in southern France, regarded Judaism as an "error and depravity of Jewish blindness . . . a damnable perfida . . . [and] a filthy Jewish superstition." His motives for halting the violence had nothing to do with his concern for Jews. Instead, he wanted to restore order to insure the ability of his royal sponsor and protector, Philip V (r. 1316–1322), to collect taxes.[52] After the riots were put down, John XXII initiated an attack on the *Talmud* and then made deadly efforts to convert Jews in southern France. In communities where Jews refused to convert, the pope ordered synagogues destroyed and forced those who remained true to their faith into exile. Then, to eliminate "the filthy Jewish superstition . . . [and replace] it with the worship of the Lord, the Holy Virgin, Mother of God, and the Saints," he built churches on the sites of the former synagogues.[53]

Philip V began his own campaign against the Jews in 1321 in response to rumors that Jews had joined with lepers to poison the wells of Christians. A royal investigation fully exonerated the Jews, but the king fined their communities a sum so large that it forced most Jews to leave the country. Several decades later, John II (r. 1350–1364) convinced some Jews to return, though Charles VI (r. 1380–1422) refused to give them new residency privileges. By this time, France was in the midst of the Hundred Years War (1338–1453) against England and its French allies. As the French slowly gained control of their country from the English, they extended their anti-Jewish policies into their newly acquired territories. Since local rulers still enjoyed considerable control over policies in these new areas of France, attitudes towards Jews varied. By the end of the fifteenth century, few Jews were left in France.

The Black Death

If Jews despaired of their deteriorating plight in certain parts of Europe, the worst was yet to come. In 1347, a bubonic plague entered Europe from Asia Minor (Turkey). As it spread northward, it became known as the Black Death (1347–1351). Though estimates vary, about a quarter to one third of Europe's population died as a result of the Black Death. As Europeans struggled with the ravages of this uncontrollable epidemic, some accused Jews of causing it.

The Jews were principally charged with spreading the plague by poisoning Christian wells throughout Europe. Their accusers argued that if the Jews were eliminated, the plague would disappear. The first mass murders of Jews took place in southern France in the spring of 1348, where the Jewish communities of Provence were annihilated. The terror soon spread to Zurich, where city officials expelled the Jews. In Basle (Basel), local mobs forced the Jews into wooden buildings and burned them alive. In 1348, Pope Clement VI (r. 1342–1352) twice reissued Innocent III's 1199 bull on the Jews and threatened to excommunicate those who mistreated them. Other leaders in Europe also

tried to protect Jews, though their efforts met with mixed success.

The persecution and murder of Jews was worse in the German states. In the winter of 1348–1349, Jews were burned alive, often in anticipation of the plague, throughout southern and central Germany. On February 14, 1349, local residents executed 2,000 Jews in Strasbourg, and the mobs involved in the murders tore the clothing off their victims trying to find hidden gold. The persecutions stopped briefly in the spring and summer of 1349; but that fall the Flagellants, a charismatic Christian group that derived spiritual satisfaction from self-beatings, revived them.

The Flagellants thought that such beatings were a way to temper God's anger, which they argued had caused the Black Death. Initially, local communities welcomed the Flagellants, who were strong in southern Germany. In the summer of 1349, a group of Flagellants, with the help of local residents, slaughtered the entire Jewish population in Frankfurt. On October 20, 1349, Pope Clement VI was prompted by similar outrages elsewhere to issue a new decree ordering churchmen to do everything possible to stop the Flagellants and their followers from, among other things, persecuting Jews. What really halted these terrible atrocities, though, was the waning of the Black Death. The massacres had devastated Germany's Jewish communities and, though some German rulers made weak efforts to convince Jews to return home, most refused.

But even with the end of the Black Death, anti-Jewish violence continued in the German states during the next century. In 1421, Viennese authorities burned two hundred Jews at the stake because of false charges that they had supplied financial and military aid to the Hussites, Czech followers of the religious dissident, Jan Hus (1369–1415). Afterwards, Austria's ruler, Duke Albert, who would later become king of Hungary, Albert I (r. 1437–1439) and Holy Roman Emperor,

Albert II (r. 1438–1439), ordered the expulsion of all Jews from Austria. He expropriated all Jewish property and ordered the children of the murdered Jews to be forcibly baptized and sent to monasteries. He later bragged: "I have warred on the Turks and encircled the Hussites, but first I burned my Jews."[54]

Within a few years, other German states and parts of Switzerland followed Austria's example and expelled their Jews. In 1475, officials in the city of Trent tried and executed its entire Jewish population on charges of murdering a Christian child. In Nuremberg, local Jews were imprisoned and their property was seized. This enabled local officials to cancel the large debts they owed local Jews, whom they expelled in 1499. The fifteen-hundred-year-old Jewish community in Regensburg fought their expulsion order in the courts and before several Holy Roman emperors for decades. One of the issues they raised was why it was permissible for Christians to practice usury and not Jews. New charges of blood libel intensified this struggle, which ended in 1519 when local leaders expelled the Jews and seized their property. They pillaged the local synagogue and turned it into a church. On the eve of the Protestant Reformation, Jews either had fled many kingdoms throughout the German states or had faced expulsion from them. Those who remained would suffer through the religious upheavals that were about to sweep Germany and other parts of Europe.

The Final Humiliation: Expulsion from Spain and Portugal

The final blow to Western Europe's Jews came in 1492 with the decision by Ferdinand and Isabella to expel Spain's Jews. Spain's Sephardic Jewish community was the largest and most prominent in Europe. It had enjoyed a "Golden Age" during the Middle Ages, but began to see its unique status suffer during the Christ-

ian wars to retake Spain from its Arab rulers, the Moors.

Though Jews remained prominent in several Spanish kingdoms through the mid-fourteenth century, the Roman Catholic Church pressured Spanish rulers to enforce many of the anti-Jewish laws prevalent in other parts of Europe. In 1391, Fernán Martínez, a prominent priest, led an attack on the Jewish quarter in Seville in Castile. According to Benzion Netanyahu, what followed "was an orgy of bloodshed and rapine on a scale that Spain's Jews had never seen before."[55] Similar anti-Jewish riots followed in Aragon, Barcelona, and elsewhere, where victims were given the choice of converting to Christianity or being put death. Though some Jews committed suicide, a considerable number chose to convert, and became known as *conversos*.

King Henry III of Castile (r. 1391–1406), troubled over the economic impact of the anti-Jewish riots, ordered the reconstruction of the destroyed Jewish communities in his kingdom. His successors, though, revived efforts forcibly to convert Spain's Jews. Many of the Jewish converts resumed their previous roles of prominence since, as Christians, they were no longer constrained by anti-Jewish restrictions. Many *conversos*, though, continued to practice Judaism in secret. Spain's traditional Christians began to refer derisively to the *conversos* as *marranos* (swine or filthy person). Greed and frustration over the dual religious practices of some *conversos* led to the final, most humiliating episode in the history of Spanish Jewry.

The status of Jews and *conversos* declined significantly throughout the fifteenth century, particularly after the Black Death, when anti-Jewish violence intensified. In 1474, Spain's monarchs, Isabella (r. 1474–1504) and Ferdinand (r. 1479–1516), asked Pope Sixtus IV (r. 1471–1484) to introduce the Inquisition into Spain. Its primary purpose was to force those *conversos* who secretly continued to practice

Judaism to give up these rites. The Inquisition also sought to deal with Muslim converts *(Moriscos)* to Christianity who continued secretly to practice Islam. *Conversos* and *Moriscos* found guilty of these crimes were severely punished. Those who refused to confess their crimes and repent were burned at the stake (the *auto–de–fé*). If, at the last minute, they confessed and repented, they were strangled before their bodies were burned.

The first Inquisition trials began in Seville in 1480 and spread slowly throughout Spain, particularly after the appointment of Tomás de Torquemada (1420–1498) as Grand Inquisitor. In time, the brutality of the Spanish Inquisition drew the attention of Popes Sixtus IV (1471–1484) and Alexander VI (r. 1492–1503), who on several occasions admonished Isabella and Ferdinand for the illegal methods of the inquisitors. In one letter, Alexander VI claimed that the Inquisition's agents were more driven by greed than concern for the souls of their victims. Ferdinand and Isabella brushed off these criticisms, and Torquemada continued his brutality unchecked.

A few prominent Jews such as Isaac Abravanel (1437–1508) and Abraham Senior (c. 1412–1493), who held prominent positions at court, were not initially affected by the Inquisition. All this changed with the conquest of Granada in 1491, the last Moorish kingdom in the Iberian Peninsula. Isabella and Ferdinand now wanted to realize the age-old goal of the *reconquista*—a purely Christian Spain. On March 30, 1492, Isabella and Ferdinand ordered all nonconverted Jews to leave Spain by July 31. This decree remained on the books in Spain until 1968. The Spanish clergy immediately began a campaign to convert Jews to Christianity. According to Howard Sachar, about a third of Spain's 150,000 Jews accepted conversion, including Abraham Senior.[56] Though the 1492 decree guaranteed the safety of the departing Jews, it forbade them to take gold, silver, or currency abroad, though they could take other property. In

1502, the Moors were given the same choice: convert or leave. A century later, they were also expelled from Spain. Over time, as many as 30,000 Jews returned to Spain as *conversos* from Portugal, joining the numerous *conversos* already there.

Most of the 100,000 Jews who left Spain went to Portugal, and others escaped to the Ottoman Empire and Eastern Europe. King João II (r. 1481–1495) agreed to let the refugees remain in his country for eight months in return for a large contribution to his treasury. Those who remained after this and had no skills valuable to the crown were made royal serfs or enslaved. When his successor, Manuel I (r. 1495–1521), tried to grant the new Jews greater freedoms, Ferdinand and Isabella intervened. They insisted that Manuel I, who was about to wed their daughter, Isabella, expel Portugal's Jews as part of the marriage agreement. In 1496, he ordered all Jews to leave the country.

The impact of the forced expulsions in Spain, Portugal, and other parts of Western and Central Europe was dramatic. The estimated Jewish population of Europe in 1490 was 600,000, with 570,000 (95 percent) living in Western and Central Europe. Two centuries later, Europe's Jewish population, which numbered 716,000 in 1700, had shifted eastward. Only 20 percent of Europe's Jews now lived in the West; the rest were in Eastern Europe and the Balkans.[57]

The Protestant Reformation

Twenty-five years after the Jews were expelled from Spain, another upheaval was to change Europe forever: the Reformation. Like most dramatic events in history, the Reformation was complex. Its background centered around centuries of growing disillusionment with a Roman Catholic Church beset by political and moral conflicts. These were compounded by a doctrinal rigidity that emphasized institutional and ritualistic practice versus a more personal approach to faith and worship. Though the Roman Catholic Church successfully weathered challenges to its authority by dissidents in the twelfth and thirteenth centuries, efforts by later reformers such as John Wyclif (1320–1384), Jan Hus (1369–1415), and Girolamo Savonarola (1453–1498) had a greater impact on a church rocked by secular challenges to its traditional authority. These were anchored by the new humanistic spirit of the Renaissance that attracted Christian thinkers such as Sir Thomas More (1478–1535) and Desiderius Erasmus (1466–1536), whose exploration of early Christian teachings and writings raised new questions about contemporary teachings in the Roman Catholic Church. These individuals all played an important role in laying the foundation for various aspects of the Protestant Reformation, though Martin Luther (1483–1546) became the central figure in this religious revolution.

Martin Luther

Martin Luther (1483–1546), a Roman Catholic Augustinian monk and a professor at Wittenberg University in Saxony, was troubled by the Roman Catholic Church's practices in Germany, particularly the sale of indulgences. According to church teachings, indulgences were good deeds performed for the church, or contributions to it, as part of an act of penance for past sins. At the time, it was even thought that indulgences could benefit someone in Purgatory, which *The Catholic Encyclopedia* describes as "a place or condition of temporal punishment for those who, departing their life in God's grace, are not entirely free from venial faults, or have not full paid the satisfaction due their transgressions."[58]

What angered Luther about the church's efforts to sell indulgences had less to do with the indulgences themselves than his conviction that salvation came solely from God as an act of mercy. For Christians, Luther would argue, it was faith, not good deeds, that

earned them salvation. Luther was particularly upset by the efforts of a Dominican friar, Johann Tetzel (1465–1519), who blended unscrupulous sales tactics with false promises about the power of indulgences in his efforts to sell them to peasants and others in the Wittenberg area. Luther responded with a diplomatic letter of protest to his archbishop, Albrecht of Brandenburg (r. 1513–1545), and enclosed ninety-five "propositions for debate for pious consideration."[59] But there was more in what became known as Luther's Ninety-five Theses than mere criticism of indulgences: Luther's ninety-five "propositions" contained the seeds of the Reformation. In them he drew attention to what he considered "an annoying and pernicious abuse in the church" that also "struck at the roots of papal sovereignty."[60] The Ninety-five Theses were soon translated into German and Luther became something of a local hero. During the next four years, an emboldened Luther expanded his attacks on the Roman Catholic Church and the papacy, and developed the cornerstone beliefs of Protestant Christianity—justification (salvation) by faith, the primacy of scripture, and the "priesthood" of all believers. Efforts to silence Luther through theological debates and other means proved fruitless, and on January 3, 1521, Pope Leo X (r. 1513–1521) excommunicated him. Charles V, the Holy Roman Emperor and Spanish king (r. 1520–1556; 1516–1556), ordered Luther arrested and his writings burned. Unlike earlier Roman Catholic dissidents, though, Luther was able to escape punishment because of the protection afforded him by Prince Frederick III (the Wise) (r. 1486–1525) of Saxony, who hid Luther in Wartburg Castle for almost a year.

Luther and the Jews

Part of the reason for Luther's success in evading imprisonment and possible death was the wide body of support he found for his ideas among the German nobility and peasantry.

The peasants misinterpreted Luther's ideas about religious freedom and individuality as a call for a solution to their longtime suffering as serfs. Though Luther was sympathetic to their plight, he spoke out harshly against a German peasant uprising in 1525, and he urged German leaders to use whatever means possible to put down the rebellion.

Like the peasants, some Jews in Europe initially saw Luther as an ally against their Roman Catholic persecutors. Sephardic *conversos* in Antwerp, for example, had some of Luther's early writings translated into Spanish. In 1523, Luther published the pamphlet, *That Jesus Christ Was Born a Jew,* which was written to counter charges that Luther denied the virgin birth of Jesus. Some Jews in Germany were heartened that Luther acknowledged Jesus as a Jew. Luther also argued that Jews were more likely to convert to his brand of Christianity than to a religion (Roman Catholicism) that had treated them so miserably. The Jews were the relatives of Jesus, Luther said, and blessed by God. Now was the time, he concluded, to begin treating Jews with true Christian love and tolerance. This would enable Jews to become aware of the true teachings of Christianity. Unfortunately, Luther was not advocating a new era of tolerance for Jews so much as a new atmosphere that would be the pathway for Jewish conversion to Protestant Christianity. Regardless, Luther's 1523 comments so moved one group of German Jews that they sent him a copy of the 130th Psalm written in German with Hebrew characters.

Over the next decade, Luther's feelings toward Jews changed when it became apparent that they were no more interested in converting to Protestant Christianity than to Roman Catholicism. When Josel of Rosheim (1478–1554), a prominent German Jewish leader, asked Luther in 1537 to try to persuade Saxony's ruler, John Frederick (r. 1532–1547), to lift an expulsion order against Jews, Luther refused. A year later, Luther unleashed a harsh attack against the Jews in his *Letter Against the Sabbathers,* a Protestant group who had adopted the Jewish sabbath as their day of worship. After his attack against the Sabbathers, Luther lashed out against the Jews, who, he claimed, were infected by devils and already judged and punished by God for their failure to convert.

As Luther aged, he intensified his diatribes against the Jews and others he viewed as his enemies. In his sermons and *Table Talk,* his published discussions with students, Luther railed against the Jews. Yet, as Richard Marius has pointed out, Luther still hoped the Jews would convert. As late as 1533, he said it was better for Jews to remain faithful to their religious traditions than to convert to Roman Catholicism. And even in the midst of some of his worst attacks on Jews late in life, Luther was able to express some sympathy for their harsh living conditions. But this did not stop his attacks against them. His worst assault came in *On the Jews and Their Lies* (1543). In it, Luther not only revived many of the mythical crimes of the Jews against Christians but also accused them of being spies for the hated Turks. He also thought it would be impossible to convert Jews to Christianity:

They are real liars and bloodhounds who have not only continually perverted and falsified all of Scripture with their mendacious glosses from the beginning until the present day. Their heart's most ardent sighing and yearning and hoping is set on the day when they can deal with us Gentiles as they did with the Gentiles in Persia at the time of Esther. [Esther, the Jewish wife of the Persian emperor Ahasuerus (Xerxes I, r. 486–465 B.C.E.), intervened to prevent the murder of Jews by Haman, a high-ranking Persian official].[61]

Consequently, Luther argued that the Jews' synagogues should be burned to the ground and their homes destroyed. He wrote that

Jews should be forbidden to own prayer books and *Talmud*s, and their rabbis forbidden to teach under threat of death. Luther added that authorities should restrict Jewish travel and that Jews should be prevented from engaging in usury. He ended his diatribe by saying that "if God were to give me no other Messiah than such as the Jews wish and hope for, I would much, much rather be a sow than a human being."[62] Diarmaid MacCulloch has called Luther's 1543 work "a blueprint for the Nazis' *Kristallnacht* of 1938."[63]

Luther followed this up with *On Schem Hemphoras and the Lineage of Christ* (1543), a coarse, vile assault against supposed Jewish claims that Jesus was a sorcerer who used the incantation "Schem Hemphoras" as part of his "routine." Luther claimed his work was inspired by a stone carving on the parish church as Wittenberg that showed a "Jewish sow" nursing her young while a rabbi looked up her rectum. Above the carving was the inscription "She Mhemphoras." To Luther, this scene represented the *Talmud*. According to Richard Marius, Christian evangelicals in Zurich considered *On Schem Hemphoras* the crudest and most vulgar work ever written by a Christian. Luther ended this distasteful attack by promising that he would "have nothing more to do with the Jews."[64]

Yet three days before his death on February 18, 1546, Luther again attacked Jews in the last sermon of his life. Essentially a summary of his 1543 writings, Luther, though still professing the need to show Jews Christian love, continued to view Jews as enemies of Christianity, who, if they could, would kill all Christians. Though attempts have been made by Roland Bainton and other Luther scholars to rationalize Luther's anti-Jewish writings and sentiments by placing them in the broader theological context of his Protestant Christian vision and concerns, the fact remains that because of his powerful role in European and German history, his eternal prominence gave a new weight to deeply ingrained anti-Jewish prejudices. Several Luther scholars argue this point. Heiko A. Oberman, for example, said that Luther's anti-Judaism became "a pawn of modern anti-Semitism," and Richard Marius argued that "it seems foolish and even immoral to seek to mitigate or explain away or cover over his [Luther's] prevailing hatred of the Jews."[65]

Julius Streicher was fond of paraphrasing Luther. According to Eliot Barculo Wheaton, the March 31, 1933, issue of *Der Stürmer* paraphrased Luther on its front page when it proclaimed: "Millions of Germans have with longing awaited the day when the German people, as a whole, would become aroused and would at last recognise [*sic*] in the Jew the world enemy. Strike down the world-enemy! *And though the world were full of devils, we must yet prevail!*"[66]

Though less virulent, some of the pro-Nazi leaders of the German Christian church were equally fond of quoting Luther. According to Wheaton, they occasionally demanded that the church "display a yea-saying, type of faith consonant with the German Luther-spirit and heroic piety."[67]

On November 10, 1933, the German Christians transformed the 450th anniversary of Luther's birth into a joint "Luther-Nazi" holiday. The new head of the pro-Nazi church in Berlin, Dr. Reinhold Krause (1893–1980), "not only demanded strict application of the 'Aryan' laws to members of the Evangelical clergy but launched a crude attack on the Old Testament. If, he said, 'we Nazis would be ashamed to buy a necktie from a Jew, how truly ashamed we would be to accept from a Jew anything inwardly religious, anything which speaks to our souls.'"

At the end of the Berlin celebrations, German Christians passed a resolution that called for "the removal of pastors 'unwilling or unable to cooperate effectively in the religious renewal of our people and the completion of the Reformation [begun by Luther] through the spirit of Nazism.'"[68]

Doris Bergen noted that, in a similar vein, a German Christian wrote to the German Foreign Ministry:

Why don't our rulers declare themselves for the *Volkskirche* [German Christian Church], which is fighting for a living Christianity? With our great leader Adolf Hitler, our previously dead church also experienced the reawakening of a vital spirit. [Julius] Streicher, the Franconian leader, said in a speech: "The murder of Golgotha is written on the foreheads of the Jews." Yes—and that is why there is a curse on that people. Jesus, however, died for us and so we should believe in him and accept him. He is the way to light, to peace and love. Only when we stand *united* in genuine faith in Christ will we defeat the priests of this world.

The Kingdom of Heaven is immanent [*sic*] in us—it must be prayed for and fought for. Martin Luther already struggled for this church for us. May we with God's help succeed, to the blessing of humanity. Amen.[69]

Bergen later explained that Nazi German Christian leaders "liked to cite Martin Luther as a precursor of their attitudes towards Jews and Judaism." To them, Luther was the "champion of antisemitism."[70] After World War II, the German (Evangelical) Church and the American Lutheran Church both condemned Luther's anti-Semitic teachings, though he remains a central figure in their faith traditions.

Zwingli, Calvin, and the Jews

As the Protestant Reformation spread to other parts of Europe, opponents of the Protestant dissidents accused them of being Judaizers, a term that harks back to the early Christian church and implies pro-Jewish religious sentiment. Ulrich Zwingli (1484–1531), a Swiss contemporary of Luther's, was a well-educated priest who had been deeply affected by the Dutch Christian humanist Desiderius

Erasmus. Zwingli, who agreed with Erasmus's call for a spiritual and moral revival within the Roman Catholic Church, did not agree with Erasmus's hatred of Jews. Zwingli started a new Protestant movement in parts of the Swiss Confederation (now Switzerland) that put an even greater emphasis on religious individuality than Luther had advocated. And though Zwingli's movement, unlike those founded by Martin Luther and John Calvin, never became a nucleus for major Protestant sects, Zwingli's emphasis on spiritual individuality, simplicity of worship, and a strong moral faith had a deep influence on Protestanism. Zwingli, who established a theocracy in Zürich, wanted to return Christianity to its early Jewish roots and simplicity. Zwingli's passion for many of the great Jewish prophets drove his ideas; indeed, he filled his sermons with references from the Old Testament, and he once told Emperor Charles V that when he reached heaven he expected to find many prominent Jewish prophets and leaders there. Zwingli's critics, particularly Luther, accused him of being a Judaizer and a heathen because of his passion for Jewish learning. Luther also said he suspected that Zwingli studied the Old Testament with Jews.

John Calvin (1508–1564), a second-generation Protestant reformer, was also accused of being a Judaizer. Calvin, a Frenchman, founded a theocracy in Geneva in the 1540s. His movement centered around the strict religious and moral teachings found in his *Institutes of the Christian Religion*. Calvinism spread throughout Europe and deeply influenced the Scottish Presbyterian Church, the Dutch Reformed Church, the English Puritans, and the French Huguenots. His opponents accused Calvin of being a Judaizer because his writings depended heavily on the Old Testament, and Calvin often reciprocated with similar accusations. Yet, in time, a subtle but important change towards Jews permeated Calvinism because of a shared tradition of persecution and a strong emphasis on Old Testament teachings. This did not, however, prevent the periodic expulsion of Jews from some Calvinist enclaves throughout Europe.

The Roman Catholic Church, the Jews, and the Counter Reformation

The Roman Catholic response to the Protestant Reformation is called the Counter Reformation, or the Catholic Reformation, which actually began in the 1490s. Once the Protestant Reformation began to spread throughout Western Europe, the Roman Catholic Church realized that its pre-Reformation reform efforts were not enough to protect it from the Protestant wave, which prompted more aggressive efforts by a series of crusading popes who sought to transform the church. The Council of Trent, which met periodically from 1545 to 1563, greatly strengthened their efforts. It initiated changes in the Roman Catholic Church that would remain in force until the Vatican II Council of 1962–1965. The Council of Trent reaffirmed the significance of the most important practices and traditions of the Roman Catholic Church. It issued decrees that emphasized the dual authority of scripture and traditions in contrast to the Protestant emphasis on the authority of the word of God in scripture. The council's decisions included the addition of the Apocrypha (Old Testament books not accepted as truly divine by Jews and Protestants) to the Roman Catholic Bible. It also accepted St. Jerome's Latin Vulgate as the official translation of the Bible, and St. Thomas Aquinas was acknowledged as the church's most important theologian.

In the early days of the Protestant Reformation, the Jewish communities in the Papal States were not persecuted. In fact, Jews throughout Italy suffered less from mistreatment than Jews in any other part of Europe. Martin Luther once remarked that there were

so many Jews in Italy that the city of Cremona in northern Italy had no more than twenty-eight Christians in it. Popes Leo X and Clement VII (r. 1523–1534) were both interested in Jewish scholarship. Pope Paul III (r. 1534–1549), who called the Council of Trent into session, welcomed recently expelled Jews and Spanish *conversos* to the Papal States.

All this changed under Pope Julius III (r. 1549–1555) and his Inquisitor General, Cardinal Giovanni Pietro Caraffa (1476–1559). Julius III approved Cardinal Caraffa's decree in 1553 that ordered the burning of *Talmud*s in Rome. After Cardinal Caraffa became Pope Paul IV (r. 1555–1559), he decreed that all Jews in the Papal States had to live in ghettos. Decades earlier, the Jews of Venice had been forced into a *Ghetto Nuovo*. Paul IV also decreed that ghetto residents could not leave the ghetto from sunset to dawn, and that each papal ghetto was to have only one synagogue for worship. Jewish men now had to wear a yellow cap, Jewish women a yellow scarf. The papacy also restricted Jews to one profession—selling used clothing—and forbade conversations with Christians. Many of these policies were soon adopted by other Italian states.

Pope Pius IV (r. 1559–1566) tried to temper some of Pope Paul IV's anti-Jewish restrictions, although he increased the size of Rome's Jewish ghetto. In time, these papal restrictions were extended to the *conversos*. In 1566, Pope St. Pius V (r. 1566–1572) ordered Jews in the Papal States to leave within three months, though he did allow Jews to remain in some Papal cities. Jews forced out of the Papal States went to other Italian cities, where they were often forced to settle in new ghettos. Pope Sixtus V (r. 1585–1590) did away with most of Pope Paul IV's anti-Jewish regulations and granted Jews new papal rights, including taxation rates similar to those of Christians.

Conclusion

During the first millenia of their existence, the Hebrews, or Jews, as they were later known, evolved from a scattered group of nomadic tribesmen into one of the Western world's most unique ethno-religious groups, in large part because of their unique, monotheistic faith: Judaism. Though unable to withstand assaults from the surrounding great powers against their ancient homeland, Israel, the Jews remained an important cultural, religious, and economic force in the Mediterranean world.

Unfortunately, much of this began to change with the coming of Christianity. Though its founder, Jesus, was himself a Jew, and, at least according to his early followers, the Jewish Messiah, most Jews rejected Jesus's messiahship. This rejection, as well as competition between Judaism and Christianity, was the basis of Christian antagonism towards the Jews. In time, the Roman Catholic Church developed an official, anti-Jewish policy towards the Jews based on the false accusation that the Jews had been responsible for the death of Jesus. Although the church tried to temper this policy with admonitions to treat the Jews with Christian kindness in the midst of its efforts to convert them, its policies condemned the Jews to an inferior role in European society. These policies, and the limitation of Jews to one occupation, moneylending, during the Middle Ages, only further isolated the Jews while breeding more hostility towards them. The Crusades transformed Europe's general dislike and distrust of Jews into something more violent, and by the end of the thirteenth century, the hatred of Jews had become so intense that most countries in Western Europe began to drive them out.

The Protestant Reformation was a bittersweet time for the Jews who remained in Europe. The Reformation's most important figure, Martin Luther, vilified them, but Protestant reformers such as Ulrich Zwingli and John Calvin helped lay the groundwork for the return of Jews to parts of Europe on the eve of the Enlightenment. The Roman Catholic Church, unfortunately, continued to see the Jews as unrepentant pagans and developed more stringent policies towards them.

SOURCES FOR FURTHER STUDY AND RESEARCH

Primary Sources

Abelard, Peter. *Collationes.* Edited and translated by John Marebon and Giovanni Orlandi. Oxford: Clarendon Press, 2001.

————. *A Dialogue of a Philosopher with a Jew and a Christian.* Translated by Pierre J. Payer. Toronto: Institute of Medieval Studies, 1979.

Augustine, Saint. *The City of God Against the Pagans.* Translated and edited by R. W. Dyson. Cambridge: Cambridge University Press, 1998.

————. *Treatises on Marriage and Other Subjects.* Translated by Charles T. Wilcox et al. In *The Fathers of the Church,* edited by Roy J. Deferrari. New York: Fathers of the Church, 1955.

Chrysostom, Saint John. *Adversos Judaeos.* http://www.preteristarchive.com/Bookstore/chrysostom_homilies_adversus_judeaus.html.

The Holy Bible Containing the Old and New Testaments: The New King James Version. Nashville, TN: Thomas Nelson, 1983.

Josephus, Flavius. *The Great Roman-Jewish War: A.D. 66–70.* The William Whiston translation as revised by D. S. Margoliouth. Edited by William R. Farmer. Gloucester, MA: Peter Smith, 1970.

"Laws of Constantine the Great, October 18, 315, Concerning Jews, Heaven-Worshipers, and Samaritans." *Heritage: Civilization and the Jews.* http://www.pbs.org/wnet/heritage/episode3/documents/documents_10.html.

Leikin, Ezekiel, ed. *The Beilis Transcripts: The Anti-Semitic Trial That Shook the World.* Northvale, NJ: Jason Aronson, 1993.

The Letters of St. Bernard of Clairvaux. Translated by Bruno Scott James. Spencer, MA: Cistercian Publications, 1998.

Luther, Martin. "On the Jews and Their Lies." *Medieval Sourcebook.* Translated by Martin H. Bertram. New York: Fordham University, 2005. http//:www.fordham.edu/halsall/basis/1543-Luther-JewsandLies-full.html.

Mendes-Flohr, Paul, and Jehuda Reinharz, eds. *The Jew in the Modern World: A Documentary History.* 2nd ed. New York: Oxford University Press, 1995.

"The Nicene Creed." *The Book of Common Prayer and Administration of the Sacraments and Other Rites and Ceremonies of the Church.* New York: Oxford University Press, 1990.

Rubin, Alexis P. *Scattered Among the Nations: Documents Affecting Jewish History, 1949 to 1975.* Northvale, NJ: Jason Aronson, 1995.

Sandmel, Samuel, M. Jack Suggs, and Arnold J. Tkacik, eds. *The New English Bible with the Apocrypha: Oxford Study Edition.* New York: Oxford University Press, 1976.

Scott, Samuel Parsons, ed. *The Civil Law: Including the Twelve Tables, the Institutes of Gaius, the Rules of Ulpian, the Opinions of Paulus, the Enactments of Justinian, and the Constitutions of Leo.* Vol. 12. Cincinnati: Central Trust Company, 1932.

Simonsohn, Shlomo, ed. *The Apostolic See and the Jews. Documents.* Toronto: Pontifical Institute of Medieval Studies, 1988.

Tacitus. *The Histories.* Translated by W. H. Fyfe. Edited by D. S. Levine. New York: Oxford University Press, 1997.

Tanakh: The Holy Scriptures. Philadelphia: The Jewish Publication Society, 1985.

"Thomas Aquinas' Letter to Margaret of Flanders." Translated by Mark Johnson. Thomistica.NET. http://www.thomistica.net/thomas-aquinas-letter-to-marg/.

The Torah: The Five Books of Moses. Philadelphia: Jewish Publication Society of America, 1962.

Secondary Sources

Bainton, Roland H. *Here I Stand: A Life of Martin Luther.* New York: New American Library, 1950.

Ben-Sasson, Haim H., ed. *A History of the Jewish People.* Cambridge, MA: Harvard University Press, 1994.

Bergen, Doris L. *The German Christian Movement in the Third Reich.* Chapel Hill: University of North Carolina Press at Chapel Hill, 1996.

Brown, Peter. *Augustine of Hippo: A Biography.* Berkeley: University of California Press, 1967.

Bryce, James. *The Holy Roman Empire.* New York: Schocken Books, 1961.

Chazan, Robert. *European Jewry and the First Crusade.* Berkeley: University of California Press, 1987.

Durant, Will. *The Age of Faith.* New York: Simon & Schuster, 1950.

———. *The Reformation.* New York: Simon & Schuster, 1957.

Eban, Abba. *Heritage: Civilization and the Jews.* New York: Summit Books, 1984.

Encyclopedia Judaica. CD ROM edition. Jerusalem: Judaica Multimedia, n.d.

Felsenstein, Frank. *Anti-Semitic Stereotypes: A Paradigm of Otherness in English Popular Culture, 1660–1830.* Baltimore: The Johns Hopkins University Press, 1995.

Fend, William Hugh Clifford. *The Rise of Christianity.* Philadelphia: Fortress Press, 1984.

Flannery, Edward H. *The Anguish of the Jews: Twenty-three Centuries of Anti-Semitism.* New York: Macmillan, 1965.

Gaer, Joseph. *The Legend of the Wandering Jew.* New York: New American Library, 1961.

Gay, Ruth. *The Jews of Germany: A Historical Portrait.* New Haven: Yale University Press, 1994.

Gibbon, Edward. *The Decline and Fall of the Roman Empire.* New York: Harcourt Brace, 1960.

Hanna, Edward J. "Purgatory." *The Catholic Encyclopedia.* Vol. 12. Online edition (2003). http://www.newadvent.org/cathen/12575a.htm.

Hsia, P. Po-chia. *The Myth of Ritual Murder: Jews and Magic in Reformation Germany.* New Haven: Yale University Press, 1988.

Johnson, Paul. *A History of the Jews.* New York: Harper & Row, 1987.

Jones, A. H. M. *Constantine and the Conversion of Europe.* New York: Collier Books, 1962.

Keller, Werner. *Diaspora: The Post-Biblical History of the Jews.* New York: Harcourt Brace & World, 1969.

Krey, August C. *The First Crusade: The Accounts of Eyewitnesses and Participants.* Princeton: Princeton University Press, 1921.

Leibowitz, Yeshaiahu. *The Faith of Maimonides.* Translated by John Glucker. New York: Adama Books, 1987.

MacCulloch, Diarmaid. *The Reformation: A History.* New York: Viking, 2003.

Marius, Richard. *Martin Luther: The Christian Between God and Death.* Cambridge, MA: Belknap Press of Harvard University Press, 1999.

Mosse, George L. *Toward the Final Solution: A History of European Racism.* New York: Harper & Row, 1978.

Netanyahu, B. *The Origins of the Inquisition in Fifteenth Century Spain.* 2nd ed. New York: New York Review of Books, 2001.

Novak, Michael. "Aquinas and the Heretics." *First Things,* no. 58 (December 1995): 1–5. http://print.firstthings.com/ftissues/ft9512/articles/novak.html.

Oberman, Heiko A. *Luther: Man Between God and the Devil.* Translated by Eileen Walliser-Schwarzbart. New York: Image Books, 1992.

_____. *The Roots of Antisemitism in the Age of Renaissance and Reformation.* Translated by James I. Porter. Philadelphia: Fortress Press, 1984.

O'Donnell, James J. *Augustine: A New Biography.* New York: HarperCollins, 2005.

Olmstead, A. T. *History of the Persian Empire.* Chicago: University of Chicago Press, 1970.

Sachar, Howard M. *Farewell España: The World of the Sephardim Remembered.* New York: Alfred A. Knopf, 1994.

Schreckenberg, Heinz. *The Jews in Christian Art: An Illustrated History.* New York: Continuum, 1996.

Smith, Helmuth Walser. *The Butcher's Tale: Murder and Anti-Semitism in a German Town.* New York: W. W. Norton, 2000.

Wheaton, Eliot Barculo. *The Nazi Revolution, 1933–1935: Prelude to Calamity.* Garden City, NY: Anchor Books, 1969.

Wigoda, Geoffrey, Fred Skolnik, and Shmuel Himelstein, eds. *The New Encyclopedia of Judaism.* New York: New York University Press, 2002.

Jews, the Enlightenment, Emancipation, and the Rise of Racial Anti-Semitism Through the Early Twentieth Century

CHRONOLOGY

—**1660–1789:** The Enlightenment

—**1689:** John Locke, *Letter Concerning Tolerance*

—**1714:** John Toland, *Reasons for Naturalizing the Jews in Great Britain and Ireland*

—**1729–1786:** Moses Mendelssohn

—**1779:** Gotthold Lessing, *Nathan the Wise*

—**1787:** Count Honoré Gabriel Victore de Mirabeau, *On Moses Mendelssohn and Political Reform*

—**1789:** French Revolution

—**1791:** French emancipation of the Jews

—**1793:** Catherine II, the Great creates the Pale of Permanent Jewish Settlement in Russia

—**1806:** Jewish Assembly of Notables meets in Paris to respond to Napoleon I's Twelve Questions

—**1807:** Jewish Grand Sanhedrin meets in Paris

—**1808:** Napoleon I issues "Infamous Decree" and creates Jewish consistory system

—**1848:** Revolutions of 1848 leads to emancipation of Jews in the German states

—**1850:** Richard Wagner publishes *Judaism in Music*

—**1858:** Charles Darwin publishes *On the Origin of Species*

—**1859:** Heinrich von Treitschke writes that the "Jews are Our Misfortune"

—**1864:** Herbert Spencer coins the phrase "survival of the fittest"

—**1879:** Wilhelm Marr coins phrase "anti-Semitism" in his *The Victory of Judaism over Germandom*

—**1880:** Eugen Dühring, *The Jewish Question as a Question of Race, Morals, and Civilization with a World Historical Answer*

—**1880s:** Georg Ritter von Schönerer founds Pan-German movement in Austria

—**1881:** Assassination of Alexander II, the "tsar liberator," in Russia

—**1881–1914:** Almost 2 million Jews flee Russia to escape *pogroms*

—**1882–1885:** Linz Program in Austria calls for removal of Jews from all walks of Austrian life

—**1883:** Francis Galton coins the phrase *eugenics*

—**1886:** Creation of German Anti-Semitic Alliance

—**1886:** Édouard Drumont publishes anti-Semitic *Jewish France*
—**1889** *(April 20):* Adolf Hitler born in Braunau am Inn, Austria-Hungary
—**1894:** Captain Alfred Dreyfus convicted of spying for Germany and sent to Devil's Island
—**1898:** Emile Zola writes "I Accuse" in defense of Dreyfus
—**1897–1910:** Karl Lueger serves as mayor of Vienna
—**1899:** Houston Stewart Chamberlain accuses Jews of destructive role in Western Civilization in
     Foundations of the 19th Century
—**1903:** Fictitious *Protocols of the Elders of Zion* published in Russia
—**1904–1905:** Dr. Alfred Ploetz, who coined the phrase *Rassenhygiene* (racial hygiene), founds
     Journal for Race and Social Biology and the Society for Racial Hygiene in Germany
—**1906:** Dreyfus found innocent and restored to active military duty
—**1913:** "Blood libel" trial of Mendel Beilis in Russia

The Jews in
Post-Reformation Europe

The dramatic religious and political upheavals that swept through Europe in the fifteenth and sixteenth centuries forever changed this part of the world. It also saw a major exodus of Jews from Western Europe to the Balkans and Eastern Europe. Poland and later Russia became the center of world Jewry. By the beginning of the eighteenth century, more than half of the world's Jews lived in Eastern Europe and the Balkans. Another third lived in the Middle East and Africa, and the rest lived in Western Europe.[1]

In Western Europe, the Enlightenment helped create a new atmosphere of tolerance that saw some Jews gain civil and political rights. In Poland, which was erased from the map of Europe in the second half of the eighteenth century, Jews faced new restrictions under Catherine II (the Great) (r. 1762–1796), who created a Pale of Jewish Settlement to restrict the movement of Russia's new Polish-Jewish population. During the next century, Europe's Jews would face a new form of prejudice that blended age-old religious animosity towards Jews with new ideas about race: anti-Semitism. In France, Germany, Austria-Hungary, and other parts of Western and Central Europe, anti-Semitism entered the political mainstream as a viable part of late nineteenth and early twentieth century discussions about

nationalism and national identity. In Russia, the traditional religious hatred of the Jews blended with anti-Semitism and erupted into a national campaign of anti-Jewish violence that saw almost 2 million Jews flee the country between 1881 and 1914. In response to international outcries against the mistreatment of Russian Jews, the tsarist secret police tapped into the new racist ideas of anti-Semitism to fabricate a document still used by anti-Semites to this day: *The Protocols of the Elders of Zion.* By the early decades of the twentieth century, traditional, religious-based attitudes towards Jews had blended with anti-Semitism to create a potent body of anti-Jewish hatred that formed the basis of Adolf Hitler's racial ideology.

The Enlightenment

The Enlightenment began with a revolution in scientific thought in the late seventeenth century. Its seeds can be traced to the works of Copernicus (1473–1543), Johann Kepler (1571–1630), Galileo Galilei (1564–1642), Francis Bacon (1561–1626), René Descartes (1596–1650), and others. Kepler and Galileo added to Copernicus's revolutionary idea that the sun was the center of the universe, a purely scientific conclusion that challenged traditional Christian teachings about the earth being the center of the universe. Bacon and Descartes, though not scientists, promoted science and rational scientific investigation as a means of understanding the world around them. Sir Isaac Newton (1642–1727) drew on the ideas of all of these figures in his *Principia Mathematica* (*Mathematical Principles of Natural Philosophy*; 1687). His law of gravity transformed Western science and prepared the way for the Enlightenment.

Two of the three principal ideas of the Enlightenment came from the Scientific Revolution. The first said that natural law governs the universe; the second emphasized that intelligence and scientific inquiry can lead to solutions and fundamental questions. John Locke (1632–1704) developed the last important concept of the Enlightenment, namely, one's environment opened the door to unlimited human improvement. He argued in his *An Essay on Human Understanding* (1689) that human knowledge is acquired through education and life experiences.[2] Locke also thought that all people had originally lived as equals in a free state. In his *Two Treatises of Civil Government* (1690), he argued that governments, which theoretically existed as the collective will of the people, had occasionally abused their power. He proposed that people had the right to change governments. Such institutions, Locke said, could have any authority over people's lives, liberty, or property without their consent.[3]

Some of the religious upheavals during and after the Reformation came when rulers or groups tried to force their religious views on others. In response, dissident religious groups such as the Puritans, Quakers, and Anabaptists called for religious freedom for all individuals. Locke wrote in his *Letter Concerning Toleration,* written in exile several years before the Glorious Revolution (1688–1689) in England, that no one in a civil society should be deprived of "civil enjoyments" because he or she belonged to another church or religion: "[N]either pagan, nor Mahometan [Mohammedan or Muslim], nor Jew, ought to be excluded from the civil rights of the commonwealth, because of his religion."[4]

The mere suggestion that Jews should not be deprived of civil rights because of their faith signaled an important change in attitudes towards Jews, particularly in England, though anti-Jewish prejudice still remained dominant in intellectual circles throughout Europe.

In his study of anti-Semitic images in eighteenth-century and early nineteenth-century English popular culture, Frank Felsenstein underscored the persistence of many medieval anti-Jewish stereotypes. In Germany, Johann Eisenmenger (1654–1704), a Hebrew scholar and Protestant professor at the University of Heidelberg, spent almost twenty years writing a massive two-volume work, *Endecktes Judenthum* (Judaism Uncovered; 1711), in shocked response to three Christian conversions to Judaism in Amsterdam, where Eisenmenger lived before his move to Heidelberg. Eisenmenger described his book, which became a seminal work for German anti-Semites well into the nineteenth century, as "a truthful and authentic account of the horrible manner in which the obdurate Jews blaspheme and dishonor the most Holy Trinity, God the Father, Son, and Holy Ghost; insult the holy mother of Christ, the New Testament, the Evangelists, and Apostles." He wrote that the "Godless Jews [had] no scruples about killing a Christian," and reported numerous instances of such fictitious acts. But Eisenmenger spent most of his time in *Endecktes Judenthum* attacking the *Talmud* because, he claimed, it promoted "immoral and even criminal behavior in relations with Christians."[5]

The growing popularity of Jewish religious studies among Christian theologians helped change intellectual attitudes towards the Jews in the eighteenth century. This did not mean that Christian scholars with an interest in Jewish studies had abandoned the idea of Jewish conversion to Christianity; they simply became sympathetic to Jewish religious and cultural traditions. Another factor that helped change attitudes towards Jews was the argument that a stronger Jewish societal presence could benefit the state. Though Jewish writers had argued this point for years, it took the support of non-Jews such as Sir Joshua Child (1658–1733/34), the head of the East India Company, and John Toland (1670–1722), a controversial supporter of Locke, to bring about real changes in attitudes towards Jews. Toland argued for full citizenship for Jews in his *Reasons for Naturalizing the Jews in Great Britain and Ireland* (1714). Consequently, countries that had struggled for their own political and religious freedoms—the Calvinist Netherlands (against Roman Catholic Spain, 1566–1609/48) and England—became the first Western European countries to allow Jews to live with a modicum of tolerance and opportunity.

But in France, the center of the Enlightenment, attitudes towards Jews were more complex. In his controversial book, *The French Enlightenment and the Jews*, Arthur Hertzberg stated that nineteenth-century racial anti-Semitism was a product of the Enlightenment and the French Revolution. He laid responsibility for this at the feet of Voltaire (1694–1778), one of the most important figures in the Enlightenment. Voltaire, Hertzberg argued, was "the major link in Western intellectual history between the anti-Semitism of classic paganism and the modern age."[6] What is disappointing about Voltaire, who had studied John Locke and Francis Bacon and was a staunch and vocal advocate for civil and religious liberties, was his attitude towards Jews. Voltaire aimed much of his criticism at Judaism, which he considered primitive and extreme. Voltaire saw Judaism as the antithesis of the rationalist, humanitarian ideals that he held so dear. In his *Dictionnaire philosophique* he blamed biblical Judaism for the fanaticism and violence so prevalent in the Christianity of his day. And though Voltaire was mildly critical of Christians who persecuted Jews in his *Essai sur les moeurs,* he also suggested, when discussing the expulsion of Jews from Spain in 1492, that they "had largely invited their fate."[7] Some scholars have argued

that Voltaire's criticism of Jews and Judaism was an oblique way of getting at Christianity and the Roman Catholic Church, which Voltaire frequently criticized. Regardless of his motivations, Voltaire seemed to buy into some of the age-old stereotypical views about Jews. Adam Sutcliffe, although disagreeing with Adam Hertzberg's ideas about Voltaire's role as a bridge to nineteenth-century racial anti-Semitism, still considered Voltaire an "obsessive and violent exponent" of anti-Jewish thinking during the Enlightenment.[8] Harvey Chisick added that it is risky to accuse Voltaire of being an anti-Semite because racial anti-Semitism did not exist at the time. But he agreed with Hertzberg that Voltaire's works "contain a veritable storehouse of anti-Jewish statements" that were later used by nineteenth- and twentieth-century anti-Semites to justify their own attitudes towards Jews.[9] Beyond this, Voltaire, who criticized many of the fundamental ideas of Christianity, embraced many of the Christian anti-Jewish arguments that had haunted Jews for centuries and made them an integral part of his attacks against Jews.

Other French Enlightenment thinkers such as Charles Louis de Secondat, Baron de Montesquieu (1689–1755), were more ambivalent in their attitudes toward Jews. Montesquieu called for greater tolerance for Jews in his *L'espirit des lois* (The Spirit of Laws; 1748), though he also criticized Judaism and Islam for their "obstinate prejudices." Later in the same work, he criticized the Inquisition in Portugal for the earlier death of a young Jewish girl. Interestingly, Montesquieu put his attack in the mouth of a Jew, who, although expressing respect for Christianity, questioned core Christian virtues of kindness: "You would have us be Christians, and you will not be so yourselves." He added, "[I]f you will not be Christians, be at least men: treat us as you would, if having only the weak light of justice which nature bestows, you had not a religion to conduct, and a revelation to enlighten you."[10]

Another French Enlightenment giant, Denis Diderot (1713–1784), included more than a hundred articles on Jews in what was the seminal work of the French Enlightenment, the twenty-eight-volume *Encyclopedie* (1751–1772). Yet despite his erudition and intellect, Diderot, as Joel Carmichael has pointed out, chose to concentrate his discussion of Jews on "nature." Diderot recognized that Jews had the right to "subsist, since they marry and have children," but thought they should live apart in French society since their "religion and that of the peoples they live among do not allow them to be absorbed by them."[11]

Given that most of eighteenth-century France's 40,000 Jews lived in poverty, why was so much attention given to this minority? Gary Kates has argued that the "Jewish question," particularly after the outbreak of the French Revolution in 1789, was a way to measure the extent of political equality and freedom in revolutionary France. But Ronald Schechter saw this differently. He wrote that Jews, at least in the minds of some eighteenth-century French political commentators, represented "what the ideal citizen was not." At the time, some French Christians still believed in St. Augustine's ideas about the Jews as a "witness people," and *philosophes,* or French intellectuals such as Voltaire, linked flaws in Christianity to its Jewish heritage. Other French writers saw Jews and the aristocracy as morally corrupt and not worthy of citizenship. For those who advocated citizen rights for Jews, it was often in the context of what citizenship could do morally to regenerate Jews "under the auspices of the state."[12]

One of Diderot's close friends and a contributor to the *Encyclopedie*, Baron Henri Dietrich d'Holbach (1723–1789), was particularly contemptuous of Jews. Like Voltaire, d'Holbach's attitudes towards Jews seemed to come from his keen dislike of Christianity, which he attacked in the *Encyclopedie* and other publications. A confirmed atheist and critic of all organized religion, d'Holbach viciously attacked Jews and Judaism in his *L'esprit du judaïsme:*

> The revolting policy of the Jewish legislator (Moses) has erected a stone wall between his people and all other nations. Since they are submissive only to their priests, the Jews have become the enemies of the human race. . . . The Jews have always displayed contempt for the clearest dictates of morality and the law of nations. . . . They were ordered to be cruel, inhuman, intolerant, thieves, traitors, and betrayers of trust. All these were regarded as deeds pleasing to God. In short, the Jews have become a nation of robbers. . . . They have become notorious for deception and unfairness in trade, and it may be assumed that if they were stronger, they would, in many cases, revive the tragedies which occurred so frequently in their country. . . . If there are also honest and just people among them (which cannot be doubted) this means that they [i.e., the few honest Jews] have rejected the principles of that law clearly aimed at creating trouble-makers and evildoers.[13]

These attitudes are troubling because they are so steadfast in the midst of one of the most vibrant intellectual movements ever to sweep Europe. And although it can be argued that such attacks on Jews and Judaism were part of the broader intellectual assault on traditional Christianity, they nonetheless helped keep alive many of the hatreds and stereotypes that had plagued Jews for centuries. Moreover, since some of the criticism of Jews came from *philosophes* later revered by German nationalists, their anti-Jewish attitudes were particularly dangerous.

Even Immanuel Kant (1724–1804), a *philosophe* who befriended prominent Jewish intellectuals such as Moses Mendelssohn (1729–1786) and Solomon Maimon (1754–1800), fell prey to some of the anti-Jewish thinking of his age. Considered by some to be the Enlightenment's most important thinker, Kant thought little of Judaism; he wrote in his *Der Streit der Fakuläten (The Conflict of the Faculties)* that Jews should "adopt publically the religion of *Jesus*." This was the only way they could be "ready for all the rights of citizenship." Kant considered that the "euthanasia of Judaism" would insure that Christianity's "ancient statutory teachings" would be removed. Kant also called for all religious sects to disappear, which would lead to "the conclusion of the great drama of religious change on earth, where there will be only one shepherd and one flock."[14]

One of Kant's disciples, Johann Fichte (1762–1814), is often seen as a dangerous anti-Semite, particularly since his works helped develop a sense of German nationalism during the next century.[15] Most often cited is Fichte's *Beiträge zur Berichtigung der öffentlichen Meinung über die Rechtmässigkeit der französischen Revolution* (Contributions to Correcting Opinion on the Rightfulness of the French Revolution; 1793), in which he claimed, among other things, that Jews were a "state within a state" and therefore could not have friendly relations with the larger state in which they resided. Fichte also mentioned other groups, such as the military, the church, and the nobility, as "states within a state."[16]

Fichte thought that Jews should have human rights, but wrote: "[T]o give them civil rights, I see no other means than that of cutting off all their heads in one night and of placing others upon their bodies in which there is not even one Jewish idea. To protect us from them, I again see no other way than of conquering their beloved country for them and to send them all there."[17]

And though, as Alfred D. Low has pointed out, Fichte later distanced himself from his anti-Jewish statements, his words nonetheless provided ample fodder for nineteenth- and twentieth-century anti-Semites. Adolf Hitler, for example, stated in a speech in 1922 that "'our German Fichte' had shared

the knowledge 'that the Jew is an alien particle, different in his nature, which is entirely harmful to the Aryan,' and 'that Judaism as a nationality opposes us as a deadly enemy, always and increasing.'"[18]

Not all Enlightenment thinkers shared these views. France's Comte Pierre Louis Roederer (1754–1835), who served as Louis XVI's *Procureur Général* (public prosecutor) and was a member of Napoleon I's Council of State, raised the question of Jewish emancipation before the Metz Royal Academy of Sciences in 1785. Roederer argued that the traditional Christian mistreatment of Jews had made them avaricious. The same year, Roederer convinced the Metz Academy to sponsor an essay contest, its entrants to answer the question "Is There Any Way of Making the Jews of France More Useful and Happier?" One of the winning essays was by Abbé Henri Grégoire (1750–1831), a Roman Catholic priest who later championed Jewish emancipation in the French National Assembly (1789–1791). His submission, *Essai sur la régénération physique, morale et politique des Juifs* (On the Physical, Moral and Political Degeneration of the Jews), argued that Christian society was responsible for Jewish faults. The Abbé noted that if roles were reversed, Christians might have worse flaws.

In 1787, the Comte Honoré Gabriel Victore de Mirabeau (1749–1791), who emerged as an important political figure during the early days of the French Revolution, wrote *Sur Moses Mendelssohn, Sur la Reforme Politique* (On Moses Mendelssohn and Political Reform), a tribute to the father of the Jewish Enlightenment, or *Haskalah*. Mendelssohn, Mirabeau wrote, was a unique example of the vast, latent resources in Europe's scattered and impoverished Jewish communities. If you wanted to make Jews better citizens, remove the restrictions and distinctions against them.

Mendelssohn, a brilliant Torah scholar, gained fame after he wrote a letter decrying the criticism of Gotthold Lessing's play *The*

Grave of Moses Mendelssohn. **Photo courtesy of David M. Crowe.**

Jews, which depicted the Jew as a sophisticated and noble individual. Mendelssohn challenged critics who said that a Jew could not be honest or noble. Lessing (1729–1781), the father of the modern German stage, was also a gifted writer and a leading intellectual. According to Hajo Holborn, Lessing's plea for religious toleration came from his belief that Judaism, Christianity, and Islam were all "individuations of the single religion that was in the beginning." Consequently, each shared a common goal, "the perfection of humanity."[19]

Lessing drew equally from the Old and New Testaments in his search for basic moral truth. His writings and plays relied heavily on the works of Baruch Spinoza (1632–1677), the most important Jewish intellectual in the seventeenth century and an important figure in the history of modern philosophy. Spinoza, an excommunicated Dutch Jew, ar-

gued that the Jewish Scriptures should be investigated with historical and scientific reasoning. In fact, Lessing's admiration for Spinoza formed the basis of his friendship with Mendelssohn.

Lessing called Mendelssohn a second Spinoza and made him the subject of his play *Nathan der Weise* (Nathan the Wise; 1779), which dealt with Christian intolerance towards other faiths, particularly Judaism. Though deeply religious himself, Lessing raised doubts about the superiority of Christianity vis-à-vis other faith traditions such as Judaism and Islam. Lessing also helped Mendelssohn publish his *Philosophische Gespräche* (Philosophical Dialogues), the first such publication by a Jew in the German language. In 1763, the Royal Academy awarded Mendelssohn a first prize for his essay on metaphysics (Immanuel Kant won second prize). Frederick II (the Great) (r. 1740–1786) was so impressed with Mendelssohn's accomplishments that he granted him special residency privileges in the Prussian capital, Berlin. Eight years later, though, the emperor rejected efforts to appoint Mendelssohn, who was now known as the "Socrates of Berlin," to the Royal Academy.

The son of a poor scribe, Mendelssohn (1729–1780) was a brilliant Judaic scholar. His translation of the Torah (1783), and later the Psalms and Song of Songs, into High German created a linguistic bridge to German culture and literature for many German Jews, and prompted some to call him the "Jewish Luther." Moreover, Mendelssohn used his gifts to argue against the terrible anti-Jewish stereotypes and criticism that continued to thrive during the Enlightenment. A devout Jew, Mendelssohn argued forcefully against efforts by a Swiss clergyman, Johann Lavater (1741–1801), to convert him to Christianity. Lavater, who greatly admired and respected Mendelssohn, publicly challenged him either to disprove Christianity or to convert. Mendelssohn responded by saying that though his faith had, like any religion, its flaws, he was as deeply committed to Judaism as Lavater was to Christianity. Mendelssohn added that no religion could claim a "monopoly on salvation" and emphasized the importance of religious and philosophical toleration.[20] He argued in his *Jerusalem oder über religiöse macht und Judentum* (Jerusalem, or, On Religious Power and Judaism; 1783) for toleration for all religions and dissident faiths. He also saw Judaism as much more compatible with Enlightenment rational thinking than Christianity.

Christian Wilhelm Dohm (1751–1820), a ministerial councilor *(Kriegsrath)* in Frederick the Great's Berlin court and an acquaintance of Mendelssohn's, seemed to share these views. In 1781, Mendelssohn asked Dohm to help write a protest for Alsatian Jews who were concerned about their lack of civil and economic rights. The result was *Über die bürgerliche Verbesserung der Juden* (On the Civil Improvement of the Jews in Germany; 1781/1783). Dohm wrote that Jewish "corruption" could be tied to their centuries of persecution. If Jews were given full civil rights, he argued, they would more readily assimilate into society. In the end, Dohm blamed "Jewish faults" on shortcomings in the Christian world. He proposed full equality for Jews, but said that, to prevent a backlash, "transitory regulations" should be adopted that would restrict their roles in certain areas of the economy, the military, and the government.[21] Dohm's work provoked considerable debate in Europe. One commentator said he was touched by Dohm's "love for the most unfortunate of the co-citizens."[22] The biblical scholar Johann David Michaelis (1717–1791), who was quite critical of Dohm's work, admitted that "he had become 'the advocate of the poorer element among the Jews.'"[23] The Swiss historian Johannes von Müller (1752–1809) applauded Dohm and suggested the translation of the works of Maimonides into German or French. But others were not so kind. H. F.

Diez, who said he was "moved" by Dohm's work, wrote in his *Über die Juden* (On the Jews) that conversion to Christianity was the key to resolving the "Jewish problem." Michaelis agreed, arguing that Jews could never become good citizens until they became Christians. Alfred D. Low concluded that the response to Dohm's *Über die bürgerliche Verbesserung der Juden* underscored "the widespread German conviction that the gulf between German Christians and Jews could be bridged only if the latter were prepared to abandon their religious identity, shed their cultural heritage, and, in effect, commit suicide as a people."[24]

The idea that successful Jewish assimilation into European society depended on conversion to Christianity remained a constant in Enlightenment thinking about the Jews, particularly among some of the continent's "Enlightened" despots. In the second part of his study, Dohm applauded the Austrian emperor Joseph II's recent Jewish decrees, particularly his 1781–1782 Edict of Tolerance, which removed many of the traditional economic, educational, and occupational restrictions against Jews without granting them full citizens' rights. Although there is no question that the emperor was driven by Enlightenment ideals of "toleration and humanity," the real purpose of his new Jewish legislation was economic—to make the Jews more effective tax-paying citizens. Jewish intellectuals such as Moses Mendelssohn, though, saw something more sinister in Joseph II's new Jewish legislation. After carefully reading the Edict of Toleration, he and Michaelis concluded that the "tendency" of the act was to "lure the Jews into the pale of the Christian church." In a letter to Dohm in early 1782, Michaelis said he was convinced the Edict was a *"political attempt at the religious improvement* of the Jews" and that it was meant "to make them into Christians within twenty, or, at most twice twenty years, i.e., by the time the present generation has died out."[25]

Joseph II (r. 1780–1792) was, if nothing else, a pragmatist, not a dreamy-eyed reformer. His Jewish decrees were part of a wide-ranging series of reforms designed to create a "perfectly uniform state" that centered around the emancipation of peasants. In 1783, he issued his *Hauptregulio* for Austria's other troubling minority, the Roma, or Gypsies, which combined earlier decrees and regulations issued by his mother, Maria Theresa (r. 1740–1780). These decrees had outlawed nomadism and forced the Roma to settle in towns and villages. Roma children older than five would be taken from their families and raised in non-Roma homes to ensure that they became good Roman Catholics, even though the empire's Roma were traditionally Christians. Austrian policies were designed to insure the complete assimilation of the Roma into imperial society in a generation or two. Only then would their troubling ways disappear.

In Prussia, Joseph II's contemporary, Frederick II (the Great), was much more restrictive in his dealings with the country's Jews. His *Generalprivilegium* of 1750 distinguished between a small group of *Schutzjuden* (protected Jews), whom the king thought could further Prussia's economic and political interests, and now acquired inheritance rights, and a larger group of unprotected Jews. During Frederick the Great's reign, authorities impoverished most of the country's Jews with a growing number of taxes. In 1787, the country's Jewish leaders told the new monarch, Frederick William II (r. 1786–1797), that the collective result of these regulations caused them to be "treated like cattle." An admirer of Mendelssohn, Frederick William abolished the Jewish head tax and also eased some earlier restrictions on Jews. A royal commission promised Jewish emancipation by the mid-nineteenth century. Frederick William II also tried to improve the status of the 128,000 Polish Jews brought into Prussia during the Partitions of Poland, which saw Prussia, in league with Russia and Austria,

erase Poland from the map of Europe from 1772 to 1795.

The status of Jews in certain parts of Europe had changed dramatically during the Enlightenment. Yet they still remained the "other," an isolated socioreligious community haunted by medieval attitudes and stereotypes that kept them separate from the larger Christian world. Yet if the Enlightenment achieved nothing else, at least it brought the "Jewish question" into the intellectual limelight of the eighteenth century. It would take the French Revolution and Napoleon I to move the debate about the role of Jews in European society to a more practical level.

The French Revolutions of 1789–1799, Napoleon I, and the Jews

The upheavals that swept France between 1789 and 1815 forever changed the status of Jews throughout Europe. By the end of the Middle Ages, almost no Jews lived in what would become modern France except for scattered border communities in Alsace, Lorraine, Avignon, Nice, and Comtat Venaissin. By 1500, no more than a few thousand Jews lived in France. Jewish numbers began to increase with the arrival of *conversos* from Portugal and Spain in the sixteenth century. More than 5,000 Jews lived in France in 1700, and by 1789, this number had grown to 40,000, more than half living in Alsace. The Sephardic Jews in southern France had prospered because of a supportive economic and intellectual environment. The Ashkenazic Jews in the country's eastern border regions did not fare as well and suffered from widespread discrimination and poverty. The 500 or so Jews living in Paris enjoyed few privileges and faced considerable restrictions on their movements and professional activities.

The divisions between France's two Jewish groups surfaced after the outbreak of the French Revolution in the summer of 1789. Soon after France's new legislature, the

National Assembly, began to meet, two delegates, Mirabeau and Abbé Grégoire, demanded that a statement about Jewish emancipation be included in the Declaration of the Rights of Man and of the Citizen, which the assembly had just begun to discuss. Initially, the assembly refused to consider such a statement until the outbreak of anti-Jewish riots in Alsace forced them to discuss the rights of Jews. Opposition from Alsatians and others who accused the Jews of greed and "separatism" initially dashed hopes of a Jewish statement in the new French declaration. This partially changed when the Sephardic community in the south demanded equal rights, which the assembly approved in early 1790. But it would be another year and a half before the French legislature approved a law granting all French Jews full emancipation. The price for such freedom was loss of Jewish community autonomy. In return, France's Jews embraced their newfound freedoms and repaid the nation with "glowing" acts of patriotism.[26] French Jews successfully weathered the numerous political upheavals that helped change the nation's political landscape during the next decade.

But the most important change for French, and later, European Jews, came during the reign of Napoleon I (Bonaparte) (r. 1799–1813/1815), who instigated a series of reforms designed to force France's Jews to assimilate into French society. Napoleon, who did not like Jews, was driven partly by complaints from Alsatian farmers who had borrowed vast sums from Jewish moneylenders to purchase estates from aristocrats who had fled the country. They complained of Jewish moneylending practices, even though more than half the country's moneylenders were Christians. Napoleon also heard complaints from French royalists who claimed that Jews remained a disloyal "nation within a nation." In response, Napoleon, who had become French emperor in 1803, adopted a series of stringent anti-Jewish laws in 1806 because, he

argued, "the evil done by the Jews comes from the very temperament of this people."[27] The worst of these laws prohibited Jews in Alsace from collecting debts for a year.

Soon after Napoleon issued this legislation, his Council of State announced the convocation of an Assembly of Jewish Notables, which would begin meeting in Paris in July 1806. At its opening session, Jewish leaders were given Twelve Questions to answer about marriage, relations with Christians, Jewish law, usury, and other matters. After considerable and thoughtful debate, the delegates assured the emperor that France's Jews were completely loyal to the state and highly moralistic. The emperor then ordered the Assembly of Notables to select members for a Grand Sanhedrin, a high Jewish court that had not met since 66 C.E. Made up principally of rabbis, Napoleon asked the Sanhedrin to confirm the Notables' responses to the Twelve Questions, which it quickly did. The Sanhedrin also acknowledged the superiority of civil courts over religious courts and encouraged Jews to participate in all aspects of French life. According to Howard Sachar, these decisions "set the tone of Western Jewish life for at least a century to come" by rejecting "corporate Jewish autonomy" and "Jewish civilization in its wider ethnic and cultural dimensions."[28]

In the spring of 1808, Napoleon's government issued three new Jewish decrees that further regulated Jewish life in France. The first, the "Infamous Decree," deprived Jews of many of the rights they had gained in 1791, particularly in Alsace and Lorraine, and forced many Jews to give up moneylending and related professions. Napoleon's other Jewish decrees dealt with the creation of a consistory system centered around a *Consistoire Israélite* that would oversee Jewish religious life throughout France. But unlike the system created for the country's Roman Catholics and Protestants, the Jews were required to pay for the consistories through a special government tax. The consistories were to act as "watchdogs" over Jewish actions and morals and make certain that the country's Jews behaved as proper Frenchmen.

Many French Jews welcomed Napoleon I's defeat in 1813 and the restoration of the Bourbon line under Louis XVIII (r. 1813–1824). The Infamous Decree expired in 1818, though a reformed consistorial system existed until 1905. The liberalization of French policies towards Jews spurred assimilation and a dramatic increase in Jewish conversions to Christianity in the first half of the nineteenth century. Yet anti-Jewish sentiment remained strong in France, particularly after the revolution of 1848 and France's humiliating defeat in the Franco-Prussian War in 1870–1871.

The Jews in Post-Napoleonic Europe

The pace of Jewish emancipation in Western Europe was uneven in the years immediately after the end of the Napoleonic Wars. In England, efforts were made to grant Jews full civil liberties. In 1833, the House of Commons passed a Jewish emancipation bill, which the House of Lords rejected. Regardless, restrictions against Jews began slowly to ease. In 1847, Lionel de Rothschild (1808–1879) was elected to the House of Commons from London, but was not permitted to take his seat until 1858 because of opposition in the House of Lords.

The status of Jews in post-Napoleonic Italy varied from kingdom to kingdom. Generally, though, Jews lived impoverished in ghettos. This was particularly true in the Papal States, where restrictions on Jews were considered an integral part of Roman Catholic teaching. Though a few popes sought to ameliorate harsh papal regulations against Jews, most embraced policies designed to restrict Jewish economic and social integration. In the nineteenth century, these policies were driven by concerns that Papal Jews were somehow tied to liberal or revolutionary movements in Italy. Jews in other parts of Italy also faced new restrictions. Fortunately, after 1815, Jewish emancipation was an important theme in Italy's *Risorgimento* (revival), which led to unification in 1860. Several important Italian revolutionary groups such as the *Carboneria* (charcoal burners) and *Giovine Italia* (Young Italy) supported Jewish emancipation.

The status of German Jews improved during the Napoleonic era, though it worsened afterwards. Between 1816 and 1824, the nationalistic writings of Fichte, Friedrich Rühs (1781–1820), and others stimulated anti-Jewish riots in many German states. Rioters in Frankfurt and other German cities attacked Jewish homes and businesses, crying, "*Hep, hep Jude verreche* (hep, hep, perish Jews)." Jews in Prussia lost many of the rights they had gained during the Napoleonic era. Despite this, Jewish life flourished in some of the German states and parts of the Austrian empire. Frankfurt, the home of the Rothschild banking empire, became the center of Reform Judaism, a movement that tried to modernize Jewish religious practices. Vienna's Jews prospered because the government officially encouraged them to become a part of Vienna's new upper middle class. Jews in other parts of the Austrian empire, though, suffered from rigid residency requirements and heavy taxation.

Much of this changed during and after the revolutions in 1848–1849. The rebellions, which began in France in early 1848, quickly spread to other parts of Europe. In France, Isaac Moïse Cremieux (1796–1880) became minister of justice in the provisional government that was set up after the overthrow of Louis Philippe (r. 1830–1848). Cremieux remained an important figure in French politics for the rest of his life and in 1860 founded *Universal Israelite Alliance*, an important international Jewish organization. On the other hand, anti-Jewish riots took place in Alsace. In Venice, the leader of the new revolutionary government, Daniele Manin (1804–1857), had Jewish roots, and two Jewish ministers served in his cabinet. Three Jews served in the legislature of the short-lived revolutionary Republic of Rome in 1848–1849. Afterwards, under the protection of French troops, Pope Pius IX (r. 1846–1878) reinstituted the Jewish ghetto in Rome and revived many of the papacy's traditional anti-Jewish restrictions there.

As revolution swept through the German states, rulers agreed to send delegates to a German Constituent National Assembly, commonly known as the Frankfurt Parliament or Assembly of 1849. This was the first time in German history that freely elected delegates had come to discuss political issues. The Frankfurt Parliament had a number of Jewish members, including the vice chairman, Gabriel Roesser. Its delegates, who came from throughout Germany, met to discuss German unification. The religious clauses of its "Law Concerning the Fundamental Rights of the German People" was the basis for the future emancipation of Germany's Jews. The same year, all German states except Bavaria granted Jews full civil rights, though during the next ten years these were weakened. Jews also played an important role in the Prussian revolution, particularly in Berlin. Frederick William IV (r. 1840–1861), who once referred to Prussia's Jews as that "contemptible Jewish clique," granted full equality to all Prussian religions in his 1848 constitution. Prussian Jewry blossomed after the revolution of 1848, though they continued to suffer from what Fritz Stern called an embattled prominence and a spirit of polite, respectable anti-Semitism.[29]

In the Austrian Empire, which suffered most from the revolutions of 1848, the new emperor, Franz Josef (r. 1848–1916), granted religious freedom to all groups, including Jews. Though Vienna remained free of anti-Jewish outbursts during the revolution of 1848–1849, anti-Jewish violence broke out in other parts of the empire. Many of Hungary's Jews supported Louis Kossuth's (1802–1894) efforts to create a separate Hungarian state, and they suffered afterwards because of this support. However, by 1860, most of the anti-Jewish restrictions in Hungary were lifted, and the country's Jews began to enjoy new professional and economic opportunities. In Bohemia and Moravia, anti-Jewish riots in 1848–1849 forced many Jews to flee to other parts of Europe. This exodus was not halted until 1867, when the *Ausgleich* created a dual, co-equal Austrian-Hungarian state under one monarch. Afterwards, the Hungarian parliament passed a Jewish emancipation bill that gave Jews full civil and political rights.

The Intellectual and Nationalistic Origins of Anti-Semitism in the Nineteenth Century

Yet at the very time Jewish emancipation bore fruit in parts of Europe, other intellectual, nationalistic, and "racial" forces would undercut the full realization of equality for Jews in Central and Western Europe. The unification of Italy and Germany between 1860 and 1871 had a profound impact on most of Europe; this was particularly true in France and Austria, countries that were humiliated in Otto von Bismarck's (1815–1898) aggressive quest for German unification.

Abroad, many of Europe's great powers were moving into Asia and Africa. Driven by new ideas of white racial superiority, Europe's great powers had taken up what Rudyard Kipling (1865–1936) called "The White Man's Burden"—the civilization of Kipling's "half devil/half child." Josiah Strong (1847–1916) said that this Anglo-Saxon move into Asia and Africa was the prelude to the "final competition of races for which the Anglo-Saxon is being schooled." Strong felt that the end result of this "competition" was the "survival of the fittest."[30] According to Peter Gay, Strong had blended together the Social Darwinism of

Herbert Spencer with new nineteenth-century concepts of racism.

But this was also a time of considerable trouble in Europe: Germany, united in 1871, slipped into two decades of depression; France continued a gradual domestic and international decline that would not end until after World War II. The British Empire was already weakening, its future collapse in sight, and the Austrian Habsburgs struggled to maintain control over their multiethnic empire. Russia's failures in the Crimean War (1853–1856) had forced Alexander II (r. 1855–1881) to abolish serfdom and initiate other reforms. After his murder in 1881, his son, Alexander III (r. 1881–1894), used harsh police-state tactics to maintain his dynasty's hold on power. Europe's "sick man," the Ottoman Empire, was gradually losing control over its vast Balkan domains.

The Industrial Revolution and the rise of modern capitalism had triggered dramatic social and economic changes throughout Europe. Although many Europeans enjoyed the benefits of industrialization and urbanization, some, particularly among the lower classes, had gained little from Europe's economic revolution. Factory workers toiled in unbearable conditions, and former peasants felt alienated towards an urban existence that was just as harsh. By the second half of the nineteenth century, social commentators began to raise questions about the negative side of modern capitalism and urbanization. They also suggested radical changes to rectify its ills.

At one extreme were the socialists and communists such as Karl Marx (1818–1883) and Friedrich Engels (1820–1895). In 1845, Engels, Marx's collaborator on most of his important works, wrote *The Conditions of the Working Class in England*, which underscored the harsh life of England's industrial workers. On the eve of the revolutions of 1848, Marx and Engels wrote the *Communist Manifesto* for the Communist League, a new organiza-

tion that wanted the *bourgeoisie* overthrown. Marx, drawing from the ideas of Wilhelm Hegel (1770–1831), viewed history through the prism of economic control and class conflict. Marx and Engels saw nineteenth-century capitalism as a stage in this conflict that would ultimately be destroyed by communism. They expanded on these ideas in their other works, particularly *Das Kapital*. Their writings became important intellectual rallying points for socialists and communists troubled by capitalism's abuses. Marx, though raised a Christian, came from a family of Jewish rabbis; later, anti-Semites would use Marx's background to claim that Marxism and communism were Jewish ideologies aimed at world domination.

Another intellectual school of thought that emerged at this time was Social Darwinism. It was loosely drawn from Charles Darwin's (1809–1882) work *On the Origin of Species by Means of Natural Selection or the Preservation of Favoured Races in the Struggle for Life* (1859). Darwin, who based his study on years of painstaking fieldwork and observation, concluded that life on earth is constantly evolving and that only those who best adapted to their environments survived. He applied this standard to all life forms. Throughout the rest of the nineteenth and early twentieth centuries, a group of writers and social commentators known as the Social Darwinists began to apply Darwin's theory to all sorts of human types and problems. Some Social Darwinists, for example, argued for greater investment in education and other reforms that would help create better human beings.

Herbert Spencer (1820–1903) embraced Darwin's ideas about natural selection and coined the phrase "survival of the fittest" to underscore the idea of racial superiority and inferiority. Whether it be humans, races, or the state, Spencer's thoughts were clear: "If they are sufficiently complete to live, they do live, and it is well they should live. If they are not sufficiently complete to live, they die, and it is best they die."[31] Racial extremists quickly embraced some of Spencer's ideas, particularly those about the "survival of the fittest." Eventually, a cottage industry emerged that used Social Darwinism to explore the dimensions of racial and ethnic diversity.

One new area of study was *eugenics* (Greek, "good birth"), a phrase coined by Francis Galton (1822–1911), Charles Darwin's cousin, in 1883. In a lecture before the Sociological Society at London University in 1904, Galton defined *eugenics* as the "science which deals with all influences that improve the inborn qualities of a race; also with those that develop them to the utmost advantage."[32]

Eugenics became an important subject throughout Europe and North America as scientists and others looked for ways to improve humankind through medical and other means. In Germany, a physician, Alfred Ploetz (1860–1940), began to use the term *Rassenhygiene* (racial hygiene) to describe the role of war, revolution, and health care in strengthening "degenerative human stock." He also suggested that inferior individuals be sent to war as "cannon fodder" to preserve the lives of racially superior individuals.[33] In 1904, Ploetz founded the *Archiv für Rassen und Gesellschaftsbiologie (Journal of Racial and Social Biology)* and, a year later, the *Gesellschaft für Rassenhygiene* (Society for Racial Hygiene). They became the principal venues for eugenics research in Germany in the years before the Great War. Ploetz's ideas found fertile ground among German racists and eugenicists, particularly after World War I. The Nazis regarded him as a pioneer of early Nazi racial ideology, and in 1936 Hitler named him an honorary professor of racial hygiene at the University of Munich; the same year, a Norwegian legislator nominated Ploetz for the Nobel Peace Prize because of his ideas about war's impact on biological reproduction.

Eugenics, though, was only one of the many schools of analysis to emerge in Europe in the second half of the nineteenth century. The common denominator among those concerned with Europe's growing problems was an effort to identify causes for what many saw as a general decline in civilized society. Some European intellectuals began to blame liberalism, socialism, and Marxism for the ills, ideas, and movements they associated with an urbanized elite. They usually linked Jews to these trends. Emancipation opened many doors for Jews in the nineteenth century and this, in turn, triggered new prejudices. The age-old stereotypes and hatreds that had haunted Jews for centuries found new life in a racist ideology that blended historic anti-Jewish and anti-Judaic feelings with questions about the threat of Jews to the greater racial health of Europe. This new anti-Jewish racial ideology was known as anti-Semitism.

Anti-Semitism, a phrase coined by the German writer Wilhelm Marr in 1879, differed from traditional Christian anti-Jewish prejudice, which viewed Jews in a religious context. Anti-Semitism, on the other hand, saw the Jews as a dangerous group not because of their faith traditions but because of certain racial characteristics. Yet Europe's anti-Semites also drew from many of the negative images and stereotypes of religious anti-Judaism.

Although racial anti-Semitism became a European-wide phenomena in the second half of the nineteenth century, Germans developed many of its core ideas. They were stimulated by the shattered dreams of German unification, which took place in the aftermath of three successful wars of unification against Denmark (1864), Austria (1866), and France (1870–1871). For many German nationalists, these swift victories and the proclamation of the Second German Reich at Versailles in early 1871 underscored the religiously blessed nature of the German people and their nation. Unification also unleashed what Dietrich Orlow called a "tasteless amalgamation of chauvinism and religiosity."[34]

After a few years of strong economic growth, Germany sank into a depression that lasted for two decades. Despite these problems, German society was dramatically transformed from a traditional agricultural society into a highly industrialized urban society. Immigrants, attracted by its wealth and power, flocked to the new state. As Germans agonized over these problems, intellectuals, nationalists, and politicians struggled with the conflict between traditional rural values in a nation that was becoming more materialistic and urbanized. The German middle class embraced Prussian militaristic values and behaviors, which further enhanced the military, which gained semiautonomous powers in the constitution of 1871. Military values now permeated every aspect of German society, a phenomena Gerhard Ritter called the "militarization of the bourgeoisie."[35] This new attitude drove Heinrich von Treitschke (1834–1896), one of Bismarkian Germany's foremost anti-Semites, to argue in his *Deutsche Geschichte in neunzehnten Jahrhundert* (History of Germany in the Nineteenth Century; 1879–1895) that military strength was the final determinant of a nation's future. Modern German anti-Semitism was born in what Fritz Stern called this era of German "cultural despair."[36]

Though the seeds of modern anti-Semitism had roots in age-old Christian attitudes towards Jews, its modern-day core developed after 1871, when German intellectuals began to discuss who and what was a German. This question was linked to the *kleindeutsch-grossdeutsch* debate in the German states in the nineteenth century. Bismarck's unification of Germany was a victory for those who wanted a *kleindeutsch* (small German) nation that excluded multiethnic Austria-Hungary. Those who supported the idea of a *grossdeutsch* (large German) state that included all Germans were frustrated with the ethnic limitations of the Second Reich. According to Karl Schleunes, the importance of this, particularly as it related to the evolution of anti-Semitism after 1871, was that it asked who did and who did not belong to the German state. For some Germans, nationality became a cultural phenomenon not necessarily tied to citizenship. Johann Gottfried Herder's ideas about language as a defining force of nationality encouraged the concept that Germany was not a mere political entity but, at least to some German nationalists, a culture state based on language and religion.

This controversy led to questions about who could and who could not be a citizen in the new German nation. Some German nationalists were particularly concerned about Jews and the question of national identity, which centered around two themes: Christianity and German patriotism. Could Jews, if they converted to Christianity and became properly "Germanized," be considered members of the German culture nation? Only Christian Germans could decide. In reality, this issue was not resolved until the Nazis took power in Germany in 1933.

Although the constitution of 1871 gave Germany's half million Jews full legal citizenship rights, some intellectuals were troubled by this, particularly during the depression of the 1870s and 1880s. Wilhelm Marr (1819–1904), who coined the term *anti-Semitism* in his pamphlet *Das Sieg des Judenthums über Germanenthum* (The Victory of Judaism over Germandom) in 1879, blamed Jews for Germany's social and economic problems and claimed they were on the verge of "Jewifying" not only Germany but the world. Marr and other German racist writers used some of Johann Gottfried Herder's (1744–1803) ideas about "humanitarian nationalism" to justify their thoughts about Jews. Herder, who developed some new definitions for nationality and culture, believed that culture had its own peculiar spirit, or *Volksgeist,* which gave it a unique language, art, and literature. Herder maintained that nationality was a living part of culture. Those who belonged to a particular nationality, the *Volk,* were joined together spiritually. Herder, unlike later German nationalists, did not see one nationality or culture as being any better than another. He argued that there was only one human race and that it was made up of a series of equal cultures. The principal determinant of nationality, Herder argued, was language. He felt that the ideal state was made up of one nationality and that mixing people of different nationalities was unnatural.

Herder had mixed feelings about Jews. As a Protestant minister, he admired their ancient writings, history, religion, and cultural traditions. Yet at the end of his section on Jews in his *Auch eine Philosophie der Geschichte zur Bildung der Menschheit* (Another Philosophy of History Concerning the Development of Mankind), he concluded that Jews had from the beginning of their history been "parasitical plants on the trunks of other nations; a race of cunning broken almost throughout the whole world; who, in spite of all oppression, have never been inspired by an ardent passion for their own honour, for a habitation, for a country, of their own."[37]

One of Marr's contemporaries, Paul Anton Lagarde (1827–1891), a biblical scholar and linguist, longed for the mythical simplicity of a Germany free of the evils of modern society, which he attributed to Jews and liberals. Lagarde was also a virulent anti-Semite, whom Fritz Stern called "the patron saint of the emergent anti-Semitic or *völkische* movements."[38] Lagarde, who was critical of racial anti-Semites, considered "Germanism" a matter of spirit, not of blood. Yet, he admitted, the "Jewish question" was a "racial question" as well, and warned of the *verjudet* ("Jewification") of Germany if Jews were allowed to remain in Germany without assimilating into German culture. And though Nazi writers later criticized Lagarde's disregard of racial theory, they adored him because of his

violent anti-Semitism and extreme German nationalism. During World War II, the *Wehrmacht* (military power; term for Germany's armed forces) distributed a special edition of Lagarde's works to German soldiers. Lagarde considered the Jews a dangerous element within German society because they possessed the very unity that the Germans lacked. He said that the Jews were "a terrible misfortune for every European people" and were the "carriers of decay and pollute every national culture." Jews, Lagarde wrote, also exploited "the human and material resources of their hosts," and destroyed "all faith." Lagarde charged the Jews with the "spread of materialism and liberalism."[39] For Lagarde, liberals were the Jews' natural allies who worked together to destroy the fabric of German society and culture. Lagarde was also a German imperialist who dreamed of a greater Germany that would expand eastward and drive the Jews and other non-German groups out of Central Europe.

Another prominent German anti-Semite was Eugen Dühring (1833–1921). Like Lagarde, Dühring was an academic whose writings gave German anti-Semitism a veneer of intellectual sophistication. And it was this, Dühring's standing as a serious scholar, that so affected Theodor Herzl (1869–1904), the Austrian founder of political Zionism. Herzl, like many liberal German-Jewish intellectuals, proudly embraced German culture and nationalism. But after reading Dühring's *Die Judenfrage als Rassen-, Sitten-, und Kulturfrage. Mit einer weltgeschichtlichen Antwort* (The Jewish Question as a Question of Race, Morals, and Civilization with a World-Historical Answer; 1880), Herzl came to the conclusion that if Dühring argued so forcefully against Jewish integration into German society there was little hope that less well-educated Germans would accept it. Dühring wrote that the only way to rid Germany of its Jewish problem was to eliminate Jews as a force in German life. Yet Dühring also alienated

Richard Wagner. Photo courtesy of David M. Crowe.

many anti-Semites with the anti-Christian tone of his *Der Ersatz der Religion durch Vollkommeneres und die Ausscheidung alles Judentums durch den modernen Völkergeist* (The Replacement of Religion by Something More Complete and the Exclusion of All Jews Through the Modern National Spirit; 1883), which argued that Christianity was a flawed form of Judaism. Dühring regarded the Old Testament as a Jewish propaganda piece. Dühring's extreme leftist tendencies and his

anti-Christian ideas kept his views on the fringe, though his call for a campaign of *Entjudung* (de-Jewification) made him attractive to German and Austrian readers.

The most prominent member of this new generation of German anti-Semites was Richard Wagner (1813–1883). Adolf Hitler put Wagner on the same pedestal as Martin Luther and Frederick the Great. Wagner was a close friend of Count Joseph Arthur de Gobineau (1816–1882), a French nobleman whose multivolume *Essai dur l'Inégalité des Race* (Essay on the Inequality of Races; 1853–1854), divided humanity into three basic races: white, black, and yellow. Wagner and other anti-Semites were particularly drawn to Gobineau's efforts to apply certain characteristics to each race. The white race, Gobineau argued, enjoyed the best qualities of the human race. Whites, he felt, were superior to the other two races and exhibited outstanding leadership and drive. Fertility was the yellow race's chief virtue and sensuality the black race's strength. Although Gobineau did not oppose racial mixing, he did feel that a great civilization's leaders needed outstanding intellectual qualities. He blamed the decline of France, which, he argued, had once been led by the Aryan whites, on blacks and Orientals. Gobineau added that these groups had also spread their "nigridity" throughout much of Europe.

Just a few years before Gobineau died, he and Wagner became friends. And though Wagner was critical of some of Gobineau's ideas, he strongly promoted Gobineau's works in Germany. Jews physically repulsed Wagner, who thought them creatively inept. He zeroed in on this theme in his 1850 essay *Das Judenthum in der Musik* (Judaism in Music). Jews, he argued, could never master any aspect of European civilization, and could, at best, only mimic it. Furthermore, assimilation or conversion would not affect Jews, who would always be "the most heartless of all human beings."[40]

On the other hand, Wagner romanticized the mythical, superior Aryan, a Sanskrit name meaning "noble" that was first used to describe Hindus and other Indo-Europeans. The term was eventually redefined to refer to an idealized, racially pure German. Wagner meant the figure of Parsifal in his opera of the same name to be the model Aryan whose life and virtues reaffirmed Christian values. Wagner wrote *Parsifal* to glorify the superior Aryan race and the *völkisch* values so impor-

tant to racial Aryanism. For Wagner, Parsifal was god-like because of his superior Aryan virtues. These were the themes that drew Adolf Hitler to Wagner's works and theories. August Kubizek, Hitler's close boyhood friend, said that Wagner's operas mesmerized the future dictator of Germany:

> During the performances, his violence left him, he became quiet, yielding and tractable. His gaze lost its restlessness; his own destiny, however heavily it may have weighed upon him, became unimportant. He no longer felt lonely and outlawed, and misjudged by society. He was intoxicated and bewitched. Willingly he let himself be carried away into that mystical universe which was more real to him than the actual workaday world. From the stale, musty prison of his back room, he was transported into the blissful regions of Germanic antiquity, that ideal world which was the lofty goal of all his endeavours.[41]

William Shirer later wrote that Hitler would occasionally say that "whoever wants to understand National Socialism must know Wagner."[42]

Political Anti-Semitism in Germany, Austria, France, and Russia Prior to World War I

By the late nineteenth century, racial anti-Semitism was widespread throughout Europe. But it was most pronounced in Germany, Austria, France, and Russia. Yet what were the practical implications of these new racist anti-Semitic ideas? When anti-Semitism entered the political mainstream in Germany and Austria, its viability was insured. The Dreyfus scandal showed how strong anti-Semitism was in France. In Russia, which had the world's largest Jewish population, traditional religious anti-Jewish ideas, in league with the new tenets of racist anti-Semitism, helped to produce an era of anti-Semitic violence not witnessed in Europe since the Middle Ages.

Germany

In 1879, Heinrich von Treitschke (1834–1896) published "Ein Wort über unser Judeten (A Word About Our Jews)" in the *Preussiche Jahrbücher* (Prussian Yearbook) in Berlin. Treitschke, who argued that anti-Semitism was a logical German reaction to the presence of this "alien" group in German society, thought that "die Juden sind unser Unglück (the Jews are our misfortune)," a phrase later favored by the Nazis, particularly in their virulent anti-Semitic newspaper *Der Stürmer*.[43] Since the infant German nation was still struggling with its own identity problems, Treitschke considered urbanized, sophisticated Jews to be particularly dangerous to contemporary Germany. In this state of weakness, Trietschke argued, German culture and society were particularly vulnerable to Jewish domination.

Conservative reaction to Bismarck's economic policies drove the anti-Semitism of Marr, Treitschke, and others. In the opinion of some anti-Semites, Bismarck was the puppet of his Jewish banker, Gerson Bleichröder (1822–1893), a view that underscored what Fritz Stern called the tragic union of anticapitalism and anti-Semitism. The new racist anti-Semitism found its first political voice in Adolf Stoecker's (1835–1909) *Christlichsoziale Arbeitspartei* (CSAP; Christian Social Workers Party). Stoecker, Wilhelm I's court chaplain, founded the CSAP in 1878. Stoecker's party promoted German nationalism, political conservatism, and Christian social consciousness. His efforts in the 1878 parliamentary elections failed miserably. In the 1881 elections, he blended the CSAP's traditional ideals with virulent anti-Semitism. Though the CSAP did not do well in the 1881 elections, its anti-Semitic themes helped pave the way for the Anti-Semites' Petition of 1881. The brainchild of Bernhard Förster (1843–1889), Ernst Henrici

(1854–1915), and Max Liebermann von Sonnenberg (1848–1911), the idea behind the petition was to help promote a national plebiscite on the "Jewish question." The petition's principal demands provided some of the basic ideas for the various anti-Semitic organizations that would crop up in the Second Reich during the next thirty years. Its essential points called for a halt or limit on Jewish immigration into Germany, a Jewish census, restrictions on substantial Jewish roles in government, and a ban on hiring Jewish teachers in the public schools. The petition's sponsors felt that it could lead to the revocation of Jewish citizenship in Germany. Though the petition garnered only 265,000 signatures, its circulation became a catalyst for Germany's budding anti-Semitic political movement. Almost half the students at the University of Berlin signed the petition, and most of Germany's educated classes supported it.

During next ten years, several anti-Semitic parties surfaced in Germany. In 1880, Henrici created the *Soziale Reichspartei* (Social Reich Party), which adopted the major themes of the Anti-Semites' Petition. A year later, Förster and von Sonnenberg founded the *Deutscher Volksverein* (German National Association), which called for the repeal of Jewish citizenship. Two distinct types of anti-Semitic movements developed in Germany during the next decade: the parliamentary anti-Semites, who sought to resolve the "Jewish question" within the context of the German constitutional and legal structure; and the more radical, revolutionary anti-Semites, who argued that Germany had to be purified of its modernistic disease before the Jews could be dealt with.

The parliamentary anti-Semites, led by von Sonnenberg and Otto Böckel (1859–1923), formed the *Deutsche Antisemitische Vereinigung* (DASV; German Anti-Semitic Alliance) in 1886. Within four years, the DASV had split into two parties, Liebermann von Sonnenberg's *Deutschsoziale Partei* (DSP; German

Social Party) and Böckel's *Antisemitische Volkspartei* (ASVP; Anti-Semitic People's Party). Later, the ASVP became part of the *Deutsche Reformpartei* (German Reform Party). Both movements blamed most of Germany's problems on the Jews, who, they asserted, had used socialism and liberalism to spread national self-doubt.

In the 1890 parliamentary elections, the ASVP and the DSP party won 5 Reichstag seats (out of 397) from Hessenland, the stronghold of the anti-Semitic political movement in Germany. Three years later, the anti-Semites won 16 Reichstag seats. This victory gave the anti-Semitic parties some respect as a viable political bloc and prompted the union of three anti-Semitic parties into the *Antisemitische Deutschsoziale Reformpartei* (ASDSRP; Anti-Semitic German Social Reform Party) in 1894. The following year, the new party developed the Erfurt Program, that blended the themes of the 1880 Anti-Semites' Petition with new demands such as the censorship of the "Jewish" press. The political anti-Semites, though, lacked organizational and economic skills, and they constantly fought among themselves. They also failed to develop a viable press, even though some German newspapers were supportive of the ASDSRP or were openly anti-Semitic. Though the anti-Semitic parties held their own in the 1895 elections, they lost 6 seats three years later and more in 1903. And though their political fortunes seemed to revive in national elections in 1907, they failed to introduce any anti-Semitic legislation in the Reichstag. They also sponsored only one successful bill: a law that required court witnesses in jury trials to take a denominational religious oath. In the 1912 elections, which the anti-Semites later termed the "Jew" elections because seven Jews were elected to the Reichstag, the ASDSRP won only 6 seats.

The limited political successes enjoyed by the Second Reich's anti-Semitic political movement are less important than its spread of anti-Semitic ideas throughout Germany. This was partly achieved through alliances between the anti-Jewish parties and other German political movements. Their most successful alliances were with the *Deutschkonservative Partei* (DKP; German Conservative Party) and the *Bund der Landwirte* (BL; Agrarian League). Adolf Stoecker, who joined the DKP after the 1881 elections, was able to persuade the conservatives to put an anti-Jewish statement in its Tivoli Program of 1892. The aristocratic BL gave informal support to the anti-Semitic parties, and the *Alldeutscher Verband*'s (ADV; Pan-German League) Heinrich Class (1868–1953) asked the new emperor, Wilhelm II (r. 1888–1918), to weaken Jewish influence domestically. The main reason the anti-Semites failed to develop stronger relations with other parties was that many Germans did not consider the "Jewish question" a serious problem.

What, then, was the impact of political anti-Semitism in the Second Reich on post–World War I Germany? According to Richard Levy, it centered around the "incessant propaganda" campaign that "helped poison German-Jewish relations and promoted an atmosphere of ready tolerance for anti-Semitism which the National Socialists were able to use effectively." The efforts of the political anti-Semites insured the viability of anti-Semitism in Germany. According to Levy, on the eve of World War I, "anti-Jewish sentiment was widespread in German life, although not as overtly a part of national politics as it had been in the 1870's or 1890's."[44]

The viability of anti-Semitism in Germany after the decline of the political anti-Semitic movement was maintained partly through the efforts of a more radical group of anti-Semites, who took control of what was left of the anti-Semitic movement in the Second Reich after 1912. The radical anti-Semites had always condemned the political anti-Semites for their activities, not their ideas. Theodor Fritsch (1852–1933), one of the important ideological bridges between pre– and post–World War I anti-Semitism, had long argued that formal political activity could achieve little against the Jews. This did not mean that the radical anti-Semites failed to see the political potential for anti-Semitism. However, they thought that what Levy called "demogogic antisemitism" had great potential "under the right conditions and with the right leadership."[45] They drew their ideas from Fritsch, Paul Lagarde, Eugen Dühring, Bernhard Förster, Friedrich Lange, and Houston Stewart Chamberlain (1855–1927).

The best-known member of this group was Chamberlain, the member of a prominent British family who married Richard Wagner's daughter, Eva, and became a German citizen in 1916. In 1899, Chamberlain wrote *Foundations of the 19th Century*, which Alfred Rosenberg (1893–1946), the early Nazi party's chief theoretician, called a *kampfbuch* (book of struggle), which helped lay the foundations for Nazism. *Foundations* looked at history through the prism of race and examined earlier developments that had a profound influence on the nineteenth century. Though Chamberlain thought that the Greeks, the Romans, and the Christians had made some contributions to Western history, it was the Germanic peoples who had saved it from total decay and collapse at the beginning of the Middle Ages. The Aryan Germans, Chamberlain argued, represented the best of civilization, but groups such as the Jews and the Slavs were civilization's most destructive forces. Christianity, Chamberlain wrote, was an example of this dichotomy. Christianity's symbolism and rich mythology represented the best of Aryan traditions. Unfortunately, Christianity's negative Jewish components robbed it of its vitality. He concluded that Jesus Christ could not have been Jewish because he was a blond, blue-eyed Nordic from Aryan Galilee. Chamberlain also developed a theory that claimed skull size could determine one's race. By 1914, *Foundations* had sold more than 100,000 copies.

Like Chamberlain, Fritsch was greatly admired by the Nazis. He published scores of anti-Semitic works during his career, including a 1924 edition of the *Protocols of the Elders of Zion*. His principal, most widely read work was the *Handbuch der Judenfrage* (Handbook on the Jewish Question), which had appeared in forty-eight editions by 1943. Adolf Hitler claimed he had read Fritsch thoroughly during his prewar years in Vienna and had drawn many of his anti-Semitic ideas from him. Julius Streicher was particularly influenced by Fritsch's prewar writings. Fritsch ran an anti-Semitic press in Leipzig, and he promoted extreme anti-Semitism in his magazine *Der Hammer: Blätter für deutschen Sinn* (The Hammer: Papers for the German Spirit). He also founded an anti-Semitic organization, the *Reichshammerbund* (Hammer League). Fritsch argued that Jews, in league with Free Masons, Roman Catholics, and Jehovah's Witnesses, were trying to gain control of governments throughout the world. He also published lists of Jews he thought were responsible for many of the major crimes in Germany. Fritsch argued that it was important to teach anti-Semitism in the public schools, and he advocated the use of revolutionary tactics to deal with the "Jewish question" and other problems caused by Jews and socialists. Fritsch opposed Germany's constitutional monarchy and said that it should be replaced with a "constitutional dictator."[46] And though Fritsch's revolutionary ideas seemed extreme in the immediate years before World War I, they gained considerable credibility in the chaotic world of postwar Germany. Fritsch's hatred of Jews, his distrust of conventional political methods and government, and his advocacy of revolutionary tactics to solve Germany's problems found new life after 1918, particularly in Adolf Hitler's infant Nazi movement.

Fritsch became a Nazi after World War I and was one of ninety-six Nazis elected to the Reichstag in 1924. Though he had misgivings about Hitler, he was revered by the Nazis for his ideas and as an *Alte Kämpfer* (Old Fighter), someone who had joined the party before Hitler's accession to power in 1933. In 1934, a member of the SA wrote these lines:

> After the war, I became very much interested in politics, and eagerly studied newspapers of all political shadings. In 1920 for the first time I read in a right-wing newspaper an advertisement for an antisemitic periodical and became a subscriber of the *Hammer* of Theodor Fritsch. With the help of this periodical, I got to know the devastating influence of the Jews on people, state and economy. I must admit today that this periodical was for me really the bridge to the great movement of Adolf Hitler.[47]

Austria-Hungary

Any study of the historical roots of the Holocaust must explore the evolution of anti-Semitism in Austria not only because it was the homeland of Adolf Hitler but also because of the important role Austrians played in the Nazi movement and the Holocaust. The Austrian-German world of Hitler's youth and early adulthood was one of uncertainty and resentment over the loss of German influence in a once great Habsburg Empire. The revolutions of 1848–1849 had underscored the serious problems of this large multiethnic empire, and the Austrian humiliation in the Austro-Prussian War of 1866 and the *Ausgleich* the following year, confirmed these weaknesses, at least in the eyes of Austrian German nationalists. They created a series of movements that looked for ways to revive Austria's lost influence and national pride. One of the most important movements to emerge was Pan-Germanism. The Pan-Germanists looked at the new German state as a role model for reviving Austrian German influence in a Habsburg empire that was principally non-German. By 1910, Germans only made up 23 percent of the Austrian empire;

Hungarians and various Slavic groups made up the rest of the population.

Georg Ritter von Schönerer (1842–1921), founded the Austrian Pan-German movement in the early 1880s. Otto von Bismarck was one of Schönerer's idols and Schönerer argued for Austrian *Anschluß* (union) with Bismarck's Germany. Schönerer thought that Germany's Hohenzollern family, not the Austrian Habsburgs, was the German people's legitimate dynasty. Schönerer declared in his *Unverfälschte Deutsche Worte* (Undiluted German Words) that Jews could not have prominent roles in his new movement. He adopted many of Richard Wagner's anti-Semitic ideas and used his music to stir crowds at his Pan-German rallies. Schönerer, who often quoted from Eugen Dührung's *Die Judefrage*, made racial anti-Semitism one of the principal ideas of the Pan-German movement.

He argued that a strong link existed between the empire's multiethnic character and its Jewish population. Schönerer glorified the virtues of the German *Volk* and argued that Jews and Germans should not assimilate. He said that Jews were totally unrelated to the German Aryans, and he thought a war against the Jews was an integral part of true Germanic nationalism. Such a campaign, Schönerer insisted, was the principal way to promote true *volkstümlich* (national convictions), which he thought should be the primary goal of the Pan-German nationalists. Germans who supported the Jews betrayed the German *Volk*. Schönerer saw this war against the Jews as a struggle not only against the Jews themselves but against Jewish liberalism and Jewish control of the press and the economy. Schönerer called the Jew "the sucking vampire" who "knocks at the narrow-windowed house of the German farmer and craftsman."[48]

Politically, Schönerer's Pan-German Party reached its peak in the election of 1887, when six Pan-Germans were elected to the *Reichsrat,* or lower house of the Austrian parliament. Some of the party's strongest support came from university students, who saw Jews as a threat to their professional wellbeing. In 1880, about 22 percent of the law school students and 38 percent of the medical students at the University of Vienna were Jewish. The idea of *Anschluß* with Germany became particularly popular among Austrian university students during this period.

In 1882, Schönerer joined other German nationalists, such as Dr. Viktor Adler (1852–1918) and Dr. Karl Lueger, in creating the Linz Program. The program called for the reorganization of the Austrian Empire to revive the power and influence of its German population. The Linz Program also advocated a number of social reforms. Three years later, Schönerer added the Aryan Clause to the Linz Program because he thought it was important to remove Jews from all areas of influence in Austrian life. Adler and other Pan-German nationalists with Jewish ancestry broke with Schönerer over this issue. From Schönerer's perspective, Jews were not true Germans. Schönerer enjoyed his greatest successes in the 1880s and held a seat in parliament, but his career declined after his arrest for assault in 1888.

His influence, though, remained strong, particularly for the young Adolf Hitler, who considered Schönerer one of his early political and ideological role models. August Kubizek, Hitler's boyhood friend, said that Germany's future dictator was a "convinced follower of Schönerer."[49] According to Brigitte Harmann, Hitler deeply admired Schönerer's persistent and "faithful adherence to his principles, and immutable love for the 'German people.'"[50] Harmann argued that Hitler's respect for Schönerer was so deep that he "not only adopted Schönerer's political principles but virtually copied them."[51] Hitler adopted Schönerer's use of the title "Führer" and his "Heil" greeting. But Hitler was also critical of some of Schönerer's ideas, particularly his struggles against non-Jewish groups. For Hitler,

there was only one enemy—the Jews. In 1938, Hitler helped publish a biography on Schönerer, and a year later he had Munich's Habsburg Square renamed Schönerer Square. In a 1942 exhibit celebrating Schönerer's birthday, the Nazis hung a quote from Hitler's idol prominently above the exhibit: "Pan-Germany is and has been my dream; and I am concluding with a *Heil* to the Bismarck of the future, the savior of the Germans and the shaper of Pan-Germany."[52]

Another important role model for Hitler was Karl Lueger (1844–1910), the anti-Semitic mayor of Vienna. Like Hitler, Lueger paid homage to Schönerer, whom he admired politically. But Hitler also noted the considerable differences between the two men. He admired Schönerer for his ideas and Lueger for his considerable political and people skills. According to Harmann, Schönerer's departure from politics helped Lueger's political rise. A master politician, Lueger differed from Schönerer in many ways. Schönerer was staunchly anti–Roman Catholic and anti-Habsburg, whereas Lueger talked of the "rechristianization" of Roman Catholic Habsburg Austria. Lueger's followers were usually religious anti-Semites, whereas Schönerer's Pan-Germans were racial anti-Semites. Lueger was involved in several anti-Semitic movements, and in 1893 he helped found Austria's *Christlichsoziale Partei* (CSP; Christian Socialist Party), the forerunner of today's conservative *Österreichische Volkspartei* (OVP; Austrian People's Party). One of the central themes of Lueger's party was the evil of modern capitalism and the Jews. To many early Christian Socialists, the two were synonymous. Given Lueger's prominence in Austrian politics, some have tried to depict Lueger as a "respectable anti-Semite." Richard S. Geehr, the editor of Lueger's private papers, would have none of this. Lueger's anti-Semitism, he argued, "betrayed criminal irresponsibility" because of the powerful role he played in Viennese politics as mayor from 1897–1910. He made Austrian anti-Semitism "an institution in its own right" and was "an authentic, if unwilling, progenitor of fascism."[53]

One of Lueger's followers, Baron Karol von Vogelsang (1818–1890), said that the decline of contemporary Austrian Christian values had prepared the way for dominant Jewish capitalism as well as Jewish materialism and liberalism. Vogelsang thought that the only way to stop the "Judaization" of Austrian society was to revive Austrian Roman Catholicism. In 1889, Lueger and Vogelsang helped form the *Vereinigte Christen* (VC; United Christians), which Lueger later transformed in his Christian Social Party. The VC's 1889 manifesto called for Jews to be excluded from law, medicine, and other professions. It also said that Jews should not be allowed to teach in Christian schools, become judges, or serve in the civil service. It also demanded that restrictions be placed on Jewish immigration into Austria. During the early stages of his political career, Lueger linked the Jewish question to liberalism and big business. Robert Wistrich and Brigitte Harmann both agree that anti-Semitism was the cement that bound together the disparate socioeconomic groups that supported Lueger's new Christian Socialist movement. For the Christian Socialists, the struggle against the Jews was a struggle for survival. In 1895, the Christian Socialists and the Pan-Germans gained control of the Vienna city government with Lueger as mayor. However, Emperor Franz Josef refused to let him take office, fearful of his anti-Semitism and demagoguery. He did permit Leuger to assume office in 1897 after being assured that his administration would be "constructive and not discriminatory."[54]

Lueger tempered some of his more extreme anti-Semitic positions in his bid to become mayor. Later, his staunchest political enemies, the Social Democrats, criticized him for having prominent Jewish friends. Lueger was a religious anti-Semite who would befriend baptized Jews as long as they were not liberals or Marxists. He explained this by saying: "I will decide who is a Jew."[55] Questions about Lueger's commitment to anti-Semitism do not alter the fact that he and his party gave anti-Semitism important respectability in Viennese society and beyond. His death in 1910 stunned the Viennese. One of the people watching as Lueger's funeral cortège moved slowly through the capital was Adolf Hitler:

> When the mighty funeral procession bore the dead mayor from the City Hall toward the Ring, I was among the hundred of thousands looking on at the tragic spectacle. I was profoundly moved and my feelings told me that the work, even of this man, was bound to be in vain, owing to the fatal destiny which would inevitably lead this state to destruction. If Dr. Karl Lueger had lived in Germany, he would have ranked among the great minds of our people; that he lived and worked in this impossible state was the misfortune of his work and himself.[56]

Hitler, who lived in Vienna from 1907 to 1913, initially supported the Pan-Germans, though he later drifted into Christian Socialism. Yet Hitler was critical of Lueger's movement. He was uncomfortable with Lueger's ties to the Roman Catholic Church and his unwillingness to embrace racial anti-Semitism and anti-Slavism. A Lueger cult developed in Austria after Hitler conquered it in 1938; and in 1943, Joseph Goebbels made the film *1910* to honor Lueger.

French Anti-Semitism and the Dreyfus Affair

Like Germany and Austria, France suffered from a distinct political, cultural, and economic malaise in the last third of the nineteenth century. It was in this atmosphere of instability and uncertainty that racial anti-Semitism took root in France. Racist justifications for hating Jews now replaced religious ones. In France, anti-Semitism was strong among leftists, who associated Jews with bourgeoisie capitalism. Pierre Joseph Proudhon (1809–1865), a prominent French revolutionary theorist, called the Jews the enemies of the human race. Alphonse Toussenel (1803–1885), the father of modern French anti-Semitism, was a follower of the utopian socialist François Charles Fourier (1772–1837). In 1844, Toussenel published a virulent anti-Semitic work titled *Les Juifs, rois de l'epoque, histoire de la féodolité financière* (The Jews, Kings of the Epoch, History of Financial Feudalism). He blamed France's mid-century problems on "usurious Jewry." Paul Mendes-Flohr and Jehuda Reinharz consider Toussenel was one of the pioneers of "a literature that linked the medieval image of the Jew as a usurer to the popular contempt for the financier and banker in the age of nascent capitalism."[57] Toussenel, an ornithologist and naturalist, used his naturalist works to criticize Jews, whom he considered "vultures." He claimed that the Rothchilds, a prominent Jewish banking family, were destroying the French countryside by building railroads. Such attitudes helped sustain the climate of anti-Semitism in France in the second half of the nineteenth century.

The works of Proudhon and Toussenel (*Les Juifs* was republished in 1886 and 1888) and others provided the intellectual underpinnings for the racial anti-Semitism that developed in France in the 1870s and afterwards. It was sustained not only by new anti-Semitic ideas from abroad but also by the political, economic, and social problems in France after its losses in the Franco-Prussian War. The collapse of Napoleon III's Second Empire unleashed political tensions that lasted for decades. The bloody Paris Commune uprisings in 1871 created conflicts between leftists, monarchists, and conservatives, and political instability remained a problem for years. Monarchists continued to promote their cause, and in the 1880s and 1890s, thousands of socialist strikes swept the country to protest France's economic problems. The Republican centrists who governed France antagonized conservatives by weakening the Roman Catholic Church's influence in politics and education. Public discontent with the government peaked in 1889 when a popular general, Georges Boulanger (1837–1891), briefly considered a coup d'état. According to Michael Burns, the Boulanger phenomenon helped introduce a new era of "militant nationalism" in France. René Rémond argued that it also helped transform the French Right in the years before the Dreyfus affair. Zeev Sternhell considered this era an initial stage in the development of French fascism.

This, combined with the collapse of the Union Générale (the Roman Catholic banking house) in 1882 and the country's general economic problems, prompted Roman Catholic–sponsored attacks against Jews. The foremost French anti-Semite at the time was Édouard Drumont (1844–1917), who was deeply influenced by the works of Toussenel. Drumont published his seminal work, *La France Juive* (Jewish France), in 1886. It quickly sold more than 100,000 copies and became the most widely read book in France. Drumont contrasted the Gallic Christian Aryan with the ugly, criminally motivated, conniving Jew. Jewish cunning, Drumont claimed, had "subjugated" French Aryans. He saw the impoverishment of the French worker and the peasant as the work of wealthy French industrialists and bankers. He claimed that Jews owned half the wealth in France. Drumont wanted an Office of Confiscated Jewish Wealth to be created so that Jewish property could be seized. This, Drumont wrote, quoting the medieval cleric Pierre the Venerable of Cluny, would "[l]et the wealth of the Jews even against their will, serve the Christian people."[58]

In 1892, Drumont began to publish *La Libre Parole* (The Free Word), a daily newspaper that blended his hatred of Jews with concerns about the poor and condemnation of modern capitalism. But it was *La Croix* (The Cross), published by the Assumptionists (the Augustinian Fathers of the Assumption), that drew the most readers. It proudly claimed to be "the most anti-Jewish newspaper in France, the one that bears Christ, the sign of horror for all Jews."[59] Both newspapers argued that all of France's troubles could be laid at the feet of the Jews.

Drumont and other French anti-Semites fed off the general public discontent over what Eugen Weber called France's "endless crisis" in the 1880s and 1890s. According to Susan Zucotti, a series of "political, social, and religious insecurities" created an environment that caused individuals across the political and social spectrum to look for scapegoats.[60] The fact that many French Jews came from Alsace, which, with Lorraine, had been lost to Germany in 1871, and spoke French with German accents, only intensified French hatred towards them. Over time, this anti-Semitic atmosphere seemed to diminish, but worsened after the outbreak of a corruption scandal in the early 1890s over French construction of the Panama Canal. *La Libre Parole* claimed that two Jews, Cornelius Herz and Baron Jacques de Reinach, were behind the scandal. Though both men were involved in the scandal, they did not cause it. Drumont, though, saw it as an opportunity to promote his anti-Semitic ideas. He argued that France's Jews, in league with Germany, England, and the United States, sought "to frustrate, weaken and isolate Catholic France." For Drumont, "the Jews were the enemy within, working to ruin France, hand in hand with the enemy outside."[61] A year later, the Dreyfus scandal broke out.

Known as *l'Affaire*, the scandal resulted from false accusations that a Jewish army officer, Captain Alfred Dreyfus (1859–1935), was spying for the Germans. Though the military had insufficient evidence for an indictment, Dreyfus, an Alsatian Jew, was court

martialed in 1894. In early 1895, Dreyfus was publicly degraded in a formal military ceremony and then sentenced to life imprisonment in France's infamous Devil's Island prison colony off the northern coast of French Guyana. Drumont, who had earlier attacked Jewish military officers in his newspaper, played a major role in whipping up public opinion against Dreyfus. Since the spying continued after Dreyfus's arrest, the head of French counterintelligence, Colonel Georges Picquart (1854–1914), discovered evidence that led him to suspect that another officer, Major Walsin-Esterhazy (1847–1923), was the spy. Colonel Picquart tried unsuccessfully to convince his superiors to reopen the Dreyfus case. When he persisted, he was transferred to remote posts in France and North Africa.

However, Picquart's suspicions were leaked to the press, and many called for a new trial. The country's right-wing press countered with reports of an international Jewish conspiracy to take control of the world. One Roman Catholic newspaper argued that the real issue was not whether Dreyfus was guilty or innocent but whether Jews and other non-Christians secretly ruled France. The French military court-martialed Major Esterhazy in 1898 and found him innocent of all charges. He left the court room after the two-day trial to shouts of "Death to the Jews" and "Long live France."[62] Esterhazy, who later admitted that he was a German spy, fled to England, where he lived for the rest of his life.

Several days after the trial, novelist Émile Zola (1840–1902), who had already published a series of articles critical of the anti-Semitism surrounding the Dreyfus case, sent a letter to the French president, François Faure (1841–1899), which the newspaper *L'Aurore* (The Dawn) published as "*J'accuse* (I accuse)" on January 13, 1898. Zola said the country's military leadership had withheld evidence in the trial that would have exonerated Dreyfus. He also noted that the military

In der Affaire Dreyfus

wird so lange weiter **enthüllt**, bis sich Juda **bis auf die Knochen** blamirt hat.

208. Kikeriki. Wien

Anti-Semitic caricature from the Viennese magazine *Kikeriki*. The text reads, "In the Dreyfus Affair, the more that is exposed, the more Judah is embarrassed." Caricature published in Eduard Fuchs, "Die Juden in der Karikatur: ein Beitrag zur Kulturgeschichte." Albert Langen, 1921. USHMM Photo No. 06333.

had acquitted Esterhazy even though they knew he was guilty. Zola's letter sparked anti-Semitic demonstrations throughout France. Thousands of people marched in protest and called for the "death of Jews." Some of the mobs destroyed Jewish storefront windows and tried to break into synagogues and Jewish homes. During the next year, France saw a wave of anti-Semitic violence and protests. At the end of 1898, *La Libre Parole* asked for contributions to help the widow of Major Hubert-Joseph, who had committed suicide after authorities learned he had forged documents in Dreyfus's trial dossier. Along with thousands of contributions, there were letters that called for the "roasting, hanging, gassing, vivisection, and massacre of Jews." Some contributors also referred to Jews as "kikes, pimps, lice, plagues, cancers, and filthy beings."[63]

Zola was soon arrested and tried for defamation. After a day-long trial, Zola and his codefendant, *L'Aurore*'s managing editor, Alexandre Bernard Perrenx, were convicted, fined, and sentenced to prison terms (one year for Zola and four months for Perrenx). As the two left the courtroom, they heard the crowd outside shouting "Death to the Jews! Long live the Army."[64] An appeals court quickly overturned the convictions. The army, though, decided to file a slander complaint against Zola and Perrenx, and both were retried and convicted in the summer of 1898. Zola fled to England, but returned to France in 1899 and continued his defense of Dreyfus. In 1902, just before his mysterious death, Zola finished *Vérité,* a novel that attacked French anti-Semitism and the Roman Catholic clergy for its role in helping spread it.

Dreyfus was retried in August 1899 after forgeries were discovered in his file. Yet, despite overwhelming evidence of his innocence, he was found guilty and resentenced to ten years in prison. President Émile Loubet (1838–1929) pardoned Dreyfus, and in 1906, a civilian court of appeals exonerated him. He was restored to full military rank and re-

ceived the Cross of the Legion of Honor. He retired from the army as a major, but returned to active duty in World War I as a lieutenant colonel.

The Dreyfus scandal dealt French anti-Semitism a severe, though not deadly blow. Publicly, it would be decades before anti-Semitism became a public force again in France. Charles Maurras (1868–1952), who founded the anti-Semitic *Action Française* in 1898, admitted that French anti-Semitism was driven partially by political opportunism. Both the Left and the Right used it in the late nineteenth century "to attract the disaffected masses and galvanize them against the common enemy, the liberal state."[65] Yet the most important effect of the Dreyfus scandal was the impact it had on conditioning "the responses of many French people who had never met a Jew and would have been astonished to be labeled antisemitic."[66] Decades after the end of the Dreyfus affair, there remained "a reservoir of antipathy to Jews in France, often stagnant and scarcely visible." It would take the crises of the 1930s to transform these vague feelings into viable political action.[67]

Russia

Nineteenth-century French anti-Semitism was driven partially by new racial ideas about Jews, but attitudes towards Jews in Russia continued to be centered on traditional Christian anti-Jewish prejudices. There were few Jews in Russia before the reign of Catherine II (the Great). Russian tsars such as Ivan IV (the Terrible) (r. 1547–1584) and Alexis (r.1645–1676) forbade Jews from living in Russia. Alexis' son, Peter I (the Great) (r. 1684/96–1725), explained that if he permitted Jews to live in his kingdom they would suffer from the animosity of the Russian people. All this changed with the Partitions of Poland (1772, 1793, 1795). Orchestrated by Russia, Austria, and Prussia, the partitions erased Poland from the map of Europe. Russia acquired much of Poland and, by 1795, had a Jewish population of 1 million. With further territorial acquisitions during the next twenty-five years, Russia had a Jewish population of 1.5 million, the largest in the world. This figure would remain stable until 1881.

The Jews of Poland and Lithuania

The nucleus of this large Jewish population initially came not from Russia but from Poland. Jews first entered Poland in the Middle Ages to escape persecution during the Crusades. In 1264, Boleslaw the Pious (r. 1221–1279), the prince of Kraków, issued the Statute of Kalisz, which granted Poland's Jews extensive religious, cultural, community, and economic freedoms not found in other parts of Europe. Subsequent Polish rulers reaffirmed the statute during the next three centuries. There were periodic efforts to repeal Jewish privileges, and Jews in Kraków and Warsaw were periodically mistreated. Polish Jews were usually treated as second-class citizens, though they were better off than Jews in other parts of Europe. The Jews in Lithuania, which joined with Poland in 1569 to become the Union of Poland-Lithuania, fared better than their Polish counterparts.

The sixteenth century is known as Poland's Golden Age, and it marked the beginning of a similar era in Polish-Jewish history. By 1578, 100,000 Jews lived in Poland-Lithuania, a figure that tripled during the next century. Though Poland's Jews made up only from 3 to 5 percent of the total population, they made up from 10 to 20 percent of the population in some Polish cities. They also became an important force in the economy, which created some problems with the local population.

In 1648, Cossacks butchered from 100,000 to 300,000 Jews during the Chmielnicki rebellion (1648–1654). It began in 1648 in response to Cossack and Ukrainian frustration about the expansionistic policies of the Polish crown and nobility. Very often, absentee Roman Catholic landlords used Jewish agents to collect oppressive feudal dues and taxes from the Orthodox Cossacks and Ukrainian peasants. Jews also rented small businesses from the same landlords. According to a Cossack folk song, "The Ukrainian Cossack, the hero bold, rides past the inn, but the Jew takes hold and will not let go. 'Rest, my Cossack, my Cossack come in, or how can I pay my master, the Pole, his rent?' And the Cossack loses his shining armor to him."[68]

Led by their *hetman* (leader), Bohdan Chmelnicki (1595–1657), Cossack units ravaged Ukraine's extensive Jewish settlements.

The Cossacks stripped the skin off one man and threw his flesh to the dogs. Others were buried alive. They stabbed infants in the arms of their mothers, and tore many to pieces like fish. Sometimes heaps of Jewish children were thrown into the water to improve fords. The [Crimean] Tatars [Cossack allies], for their part, made prisoners of the Jews; but they, too, raped women before the eyes of their husbands and took away the most beautiful for slaves and concubines. The Cossacks everywhere behaved in no less cruel a fashion toward the Poles, especially the priests.[69]

The rebellion ended after Russia stepped in to help the Cossacks. This marked the beginning of Russia's absorption of Ukraine, which was completed after the defeat of Poland-Lithuania in 1667. Poland-Lithuania's Jewish communities were devastated by these conflicts and many Jews fled westward, never to return. Though the region's Jews recovered demographically, the two decades of conflict had robbed these communities of their vitality. Poland-Lithuania's Jewish communities became increasingly fractionalized and affected by new messianic religious movements.

The most enduring of these movements centered around the Ba'al Shem Tov (Master of the Good Name), or, as he is known to his followers, the Besht. Born Israel ben Eliezer (1698/1700–1761), the Besht founded one of modern Judaism's most dynamic sects, Hasidism. The Besht, drawing partly on the mystical doctrines of *Kabbalah,* wanted to spread the joy and dynamism of Judaism and take it out of its scholarly cocoon. He taught his followers to love God, Israel, and Torah. He emphasized the joy of belief and worship as well as the importance of prayer and a moral life. The Besht's ideas quickly spread throughout Poland-Lithuania because of the simplicity of his teachings.

The powerful *Gaon* of Vilna (Vilnius, Wilno), Elijah ben Solomon (1720–1797), challenged Hasidism's remarkable successes in Poland, particularly when the movement tried to move into Lithuania. Vilna, Lithuania's historic capital, had become an important Jewish legal and educational center by the seventeenth century. The *Gaon,* a scholarly, ascetic man, taught that study of Torah was core to man's soul. He insisted on strict adherence to Jewish law and practice. The *Gaon* became a bitter opponent of Hasidism because he thought it was an undisciplined movement that trampled on rabbinic teachings. He also feared that Hasidism would divide the Jewish people. In the midst of all of this, Poland-Lithuania's Jewish population continued to grow. There were 750,000 Jews in the country (550,000 in Poland, 200,000 in Lithuania) when Catherine the Great came to power in 1762. Little did Poland-Lithuania's Jews know that by the end of the century, they would be living in the vast Russian Empire.

The Jews in Postpartition Russia

Catherine II, the Great (r. 1762–1796) oversaw Russia's acquisition of much of Poland-Lithuania between 1772 and 1795. A German and a child of the Enlightenment, Catherine the Great accepted some of the more tolerant Enlightenment attitudes towards Jews. Soon after she came to power, Catherine gave some thought to allowing Jews to settle in Russia,

though she quickly backed away from this idea when she realized there was strong public and religious opposition to such a move. After the First Partition of Poland in 1772, the empress decided to integrate all her new Polish-Lithuanian subjects directly into the larger Russian population without legal or ethnic distinction. However, before the Second Partition in 1793, various Moscow businessmen petitioned the empress to place restrictions on new Jewish businessmen in the city. Catherine responded by creating what later became known as the *Cherta postoiannoi evreeskoi osledosti* (Pale of Permanent Jewish Settlement), a large swath of Russian territory on Russia's western borders that stretched from the Baltic to the Black Sea. The Jewish population in the ever-expanding Pale, which came to include parts of modern-day Latvia, Lithuania, Belarus, Poland, Moldova, and Ukraine, grew from 1.5 million in 1825 to almost 5 million by 1897. Overall, Jews, who lived primarily in the Pale's urban areas and *shtetl*s, or small towns, never made up more than 11.6 percent of the Pale's population. Restrictive tsarist policies, driven by the idea that Jews were immoral and culturally decadent exploiters, kept most Jews in the Pale impoverished.

Jewish life and culture was vibrant in the Pale. In 1804, a government *ukaz* (decree), "*Polozhenie dlia evreev*" (The Status of Jews), criticized the *kahal* (Jewish community governance system) and the network of rabbis that dominated Russia's religious communities. The *ukaz* said that the Pale's Jews would remain backward and poor as long as they refused to embrace Russian culture, education, and Orthodox Christianity. Until that time, the Russian state felt justified in maintaining policies designed to keep Jews from harming the empire's Orthodox Christians. The statute did, though, allow Jews to buy uncultivated land and lease it for farming. It also removed the double taxation standard for those who did not farm. Regardless, most

The Pale of Jewish Settlement.

Jews in the Pale eked out a living as tailors, cobblers, petty tradesmen, and inn keepers. And though most Jews in the Pale were poor, the diversity of their economic activity raised general standards of living above that in other parts of the empire. From the end of the Napoleonic Wars until 1881, tsarist policies towards Jews wavered between greater restrictions on their movement and autonomy and modest periods of renewed rights. Religious and social anti-Jewish prejudice remained strong throughout this period.

There was a hint of change during the reign of Alexander II (r. 1855–1881), the Tsar Liberator, who emancipated Russia's serfs in 1861. He initiated important government, economic, and social reforms that modestly helped improve the status of Jews. Jews were now subject to the normal military draft and religious authorities became less aggressive in their efforts to convert Jews to Russian Orthodox Christianity, though assimilation remained an important part of government Jewish policy. Residency requirements were eased in some cities, and, though still not emancipated, Jews began to play a more important role in Russian business, society, and culture.

As talk of Jewish emancipation spread, an upsurge in virulent anti-Jewish sentiment surfaced, particularly after the failed Polish rebellion of 1863. Months before, the Jews in Congress Poland, the semi-autonomous, Russian-dominated kingdom in the Warsaw-Lublin area, had been emancipated. After the tsar crushed the rebellion, he outlawed the official use of Polish and did away with what little autonomy remained in Congress Poland. This action led to an upsurge of anti-Russian and anti-Jewish sentiment there, even though some Jews had fought side-by-side with the Poles in 1863 and had identified closely with Polish national aspirations. Elsewhere, the 1863 Polish rebellion brought a wave of Russian nationalism.

In this atmosphere there developed a new, more vicious strain of anti-Jewish feeling that was fueled by several writers, particularly Iakov Brafman (1825–1879), a Jew who had converted to Russian Orthodoxy, and Ippolit Liutostanskii (1835–1915), a defrocked Roman Catholic priest. Brafman's most important work was *Kniga Kagal* (The Book of the Kahal), which claimed that Russian *kahals* had joined other Jewish community organizations worldwide to create a Talmudic Republic seeking the "subjugation of the Christian world to Jewish hegemony and exploitation."[70]

Brafman's works stimulated an outpouring of anti-Jewish articles and books in the 1860s and 1870s that claimed Jews took advantage of poor Christians. One of Russia's greatest writers, Fyodor Dostoevsky (1821–1881), thought that Jews wanted to "exterminate or enslave the non-Jewish populations of the world."[71] Konstantine P. Pobedonostsev (1827–1907), an influential minister in the governments of Alexander III (r. 1880–1894) and Nicholas II (r. 1894–1917), wrote Dostoevsky:

What you write about the Yids is completely just. They have engrossed everything, they have undermined everything, but the spirit of the century supports them. They are at the root of

the revolutionary socialist movement and of regicide, they own the periodical press, they have in their hands the financial markets, the people as a whole fall into financial slavery to them; they even control the principles of contemporary science and strive to place it outside of Christianity. And on top of all that—whenever anyone raises a question about them a shower of voices rises in favor of the Jews in the name of civilization and tolerance, of indifference to faith. Among the Roumanians and Serbs [who, like the Russians, were Orthodox Christians], and among us as well, no one dares to say a word about the simple fact that the Jews have won ownership of everything. Even our press is becoming Jewish.[72]

In 1876, Ippolit Liutostanskii published *Ob upotreblenii evreiami kristianskoi krovi dlia religioznykh tseli* (Concerning the Use of Christian Blood by the Jews), which revived the "blood libel" charge against the Jews. Grand Prince Alexander Alexandrovich, who was soon to become Tsar Alexander III, sent Liutostanskii a note congratulating him for his work. Liutostanskii followed this up with another inflammatory work, *Talmud I Evrei* (The *Talmud* and the Jew). Jewish critics noted that Liutostanskii drew most of his material from Western European anti-Semites and knew little about Jews or Judaism. Regardless, Luitostanskii's works, along with those of Brafman, formed the nucleus of a growing body of anti-Jewish and anti-Semitic works in Russia that helped transform official and public attitudes towards Jews through the end of the tsarist era. Their works also helped lay the groundwork for the violent anti-Semitic pogroms that took place after the assassination of Alexander II on March 1, 1881.

Several days after the assassination, several newspapers accused Jews of the tsar's murder, even though only one Jew, Gesya Gelfman (1852/55–1882), was among the conspirators. What followed were a series of pogroms (Russian, *pogromit*, to break or to smash), or anti-Jewish riots, that resulted in the widespread destruction of Jewish property and homes. Local police and officials were deliberately slow to respond to the mass violence. A shocked Alexander III (r. 1881–1894) ordered an investigation, which officials described as peasant reactions to Jewish exploitation. In May 1882, the government enacted a series of May Laws that prevented Jews from settling in towns and villages. Three years later, the government adopted a *numerus clausus* law that limited the number of Jewish students who could attend schools in the Pale. Other restrictions soon followed that limited Jewish professional development.

The pogroms stunned Russia's Jewish community. Over the next few decades, Russia's Jews felt increasingly trapped in a country troubled by serious economic and social problems. Moreover, Alexander III's successor, Nicholas II (r. 1894–1917), expanded his father's anti-Jewish policies. Soon after he came to power, Nicholas placed new restrictions on Jewish professional and educational opportunities and did little to stop new pogroms in the early years of the twentieth century.

The open involvement of the police and military in the pogroms was particularly troubling. Oddly enough, Nicholas II and his officials blamed the Jews for the pogroms. According to Shlomo Lambroza, the official view was that Russia's Jews were a parisitic element in the Russian Empire who lived off the hard-earned wages of the *narod* (people) and secretly conspired with revolutionary cadres to overthrow the Romanov dynasty. Such a perspective, of course, was unfounded. Jews throughout the Pale were as poor as, or poorer, than their Russian counterparts. And few Russian Jews were involved in revolutionary activities. The publication of more than 14 million copies of 2,837 anti-Semitic books and pamphlets in Russian between 1905 and 1916 kept the anti-Semitic violence alive during this period. Nicholas II supposedly contributed more than 12 million rubles ($6.2 million) to this effort.

The Jewish reaction to the violence was multifaceted. From 1881 to 1914, almost two million Jews fled Russia, about three quarters of them settling in the United States. Organizations such as Theodor Herzl's Zionist Organization (today, World Zionist Organization) encouraged migration and promoted the restoration of a Jewish homeland in Palestine. Other groups such as the *Algemeyner Yidisher Arbeter Bund in Lite, Polyn un Rusland* (General Jewish Labor Union of Lithuania, Poland, and Russia), or Jewish Bund, became involved in labor organization and Jewish political activity. These developments emboldened many Jews to become more aggressive in their response to the violence and discrimination. According to Alexander Orbach, these developments helped Jewish liberals and workers forge a new "Jewish national identity."[73]

Perhaps nothing better symbolized official attitudes towards Russia's Jews than the trial of Mendel Beilis (1874–1934) in 1913 for blood libel murder. The trial, which took place in the fall of 1913, drew international attention. The prosecution used fabricated evidence to claim that Beilis had murdered a thirteen-year-old school boy, Andriusha Yushchinskii, and had mixed his blood with unleavened Passover bread. The police, though, discovered that thieves had murdered Yushchinskii, not Beilis. The mastermind behind the trial was Ivan Shcheglovitov (1861–1918), Nicholas II's minister of justice. A virulent anti-Semite, Shcheglovitov used the trial to curry favor with the tsar, who also hated Jews. The prosecution spent two years trying to find evidence against Beilis and to prove that Russia's Jews practiced blood libel. By the time the trial began, Shcheglovitov and most officials involved in the case knew that Beilis was innocent. Consequently, Shcheglovitov did everything possible to rig the proceedings. Regardless, the hand-selected jury found Beilis innocent. Afterwards, the judge, who supported the government's case, asked the jury to consider the claim that Yushchinskii's body was found on the grounds of the Jewish-owned brick yard where Beilis worked and had lost "five glasses of blood." The majority of the jurors voted to support this contention, which allowed Russia's anti-Semites to claim that the jury had proved that a blood libel murder had indeed taken place, even if the court could not determine who had committed the crime.

The Protocols of the Elders of Zion

It was in this environment that one of the most virulent anti-Semitic documents ever written surfaced: *Protokoly sionskikh mydretsov (The Protocols of the Elders of Zion)*. Adolf Hitler considered the protocols, a fictitious Jewish blueprint for world domination, essential in proving his claim that Jews were out to control the world. This, from Hitler's perspective, was the ultimate Jewish crime. He wrote that "it is completely indifferent from what Jewish brain these disclosures originate; the important thing is that with positively terrifying certainty they reveal the nature and activity of the Jewish people and expose their inner contexts as well as their ultimate final aims."[74]

The author of the *Protocols* was Piotr Rachkovskii, the head of the tsarist secret police, the *Okhrana*, in Europe. Inspired by Édouard Drumont's *La France Juive*, Rachkovskii (1853–1910), working with a team of forgers, wrote the *Protocols* to discredit Russian revolutionaries in Europe and "to incite Russians against Jews."[75] Sergei Witte (1849–1915), Nicholas II's minister of finance and chair of the tsar's Council of Ministers, was worried that, if widely distributed, the *Protocols* might further incite anti-Semites in Russia; he therefore asked a well-known attorney, Henry Sliosberg, to determine whether the document was authentic. Sliosberg concluded that the *Protocols* were a "crude forgery" that "was virtually ignored by both official and aristocratic Russian society."[76]

This did little to stop the serialized publication of the *Protocols* in Pavel Khrushevan's

(1860–1909) anti-Semitic newspaper, *Znamya* (The Banner) in 1903. Coming on the heels of a terrible pogrom in Kishnev, Bessarabia, Khrushevan also published another fictitious document, "The Rabbi's Speech," that had been used to stir up the anti-Semites on the eve of the Kishinev pogrom. Two years later, in the midst of the 1905 revolution, the tsar's Censorship Committee approved the publication of the *Protocols* as an addendum to the third edition of Sergei Nilus's *Velikoe v malom* (The Great in the Small).[77] Though the committee members doubted the *Protocol*'s authenticity, they were deeply influenced by the tsar's sister-in-law, Grand Duchess Elizabeth Fyodorovna (1864–1918; St. Elizabeth, Russian Orthodox Church), who pushed to have the *Protocols* published.

Though later editions appeared in Russia, it was not until after World War I that the *Protocols* became widely distributed internationally. In 1920, Ludwig Müller, using the pseudonym Gottfried zur Beek, published the first German edition of the *Protocols, Die Geheimnisse der Weisen von Zion*. During the next thirteen years, it went through thirty-three editions.

Alfred Rosenberg (1893–1946), an early Nazi Party member, party theoretician, and editor of the party newspaper *Völkischer Beobachter* (People's Observer), published the *Protocols* in 1924. This was a seminal work for the Nazis, who found it helped support their claim that the Jews were responsible for all of Germany's problems.

But it was not just Russian and German extremists who were enamored with the *Protocols*. No less a figure than the American industrial giant Henry Ford (1863–1947) was equally moved by the *Protocols*. Ford was convinced that the *Protocols* were authentic and, as early as 1920, began to publish a series of articles on the threat of international Jewry in the *Dearborn Independent*. Ford later had these reprinted in his four-volume *The International Jew*. Ford accepted all the *Protocols*' hateful stereotypes of the Jews, particularly the idea that Jews controlled the world's wealth. He also wrote "that the Bolshevik revolution was a carefully groomed investment on the part of International Jewish Finance."[78] Adolf Hitler, who considered Ford a great man because of his stand against the Jews, agreed with Ford about the threat of Jewish Bolshevism, an important Nazi ideological theme in the 1920s.

The spread of the *Protocols,* particularly in the 1930s, deeply troubled many Jews, and in 1934 they sued the pro-Nazi distributors of the *Protocols* in South Africa and Switzerland. The South African case ended quickly when the court rejected the idea of an international Jewish plot to destroy Christianity. All three defendants in the trial were found guilty, and one was sentenced to a lengthy prison term. The Swiss trial, which addressed the *Protocols* and an anti-Semitic article in the Swiss Nazi newspaper *Der Eidgenossen* (the Confederation), examined four central issues: plagiarism, the authenticity of the *Protocols,* their authorship, and whether they should be considered *Schundliteratur* (obscene or trashy literature). The court explored the full history of the *Protocols* and heard many witnesses who had firsthand knowledge about their origins. In the spring of 1935, Judge Walter Meyer ruled that the *Protocols of the Elders of Zion* were not only a forgery but also obscene literature. He added:

> I hope that a time will come when nobody will understand how in the year 1935 almost a dozen sane and reasonable men would for 14 days torment their brains before a Berne court over the authenticity of these so-called *Protocols,* these *Protocols* which, despite the harm they have caused and may yet cause, are nothing more than ridiculous nonsense.[79]

This did not end the matter because the three defendants in the case appealed the decision. Two years later, a Swiss appeals court overturned Meyer's decision on the grounds that even though the *Protocols* were wrong they could not be considered obscene or pornographic. The appellate court agreed that the authenticity of the *Protocols* had not been proven in the 1935 trial. They concluded their decision by calling the *Protocols* "immoral literature," and they warned that anyone who distributed them in Switzerland would be brought to court for disseminating these crude, "libelous and insulting writings."[80]

The general international condemnation of the *Protocols* evidently concerned Adolf Hitler. In the dark days after the German debacle at Stalingrad in 1943, Joseph Goebbels, Hitler's Reich minister for *Volk* enlightenment, noted that he had recently reread the *Protocols* and considered them as useful "as they were when published for the first time." He referred to the original Swiss court decision and quoted from it. He added that he had discussed the Swiss decision earlier in the day (May 13, 1943) with Hitler, who considered the *Protocols* "genuine." Hitler told Goebbels that he considered Jews to be "parasites" who threatened Western society. There was "no other recourse left for modern nations except to exterminate the Jew." He added that there was "no hope of leading the Jews back into the fold of civilized humanity by exceptional punishments" and that "[t]hey will forever remain Jews just as we are forever members of the Aryan race."[81]

Conclusion

The new influx of Jews into Europe after the Reformation opened new doors of opportunity for them but also created new problems. This was particularly true during the Enlightenment. In many ways, discussions about Europe's Jews became a measure of how willing countries were to support the era's newfound political, economic, and social freedoms. Though a handful of intellectuals proposed full emancipation for Jews, most saw the Jews as a threatening "state within a state" who could enjoy full rights only after they had converted to Christianity and fully assimilated into European society.

Napoleon I (Bonaparte) set the tone for national Jewish policy during his long reign. Though earlier French revolutionaries had grudgingly granted French Jews full citizenship rights, Napoleon, who disliked Jews, sought to curb many of their privileges. A grand social engineer, Napoleon I wanted to destroy traditional Jewish community and religious autonomy and force France's Jews to become Frenchmen first. Though not an advocate of conversion as the path to assimilation, he sought assurances from France's Jewish leadership that their first loyalty was to their nation, and not to their faith. His efforts set the tone for Jewish assimilation policies throughout Europe for the next century.

Jewish emancipation, in league with the upsurge in nationbuilding throughout the nineteenth century, had positive and negative dimensions, particularly when blended with growing urbanization and industrialization throughout Europe. As European societies struggled with the problems associated with these issues, medieval stereotypes concerning Jews surfaced: Jews were accused of controlling Europe's capitalist wealth. Since capitalism was seen by some as the root of nineteenth-century Europe's many problems, Jews once again were cast as scapegoats for the world's ills. Jews came to be viewed as dominating capitalists tied to such leftist movements as liberalism, socialism, and Marxism.

These attitudes were particularly true for Europe's new anti-Semites, a vague group of nationalist racists who blended distorted interpretations of Social Darwinism with age-old prejudices against Jews. Though they usually operated on the political fringe in most European countries, the anti-Semites were able to tap into a growing body of disillusionment throughout Europe that anguished over the loss of traditional Christian rural values in an increasingly complex, impersonal world.

Anti-Semitism was particularly vibrant in Germany, Austria, France, and Russia, where traditional anti-Jewish sentiment blended with anti-Semitic ideas from abroad. The anti-Semitic movements in Germany and Austria were particularly important because they helped create the environment that Adolf Hitler used so successfully in the 1920s and 1930s to develop his Nazi movement. In France, anti-Semitism was used by the Left and the Right to make gains politically. The Dreyfus scandal underscored the degree to which anti-Semites were willing to go to further their political ambitions. In Russia, anti-Jewish prejudice remained a vibrant part of official policy and helped produce the last major blood libel trial in Europe. But, more important, anti-Jewish violence became a watchword of state policy that, in response to international outcries over Russia's violent pogroms, produced the most vile, insidious anti-Semitic work in history prior to Adolf Hitler's *Mein Kampf*, the *Protocols of the Elders of Zion*.

SOURCES FOR FURTHER STUDY AND RESEARCH

Primary Sources

Albert, Phyllis Cohen. *The Modernization of French Jewry: Consistory and Community in the Nineteenth Century*. Hanover, NH: Brandeis University Press and University Press of New England, 1977.

Drumont, Édouard. *La France juive: Essai d'histoire contemporaine*. Paris: Flammarion, 1886.

Fichte, Johann Gottlieb. *Addresses to the German Nation*. Translated by R. F. Jones and G. H. Turnbull. Westport, CT: Greenwood Press, 1979.

———. *Johann Gottlieb Fichte's sämmlitche Werke*. Vol. 4. Berlin: Verlag von Veit und Comp., 1845.

Ford, Henry Sr. *The International Jew*. 4 vols. Boring, OR: 1920.

Galton, Francis. "Eugenics: Its Definition, Scope, and Aims." *American Journal of Sociology* 10, no. 1 (July 1904): 1–21. http://galton.org/essays/1900–1911/galton–1904-amjourn-soc-eugenics-scope-aims.htm.

———. *Memories of My Life*. London: Metheun, 1908.

Geehr, Richard S., ed. and trans. *"I Decide Who Is a Jew": The Papers of Dr. Karl Lueger*. Washington, DC: University Press of America, 1982.

Goebbels, Joseph. *The Goebbels Diaries, 1942–1943.* Edited and translated by Louis P. Lochner. Garden City, NY: Doubleday & Company, 1948.

Herder, Johann Gottfried von. *Reflections on the Philosophy of the History of Mankind.* Chicago: University of Chicago Press, 1968.

Hitler, Adolf. *Mein Kampf.* Translated by Ralph Manheim. New York: Houghton Mifflin, 1943.

d'Holbach, Baron Paul Henri Thiry. *L'espirit du judaïsme, ou examen raisonné de la loi de Moyse, et de son influence sur la religion chrétienne.* London: 1770.

Holborn, Hajo. *A History of Modern Germany, 1648–1840.* Princeton: Princeton University Press, 1982.

Jospe, Eva, ed. *Moses Mendelssohn: Selections from His Writings.* New York: Viking Press, 1975.

Kant, Immanuel. *The Conflict of the Faculties* [Der Streit der Fakultäten]. Introduced and translated by Mary J. Gregor. New York: Abaris Books, 1979.

Kubizek, August. *The Young Hitler I Knew.* Translated by E. V. Anderson. Cambridge, MA: Riverside Press, 1955.

Lessing, Gotthold Ephraim. *Nathan the Wise.* Translated, edited, and with an introduction by Ronald Schechter. Boston: Bedford/St. Martin's Press, 2004.

Levy, Richard S. *Antisemitism in the Modern World: An Anthology of Texts.* Lexington, KY: D. C. Heath, 1991.

Locke, John. *An Essay Concerning Human Understanding.* Abridged and edited with an introduction and notes by Kenneth P. Winkler. Indianapolis: Hackett, 1996.

_____. *Two Treatises of Government and a Letter Concerning Toleration.* Edited by Ian Shapiro. New Haven: Yale University Press, 2003.

Mendelssohn, Moses. *Jerusalem or On Religious Power and Judaism.* Translated by Allan Arkush. Hanover, NH: Brandeis University Press, 1983.

_____. *Philosophical Writings.* Translated and edited by Daniel O. Dahlstrom. Cambridge: Cambridge University Press, 1997.

Mendes-Flohr, Paul, and Jehuda Reinharz. *The Jew in the Modern World: A Documentary History.* 2nd ed. Oxford: Oxford University Press, 1995.

Montesquieu. *The Spirit of Laws.* Edited and with an introduction, notes, and appendices by David Wallace Carrithers, together with an English translation of *An Essay on Causes Affecting Minds and Characters (1736–1743).* Berkeley: University of California Press, 1977.

Ole, Peter Grell, and Roy Porter. *Toleration in Enlightenment Europe.* Cambridge: Cambridge University Press, 2000.

Tama, M. Diogene. *Transactions of the Parisian Sanhedrin or Acts of the Assembly of Israelitish Deputies of France and Italy; Convoked at Paris by an Imperial and Royal Decree, Dated May 30, 1806.* London: Charles Taylor, 1807.

Wagner, Richard. *Judaism in Music* [Das Judenthum in der Musik]. Translated by William Ashton Ellis. http://reactor-core.org/judaism-in-music.html.

Secondary Sources

Albert, Phyllis Cohen. *The Modernization of French Jewry: Consistory and Community in the Nineteenth Century.* Hanover, NH: Brandeis University Press, 1977.

Altmann, Alexander. *Moses Mendelssohn: A Biographical Study.* Tuscallosa: University of Alabama Press, 1973.

Arkush, Allan. *Moses Mendelssohn and the Enlightenment.* Albany: State University of New York Press, 1994.

Baldwin, Neil. *Henry Ford and the Jews: The Mass Production of Hate.* New York: PublicAffairs, 2001.

Baron, Salo W. *The Russian Jew Under Tsars and Soviets.* New York: Schocken Books, 1987.

Ben-Itto, Hadassa. *The Lie That Wouldn't Die: The Protocols of the Elders of Zion.* London: Vallentine Mitchell, 2005.

Ben-Sasson, Haim H. *A History of the Jewish People.* Cambridge: Cambridge University Press, 1976.

Berk, Stephen M. *Year of Crisis, Year of Hope: Russian Jewry and the Pogroms of 1881–1882.* Westport, CT: Greenwood Press, 1985.

Bredin, Jean-Denis. *The Affair: The Case of Alfred Dreyfus.* Translated by Jeffrey Mehlman. New York: George Braziller, 1986.

Brenner, Michael, Vicki Caron, and Uri R. Kaufmann, eds. *Jewish Emancipation Reconsidered: The French and German Models.* London and Tübingen: Leo Baeck Institute and J. C. B. Mohr, 2003.

Burns, Michael. *France and the Dreyfus Affair: A Documentary History.* Boston: Bedford/St. Martin's Press, 1999.

_____. *Rural Society and French Politics: Boulangism and the Dreyfus Affair: 1886–1900.* Princeton: Princeton University Press, 1984.

Byrnes, Robert F. *Pobedonostsev: His Life and Thought.* London: Indiana University Press, 1968.

Carmichael, Joel. *The Satanizing of the Jews: Origin and Development of Mystical Anti-Semitism.* New York: Fromm International, 1992.

Chisick, Harvey. "Ethics and History in Voltaire's Attitudes toward the Jews." *Eighteenth Century Studies* 35, no. 4 (Summer 2002): 577–600.

Cornwell, John. *Hitler's Scientists: Science, War and the Devil's Pact.* New York: Viking, 2003.

Cushing, Max Pearson. *Baron d'Holbach: A Study of Eighteenth Century Radicalism in France.* New York: Columbia University, 1914.

Davies, Alan. *Infected Christianity: A Study of Modern Racism.* Kingston, ON: McGill-Queen's University Press, 1988.

Evans, Richard J. *The Coming of the Third Reich.* New York: Penguin, 2004.

Feiner, Shmuel. *The Jewish Enlightenment.* Translated by Chaya Naor. Philadelphia: University of Pennsylvania Press, 2004.

Fischer, Klaus. *The History of an Obsession: German Judeophobia and the Holocaust.* New York: Continuum, 1998.

Gay, Peter. *The Cultivation of Hatred: The Bourgeoisie Experience, Victoria to Freud.* New York: W. W. Norton, 1993.

Geehr, Richard S. *Karl Lueger: Mayor of Fin de Siècle Vienna.* Detroit: Wayne State University Press, 1990.

Graetz, Michael. *The Jews in Nineteenth Century France.* Translated by Jane Marie Todd. Stanford: Stanford University Press, 1996.

Halasz, Nicholas. *Captain Dreyfus: The Story of a Mass Hysteria.* New York: Simon & Schuster, 1955.

Hamann, Brigitte. *Hitler's Vienna: A Dictator's Apprenticeship.* Translated by Thomas Thornton. New York: Oxford University Press, 1999.

Hertzberg, Arthur. *The French Enlightenment and the Jews.* New York: Columbia University Press, 1968.

Israel, Jonathan I. *Radical Enlightenment: Philosophy and the Making of Modernity, 1650–1750.* Oxford: Oxford University Press, 2001.

Jackson, Samuel Macauley, and Lefferts Augustine Loettscher, eds. *The New Schaff-Herzog Encyclopedia of Religious Knowledge.* New York: Funk and Wagnalls, 1908.

Jaher, Frederic Cople. *The Jews and the Nation: Revolution, Emancipation, State Formation, and the Liberal Paradigm in America and France.* Princeton: Princeton University Press, 2002.

Klier, John D., and Shlomo Lambroza, eds. *Pogroms: Anti-Jewish Violence in Modern Russian History.* Cambridge: Cambridge University Press, 1992.

Kobler, Franz. *Napoleon and the Jews.* New York: Schocken Books, 1976.

Laquer, Walter. *A History of Zionism.* New York: Schocken Books, 1976.

Levy, Richard S. *The Downfall of the Anti-Semitic Political Parties in Imperial Germany.* New Haven: Yale University Press, 1975.

Mack, Michael. *German Idealism and the Jew: The Inner Anti-Semitism of Philosophy and German Jewish Responses.* Chicago: University of Chicago Press, 2003.

Malino, Frances. *A Jew in the French Revolution: The Life of Zalkind Hourwitz.* Oxford: Blackwell, 1996.

Marrus, Michael, and Robert O. Paxton. *Vichy France and the Jews.* Stanford: Stanford University Press, 1995.

Nicholls, William. *Christian Antisemitism: A History of Hate.* Northvale, NJ: Jason Aronson, 1993.

Orlow, Dietrich. *A History of Modern Germany.* Englewood Cliffs, NJ: Prentice-Hall, 1987.

Palmer, Alan. *Twilight of the Habsburgs: The Life and Times of Emperor Francis Joseph.* New York: Grove Press, 1994.

Rémond, René. *The Right Wing in France from 1815 to de Gaulle.* Philadelphia: University of Pennsylvania Press, 1965.

Robertson, Ritchie. *The "Jewish Question" in German Literature, 1749–1939.* Oxford: Oxford University Press, 1999.

Sachar, Howard M. *A History of the Jews in the Modern World.* New York: Alfred A. Knopf, 2005.

Schechter, Ronald. "The Jewish Question in Eighteenth-Century France." *Eighteenth-Century Studies* 32, no. 1 (Fall 1998): 84–91.

Shirer, William L. *The Rise and Fall of the Third Reich: A History of Nazi Germany.* New York: Simon & Schuster, 1960.

Sorkin, David. *Moses Mendelssohn and the Religious Enlightenment.* Berkeley: University of California Press, 1996.

Stearns, Peter N., ed. *Encyclopedia of European Social History from 1350 to 2000.* 6 vols. Detroit: Charles Scribner's Sons, 2001.

Stern, Fritz. *The Politics of Cultural Despair: A Study in the Rise of the Germanic Ideology.* Garden City, NY: Anchor Books, 1965.

Sternhell, Zeev. *La droitte révolutionnaire (1885–1914): Les origines française du fascisme.* Paris: Éditions du Seuil, 1978.

Timms, Edward, and Andrea Hammel, eds. *The German-Jewish Dilemma from the Enlightenment to the Shoah.* Lewiston, KY: Edward Mellen Press, 1999.

Wistrich, Robert S. *The Jews of Vienna in the Age of Franz Joseph.* Oxford: Oxford University Press, 1990.

Zuccotti, Susan. *The Holocaust, the French, and the Jews.* Lincoln: University of Nebraska Press, 1993.

CHAPTER 3

The World of Adolf Hitler, 1889–1933

War, Politics, and Anti-Semitism

CHRONOLOGY

—**1889:** Adolf Hitler born in Braunau am Inn, Austria, on April 20
—**1907–1908:** Hitler fails in efforts to study art and architecture at Academy of Fine Arts in Vienna
—**1909–1913:** Hitler lives in Vienna selling postcards and small portraits; influenced by ideas of prominent Austrian anti-Semites, George Ritter von Schönerer and Karl Lueger
—**1913:** Hitler flees Vienna for Munich to escape Austrian draft
—**1914–1918:** Hitler serves in Bavarian Reserve Infantry Regiment 16 during World War I; wins two Iron Crosses for bravery
—**1918** *(November 11)*: Armistice ends World War I
—**1919** *(January 5)*: *Spartikist* communist uprising in Berlin
—**1919:** Creation of Weimar Republic; Bavarian Soviet Republic surfaces briefly in spring
—**1919** *(June 28)*: Treaty of Versailles signed
—**1919:** Hitler becomes spy for Reichswehr; delivers army lectures to soldiers on anti-Bolshevism and anti-Semitism
—**1919** *(September 12)*: Hitler attends meeting of anti-Semitic German Workers Party; joins few days later
—**1920** *(February 24)*: Hitler presents 25-point party program with strong anti-Semitic themes; Party soon renamed National Socialist German Workers Party (Nazi)
—**1921** *(July)*: Hitler becomes head of Nazi Party
—**1922** *(January 12)*: Hitler sentenced to 3 months imprisonment for political harassment
—**1922:** Nazis join other right wing groups in rally against "Jewish Bolshevism"
—**1922** *(October 28)*: Benito Mussolini's mythical "march on Rome"
—**1923** *(January 11)*: French and Belgian troops occupy Rhineland
—**1923** *(November 8–9)*: Hitler's failed Beer Hall Putsch in Munich
—**1924** *(February 24)*: Hitler's treason trial begins in Munich; Hitler sentenced to 5 years imprisonment; dictates first volume of *Mein Kampf*
—**1924** *(May)*: Nazis, in league with *Völkischer-Nationaler Bloc*, win 32 Reichstag seats

—1924 *(August)*: Allied Dawes Plan helps resolve reparations crisis for Germany
—1925: Paul von Hindenburg wins Weimar presidency
—1925: SS created; Hitler released from prison in December; begins rebuilding Party
—1927: Beginning of German agricultural depression
—1928: Nazis lose 20 seats in Reichstag elections
—1928: Hitler dictates *Second Book*; further develops ideas about *lebensraum* and war against Jews
—1929: Nazis join right-wing national protest against Young Plan
—1930: Nazis win 107 Reichstag seats
—1931: Hitler joins other right wing party leaders in *Harzburger Front*
—1932: Hitler twice runs unsuccessfully for president against Hindenburg
—1932: Nazis win 230 Reichstag seats; Hindenburg refuses to name Hitler chancellor
—1932 *(November)*: Nazis lose seats in Reichstag elections
—1933 *(January 30)*: Hitler becomes chancellor of Germany

Anti-Semitism was an integral part of Adolf Hitler's political philosophy, which permeated everything associated with Nazism. Given the centrality of Adolf Hitler to Nazism in Germany, it is reasonable to examine the origins of Hitler's deep hatred of the Jews. Was he born into a family of anti-Semites or was his hatred of Jews born of life experiences? Moreover, were Hitler's attitudes towards Jews psychological responses to his own neuroses, or was Hitler simply a product of his times? It is impossible to answer all these questions completely since many of the clues to Adolf Hitler's virulent hatred of the Jews was wrapped up in his distorted psychological makeup. Yet a careful look at his life, writings, and speeches before his rise to power in 1933 provides insight into the origins of his strong feelings towards this group.

Adolf Hitler: Family Roots and Questions of Jewish Ancestry

Adolf Hitler was born on April 20, 1889, in Braunau am Inn, Austria. His father, Alois Hitler (1837–1903), was an ambitious, successful official in the Austro-Hungarian customs service. Hitler's mother, Klara Pölzl (1860–1907), was Alois's third wife. By the time Adolf Hitler was born, two brothers and a sister had already died of childhood diseases; consequently, his mother spoiled him

because he was her only remaining son. Hitler also had a younger sister, Paula (1896–1960), one of the few relatives with whom Hitler had close relations. He also had a half-brother and half-sister from his father's earlier marriages.

A look back into Adolf Hitler's family tree shows a complex family lineage that was a growing embarrassment to Hitler, particularly in the immediate years before he became German chancellor. Of particular concern were rumors of Jewish ancestry. The origin of the stories about Hitler's Jewish roots go back to his paternal grandmother, Maria Anna Schikelgruber (1796–1847), who was unmarried when she gave birth to Hitler's father in 1837. He was baptized as Alois Schikelgruber and listed on the church registry as "illegitimate." Five years later, Maria married Johann Georg Hiedler (1792–1857), though Alois retained his mother's maiden name until 1876. At that time, his stepfather urged Alois to adopt his name legally and so enhance his budding career in the Austrian customs service. On June 6, 1876, Johann declared that Alois was his real son, and he had this change recorded in the local church registry. The parish priest mistakenly wrote "Alois Hitler" in the registry and changed the citation from "illegitimate" to "legitimate" by Alois's name. Three illiterate witnesses signed their names with an X. The parish priest also forgot to sign and date the change.

After World War II, Hans Frank (1900–1946), the Nazis' top lawyer and governor general of the Holocaust's principal killing ground, the General Government, wrote in his prison memoirs, *Im Angeschicht des Galgens* (In Sight of the Gallows), that in the early 1930s Hitler asked him to investigate the rumors about his Jewish roots. According to Frank, three men were possibly Alois Hitler's real father—Johann Georg Hiedler; his brother, Johann Nepomuk Hüttler/Hiedler (1807–1888); and a wealthy Graz Jew, Frankenberger. According to Frank, who wrote his account during the Nuremberg trials, Hitler's grandmother, Maria, had worked for the Frankenberger family in Graz when Alois was conceived. Frank added that the elder Frankenberger sent Maria Schikelgruber regular child support payments until Alois was fourteen years old.

Hitler told Frank that his father and grandmother claimed that Frankenberger was not his grandfather. But, he added, his grandmother and her husband were so poor that they had "conned" Frankenberger into thinking he was Alois's father so that he would pay them child support. Later investigations by the Gestapo into this matter found no new evidence to the claim that Hitler had a Jewish grandfather. In fact, according to Ian Kershaw, no Jews lived in Graz in 1837. In the end, it is impossible to determine who Alois Hitler's father was. But "whoever he was, [he] was not a Jew from Graz."[1]

Robert G. Waite concluded in his *The Psychopathic God: Adolf Hitler* that the German dictator was concerned about the impact of these charges on his political career:

He expressed his apprehension in many ways. Over and over again, in public speeches and private conversations, he stressed the dangers of "blood poisoning" and thereby demonstrated that he could not get the idea out of his mind: "Alone the loss of purity of the blood destroys the inner happiness forever; it eternally lowers man, and never again can its consequence be removed from body and mind." He felt the need to atone for bad blood. Unable to bring himself to admit directly his own family's "guilt," he used the defense of universalising the "sin" by claiming that *all* Germans were involved. Thus the poisoning of German blood became the "original sin" of all humanity. To an intimate he said, "All of us are suffering from the ailment of mixed, corrupted blood. How can we purify ourselves and make atonement?" To another associate on a different occasion he suggested that the Jewish blood of Jesus was a special curse. "In the Gospels the Jews call to Pilate when Pilate hesitated to crucify Jesus: 'His blood comes over us and over our children.' I must perhaps fulfill this curse." One of the reasons he gave for not marrying and having children was his fear of tainted blood and a family history of feeble-mindedness: "The offspring of the genius have great difficulties in life. Everyone expects that they will have the same abilities as their famous parent. But that seldom happens. Besides they would all be feeble-minded."[2]

Yet if Hitler's concerns over blood-defilement were rooted in his family's history, they rested not only on suspicions about his own Jewish ancestry and his father's illegitimacy but also on the fact that his mother, Klara Pölzl, was the granddaughter of one of Alois Hitler's three possible fathers, Johann Nepomuk Hüttler/Hielder. If Johann Hüttler was Alois Hitler's father, it would mean that Adolf Hitler's grandfather on his father's side was the same person as his great-grandfather on his mother's side. From 1930 on, Hitler showed growing uneasiness about his family's past. He was particularly sensitive about German women younger than forty-five working as servants for Jews, and he put such restrictions in the 1935 Nuremberg *Blutschutzgesetz* (Law for the Protection of German Blood and Honor). In 1942, he ordered the destruction of his mother's village of Spital after learning that a local administrator had put up a sign saying that Hitler had once lived there. The area was later transformed into a military training preserve. Yet Hitler's efforts to cloud his past also enabled him to build new myths to fill voids surrounding the mysteries of his origins.

Hitler's Early Life

Adolf Hitler's young life was reasonably stable and prosperous. He wrote in his political memoir, *Mein Kampf,* that his "father [was] a dutiful civil servant, my mother giving all her being to the household, and devoted to us children in eternal, loving care."[3]

Alois Hitler, though strict and occasionally bad-tempered, was a successful customs official who provided his family with a comfortable lifestyle. There is no evidence to show that as a child Adolf Hitler was excessively mistreated by his father; in fact, because his father was so committed to his career and family and had successfully overcome childhood poverty, Hitler gave him a great deal of respect. Hitler was particularly close to his mother, Klara, who doted on the young Adolf.

As a young schoolboy, Adolf Hitler was a well-adjusted and good student. He attended the local Roman Catholic primary school in Lambach am Traun, and he sang in the choir. His interest in school faded after the family moved to a farm near Linz in 1898; in 1905, he left school forever. According to one of his teachers, the young Adolf Hitler was intelligent but undisciplined and lazy.

During this period the fifteen-year-old Hitler met August Kubizek (1888–1956), who became his steadfast friend from late 1904 until the summer of 1908. Kubizek's memoir, *Adolf Hitler Mein Jugendfreund* (Adolf Hitler My Childhood Friend), provides us the first glimpse of the future German dictator as a teenager. Kubizek also lived briefly with Hitler in Vienna in 1908. And although one should approach Kubizek's account with some cau-

tion, the memoirs do provide insight into the mind and heart of Adolf Hitler. Kubizek presented Adolf Hitler between the ages of fifteen and nineteen as a shy, insecure young man who hid his insecurities behind a façade of self-confidence that bordered on arrogance.

Kubizek and Hitler got along because Kubizek simply gave into all of Hitler's whims and emotional outbursts. Early in their relationship, Kubizek described Hitler as "exceedingly violent and high strung." He was also impatient, and "everything aroused his interest and disturbed him." He was also incredibly "firm, inflexible, immovable, obstinately rigid." Kubizek was just the opposite: He was a "patient listener" and never challenged or questioned Hitler.[4] Initially, these two very different personalities shared one thing in common: music, particularly Wagnerian opera, their favorite being *Lohengrin*. As he did with most things that interested him, Hitler embraced opera with an impassioned earnestness; for Kubizek, this trait was Hitler's "most striking quality."[5]

Other than Kubizek, Hitler was closest to his mother and always carried a portrait of her with him. He also seemed to have a warm relationship with his younger sister Paula, though his deepest affection went to a distant love, Stephanie, whom Hitler shyly adored from afar. Though he never had the courage to approach or speak to Stephanie, he was convinced that she was just as deeply in love with him. When he left for Vienna in 1906, he asked Kubizek to send him reports about her. These were to be based on Kubizek's observations of Stephanie while she took long strolls in the evening. The important aspect of this story is that it shows the delusional nature of Hitler's thinking. There was truth and there was reality. But then there was Adolf Hitler's truth and Adolf Hitler's reality, and they were often quite different.

It is difficult to come away from Kubizek's account with any real sense of Hitler's political or racial views. Kubizek knew him as a teenager and only hinted about the future German politician's thoughts and ideas. He wrote that even then Hitler hated the multiethnic Austrian Empire and that he identified more closely with the German Second Reich. But at this stage in his life, politics for Hitler was "only an exercise in the realm of ideas."[6]

One of the criticisms of Kubizek's memoirs is that he used *Mein Kampf* to fill the gaps in Hitler's life during this period. He blended sections of *Mein Kampf* with his own memories to discuss Hitler's anti-Semitism, which he said was "already pronounced" by the time Hitler moved to Vienna in 1906. Since few Jews lived in Linz, Kubizek was not certain where such feelings came from. Perhaps, Kubizek suggested, he got it from his father, though Hitler wrote in *Mein Kampf* that he never heard his father use the word *Jew* at home.

Other than opera, Hitler's other great interest at this time was painting and architecture. Painting was nothing more than a hobby, but architecture appealed to Hitler's grandiose way of looking at the world. During the four years that Kubizek knew Hitler, the future dictator never worked. Instead, he spent most of his time reading and developing grand architectural designs for rebuilding Linz and Vienna.

In the spring of 1906, Hitler made his first trip to Vienna, the Austrian capital. He returned in 1907 determined to study at the *Akademie der bildenden Künste* (Academy of Fine Arts). Funded by a generous loan from his Aunt, Johanna Plözl (1863–1911), Hitler returned to Vienna despite his mother's illness with breast cancer. Hitler failed the entrance exam to the academy and soon returned to Linz to care for his mother, who died at the end of 1907. "I have never seen anyone so prostrate with grief as Adolf Hitler," wrote Klara's physician, Dr. Eduard Bloch.[7] Hitler did not mention in *Mein Kampf* that Dr. Bloch was Jewish. Bloch fled Germany in 1940 for the United States and died in the Bronx in 1945.

Hitler, determined now to enter the *Akademie* as an architecture student, returned to Vienna and convinced Kubizek, a promising young musician, to join him. Kubizek quickly gained entrance into the *Wien Konservatorium* (Vienna Conservatory), but Hitler failed to convince the *Akademie* even to give him another entrance exam. For a while, Hitler told Kubizek that he had been accepted by the *Akademie*. When Kubizek returned to Linz for a vacation, Hitler abandoned their joint apartment and disappeared into the depths of Austria's poverty-stricken underworld. Kubizek would not see Hitler again until 1938.

Hitler's Vienna Years

The impact of Adolf Hitler's years in Vienna on the future dictator are difficult to gauge. We know, of course, that he was influenced by the ideas and politics of two prominent Viennese anti-Semites, Georg Ritter von Schönerer and Karl Lueger. Hitler later wrote that he first became aware of the two greatest threats to the German people—Marxism and Jewry—in Vienna. Kubizek also claimed that Hitler's interest in politics developed during this period, though he seemed more concerned about the plight of the Germans in multiethnic Vienna than Jews or Marxism. On the other hand, Kubizek also claimed that Hitler did become interested in the city's "Jewish problem," particularly as it related to Jews from Eastern Europe.

Yet Hitler, who survived in Vienna between 1909 and 1913 by selling small paintings and postcards, did a lot of business with Jewish art dealers, who bought and sold his work. One of his friends, Reinhold Hanisch (1884–1937), said that Hitler felt that Jews were "better businessmen and more reliable customers than 'Christian dealers.'"[8] So although it would be safe to say that the seed for Hitler's anti-Semitism was planted in Vienna, it was his antichurch and anti-"Reds" views that really developed there. He drew these ideas from the works of Schönerer and other Pan Germanists. But Hitler also came away from Vienna with little sympathy for the poor or the working classes; instead, his experiences strengthened his attitudes about "survival, struggle, and 'every man for himself.'"[9]

Hitler, Munich, and German Anti-Semitism

In time, Hitler came to despise Vienna and Austria and decided to move to Munich and Germany; prompting the move was a sizeable inheritance from his father's estate and an attempt to avoid Austrian military service. Hitler considered his fourteen months in the Bavarian capital before the outbreak of World War I "the happiest and by far the most contented of [his] life." He called Munich "a German city" as opposed to Vienna, which he called a "Babylon of races."[10]

Yet this was also a lonely time for Hitler; he spent most of his energies dealing with Austrian military authorities, who had been looking for him for four years. He finally returned to Austria in early 1914 for an army physical, which he failed. Within seven months, though, Adolf Hitler was in the army, not as an Austrian, but as a German.

There is nothing to indicate that Hitler's life was any better in Munich, particularly given his Austrian draft problems. He continued to survive as an itinerant artist, and, though he no longer dreamed of becoming a professional artist, he still talked of becoming an architect. Pre–World War I Munich was a vibrant city that celebrated its great collection of writers, artists, and political eccentrics who lived and worked there. Some of Richard Wagner's most important operas opened there, and artists such as Vassili Kandinsky (1866–1944) and Paul Klee (1879–1940) drew their inspiration from the city. German literary giants such as Thomas Mann (1875–1955) and Rainer Maria Rilke (1875–1926) lived and wrote in Munich. Hitler was attracted to the city partially because of its accepting intellectual atmosphere

and its true sense of Germanness; nonetheless, Vienna had impressed him more.

Unlike Vienna, Munich did not have a strong anti-Semitic heritage. During the heyday of German political anti-Semitism from 1893 until 1912, Bavaria's ruling *Zentrum* (Catholic Center Party) and Catholic Church leaders were able successfully to keep Germany's major anti-Semitic parties from making significant inroads in the state. This had more to do with politics than any strong Catholic moral reaction against anti-Semitism. Yet, according to Breslau's (today, Wrocław, Poland) *Jüdische Volksblatt* (Jewish Newspaper): "It would be unjust not to concede that our co-religionists in Bavaria have fared quite well under the rule of the Center party."[11]

This, of course, did not mean that anti-Semitism was nonexistent in Bavaria. The *Allgemeine Zeitung des Judenthums* (Universal Newspaper of Jewry), which served as a watchdog for German Jewish rights, received frequent complaints about anti-Semitism in Bavaria. Yet, though Bavaria was Germany's second largest state, less than 10 percent of the country's Jewish population (615,021 in 1910) lived there. Moreover, many Bavarian Jews were Orthodox, and were less likely to assimilate through intermarriage than other German Jews. By 1912, almost 12 percent of Germany's Jews had married non-Jews, whereas only about 5 percent of Bavaria's Jews had married outside their faith. Consequently, the more tolerant, intellectual atmosphere in Bavaria, the efforts of the *Zentrum* and church to halt significant incursion by anti-Semitic parties into Bavaria, and the small size of the Jewish community served to make Bavaria a more stable environment for Jews than other parts of Germany.

These factors might explain Hitler's lack of significant reference in *Mein Kampf* to domestic politics in Munich and Bavaria in the days before World War I, but they are only small factors in the way political and societal anti-Semitism in Germany evolved during

Adolf Hitler attends a rally in the Munich Odeonsplatz to celebrate the declaration of war in 1914. USHMM Photo No. 08039, courtesy of William O. McWorkman.

the Second Reich. This development would later have an impact not only on Adolf Hitler but on the entire Nazi movement in the years after the World War I.

Hitler and World War I

World War I was a "godsend" for Adolf Hitler.[12] Until 1939, the so-called Great War (1914–1918) was the most devastating war in European history. Though its roots lie deep in the nationalistic and imperialistic conflicts that swept Europe and the world in the second half of the nineteenth century, it was more immediately triggered by a regional conflict between Austria-Hungary and Serbia in the Balkans, particularly the assassination of the heir to the Austro-Hungarian throne, Archduke Franz Ferdinand (1863–1914), by a Serb nationalist in Sarajevo on June 28, 1914. The behind-the-scenes maneuvering of both sides' most prominent allies—Germany (Austria-

Hungary) and Russia (Serbia)—exacerbated this conflict. On July 3, 1914, Kaiser Wilhelm II (r. 1888–1918) gave the Austrians a "blank check" to pursue whatever policy necessary to bring the Serbs to heel and curb Russia's ambitions in the Balkans. When tsarist Russian forces mobilized on July 28, 1914, in reaction to an Austro-Hungarian declaration of war against Serbia, the Germans warned the Russians that if they did not back down they risked war. When the Russians refused to demobilize on August 1, Germany declared war. Two days later, Germany declared war on France after Paris refused to declare its neutrality. The following day, Germany invaded neutral Belgium and Luxembourg, prompting a British declaration of war.

For Adolf Hitler, the outbreak of war was a time of great excitement. He had followed the developing events closely since late June, and the news of war filled him with a highly emotional, almost religious fervor: "To me those hours seemed like a release from the painful feelings of my youth. Even today I am not ashamed to say that, overpowered by stormy enthusiasm, I fell down on my knees and thanked heaven from an overflowing heart for granting me the good fortune of being permitted to live at this time."[13]

For the future dictator of Germany, a war that cost 1.6 million German lives and left 4.4 million German wounded was much more than a mere armed struggle; it was a battle for Germany's survival. On August 5, Hitler tried to join the First Bavarian Infantry Regiment but was turned away. Eleven days later, he was ordered to report for duty and was assigned to Bavarian Reserve Infantry Regiment 16. After completing basic training, he was shipped to the western front, where he took part in the first battle of Ypres. After four days of fighting, only 611 men remained out of the original 3,600 soldiers in his unit. On November 3, 1914, Hitler was promoted to corporal. Despite the horror and bloodshed, Hitler thrived in the trenches. There is no question from the numerous accounts of comrades and officers that he was quite brave, though some questioned his leadership skills. Hitler won two Iron Crosses for bravery during the war [Second Class in 1914 and First Class in 1918] as well as the Military Cross Third Class with Swords (1917) and the Regimental Award for Outstanding Bravery (1918). As Führer, he wore only the highly prized Iron Cross First Class. The officer who nominated him for this medal, *Leutnant* Hugo Guttmann, was Jewish.

In many ways, Hitler was a soldier's soldier. He served as a courier between frontline units and the rear, perfect for an individual who scorned the senseless banter of the trenches. His sergeant, Max Amann (1891–1957), who later headed the Nazis' press empire, nominated Hitler for promotion to *Unteroffizer* (noncommissioned officer), which the future German dictator turned down because he wanted to remain with his unit.

In the trenches, Hitler talked fanatically about the pursuit of the war and was critical of anyone not deeply committed to Germany's war effort. He was particularly critical of soldiers who used their wounds as an excuse to avoid combat. In the fall of 1916, he was wounded in the thigh and spent two months at a hospital near Berlin. Later, he recuperated in Munich. Public disillusionment with the war was widespread, and he later noted that he was shocked by the attitudes and conditions in his beloved Munich, which he blamed on the Jews. And although there are some questions about whether Hitler had fully developed his deeper anti-Semitic prejudices by this time, there is no doubt that his days in Berlin and Munich in 1916–1917 helped strengthen his growing hatred of Jews whom he would, in time, blame for all of Germany's ills.

Hitler returned to his unit in the spring of 1917, only months after German forces had failed to make a breakthrough against the Allied lines in the Verdun region. As German submarines began a new round of unlimited warfare around the British Isles, the French mounted major offenses in the west. Though the German submarines did not, as hoped, bring Great Britain to its knees, the collapse of the tsarist regime of Nicholas II in March 1917 and the growing chaos among Russian forces along the eastern front provided the German armed forces new opportunities. Unfortunately, as Germany made increasing gains against the weakened and dispirited Russian forces, the United States hesitatingly entered the war in April 1917 in response to the new unlimited German submarine warfare campaign in the Atlantic. Russia's departure from the war in the spring of 1918 after the Treaty of Brest-Litovsk (March 3, 1918) left Germany in control of much of western Russia. Emboldened by their victory over Russia, Germany's military leaders decided to mount a major offensive on the western front. Led by *Generalquartiermeister* Erich

Ludendorff (1865–1937), the Germans mounted four massive attacks in France from March 21 to July 17, 1918. In the Aisne offensive from May 27 to June 6, the Germans came within thirty-seven miles of Paris. However, the lack of adequate reserve troops and supplies, combined with the growing contribution of American forces and supplies, neutralized early German successes. By late July 1918, Allied forces under *Generalissimo* Ferdinand Foch (1851–1929) began a counteroffensive that would ultimately lead to the war's end. As Allied forces slowly pushed German troops from France in the fall of 1918, Hitler was gassed near Ypres and hospitalized for blindness. As he struggled with the prospect that his sight might not return, he learned of the armistice of November 11, which signaled Germany's defeat, and the earlier abdication of Kaiser Wilhelm II. The news stunned and angered Hitler, who cried for the first time since his mother's funeral.

Hitler, Versailles, and the Early Weimar Republic

Germany's humiliating defeat scarred Hitler in a transformative way, since it confirmed his deep suspicions about the dark forces affecting domestic and international politics. Though *Mein Kampf* is essentially a testament of hindsight, Hitler said that the trauma of defeat convinced him that it was caused by German Jews who stabbed the Second Reich in the back. Moreover, Hitler wrote, Germany's defeat opened the path to his true calling—politics.

The collapse of Germany's war effort shocked many Germans, who were unaware of the seriousness of Germany's military failures throughout the spring and summer of 1918. By August 1918, Germany's military leaders, led by Ludendorff, began to distance themselves from the inevitable military defeat as Reichstag leaders struggled with the prospect of an armistice. In the fall of 1918, parliamentary leaders suggested political re-

forms that would transform Germany into a constitutional monarchy in response to demands throughout Germany for bold political reform. However, just days before the November 11 armistice, Wilhelm II reneged on an earlier promise to support these changes. Germany's new chancellor, Prince Max von Baden (1867–1929), forced the kaiser to abdicate. He then asked Friedrich Ebert (1871–1925), the head of the *Sozialdemokratische Partei* (SPD; Social Democratic Party), to succeed the monarch as Reich Chancellor. As Ebert struggled to form a new government, he and his political allies faced various problems, including the armistice and growing political, social, and economic chaos throughout a defeated Germany.

Political opposition to the war had grown slowly and radically as the war progressed. By 1916, Rosa Luxemburg (1870–1919) and Karl Liebknecht (1871–1919), who later helped found the *Kommunistische Partei Deutschlands* (KPD; Communist Party of Germany), were calling for violent revolution throughout Germany. The following year, political strikes spread throughout Germany, stimulated partly by the Russian revolutions that toppled Tsar Nicholas II (the February Revolution) and brought the Bolsheviks to power (the October Revolution). In January 1918, 120,000 munitions workers went on strike to protest the war and the Prussian political system.

Revolutionary violence was particularly widespread in Bavaria, where Hitler was stationed after the war. The political vacuum in Munich enabled a revolutionary government under Kurt Eisner (1867–1919), a Jewish peace activist, to take power on November 7, 1918; the abdication of King Ludwig III (r. 1913–1918) followed. In state elections two months later, Eisner's *Unabhängige Sozialdemokratische Partei Deutschlands* (USPD; Independent Democratic Socialist Party of Germany) suffered a major defeat. Bavaria slipped into chaos after Eisner's assassination on February 21, 1919. Left-wing extremists, fearing a rightist coup, imposed martial law throughout the country and prepared to make Bavaria a communist state. A *Bayerische Räterepublik* (Bavarian Soviet Republic) emerged from this chaos in the spring of 1919. From Adolf Hitler's perspective, this amounted to "a passing rule of the Jews," which he thought "had been the original aim of the instigators of the whole revolution."[14]

Though short lived, the *Räterepublik* helped create a paranoid fear of communism in the minds of middle-class Germans throughout Bavaria. Furthermore, the effective destruction of the *Räterepublik* from April 30–May 1, 1919, by the army and right-wing *Freikorps* (Free Corps; private units made up of former soldiers) troops and the resulting White Terror helped transform Munich into a bastion for right-wing nationalist groups. These groups claimed they had saved Munich and Bavaria from "alien—Bolshevik and Jewish—forces" who wanted to control the government and the very soul of Christian Bavaria. It is small wonder that Munich became the city of Adolf Hitler's political awakening.[15]

Similar revolutionary outbursts took place elsewhere in Germany, particularly in Berlin, where leftist political factions tried to create a German Socialist Republic run by workers and soldiers' councils. On January 5, 1919, a six-day *Spartikist* communist rebellion that broke out in the German capital just two weeks before national elections for a constitutional assembly was successfully put down by the army and *Freikorps* units. Two months earlier, the army had made an agreement with Chancellor Ebert that promised no government interference in military affairs in return for the military's support of his government. This, unfortunately, continued the imperial tradition of allowing the military to function as a "state within a state." Fourteen months later, Berlin was rocked again by revolution—the right-wing-inspired Kapp-Lüttwitz putsch (coup). Several *Freikorps* units seized control of Berlin and Bavaria after they learned that the govern-

ment of Philip Scheidemann (1865–1939) intended to dissolve their units. Though the Berlin putsch failed in a few days, the Bavarian coup toppled the government of Johannes Hoffmann (1867–1930), replacing it with a military-backed premier, Gustav von Kahr (1862–1934), who helped transform Bavaria into a haven for right-wing groups.

These upheavals underscored the difficult political, economic, and social problems that Germany faced in the months and years after World War I. Meanwhile, German politicians struggled to create a new democratic state in Germany—the Weimar Republic. Created in the aftermath of national constituent assembly elections in early 1919, the new German democracy had a constitution that gave Germany a parliamentary system based on French and British models. It centered around a *Reichstag* elected to four-year terms by universal suffrage. A second legislative body, the *Reichsrat*, consisted of delegates appointed by Germany's fifteen new *Länder*, or states. The Executive Branch would be led by a *Reichspräsident*, who was elected to a seven-year term. The president would represent Germany in foreign affairs, appoint the chancellor, and be commander-in-chief of the armed forces.

The president would also have the right to dissolve the Reichstag and to invoke Article 48, which gave the president the right to use the military to enforce a state's constitutional obligations. He could also suspend many basic civil rights throughout Germany without the approval of the Reichstag when "public order and security are seriously disturbed or endangered."[16] The president could also use the armed forces to back up this presidential state of emergency. The chancellor had to countersign all the president's emergency decrees or orders. The Reichstag could override such decrees or orders, though the president could neutralize such efforts by dissolving the legislature and calling for new elections. Unfortunately, Article 48 would later be used to undermine the very democratic system it was

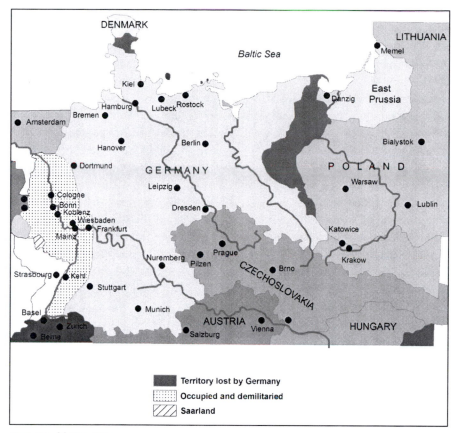

DENMARK

Baltic Sea

LITHUANIA
Memel

Kiel

Hamburg Lubeck Rostock
Bremen   Danzig   East
Amsterdam   Prussia

Hanover   Berlin   Bialystok

Dortmund   GERMANY   P O L A N D
Leipzig   Warsaw
Cologne
Bonn   Dresden   Lublin
Koblenz
Wiesbaden
Mainz Frankfurt   Katowice

Nuremberg   Prague
Strasbourg   Pilzen   Krakow
Kehl   CZECHOSLOVAKIA   Brno
Stuttgart

Basel   Munich
Zurich   AUSTRIA   HUNGARY
Berne   Salzburg   Vienna

■ Territory lost by Germany
▦ Occupied and demilitaried
▨ Saarland

Post-World War I Germany.

designed to protect. The new Weimar constitution also guaranteed full civil, property, and religious rights to all German citizens. Although the new constitution was not perfect, it was a democratic document that could have become the foundation for democracy in Germany for decades. Unfortunately, the events of the next fourteen years seriously undermined this democratic experiment and helped pave the way for the dictatorship of Adolf Hitler.

While Weimar politicians worked on the new constitution, the Allied powers put the finishing touches to the controversial Treaty of Versailles. Hitler later called it a *"Diktat"* and an "instrument of boundless extortion and abject humiliation" for the German people.[17] And though the Allies concluded separate peace treaties in Paris at the end of World War I with each of the Central Powers (Germany, Austria,

Hungary, Bulgaria, and Turkey), they considered the Treaty of Versailles with Germany the principal treaty because it dealt with, at least from their perspective, the war's main villain, Germany. The sudden end of the war, the growing specter of communist revolution in Europe, particularly after the dramatic successes of Vladimir Ilyich Lenin's (1870–1924) Bolsheviks in Russia in late 1917, and uncertainty over the direction of the planned negotiations with Germany prompted the Allies to produce a dictated settlement that stunned most Germans. But the victors were also motivated by revenge, fear of German military and economic resurgence, and the desire to have Germany repay the winning side for their huge war losses. The French government, for example, insisted on a buffer state along the Rhine River between France and Germany, and wanted the return of Alsace-Lorraine, which Germany had seized at the end of the Franco-Prussian War. The British and the Americans, led by David Lloyd-George (1863–1945) and President Woodrow Wilson (1856–1924), who insisted on the inclusion of the League of Nations in the treaty, argued that German arms reduction was essential to future European peace and stability.

The result was a weighty, 450-article document that began with the League of Nations Covenant and concluded with mandates for German colonies. The clauses that initially infuriated most Germans were those dealing with war criminals. Article 227 accused the kaiser, Wilhelm II, of "a supreme offence against international morality and the sanctity of treaties," and created an Allied tribunal to try him for such crimes.[18] But the most controversial section of the treaty was Article 231, the "war guilt" clause, which forced Germany to accept responsibility for itself and its allies for "causing all of the loss and damage to which the Allies and Associated Governments and their nationals have been subjected as a consequence for the war."[19] The most significant clauses of the treaty transferred Alsace-Lorraine to France and Eupen-Malmedy to Belgium. France also got the Saar coal mines as reparations, and the Allied powers were to occupy the mineral-rich Saar Basin for fifteen years. A plebiscite would later determine whether the region would be returned to Germany. Germany also lost all its colonies in Asia and Africa. In addition, the treaty created a Polish Corridor out of German territory to give the new Polish state access to the Baltic Sea. East Prussia, the mythical homeland of the Teutonic Knights, was now separated from Germany by Polish territory. The treaty made the important German port, Danzig (Polish, Gdansk), a "Free City" under League of Nations control to give the Poles an operable port on the Baltic, though the city remained predominantly German.

The treaty reduced the *Reichswehr* (Reich Defense Forces) to 100,000 men (including officers). It also required twelve years of volunteer service for enlisted men and twenty-five years for officers to prevent a buildup of strong reserve forces. The treaty abolished the German General Staff and forbade offensive weapons of war such as submarines, airplanes, and blimps. A Reparations Commission was set up to determine how much Germany would have to pay the Allies in reparations. In 1921, the commission concluded that Germany owed the Allies 132 billion gold marks ($31.4 billion). Given the complex repayment schedule, the actual figure was probably between 25 and 35 billion gold marks, a sum Germany's leaders thought they could pay.

The treaty stunned the Germans and created a crisis for Chancellor Philipp Scheidemann's new government, which immediately objected to most of the terms. Scheidemann argued that they were too harsh and that the treaty violated the spirit of Woodrow Wilson's Fourteen Points (presented to the U.S. Congress on January 18, 1918). Though the Allied powers agreed to some minor changes, they informed the German government that it had two choices: sign the treaty or risk invasion. The Treaty of Versailles was formally signed on June 28, 1919.

During the next fifteen years, a cottage industry in Germany explored the complex issues surrounding the war, its causes, and the Treaty of Versailles. Germany's military leadership, trying to preserve some remnant of its traditional "state within a state" status, began to embrace the *Dolchstoßlegende* ("stab in the back" myth or legend), which blamed Germany's defeat on the "November Criminals," or politicians who had signed the armistice in 1918. This myth was partially fueled by the Allied decision on November 1, 1919, to ask the new Weimar Republic to turn over 830 Germans, including Paul von Hindenburg and his second-in-command, Erich Ludendorff, for war crimes trials. Berlin refused, but did offer to try each of the politicians and military figures suspected of war crimes before Germany's *Reichsgericht* (Supreme Court) in Leipzig.

Though the Allies soon dropped the matter, the Weimar government did open an investigation into who was responsible for the war, and they questioned many of those accused of war criminality, including Hindenburg and Ludendorff. Both men had begun to embrace some tenets of the *Dolchstoßlegende* before the war ended. In a letter to the kaiser on October 24, 1918, Hindenburg criticized the impact of defeatist speeches in the Reichstag on the military and said in his memoirs that the revolution in Germany "destroyed the very backbone of the Army, the German officer." As revolution swept Germany, Hindenburg wrote, it "pressed the thorny crown of martyrdom" on the "bleeding head" of the German officer.[20]

Ludendorff, one of the leaders of the nationalist right after the war and a partner in Hitler's failed Beer Hall Putsch in 1923, suffered a nervous breakdown in the summer of 1918 and on September 29 called for an armistice with the Allies. He resigned his commission in late October and fled to Sweden. Later, he decried the postarmistice atmosphere in Germany: "[O]rder in state and society vanished. All authority disappeared. Chaos, Bolshevism, terror, un-German in name and nature, made their entry into the German fatherland."[21]

On November 18, 1919, Hindenburg told the investigative commission in Berlin that the "German army had been stabbed in the back," a phrase used earlier by two British generals to explain the reason for Germany's surprise defeat.[22] Hindenburg's words became an integral part of right-wing nationalist explanations for the defeat in 1918 and was quickly linked to the "November Criminals" who had signed the armistice and the hated *Diktat* of Versailles. Adolf Hitler, who had remained in the army until 1920, quickly

embraced the *Dolchstoßlegende*, which he ultimately blamed on "the international Jew."[23] In a speech in Munich on April 17, 1923, Hitler charged that wartime Germany was really run by "a whole brood of Hebrews" who were responsible for Germany's defeat.[24] Several months later, he blamed Germany's postwar problems on the decisions of the "November Criminals" and claimed that its subservient spirit still guided Weimar politicians.[25] In reality, there had been no "stab in the back." But the idea entered the mythology of right-wing movements that cropped up all over Germany after the war; eventually, the idea that a Jewish-led cabal had orchestrated Germany's defeat in World War I and was still the guiding spirit in Weimar Germany became one of the central themes in Nazi propaganda.

Hitler, the Early Nazi Party, and Anti-Semitism

Unlike the millions of German soldiers who faced unemployment at the war's end, Adolf Hitler made an easy transition from life as a soldier to that of a politician. After his release from the hospital in November 1918, Hitler served first in a reserve unit and then as a guard at the Traunstein POW camp in southeastern Bavaria. Two months later, the army transferred him to Munich to await discharge. In the interim, his unit elected him their *Vertrauensmann* (representative) to Munich's new socialist government. As Ian Kershaw pointed out, Hitler's first foray into politics had little to do with sympathy for the governing Social Democrats. It was, he argued, nothing more than "sheer opportunism aimed at avoiding for as long as possible demobilization for the army."[26]

After the collapse of the Munich Soviet in May 1919, the military occupied the city. *Reichswehr* commanders wanted to know which soldiers had supported the Socialists and also began to sponsor a series of "anti-Bolshevik" courses in their units. Adolf Hitler was one of the soldiers chosen both to spy on their comrades and to teach the courses that blended "anti-Bolshevism" with German nationalism. As part of his training, Hitler heard lectures from "experts" in Munich. It was here that Hitler discovered his natural talents as a public speaker. The army also recognized his skills and made him one of twenty-six instructors who would lecture units on nationalism and anti-Bolshevism.

Anti-Semitism was one of the central topics of Hitler's army lectures. In fact, his attacks on Jews were so virulent that one of his commanders asked him to tone down his comments because he was afraid they might trigger actions against Jews. Once he had completed his series of lectures, Hitler began to spy on a number of left- and right-wing political groups in Munich. On Friday, September 12, 1919, Hitler attended a meeting of the *Deutsche Arbeiterpartei* (DAP; German Workers Party). The DAP was founded in early 1919 by Anton Drexler (1884–1942) and Karl Harrer (1890–1926), both members of the right-wing *Thule Gesellschaft* (Thule Society), which included future prominent Nazis and used the swastika as its symbol. Drexler dreamed of a *völkisch* German state that would be free of Jews, Slavs, communists, pacifists, and any other alien group or ideology that would hinder the revival of German national spirit. Another early DAP member, Gottfried Feder (1883–1941), whom Hitler greatly admired, blamed the Jews for postwar Germany's economic collapse. Hitler devoted the last lines of *Mein Kampf* to Dietrich Eckart (1868–1923), another early DAP member known for his anti-Semitism and anti-Bolshevism. Hitler called Eckart an early party hero "who devoted his life to the awakening of his, our people, in his writings and his thoughts and finally his deeds."[27] Eckart edited the DAP's *Münchener Beobachter* (Munich Observer), which later became the Nazi Party's most important newspaper, the *Völkischer Beobachter* (People's Ob-

server). Alfred Rosenberg, who later became the Nazi Party's unofficial philosopher and foreign policy expert, became chief editor of the *Völkischer Beobachter* in 1921. Rosenberg, like Eckart, was one of Hitler's early political and ideological mentors.

At the end of the September 12 meeting, Hitler spoke heatedly against one of the ideas discussed at the gathering—Bavarian unification with Austria. Drexler was so impressed by Hitler's comments that he asked him to join the party, which Hitler did a week later. Drexler later challenged Hitler's claim that he was party member no. 7. Joachim Fest attributed Hitler's early success in the DAP to the great amount of free time he enjoyed. Ian Kershaw, though, thought that Hitler's contributions were more significant. His gift, Kershaw concluded, was his ability "to advertise unoriginal ideas in an original way." But, he added, "Hitler was more of a propagandist than an original thinker."[28] Whatever his strengths, Hitler helped transform the DAP from a smallish, obscure nationalist organization into a mainstream group through his rabble-rousing anti-Semitic speeches. Party membership rose from 190 members in January 1920 to 3,300 by August 1921. In July 1921, Hitler said that he was, for all practical purposes, "the [renamed] NSDAP." He was "its voice, its representative figure, its embodiment," and he was able to use these claims to gain full control over the party.[29]

Anti-Semitism was a central theme in Hitler's oratorical repertoire. In the fall of 1919, in response to a question from one of his officers about his views on Jews, Hitler wrote that the Jewish question should be approached factually, not emotionally. Jews, he argued, were a race and not a religious group. Jews were driven by two things, power and money; as a result, they became "a racial tuberculosis of the nations."[30] Emotional anti-Semitism sought solutions through pogroms, Hitler continued.

"Rational anti-Semitism [by contrast] must lead to a systematic and legal struggle against, and eradication of, what privileges the Jews enjoyed over other foreigners living among us (Alien Laws). Its final objective, however, must be the total removal of all Jews from our midst."[31] This could only be achieved by a "government of national strength."[32] Germany's current leadership, he argued, would never do this because they were obligated to serve Jewish interests. Hitler continued his "eradication" theme in *Mein Kampf* a few years later. In comments about the Marxist traitors, which, he claimed, were behind Germany's defeat in World War I, he stated:

[If] twelve or fifteen thousand of the Hebrew corrupters of the people had been held under poison gas, as happened to hundreds of thousands of our very best German workers in the field, the sacrifice of millions at the front would not have been in vain. On the contrary: twelve thousand scoundrels eliminated in time might have saved the lives of a million real Germans, valuable for the future.[33]

In a speech before a DAP rally in Munich in February 1920, Hitler read the new party program. Though modestly revised over the years, its points were declared inviolable in 1926. The 25-point program directly and indirectly addressed the "Jewish question."

Only members of the nation may be citizens of the State. Only those of German blood, whatever their creed, may be members of the nation. Accordingly, no Jew may be a member of the nation.

Noncitizens may live in Germany only as guests and must be subject to laws for aliens.

We demand that the State shall make it its primary duty to provide livelihood for its citizens. If it should prove impossible to feed the entire population, foreign nationals (noncitizens) must be deported from the Reich.

All non-German immigration must be prevented. We demand that all non-Germans who entered Germany after 2 August 1914 shall be required to leave the Reich forthwith.[34]

In a speech on September 18, 1922, Hitler complained again about the Jews and the "November Criminals," who, he said, should be hanged as traitors. He then demanded "immediate expulsion of all Jews who [had] entered Germany since 1914, and of all those, too, who through trickery on the Stock Exchange or through other shady transactions [had] gained their wealth."[35]

Other points in the DAP program made veiled allusions to Jewish crimes or threats to German society:

In view of the enormous sacrifices of life and property demanded of a nation by any war, personal enrichment from war must be regarded as a crime against the nation. We demand therefore the ruthless confiscation of all war profits.

We demand the creation and maintenance of a healthy middle class, the immediate communalising of big department stores, and their lease at a cheap rate to small traders. . . .

We demand a land reform suitable to our national requirements, the passing of a law for the expropriation of land for communal purposes without compensation. . . .[36]

In 1928, Hitler stated that point 17 on land reform was aimed at Jewish companies who had acquired land illegally.

We demand the ruthless prosecution of those whose activities are injurious to the common interest. Common criminals, usurers, profiteers, etc., must be punished with death, whatever their creed or race.

We demand legal warfare on deliberate political mendacity and its dissemination in the press.

A. that all editors of, and contributors to newspapers appearing in the German language must be members of the nation;

B. that no non-German newspapers may appear without the express permission of the State. They must not be printed in the German language.

C. that non-Germans shall be prohibited by law from participating financially in or influencing German newspapers, that the penalty for contravening such a law shall be the suppression of any such newspaper, and the immediate deportation of the non-Germans involved.

We demand freedom for all religious denominations in the State, provided they do not threaten its existence nor offend the morals feelings of the German race.

The Party, as such, stands for positive Christianity, but does not commit itself to any particular denomination. It combats the Jewish-materialist spirit within and without us, and it is convinced that our nation can achieve permanent health only from within on the basis of the principle: *The common interest before self-interest.*

The leaders of the party promise to work ruthlessly—if need be to sacrifice their very lives—to translate this programme into action.[37]

In 1922, Hitler explained that "extremes must be fought by extremes." He added: "Against the infection of materialism, against the Jewish pestilence we must hold aloft a flaming ideal. And if others speak of the World and Humanity we say The Fatherland—and only the Fatherland!"[38]

Hatred and fear of communists and Jews were common themes among right-wing nationalists throughout Germany during this period. The fear of Bolsheviks and communists was particularly strong in the immediate years after the Bolshevik seizure of power in Russia and the deadly civil war that followed between 1918 and 1921. Communist efforts to initiate Bolshevik-style revolutions in Germany in the early years after the end of World War I only exacerbated these fears. For Hitler, though, his hatred and fear of Jews predated his concerns about Bolsheviks and communists. In 1922, he joined other nationalist group leaders at a rally whose theme, "'For Germany—Against Berlin,'" was directed at "the approaching Jewish Bolshevism under the protection of the Republic."[39]

Over the next few years, Hitler blended his deep anti-Semitism with his hatred of communism and the desire for greater *lebensraum* (living space) into a world view that found voice in his biographical treatise, *Mein Kampf.* Hitler considered Marxism a Jewish doctrine that "systematically [planned] to hand the world over to the Jews."[40] In many ways, Hitler was already convinced that Jews dominated most facets of German culture and society. He pointed to the *Protocols of the Elders of Zion* as evidence of Jewish goals and proclaimed: "*[B]y defending myself against the Jew, I am fighting for the work of the Lord.*"[41] He pointed to Russia as an example of Jewish efforts to dominate society. He claimed that Jews (i.e., the Bolsheviks) had recently murdered 30 million people "to give a gang of Jewish journalists and stock exchange bandits domination over a great people."[42] One of Nazism's principal goals, Hitler declared, was to destroy "Jewish Bolshevism" and provide the Nazis with the *lebensraum* they needed to create a super Aryan race. This end could be achieved only through a "war of extermination"; the ultimate goal of the war was the "annihilation and extermination of the Marxist *Weltanschauung* (world view)," which in Hitler's mind was synonymous with "the Jew."[43]

Hitler's racial and political theories matured as he began to reform the DAP, which was renamed the *Nationalsozialistische Deutsche Arbeiterpartei* (Nazi; NSDAP; National Socialist German Workers Party) in early 1920. He quickly instituted military-style reforms that brought better discipline and organization to the party. He also played an important role in developing the symbols and mythology that became so important to later party practice and tradition. The inverted cross, or swastika, was chosen because of its ancient, mystical symbolism. According to Hitler, the black swastika, laid upon a white circle surrounded in red, symbolized the core ideals of the Nazi movement: "In the red we see the social ideal of the movement, in the white the national idea, in the swastika the mission of the fight for the victory of Aryan man, and at the same time also the victory of the idea of creative work which in itself is and always will be anti-Semitic."[44]

Using a successful blend of radical oratory that at times was spellbinding, strong organizational skills, and a growing body of racist propaganda and mythical, nationalistic symbols, Hitler and the Nazi leadership gradually transformed the Nazi Party into an organization that appealed to many Germans, particularly the lower middle classes. Many of Hitler's early sympathizers were small merchants and craftsmen who felt threatened by Germany's Jewish businessmen. German big business also gave some insignificant support to the early Nazi movement.

Hitler surrounded himself with radical anti-Semites such as Ernst Röhm (1887–1934), who later commanded the SA (*Sturmabteilung*; Storm Detachment), initially the most militant anti-Semitic paramilitary organization in the party, and Hermann Göring (1893–1946), a World War I ace who later became Hitler's heir-designate. Rudolf Hess (Heß; 1894–1987), Hitler's private secretary and deputy party leader, tirelessly promoted Hitler's ideas, particularly anti-Semitism. Perhaps the most anti-Semitic figure in Hitler's inner circle was Julius Streicher, a crude, brutal, sexual deviant who founded *Der Stürmer* in 1923 and used it to promote the Nazi Party's anti-Semitism. Equally important was Joseph Goebbels (1897–1945), Hitler's future propaganda minister, who walked with a limp because of a club foot. Otto Strasser (1897–1974), his brother, Gregor Strasser (1892–1934) and Ernst Hanfstaengel (1887–1975) were other important early party members.

Binding this diverse collection of radicals together was their strong sense of German patriotism, hatred of the Jews, great dislike of Weimar democracy, and the fear of communism. In his first two years as head of the Nazi movement, Hitler used these themes to expand party membership. SA violence also helped give party rallies and events a reputation for rowdiness. On January 12, 1922, Hitler was sentenced to three months in prison for disrupting the meeting of a political rival. After a month in jail, Hitler returned to the streets to rouse Germans to battle against what he claimed were Jewish-dominated governments in Munich and Berlin. The more extreme his speeches, the more attractive he seemed to Germans frustrated over Germany's serious political and economic problems.

When the German government borrowed heavily to make its early Versailles debt payments, it started a period of inflation that the Weimar government later used to underscore what many Germans felt was Allied insensitivity to Germany's depressed economy. The German mark rose from 8.4 marks to the dollar in 1919 to 18,000 marks to the dollar by early 1923. The Allies were annoyed with the Weimar government for dragging its feet in making timely reparations payments; and right-wing nationalists were angered by the government's efforts to promote a policy of payment "fulfillment," meaning an attempt to pay something to weaken Allied insistence on full payments, because they opposed such payments. Three of them assassinated Foreign Minister Walther Rathenau (1867–1922), a Jew, on June 24, 1922, believing, like Hitler, that Jews and "Reds" were the cause of Germany's problems and defeat in World War I. As tensions rose, the government tried unsuccessfully to borrow money to pay a portion of the 1922 Versailles payment. When the Germans delayed the reparations delivery of coal and telegraph poles, a frustrated Allied Reparation Commission sent French and Belgian troops into the Ruhr Valley area on January 11, 1923, to insure the timely delivery of reparation goods. The government of Chancellor Wilhelm Cuno (1876–1933) immediately asked all Ruhr Germans passively to resist the Franco-Belgian occupation, a campaign that quickly spread throughout Germany. On March 31, French troops fired on striking workers at the Krupp factories in Essen, killing thirteen and wounding thirty. Two days later, the French executed Albert Leo Schlageter (1894–1923) for sabotage. The Nazis immediately transformed him into a nationalist martyr.

The occupation of the Ruhr was the worst crisis Germany had faced in the interwar period before the Depression. On the day of the occupation, Hitler delivered a speech titled "The November Criminals." He blamed the Jews for Germany's inability to resist the occupation and said they were trying to push Germany into a war it could not win. He then ordered all Nazis not to take part in the passive resistance campaign. *Völkischer Beobachter* also attacked Cuno's idea of a "united front" against the occupation and said that German traitors should first be dealt with before anything could be done against the French and the Belgians. Hitler later wrote that the crisis could have been avoided with "the elimination of the Marxist poison from [the] national body in 1918."[45] For the Nazis, of course, the "November Criminals," traitors, and Marxists were all Jews.

The passive resistance campaign was not successful and to support the campaign the government adopted inflationary fund-raiding policies. Between 1922 and 1923, the German budget deficit rose from 6.1 billion marks to 11.7 billion marks. The government responded by printing worthless marks that saw the mark drop from 40,000 to the dollar at the beginning of the Ruhr crisis to 4.2 trillion marks to the dollar by the end of 1923. In the midst of the crisis, Cuno resigned, replaced by Gustav Stresemann (1878–1929), who became chancellor and foreign minister. Stresemann announced an end to the passive resistance campaign and pledged Germany's commitment to repay its war debts. Stresemann, the architect of Germany's postwar recovery, stabilized the economy with a blend of new taxes, reduced government expenditures, and a new currency, the *rentenmark,* which was based on the value of all property in Germany.

Stresemann's controversial moves doomed his chancellorship, which lasted only three months, though he remained foreign minister. It was in this position that he enjoyed his greatest achievements. He was able to persuade the Allies to agree to the restructuring of Germany's reparations debt through the Dawes Plan in 1924, which opened the door to the Locarno treaties in 1925; these treaties normalized Allied relations with Germany, settled Europe's Versailles boundaries, and led to Germany's admission to the League of Nations the following year. Meanwhile, Stresemann negotiated the withdrawal of the French and the Belgians from the Ruhr.

Hitler thought little of Stresemann's efforts; he felt that the foreign minister, along with Cuno and other German politicians, was leading Germany down the *"Via dolorosa (leidensweg)* [the way of the cross in Jerusalem], to the dictatorship of a Jewish lord of finance."[46] Consequently, it should come as no surprise that Hitler and other German nationalists were deeply affected by Benito Mussolini's (1883–1945) mythical "March on

Rome" in late October 1922, which led to his appointment as prime minister of Italy. This prompted right-wing groups throughout Germany, particularly in Bavaria, to talk of a similar "March on Berlin." Hermann Esser (1900–1981), the managing editor of the *Völkischer Beobachter,* told a crowd a week after Mussolini's "march" that "Germany's Mussolini is called Adolf Hitler."[47] This marked the beginning of what became the "Führer cult of personality." Hitler now saw himself as the special person, who, like Mussolini, could transform the face of Germany.

Hitler's moment came in the fall of 1923 in the midst of efforts by the Stresemann government to restrict the activities of the Nazis and similar groups throughout Bavaria and Germany. In league with members of the *Deutscher Kampfbund* (German Combat League), a coalition of right-wing paramilitary organizations, a decision was made to take advantage of the financial and political crisis in Germany to move first against the Bavarian government in Munich as a prelude to a "March on Berlin." Though Hitler was considered the head of the *Kampfbund,* Erich Ludendorff was seen as Germany's future dictator. The result was the mythical Beer Hall Putsch of November 8–9, 1923. Armed police quickly dispersed the marchers, though the infamous putsch would go down in the annals of Nazi mythology as a major turning point in its history.

Hitler, Ludendorff, and several other putsch leaders were arrested, imprisoned, and put on trial for treason. The government also outlawed the Nazi Party. When the judges allowed Hitler to use the trial as a soap box to voice his radical ideas, he became a household word throughout Germany. The judges acquitted Ludendorff and sentenced Hitler to five years in prison. Hitler spent his thirteen months in Landsberg Prison outside Munich dictating his political autobiography, *Mein Kampf* (My Struggle), and reflecting on the future direction of the outlawed Nazi movement, now in the hands of Alfred Rosenberg.

Sympathetic jailers gave Hitler and the forty Nazis imprisoned with him full run of the prison, which Klaus Fischer described as a "beehive of [Nazi] party activity."[48] After his release in late December 1924, Hitler found his movement in disarray and quickly convinced the government to lift its ban against the party. On February 26, 1925, he published an article in the *Völkischer Beobachter* proclaiming that "the newly awakened NSDAP," in league with the Christians of Germany, should join together "in the common fight against the power which is the mortal foe of Christianity."[49] The foe he referred to, of course, was "Jewish Bolshevism."

The reorganization of the party placed more and more authority in Hitler's hands. The result was the creation of the *Führerprinzip* (leader principle), which emphasized that one leader—Adolf Hitler—should wield sole power over all party matters. These changes came in the midst of the Weimar Republic's brief "golden age," which saw Nazi political fortunes wane nationally between 1925 and 1929. In May 1924, the Nazis, in league with the *Völkisch-Nationaler Bloc,* garnered almost 2 million votes and 32 seats (out of 472) in Reichstag elections. The Nazis lost 18 seats in the national elections eight months later; in 1928, it lost another 2 seats. Undeterred, Hitler continued with his reorganization of the party, which saw membership grow from 27,000 in 1925 to 108,000 on the eve of the Depression in 1929.

Part of the party's new appeal was its large array of new organizations for students, professionals, and women. The SA now became the party's *Hilfstruppe* (auxiliary troop), though SA members saw themselves as the vanguard of the Nazi revolution, and violence as the principal means of promoting the party's racial ideals and propaganda. In April 1925, Hitler created a new paramilitary unit, the SS (*Schutzstaffel*; defense or protection guard) out of his personal body guard unit, the *Stoßtrupp Adolf Hitler* (Shock Troop

Adolf Hitler gives a speech at the third Nazi Party Congress in Nuremberg, 1927. USHMM Photo No. 09730, courtesy of Joanne Schartow.

Adolf Hitler). The SS would become not only the racial vanguard of the Nazi Party but also its Praetorian Guard.

Hitler used this time in the "political wilderness" to further develop his political theories, particularly those dealing with *lebensraum* and eastward expansion. Anti-Semitism remained central to all Nazi thinking, though Hitler increasingly began to put his pathological hatred of Jews into a more Marxian context, probably because of his thoughts on eastward expansion and Russia. He wrote in the *Völkischer Beobachter* in 1927 that the "Jew is and remains the world enemy and his weapon, Marxism, a plague of mankind."[50]

In 1928, Hitler dictated a sequel to *Mein Kampf*, his *Zweites Buch* (Second Book), in which he discussed the keys to the survival of a people. The most important thing, he argued, was "the will to preserve itself and the vital strength that is available to do so." He ar-

gued that Germany's "internal racial fragmentation" and its effect on the military in World War I had caused Germany's defeat. The German army, he continued, understood that they were motivated by higher ideas of nationhood and honor, values contemporary politicians and Jews had never understood. Hitler pledged that once the Nazis came to power, he would restore "the people's value in itself, the personal qualities present, and a healthy preservation drive" to draw the state and people back together as one.[51]

If Hitler's goal domestically was to restore the honor and racial purity of the German nation, internationally it would need land to thrive. Part of the reason for international expansion was to unite all ethnic Germans in one state. But beyond that, Hitler argued, was the need for *lebensraum*, which was available only in the East. Gaining *lebensraum* in the East had to become Germany's sole foreign policy goal, and it would require building a great land army. To achieve this, the nation and people must be pure and racially strong because they would have to struggle against Germany's greatest enemy—the Jews. Hitler repeated his traditional charges that the Jews were a parasitic people who sought, through "the denaturalization and chaotic bastardization of other peoples," to destroy all non-Jews. "The Jewish international struggle will therefore always end in bloody Bolshevization."[52]

After the Nazi election failures in 1928, Hitler ordered the party to place more emphasis on small-town and peasant voters in the countryside. Farmers had begun to suffer economically as early as 1927 from an international agricultural depression and they were vulnerable to Nazi propaganda that blamed Jewish bankers and a Weimar government controlled by communists for their problems. Lower-middle-class businessmen in Germany's small towns were swayed by similar Nazi themes about Jews and communists. The Nazis depicted department stores that were even partly owned by Jews as threats to the small businessman. The Nazis promised a return to a premodern, traditional Germany where such abuses would not have been permitted. The Nazis also successfully appealed to impressionable university students, and, by 1930, many had joined the Nazi Party. This partly explains the tremendous youthfulness of the Nazi movement, which had an average member age of thirty by 1930. Though the Nazi Party remained primarily a male, lower-middle-class movement, a disproportionate number of higher party leaders were drawn from the upper middle class. Women made up only 10 percent of party membership as late as 1937, though these figures had more than tripled by 1944.

The German economy was already in trouble before the United States stock market crash in 1929, which deeply affected Germany. But what helped put the Nazis back onto the political map was their support of Alfred Hugenberg's (1865–1951) campaign to persuade the government to reject the Young Plan (June 7, 1929). This was an American-driven reparations restructuring plan that spread Germany's Versailles debts over fifty-nine years in return for the promise of an Allied withdrawal from the Rhineland five years early. Hugenberg, the wealthy, influential head of the right-wing, monarchist, anti-Semitic *Deutschnationale Volkspartei* (DNVP; German National Peoples Party), rejected both the Treaty of Versailles and the Weimar constitution. He convinced Hitler to join his efforts to hold a national plebiscite on the Young Plan on December 22, 1929. Though the referendum failed miserably, the campaign gave the Nazis a newfound respectability, which translated into considerable political gains in local and state elections at the end of 1929. Party membership also grew from 108,000 in late 1928 to 178,000 by the end of the following year. The SA now had 100,000 members, making it as large as the *Reichswehr*.

What followed for Hitler and the Nazi Party during the next three years was nothing short of a political miracle fueled by the deepening Depression and the institution of government by presidential decree. Yet the dramatic political revival of the Nazis also came about because Hitler's earlier reforms put the Nazi Party in an opportune position to take advantage of Germany's dramatic economic and political woes. The Depression had a devastating impact on a Germany already weakened economically, politically, and socially. Official unemployment figures rose from 8.5 percent (1.3 million) of the working force in 1929 to 29.9 percent (6 million) by the fall of 1932. In reality, these figures were much higher when the hidden unemployed were counted. German exports fell from 12.3 billion marks ($2.9 billion) in 1928 to 5.7 billion ($1.3 billion) marks two years later. Imports suffered similar declines (14 billion marks [$3.3 billion] in 1928 to 4.7 billion [$1.1 billion] in 1932), and the country's national income fell by 20 percent during the same period. By March 1930, political infighting over a solution to Germany's unemployment and economic problems paralyzed the Reichstag.

On March 17, 1930, the coalition government of Hermann Müller (1876–1931) collapsed, which paved the way for a new era in Weimar politics centering around the figure of the country's aging war hero and president, Paul von Hindenburg. No friend of Weimar democracy, Hindenburg chose to bypass the traditional parliamentary system to deal with the country's political and economic problems. He did this by using Article 48 of the Weimar constitution. The invocation of Article 48 in the early years of the Weimar Republic established a dangerous precedent that Hindenburg used to bypass the Reichstag, thus weakening parliamentary government. Adolf Hitler would later use Article 48 to create the foundations of his dictatorship.

Hindenburg appointed three chancellors from March 1930 to January 1933—Heinrich Brüning (1885–1970), Franz von Papen (1879–1969), and Kurt von Schleicher (1882–1934). Each was a conservative disdainful of parliamentary democracy and each hoped to transform the Weimar democratic system into an authoritarian regime that would restore Germany to its prewar prominence. The neutralization of the traditional political parties and the growing inability of the three chancellors to resolve Germany's desperate economic and social problems saw some voters shift their loyalties to some of Germany's extremist parties such as the communists and the Nazis. This did not mean, of course, that Germany's mainstream political parties, the Social Democrats and the Catholic Center Party, totally collapsed. Their inability to work out viable coalitions in the face of presidential rule, however, created a dramatic increase in voter support for the Nazis, who tried to frighten voters by pointing to the growing power of German communists. The Nazis' intention was to raise anew fear of a Soviet-sponsored takeover of the German state.

As a result, the Nazis won dramatic political successes in national, regional, and local elections from the fall of 1929 through the summer of 1930. Backed by a sophisticated national political organization, the Nazis got 6.5 million votes in the September 14, 1930, Reichstag elections, winning 107 seats. Most of this increase was at the expense of the mainstream political parties except for the communists, who acquired 77 seats, an increase of one third over 1928 figures. The growing power of the communists played directly into the Nazis' hands, who talked constantly of the growing threat of international Jewish-dominated communism. In contrast, the Nazis promised they would restore traditional German values and make Germany a great nation again when they came to power.

The Jewish question was not prominent in Nazi campaigning during the fall 1930 Reichstag elections. Instead, Hitler emphasized *lebensraum* and promised to build a new Germany on the bones of the decaying Weimar Republic. It would be a state based on firm Aryan racial ideals that would restore Germany to international prominence. During an interview with *The Times* (London) on October 15, 1930, Hitler claimed that the party rejected anti-Semitism and wanted nothing to do with pogroms. Nazi doctrine, he told the reporter, was "Germany for the Germans." The party would base its attitude towards Jews on how Jews viewed this doctrine. But, he added, "if Jews associated themselves with Bolshevism, as many unfortunately did, they would be regarded as enemies." The Nazi Party, Hitler concluded, was opposed to violence but would defend itself if attacked.[53]

Violence, unfortunately, was now a hallmark of Nazi electioneering. And Hitler, as hard as he tried, could not help but tie Jews to Bolshevism and communism. He remained as anti-Semitic as ever. In the midst of a power struggle between Joseph Goebbels and Otto Strasser in the spring of 1930, Hitler called Strasser "an intellectual Jew, totally incapable of organization, a Marxist, of the purest ilk."[54] Hitler often disguised his anti-Semitism as "anti-Bolshevism." On October 5, 1930, Brüning, who was about to begin his second term as chancellor, met with Hitler to ask that he halt his attacks against the government. Brüning later wrote that he was surprised by how many times Hitler talked about "annihilating" his political enemies as well as the Soviet Union, "the home of Bolshevism."[55] Ten days later, during his interview with the reporter from *The Times*, Hitler stated that if the Bolsheviks ever took over Germany, Western civilization would be destroyed.

The Nazis did not rest on their laurels after their dramatic Reichstag victory in 1930. Nazi political fortunes were now tied directly to the decaying economy and the seeming failure of the Brüning government to address or solve the country's problems. Equally important was the damage Brüning did during this period to democratic institutions of the Weimar state. He invoked Article 48 more than forty-five times between 1930 and 1931. The Nazis responded with a "perpetual campaign" that centered around continual propaganda assaults against the government. The growth in party membership, which rose from 108,717 to almost 1.5 million between 1930 and the end of 1932, reflected the campaign's success.[56] This increase translated into considerable political gains in local elections in 1931. Hitler further strengthened his national political image by joining the *Harzburger Front* in the fall of 1931, which was led by Hugenberg, Hitler, and other prominent right-wing leaders. Though the front was meant to unite these movements into a "National Opposition" campaign against Brüning, it did little more than help Hitler burnish his reputation as the country's most dynamic politician; indeed, his national prominence finally forced him to consider running for the presidency in 1932 against President Hindenburg.

Hitler did well in the first round of the presidential election on March 13, garnering 11.3 million votes. More than 18.6 million Germans voted for Hindenburg, and Ernst Thälman, Hitler's hated enemy and head of the *Kommunistische Partei Deutschlands*, got almost 5 million votes. Because no candidate got a majority of the votes, a second election was held on April 10. Hindenburg and Hitler's numbers increased to 19.3 million and 13.4 million respectively, but Thälman's vote totals dropped to 3.7 million. Though Hitler lost to the storied Hindenburg, the presidential elections made him a legitimate national politician. Although the Nazis seemed to have hit a political wall when it came to national support (their vote totals in the presidential and state elections in 1932 hovered between 35 and 38 percent), they were able to use the collapse of parliamentary government in the summer and fall of 1932 to their advantage.

Soon after his reelection, Hindenburg dismissed Brüning and replaced him with von Papen, who shared Brüning's dislike of Weimar democracy. Influenced partly by the growing unpopularity of von Papen's government, the Nazis hoped to increase their vote totals in new Reichstag elections in the summer of 1932. To help their cause, they began a reign of terror against the communists that brought the country close to civil war. Germany was now slowly drifting towards dictatorship by presidential decree. This was certainly on the mind of General Kurt von Schleicher, a close adviser to Hindenburg as minister of defense from June 1932 until January 1933. Schleicher, who was later murdered, along with his wife, in the 1934 Röhm Purge, wanted to create "an authoritarian regime, resting on the Reichswehr, with support from the National Socialists."[57] Schleicher, mindful of the voting strength of the Nazis and the 400,000-member SA, thought he could control Hitler by bringing him into a ruling coalition. It was a serious miscalculation. Hitler sought full control of the government and hoped the summer's Reichstag elections would bring the Nazis to power.

Though their vote totals were impressive, the Nazis garnered only 37.3 percent of the popular vote, enough to win 230 seats in the Reichstag. Though they more than doubled their Reichstag seats, their numbers were not sufficient to give them full control of the government. A disappointed Hitler met with Schleicher, who seemed to agree to Hitler's demands for the chancellorship and nine of the cabinet's fourteen seats. Hindenburg, though, refused to support Hitler as chancellor, commenting that "it would be a fine thing indeed were he to make the 'bohemian corporal' Reich Chancellor."[58] Hindenburg first met Hitler in the fall of 1931, and later said: "This Bohemian corporal wants to become Reich Chancellor? Never! At most he could be my Postmaster General. Then he can lick me on the stamps from behind."[59]

Hitler, as he often did, twisted the truth by claiming that he had rejected offers to join the cabinet. He continued to insist on nothing less than the chancellorship, and he spent much of the fall campaigning for new Reichstag elections on November 6.

In early October he met with a group of his supporters in his Munich apartment and discussed Nazi goals once they came to power. Nazism was a new faith, he declared, that would replace Christianity with a new "Deutsche Kirche (German church)." If Luther were alive, Hitler noted, he would bless this new "church." But it was not the church but the Jews and Marxists who were the Nazis' principal enemies. Once they were destroyed, he proclaimed, the Nazis would go to war against the Christian church and replace it "with our own temples, our own shrines." He blamed the church for its denial of "racialism," "suicidal tolerance," and the "French Revolution, Bolshevism, all of Marxism." It was "the tragedy of the Germanic world that no German 'Heiland [savior or redeemer]' was born among us; that our organic spiritual evolution was suddenly violently interrupted; that Jesus was judaized, distorted, falsified, and an alien Asiatic spirit was forced upon us. That is a crime we must repair."[60]

On the eve of the November Reichstag election, Goebbels predicted a defeat for the party. The Nazis lost 2 million votes, and their percent of the total vote dropped from 37.4 percent the previous summer to 33.1 percent in November. The middle-class voter was beginning to have second thoughts about Hitler and the Nazis. But the election also intensified the political crisis in government, which would ultimately benefit Hitler. Von Papen now tried to establish a presidential government by doing away with the Weimar constitution. Von Schleicher countered this by floating a game plan that would undercut von Papen's efforts and create a new, workable political alliance in the Reichstag. In early December 1932, von Schleicher convinced Hindenburg to appoint him as chancellor and dismiss von Papen. Von Schleicher then offered the vice chancellorship to an old Nazi rival of Hitler's, Gregor Strasser (1892–1934), in an effort to split and weaken the Nazi Party. Hitler angrily accused Strasser of trying to rob him of the chancellorship and forced him to refuse von Schleicher's offer. Strasser resigned from the party and was murdered for his treachery during the Röhm Purge. Von Papen countered Schleicher's efforts by offering Hindenburg a united rightist front headed by Hitler and the Nazis. Hindenburg, already dissatisfied with Schleicher because of earlier moves against von Papen, still hesitated to appoint Hitler chancellor until von Papen convinced him that if they gave Hitler only three cabinet seats, including the chancellorship, they could easily control him. Von Papen would serve as vice chancellor and Reich Commissioner for Prussia. Von Papen told Hindenburg that this would enable him to create a conservative majority in the Reichstag and end rule by presidential decree. Von Schleicher resigned as chancellor on January 28, 1933, and two days later Hindenburg appointed Adolf Hitler the chancellor of Germany. Von Papen, who became Germany's ambassador to Austria in 1934 and later Turkey from 1938 to 1944, later wrote that he and others "underrated Hitler's insatiable lust for power as an end in itself."[61] In underestimating Hitler, von Papen, Hindenburg, and others effectively destroyed all hope for democracy in interwar Germany. But no one ever dreamed of the horror that was soon to follow.

Conclusion

The seeds of Adolf Hitler's deep, obsessive hatred of the Jews were planted during his years in Vienna, though it took them years to mature. Although it could be argued that Hitler's anti-Semitism was born partially of political opportunism, there is no question that he was deeply affected by the ideas and writings of German nationalists such as George Ritter von Schönerer and others. Whatever the source of his deep hatred of the Jews, we know that by the fall of 1919 Hitler's anti-Semitism was virulent enough to trouble his military superiors.

Hitler found a ready home for his anti-Semitic ideas in the *Deutsche Arbeiterpartei*, which later became the Nazi Party. Hitler and the DAP's leaders shared a common hatred of Jews, and he quickly emerged as his party's most vocal anti-Semite. Over time, Hitler's anti-Semitism deepened as he transformed the Nazi Party into a vehicle for his racial and political ideas. From Hitler's perspective, the Jews, which he gradually linked with communism and Bolshevism, were the cause of all that had gone awry in Germany since the outbreak of World War I. The Jews, and their principal movement, communism, were, in Hitler's eyes, the Nazis' primary racial and political enemy.

He expanded the theme of Jewish Bolshevism in his *Second Book,* where he married his racial ideas with his foreign policy goals of *lebensraum* in the East. To prepare for this eastward thrust, Hitler argued, Germany had to strengthen itself racially, which would require a campaign against the Aryans' greatest enemy—the Jews.

Yet anti-Semitism was not what drew the average voter to Hitler and the Nazis, though it certainly was a factor. What really opened the door for the Nazis was a peculiar blend of economic and political chaos, which, when combined with widespread disillusionment with the Weimar democratic experiment and a desire to restore German national pride, created the peculiar environment that helped Hitler seize power as a theoretically weak chancellor. Pre–World War II Germany's last democratic leaders quickly discovered that they had miscalculated Hitler's political determination.

More important, many in Germany had failed completely to understand Hitler's deep hatred of the Jews and his determination, if given power, to do everything he could to drive them from Germany. Yet if anyone other than his followers had paid more attention to what Hitler and the Nazis had said about the Jews since the early 1920s, they would not have been surprised by the actions taken against the Jews in the months and years after Hitler's accession to power in early 1933. From Hitler's perspective, a campaign against the Jews was an essential part of the war for Aryan survival and expansion.

SOURCES FOR FURTHER STUDY AND RESEARCH
Primary Sources

Baynes, Norman H., ed. *The Speeches of Adolf Hitler, April 1922–August 1939.* 2 vols. New York: Howard Fertig, 1969.

"The Constitution of the German Confederation of August 11, 1919." http://web.jjay.cuny.edu/jobrien/reference/ob13.html.

Hindenburg, Marshal von. *Out of My Life.* Translated by F. A. Holt. London: Cassell, 1920.

Hitler, Adolf. *Hitler's Letters and Notes.* Compiled by Werner Maser. Translated by Arnold Pomerans. New York: Bantam Books, 1976.

———. *Mein Kampf.* Translated by Ralph Manheim. Boston: Houghton Mifflin, 1943.

Hubatsch, Walther. *Hindenburg und der Staat: Aus den papieren des Generalfeldmarschalls und Reichspräsidenten von 1878 bis 1934.* Berlin: Musterschmidt-Verlag, 1966.

Kubizek, August. *The Young Hitler I Knew*. Translated by E. V. Anderson. Cambridge, MA: Riverside Press, 1955.

Ludecke, Kurt Georg Wilhelm. *I Knew Hitler: The Story of a Nazi Who Escaped the Blood Purge*. London: Jarrolds, 1938.

Ludendorff, Erich von. *Ludendorff's Own Story, August 1914–November 1918*. 2 vols. Freeport, NY: Books for Libraries Press, 1971.

Maser, Werner, ed. *Hitler's Letters and Notes*. Translated by Arnold Pomerans. New York: Bantam Books, 1976.

Noakes, Jeremy, and Geoffrey Pridham, eds. *Nazism: A History in Documents and Eyewitness Accounts, 1919–1945*. Vol. 1, *The Nazi Party, State and Society, 1919–1939*. New York: Schocken Books, 1984.

Von Papen, Franz. *Memoirs*. Translated by Brian Connell. New York: E. P. Dutton, 1953.

The Treaty of Versailles (June 28, 1919). Part 7. Penalties. Article 227 and Part 8. Reparation Section. General Provisions. Article 231. http://history.acusd.edu/gen/text/versailles/ver231.html.

Weinberg, Gerhard L. *Hitler's Second Book: The Unpublished Sequel to Mein Kampf*. Translated by Krista Smith. New York: Enigma Books, 2003.

Secondary Sources

Barraclough, Geoffrey. *The Origins of Modern Germany*. New York: Capricorn Books, 1963.

Bessel, Richard. *Germany After the First World War*. Oxford: Clarendon Press, 1993.

Buse, Dieter K., and Juergen C. Doerr, eds. *Modern Germany: An Encyclopedia of History, People, and Culture, 1871–1990*. 2 vols. New York: Garland, 1998.

Childers, Thomas. *The Nazi Voter: The Social Foundations of Fascism in Germany, 1919–1933*. Chapel Hill: University of North Carolina Press, 1983.

Eyck, Erich. *From the Collapse of the Empire to Hindenburg's Election*. Vol. 1 of *A History of the Weimar Republic*. Translated by Harlan P. Hanson and Robert G. L. Waite. New York: Atheneum, 1970.

———. *From the Locarno Conference to Hitler's Seizure of Power*. Vol. 2 of *A History of the Weimar Republic*. Translated by Harlan P. Hanson and Robert G. L. Waite. New York: Atheneum, 1970.

Fest, Joachim C. *Hitler*. Translated by Richard and Clara Winston. New York: Harcourt Brace Jovanovich, 1974.

Fischer, Klaus. *Nazi Germany: A New History*. New York: Continuum, 1995.

Fowler, E. W. W. *Nazi Regalia*. Secaucus, NJ: Chartwell Books, 1992.

Gellatey, Robert. *Backing Hitler*. Oxford: Oxford University Press, 2001.

Grathwol, Robert P. *Stresemann and the DNVP: Reconciliation or Revenge in German Foreign Policy, 1924–1928*. Lawrence: The Regents Press of Kansas, 1980.

Hamilton, Richard F. *Who Voted for Hitler*. Princeton: Princeton University Press, 1982.

Halperin, S. William. *Germany Tried Democracy: A Political History of the Reich from 1918 to 1933*. New York: W. W. Norton, 1965.

Hildebrand, Klaus. *The Third Reich*. Translated by P. S. Falla. London: George Allen & Unwin, 1984.

Holborn, Hajo. *A History of Modern Germany: 1840–1945*. Princeton: Princeton University Press, 1982.

Kershaw, Ian. *Hitler: 1889–1936 Hubris*. New York: W. W. Norton, 1999.

Kirk, Tim. *The Longman Companion to Nazi Germany*. London: Longman, 1995.

Large, David Clay. *Where Ghosts Walked: Munich's Road to the Third Reich*. New York: W. W. Norton, 1997.

Levy, Richard S. *The Downfall of the Anti-Semitic Political Parties in Imperial Germany*. New Haven: Yale University Press, 1975.

Macdonogh, Giles. *The Last Kaiser: The Life of Wilhelm II*. New York: St. Martin's Press, 2000.

Orlow, Dietrich. *A History of Modern Germany: 1870 to Present*. Englewood Cliffs, NJ: Prentice-Hall, 1987.

Overy, Richard. *Goering*. London: Phoenix Press, 1984.

Spielvogel, Jackson J. *Hitler and Nazi Germany: A History*. 3rd ed. Upper Saddle River, NJ: Prentice Hall, 1988.

Tipton, Frank B. *A History of Modern Germany Since 1815*. Berkeley: University of California Press, 2003.

Waite, Robert G. L. *The Psychopathic God: Adolf Hitler*. New York: Basic Books, 1977.

Wheeler-Bennett, John W. *Hindenburg: The Wooden Titan*. London: Macmillan, 1967.

Wright, Jonathan. *Gustav Stresemann: Weimar's Greatest Statesman*. Oxford: Oxford University Press, 2002.

Zentner, Christian, and Friedemann Bedürftig, eds. *The Encyclopedia of the Third Reich*. Translated by Amy Hackett. New York: Da Capo Press, 1997.

CHAPTER 4

The Nazis in Power, 1933–1939

Eugenics, Race, and Biology;
Jews, the Handicapped, and the Roma

CHRONOLOGY

--**1871:** Article 175 of German Criminal Code makes homosexuality a crime
--**1904–1905:** Dr. Alfred Ploetz founds *Journal for Racial and Social Biology* and *Society for Racial Hygiene*
--**1905:** *Zigeuner-Buch* published by Gypsy Information Agency under Alfred Dillmann
--**1919:** Dr. Magnus Hirschfeld opens Institute for Sexual Science in Berlin
--**1920:** *Permission for the Destruction of Life Unworthy of Life* published
--**1925:** *The Problem of Curtailment of Life Unworthy of Life* published
--**1929:** Bavarian *Ziguenernachrichtendienst* becomes national clearing house for Roma issues
--**1930** *(December 31)*: Pope Pius XI issues *Casti Connubi*
--**1933** *(January 30)*: Adolf Hitler becomes Chancellor of Weimar Germany
--**1933** *(February 4)*: "Decree for the Protection of the German People"
--**1933** *(February 27)*: Reichstag fire
--**1933** *(February 28)*: *Reichstagsbrandverordnung* suspends many civil rights in Germany
--**1933** *(March 5)*: Reichstag elections; Nazis win 43.9 percent of vote
--**1933** *(March 21)*: Dachau concentration camp opened outside of Munich
--**1933** *(March 23)*: Reichstag passes Enabling Act
--**1933** *(April 1)*: National boycott of Jewish businesses
--**1933** *(April 7)*: Law for the Restoration of the Professional Civil Service
--**1933** *(May 6)*: National book burning of decadent books
--**1933** *(July 14)*: Sterilization law
--**1933** *(August 7)*: Haavara agreement
--**1933** *(November 8)*: Joseph Goebbels creates Reich Chamber of Culture
--**1934** *(June 30)*: Röhm Purge/Night of the Long Knives
--**1934** *(August 2)*: Death of President Hindenburg; Hitler combines chancellorship with presidency

——**1935:** Dr. Helmuth Unger publishes *Mission and Conscience*

——**1935** *(March 1)*: Saarland reunited with Germany

——**1935** *(September 15)*: Nuremberg Laws

——**1935** *(October 15)*: Marital Health Law

——**1936:** Reich Central Office for Combating Homosexuality and Abortion opened

——**1936:** Reich Center for Combating Gypsy Nuisance opened

——**1936:** Olympic Games (February 6–16, Garmisch-Parenkirchen); (August 1–16, Berlin)

——**1936** *(March 7)*: Occupation of Rhineland

——**1938** *(March 12)*: *Anschluß* with Austria

——**1938** *(July 6–15)*: Evian Conference

——**1938** *(September 29)*: Munich Accord awards Sudetenland to Germany

——**1938** *(November 9–10)*: *Krystallnacht*

——**1938** *(December 8)*: Heinrich Himmler issues decree Combating the Gypsy Plague

——**1939** *(January 21)*: Hitler tells Reichstag that Jews will be annihilated if war comes

——**1939** *(March 14)*: Germany invades remnant of Czechoslovakia

——**1939** *(May 13–June 17)*: *St. Louis* incident

——**1939** *(September 1)*: Germany invades Poland

The Jewish question was an important part of Nazi theoretical writings and propaganda well before Adolf Hitler's accession to power on January 30, 1933, as Weimar Germany's chancellor. Once Hitler took office, the "Jewish question" moved from the abstract world of Nazi theorizing into practical politics. Yet, in exploring the evolution of a Nazi plan for dealing with Germany's Jewish population, one must always remember that this issue, though seminal to Nazi ideology, had to be filtered through the maze of political considerations that governed much of what Hitler and the Nazi Party did during the early years in power. Until Hitler completed his *Gleichschaltung* (reordering or coordination) policy of completely nazifying Germany, he had to weigh his desire to strike forcefully against Germany's Jewish population with the practical realities of political power. These goals often conflicted with the more extreme, revolutionary factions within the Nazi movement who saw Hitler's appointment as chancellor as the signal for a war against the Jews. Throughout the German domestic phase of the Holocaust from January 30, 1933, until September 1, 1939, the Nazi campaign against the Third

Reich's Jews was complicated by the realities of domestic and international politics.

The Germans also victimized other groups and minorities during this phase of Hitler's reign, though Jews remained the principal target of the Nazis. Such policies ranged from ongoing harassment, the removal of citizenship rights, imprisonment, forced labor, sterilization, and murder. In many ways, the German campaign against the Jews and other groups can best be understood as an assault against all of European history's traditionally mistreated groups—the Jews, the Roma (Gypsies), the handicapped, the mentally ill, Afro-Germans, gays, religious and political dissidents, and others. The Nazi victory in Germany destroyed traditional, though often unpracticed, societal values anchored in the Judaeo-Christian ideal of humane compassion. The Nazis replaced this ethical tradition with a quasi-religious, amoral value system that promoted some of European society's worst prejudices. Brutal, animalistic instincts overcame any sense of moral restraint. The policies and practices devised to deal with the Nazis' various racial, biological, and political enemies in the first six years of the Hitler state were the precursors of the more deadly experiments against Jews and other minorities that took place during World War II.

Germany's Interwar Jewish Community

One of the myths propagated by the Nazis in their drive for power was the dominating presence of the German Jew, particularly in the German economy. The Nazis depicted Germany's Jewish community as a force determined to destroy the fabric of German society and culture, yet the reality is much different. Germany's Jewish community, which had peaked in 1925 at 568,000, numbered from 523,000 to 525,000 in 1933, and made up just 0.76 percent of the population of 66.1 million. Almost a third of Germany's Jews lived in Berlin; the rest lived in large and small urban areas throughout the country. German Jews did make up a disproportionate percent of the legal (16 percent) and medical professions (10 percent), and from 3 to 5 percent of the country's writers and journalists, accountants, and performing artists. More than 137,000 Jews were involved in business, the vast majority of them in small-scale merchandising. Only 2 percent of the country's bankers and stockbrokers were Jewish, a statistic that contradicted the Nazi claim that Jews controlled this vital part of the German economy. The only segment of the Germany economy in which the Jews played a predominant role was in the department store business (i.e., Tietz, Wertheim, Karstadt). The Nazis so detested these Jewish businesses, which they saw as symbols of Jewish modernism and economic domination, that they even mentioned them in the 1920 Party platform: "We demand the creation and maintenance of a healthy middle class, the immediate communalising of big department stores, and their lease at a cheap rate to small traders, and that the utmost consideration shall be shown to all small traders in the placing of State and municipal orders."[1]

Yet, as the Nazis learned during their early months in power, Jewish department stores were often controlled by non-Jewish German banks or foreign business concerns.

The Nazis also hated what they perceived to be the Jewish-controlled press; in fact, some of Germany's most respected journalists were Jewish. And although it is true that Jews owned some of Germany's more prominent newspapers such as the *Vossiche Zeitung* in Berlin and the *Frankfurter Zeitung,* neither paper ever had a circulation of more than 100,000 apiece. Moreover, Alfred Hugenberg (1865–1951), the head of the DNVP, an erstwhile political ally of Hitler's and the minister for economics and food in Hitler's first cabinet, owned a media conglomerate that controlled half of Germany's newspaper industry. Hugenberg was also the director of the Krupp industrial empire. But the Nazis, who viewed the press as an essential propaganda outlet for their own views, were paranoid about any perceived Jewish domination of this important media source. The longest article (no. 23) in the party program decreed that all German newspaper editors and contributors had to be "members of the nation." Moreover, the program stated, it should be illegal for "non-Germans" to own German newspapers or to influence them in any way. Anyone who violated such a law would be immediately deported; in fact, the "publishing of papers which are not conducive to the national welfare must be forbidden."[2]

In reality, Germany's Jewish community was a loyal, well-integrated part of German society. More than 80,000 Jews had served in the kaiser's armies in World War I; 12,000 had died serving their country. Thirty-five thousand German Jewish soldiers had been decorated for bravery during the war. By the time the Depression reached Germany, 23 percent of Germany's Jews had married non-Jews. These intermarriage figures were higher in Germany's larger cities. Unfortunately, though intermarriages represented strong

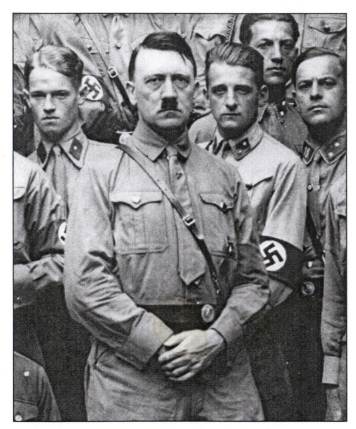

Hitler poses with a group of SS members after becoming Chancellor, 1933. USHMM Photo No. 24532.

assimilationist trends among Germany's Jewish community and reflected the growing opportunities for German Jews in the Weimar Republic, the Nazis viewed such unions as a dire threat to Aryan racial purity.

The Nazification of Germany and the "Jewish Question": 1933–1935

The "Jewish question" was a very important issue in the early days of Nazi power. Several months before Hitler became chancellor, a Nazi position paper laid out the basic aim of the Nazi Party if it should come to power: "Should the NSDAP receive an absolute majority [in the November 1932 Reichstag elections], Jews will be deprived of their rights by legal process. If, however, the NSDAP receives power only through a coalition, the rights of

German Jews will be undermined through administrative means."[3] Yet Adolf Hitler's first instincts after he became chancellor was to secure firm Nazi control of the government and then the country. And he was astoundingly successful.

When Hitler came to power, the Nazis held only three seats (Hitler, chancellor; Wilhelm Frick, interior; Hermann Göring, without portfolio) in a twelve-man cabinet and controlled a third of the seats in the Reichstag. To secure a Reichstag majority, Hitler called for new Reichstag elections, which he hoped would be Germany's last democratic election. In the interim, Hitler worked to strengthen the Nazis' political base throughout the country and used Nazi control of the police in Prussia (which made up 60 percent of Germany) and elsewhere to intimidate opponents. The mysterious Reichstag fire of February 27, 1933, greatly enhanced Nazi efforts to control state and local governments throughout the rest of Germany. The day after the fire, Hitler convinced Hindenburg to issue the *Reichstagsbrandverordnung* (Reichstag Fire Decree; *Verordnung des Reichspräsidenten zum Schutz von Volk und Staat,* Decree of the Reich President for Protecting the German *Volk* and the State), which suspended many civil rights and gave Hitler's government the right to govern any state that could not maintain public order. The SA was now sent throughout Germany to create disorder, and Wilhelm Frick (1877–1946), Hitler's interior minister, responded quickly by placing state and local governments under Nazi administrators.

Consequently, when new Reichstag elections took place on March 5, the Nazis had already taken over many important national

Hitler and Hindenburg, 1933. USHMM Photo No. 24538.

and regional administrative positions. Yet the Nazis only got 43.9 percent of the vote in an election that drew 88 percent of the country's eligible voters. The communists got 12.3 percent of the vote, the Social Democrats 18.3 percent, the Catholic *Zentrum* 11.2 percent, and Hugenberg's DNVP 8 percent. The Nazis pieced together a coalition with the DNVP that barely gave them a parliamentary majority. But after the elections and before the opening of the Reichstag in Berlin on March 21, the Nazis moved quickly throughout Germany to seize control of governments not already under party control. Hitler then began to prepare for passage of the *Ermächtigungsgesetz* (Enabling Act; *Gesetz zur Behebung der Not von Volk und Reich*; Law to Relieve the Distress of the *Volk* and Reich), which would allow the government to issue laws and decrees for four years without Reichstag approval.

But to pass this law, Hitler needed to control two thirds of the seats in the Reichstag. Since February, the Nazis had used Hindenburg's *Reichstagbrandverordnung* to intimidate

opponents, particularly the communists, during the election campaign. What followed was a Nazi reign of terror against the communists and others who opposed Hitler's movement. As part of this campaign, the Nazis created a network of wildcat detention centers to imprison their political opponents. On March 21, 1933, the *Münicher Neueste Nachrichten* and other newspapers published a communiqué from Heinrich Himmler, the *Reichsführer SS-* and *Kommisarischer Polizeipräsident der Stadt München*, announcing the creation a *Konzentrationslager* (*KZ*; concentration camp) outside the village of Dachau, near Munich. The camp, which, when completed, could hold 5,000 prisoners, was meant for communists, Social Democrats, and anyone else who "endangered state security." The opening of the camp, Himmler proclaimed, was done "without regard to any petty considerations and [we] are convinced they will have a calming effect upon the nation in whose interest we have acted."[4] By midsummer, the Nazis held 27,000 Germans in protective custody. *SS- Oberführer* (later *Obergruppenführer*) Theodor Eicke (1892–1943) became Dachau's first commandant. He so impressed Himmler with his work at Dachau that in 1934 he was made *Inspekteur der Konzentrationslager und Führer der SS- Wachbände* (Inspector of Concentration Camps and Führer of the SS-Guard Units), which later became known as the *Totenkopfverbände* (Death's Head Units). Eicke developed a rigid camp administration system that became the model for other camps throughout Germany and Nazi-occupied Europe.

Soon, the Nazis began to imprison groups they considered "asocial" (or habitual) criminals. By 1935, six concentration camps were open throughout the Third Reich—Dachau, Sachsenhausen, Oranienburg, Lichtenburg, Esterwegen, and Columbia Haus. In 1936, Hitler squelched talk of eliminating these camps and ordered that they remain open.

It was in this atmosphere that Hitler was able to convince a hesitant Roman Catholic *Zentrum* Party to join his coalition by promising to protect the Roman Catholic Church in Germany. Though this still did not give Hitler his two thirds majority, the Nazi leadership was certain that the Reichstag's eighty-one communist delegates, most of whom were in jail or in exile abroad, would not appear when the vote was taken for the Enabling Act on March 23. The Social Democrats were the only party to oppose the Enabling Act, which passed by 441 to 94.

This act marked the end of democracy in interwar Germany and gave Hitler firm control of the German government. According to Ian Kershaw, what made Hitler's victory possible "were important strands of continuity in German political culture stretching back beyond the First World War—chauvinistic nationalism, imperialism, racism, anti-Marxism, glorification of war, the placing of order above freedom, caesaristic attractions of strong authority—as well as the specific and more short-term consequences of the multi-layered crises that afflicted Weimar democracy from the start."[5]

Hitler's genius, of course, was his ability "to bind together for a time all of the strands of continuity with 'old Germany.'"[6] Racism, particularly anti-Semitism, remained an important part of Nazi thinking at this time and would become a central issue in the early months of Nazi power.

Jews suffered quite a bit during this period, particularly at the hands of the SA, the most violent anti-Semitic group in the Nazi movement. Local SA units attacked Jewish businesses and initiated boycotts of Jewish businesses and department stores. They also kidnapped Jews for ransom and enjoyed humiliating Jews in public. These uncoordinated SA acts occasionally created conflicts with local police units and compromised Nazi efforts nationally to maintain law and order. They also created a dilemma for Hitler and the Nazi leadership: On the one hand, they could not allow the SA to continue to create public disorder; on the other, since the SA was an important element in the Nazi revolution, a way had to be found to temper its excesses without destroying its revolutionary, anti-Semitic zeal. Consequently, on March 28, 1933, Hitler declared an indefinite nationwide boycott of Jewish businesses and professional activities, to begin on April 1. He appointed Julius Streicher as head of a *Zentralkomitee zur Abwehr der jüdische Greuel und Boykotthetze* (Central Committee for Defense Against Jewish Atrocity and Boycott Propaganda), which would organize the boycott. Several days earlier, Hermann Göring told Germany's Jewish leaders that he could no longer guarantee their community's safety, and he blamed the Jews for the boycott. Germany's Jews, he told them, were responsible for the growing American and British press attacks against the Nazi regime, particularly calls for a boycott of German goods abroad. Joseph Goebbels, Hitler's propaganda chief, told Party organizations:

SA members boycott Jewish Store in Kaiserslautern, 1933. Sign caption
reads: "Germans. Do Not Buy From Jews!" USHMM Photo No. 37350,
courtesy of Stadtarchiv der Stadt Kaiserslautern.

National Socialists, you performed the miracle of overthrowing the November state in a single attack; you will solve this second assignment in similar fashion. Let international Jewry be put on notice. . . . We took care of the Marxist agitators in Germany, and they won't force us to our knees, even if they now carry on from abroad their criminal treachery against the *Volk*. National Socialists! Saturday, at the stroke of ten, the Jews will find out whom they've declared war on![7]

Local party organizations did everything possible to insure the boycott of all Jewish businesses, though those owned by foreign Jewish interests were to be left alone. At the

last minute, Hjalmar Schacht (1877–1970), president of the *Reichsbank*, Foreign Minister Konstantin von Neurath (1873–1958), who had recently joined the Nazi Party and the SS, and even President Hindenburg tried to convince Hitler to call off the boycott because of its potential impact on the economy. Mindful that the American, British, and French governments had just announced their refusal to join in a boycott of German goods, Hitler compromised and decided to hold a one-day boycott on April 1. He added, though, that if the "'horror agitation'" from abroad did not cease, the boycott would resume on April 5.[8]

Public support for the boycott was mixed, and the SA, who used the occasion as "a cover for plundering and violence," carried it out unevenly. The Nazi press claimed the boycott was a success, though the *New York Times* accused the Nazis of acting "blindly and . . . with a touch of insanity." On the other hand, the *Christian Science Monitor* blamed the boycott on exaggerated American Jewish reports about the mistreatment of German Jews. Other foreign press reports tended to excuse Nazi excesses as immature acts of revolutionary zeal.[9]

Since many of the boycotted businesses were jointly owned with non-Jews, these co-owners had to be protected from boycott protests. During the next few months, Hitler's government grudgingly had to loan the Tietz and Karstadt chains millions of *Reichsmarks* to prevent them from going under and to save thousands of non-Jewish German jobs. The boycott traumatized Germany's Jewish community, whose members began slowly to realize that this "was a Germany in which they could no longer feel 'at home,' in which routine discrimination had been replaced by state-sponsored persecution."[10]

Such fears grew in the next seven months as the Nazis passed laws that greatly limited the role of Jews in German professional and educational life. This legislation was part of Hitler's *Gleichschaltung* efforts to nazify Germany completely. Between April and July 1933, the Nazis eliminated the state legislatures and replaced them with *Reichstatthälter* (Reich governors). The government outlawed trade unions in May, and during the next two months did away with all political parties except the Nazi Party. Increasingly, German professionals were drawn into the Nazi orbit and forced to join Nazi-sponsored organizations for teachers, lawyers, physicians, and others. The Nazis also tried to control Germany's churches, Roman Catholic and Protestant, but success was mixed.

Traditionally, Germany's Roman Catholic Church had opposed the Nazis more staunchly than the country's Protestants. This changed

with the signing of the *Reichskonkordat* (Reichs Concordant) between the Vatican and Germany on July 8, 1933, that guaranteed the sanctity of the Roman Catholic Church in Germany in return for recognition of Hitler's government. Perhaps its most important feature, at least from Hitler's perspective, was the "exclusion of the clergy from politics."[11] According to James Carroll, the *Reichskonkordat* "effectively removed the German Roman Catholic Church from any continued role of opposition to Hitler."[12] This was doubly so given the Roman Catholic *Zentrum*'s earlier decision to support Hitler's efforts to pass the Enabling Act. When violations of the *Reichskonkordat* did occur, church leaders tended to fall back on its terms in protest. In the end, German Roman Catholic leaders were more concerned about protecting the church's institutions than non–Roman Catholic victims of Nazi persecution.

Germany's Protestants were more difficult to deal with even though Protestants in general had been less critical of the Nazi movement in the years before 1933 than the country's Roman Catholics. There was widespread resistance to Nazi efforts to force German Protestants into a united *Deutsche Christen* (German Christian) church under *Reichsbischop* Ludwig Müller (1883–1945). In the fall of 1933, Pastor Martin Niemöller (1892–1984), an early supporter of the Nazi movement, and several colleagues formed the *Pfarrernotbund* (Pastors' Emergency League) after German Christians tried to impose the *Arierparagraph* (Aryan Paragraph), which forbade Jews from participating in any organization or having any role in public life. In time, this opposition group, which did not staunchly oppose the German Christians' racial ideas or its anti-Semitism, became the *Bekennende Kirche* (Confessing Church), the principal opposition movement against the *Deutsche Christen* church.[13]

Niemöller, a hero to Protestants worldwide because of his arrest, show trial, and imprisonment in 1937 as Hitler's "personal prisoner," later explained that he opposed the Aryan Paragraph because it "would effectively negate the teaching of baptism."[14] Niemöller, an avowed anti-Semite, thought that the church had to endure "Jewishness" as a "disagreeable fact" to show that it was "a community that transcends national groups."[15] As late as 1935, Niemöller told his congregation in Dahlem, a suburb of Berlin, that "the Jews have caused the crucifixion of God's Christ. . . . They bear the curse, and because they rejected the forgiveness, they drag with them as a fearsome burden the unforgiven blood-guilt of their fathers."[16] It was not until later that Niemöller gave any hint that he had changed his mind about this issue.

There were, of course, Protestant church leaders who did speak out against German anti-Semitism. Dietrich Bonhoeffer (1906–1945), a leading Protestant theologian and church leader executed for his involvement in the plot to kill Hitler in the summer of 1944, was one of the few Confessing Church leaders to speak out against the racist implications of Nazi teachings. He considered Hitler's accession to power "an end to the church in Germany." He strongly opposed the Aryan Paragraph because he thought that keeping Jewish Christians from the "pastoral office" put them in an inferior position in the church. He considered supporters of the Aryan Paragraph "weak of faith."[17] And though Bonhoeffer never gave up his belief that Jews should covert to Christianity, in 1938 he wrote that God viewed synagogue and church equally. Jews, he argued, were "'brothers of Christians' and 'children of the covenant.'"[18] Bonhoeffer was deeply affected by the *Kristallnacht* pogrom in 1938 and later became involved in efforts to save Jews, most of whom were converts to Christianity, as part of his larger involvement in the anti-Nazi movement. The Gestapo arrested him in 1943 for these activities and charged him for this and various intelligence-related religious

crimes. Moved from prison to prison, he was ultimately executed on April 9, 1945, at the Flossenbürg concentration camp.

In the midst of their efforts to nazify Germany's churches, the government implemented a series of laws with serious consequences for the country's Jews. The first was the April 7, 1933, *Berufsbeamtengesetz* (Professional Civil Service Law; *Gesetz zur Wiederherstellung des Berufsbeamtentums;* Law for the Restoration of the Professional Civil Service), which made it legal to dismiss anyone who joined the Weimar civil service after November 9, 1918, or lacked proper credentials or training. It permitted the removal of anyone who might not be completely loyal to the Nazi regime because of past political affiliations and it also gave authorities the right to dismiss anyone who was not an Aryan. Three days before the law went into effect, President Hindenburg wrote to Hitler and complained about earlier dismissals and harassment of Jewish civil servants, judges, and lawyers who had served in the armed forces during World War I, or were sons or had sons who had suffered in the war. Hindenburg called such mistreatment "intolerable" and asked Hitler to allow these Jews to keep their government jobs. Consequently, the law allowed exemptions for all war veterans, whether they were Jewish or not, as long as they were professionally qualified and politically reliable. And since the law applied only to the upper ranks of the civil service, it had little practical impact on lower-level Jewish civil servants.

The Reichstag's *Gesetz betreffend die Zulassung zur Anwaltschaft* (Law Concerning Admission to the Legal Profession) of the same date also included veterans' exemptions but affected only a sixth of Germany's 18,000 lawyers and judges. The same was true of the *Verordnung über die Zulassung von Ärzten zur Tätigkeit bei den Krankenkassen* (Decree Regarding Physicians' Services with the National Health Service; April 22, 1933), which said that patients who were treated by non-Aryan physicians would not be covered by German national health insurance. This law affected only about 25 percent of the Jewish doctors who worked for the National Health Service because of the Hindenburg exemptions, though it did severely weaken Germany's Jewish medical community.

The April 25 *Gesetz gegen die Überfüllung deutscher Schulen und Hochschulen* (Law Against the Overcrowding of German Schools) had a much more devastating impact on the country's urban-based Jewish community because it limited Jewish enrollment in postprimary German schools to 1.5 percent of the total enrollment. Exceptions were in cities where Jews made up 5 percent of the population. But even then, Jews could make up no more than 5 percent of a city's school population. Hindenburg's exemptions also applied here: Jewish communities throughout Germany now had to create alternative schools, and Jewish children who remained in German schools had to suffer through the growing nazification of the curriculum and its anti-Semitic themes.

That summer, the Reichstag passed other laws that affected Jews. These new regulations gave authorities the right to seize the property of any organization and revoke the citizenship of anyone the government deemed unfit for citizenship. Aimed primarily at the country's 150,000 East European Jews who had entered Germany after the war, the *Ausbürgerungsgesetz* (Denaturaliztion Law; *Gesetz über den Widerruf von Einbürgerungen und die Aberkennung der deutscher Staatsangehörigkeit;* Law on the Revocation of Naturalization and the Annulment of German Citizenship) was strengthened a year later by the *Gesetz über die Reichsverweisungen* (Law Regarding Expulsion from the Reich).

The Nazis also initiated a campaign against Jewish intellectuals, writers, and artists, whose works they considered decadent. On May 10, 1933, the Nazis sponsored a massive book burning of works by Jewish, foreign, and other "undesirable" authors. Six months later, Joseph Goebbels created the *Reichskulturkammer* (Chamber of Culture), which had seven chambers for film, music, theater, the press, writing, fine arts, and radio. In his address marking the opening of the *Reichskulturkammer* in the hall of the Berlin Philharmonic on November 8, 1933, Goebbels talked of a "great German awakening of our times" that would culturally bring forth the "healthy instincts of the *Volk.*"[19] Any artist who wanted to work in Nazi Germany had to apply to his or her particular chamber for permission to work. Goebbels felt strongly that Jews should not play any role in German cultural life. Over the next year, he excluded numerous Jewish artists, journalists, and musicians from playing active roles in their professions. He fired Otto Klemperer (1885–1973), the conductor of the Berlin State Opera, in late 1933 because he was Jewish. Klemperer soon joined other distinguished Jewish musicians, artists, and intellectuals in exile.

Germany's Jewish community looked for a silver lining in all this. They were deeply patriotic and concerned about the devastating impact of flight from Germany. By the end of 1933, there seemed to be a lull in the Nazis' anti-Semitic furor. Earlier that summer, Rudolf Hess had ordered Julius Streicher's *Zentral Komitee* to limit its anti-Semitic activities to the investigation of Jewish corruption in Germany; and in September, Goebbels told party members at the Nuremberg rally that domestic and international pressures made it difficult to pursue more rigorous anti-Semitic policies. Goebbels later noted in his diary that Hitler had forced him to moderate his statements about the Jews in his Nuremberg speech. On December 7, 1933, Hitler's government announced that it would not apply business restrictions to non-Aryans. A few weeks earlier, Germany's most prominent Jewish newspaper, the *Jüdische Rundschau* (Jewish Review), had observed:

Joseph Goebbels urges Germans to support Jewish boycott, 1933. USHMM Photo No. 44203, courtesy of National Archives and Records Adminstration, College Park.

If we look at the events of the past year, we must note that many German Jews have lost their economic base for existence. Yet it appears from the pronouncements of authoritative sources that in the future our economic existence will be guaranteed, though limited, by the new legal situation. . . . In this light we can understand Dr. Goebbels remark [in his September Nuremberg speech] that what needs to be solved concerning the Jewish question has been solved by the government.[20]

By this time, about 37,000 Jews had fled Germany. Another 23,000 left in 1934. Heartened by what seemed to be an end to more virulent forms of anti-Semitism in Germany and the revival of the economy, 10,000 German Jews returned to the Third Reich in 1935. Those who had gone abroad found a Europe ravaged by the Depression and surging anti-Semitism.

The only exceptions were the 16,000 Jews who had left for Palestine between 1933 and 1934, aided in part by the *Haavara* (transfer) agreement of September 1933 between Germany and the Jewish Agency (JA) in Palestine. The JA was the administrative wing of the Zionist Organization in Palestine, and was created after the League of Nations issued its Mandate for Palestine on July 24, 1922. The mandate incorporated the earlier Balfour Declaration, which recognized the Jewish people's historic ties with Palestine as the basis for a future Jewish homeland. By the spring of 1933, the JA, which was responsible for day-to-day Jewish affairs in Palestine, had become the principal bargaining agent for the Jews. The *Haavara* accord allowed German Jews to transfer their assets into a special German account that would permit them to get half their resources back when they entered Palestine; the JA used the other half to help pay for German goods. Since Nazi regulations forced anyone leaving Germany to leave most of their assets behind, the *Haavara* accord allowed Jews who fled to Palestine to protect some of their assets.

The return of more than 16 percent of the German Jews who had left the Third Reich in 1933 and 1934, though, did not mean that German Jews were comfortable with their restricted status. One woman recorded a conversation in the spring of 1935 between German Jews about a Jewish physician who had recently left Germany:

> The women protested strongly: they found that it took more courage to go than to stay. . . . "Why should we stay here and wait for our eventual ruin? Isn't it better to go and build up a new existence somewhere else, before our strength is exhausted by the constant physical and psychic pressure? Isn't the future of our children more important than a completely senseless hold out. . . ." All the women, without exception, shared this opinion . . . , while the men, more or less passionately, spoke against it. Also, on the way home, I discussed this with my husband. Like all other men, he simply couldn't imagine how one could leave one's beloved homeland and the duties that fill a man's life. "Could you really give that all up . . . ?" The tone of his voice told me how upset he was at the mere thought of this. "I could," I said, without hesitating a second.[21]

Part of the reason for the decline in violent anti-Semitism in Germany at this time centered around Hitler's efforts to consolidate his dictatorship. The one institution that Hitler had not been able to win over fully was the military. *Reichswehr* leaders were particularly concerned with the growing strength of the SA, which had grown to 2.5 million by early 1934. Ernst Röhm, the head of the SA, was open about the SA becoming the nucleus of a new German army and thought that Hitler had turned his back on many of the revolutionary ideals of the Nazi movement. Hitler did not support Röhm's ideas about the SA and the army because he was afraid this would threaten his power base. Hitler knew that President Hindenburg was in failing health; he also realized that if he wanted to assume the presidency after Hindenburg's death he would have to rein in the SA to get the military's support for this move. Sensitive to Hitler's goals, Himmler, Göring, and other Nazi leaders convinced Hitler that the SA was planning a coup against him, which was not true.

On June 30, 1934, Hitler personally oversaw the arrest of Röhm and other SA leaders at a resort in Bavaria, instigating what became known as the Röhm Purge or "Night of the Long Knives." Hitler and the Nazi leadership used the Röhm Purge to settle scores against from eighty-five to a hundred political enemies throughout Germany. Though initially hesitant, Hitler finally ordered Röhm's murder and ordered Theodor Eicke, Dachau's commandant, to take care of the matter. When Röhm refused to take his own life, Eicke had one of his aides shoot him. The press explained that the Führer had no recourse but to move against a band of traitors and homosexual deviants.

The SA now became nothing more than a Nazi "military sports and training body."[22] Heinrich Himmler moved quickly to make the SS Nazi Germany's top paramilitary organization. Several days after the Purge, Hindenburg wired Hitler his thanks for this move: "From the reports placed before me I learn that you, by your determined action and your brave personal intervention, have nipped treason in the bud. You have saved the German nation from serious danger. For this I express to you my most profound thanks and sincere appreciation."[23]

Hitler now had the military leadership in his back pocket. A month later, President Hindenburg died. Within an hour of his death, Hitler had assumed the German presidency and combined his office with the chancellorship. Officially, Hitler now became the Führer and Reich chancellor. On the day of Hindenburg's death (August 2, 1934), every member of the armed forces was required to swear the following oath to Adolf Hitler: "I swear before God this sacred oath: I will render unconditional obedience to Adolf Hitler, the Führer of the German nation and people, Supreme Commander of the Armed Forces, and will be ready as a brave soldier to risk my life at any time for this oath."[24]

Civil servants were soon required to take a similar oath of loyalty to Hitler. The Nazis transformed Hindenburg's August 6 funeral into a Nazi mass; thirteen days later, Hitler held a plebiscite on the question of the Führer's assumption of the Reich presidency. More than 84 percent of those who voted approved of this move. Hitler celebrated his victory at the Nuremberg *Parteitage* (party days) rally two weeks later. In a spectacle immortalized in filmmaker Leni Riefenstahl's (1902–2003) *Triumph des Willens* (Triumph of the Will), *Gauleiter* Adolf Wagner (1890–1944) proclaimed: "The German form of life is definitely determined for the next thousand years. The Age of Nerves of the nineteenth century has found its close with us. There will be no other revolution in Germany for the next one thousand years!"[25]

The Jewish question remained on the back burner, but not for long. On January 13, 1935, the Nazi-supported *Deutsche Front* garnered more than 90 percent of the vote in a plebiscite in the Saarland, an area placed under French control in the Treaty of Versailles, that supported reunification with Germany. On March 1, 1935, the Saarland was reunited with Germany; two weeks later, Hitler announced that Germany would reinstate the draft, despite recent pledges to honor the Treaty of Versailles. Hitler had already begun a rearmament program that would be the first step in his plan to acquire *lebensraum* for his future German empire,

and reviving the draft was a key element in his plans. Europe's major powers voiced shock and disapproval, but little else. Great Britain quickly signed a naval accord with Germany that indirectly approved Hitler's rearmament plans. Emboldened by these domestic and international victories, Hitler and the Nazi Party were now ready to revisit the Jewish question. Within a few months, the relative calm that had deluded Germany's Jewish community ended.

In some parts of Germany, anti-Semitic violence had continued unabated, and by early spring 1935, prominent party leaders began verbal assaults against Germany's Jews. When the SS, the SA, and the *Hitlerjugend* (HJ; Hitler Youth) began personal attacks against Jews, signs cropped up throughout the country stating *Juden sind hier unerwünscht* (Jews Not Wanted Here). According to Ian Kershaw, Nazi radicals concluded that "they were being given the green light to attack Jews in any way they saw fit."[26] Most of the violence came from party groups. The average German was too worried about the country's continued economic malaise to care much about the increase in anti-Semitic violence. In fact, the attacks against Jews intensified public criticism of the Nazi Party, but not because of any sympathy for the Jews.

The Nuremberg Laws

In the fall of 1935, Hitler ordered that a series of laws be created to better define the status of the Jews in Germany, particularly as it related to intermarriage and citizenship. This legislation, collectively known as the Nuremberg Laws, was a response to a growing body of demands from party radicals such as Julius Streicher and Heinrich Himmler who wanted the legal status of Germany's Jews clarified. Dr. Gerhard Wagner (1888–1938), the *Reichsärzteführer* (Reich Physicians Leader) of the *Nationalsozialistischer Deutscher Ärztebund* (National Socialist German Physicians' League), also played an important role in pushing for a new body of laws dealing with the Jews.

In the summer of 1933, *Deutsches Ärzteblatt* (German Physicians' Journal), the journal of the *Deutscher Ärztebund,* called for the outlawing of marriages between Jews and non-Jews. Other medical journals voiced similar support for such a ban partly because many German physicians resented the prominence of Jewish physicians in the medical profession. This resentment partly explains the high percentage (44.8 percent) of physicians who joined the Nazi Party; in fact, so many German physicians had applied for party membership by the end of 1933 that the Nazi Party halted the application process until it could deal with the backlog. The Nazis' racial policies and experiments provided new medical opportunities that never existed in the Weimar Republic and explains why the number of physicians in the Third Reich grew from 51,500 in 1933 to 59,454 in 1939, and continued to increase during the war. Hitler underscored the importance of physicians to the Nazi regime in an address to members of the newly formed *Deutscher Ärztebund* in 1933: "You, you National Socialist doctors, I cannot do without you for a single day, not a single hour. If not for you, if you fail me, then all is lost. For what good are our struggles, if the health of our people is in danger?"[27]

In early 1935, the party newspaper, *Völkischer Beobachter,* announced that each German would be required to carry an *Ariernachweis* (Aryan health certificate). Several months later, Wilhelm Frick (1877–1946), the minister of the interior, proclaimed that the state now considered marriages between an Aryan and a Jew to be racial and not religious. Frick ordered all health offices throughout the Reich to create special counseling centers to oversee all marriage requests and to assemble a genealogical archive for the entire country. Seven months later, Frick told state marriage bureaus to delay all mixed-marriage applications because the government would soon

issue new regulations concerning such unions. As anti-Semitic violence spread throughout the country, some of Germany's economic leaders argued that new anti-Jewish legislation would temper some of this violence because it was hurting Germany's economy. The Nuremberg Laws were written partly in an attempt to resolve the conflict between party radicals like Streicher who were continuing to wage war against the Jews in the streets and those who were concerned about the impact of such violence on the German economy.

The result was the Nuremberg Laws, which, though completed during the final days of the Nuremberg *Parteitage* (September 8–15, 1935), were based on earlier legal concepts and ideas discussed in the upper echelons of the party. Hitler had already indicated his resolve to "nip in the bud" any danger that threatened the nation, and he explicitly named "Jewish Marxism" as one of those dangers.[28] On September 12, Gerhard Wagner announced that a *Blutschutzgesetz* (Law to Protect German Blood) would soon appear; two days later, Hitler ordered the Interior Ministry to prepare a law dealing with marriages between Aryans and non-Aryans that he could present to the Reichstag before the end of the *Parteitage.*[29] Hitler rejected the original drafts as too lenient and then insisted on adding a new law dealing with Reich citizenship. Ultimately, Hitler presented two laws to the Reichstag on September 15 that became collectively known as the Nuremberg Laws, the *Blutschutzgesetz* (*Gesetz zum Schutz des deutschen Blutes und der deutschen Ehre*; Law for the Protection of German Blood and Honor) and the *Reichsburgergesetz* (Reich Citizenship Law).

The *Reichsburgergesetz* stated that only someone of German or related blood who was willing to serve the German people and the Reich could be a *Reichsbürger* (citizen of the Reich), a status affording that individual "full political rights." Others could enjoy sta-

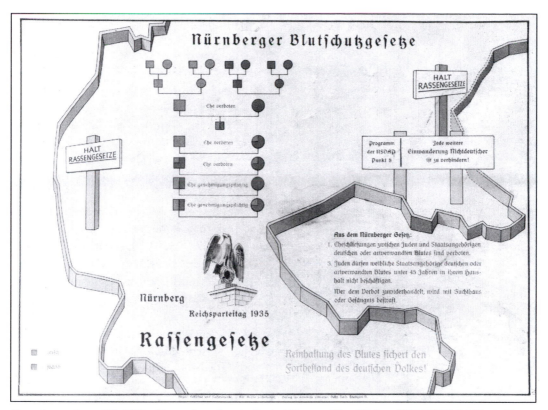

Eugenics poster entitled "The Nuremberg Law to Protect German Blood," circa 1935. USHMM Photo No. 94188, courtesy of Hans Pauli.

tus only as *Staatsangehöriger* (subject of the state), meaning they received the "protection of the German Reich" and had particular obligations to the Reich.[30] The *Blutschutzgesetz* outlawed marriages and extramarital relations between Aryans and Jews and forbade Jews from employing in their households female Aryans younger than forty-five, possibly a throwback to rumors that Hitler's grandmother, Maria Schikelgruber, had supposedly worked for a Jewish household in Linz. Jews were also not allowed to fly Nazi flags.

The first two laws, only skeletal in outline, were later expanded through supplemental decrees to deal fully with various aspects of Nazi policy towards the Jews. The Interior Ministry would issue thirteen supplementary decrees to the *Reichsburgergesetz* between 1935 and 1943 and one for the *Blutschutzgesetz*. The most important supplements to the *Reichsburgersgesetz*

extended its coverage to *Jewish Mischling* and defined a Jew as someone with "at least three grandparents who are racially full Jews." A Jewish *Mischling* was someone with two full-blooded Jewish grandparents who were members of the Jewish religious community when the Nuremberg Laws came into effect, was married to a Jew at the time, was the offspring of such a marriage, or was the offspring of an extramarital relationship with a Jew after July 31, 1936. Other supplements ordered that Jewish civil servants be forcibly retired at the end of 1935, and forced Jewish physicians and attorneys to give up their licenses. Those allowed to continue to practice could treat or serve other Jews only. In early 1936, Rudolf Hess estimated that from 400,000 to 500,000 people in Germany were full or three-quarters Jewish and another 300,000 were quarter- or half-Jewish *Mischling*.

Poster advertising special edition of "Der Stürmer" on "Rassenschande" (race pollution), circa 1935. USHMM Photo No. 32615, courtesy of Deutsches Historisches Museum GmbH.

On October 18, 1935, the government issued a third law that complemented the Nuremberg Laws, the *Ehegesundheitsgesetz* (Marital Health Law; officially, *Gesetz zum Schutze der Erbgesundheit des Deutschen Volkes*; Law for the Protection of the Genetic Health of the German People). It required couples who wished to marry to acquire a *Ehetauglichkeitszeugnis* (certificate of fitness to marry) from public health officials. Before the authorities could issue such a certificate, they had to determine whether either applicant might "racially damage" the marriage because of a history feeblemindedness, epilepsy, venereal disease, or other "racially" contagious diseases. The *Ehegesundheitsgesetz*

gave officials the right to register and exclude "'alien' races and the 'racially less valuable' from the 'national community.'" The *Ehegesundheitsgesetz* would in time allow Nazi officials to register most of the German population and so identify those who were members of "alien" races or were "racially damaged."[31]

One of those targeted "alien" groups were the *Zigeuner* (Gypsies) or Roma. On November 26, 1935, the Interior Ministry issued special decrees to include the *Zigeuner* in the *Reichsburgergesetz*. One, on November 26, 1935, identified "Gypsies, Negroes and their Bastards" as pollutants of Aryan blood because of their *artfremdes blut* (alien blood) and banned marriages between Aryans and these groups. And even though the Roma did not technically lose their *Reichsbürger* status until 1943, the state moved quickly to deprive them of other rights. On December 1, 1935, Frick published an article in the *Deutsche Juristen-Zeitung* in which he noted that, like Jews, Roma and Negroes could not become German citizens. Five weeks later, his office issued a decree stating that "besides the Jews, normally the Gypsies belong to the alien races in Europe." In March, Frick ordered all *Zigeuner* and *Zigeunermischlinge* stricken from voter rolls throughout Germany. The following year, the *Wehrmacht* (military or defense power), the new name for the German armed forces, decreed that Roma could not serve in the military, though hundreds did through the early years of World War II.[32]

The German medical community applauded the Nuremberg Laws. The *Deutsches Ärzteblatt* said the new laws would protect Germany from "alien races" and purify the *völkisch* soul of the Third Reich. The journal was particularly complimentary of the *Ehegesundheitsgesetz*, which, it claimed, would insure the health of the Aryan German people for generations to come. Hitler shared these views and firmly believed in racial laws that prevented the defilement of German

Aryan blood by racial inferiors. He told a United Press reporter in November 1935 that the Nuremberg Laws were meant to protect the German people from the negative influence of Jews and Jewish Bolshevism. In fact, he said, the Nuremberg Laws protected Jews because, since their passage, anti-Semitic agitation had declined. At the same time, Hitler warned that his government would pass new legislation to protect the nation if the country's Jewish community began to cause trouble again.

Germany's Jewish community hoped this meant an end to the recent upsurge in violent anti-Semitism. In late September 1935, the *Reichsvertretung der Juden in Deutschland* (Reich Representative of German Jews in Germany), the pre-1939 de facto representative body for the Third Reich's Jewish community under Rabbi Leo Baeck (1873–1956) and Otto Hirsch (1885–1941), announced it would try to seek a *modus vivendi* with the Nazis. The *Reichsvertreutung*'s leadership hoped the Nuremberg Laws would be the pathway to this new relationship with Germany's Nazi leaders.

Hitler and Goebbels sign autographs for members of Canadian Figure Skating Team, Garmisch-Partenkirchen, 1936. USHMM Photo No. 02322A, courtesy of National Archives and Records Administration, College Park.

The Nazi Aryan Olympics (1936)

The reality, of course, was quite different. Although there was another lull in the Nazis' virulent campaign against the Jews, particularly in 1936 as they focused their attention on the Rhineland crisis and the Olympic Games in Garmisch-Partenkirchen in February and Berlin in August, less public efforts continued to limit the role of Jews in German society. Josef Goebbels, for example, continued his *Entjudung* (dejudaization) campaign against Jewish intellectuals and artists through his Reich Chamber of Culture. Hitler, who supported Goebbels's efforts, initially thought of suspend-

ing this campaign as his government prepared for the reoccupation of the Rhineland and the 1936 Olympics. He changed his mind after the murder of Wilhelm Gustloff (1895–1936), the Nazis' top leader in Switzerland, by a Jewish student in early 1936. Hitler bitterly attacked the Jews in a speech at Gustloff's funeral on February 12. He claimed that the Jews had murdered scores of Nazis over the years, acts he attributed to the "hate-filled power of our Jewish enemy," and pledged: "[T]his deed shall fall upon the doer."[33] Although Hitler permitted Goebbels to continue his *Entjudung* efforts by expanding his prohibition against Jewish membership in the Chamber of Culture, he banned "individual actions" against Jews.[34]

Hitler's restraint was closely linked to plans for his boldest international gamble to date—the illegal occupation of the Rhineland, which took place on March 7, 1935. Though the French could easily have stopped the occupation, they did nothing. German public opinion soared, and Ian Kershaw claims that this victory cemented Hitler's belief in his own infallibility. He now truly saw himself as Germany's messiah.[35]

But the Nazis were concerned about international reaction to the Rhineland occupation and did everything they could to diffuse it. In a speech to the Reichstag on March 7, Hitler reminded the French about how well their athletes had been treated at the Winter Olympics in Garmisch-Partenkirchen in February. Before they began, Hitler had ordered the removal of all anti-Semitic signs in Garmisch and now planned to do the same thing throughout Germany in preparation for the XI Olympiad Summer Games (August 1–16, 1936) in Berlin. Party officials also ordered police in the capital to round up hundreds of Roma and send them to a special camp near Marzhan to keep them out of the public eye. Hitler wanted the XI Summer Olympiad to show the world a new, prosperous, stable Germany, despite efforts in the United States and elsewhere to mount a boycott of the Nazi Olympics.

Soon after Hitler came to power, the *Deutscher Reichsbund für Leibesübungen* (DRL; German Reich League for Physical Exercises) under *Reichssportführer* Hans von Tschammer und Osten (1887–1943) banned non-Aryans from participation in DRL-sponsored sports. This meant that several world-class Jewish athletes, such as Erich Seelig, a boxer; Dr. Daniel Prenn, Germany's top tennis player; and Gretel Bergmann (1914–), a high-jumper, could no longer be members of Germany's national sports teams. They could now participate only in sports activities sponsored by Jewish sports clubs such as Maccabee and *Der Schild* (The Shield), whose facilities were inferior to those funded by DRL. Johann

"Rukelie" Trollmann (1907–1943), a Roma and Germany's middleweight boxing champion, was also excluded from DRL-sponsored activities and facilities. Trollmann, who was later sterilized, served in the Wehrmacht on the eastern front. In 1943, he was sent to the Neuengamme concentration camp, where he was murdered because he was a Roma.

Germany was awarded the Olympic Games in 1931 to signal its return to international normalcy. After Hitler came to power two years later and began to persecute Jews, questions were raised in the United States and elsewhere about the wisdom of holding the Olympics in Germany. The American Jewish Committee and the Jewish Labor Committee strongly supported a boycott, and prominent American political leaders such as Al Smith (1873–1944), the governor of New York, also supported the boycott. The prominent Roman Catholic journal, *Commonweal*, said that such a boycott would "set the seal of approval upon the radically anti-Christian Nazi doctrine of youth."[36] Individual Jewish athletes from the United States and Europe chose personally to boycott the 1936 Olympics.

Despite considerable international pressure to boycott the 1936 Olympics, the International Olympic Committee (IOC) decided to go ahead with the games. It expelled Ernest Lee Jahncke (1877–1960) for publicly opposing this move and replaced him with Avery Brundage (1887–1975), president of the American Olympic Committee. Brundage, who created an uproar in 1972 when, as president of the IOC, he refused to cancel the Munich Olympics after the kidnapping and murder of nine Israeli athletes by Arab terrorists, charged in 1935 that a "Jewish-Communist" conspiracy was behind the American boycott effort; he added that politics had no place in sports and advised American athletes to avoid being drawn into "the present Jew-Nazi altercation" in Germany.[37]

In response to boycott threats, the Nazis promised not to keep Jews from participating in the games or being part of German Olympic teams. And there were several Jews on Germany's Olympic squads. Helene Mayer (1910–1953), who was half Jewish and who had won a gold medal for Germany in the 1928 Olympics, was a member of the German fencing team. Rudi Ball (1910–1975) was a half-Jewish hockey player who played on the German national team in the 1936 Winter Olympics. Captain Wolfgang Fürstner (?–1936) was asked to build, organize, and run the Olympic Village in Berlin. He committed suicide two days after the Olympics ended when he learned he had been dismissed from the army because of his Jewish background.

The 1936 Olympic games were a Nazi spectacle brilliantly orchestrated by Goebbels and Hitler's personal architect, Albert Speer (1905–1981). A year earlier, Goebbels had commissioned Leni Riefenstahl to film the Berlin games; the result was *Fest der Völker* (Festival of the People) and *Fest der Schönheit* (Festival of Beauty). Goebbels broadcast the games worldwide on radio and locally on television. The games took place in a massive new stadium that was meant to reflect a spirit of *Volksgemeinschaft* (people's community). Even Hitler, who disliked sports, was drawn to the sixteen-day event. Some national teams were so caught up in Goebbels's spectacle that they gave Hitler the Nazi-style Olympic salute as they passed him on the reviewing stand during the opening ceremonies. The American team, which included African American and Jewish athletes, refused to afford Hitler this "honor."

But the fourteen medals won by African Americans and the fourteen won by Jewish athletes and athletes of Jewish descent thwarted Hitler's dream that the games would fully underscore Nazi racial superiority. This was particularly true of Jesse Owens (1913–1980), the gifted African American runner who won gold medals in the 100-meter and 200-meter events, the high jump,

and the 400-meter relay. But Owens's achievements were marred when Avery Brundage replaced two Jewish members of the American relay team, Marty Glickman (1917–2001) and Sam Stoller, with Owens and another African American athlete, Ralph Metcalfe (1910–1987).

One of the myths that emerged during the 1936 Olympics was that Hitler refused to shake hands with any of the African American athletes who won medals. Jesse Owens, though, said in his memoirs that Hitler rose and waved to him on one occasion when he passed by the reviewing stand. At the beginning of the games, Count Henri Baillet-Latour (1876–1942), the president of the IOC, told Hitler that either he had to shake the hands of all the athletes who had won medals or he had to shake none. Hitler chose not to shake the hand of any Olympian, but this did not prevent him from expressing his dismay at the success of the African American athletes. He told Baldur von Schirach (1907–1974) the *Reichsjugendführer* (Reich Youth Führer) that the "Americans ought to be ashamed of themselves for letting their medals be won by Negroes."[38]

Despite these setbacks, the 1936 Olympic games in Germany were a tremendous propaganda success. Germany won eighty-nine medals, including thirty-three gold medals, and the United States won fifty-six medals, twenty-four of them gold. The games achieved everything that Hitler and Goebbels had hoped for, and, at least temporarily, seemed to temper some of the harsher international criticism of the Third Reich. President Franklin Roosevelt (1882–1945) told Rabbi Stephen S. Wise (1874–1949), a prominent American Jewish leader deeply involved in the Olympic boycott movement, that he had heard that Germany's synagogues had been full during the Olympics and that life had returned to normal for the Third Reich's Jews. Wise and others, though, knew the truth. The American journalist William

Shirer (1904–1993), for example, reported that nothing had really changed and that the Olympics simply masked the "degrading transformation of German life."[39] A handful of other foreign observers drew similar conclusions, though most people who attended the games saw what they wanted to see. It was easier to accept Nazi Germany as a modern, strong, revitalized nation than as a police state driven by dark, racist ideals.

Aryanization and the Road to *Kristallnacht*

Several days after the Olympics ended, Hitler issued a special memo detailing the general economic and rearmament ideas that would form the basis of his new Four-Year Plan. Germany's future greatness, Hitler argued, could be achieved only by acquiring *lebensraum* to expand its population and gain new raw material resources. Without this, Hitler thought, Germany would be swallowed up by the Jewish-controlled Soviet Union. Since *lebensraum* was a long-range goal, something had to be done immediately to give the Reich the economic resources it needed to build a first-class military. The Four Year Plan, under Hermann Göring, was designed to do just that.

The plan in turn raised questions about the role of Jews in the German economy. Some Nazi economic leaders such as Hjalmar Schacht (1877–1970), the head of the *Reichsbank,* argued against the complete Aryanization of Jewish property because of its negative economic consequences. When the Nazis came to power, there were approximately 50,000 Jewish businesses in Germany. By the summer of 1938, only about 9,000 Jewish firms were still operating.[40] The continued existence of such a large number of Jewish firms angered radical Nazi leaders. Yet as long as Aryanization was linked to the accessibility of Jewish resources as a negotiating factor in forced Jewish emigration from Germany, it would be difficult for party leaders to take

over Jewish property nationwide. Moreover, as long as more reasonable figures—such as Schacht—continued to have a say in German economic matters, eliminating the continuing Jewish presence in the German economy would be difficult.

There were also questions about the wisdom of Jewish emigration. In the fall of 1937, Herbert Hagen (1913–1985), the head of the SD's (*Sicherheitsdienst*; intelligence organization for the SS and the Nazi Party) Department II/112, which included Adolf Eichmann (1906–1962), presented a report on Jewish emigration to Palestine. Hagen, who had just returned from a month-long fact-finding visit to Palestine and the Middle East with Eichmann, noted that the British government's recent Peel Commission report, which proposed the creation of separate Jewish and Arab states in Palestine, posed new problems for Nazi emigration planners. If the British did permit the creation of an independent Jewish state, it could grant special minority status to German Jews and use its diplomatic powers to strengthen the ongoing international Jewish boycott against Germany. Hagen concluded, though, that the Reich should continue to work with Zionists to promote Jewish emigration from Germany and to "reduce the assimilationist elements in German Jewry."[41]

Yet the presence of a large Jewish population with a continuing role in the German economy contradicted German Aryan ideals. This would begin to change in 1937 as Hitler started to prepare for war. Strengthened by Schacht's resignation, Göring and Reinhard Heydrich (1904–1942), now *Chef der Sicherheitspolizei und des SD* (Chief of the Security Police and the SD), began to push for a program of greater Aryanization of Jewish property. These efforts were partially driven by Eichmann's success in Austria after the *Anschluß* (union) on March 12, 1938. This began with Heydrich's request that Eichmann gather material for a memorandum on Jewish emigration in Europe. Eichmann, who had grown up in Linz, Austria, arrived in Vienna a week after *Anschluß*. He quickly created a *Zentralstelle für jüdische Auswanderung* (Central Office for Jewish Emigration), which would become the model for similar Nazi-sponsored Jewish councils in other parts of Nazi-occupied Europe. The *Zentralstelle* was staffed by Jews who, under Eichmann's supervision, oversaw the administrative and economic aspects related to the forced emigration of Austria's 200,000 Jews. Eichmann, who now had sole control over Austria's Jews, gave them a choice—emigrate or go to a concentration camp. He backed this ultimatum up with a steady campaign of "discrimination and terror." By the end of September 1938, Eichmann reported that 50,000 Jews had left Austria. His superiors in Berlin were duly impressed and promoted him to *SS- Obersturmführer.*[42]

The *Anschluß* also spurred international interest in Jewish emigration from the Greater Reich. President Roosevelt called for an international conference to discuss ways of dealing with Jewish emigration from Germany and Austria. The result was the Evian Conference, which took place in Evian, France, from July 6 to July 15, 1938. Though the conferees created an Intergovernmental Committee on Refugees (ICR) to help deal with the refugees from the Reich, most of the thirty-two conferee nations refused to accept any new Reich Jews. The United States agreed to make its current annual quota of 27,370 refugees from Germany and Austria available to Jews, but the British refused to accept any new Jewish emigrants into Palestine or Britain itself. This failure to act on the Jewish refugee problem emboldened Nazi leaders to take more aggressive action against the 500,000 Jews who remained in the Third Reich.

In Germany, Julius Streicher initiated an anti-Jewish boycott in Nuremberg at the end of 1937. During the next four months, Göring issued various laws and decrees that made it more difficult to hide a Jewish presence in any business. The series of violent anti-Jewish boycotts that now broke out helped intensify the campaign of forced Aryanization; as a result, the government took over 80 percent of the remaining firms with Jewish interests. On March 28, 1938, the *Gesetz über den rechtlichen Status der Jüdischen Religionsgemeinschaften* (Law Concerning the Legal Status of Jewish Religious Communities) deprived these communities of legal protection. Nazi authorities also began to strike out at Germany's large foreign Jewish community, particularly the country's 70,000 Polish Jews. In the summer of 1938, Nazi vandals defaced synagogues and Jewish cemeteries but also destroyed synagogues in Munich and Nuremberg. The Gestapo arrested 1,500 Jewish "asocials" on trumped-up charges and sent them to the Buchenwald concentration camp near Weimar. In August, the government decreed that all Jews had to add either "Israel" or "Sara" to their names; later, at Swedish and Swiss instigation, they had to have a red "J" (Juden) stamped on their passports.

This new wave of anti-Semitic violence angered Göring, who supported "orderly" legal moves against the Jews. He complained to Hitler, who ordered a halt to the "wildcat" violence, promising soon to resolve the "Jewish question." But opinions differed widely in the upper echelons of the party about how best to deal with this problem. Party radicals such as Goebbels saw violence and boycotts as a key to resolving this matter, but Göring, Heydrich, Eichmann, and others sought a more orderly, stable solution to the "Jewish problem." The *Kristallnacht* pogrom in November 1938 would bring the matter to a head and forever change Germany's policies towards the Jews.

All this has to be viewed through the prism of Nazi international goals and achievements, all of which were intricately linked to Nazi

„Wenn ihr ein Kreuz seht, dann denkt an den grauenhaften Mord
der Juden auf Golgatha..."

Drawing from Julius Streicher's *The Poisonous Mushroom*. Caption reads: "When you see the Cross, remember the gruesome murder by the Jews on Golgotha." Source: *Der Giftpilz*. Public domain.

racial policy domestically. Ian Kershaw thinks the driving force behind this ideological marriage was Himmler and his SS leadership, who "were now looking to territorial gains to provide them with opportunities for ideological experimentation on the way to the fulfillment of the vision of a racially purified Greater German Reich under the heel of the chosen caste of the SS élite."[43] The SS leadership was ecstatic about Hitler's successes in Austria and the Sudetenland, where, in the fall of 1938,

Britain and France orchestrated the German takeover of this portion of Czechoslovakia in response to Hitler's threats to go to war over fabricated charges concerning the mistreatment of Sudeten Germans in Czechoslovakia.

The SS, which saw itself as the symbol and guardian of Nazi racial ideology and purity, "saw as their mission" the "ruthless eradication of Germany's ideological enemies." In early November 1938, Himmler made a declaration to the SS leadership:

We must be clear that in the next ten years we will certainly encounter unheard of critical conflicts. It is not only the struggle of the nations, which in this case are put forward by the opposing side merely as a front, but it is the ideological *(weltanschauliche)* struggle of the entire Jewry, freemasonry, Marxism, and churches of the world. These forces—of which I presume the Jews to be the driving spirit, the origin of all negatives—are clear that if Germany, and Italy are not annihilated, *they* will be annihilated *(vernichtet werden)*. That is a simple conclusion. In Germany the Jew cannot hold out. This is a question of years. We will drive them out more and more with an unprecedented ruthlessness.[44]

Kristallnacht (Crystal Night) or "Night of the Broken Glass," took place in this ideologically charged atmosphere. It began officially on November 9 (which was also the fifteenth anniversary of Munich Beer Hall Putsch), two days after Herschel Grynszpan (1921–1942?) shot a lower-level German diplomat, Ernst vom Rath (1909–1938), in Paris in retaliation for the humiliating expulsion of Grynszpan's parents, along with 16,000 other Polish Jews, to Poland in late October. After the shooting, the German press incited widespread attacks against the Jewish community. When they learned of vom Rath's death on the ninth, the Nazi leadership transformed these "wildcat" assaults against Jews and their property into an officially sponsored pogrom. In the next few days, Nazi thugs destroyed or damaged more than 1,500 synagogues and thousands of Jewish businesses and homes. They also murdered scores of Jews and severely injured many more. By November 16, the Gestapo had rounded up 30,000 Jewish males and sent them to the Dachau, Buchenwald, and Sachsenhausen concentration camps. Reinhard Heydrich estimated that Jewish property losses totaled 200 million *Reichsmarks* ($80 million), which the German insurance industry later lowered to 39 million *Reichsmarks*

($15.6 million). Included in this figure was 3.5 million *Reichsmarks* ($1.4 million) in goods looted from Jewish businesses and homes.

The international reaction to *Kristallnacht* concerned many Nazi leaders. Walther Funk (1890–1960), the Reich economics minister, was furious with Goebbels; and Joachim von Ribbentrop (1893–1946), Hitler's foreign minister, worried about the impact of the pogrom on German foreign policy. Goebbels issued a press statement on November 10 that was meant to help assuage some of these concerns:

> The justifiable and understandable indignation of the German people at the cowardly murder of a German diplomat in Paris manifested itself in a wide degree last night. In numerous towns and villages of the Reich, reprisals were carried out against Jewish buildings and places of business.
>
> The whole population is now strictly enjoined to abstain from all further action of whatsoever nature against the Jews. The final reply to all Jewish outrage in Paris will be given to the Jews by legal means, i.e., by decree.[45]

The pogrom also angered Göring, who moved quickly to reassert control over Jewish policy. On November 12, Göring held a meeting of the top Nazi leadership at his Air Ministry to discuss future Jewish policy. He used the meeting to reassert his control over Aryanization and emphasized the need to coordinate Jewish policy. He was extremely critical of uncoordinated anti-Semitic violence because it damaged the economy. Goebbels, who at times seemed more interested in putting parking lots on the sites of some of the burned synagogues, wanted to ban Jews from all public places where "they might cause provocation," including German forests:

> "Herds of Jews are today running around in the Grünewald" [Goebbels said]. "That is a constant provocation—we shall have constant incidents. What the Jews do is so

Front page of *Der Stürmer* proclaiming the "crucifixion" of Ernst vom Rath by Herschel Grynszpan. At the bottom is the phrase, "The Jews Are our Misfortune." Circa 1939. USHMM Photo No. 31520, courtesy of Virginius Dabney.

provocative that it constantly comes to blows." "Well then," Göring responded with heavy sarcasm, "we shall have to give the Jews a certain part of the forest, and rangers will see to it that the various animals which are damnably like the Jews—the elk has a hooked nose, too—go into the Jewish enclosure and settle down among them."[46]

The group also discussed creating ghettos for Jews, and Heydrich suggested that Jews be required to wear special armbands. Heydrich reminded the conferees of Eichmann's successes in Austria. The Nazi leaders also spent a great deal of time discussing who would pay for the *Kristallnacht* damages: Göring insisted that Germany's insurance companies pay

Jews for their losses, which the government would then seize. Goebbels proposed a Jewish "Atonement Fine" of 1 billion *Reichsmarks* ($401 million) for the vom Rath murder and *Kristallnacht*.

After the meeting, Göring issued several decrees that imposed the 1 billion *Reichsmarks* fine on the Jewish community and required Jews to pay for the damage to their property. He also decreed that Jews be excluded from having a role in the German economy after January 1, 1939. Three weeks later, Göring ordered Heydrich to create and head a Reich-wide copy of Eichmann's *Zentralstelle für jüdische Auswanderung*. Other decrees issued in early 1939 prevented Jews from using the German courts to seek redress from *Kristallnacht* damages. The government also ordered the closing of all Jewish organizations except for the *Zionistische Vereinigung für Deutschland* (Zionist Federation for Germany), which was considered important to Jewish emigration. In July 1939, the Nazis created a new organization to represent Reich Jewry, the *Reichsvereinigung der Juden in Deutschland* (Reich Association of Jews in Germany). The government also shut down all Jewish newspapers except for the *Jüdische Nachrichtenblatt* (Jewish Newsletter).

International reaction to *Kristallnacht* ranged from extreme outrage to tempered concern. In the United States, the German ambassador, Hans Dieckhoff (1884–1952), called American reaction a "hurricane raging," and New York Mayor Fiorello La-Guardia (1882–1947) created a special "Nazi Guardian Squad" made up of twelve Jewish policemen to guard the German consulate.[47] British reaction was equally harsh, though elsewhere in Europe public outrage was tempered by political or diplomatic considerations. Many American papers blamed *Kristallnacht* on Neville Chamberlain's misguided appeasement policy. Yet most reports failed to understand the deadly implications

of *Kristallnacht*. Many newspapers blamed Nazi leaders, not the German public, for the pogrom's excesses.

In fact, *Kristallnacht* outraged and frightened many Germans who had previously been generally supportive of Hitler's less violent anti-Semitic policies. David Bankier noted that the vast majority of Germans had previously supported government efforts to isolate Jews socially and to eliminate them from the German economy. Others, though, had continued to frequent Jewish businesses throughout the 1930s, though more as an anti-Nazi gesture than as a pro-Jewish statement. By the fall of 1938, the average German was far more worried about the coming of war than the plight of Jews. The November 9–10 pogrom changed all that. Many Germans condemned the indiscriminate violence and felt physically threatened by Hitler's regime, and they feared they could be next. Some intellectuals even sent letters of shame to the British embassy in Berlin after *Kristallnacht*.[48]

Such reactions, though, did little to sway the German leadership from its new anti-Jewish course, particularly when it became clear that most countries would do little more than issue diplomatic protests to voice their disapproval of what took place during *Kristallnacht*. And Goebbels warned a group of foreign journalists on November 11 that if ongoing Jewish-sponsored international press criticism of Germany, particularly in the United States, continued, it would backfire. Such criticism, he added, could "be digging the graves of the Jews in Germany."[49] The Third Reich would not be pressed by foreign interests, Goebbels raged. The plight of Germany's Jews, he said, would be tied directly to their own behavior and to that of foreign Jews.

Hitler continued this line of thinking in a conversation with the Czech foreign minister, Edvard Beneš (1884–1948), on January 21, 1939. He said he would destroy the Jews and not allow them to stab Germany in the back as they had done at the end of World War I. And nine days later, in a speech before the Reichstag, Hitler proclaimed:

> Europe cannot find peace until the Jewish question has been solved. It may well be that sooner or later an agreement may be reached in Europe itself between nations who otherwise would not find it so easy to arrive at an understanding. There still exists sufficient land on this globe.
>
> One thing I should like to say on this day which may be memorable for others as well as for us Germans. In the course of my life I have very often been a prophet, and have usually been ridiculed for it. During the time for my struggle for power it was in the first instance only the Jewish race that received my prophecies with laughter when I said I would one day take over the leadership of the State, and with it that of the whole nation, and that I would then among other things settle the Jewish problem. Their laughter was uproarious, but I think that for some time now they have been laughing on the other side of their face. Today I will once more be a prophet: if the international Jewish financiers in and outside of Europe should succeed in plunging the nations once more into a world war, then the result will not be the Bolshevizing of the earth, and thus the victory of Jewry, but *the annihilation of the Jewish race in Europe!*[50]

By this time, Hitler was planning the takeover of the rest of Czechoslovakia and was preparing for war. Yet what did he mean by the "annihilation" of the Jews? There is no documentation that points to a German game plan to destroy the Third Reich's Jews at this time. Yet words such as "annihilation," particularly when combined with the success of the *Kristallnacht* pogrom, represents an important shift in German thinking about the "Jewish question." This was no doubt

partly driven by Hitler's successful international gambles, which fed his growing sense of invincibility.

The Nazis now sought new havens for Reich Jews, though few countries were willing to accept new immigrants, despite efforts by Jewish organizations in the United States, Great Britain, Palestine, and elsewhere to pressure their respective governments to increase their Jewish quotas. The British government did set up the *Kindertransport* network, which brought 10,000 German Jewish children to Great Britain but refused to allow another 21,000 children to enter Palestine. Regardless, about 36,000 Jews were able to flee Germany in 1938 and 77,000 in 1939. But for those unable or unwilling to leave, life became increasingly difficult.

Viktor Klemperer (1881–1960), a secular Jew and a professor of romance languages at the Dresden Technical Institute, wrote in his diary that Jews found the atmosphere in post-*Kristallnacht* Germany "crushing" and chaotic. A friend suggested they sell everything and leave since "everything is lost." And though Klemperer chose to remain in Germany, he noted that life for Jews who remained was one of "deadening wretchedness" and growing impoverishment.[51] Many of those who left the country during this period were young, and almost 60 percent of those who remained were elderly and poor.

Perhaps no event symbolized the frightening efforts of German Jews seeking refuge abroad more than the *St. Louis* tragedy. On May 13, 1939, the SS *St. Louis* left Hamburg, Germany, with 937 Jews on board, for Cuba. Of this number, 734 possessed American immigration documents that would allow them to settle in the United States over a three-year period. Sadly, the day before the *St. Louis* sailed, the ship's owners learned that the Cuban government had invalidated these temporary travel documents; this meant that the passengers would need full Cuban visas for entry, information that was never shared

Jewish refugees aboard SS *St. Louis* in Havanna, 1939. USHMM Photo No. 11291, courtesy of National Archives and Records Administration, College Park.

with them. Once the *St. Louis* reached Havana, Cuban officials demanded a "bond" of $465,000 before the passengers were allowed to disembark. Efforts by the American Jewish Joint Distribution Committee (AJJDC) to negotiate a settlement failed because it could not raise the funds demanded by corrupt Cuban officials. A handful of passengers somehow managed to disembark, though most were forced to remain on board.

As negotiations continued between the AJJDC and the Cuban government, the *St. Louis* was forced to leave Cuba. When it entered U.S. waters, the U.S. Coast Guard cutter *244* shadowed it as it moved up the Florida coast. Negotiations with the Cuban government ultimately fell through despite an AJJDC offer of $443,50000 for the remaining 907 passengers and 150 Jews on two other ships. Corruption and a groundswell of anti-Semitism in Cuba had sunk the deal. On June 7, the *St. Louis* sailed slowly for Hamburg, but

Captain Gustav Schröder, whom Yad Vashem later named a Righteous Among the Nations (Righteous Gentile) for his kindness towards his passengers, considered beaching his vessel on the coast of England. In desperation, the ship's passengers wired President Roosevelt directly, asking for help. The telegram noted that more than four hundred of the *St. Louis*'s Jewish refugees were women and children. The White House did not respond. On June 10, a *New York Times* editorial captured the tragic essence of the *St. Louis*' odyssey:

It is hard to imagine the bitterness of exile when it takes place over a faraway frontier. Helpless families driven from their homes to a barren island in the Danube, thrust over the Polish frontier, escaping in terror of their lives to Switzerland or France, are hard for us in a free country to visualize. But these exiles floated by our own shores. Some of them are on the American quota list and can later be admitted here. What is to happen to them in the interval has remained uncertain from hour to hour. We can only hope that some hearts will soften somewhere and some refuge be found. The cruise of the *St. Louis* cries to high heaven of man's inhumanity to man.[52]

Fortunately, the AJJDC was able to negotiate a settlement with the British, French, Dutch, and Belgian governments to accept the *St. Louis*'s Jewish refugees. At the time, no one could foresee the tragic consequences for those Jews sent to France (224), Belgium (211), and the Netherlands (181) after the ship landed in Antwerp, Belgium, on June 17, 1939. Most of the Jews sent to these countries would later be murdered by the Germans or their collaborators, but those sent to England survived.

Several days before the *St. Louis* landed in Antwerp, SD Section II 112 issued a report criticizing various Jewish organizations and countries that had closed their doors to Jewish refugees. As Hitler eyed Poland as his next victim, which had a Jewish population of over 3 million, Nazi leaders searched for new ways to deal with its unwanted, growing Jewish population.

The Early Campaign of Forced Sterilization

The "Jewish question" was the most important issue in a body of Nazi ideology that embraced all the collective historic, racial, ethnic, and other prejudices in Western tradition. And though Nazi Germany was foremost a "racial state," its web of hatred and prejudice reached far. Each group caught in this web faced the complexity of various Nazi policies designed to weaken or reduce that particular group's threat to German society. The first group the Nazis aggressively dealt with in the months after Hitler came to power in early 1933 were the handicapped or the disabled. The Germans also sterilized many of the

Reich's blacks, or Afro-Germans, and scores of Roma.

The idea of sterilizing the mentally and physically handicapped or disabled had deep roots in nineteenth- and early twentieth-century scientific thinking and practice. By the time Adolf Hitler had come to power, more than half of the American states had laws on the books that permitted the forced sterilization of those who suffered serious mental illnesses. Many other countries adopted similar laws in the 1930s. German racial scientists in the Second Reich and the Weimar Republic had advocated sterilization for years. Hitler supported this practice; in *Mein Kampf*, he wrote:

It is a half-measure to let incurably sick people steadily contaminate the remaining healthy ones. This is in keeping with the humanitarianism which, to avoid hurting one individual, lets a hundred others perish. The demand that defective people be prevented from propagating equally defective offspring is a demand of the clearest reason and if systematically executed represents the most humane act of mankind. It will spare millions of unfortunates undeserved sufferings, and consequently will lead to a rising improvement of health as a whole. . . . For, if necessary, the incurably sick will be pitilessly segregated—a barbaric measure for the unfortunate who is struck by it, but a blessing for his fellow men and posterity. The passing pain of a century can and will redeem millenniums from suffering.[53]

After considerable debate in the summer of 1932, the *Reichsärztekammer* (German Medical Association) and the Prussian *Landesgesundheitsrat* (Health Council) agreed to send the Reichstag a law for the voluntary and physician-supervised sterilization of the handicapped. Though it never became law during the Weimar era, the *Landesgesundheitsrat* sterilization proposal became the basis for the Nazis' more extensive Sterilization Law the following summer.

On July 14, 1933, the Reichstag passed Germany's first sterilization law, the *Gesetz zur Verhütung erbkranken Nachwusches* (Law for the Prevention of Genetically Diseased Offspring), which allowed the forced sterilization of handicapped individuals suffering from hereditary diseases such as feeblemindedness, schizophrenia, manic depression, epilepsy, Huntington's disease, blindness, deafness, physical deformities, and extreme alcoholism. Five months later, two new laws, the *Gesetz gegen gefährliche Gewohnheitsverbrecher* (Law Against Dangerous Habitual Criminals) and the *Gesetz von Maßnahmen für Sicherheit und Reform* (Law on Measures of Security and Reform), which expanded the list of victims to include "asocials," particularly the Roma, or Gypsies. These laws also gave courts the power to place "asocials" in mental hospitals. Habitual criminals could now expect longer prison terms, and sexual deviates could be castrated. The 1935 *Ehegesundheitsgesetz* (Marital Health Law) was designed to keep those afflicted with serious hereditary deficiencies from marrying "genetically" healthy Germans.

Eleven days after the Reichstag passed the sterilization law, the government created the *Erbgesundheitsgericht* (Hereditary Health Courts), which were made up of two physicians and a lawyer, to review the sterilization recommendations of health-care professionals. From 1933 to 1945, the government sterilized from 375,000 to 400,000 Germans, most of them between 1934 and 1937. The *Erbgesundheitsgericht* system grew to about 1,700 courts; most of those sterilized had low IQs (officially, *Schwachsinnige;* "feebleminded person"). Next were those suffering from schizophrenia, epilepsy, or severe alcoholism. Though families could challenge sterilization decisions, only 11 percent of these decisions were ever overturned. Tubal ligations and vasectomies were the most common forms of sterilization,

though German physicians also experimented with x-rays and other methods.

The Germans also sterilized many of the Reich's *Rheinlandebastarde* (Rhineland bastards), a reference to the offspring of French African troops who helped occupy the Rhineland in the 1920s. Clarence Lusane estimates that about 20,000 people of African descent lived in Germany when Hitler came to power in 1933.[54] Hitler hated blacks, particularly the *Rheinlandebastarde,* and referred to them frequently in *Mein Kampf.* Jews, he claimed, had brought "Negroes" into the Rhineland deliberately to "bastardize" the white race. He viewed blacks as "half apes" and considered educated blacks no better than trained poodles. He blamed the French for bringing blacks into Europe:

> For this very reason, France is and remains by far the most terrible enemy. This people, which is basically becoming more and more negrified, constitutes in its ties with the aims of Jewish world domination an enduring danger for the existence of the white race in Europe. For the contamination by Negro blood on the Rhine in the heart of Europe is just as much in keeping with the perverted sadistic thirst for vengeance of this hereditary enemy of our people as is the ice-cold calculation of the Jew thus to begin bastardizing the European continent at its core and to deprive the white race of the foundations for a sovereign existence through infection with lower humanity.[55]

In 1927, Bavarian officials unsuccessfully proposed the sterilization of *Rheinlandbastarde* children, which the *Reich Gesundheitstamt* (Reich Health Office) rejected because it might alienate their white German mothers. Soon after the Nazis came to power, Hermann Göring ordered the registration of all *Rheinlandbastarde* in the Rhineland, and had 145 *Rheinlandbastarde* children examined to determine their racial characteristics.

In 1935, authorities decided to sterilize all *Rheinlandbastarde* children because, they argued, they were the product of rape or of mothers who were prostitutes. Two years later, the Gestapo arrested all *Rheinlandbastarde* and turned them over to its Special Commission No. 3, which was set up to oversee the secret sterilization of the Reich's *Rheinlandbastarde* children. Between 1935 and 1937, the Gestapo sterilized 385 *Rheinlandbastarde*. It briefly halted these sterilizations in 1937 because of international concern over the impact of such actions on important foreign non-Aryans living in the Third Reich at the time. The Gestapo resumed the forced sterilizations later that year, though it is difficult to determine how many *Rheinlandbastarde* the Gestapo ultimately sterilized during the Holocaust.

Euthanasia: Theory and Nazi Practice

Sterilization, though, did not completely offer the Nazis a satisfactory solution to their concerns over the threat of groups and individuals they deemed *Lebensunwertes Lebens* (lives unworthy of life). Euthanasia did. The idea of euthanasia—from the Greek *eu thanatos*, meaning "good death"—had roots that went back to the ancient world. The Roman historian Suetonius (c. 71–c. 135 C.E., Gaius Suetonius Tranquillus) first coined the word, which at the time meant allowing a patient to die simply by not treating his or her illness. The medieval Roman Catholic Church condemned euthanasia because it thought that only God had power over life and death. The church also argued that suffering was an integral part of salvation and that euthanasia interfered with God's will. Islam had similar teachings on euthanasia. Sir Francis Bacon (1561–1626) revived the term and emphasized the important role of the physician in euthanasia. Yet, as the Prussian physician Christoph Wilhelm Hufeland (1762–1836) argued:

[The doctor] should and must do nothing other than maintaining life; it is not up to him whether that life is happy or unhappy, worthwhile or not, and should he incorporate these perspectives into his trade the consequences would be unforeseeable and the *doctor could well become the most dangerous person in the state*; if this line is crossed once, with the doctor believing he is entitled to decide upon the necessity of a life, then it only requires a logical progression for him to apply the criteria of worth, and, therefore, unworth, in other instances.[56]

Yet another nineteenth-century German essayist, Adolf Jost, argued in his *Das Recht auf den Tod* (The Right to Death) that the state, not the individual or the physician, should have ultimate control over life and death. He thought the principal consideration in determining the fate of the incurably ill was the impact their deaths would have on the overall health of the *Volk*. Jost added that the state made such decisions during wartime, when it sacrificed the lives of some for the benefit of the nation.

By the early twentieth century, the idea of euthanasia had become part of the larger discussion of eugenics in Germany. In 1904 and 1905, Dr. Alfred Ploetz, who began to use the term *Rassenhygiene* to describe the role of war, revolution, and health care in strengthening "degenerative human stock," founded the *Archiv für Rassen und Gesellschaftsbiologie* (Journal for Racial and Social Biology) and the *Gesellschaft für Rassengygiene* (Society for Racial Hygiene), which became the principal venues for the study of eugenics in Germany before World War I. The Nazis regarded him as a pioneer in this field and Hitler made him an honorary professor of racial hygiene at the University of Munich in 1936.

But at the end of World War I, practical concerns drove the German medical community to raise questions about the costs involved in keeping alive those with serious illnesses. Such questioning, of course, took place in the midst of the larger debate about eugenics, euthanasia, and the sterilization of the "genetically diseased." During World War I, about a third of the inmates in Germany's mental institutions died, half of them from malnutrition. In 1920, Karl Bonhoeffer (1868–1948), the chairman of the *Deutsche Gesellschaft für Psychiatrie* (German Psychiatric Association), noted that some German psychiatrists had allowed mental patients to starve to death to preserve food for the war effort. The same year, Karl Binding (1841–1920), a renowned professor of law, and Alfred Hoche (1856–1944), a psychiatrist, discussed euthanasia in their study *Die Freigabe der Vernichtung lebensunwerten Lebens* (Permission for the Destruction of Life Unworthy of Life). Binding proposed laws that would permit the "mercy killing" of those he considered *Lebensunwertes Lebens*—the "incurable idiots"—and brain-damaged "human vegetables." Hoche and Binding argued that such individuals were *Ballastexistenzen* (unnecessary lives) and a drain on German society. Their ideas appalled many German physicians. Yet Dr. Ewald Metzler, the director of the Katharinhof mental institution in Saxony, responded in *Das Problem der Abkürzung 'lebensunwerten' Lebens* (The Problem of Curtailment of Life Unworthy of Life; 1925) that three-quarters of the parents of handicapped children he had surveyed supported euthanasia if their children suffered severe physical and mental pain or if the parents were no longer able to care for their children.

The rising costs of caring for mental patients, coupled with their increasing numbers, also affected attitudes on euthanasia. Between 1924 and 1929, the number of mental patients in Weimar Germany grew from 185,387 to more than 300,000, but the number of institutions open to care for these patients remained about the same. In 1928, the *Gesellschaft für Geisteshygiene* (Society for Mental Hygiene) discussed eugenic measures

to deal with serious mental illness, alcoholism, and crime in German society. Ongoing government cuts during the early 1930s brought new demands from mental health-care professionals to adopt eugenic methods to deal with the economic crises facing their institutions. While they searched desperately for ways to deal with the situation, they gave more thought to selective sterilization as a solution to Germany's long-range mental health problems. This method would involve not only the severely handicapped who lived in special institutions but also mentally and physically challenged individuals who lived with their families.

Adolf Hitler spoke about this problem in a speech before the *Parteitage* rally in Nuremberg on August 5, 1929:

> If Germany was to get a million children a year and was to remove 700–800,000 of the weakest people then the final result might even be an increase in strength. The most dangerous thing is for us to cut off the natural process of selection and thereby gradually rob ourselves of the possibility of acquiring able people. . . . As a result of our modern sentimental humanitarianism we are trying to maintain the weak at the expense of the healthy. It goes so far that a sense of charity, which calls itself socially responsible, is concerned to ensure that even cretins are able to procreate while more healthy people refrain from doing so, and all that is considered perfectly understandable. Criminals have the opportunity of procreating, degenerates are raised artificially and with difficulty. And in this way we are gradually breeding the weak and killing off the strong.[57]

In 1932, psychiatrist Berthold Kihn (1895–1964) argued in the *Allegemeine Zeitschrift für Psychiatrie* (Universal Journal of Psychiatry) that Germany's financially strapped mental health system required radical solutions. He said there were four ways to insure the health of the German nation: "Eugenic marriage counseling and prohibition of unions between the 'unfit'; the 'destruction of life unworthy of life'; the isolation in asylums of people deemed unfit to reproduce; and castration or sterilisation for those whose progeny society deemed undesirable."[58]

Kihn added that it cost Germany 150 million *Reichsmarks* ($35.3 million) annually to deal with the country's 30,000 "idiots." These funds, Kihn argued, could be better spent elsewhere if the states euthanized the 30,000 "idiots." He concluded, though, that Germany was not ready for euthanasia. The next best thing to do with these "idiots," he suggested, was to sterilize them humanely. Kihn's views were considered quite controversial and German physicians were split over solutions to the mental health-care crisis. For ethical or professional reasons, some opposed any form of sterilization or euthanasia; others supported sterilization and other eugenic solutions.

The Roman Catholic Church and Protestant denominations were also important forces in the eugenic debate. Pope Pius XI's (r. 1922–1939) 1930 encyclical *Casti Connubi* (On Christian Marriage), laid the ethical groundwork for Roman Catholic opposition to any eugenic solution to mental and physical disease or deformities, though it did not keep individual Roman Catholics from supporting such measures. On the other hand, many German Protestants supported voluntary sterilization as a positive measure that would benefit future generations. Both religious groups would later oppose Nazi "euthanasia" programs.

In the early years of the Nazi regime, the government sterilized tens of thousands of mentally and physically challenged Germans. However, Hitler never forgot about "euthanasia." Dr. Karl Brandt (1904–1948), Hitler's personal physician, claimed that the Führer had decided to adopt a "euthanization" program for the mentally ill before he came to power. Hitler and others also discussed "euthanasia" as part of the broader talks about the 1933 sterilization law. In a speech during the *Parteitage* that year, Dr. Gerhard Wagner, the head of the German Physicians' League, said that a society that put "the sick, the dying, and the unfit on a par with the healthy and the strong" was dangerous. Wagner decried the vast sums spent in Germany over the previous seventy years on "genetic inferiors," and said the trend was being reversed. Several years later, Hitler told Wagner that "if war should break out, he would take up the euthanasia question and implement it . . . because the Führer was of the opinion that such a problem would be easier and smoother to carry out in wartime, since the public resistance which one could expect from the churches would not play such a prominent role amidst the events of wartime as it otherwise would."[59]

The same year (1935), Dr. Hellmuth Unger (1891–1953), an ophthalmologist, published a widely read novel, *Sendung und Gewissen* (Mission and Conscience), about a physician, Dr. Terstegen, whose wife, a gifted pianist, asked him to end her life because she suffered from multiple sclerosis. He gives her an overdose of morphine, while a family friend, also a physician, plays the piano to relax the victim. Tergstegen is put on trial for murder. A jury, though, finds him not guilty, concluding that what he did was an act of mercy, not of murder. At a poignant scene in the book, Unger, quoting the Swiss Renaissance physician, Paracelsus (1493–1541), proclaims that "medicine is love."[60] Wagner was so taken by Unger's novel that he ordered it made into a film, which Goebbels released in 1941 as *Ich Klage an!* (I accuse). Unger later became an adviser to the children's "euthanasia" program.

It was not until the end of 1938 that more serious thought was given to the "euthanasia" issue. And though serious planning for the "euthanasia" program began before the war

Roma children doing their homework in a Roma camp, Berlin. Source: *Gypsies: Their Life and Customs*, Martin Friedrich Block. AMS Press Inc., 1939.

broke out, the Nazis used the war as a cover to begin the first mass murder of the Holocaust—the T-4 "euthanasia" program.

The Roma (Gypsies)

The Roma (singular Rom), or as they are more commonly known in the English-speaking world, the Gypsies, entered Europe in the late Middle Ages from India. Many early chronicles referred to the Roma as "Egyptians," which is the origin of the term "Gypsy." In the non-English-speaking world, the Roma are known as *Zigeuner, cigán, cigány, tsiganes,* and similar terms. These words come from the Byzantine Greek word, *Atsínganoi,* meaning itinerant wanderers and soothsayers. The Roma prefer a name of their their own choosing, since "Gypsy" and derivatives of *Atsínganoi* are riddled with negative stereotypical meanings. Today, they prefer the term Roma (men or husbands) or Romani, an adjectival form of Roma, which comes from their own language, Romani.

The Roma settled primarily in the Balkans, where they lived as nomads who plied their skills as respected gunsmiths, metal smiths, equine specialists, and musicians. The only exception was in Romania's historic provinces, Wallachia and Moldavia, where they were enslaved to retain their valuable skills. Attitudes towards the Roma began to change during the Ottoman Turkish conquest of the Balkans in the fifteenth and sixteenth centuries. When the Roma began to migrate out of this troubled area, they met a harsh body of laws and restrictions that deeply affected their movements and settlement patterns; this was particularly true in the German states, which were plagued by the upheavals of the Reformation and the distant Ottoman conquests. Local officials and rulers implemented laws that exacted harsh punishments, including branding and executions, for nomadic Roma traveling through their kingdoms. This began to change in the eighteenth century as more and more German states adopted the *kamerialist,* or mercantilist, policies of the Austrian emperors Maria Theresa (1740–1780) and Joseph II (1780–1790), who wanted the Roma to settle and become good tax-paying Austrian Roman Catholics. These policies did little, though, to change public attitudes towards the Roma.

In the second half of the nineteenth century, a new Roma migration began in the aftermath of the Romanian Roma's emancipation and the wars of liberation that swept through the Balkans. Though Balkan Roma now spread throughout Europe, few settled in the new German state: The Roma there were viewed as an asocial, thievish group of irresponsible nomads. In response to growing complaints about vagrants in rural areas, particularly Roma, Otto von Bismarck, the "Iron Chancellor" and architect of German unification, sent a letter to state officials in 1886 that addressed these problems. He stated that it was important to distinguish between the Sinti, native-born Roma who had lived in Germany for centuries, and the Roma, nomads who had recently arrived from Eastern Europe. Armed with earlier legislation that gave local officials the right to deport Roma, they began a crackdown against Roma and Sinti throughout Germany. Some were deported and others were jailed or fined for petty theft and other crimes. The government outlawed nomadism and initiated efforts to take Roma children from their parents and place them in state-run schools. Local politicians in Swabia organized a conference to discuss "Gypsy scum" and suggested, among other things, the use of church bells to warn inhabitants of Roma in the area.

In the spring of 1899, Bavarian police created a special Roma unit, the *Zigeunernachrichtendienst* (Gypsy Information Agency), commanded by Alfred Dillmann. This unit began to collect fingerprints, family information, photographs, and other data on the Roma and Sinti in Bavaria. The state conducted a Roma and Sinti census in 1905, and

Dillmann's office encouraged local residents to inform his office of Roma or Sinti activities. Dillmann put all the information he had gathered on Bavarian Roma into one volume, the *Zigeuner-Buch* (1905). His study, which contained information about 3,350 Roma and Sinti, claimed that they were a plague upon society because they were "a morally inferior and criminally inclined" group.[61] The *Zigeuner-Buch* included detailed genealogies on all the Roma and Sinti listed, including criminal records and arrest photographs.

Two years earlier, the state of Württemberg issued a decree, *Bekämpfung des Zigeunerwesens* (Combatting the Gypsy Nuisance), that limited the number of licenses for "itinerant trade" and required local police to travel with local Roma and Sinti groups from district to district. It also ordered local officials forcibly to remove children from nomadic Roma and Sinti homes and place them in local schools. In 1905, Württemberg officials also outlawed traveling in groups, or, as they put it, in "hordes."[62] In 1904, Prussia began a crackdown on Roma and Sinti nomadism and placed restrictions on Roma labor. Two years later, Prussia's Ministry of the Interior issued its own *Bekämpfung des Zigeunerunwesens* regulations: Anyone who wanted to work in Prussia was required to obtain a new permit. To acquire one, applicants had to prove they were legal residents, had no criminal record, and possessed adequate funds to pay taxes and properly educate their children. Officials hoped these regulations would limit the number of Roma and Sinti who applied for work permits and force those unable to meet the requirements out of Prussia.

Many Roma fled Germany at this time, though, at least in the eyes of German officials, they still remained a problem. In 1911, the Bavarian Ministry of the Interior invited representatives from Germany to Munich to discuss a nationwide coordination of efforts against the Roma and Sinti. The two-day meeting (December 18–19) addressed issues raised in a memo prepared by the Munich state police stating that "there existed few pure Gypsies and that it was therefore the Gypsies' way of life, their occupation and nomadic lifestyle, and not membership in a tribe or race, that should be the decisive criteria" in determining who was a Roma. Some delegates thought this definition "too broad" and insisted on a more limited one, which the conferees ultimately agreed to. The new definition stated that Roma were "in the eyes of the police, those who are Gypsies according to the teachings of ethnology as well as those who roam about in the manner of Gypsies."[63]

German officials did not revisit the "Gypsy Question" until after World War I. In 1926, the Bavarian parliament passed the controversial *Gesetz Bekämpfung von Zigeunen, Laufahren und Arbeitscheuneswesens* (Law for Combating Gypsies, Vagrants, and the Work-Shy), which linked the Roma with other groups in Bavaria because of their lifestyle, not their ethnicity, an approach the Nazis later used. The legislation's sponsors noted: "These people are by nature opposed to all work and find it especially difficult to tolerate any restriction of their nomadic life; nothing, therefore, hits them harder than loss of liberty, coupled with forced labour."[64]

It required nomadic Roma and Sinti to obtain a special travel permit annually. Children could not travel with their parents unless special arrangements had been made for their schooling. "Itinerants" were also forbidden to travel in groups, or "hordes." The police were authorized to deal with "itinerants" who had criminal records, and they could place anyone older than sixteen who could not produce "proof of regular work" in a state workhouse for up to two years.[65] A year later, the Prussian government ordered that nomadic Roma and Sinti and "Gypsy-like itinerants" be fingerprinted, a policy soon adopted throughout Germany.[66]

In 1929, Bavaria's *Zigeunernachrichtendienst* became the national clearinghouse for Roma and Sinti throughout Germany. Within a year, the *Zigeunernachrichtendienst* had collected files on 19,000 of Germany's 20,000 to 26,000 Roma and Sinti. By the end of the Weimar era, a vast body of anti-Roma and anti-Sinti laws and regulations were in place to fight what many viewed as one of Germany's most serious problems—the "Gypsy nuisance." The Nazis would use this as the basis for their ongoing campaign against the Roma and Sinti from 1933 to 1945.

Initially, the Nazis felt these laws and regulations, in league with the files of the *Zigeunernachrichtendienst* in Munich, were sufficient to deal with what they termed the "*Zigeunerplage* (Gypsy plague)." What changed for the Roma was the intensification of harassment policies throughout Germany. The *Zigeunernachrichtendienst*, which was at the forefront of these policies, was constantly prodding state officials to intensify their efforts against the "Gypsy race."

In 1936, German officials created the *Reichszentrale zur Bekämpfung des Zigeunerwesens* (Reich Center for Combating the Gypsy Nuisance) in Berlin, which took over the work of the *Zigeunernachrichtendienst*. The *Reichszentrale* quickly ordered that Roma nationwide be settled in *Zigeunerlager* (Gypsy concentration camps); these were located in Cologne, Düsseldorf, Frankfurt, Berlin, and elsewhere. The largest camp, which was built on the site of a former sewage disposal dump, was in the Berlin suburbs at Marzahn and was set up on the eve of the 1936 Olympics to hide the Roma from international view. Before the Nazi Olympics opened, police throughout Prussia raided Roma camps and homes and forced-marched six hundred of them to Marzahn.

Special supplements to the Nuremberg Laws and other decrees strengthened German efforts against the Roma and Sinti. One banned all interracial marriages between

Aryans and "Gypsies, Negroes and their bastards" because they were "polluters" of German blood. The only exceptions were for Roma and Sinti who had only "a quarter or less of alien blood."[67] From the Nazis' perspective, the Roma and Sinti, like the Jews and blacks, possessed *artfremdes blut* (alien blood) and were a dire threat to Aryan racial purity. Wilhelm Frick, Hitler's interior minister, applied the same standards when it came to questions about Roma and Sinti citizenship, meaning that no Roma could be a German citizen because of his or her *artfremdes blut*. Instead, like Jews, they could possess only *Staatsangehöriger* (subject of the state) status. Later decrees deprived the Roma of all voting rights and forbade them to serve in the military.

Missing from all this were details concerning the "racial" makeup of the Roma and Sinti population in Germany. Consequently, in 1936, the *Reichsgesundheitsamt* (Reich Health Office) created the *Rassenhygienischen und bevölkerungsbiologischen Forschungsstelle* (Research Institute for Racial Hygiene and Population Biology), which became the principal German research institute on the Roma. The director, Dr. Robert Ritter (1909–1950), held a doctorate in educational psychology from the University of Munich and an MD from the University of Heidelberg. His principal assistant at this time was Eva Hedwig Justin (1909–1966), whose 1943 PhD thesis, *Lebensschicksale artfremd erzogener Zigeunerkinder und ihrer Nachkommen* (The Fate of Gypsy Children with Well-Developed Alien Blood and Their Offspring), dealt with her work with Roma children.

The purpose of the *Zigeuner Forschungsstelle* was to gather data on the Roma and Sinti and other asocials to determine who was a "Gypsy." This information would aid the writing of a "Gypsy law" and help authorities decide whether the Roma and Sinti should be sterilized under the 1933 sterilization law. Ritter's team ranked Roma and Sinti according to blood purity; to determine the proper category for each Roma, the investigators went back four generations. In 1941, after several revisions, the team developed a detailed racial classification system for their subjects. There were five categories, ranging from Z for *Vollzigeuner* (full-blooded Gypsy) to *Nicht-Ziguener* (non-Gypsy). In between were three listings for Gypsy: *Zigeunermischling* + (ZM+; five or more Gypsy great-grandparents); *Zigeunermischling-* (ZM-; four Gypsy great-grandparents); and *Zigeunermischling* (ZM; four Gypsy grandparents). Roma and Sinti ZM were further classified as ZM first class (ZM1) if one parent was a pure Roma or Sinti and the other an Aryan, or ZM second class (ZM2) if one parent was a ZM1 and the other parent an Aryan.[68]

Ritter had argued as early as 1935 that only about 10 percent of Germany's Roma and Sinti were true Roma. "Pure race Gypsies [*Reinrassige* or *Stammechte Zigeuner*]," he concluded, were "no danger to the German people," and should be able to continue their traditional way of life. He also felt that there were no pure Roma life in Europe, and all Roma were tainted "racially." He also accepted the general view of most German anthropologists that the Roma were not Aryans; instead, like the Jews, they were "an Oriental-West Asia mixture of races."[69] This racial mixing, Ritter thought, was the reason for most German Roma and Sinti's asocial, animalistic behavior.

In 1938, Ritter wrote two articles analyzing the "Gypsy problem" and suggesting possible solutions. He said that past policies dealing with the Roma had failed because they were aimed at making the Roma sedentary. "Here," he wrote, "we know clearly that we are dealing with primitive nomads of an alien race whom neither education nor penalties can make sedentary citizens."[70] He argued that the Roma should be allowed to continue their nomadic ways, though they should also be kept from the rest of the German population.

It was essential, though, that all Roma have steady, honest work. The most difficult groups to deal with were the *Zigeunermischlinge* and the *Jenische* ("White Gypsies"), whom Ritter considered "a population of criminal clans and asocial elements." He suggested sterilizing these groups and moving them to "closed colonies."[71] Sterilization, Ritter hoped, would eliminate the Roma *mischlinge* within a generation.

Ritter's ideas met with widespread support from Germany's political leaders and scientific community. Although most agreed with Eva Justin, who wrote in 1943 that the "Gypsy problem" differed from the "Jewish problem" since "the 'Gypsy breed' *(Zigeunerart),* in contrast to the Jewish intellectuals *(jüdischen Intelligenz),* could not undermine or endanger the German people."[72] But not all German racial scientists agreed with Justin's ideas about the diminished Roma and Sinti threat. *SS- Obersturmführer* Dr. Carl-Heinz Rodenberg (1904–), Nazi Germany's infamous "homo-hunter," argued that the Roma, like the Jews, were a social and a biological threat to German society because they were both "'a biological foreign body' that 'has a destructive influence on our body politic, integrated in terms of race and blood.'"[73]

Prodded by Ritter's work and reports from the *Reichszentrale* in Berlin, Heinrich Himmler issued Nazi Germany's first major decree on the Roma "problem," *Bekämpfung der Zigeunerplage* (Combating the Gypsy Plague), on December 8, 1938. It dealt not only with Nazi Germany's handful of Sinti but also with Roma *Mischlinge* and those who lived a "Roma way of life." The decree stated that each group had to be dealt with separately *"bei der endgültigen Lösung der Zigeunerfrage* (in the final solution of the Gypsy question)."[74] To determine these differences, the police were to register Roma and Sinti older than six years as well as all those who lived as Roma-like itinerants. This information was to be sent to the *Zentralstele* in Berlin. Ex-

perts with the *Reichskriminalpolizei* (Kripo; Reich Criminal Police) would then determine their racial category by thoroughly examining everyone covered by Himmler's decree. To gather this information, Kripo could arrest, if necessary, those suspected of being Roma or itinerants.

Himmler's decree also required all Roma to carry identification papers that designated their specific racial status and lifestyle. The decree included traditional restrictions on Roma and Sinti occupations and travel, and foreign Roma were to be expelled or prevented from entering Germany. Local Kripo offices were to keep detailed records on Roma and Sinti births, deaths, and marriages, and were to send this information to Kripo headquarters in Berlin. All categories of Roma and Sinti and itinerants were now subject to the *Blutschutzgesetz* (Law for the Protection of German Blood and Honor), meaning that they could not marry until they had completed an *Ehetauglichkeitszeugnis* (marriage suitability certificate). Finally, Himmler's decree required that all local and state laws or regulations dealing with the Roma had to be changed to reflect the December 8 regulations, which would govern Roma policy throughout the Greater Reich. Nazi Roma policy was now to be solely a function of the national government.

On March 1, 1939, Reinhard Heydrich (1904–1942), now the *Chef der Sicherheitspolizei und der SD* (Chief of the Security Police and the SD), issued regulations for implementing Himmler's December 8 decree. Every Kripo office would now have to appoint a Roma specialist, and each Kripo region would have to open a special Roma and Sinti department. Heydrich ordered Kripo to issue new identity cards in colors distinguishing each category of Roma and Sinti. Pure Sinti would have brown cards; Roma *Mischlinge* would have a brown card with a blue stripe. Those who lived a Roma-like itinerant lifestyle would have a gray card. Heydrich explained that although Germans respected foreign races, the Reich had to develop policies to resolve the country's Roma and Sinti problem. These included isolating the Roma and Sinti from the German people, preventing marriage between Aryans and Roma, and regulating the lifestyle of pure Sinti and Roma *Mischlinge*. He promised that a law would be written to provide the legal basis for these regulations, though it never was. Nazi Germany's future Roma and Sinti policies now depended upon the work of Robert Ritter and the whims of Heinrich Himmler.

Yet well before Himmler's December 8 decree was implemented, Roma and Sinti throughout the Greater Reich were being subjected to intensified police harassment and internment in the growing network of *Zigeunerlager*. Although most camps blended traditional barracks with Roma and Sinti caravans for housing, the *Zigeunerlager* in Düsseldorf was the first to house Roma and Sinti in barracks only:

> From the very beginning the inmates of the camp were guarded by a warden who lived in the guard room. In addition, a neighbouring police officer kept the camp under continual surveillance. Anyone who wanted to go in or out had to report to the warden. Internees could only shop on a certain day in a small shop near the camp. After 9:00 P.M. no one could leave the living huts and there were sporadic spot-checks to moniter this. Every morning a roll call was held in which everyone had to take part. Non-Gypsies were not allowed into the camp. Anyone who, in the opinion of the police, had behaved in an unruly manner was locked up in the guardroom and generally held under arrest for many days. Often Sinti and Romanies were brutally beaten by the supervisor and quite often the guard dogs were set on the inmates.[75]

The Roma and Sinti lost all sources of income once they were put in the camps. The government now forced them to live on state welfare, which was cut in half because they were considered "asocials." As Roma and Sinti impoverishment intensified, one official report from the Marzhan *Zigeunerlager* noted: "[T]hey get, however, so little pay that they cannot live on it, so the danger arises that, through constant undernourishment, they will fall ill, this giving rise to intolerable conditions."[76] Consequently, more and more Roma and Sinti found work in forced labor situations, public works projects, and factories. Officials threatened those without jobs with incarceration in *Konzentrationlager* (KZ; concentration camps), where conditions were even worse than in the *Zigeunerlager*. In June 1938, scores of unemployed Roma and Sinti were sent to concentration camps as part of *Aktion Arbeitsschen Reich* (Reich Action Workshy). As World War II approached, Nazi Germany had firmly established policies for dealing with the Roma and Sinti that centered around forced sterilization or incarceration in *Zigeunerlager* or concentration camps. Such policies were designed slowly to eliminate them as a people.

Homosexuals, or Gays

Homosexuals were another of Nazi Germany's victim groups. The Nazis detested homosexuals because of their "socially aberrant behavior." Homosexuality was socially condemned during the Second Reich, although homosexuals felt more comfortable about not hiding their sexual preferences during the early years of the Weimar era. This attitude would change as conservative governments adopted more restrictive policies towards this group. After World War I, Dr. Magnus Hirschfeld (1868–1935), long an advocate for homosexual rights, founded the *Institut für Sexualwissenschaft* (Institute for Sexual Science) to act as a center for the reform of anti-homosexual laws in postwar Germany. His principal target was Article 175 of the 1871

German students march in front of Hirschfeld's Institute for Sexual Science, May 6, 1933. USHMM Photo No. 01625, courtesy of National Archives and Records Administration, College Park.

Reichsstrafgesetzbuch (Reich Criminal Code), which criminalized homosexual activity. Nazi Reichstag member Wilhelm Frick, who later became Hitler's interior minister, criticized Hirschfeld's efforts in a speech before the Reichstag in 1927. Homosexuals, he argued, "should be prosecuted with all severity, because such vices will lead to the downfall of the German nation."[77] And, Frick asked, who was to blame for this problem? "Naturally it is the Jews, Magnus Hirschfeld and his racial comrades, who have taken the lead and are trying to break new ground, just as in general the whole of Jewish morality has ruined the German people."[78]

This charge was repeated in an August 2, 1930, article in the *Völkischer Beobachter*: "'Since all the foul urges of the Jewish soul' come together in homosexuality, the 'law should recognize them for what they are—

utterly base aberrations of Syrians, extremely serious crimes that should be punished with hanging and deportation.'"[79]

It is not surprising, then, that when the National Socialists came to power in early 1933, Germany's homosexuals expected the worst. Attacks on homosexual bars began almost immediately, and German homosexuals, principally men, learned to avoid such places and to refrain from public displays of homosexual behavior. On May 6, 1933, as part of a national campaign to burn books of an "unGerman spirit," students from the Berlin *Institut für Leibesübungen* (Institute for Physical Exercise) joined with SA units in an attack on Hirschfeld's *Institut*. They destroyed 10,000 books, some in a huge bonfire four days later.

The following year, Joseph Goebbels played up the homosexuality of Ernst Röhm and other SA leaders partially to justify the "blood purge" of the SA during the "Night of the Long Knives." This prompted Himmler to move more forcefully against German homosexuals. The Gestapo set up a special division to deal with homosexuals and ordered police units from throughout Germany to send the new division their homosexual "pink lists": files on suspected male homosexuals that the police had been compiling since 1900. On September 1, 1935, German officials issued a revision of Article 175 of the criminal code, which greatly broadened the definition of unnatural acts between males to include any sort of physical contact. Clause 175a proscribed from three months to ten years imprisonment for those engaging in homosexual prostitution and for those committing sex acts with a person in a citizen's employ or service, or with someone younger than twenty-one. These changes, in league with an earlier amendment on sex offenses, expanded the rights of judges to rule on such offenses even if no law was "applicable to the act."[80]

The following year, Himmler created the *Reichszentrale zur Bekämpfung der Homosexualität und Abtreibung* (Reich Central Office for the Combating of Homosexuality and Abortion). From 1936 to 1938, this special Gestapo office (Special Office IIS), was run by *SS- Sturmbannführer* Josef Meisinger (1899–1947), who was executed in Poland in 1947 as the "butcher of Warsaw." In a speech to medical experts in the spring of 1937, Meisinger called homosexuality "alien in kind to the Nordic race" and a crime that weakened a nation and affected its "military capacity." He considered homosexuality and abortion political problems of the highest order. Homosexuals, he argued, could become "useful members of the national community with 'firm education and order.'" He saw lesbianism as a sexual aberration caused by a lack of male companionship and im-

proper upbringing. If given the chance "to assume the purpose given them by nature," most lesbians, Meisinger thought, would quickly return to a heterosexual lifestyle.[81]

A year later, Himmler addressed a group of SS generals about the problem with homosexuals:

If you take further into account the fact I have not yet mentioned, namely that with a static number of women, we have two million too few on account of those who fell in the war, then you can well imagine how this imbalance of two million homosexuals and two million war dead, or in other words a lack of about four million capable of having sex, has upset the sexual balance sheet of Germany, and will result in a catastrophe.

Therefore we must be absolutely clear that if we continue to have this burden in Germany, without being able to fight it, then that is the end of Germany, and the end of the Germanic world.[82]

The *Reichsführer SS* added that if a homosexual was caught in the SS, and he admitted that there was usually a case a month, the SS man would be publicly "degraded, expelled, and turned over to the courts." Once he had served his time in prison, he would be taken to a concentration camp and shot "while attempting to escape." This, Himmler said, would insure that the "good blood, which we have in the SS, and the increasing healthy blood which we are cultivating for Germany, will be kept pure."[83]

In 1937, the government mounted an extremely aggressive campaign against male homosexuals throughout Germany. Estimates are that German authorities arrested 100,000 homosexuals between 1933 and 1945 and sentenced half of them to prison terms. Most of these arrests and convictions took place between 1937 and 1939. Many homosexuals served their terms in regular prisons, but from 5,000 to 15,000 were sent to concentration camps. Though it is difficult to estimate how many homosexuals died in concentration camps, some suggest a figure as high as 60 percent. Camp authorities forced homosexuals to wear special identifying badges, such as pink triangles, a requirement that resulted in brutal mistreatment from guards and inmates. Some homosexuals were also victimized in medical experiments that included castration. In Buchenwald, *SS- Sturmbannführer* Dr. Carl Peter Vaernet (1893–1965), a Dane, performed experimental surgery on homosexuals to try to make them heterosexuals. Though Vaernet claimed all his operations were a success, Himmler was suspicious; in 1944, he ordered that Vaernet's patients be sent to the brothel at Ravensbruck women's camp to see whether they were now truly heterosexual. No documentation exists about the fate of these victims.

Conclusion

What is important about the various legal, social, economic, eugenic, and other policies adopted by the Nazi leadership between 1933 and 1939 against the Jews, the Roma and Sinti, the handicapped, Afro-Germans, and homosexuals was their collective significance to future German efforts to be rid of groups deemed a threat to German society and Aryan racial purity.

The Nazis considered the Jews the most threatening of these groups and developed policies designed to rip them from the fabric of German society and force them to leave the Reich. When laws and other restrictions, coupled with on-again, off-again waves of anti-Semitic violence did not work, Germany's rulers embraced Adolf Eichmann's brutish tactics used so successfully in Austria. These new efforts peaked in late 1938 during *Kristallnacht,* an anti-Semitic reign of terror that forever transformed Nazi policies towards the Jews. Hitler, no doubt emboldened by his incredible international successes in Austria and the Sudetenland the year before, warned the world in early 1939 that if war came, the Jews would be annihilated.

The Nazis also viewed other groups such as the Roma and Sinti and Afro-Germans as threats to the Aryan racial pool, though they were not despised and feared like the Jews. Because of their smaller numbers, Germany's leaders thought they could wipe out these groups by using eugenic methods such as sterilization. The same was true of the handicapped, whose crimes were not racial but hereditary. From the Nazi perspective, the mentally challenged and the disabled were not only potential threats to Aryan racial purity but also an economic burden on German society. To address the long-range threat from such individuals, the Germans fell back on pre-Nazi ideas about sterilization to develop an extensive program of forced sterilization and so rid German society of this genetic threat in a generation or two. Homosexuals, particularly males, were also viewed as a threatening element in German society, but this was more from traditional prejudice and the feeling that their sexual preferences prevented them from producing offspring.

The successes and failures of these efforts to eject, isolate, or neutralize the perceived harm that each of these racial, biological, or lifestyle threats might cause German society and Aryanism provided the basis for Nazi Germany's next round of experimentation in the early years of World War II. Again, emboldened by a growing sense of invincibility both domestically and internationally, Nazi Germany's leadership now began to experiment with much more deadly policies designed to rid Germany and European society of groups seen as a threat to core Nazi racial, ideological, and societal goals.

SOURCES FOR FURTHER STUDY AND RESEARCH

Primary Sources

Baynes, Norman H., ed. *The Speeches of Adolf Hitler, April 1922–August 1939*. Vol. 1. New York: Howard Fertig, 1969.

Bonhoeffer, Dietrich. *Letters & Papers from Prison*. Edited by Eberhard Bethge. Enlarged ed. New York: Touchstone, 1997.

The Buchenwald Report. Translated and edited by David A. Hackett. Boulder: Westview Press, 1995.

Casti Connubi: Encyclical of Pope Pius XI on Christian Marriage. http://www.vatican.va/holy_father/pius_xi/encyclicals/documents/hf_pxi_enc_3112 1930_c [accessed July 3, 2006].

Hirschfeld, Magnus. *The Homosexuality of Men and Women*. Translated by Michael A. Lombardi-Nash. Amherst, NY: Prometheus Books, 2000.

Hitler, Adolf. *Mein Kampf*. Boston: Houghton Mifflin, 1943.

James, Eldon R., ed. *The Statutory Criminal Law of Germany*. Washington, DC: The Library of Congress, 1947.

Klemperer, Victory. *I Will Bear Witness: A Diary of the Nazi Years, 1933–1941*. Translated by Martin Chalmers. New York: Random House, 1998.

Ludecke, Kurt G. *I Knew Hitler: The Story of a Nazi Who Escaped the Blood Purge*. London: Jarrolds, 1938.

The New York Times, June 10, 1939.

Noakes, Jeremy, and Geoffrey Pridham, eds. *The Nazi Party, State and Society, 1919–1939*. Vol. 1 of *Nazism, 1919–1945: A History in Documents and Eyewitness Accounts*. New York: Schocken Books, 1984.

_____, eds. *Foreign Policy, War and Racial Extermination*. Vol. 2 of *Nazism, 1919–1945: A History in Documents and Eyewitness Accounts*. New York: Schocken Books, 1988.

Owens, Jesse, and Paul G. Neimark. *The Jesse Owens Story*. New York: Putnam, 1970.

Rittner, Carol, and John K. Roth, eds. *Different Voices: Women and the Holocaust*. New York: Paragon House, 1993.

Rose, Romani, ed. *Der Nationalsozialistische Völkermord an den Sinti und Roma*. Heidelberg: Documentations- und Kulturzentrum Deutscher Sinti und Roma, 2003.

Schleunes, Karl A., ed. *Legislating the Holocaust: The Bernhard Loesener Memoirs and Supporting Documents*. Translated by Carol Scherer. Boulder: Westview Press, 2001.

Shirer, William L. *The Nightmare Years, 1930–1940*. Boston: Little, Brown, 1984.

Unger, Hellmuth. *Sendung und Gewissen*. Berlin: Brunnen Verlag, 1935.

Secondary Sources

Bankier, David. *The Germans and the Final Solution: Public Opinion Under the Nazis*. Oxford: Blackwell, 1996.

Barnett, Victoria. "Dietrich Bonhoeffer." http://www.ushmm.org/bonhoeffer. N.d.

_____. *For the Soul of the People: Protestant Protest Against Hitler*. New York: Oxford University Press, 1992.

Bauer, Yehuda. *Jews for Sale: Nazi-Jewish Negotiations, 1933–1945*. New Haven: Yale University Press, 1994.

Berben, Paul. *Dachau, 1933–1945: The Official History*. London: Comité International de Dachau, 1975.

Bergen, Doris. *Twisted Cross: the German Christian Movement in the Third Reich*. Chapel Hill: University of North Carolina Press, 1996.

Bethge, Eberhard. *Dietrich Bonhoeffer: A Biography*. Edited by Victoria Barnett. Rev. ed. Minneapolis: Fortress Press, 2000.

Black, Edwin. *War Against the Weak: Eugenics and America's Campaign to Create a Master Race*. New York: Four Walls Eight Windows, 2003.

Burleigh, Michael. *Death and Deliverance: 'Euthanasia' in Germany 1900–1945*. Cambridge: Cambridge University Press, 1994.

_____. *The Third Reich: A New History*. New York: Hill and Wang, 2000.

Burleigh, Michael, and Wolfgang Wippermann. *The Racial State: Germany 1933–1945*. Cambridge: Cambridge University Press, 1991.

Campt, Tina M. *Other Germans: Black Germans and the Politics of Race, Gender, and Memory in the Third Reich*. Ann Arbor: University of Michigan Press, 2004.

Carroll, James. *Constantine's Sword: The Church and the Jews*. Boston: Houghton Mifflin, 2002.

Cesarani, David. *Becoming Eichmann: Rethinking the Life, Crimes, and Trial of a "Desk Murderer."* Cambridge, MA: Da Capo Press, 2006.

Crowe, David M. "The Roma Holocaust." In *The Holocaust's Ghost: Writings on Art, Politics, Law and Education*, edited by F. C. DeCoste and Bernard Schwartz, 179–202. Alberta: University of Alberta Press, 2000.

Dippel, John U. H. *Bound Upon a Wheel of Fire: Why So Many German Jews Made the Tragic Decision to Remain in Nazi Germany.* New York: Basic Books, 1996.

Distel, Barbara, and Ruth Jakusch, eds. *Concentration Camp Dachau, 1933–1945.* Munich: Comité International de Dachau, 1978.

Evans, Richard J. *The Coming of the Third Reich.* New York: Penguin, 2004.

_____. *The Third Reich in Power.* New York: Penguin, 2005.

"Euthanasia." *UK Rights* (the online newspaper of UKCHR). http://www.ukcouncilhumanrights.co .uk/euthanasia.html.

Fings, Karola, Herbert Heuss, and Frank Sparing, eds. *From 'Race Science' to the Camps: The Gypsies During the Second World War.* Hatfield, UK: University of Hertfordshire Press, 1997.

Fischer, Klaus P. *The History of an Obsession: German Judeophobia and the Holocaust.* New York: Continuum, 1998.

_____. *Nazi Germany: A New History.* New York: Continuum, 1995.

Friedlander, Henry. *The Origins of Nazi Genocide: From Euthanasia to the Final Solution.* Chapel Hill: University of North Carolina Press, 1995.

Friedländer, Saul. *Nazi Germany and the Jews.* Vol. 1, *The Years of Persecution.* New York: HarperCollins, 1997.

Gerlach, Wolfgang. *Als die Zeugen schwiegen: Bekennende Kirche und die Juden.* Berlin: Institut Kirche u. Judentum, 1993.

Gilbert, Martin. *Kristallnacht: Prelude to Madness.* New York: HarperCollins, 2006.

Grau, Günter. *Hidden Holocaust? Gay and Lesbian Persecution in Germany, 1933–1945.* Translated by Patrick Camiller. London: Cassell, 1995.

Gross, Larry, and James D. Woods, eds. *The Columbia Reader on Lesbians and Gay Men in Media, Society, and Politics.* New York: Columbia University Press, 1999.

Hake, Sabine. *Popular Cinema of the Third Reich.* Austin: University of Texas Press, 2001.

Hart-Davis, Duff. *Hitler's Games: The 1936 Olympics.* New York: Harper & Row, 1986.

The Jewish Virtual Library. "The Nazi Olympics." http://www.jewishvirtuallibrary.org/jsource/ Holocaust/olympics.html.

Kershaw, Ian. *Hitler: 1889–1936 Hubris.* New York: W. W. Norton, 1999.

_____. *Hitler: 1936–1945 Nemesis.* New York: W. W. Norton, 2000.

Klee, Ernst. *"Euthanasie" im NS-Staat: Die "Vernichtung lebensunwerten Lebens."* Frankfurt: Fischer Taschenbuch Verlag, 2004.

Lewy, Guenther. *The Catholic Church and Nazi Germany.* New York: McGraw-Hill, 1964.

_____. *The Nazi Persecution of the Gypsies.* New York: Oxford University Press, 2000.

Lifton, Robert Jay. *The Nazi Doctors: Medical Killing and the Psychology of Genocide.* New York: Basic Books, 1986.

Lipstadt, Deborah E. *Beyond Belief: The American Press & the Coming of the Holocaust, 1933–1945.* New York: Free Press, 1986.

Lively, Scott, and Kevin Abrams. *The Pink Swastika: Homosexuality in the Nazi Party.* Keizer, OR: Founders, 1995.

Lusane, Clarence. *Hitler's Black Victims: The Historical Experiences of Afro-Germans, European Blacks, Africans, and African Americans in the Nazi Era.* New York: Routledge, 2003.

Margalit, Gilad. *Germany and Its Gypsies: A Post-Auschwitz Ordeal.* Madison: University of Wisconsin Press, 2002.

McClellan, David. *Karl Marx: His Life and Thought.* New York: Harper & Row, 1973.

Michael, Robert. "Theological Myth, German Anti-Semitism and the Holocaust: The Case of Martin Niemöller." In vol. 2 of *Holocaust and Genocide Studies,* edited by Yehuda Bauer, 105–122. New York: Oxford University Press, 1987.

Morse, Arthur D. *While Six Million Died: A Chronicle of American Apathy.* New York: Hart, 1968.

Plant, Richard. *The Pink Triangle: The Nazi War Against Homosexuals.* New York: Henry Holt, 1986.

Proctor, Robert N. *Racial Hygiene: Medicine Under the Nazis.* Cambridge, MA: Harvard University Press, 1988.

Read, Anthony, and David Fisher. *Kristallnacht: The Unleashing of the Holocaust.* New York: Peter Bedrick Books, 1989.

Reuth, Ralf Georg. *Goebbels.* Translated by Krishna Winston. New York: Harcourt, Brace & World, 1993.

Rose, Romani, and Walter Weiss. *Sinti und Roma im 'Dritten Reich.'* Göttingen: Lamuv Taschenbuch, 1991.

Schleunes, Karl A. *The Twisted Road to Auschwitz: Nazi Policy Toward German Jews, 1933–1939.* Urbana: University of Illinois Press, 1990.

Schwab, Gerald. *The Day the Holocaust Began: The Odyssey of Herschel Grynszpan.* New York: Praeger, 1990.

Shirer, William L. *The Rise and Fall of the Third Reich: A History of Nazi Germany.* New York: Simon & Schuster, 1960.

Spielvogel, Jackson J. *Hitler and Nazi Germany: A History.* 3rd ed. Upper Saddle River, NJ: Prentice Hall, 1996.

Steigmann-Gall, Richard. *The Holy Reich: Nazi Conceptions of Christianity, 1919–1945.* Cambridge: Cambridge University Press, 2003.

Thomas, Gordon, and Max Morgan-Witts. *Voyage of the Damned.* 2nd ed. Belton, UK: Dalton Watson Fine Books, 1994.

United States Holocaust Memorial Museum. *Deadly Medicine: Creating the Master Race.* Washington, DC: United States Holocaust Memorial Museum, 2004.

_____. *The Nazi Olympics: Berlin 1936.* Washington, DC: United States Holocaust Memorial Council, 1997.

Wheeler, John W. *Hindenburg: The Wooden Titan.* London: Macmillan, 1967.

Willems, Wim. *In Search of the True Gypsy: From Enlightenment to Final Solution.* Translated by Don Bloch. London: Frank Cass, 1997.

Zimmermann, Michael. *Rassenutopie und Genozid: Die nationalsozialistische "Lösung der Zigeunerfrage."* Hamburg: Hans Christians Verlag, 1996.

CHAPTER 5

Nazi Germany at War, 1939–1941

"Euthanasia" and the Handicapped; Ghettos and Jews

CHRONOLOGY

- **1939:** Children's "euthanasia" program created
- **1939:** Secret Nazi-Soviet Pact signed in Moscow
- **1939 (*September 1*):** Germany invades Poland; *Einsatzgruppen* begin terror campaign against Polish civilians
- **1939 (*September 1*):** Adolf Hitler authorizes the T-4 adult "euthanasia" program
- **1939 (*September 17*):** Soviet forces begin occupation of eastern Poland
- **1939 (*September 21*):** Reinhard Heydrich writes "The Problem of the Jews in the Occupied Areas"
- **1939 (*September 27*):** Reich Security Main Office (RSHA) created to oversee all Nazi police organizations
- **1939 (*September 27*):** Heydrich meets with RSHA chiefs to discuss transfer of Reich Jews and Roma to Poland
- **1939 (*September 29*):** Wehrmacht orders seizure of Jewish property
- **1939 (*October*):** Adolf Eichmann orders shipment of Reich Jews to Poland as part of Nisko Plan; halted by Heinrich Müller, head of Gestapo
- **1939 (*October 26*):** General Government created with Hans Frank as *Generalgouverneur*
- **1939 (*October 26*):** Frank orders that all Jewish males from fourteen to sixteen be available for forced labor
- **1939 (*November*):** All Jewish assets frozen in General Government
- **1939 (*November 1*):** Hermann Göring creates Main Trusteeship Office East
- **1939 (*November 28*):** Frank orders ghettos opened throughout General Government
- **1939 (*December 12*):** All Jews ordered to do two years of forced labor in General Government
- **1940 (*February 8*):** Łódź ghetto opened with Mordechai Rumkowski as head of *Ältestenrat*
- **1940 (*spring*):** Göring resumes transports to General Government
- **1940 (*spring*):** Reich Roma (2,500) shipped to General Government
- **1940 (*spring*):** Operation A-B. Thousands of Polish political, religious, cultural figures murdered
- **1940 (*May 18*):** Jews ordered to leave Kraków, capital of General Government

—**1940** *(May)*: Himmler writes "Some Thoughts on the Treatment of the Alien Population in the East"

—**1940** *(June)*: Franz Rademacher and Adolf Eichmann develop separate Madagascar plans for Jewish settlement

—**1940** *(September 8)*: Hans Biebow becomes manager of Łódź ghetto

—**1940**: Göring orders all remaining Jewish property in General Government seized

—**1940**: Hans Frank orders creation of Warsaw ghetto with Adam Czerniaków as head of *Judenrat*

—**1940** *(November 25)*: Jews forbidden to enter Kraków

—**1941** *(March 3)*: Otto Wächter orders creation of Kraków ghetto in Podgórze

—**1941** *(August)*: SS creates 14f13 "euthanasia" program in concentration camps

—**1941** *(August 13)*: Bishop Dr. Antonius Hilfrich protests T-4 program

—**1941** *(fall)*: Roma compound opened in Łódź ghetto

—**1941** *(fall)*: T-4 program shut down; specialists sent to East to help develop Final Solution

—**1941** *(November)*: Thousands of Roma (4,996) sent to Łódź ghetto; murdered in Chełmno in early 1942

The German invasion of Poland on September 1, 1939, marked a dramatic turning point in the Third Reich's campaign against its various racial and biological enemies. Using war as a cover and emboldened by earlier domestic and international successes, German leaders initiated a series of campaigns in Germany and Poland designed to "euthanize" selected groups of handicapped individuals; murder Polish intellectuals, politicians, and religious leaders; and isolate Jews from the rest of Polish society. This chapter will explore these efforts and the impact they had not only on their victims but also on Nazi Germany's evolving racial and biological policies.

The seeds for Nazi Germany's "euthanasia" programs were planted during the discussions over the costs and other issues concerning the care of those with severe physical and mental handicaps in the years preceding World War II. Yet what was involved was not euthanasia in the traditional sense, but a program that Henry Friedlander calls the "systematic and secret execution" of the handicapped or the disabled.[1] "Euthanasia" became the German euphemism for this program of institutionalized murder.

The successful program to sterilize the handicapped and the *Rheinlandbastarde* from 1934 onwards emboldened the Nazi leadership to experiment with a more truly eliminationist policy against those they determined to be *Lebensunwertes Lebens* (lives unworthy of life), or people who lived *Ballastexistenzen* (unnecessary lines). Because of the great success of the Nazi sterilization program, it was easy to move from sterilizing those deemed eugenically unfit to a wartime policy that called for the state murder of those considered racially or "genetically inferior." Tragically, the programs and specialists developed and trained in this new phase of the Holocaust would later provide the nucleus of the more deadly mass murder campaign against the Jews and the Roma.

Children's "Euthanasia" Program

The idea for the children's "euthanasia" program came from a letter written by the Knauers to Adolf Hitler. Encouraged by their child's grandmother, they asked permission to "euthanize" their newborn infant. The parents had taken the child to Leipzig University's *Universitätkinderlinik* (University Children's Clinic) and asked its director, Dr. Werner Catel (1894–1981), to "euthanize" their infant. The father told Catel that he wanted the child "put to sleep" because its condition was causing his wife a lot of mental anguish. When Catel refused, the parents wrote to Hitler. The Führer, who had already received similar appeals, asked his personal physician, *SS- Obersturmführer* Dr. Karl Brandt (1904–1948), to go to Leipzig

MURDER OF THE HANDICAPPED

View of the "Murder of the Handicapped" exhibit, United States Holocaust Memorial Museum, 1995. USHMM Photo No. N02413, Photographer: Edward Owen.

and examine the Knauer child. He also authorized Brandt to "euthanize" the child if he felt the infant eugenically warranted death. After a brief examination, Brandt executed Hitler's "euthanasia" order and had the child put to death.[2] Hitler later asked Brandt and *SS- Obergruppenführer* Philipp Bouhler (1899–1945), the head of the *Führerkanzlei* (Chancellery of the Führer), to develop a program that would "euthanize" other German children afflicted with serious physical and mental handicaps.

In early 1939, Bouhler assigned three men from Hitler's chancellery—Viktor Brack (1904–1948), head of the *Führerkanzeli's* Central Office II (State and Party Affairs), and two of Brack's subordinates, Hans Hefelmann (1906–1986) and Richard von Hegener (1905–1981) to begin work on highly secret plans for a children's "euthanasia" program.

The group that oversaw this planning was known as the *Reichsansschuss zur Wissenschaftlichen Erfassung von erb- und anlagebedingten schweren Leiden* (Reich Committee for the Scientific Registration of Severe Hereditary Ailments). Several prominent physicians joined this committee, including Dr. Herbert Linden (1899–1945), who was in charge of the *Reichsministerium Innern's* (Ministry of the Interior) state hospital and nursing home network. As planning moved ahead in the first half of 1939, Linden was joined by five more prominent physicians: Karl Brandt, Werner Catel, Hans Heinze (1895–1983), Hellmuth Unger (1891–1953), and Ernst Wentzler (1891–1973). Each of these men had early supported the idea of "euthanizing" children. Dr. Catel held a chair in pediatrics at Leipzig University and was director of its children's clinic, positions he retained after the war. Dr. Heinze, a psychologist and neurologist, was director of the state hospital in Brandenburg-Görden, one of the most renowned institutions in Germany. He set up a special children's "euthanasia" ward at his hospital and also opened a gruesome "euthanasia" research center there. Dr. Wentzler was a successful Berlin pediatrician who ran a private children's clinic in the German capital. He later opened a special children's "euthanasia" ward at his facility in Berlin.

Two weeks before Germany invaded Poland, the Reich Committee circulated a secret decree through the Ministry of the Interior's network that ordered physicians and midwives to report children who were younger than three and suffered the following medical problems:

1. Idiocy as well as Down syndrome (especially cases also involving blindness and deafness)
2. Microcephaly (abnormally small head size)
3. Severe or progressive hydrocephalus (enlarged head caused by excessive fluid in the brain cavity)
4. All deformities, especially missing limbs and severely defective closure of the head and the vertebral column
5. Paralysis, including Little's disease (spastic diplegia)

The ministry attached a one-page form to the decree that made it appear as if the information was needed for scientific research. The form asked for the gender and age of each child three and younger, as well as details about the child's illness, the nature of its hospital care, and a prognosis for the long-range outcome of such care. Physicians and midwives were to submit the completed one-page form to their local public health officer, who would then send it to the Reich Committee's post office box 101, Berlin W 9. Midwives received a stipend of 2 *Reichsmarks*

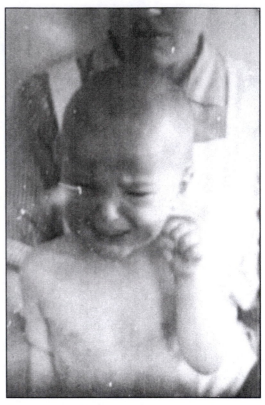

Richard Jenne, last child murdered at Kaufbeuren-Irsee "Euthanasia Center," 1945. USHMM Photo No. 78606, courtesy of National Archives and Records Administration, College Park.

($.80) for each form they filled out. The following summer, the Reich Committee decided that the original form asked for too little information and adopted a new, more thorough form that requested medical history information about the child's family members as well as the parents' address and religion.

Once they received the forms, Catel, Heinze, and Wentzler decided whether to "euthanize" the children in question. Their work was quite simple. After reviewing the forms, they marked those they decided fit for "euthanization" with a plus (+); those to be spared they marked with a minus (–). If they were uncertain about the fate of a child, the physicians simply wrote *Beobachtung* (observation) on the form. They all used the same form to record their decisions.

Heinze opened the first children's "euthanasia" ward at his hospital in Brandenburg-Görden. Authorities opened the second, Am Spiegelgrund, in the large Viennese state hospital, Am Steinhof. During the next year, the Reich Committee opened twenty other children's "euthanasia" wards throughout Greater Germany. Killing methods differed from hospital to hospital. Dr. Heinze, for example, preferred slow injections of poison over a long time, but Dr. Hermann Pfannmüller (1886–1961), the director of the suburban Munich hospital, Eglfing-Haar, slowly starved his children to death. Pfannmüller, a psychiatrist and early Nazi Party member, was so enthusiastic about his work that he led tours of his facility throughout the war and proudly showed off his murderous skills. Ludwig Lehner, a school teacher from Bavaria, described the tour he took in the fall of 1939:

During my tour, I was eyewitness to the following events: After visiting a few other wards, the institution's director himself, as far as I remember he was called Pfannmüller, led us into a children's ward. This hall impressed me as clean and well-kept. About 15 to 25 cribs contained that number of children, aged approximately one to five years. In this ward Pfannmüller explicated his opinions in particular detail. I remember pretty accurately the sense of his speech, because it was, either due to cynicism or clumsiness, surprisingly frank: "For me as a national Socialist, these creatures (meaning these children) obviously represent only a burden for our healthy national body [*Volkskörper*]. We do not kill (he might also have used a euphemism instead of the word "kill") with poison, injections, etc., because that would only provide new slanderous campaign material for the foreign press and certain gentlemen in Switzerland [the Red Cross]. No. our method is, as you can see, much simpler and far more natural." As he spoke these words,

[Pfannmüller] and a nurse from the ward pulled a child from its crib. Displaying the child like a dead rabbit, he pontificated with the air of a connoisseur and a cynical smirk something like this: "With this one, for example, it will still take two or three days." I can still clearly visualize the spectacle of this fat and smirking man with the whimpering skeleton in his fleshy hand, surrounded by other starving children. Furthermore, the murderer then pointed out that they did not suddenly withdraw food, but instead slowly reduced rations.[3]

Pfannmüller, who was accused of the deaths of more than 3,000 of his patients, was tried for his war crimes in Munich in 1951 and sentenced to one to five years in prison.

By the end of 1940, the Reich Committee was allowing physicians to "euthanize" children older than three; and several weeks after the invasion of the Soviet Union on June 22, 1941, it expanded the program to include all school children who had any sort of disability. Their teachers were now required, under penalty of a fine (150 *Reichsmarks*), to report such children to their local health office. Two years later, the Reich Committee ordered the "euthanization" of children who had no deformities or disabilities but belonged to "unwanted races." In the spring of 1943, Jewish children, who previously were felt to be unworthy of mercy killing, were now murdered at the adult "euthanasia" centers at Hadamar. It is estimated that the Germans murdered more than 5,000 children in the children's "euthanasia" program during the war.

In obtaining permission to send children to these wards, the Reich Committee's representatives deceived many parents, often promising a cure for their children's ailments. Though some parents protested, Reich Committee officials were usually successful in pressuring them to agree to their children's admission to these special wards because they were unaware that the facilities existed to kill their children. Few parents knowingly agreed to have their children "euthanized." After the child's death, a standard form letter was sent to the parents informing them that their child had died rather suddenly of a fictitious ailment. The letter also informed the parents that their child's body had been cremated because of fear of an epidemic, an ongoing rationale and concern of the Germans as their murderous programs spread throughout Europe.

Adult "Euthanasia" Program

Six weeks before the invasion of Poland, Hitler met with Dr. Leonardo Conti (1900–1945), the *Reichsärzteführer* (Reich Physicians Leader), Martin Bormann, Hitler's major domo and later head of the *Parteikanzlei* (Party Chancellery), and Hans Heinrich Lammers (1879–1962), head of the *Reichskanzlei* (Reich Chancellery). Michael Burleigh wrote that

> [Hitler] regarded it as right that the worthless lives of seriously ill mental patients should be got rid of. He took as examples the severe mental illnesses in which the patients could only be kept lying on sand or sawdust, because they perpetually dirtied themselves, cases in which these patients put their own excrement in their mouths as if it were food, and things similar. Continuing from that, he said that he thought it right that the worthless lives of such creatures should be ended, and that this would result in certain savings in terms of hospitals, doctors and nursing staff.[4]

Afterwards, Hitler made Philipp Bouhler head of the adult "euthanasia" program, bypassing Conti. The Führer was afraid that if he put Conti in this position, it would have given his mentor, Bormann, full control over the program.

Bouhler, using the administrative structure already in place for the children's "euthanasia" program, brought more physicians onboard with specialities other than children's pediatrics. The adult "euthanasia" program was housed in a former Jewish villa at No. 4 Tiergarten Straße, thus its code name T-4. Bouhler and Karl Brandt were Hitler's link to the T-4 program, and Viktor Brack, an early Nazi who had once served as Himmler's driver and, later, as Bouhler's assistant, ran the T-4 program's daily operations. Dr. Werner Heyde (1902–1964), a rising Nazi psychiatrist and a protégé of Theodor Eicke, the commandant of Dachau, became the guiding medical hand of the adult "euthanasia" program. Heyde's Nazi connections had already earned him a chair in psychiatry at the University of Würzburg. Bouhler, Brandt, and Heyde put together a team of physicians that included Drs. Wenzler and Unger from the children's "euthanasia" program. This group of medical specialists met throughout August and September 1939 to work out the details of their new killing operation.

It was difficult to convince some physicians to join the program since they feared they could be prosecuted for murdering patients. Hitler was unwilling to make "euthanasia" legal because he was afraid that such legislation would rob the program of its secrecy. But Bouhler was able to persuade Hitler to sign an order in October 1939 (backdated to September 1, 1939), authorizing "euthanasia" murder. This document was used to convince physicians that they would not face criminal charges for their actions. It read:

[LETTERHEAD: A. HITLER]
BERLIN, 1 SEPT. 1939

Reichsleiter Bouhler and Dr. Brandt, M.D., are charged with the responsibility of enlarging the authority of certain physicians to be designated by name in such a manner, so that persons who, according to human judgment, are incurable can, upon a most careful diagnosis of their condition of sickness, be accorded a mercy death.

[signed] A. Hitler[5]

Registration Form 1   To be typewritten

Current No._____

  Name of the Institution :_____

  At : _____

Surname and Christian name of the patient :_____

At birth_____

Date of birth :_____Place :_____District :_____

Last place of residence_____District :_____

Unmarried, married, widow, widower, divorced :_____

Religion :_____ Race* :_____

Previous profession :_____Nationality :_____

Army service when? 1914–18 or from 1–9–39_____

War injury (even if no connection with mental disorder) Yes/No_____

How does war injury show itself and of what does it consist?_____

_____

Address of next of kin :_____

Regular visits and by whom (address) :_____

Guardian or nurse (name, address) :_____

Responsible for payment :_____

Since when in Institution_____

Whence and when handed over :_____

Since when ill :_____

If has been in other institutions, where and how long :_____

Twin? Yes/No_____ Blood relations of unsound mind :_____

Diagnosis : _____

Clinical description (previous history, course, condition ; in any case ample data
  regarding mental condition) :_____

_____

Very restless? Yes/No_____Bedridden? Yes/No_____

Incurable physical illness : Yes/No (which)_____

Schizophrenia : Fresh attack_____Final condition_____Good recovery_____

Mental debility : Weak_____Imbecile_____Idiot_____

Epilepsy : Psychological alteration_____Average frequency of the attacks_____

Therapeutics (insulin, cardiazol, malaria, permanent result : _____
  Salvarsan, etc. when?)_____ Yes/No_____

Admitted by reason of par. 51, par. 42b German Penal Code, etc. through_____

_____

Crime :_____Former punishable offenses :_____

Manner of employment (detailed description of work) :_____

Permanent/Temporary employment, independent Worker? Yes/No_____

Value of work (if possible compared with average performance of healthy
  person)_____

  This space to be left blank.

                ----------------------Place, Date_____

                        Signature of the head doctor or his repre-
                        sentative (doctors who are not phychia-
                        trists or neurologists, please state same).

_____

*German or of similar blood (of German blood), Jew, Jewish mixed breed Grades I or II,
Negro (mixed breed).

Form to be used by physicians to determine degree of mental or physical disabilities. Source: *Trials of War Criminals Before the Nuremberg Military Tribunals.* Public Domain.

For safe keeping, the original was kept in the Reich chancellery, but copies were shown to physicians under consideration for T-4 duty.

On September 21, 1939, the Reich Ministry of the Interior ordered regional governments to send it a list by October 15 of all state hospitals in their jurisdictions that housed patients afflicted with serious mental problems, epilepsy, or low IQs. Each hospital was sent a one-page form that listed detailed questions about the individual hospital, its proximity to reliable transportation, and how many criminal and Jewish patients it was treating. Each hospital also received individual reporting forms for these patients. Administrators were asked to supply the date of institutionalization and ample information on a patient's "mental condition." The form also had questions about a patient's "incurable physical illness" as well as his or her mental problems such as schizophrenia, "mental debility," imbecility, idiocy, and epilepsy. It also asked about the effectiveness of various medications on a given patient's condition and whether the patient had been admitted for criminal behavior or had a criminal record. Finally, there was a question about a patient's employment record, its purpose being to determine whether a patient was asocial or "work shy."[6]

Bouhler's office then chose a group of ideologically reliable physicians to review these forms. Each physician could decide whether or not to participate in the program. Few refused. Their decisions for murdering adults followed much the same format and ideological guidelines for "euthanizing" children—those selected for "mercy" killing were individuals they considered Lebenswertes Lebens living Ballastexistenzen.[7]

One of the most important aspects of the T-4 program, particularly as it related to the broader mass murder of Jews, Roma, Poles, Russians, and others, was the complex technology and expertise developed to insure the program's success. Between the fall of 1939 and August 1941, when Hitler ordered the program ended, the Germans murdered from 70,000 to 80,000 handicapped adults. A program this extensive and secretive needed a sophisticated and technologically advanced machinery of death to deal with so many victims. Early on, possibly because of a suggestion from Hitler (who kept tabs on the T-4 program through Brandt and Bouhler), the T-4 leadership decided that gassing was the most efficient way to kill its victims. Sometime in late December 1939 or January 1940, the SS conducted a gassing demonstration for Bouhler, Brandt, Conti, Heyde, Brack, and others; the gas chamber, which had been specially built for the occasion, was housed in an old jail in Brandenburg, near Berlin. Brandt and Conti personally injected several handicapped patients with Barbituric acid to show the inefficiency of this type of "euthanasia." Eight patients were then gassed with carbon monoxide. The unsuspecting inmates died much more quickly, which pleased the gathered Nazi dignitaries.

Once T-4 officials had chosen the means of death, they opened six "euthanasia" killing centers; these were located at Brandenburg, Grafeneck (near Stuttgart), Bernburg (near Dessau), Hadamar (near Wiesbaden), Hartheim (near Linz, Austria), and Sonnenstein (near Dresden). They closed the centers at Grafeneck and Brandenburg at the end of 1940 because of local concern about their activities. By the time Hitler shut the program down, only four centers were in operation. Bouhler built each of the death centers, except Sonnenstein, at former hospitals, and outfitted them with gas chambers and crematories to burn the bodies. The industrial giants BASF and I. G. Farben developed the gas used in the chambers. T-4 officials were insistent on efficiency and secrecy, and they did everything possible to delude the patients. A physician gave victims phony medical examinations beforehand and did everything possible to soothe them before they were put into the gas chamber. The examination also enabled physicians to identify gold fillings in the victim's teeth, which would be extracted after death. After the exam, the patients were told they were going to take a shower. Orderlies sedated potentially troublesome patients before their gassing. They also used other ruses to coax suspicious patients into the gas chambers.

Depending on the facility, T-4 teams could gas from 25 to 150 patients at a time. After the gold was removed from victims' teeth, some bodies were sent to the crematory, others were autopsied or used for medical experiments. The entire process usually took less that twenty-four hours. Relatives were then sent a letter informing them that their loved one had died suddenly despite medical efforts to save him or her. The body, the letter explained, had been cremated for public-health reasons. Relatives had fourteen days in which to request an urn containing their family member's ashes, which would be sent to a designated cemetery. If the family failed to respond in the allotted time, the ashes would be interred in a mass grave. In reality, even if the relatives did request the ashes in a timely manner, what they got were not the remains of the actual loved one because the T-4 centers cremated many bodies at a time: The ashes they received came from a large, common pile.

Despite efforts to mask the deadly work of the T-4 centers, public knowledge was widespread, particularly in the communities where the centers were located. Some families began to note inconsistencies in the death notices; others received two urns for one dead relative, or the ashes of a male relative with a hairpin. Eventually, Germany's churches began to protest the killings because they controlled many of the institutions that housed the T-4 victims. In fact, half of those murdered in the T-4 program between 1939 and 1941 were patients housed in Protestant or Roman Catholic institutions. Most religious protests were conducted behind closed doors and through official channels. Dr. Antonius Hilfrich (1873–1947), the Roman Catholic bishop of Limburg, wrote to Wilhelm Frick, the interior minister, on August 13, 1941, asking his help in stopping a program that "all God-fearing men consider . . . a crass injustice."[8] Ten days earlier, the Roman Catholic bishop Clemens August Graf von Galen (1878–1946), long a critic of Nazism and the Nazi regime, spoke out forcefully against the T-4 program in a sermon he delivered at the Lambertikirche. He began by reminding the congregation that premeditated murder was still illegal under the Reich Criminal Code. He went on:

> [I]f you establish and apply the principle that you can kill "unproductive" fellow human beings then woe betide us all when we become old and frail! If one is allowed to kill the unproductive people then woe betide the invalids who have used up, sacrificed and lost their health and strength in the productive process. If one is allowed forcibly to remove one's unproductive human beings then woe betide loyal soldiers who return to the homeland seriously disabled, as cripples, as invalids.
>
> Woe to mankind, woe to our German nation if God's holy commandment "Thou shalt not kill," which God proclaimed on Mount Sinai amidst thunder and lightning, which God our Creator inscribed in the conscience of mankind from the very beginning, is not only broken, but if this transgression is actually tolerated and permitted to go on unpunished.[9]

Though some believe that Bishop Galen's sermon caused Hitler to order the program shut down, it had little to do with it. According to Michael Burleigh, Hitler had already decided to close the adult T-4 program because it had exceeded its goal of killing one mentally and physically challenged person for every thousand Germans. Moreover, by the fall of 1941, many T-4 personnel were being sent to the eastern front, where the Germans were beginning to experiment with a mass murder program designed to kill all the Jews of Europe—the Final Solution. These experts were needed to insure the success of the program.[10] Some T-4 specialists such as Christian Wirth (1885–1944; Bełżec), Franz Stangl (1908–1971; Sobibór and Treblinka), Dr. Franz Reichleitner (1906–1944; Sobibór), and Dr. Imfried Eberl (1910–1948; Treblinka) became death camp commandants, and almost ninety others helped run some of the death camps.

Even though Hitler had officially shut down the T-4 program in August 1941, the SS began a new "euthanasia" program, "14f13," in the concentration camps earlier that spring, which had the same goals as the T-4 program. "Euthanasia" killings also continued in Germany and included patients whose eugenic "crime" was nothing more than bed-wetting or being a nuisance. By the fall of 1941, *Einsatzgruppen* units began to murder inmates in asylums in the Soviet Union, and there is evidence that at least 40,000 inmates in mental institutions in Vichy, France, died of deliberate starvation and hypothermia during the war. Overall, from 200,000 to 250,000 Germans and others were murdered in the Third Reich's various "euthanasia" programs.

The Road to War and the German Invasion of Poland

In the mid-1930s, British and French leaders started to pursue a policy of appeasement towards Germany because they not only feared another war but had convinced themselves that Adolf Hitler was a rational man of peace who was simply trying to rectify the wrongs done Germany after World War I. This policy reached its zenith in the fall of 1938 when the Allies awarded Germany the Sudetenland, a part of Czechoslovakia that had a large German population. The day after signing the Munich Accord, Hitler and Britain's prime minister, Neville Chamberlain (1869–1940), promised to do everything possible to insure peace in Europe. Five and a half months later, German troops marched into what remained of the Czech lands. Europe's leaders now realized that war was inevitable. Though most thought that Romania would be Hitler's next target because of its oil reserves, it became apparent by the end of March 1939 that Poland would be his next victim.

As Britain, France, and the Soviet Union searched for ways diplomatically and militarily to thwart a German invasion of Poland in the spring and early summer of 1939, the Wehrmacht moved ahead with plans for the invasion of Poland. As Anglo-French-Soviet talks faltered in the spring and summer of 1939 because the Soviets insisted on the right to move into countries on Stalin's western frontier that he suspected of being in the German camp, Moscow and Berlin began low-level discussions that led on August 23, 1939, to a nonaggression treaty that had a secret protocol. In the accord, Germany and the Soviet Union divided Eastern Europe into separate German and Soviet spheres of influence, with eastern Poland becoming part of the Soviet sphere. The Soviet Union now became an active, though belated, partner with Germany in the invasion of Poland a week later.[11]

Two days after the conclusion of this treaty, the *Oberkommando der Wehrmacht* (OKH, Wehrmacht High Command) under *Generaloberst* Wilhelm Keitel (1882–1946) issued the order for the invasion of Poland. On August 31, special SD, SS, and *Abwehr* (Wehrmacht military counterintelligence) units dressed in Polish uniforms launched phony assaults along the German-Polish border, thus giving Hitler his "justification" for war. The following day, September 1, 1939, Hitler told the Reichstag that Germany had to respond to fourteen "border incidents" of the previous night, even though he had signed the final directive for the attack on Poland at noon on August 31.[12] Seventeen hours later, five German armies moved into Poland. During the next few days, Hitler, who in early 1938 had become supreme commander of the Wehrmacht, rejected British and French demands to withdraw from Poland as a prelude to negotiations. On September 3, London and Paris declared war on the Third Reich. By the time that Soviet forces, after considerable German prodding, began to occupy their portion of eastern Poland on September 17, the Wehrmacht had almost completed its conquest

SS troops lead Polish citizens to execution site in Palmiry forest near Warsaw, 1939. USHMM Photo No. 50649, courtesy of Instytut Pamieci Narodowej.

of Poland and the destruction of Poland's once proud military forces. Though some Polish units escaped into neutral territory, the Germans defeated those that remained in Poland by October 6.[13]

At the time, Poland had a population of 35,340,000, including from 3.3 to 3.5 million Jews. After Germany and the Soviet Union formally agreed to the final boundaries of Poland on September 22, Germany got a little less than half of the country, with a population of 22,250,000 Poles. About 2 million Jews were trapped in German-occupied Poland, and the rest, including from 300,000 to 350,000 Jews who fled eastward after the German invasion, lived in the Soviet portions of occupied Poland.

Racial War in Poland: Polish Christians

Hitler regarded ethnic Poles as that "dreadful [racial] material" who stood in the way of his dreams of a greater Aryan-pure Germany. He considered Poland's Jews "as the most horrible thing imaginable."[14] On August 22, 1939, Hitler told his Wehrmacht commanders that they were to kill "without pity or mercy all men, women, and children of Polish descent or language." He added: "Only in this way can we obtain the living space [*lebensraum*] we need."[15] Hitler said that once the invasion of Poland began, "whatever we have now discovered in the way of a Polish ruling class must be liquidated; whatever grows again we must take into our safekeeping and eliminate in due course."[16]

The reason for this policy was threefold: to destroy all vestiges of Polish nationalism; to prevent the country's leadership from mounting an effective resistance campaign against the German occupation; and, finally, to use what he hoped was to become a leaderless Polish peasant and worker class as forced laborers in German industry and agriculture.

Consequently, during the six years the Germans occupied Poland, they waged two wars against the Polish population—one against

Polish Jews, the other against Polish Christians. Once in Poland, the Germans were determined to destroy the intellectual, political, and religious leadership of the country and to remove the Jews from what remained of Polish society. Specially trained *Einsatzgruppen* (special task or action groups; *Einsatzgruppen der Sicherheitsdienstes* [SD] *und der Sicherheitspolizei* [Sipo]), made up of 4,250 men from the SD, Sipo, and the SS, were sent into Poland to combat "hostile elements." The *Einsatzgruppen* were first used in the invasion of Austria in 1938 to oversee security, meaning the roundup and imprisonment of Nazi opponents until permanent SD and Sipo offices could be opened. The Germans used *Einsatzgruppen* in all subsequent major military campaigns in Europe, though their tasks varied from country or region where they operated. In the Czech lands (Bohemia and Moravia), Poland, and the Soviet Union, for example, their mission was to neutralize or eradicate all societal elements deemed racially or physically dangerous to the German control of each occupied country or region. Before the death camp system of the Final Solution was created, these units were Germany's principal killing squads in the Soviet Union.[17]

Five *Einsatzgruppen* swept into Poland on the heels of the Wehrmacht in early September 1939. What followed was an "orgy of atrocities" that put earlier Nazi brutalities in the Greater Reich "completely in the shade."[18] The Germans were determined to wipe out Poland's religious, political, and intellectual leaders as well as the nobility. By the end of 1939, the Wehrmacht and the *Einsatzgruppen* had shot 50,000 Polish civilians, 7,000 of them Jews, numbers that support what Alexander Rossino calls "the decidedly anti-Polish, and not anti-Jewish, animus of the killing program of the SS in those early months of the war."[19] Some of the worst killing took place in Bydgoszcz, where the *Black Book of Poland* estimates the Germans murdered 10,000 civilians between September 1939 and early 1940. One Danish newspaper called the murders "a war of extermination against the Poles."[20] In the spring of 1940, the Germans executed several thousand more Polish political, religious, and cultural leaders during Operation A-B (*Ausserordentliche-Befriedungsaktion*; extraordinary pacification action).

The Germans were particularly brutal in their treatment of the Roman Catholic Church because they saw it as an integral part of Polish national identity. During the war, the Germans sent 3,646 Polish priests (out of 11,300) and 1,117 nuns (out of 17,000) to concentration camps. More than 2,600 priests and 263 nuns would die in these camps, most of them in Dachau. The Germans would kill hundreds more during the invasion and occupation. The German goal was the destruction of Polish Roman Catholicism. The Germans imprisoned most of the priests in the Wartheland (Warthgau), one of two areas in western Poland integrated directly into the Third Reich. Church property that was not stolen or destroyed was desecrated. The Germans forced the monks at the monastery in Radecznica to leave and then tore it apart in their search for valuables. They stole all the monastery's gold and jewels and warned the monks to tell no one of the thefts "under penalty of death."[21]

The Germans also closed many churches in occupied Poland; they placed severe restrictions on those allowed to remain open. According to one report, to survive, the church was "forced to withdraw back to the catacombs." German efforts to destroy Polish Roman Catholic zeal through murder, deportations, and intimidation did not work. Church leaders were able to report that the enthusiasm of the clergy "[was] marvelous, the piety of the faithful greater than ever, the devotion to the church heroic."[22]

One of those who was actively involved in the underground church and other illegal activities was Karol Józef Wojtyła (1920–2005), a forced laborer by day and co-creator of an illegal theater group by night. In 1942, Wojtyła entered Kraków's underground Roman Catholic seminary to study for the priesthood, and he attended classes at the illegally reopened underground Jagiellonian University. After his ordination in 1946, he taught at Catholic University in Lublin; there, he gained a reputation as a brilliant scholar, which led to his appointments as Kraków's auxiliary bishop in 1958 and bishop five years later. He became a cardinal in 1967, and pope eleven years later. The first person he officially received in private audience after his coronation as Pope John II (r. 1978–2005) was a close childhood friend, Jerzy Kluger (1920–), who was Jewish.

German racial policy in Poland towards Christians and Jews, driven in part by Heinrich Himmler's ideas about ethnic cleansing, racial purity, and the need to expand Germany's Aryan racial pool, evolved slowly over several years. In late October 1939, Himmler issued a controversial order suggesting that the SS and the police try to father as many children as possible to offset the loss of "the best German blood" during the war. In the spring of 1940, Himmler gave a series of lectures to military, industrial, and Nazi Party leaders in which he emphasized the dangers of "racial mixing" in the newly occupied territories and outlined his plans for Poland's Germanization. He thought the best way to deal with the problem of "racial mixing" was to eliminate the leadership of these dangerous groups. In one speech, Himmler said that other solutions could include the mass murder of entire populations and the deportation of racial inferiors to the General Government. For the moment, though, he preferred the first option.[23]

After an inspection tour in Poland in early May 1940, Himmler wrote a highly secret memorandum, *Denkscrhift Himmlers über die Behandlung der fremd völkischen im Osten* (Some Thoughts on the Treatment of the Alien Population in the East). He mentioned not only Poles and Jews but also Ukrainians, White Russians (Belorussians), and various others. He planned to keep these groups disunified by breaking them into as many "splinter groups as possible." On the other hand, he wanted to use their leaders as "policeman and mayors," an idea that contradicted his earlier statements about eliminating the leaders of the "alien" peoples. He thought that groups such as the Jews would disappear through large-scale emigration to Africa or "some colony." And though it would take longer, Himmler also hoped the Poles would disappear as a people.[24]

In the interim, Himmler wanted to limit public education for these groups' youth, teaching them only how to count to five hundred and to write their names. He did not think they should be taught to read. The ultimate goal of such schooling was "to teach that it is God's commandment to be obedient to the Germans and to be honest, hard working, and well-behaved."[25] If parents wanted to educate a child further, they would have to apply to SS officials in the occupied territories for a decision about whether the child in question was racially qualified for such education. If the answer was yes, the child would be sent "indefinitely" to school in Germany. Given that the Germans considered only about 3 percent of the Polish population fit for Aryanization, Himmler could expect few applications from Polish parents.

Even if Polish parents did not apply for Aryanization, he proposed that the SS begin its own program of determining which Polish young people had "valuable blood." Once Poland had been emptied of these special children, what remained would be an "inferior remnant," a "leaderless labouring class" that could provide Germany with a cheap source of labor for agriculture, industry, and "special work projects."[26] During the war, the Germans kidnapped almost 4,500 Polish children for possible adoption by German parents as part of the SS *Lebensborn* (Fount of Life) program. Another 45,000 Polish children were taken to orphanages or placed in foster homes in areas under German occupation.

Using conquered peoples as a cheap source of labor had been an integral part of German prewar economic planning. As the war progressed, the Germans relied more and more on forced and slave labor to keep their economy going. They employed 9.5 million foreigners and POWs as forced or slave laborers between 1939 and 1945. In addition, the Germans used 700,000 Jewish slave laborers in factories in Poland, though their numbers declined rapidly because slave labor was intended to be a slow means of death for Jews. By the fall of 1944, 1.7 million Poles were working in forced-labor situations throughout the Third Reich, most of them as farm laborers. The Germans also used many of the tens of thousands of Poles in concentration or other camps in forced- or slave-labor situations.

Marian Dąbrowski was taken from an orphanage in Bydgoszcz to East Prussia, where he was forced to work as a farm laborer in Elbing. He worked for Erich Salwey, who considered Poles racial inferiors. Salwey forced Marian to work in below-freezing temperatures during the winter without gloves. Marian and the other children who worked for Salwey suffered from frostbite. As Marian wrote after the war: "[W]e used to pull down our sweater sleeves over our hands, but this was hopeless. Eventually we made crude mittens out of rags to protect our already sore hands." Marian lived in a "small cubbyhole in the stable" and was forced to wear a *P* on his clothing. He subsisted on "watery soup" and bread as well as cream that he stole from milk churns.[27]

It is estimated that from 1.8 to 1.9 million Polish Christians died during World War II. Although this figure is lower that the traditional 1947 Polish estimate of 3 million, it nevertheless shows how brutal the German occupation of Poland was from 1939 to 1944, particularly when you add the 3.2 million

Polish Jews who were murdered during this period. Though estimates vary, from 17 to 18 percent of Poland's prewar population died as a result of the German occupation policies during World War II.

Some of the deaths took place during the massive deportations in those parts of Poland integrated into the Third Reich or in the General Government. By the end of 1940, the SS had forced 325,000 Poles and Jews out of the Wartheland into the General Government and had taken their property and most of their personal belongings. Many elderly Poles and children died in temporary transit camps en route. The deportations often began without warning and occasionally took place in freezing temperatures. It was not uncommon to find the frozen bodies of children and the elderly in the transport trucks. Between 1941 and 1943, the Germans expelled another 155,000 Poles in the Wartheland and the General Government; many expellees were sent to the Auschwitz or Majdanek concentration camps. Overall, the Germans uprooted about a million Polish Christians and Jews and sent most of them into the General Government. Many of their homes were taken over by about 400,000 to 750,000 *Volksdeutsche* (ethnic Germans) as part of Himmler's resettlement program in occupied eastern territory.

The Creation of the General Government: Nazi Germany's "Racial Laboratory"

In the midst of the Germans' brutal campaign against Poland's Christians and Jews, Hitler approved the creation of the *Generalgouvernement für die besetzten polnischen Gebiete* (General Government for the Occupied Areas of Poland). The General Government would become not only Nazi Germany's racial laboratory but also a dumping ground for those in Europe deemed *untermensch* or *Lebensunwertes Leben*. It would also be one of

Nazi Germany's principal killing fields (the other was the Soviet Union) during the Holocaust because it was here that the Germans opened five of their six Final Solution death camps.

Once the military had conquered Poland, it turned control of German-occupied Poland over to civilian and party administrators. The government integrated portions of western Poland directly into the Greater Reich as the *Reichsgau Danzig Westpreussen* and the *Reichsgau Wartheland*. What remained of German-occupied Poland, the districts of Warsaw, Radom, Lublin, and Kraków, became the General Government. After the invasion of the Soviet Union in 1941, a fifth district, Galicia, with its capital in Lvov (Lviv; Lwow; Lemberg), was added to the General Government. Kraków was chosen as the General Government's capital to rob Warsaw of its traditional historical and nationalistic importance to Poles.

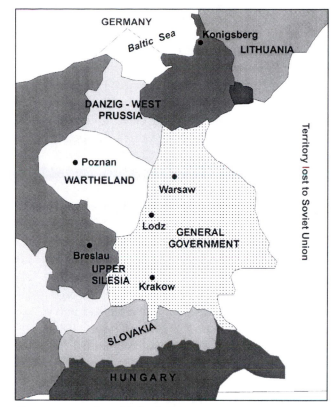

German occupation of Poland, 1939.

In late September 1939, Alfred Rosenberg, the head of the *Aussenpolitisches Amt der NSDAP* (Foreign Policy office of the NSDAP [Nazi Party]), noted in his diary a recent conversation he had had with Hitler about Poland. The Führer, he wrote, considered Poles

a thin Germanic layer, underneath frightful material. The Jews, the most appalling people one can imagine. The towns thick with dirt. He's learnt a lot in these past few weeks. Above all, if Poland had gone on ruling the old German parts for a few more decades everything would have become lice-ridden and decayed. He wanted to split the territory into three strips: 1. Between the Vistula and the Bug: this would be for the whole of Jewry (from the Reich as well) as well as all other unreliable elements. Build an insuperable wall on the Vistula—even stronger than the one in the west. 2. Create a broad cordon of

territory along the previous frontier to be germanized and colonized. This would be a major task for the whole nation: to create a German granary, a strong peasantry, to resettle good Germans from all over the world. 3. In between, a form of Polish state [*Staatlichkeit*]. The future would show whether after a few decades the cordon of settlement would have to be pushed further forward.[28]

Several weeks later, Hitler told Wehrmacht and party leaders that Poland was not to be treated like a German province, nor was it to have a strong economy. He intended the quality of life for the Poles there to be low, and he viewed the General Government as a primary source for forced labor. German efforts there should be considered a *Volkstumskampf* (ethnic struggle) to be carried out without "legal restrictions." Nazi control of this part of Poland would allow the party to "purify the Reich area too of Jews and Po-lacks." German activity in the General Government, Hitler told the gathering, was "the devil's work."[29]

On October 26, Hitler appointed Dr. Hans Frank (1900–1946) as *Generalgouverneur* (Governor General) of the General Government. Though there were three competing centers of power in the General Government—the government, the Wehrmacht, and the SS—it was the SS, which considered the General Government its special "racial laboratory," that wielded the greatest authority there. And though Frank could hold his own against the Wehrmacht, he was, according to Hans Umbreit, "on a losing ticket from the start" when it came to Himmler and the SS.[30] In late September 1939, Himmler had masterfully consolidated his control over all the central offices of Sipo, which included the Gestapo, Kripo, the *Grenzpolizei* (Green, or Border, Police), and the SD into the newly created *Reichssicherheitshauptamt* (RSHA; Reich Main Security Office), which he placed under Reinhard Heydrich. Several weeks later, Himmler also became the *Reichskommissar für die Festigung des deutschen Volkstums* (RKFDV; Reich Commissioner for the Fortification of the German Volk-Nation), a position that gave him considerable authority to press his claim as the guardian of police and political authority in the Nazis' new "racial laboratory." Himmler's closeness to Hitler also strengthened his hand when it came to dealing with racial and other questions in the General Government.[31]

Himmler's top official in the General Government was the *Höhrere SS- und Polizeiführer* (HSSPF; Higher SS and Police Leader), who oversaw the various branches of the RSHA there.[32] During the war, Himmler tried to expand the role and powers of the HSSPF to include authority over all political and racial matters in the General Government. As a result, Himmler and his subordinates became Frank's principal competitors for power and

authority in what commonly became known to many Nazi leaders as the "Frank-reich."[33]

The Jews in Interwar Poland

One of the most controversial issues in Holocaust studies is the relationship between Poles and Jews before and during World War II. According to Celia S. Heller, a direct line has been drawn between this period and the Holocaust, a viewpoint that many Poles deeply resent: "It would be senseless for me to try to convey the horrors of the violence against Jews during World War I and the immediate postwar period to those of the Holocaust and post-Holocaust generations who have become accustomed to the sight and sound of the ultimate horrors."[34]

The traditions of Polish anti-Semitism, particularly during the interwar period, are at the heart of the controversy. Norman Davies tried to put the treatment and status of Jews in interwar Poland into what he called a "meaningful perspective": "In a new, multinational society, intercommunal antipathies were commonplace, and the Jews were not exempt from the irritations and antagonisms which divided every ethnic group from the others. Yet it must be stressed that the pressures and discriminations to which the Jews were exposed were nothing exceptional."[35] The Jewish perspective on this, of course, is quite different.

The key here is the question of victimization. Wojciech Raszkowski argued that the differences arose from the assumption made on both sides "that they have been the innocent victims of history." Poles who take this position, he noted, feel that in light of "all the misfortunes and suffering they bore during World War II it is unfair to mention any wrong doing by any Pole." Jews who play the victim card, he added, "claim that the Holocaust has been such an unprecedented tragedy that any mention of Jewish guilt is horrendous."[36]

The only problem with this argument is that it assumes some Jewish role in the Jews' own victimization, a point alluded to by Roman Dmowski (1864–1939), one of Poland's most important right-wing politicians in the interwar period: "In the character of this race [the Jews] so many different values, strange to our moral constitution and harmful to our life, have accumulated that assimilation with a larger number of Jews would destroy us, replacing with decadent elements those young creative foundations upon which we are building the future."[37] A commentator later noted that Dmowski felt that "Jews were in more complete control over the Poles' economic life than the foreign conquerors [the Soviets, who had briefly conquered parts of Poland during the Civil War] were over their political life, and his anti-Jewish sentiments were far stronger than his feelings against the conquerors."[38] Dmowski's ideas were based on the incorrect perception that Jews were a wealthy urban elite that dominated Polish business and commerce. In reality, most Polish Jews were simply small-business owners; for example, almost a fifth of the Jews who worked in mining and industry owned "small and technologically obsolescent sweatshops and handicraft establishments."[39] And a third of Poland's Jews lived below the poverty line and relied on charity to survive.

This situation got worse after the death of Marshal Józef Piłsudski (1867–1935), the most dominant figure in Polish politics during the interwar period. Many Jews viewed Piłsudski, a socialist revolutionary turned soldier, politician, and, after 1926, dictator, as their friend and benefactor.

This "springtime" in Polish-Jewish relations did not last long. The Depression and the weakening of Poland's democratic institutions hurt the Jews' economic status and political influence. The drift rightward in the 1930s, particularly after Piłsudski's death in 1935, saw a return to a more virulent form of public and official anti-Semitism. His succes-

sors adopted anti-Semitic economic policies designed to weaken the role of Jews in the economy and the professions. When the government placed *numerus clausus* restrictions on Jewish university students, Jewish total university enrollment dropped from 20.4 percent in 1928–1929 to 9.9 percent in 1937–1938. Anti-Semitic violence was particularly widespread in some universities, and in some university classrooms Jewish students were often forced to sit in "ghetto" seats. Although this new upsurge in anti-Semitism could be explained as a reaction to the social and economic dislocations caused by the Depression, its roots could be found in a deeper religious hatred of Jews and in stereotypical fears that "the Poles might become a nation of peasants, proletarians, and officials while the Jews flooded commerce and the free professions."[40] But as war threatened, some politicians realized that growing anti-Semitic violence could backfire if it empowered the Right to broaden their attacks against other groups and institutions in Poland. And, of course, there was fear that if anti-Semitism worsened, Poland could become like Nazi Germany. Yet when war came, Poland's loyal Jewish community supported their country: In the fall of 1939, 200,000 Jewish soldiers fought valiantly against the Germans.

The War Against the Jews in Poland

Within a week after the invasion began, the Germans ordered Jewish businesses in areas under their control to display the blue Star of David. In late October, authorities began to require Jews in Breslau (today, Wrocław, Poland) to wear a yellow triangle, a regulation extended to Łódź and Kraków in mid-November. On November 23, 1939, Hans Frank ordered all Jews in the General Government to begin wearing a four-inch-wide white armband with the Star of David on the right sleeve of all clothing by December 1, 1939.

Jewish man is forced to cut off beard of another Jew in Tomaszow Mazowiecki, 1939. USHMM Photo No. 50978, courtesy of Instytut Pamieci Narodowej.

Two months earlier, Reinhard Heydrich met with *Einsatzgruppen* leaders in Berlin and on September 21 followed up with a memo that dealt with the "Jewish Question" in the occupied territories that became the blueprint for future German policies towards Jews in Poland. Heydrich began by reminding everyone who attended the meeting that "the *overall measures envisaged* (i.e., the final goal) must be kept secret." The first task of *Einsatzgruppen* commanders, Heydrich wrote, was quickly to move Jews in small towns and villages in the countryside to larger cities. He wanted either to "liberate" Danzig, West Prussia, and eastern Upper Silesia, areas to be integrated directly into the Greater Reich, of Jews, or to put them into "a few cities as concentration points." Jewish communities of five hundred or fewer residents were to be dissolved.[41]

Heydrich then ordered the creation of *Judenrat* (Council of Jewish Elders) in each new Jewish community, each one to consist of twenty-four "leading persons and rabbis." *Einsatzgruppen* commanders were to warn *Judenrat* members that they would exact harsh penalties for acts of sabotage against the Germans and explained that Jews were concentrated in larger cities because they had "played a major part in ambushes and plundering" throughout Poland. For security purposes, restrictions would limit Jewish movement outside the new ghettos. He added that all measures dealing with this matter had to be done in "closest agreement and cooperation" with German civilian and military authorities. It was also important "that the economic exploitation of the occupied territories [did] not suffer as a result of these measures." Jews involved in businesses that supplied the Wehrmacht or were vital to the Four-Year Plan should be left alone temporarily, though all Jewish businesses should be Aryanized as quickly as possible.[42]

Heydrich further clarified Nazi goals in a meeting with RSHA department heads six days later, and for the first time he also mentioned the Roma. Hitler, he told them, had approved the creation of the "foreign Gau [General Government]." He expected it would take about a year to move all Jews into the "foreign Gau," where they would be put in ghettos "in order to ensure a better chance of controlling them and later of removing them." The RSHA's most urgent task was the removal of Jews from the countryside as "small traders." The only exceptions were those Jews involved in the provisioning of Wehrmacht units. Heydrich ended the meeting with the followings order:

1. Jews out of the towns as quickly as possible
2. Jews out of the Reich into Poland
3. The remaining Gypsies also to Poland
4. The systematic evacuation of the Jews from German territory via goods trains[43]

The Physical and Economic Exploitation of the Jews in the General Government

The Germans began the physical and economic exploitation of Poland's Jews immediately after they invaded Poland. On September 21, Dr. Marek Bieberstein, the head of Kraków's new *Judenrat*, told the city's Jews that they would have to fill in the various antiaircraft ditches throughout the city. This was the beginning of the German forced- and slave-labor practices that transformed the General Government's Jews into slaves of the Third Reich. Once Hans Frank was in power, his administration decreed that all Jews between twelve and sixty were obligated to work two-year terms in a forced-labor camp. Frank's subordinate, *SS-Gruppenführer* Otto Wächter (1901–1949), the governor of the Kraków district, decreed on November 18, 1939, that all Jews in his district older than twelve were required to wear a highly visible white band with a blue Star of David sewn on

it. Wächter added that the white band had to be 10 centimeters wide and the star had to be 8 centimeters in diameter. The Kraków governor defined a Jew as someone "who is or was a believer in the Jewish faith" and also someone whose mother or father "is or was a believer in the Jewish faith." This dictum included not only permanent Jewish residents of Kraków but also temporary ones.[44]

But the worst was yet to come. There followed a series of decrees and regulations that stripped Jews of their homes, businesses, and personal property. Jews had already lost many of their possessions during the random military and civilian plundering that took place during the invasion and occupation of Poland in September 1939. On September 29, for example, the military issued a decree that allowed the immediate seizure of property owned by absentee owners or that was improperly managed. This became a pretext for the seizure of much Jewish property.[45]

Göring and Himmler both claimed they had the authority to seize property for the good of the Reich without consideration of compensation. The military and the police, and occasionally bold civilians, had no qualms about raiding a Jewish business, factory, or home and stealing everything inside. Stella Müller-Madej tells of one such incident in her memoirs. Early one November morning in 1939, three SS men entered her family's modern and spacious apartment in a predominantly Polish neighborhood. At first, the Germans thought they had the wrong apartment because it was so elegant; also, Stella's mother, Bertha, a German Jew with blond hair and green eyes, spoke "impeccable" German. Bertha politely informed the SS officer that she was Jewish. After a moment of hesitation, the SS officer informed Bertha that her family had half an hour to vacate the apartment. They could take nothing with them. The officer assured the family that they would receive a detailed inventory of everything in the apartment. The family quickly dressed and put on extra layers of clothes. Bertha was also able to sneak a few items from her jewelry box, although she was sure that the Germans would keep their word about a receipt for the confiscated items. Of course, they never got a receipt; they lost everything they owned that day. Such tragic stories were repeated time and again throughout German-occupied Poland during the first year of the war.[46]

In November, the Germans froze all Jewish and foreign assets in banks and other financial institutions and permitted them to keep only 2,000 złótys ($625) in cash. In Kraków, for example, the Germans entered Jewish homes throughout the city in early December and brutally confiscated anything collectively valued above 2,000 złótys ($625). Several days earlier, the Germans seized all Jewish motor vehicles. On January 24, 1940, authorities gave Kraków's Jews five weeks to register their remaining property. They were also told not to change their addresses.[47]

On November 1, 1939, Hermann Göring created the *Haupttreuhandstelle Ost* (HTO; Main Trusteeship Office East), which would have offices throughout German-occupied Poland. Göring's directive, which he later clarified in early 1940, recognized two methods of property seizure based on property rights—*beschlagnahmt* (taking over) and *einzeihung* (confiscation). The HTO could "take over" or "confiscate" any property deemed important to the public interest. Local HTO offices would then be responsible for overseeing the stolen property and putting it in the hands of carefully selected German *Treuhänder* (trustees). Polish property that was not officially registered with the Germans was considered "ownerless" and was subject to HTO seizure. Jewish property seized by the HTO, the military, or other organs of state for "the benefit of the Reich" was not bound by Göring's directives. For Jews, the only things exempt from seizure were invaluable personal items.[48]

On September 17, 1940, Göring ordered the immediate confiscation of all remaining Jewish property in Poland with the exception of personal belongings and 1,000 *Reichsmarks* ($400) in cash. These regulations were enforced unevenly throughout German-occupied Poland. In Kraków, for example, the new rule was applied only to homes that brought in a rent of over 500 złótys ($156.25) a month. Yet most of the private property seized in Poland by the Reich was Jewish-owned. The only exception was state-owned Polish property, which, Frank declared in the fall of 1940, was now the property of the General Government. At the end of 1941, Germans only owned 157 private businesses out of 2,973 in Kraków. Christian Poles owned the rest.[49]

The Nisko Plan, the Lublin Reservation, and Madagascar

Once the Germans had solidified their control over Poland, they began to discuss what to do with its large Jewish population. Initially, they thought of ghettos as temporary urban concentration centers for Jews, Roma, and other racial undesirables from throughout German-occupied Poland and the Greater Reich. They also hoped the ghettos would supply Germany with a source of cheap labor. But at a meeting with officials from the Radom district on November 25, 1939, Hans Frank was explicit: "We won't waste much time on the Jews. It's great to get to grips with the Jewish race at last. The more that die the better; hitting them represents a victory for our Reich."[50]

Top Nazi leaders first discussed ghettoizing Jews during Hermann Göring's post-*Kristallnacht* meeting on November 12, 1938. When the war broke out, Adolf Eichmann, who had been sent to Prague in the spring of 1939 to oversee the deportation of Czech Jews, devised a scheme to transport Jews from Vienna, Upper Silesia, and the new Protectorate of Bohemia and Moravia, and later Katowice, to a temporary camp in Nisko near Lublin. Eichmann, who was made head of the Gestapo's *Reichszentralstelle für jüdische Auswanderung* (Reich Central Office for Jewish Emigration; Section IVD4) in October 1939, planned to ship 300,000 Jews from the Greater Reich to the Lublin region. But just as the first transports were leaving, *SS- Brigadeführer* Heinrich Müller (1900—missing since 1945), the head of the Gestapo, ordered them halted. Eichmann, who was in Nisko at the time proudly awaiting the first transport of Jews, did everything possible to revive his program and managed to ship several thousand Jews to a temporary camp near Nisko before Müller finally ended it. His plan had fallen prey to military concerns over tying up vital rail lines for civilian transport and practical concerns about simultaneously moving large numbers of ethnic Germans into Poland while deporting hundreds of thousands of Jews eastward. But Eichmann's Nisko scheme did show Nazi leaders that, with little cost, they could forcibly deport Jews to Nazi Germany's new "racial laboratory."

Concerns over efforts to ship Jews to the General Government did prompt Hermann Göring to decree that Hans Frank had to approve all further transports. Later, Göring declared that he would have final say on all transports eastward; after discussions with Frank in the spring of 1940, he allowed the shipment of Jews and Poles out of those parts of Poland recently integrated into the Reich and other parts of Europe into the General Government.

The Madagascar Plan

As German leaders struggled with their "convulsive population policy," they began to look for other deportation alternatives, particularly during the conquest of much of Atlantic Europe (Norway, Denmark, the Netherlands, Luxembourg, Belgium, and France) in the late spring and early summer of 1940.[51] One scheme that gained brief currency among Nazi Party leaders was the Madagascar Plan, which envisioned the shipment of 4 million European Jews to the French colony of Madagascar, off the southeastern coast of Africa. The idea of Madagascar as a place of Jewish settlement can be traced back to the late nineteenth century. By the 1930s, officials in Poland, France, Great Britain, and even the American Jewish Joint Distribution Committee, looked briefly at this idea. Poland and France entered into discussions about Madagascar in 1937–1938, though their talks came to nothing. Nazi leaders also gave some thought to the idea, but they never seriously considered it until the summer of 1940, when they faced the prospect of dealing with 565,000 more Jews in the recently conquered states of Atlantic Europe. In light of the problems with deportations to the General Government, creating a large settlement area for Jews in Madagascar now seemed a possible solution to the Reich's growing Jewish population. In the midst of the invasion of Norway and Denmark in late April 1940, Himmler's RSHA sent out a directive emphasizing the importance of deporting Jews from the Reich, but it discouraged the idea of emigration to Palestine or the General Government. On June 3, Franz Rademacher (1906–1973), the head of the *Auswärtige Amt*'s (Foreign Office) Jewish desk, wrote a memo to his boss, Martin Luther (1895–1945), the head of the *Auswärtige Amt*'s *Deutschlandabteilung* (Germany Division), about the need, in light of the "imminent victory" in France, to solve "the Jewish question in Europe." He thought the *Auswärtige Amt*'s role was to reach either a peace settlement or other agreements in Europe that dealt with this issue and provided "the necessary territory for settling the Jews."[52]

He envisaged setting up an international bank that would use Jewish resources for such a move, and suggested Madagascar,

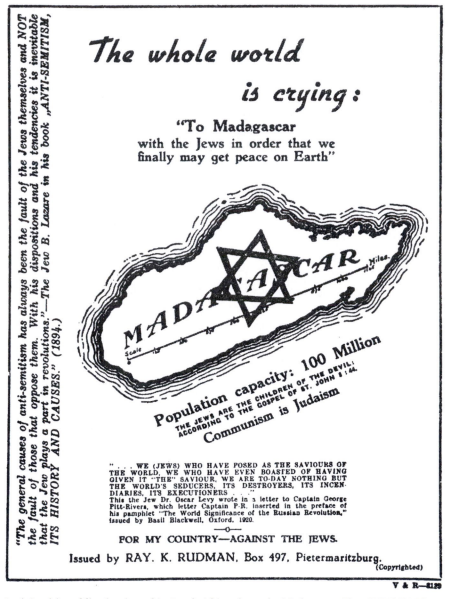

Anti-Semitic publication issued in South Africa about the Madagascar Plan. USHMM Photo No. 63662, courtesy of Tine Thevenin.

which Germany could acquire from France as a mandate. The *Kriegsmarine* (navy) could use part of the island for bases; the rest would be used to settle Jews from Nazi-occupied Europe. The SS, which would control the Jewish settlement area in Madagascar, would allow the Jews to set up their own administrative system. Such a plan, Rademacher argued, would prevent the Jews from setting up a separate state in Palestine and also show the world "the generosity which Germany shows the Jews by granting them self-government in the fields of culture, economics, administration, and justice."[53] When Heydrich heard about Rademacher's memo, he reminded Joachim von Ribbentrop (1893–1946), Germany's foreign minister, that Göring had put him in charge of Jewish emigration earlier that year. Ribbentrop told Rademacher that he should work closely with Heydrich's offices on all future plans for deporting Jews from Europe.

As news of the Madagascar plan spread among the Nazi leadership, Rademacher and Eichmann worked on separate plans to create a Jewish settlement area on the French island. Rademacher's plan centered on demographic and economic issues; Eichmann's scheme dealt with the practical and political aspects of sending 4 million European Jews to Madagascar over a four-year period. Eichmann included detailed preparation instructions for agencies throughout Europe that discussed, among other things, the sale of Jewish property, registration, and the occupations of the first Jews selected for Madagascar resettlement. But unlike Rademacher's plan, which envisioned a semiautonomous Jewish region under SS control, Eichmann's program called for a "police state" in which Jewish organizations would exist, as they did in the emerging ghettos of German-occupied Poland, simply to carry out SS orders. Eichmann also envisioned shipping all of the Jews of Europe, including those in Great Britain, "to a colonial territory." Once Eichmann had completed his report, *Reichssicherheitshauptamt: Madagaskar Projekt* (RSHA: Madagascar Project), he had it printed in a brochure, complete with maps and a table of contents.[54]

Yet the Madagascar Plan never got beyond the discussion stage and literally died a slow death on Heydrich's desk. The failed German assault against Great Britain, which robbed Germany of England's vast naval resources so important to the transfer of Jews to Madagascar, effectively killed the plan; but as late as the spring of 1942, Joseph Goebbels noted in his diary that Hitler still intended to throw the Jews out of Europe and would perhaps send them to Madagascar. He added: "[T]here can be no peace in Europe until the Jews are

eliminated from the continent."[55] Several months later, the British began their invasion of this strategic African island. By then, the Germans had already adopted an alternative strategy for dealing with the "Jewish question"—the Final Solution.

The Creation of the Ghettos in German-Occupied Poland

As German leaders struggled to develop a viable Jewish deportation plan, they also agonized over the question of ghettoization. From the outset, the Germans thought it was essential that Jewish community leaders play a role as liaisons between party and government functionaries in occupied Poland. Reinhard Heydrich paid a great deal of attention to the *Judenräte* (Jewish Councils; *Judenrat*, singular) in his September 21, 1939, memo to *Einsatzgruppen* leaders. Hans Frank further clarified the role of the *Judenräte* in his November 28, 1939, decree ordering their creation throughout the General Government. He declared that Jewish communities of fewer than 10,000 people would have a twelve-member *Judenrat*, and those of more than 10,000 would have a twenty-four member Jewish Council. According to Frank: "The Jewish Council is obliged to receive, through its chairman or his deputy, the orders of German official agencies. Its responsibility will be to see to it that the orders are carried out completely and accurately. The directives which the Council may issue in the execution of German orders must be obeyed by all Jews and Jewesses."[56] The creation and activities of the *Judenräte*, or, as they were known in Łódź, Kovno, and other ghettos, the *Ältestenrate* (Councils of Elders), would become one of the Germans' most controversial decisions. Initially, many Jewish leaders rejected appointment to a *Judenrat* because they thought they would be collaborating with the Germans; others saw membership as a way of helping their community. A few *Judenräte* members saw membership as an opportunity for self-aggrandizement. Regardless, the Germans used the *Judenräte* and *Ältestenrate* as their principal institutions for administering the ghettos.

German authorities began to use the *Judenräte* to do their bidding soon after they conquered Poland. The *Judenräte* became responsible for conducting a December 1939 Jewish census and were responsible for rounding up Jewish workers for forced-labor battalions. The Germans also required that they help gather information on Jewish property and financial holdings, information used later in seizing these resources.

Yet before the Germans could begin effectively to use the *Judenräte* and the *Ältestenrate,* they first had to face the problems of opening ghettos in occupied Poland. This involved locating property for the ghettos themselves, moving populations, and developing regulations dealing with life and work in the ghettos. They also had to create a German ghetto administration system in Germany and in the occupied territories. But the biggest problem confronting the Germans was the struggle between what Christopher Browning calls the "attritionists" and the "productionists." The attritionists saw ghettos as a means of slow death for the Jews, but the productionists hoped the ghettos would become a source of cheap slave labor valuable to an expanding and sometimes troubled German war economy.[57]

Łódź (Litzmannstadt): Jews and Roma

Łódź, which is about 75 miles southwest of Warsaw, became part of the Wartheland after the German conquest of Poland. It had a prewar Jewish population of 223,000, the second largest in Poland after Warsaw. Łódź was an important Jewish cultural center as well as home to various prosperous Jewish businesses, particularly textiles. The Germans occupied

Łódź on September 8, 1939, and two months later it officially became part of the Wartheland. In the spring of 1940, the Germans renamed the city Litzmannstadt. Soon after they had taken over the city, the Germans initiated a reign of terror against the city's Jews: They looted homes and businesses and placed restrictions on Jewish business and commerce. Dawid Sierakowiak (1924–1943) described in his diary the horrors many Jews faced in the early days of the German occupation:

> People are being seized again for forced labor; beatings and robbings. The store where my father works had also been robbed. The local Germans do whatever they wish. There are numerous stories of how they treat Jews at work; some Germans treat them very well, while others bully them sadistically. At one place, for example, the Jewish employees were ordered to stop work, undress, and face a wall. Then they were told that they would be shot. Indeed, they were aimed at with great precision. No one was hurt, but this procedure was repeated several times and it threw most of the Jews completely off balance—that's what Łódź Nazis can do.[58]

Initially, the Germans planned to deport most of the city's Jews to other parts of the Wartheland or the General Government. Once the city was formally integrated into the Wartheland on November 9, the Germans began a new campaign of terror against Łódź's Jews and Poles. They destroyed all of the city's synagogues and made Jews wear yellow armbands; the armband was soon changed to a yellow Star of David that Jews had to display on the right front and rear of their clothing. The Germans also imprisoned several thousand Poles and Jews. This new reign of terror triggered a new migratory wave of Jews out of the city, and by the time the ghetto was finally sealed off on April 30, 1940, there were only 162,000 to 164,000 left in Łódź.

The idea of a ghetto in Łódź was a stopgap measure devised by *SS- Obergruppenführer* Arthur Greiser (1897–1946), the *Statthalter* (governor) of Wartheland, who was frustrated by the inability to move the city's Jews to the General Government. Since he was convinced that Łódź's Jews had hoarded great wealth before the war, he intended to put them into a ghetto and so force them to use their resources to buy food. Once they were destitute, he would send them to the General Government.

In mid-October, the Germans appointed the controversial Mordechai Rumkowski (1877–1944) to head the Łódź *Ältestenrat*. A month later, Friedrich Übelhör, the *Regierungspräsident* of the Kalisz-Łódź district, proposed creating a "closed ghetto" in his memo titled "Establishment of a Ghetto in the City of Łódź." He planned to open it in the Baluty section of the city, where many poor Jews already lived. He also suggested that a second ghetto be created for Jews fit for forced labor. Übelhör noted that the ghetto would require a considerable amount of administrative work and coordination among various branches of the party and government; consequently, he created a special team of representatives from the SS, RSHA, and various government agencies to draw up a plan for the ghetto. He concluded his memo by saying that "the creation of the ghetto is, of course, only a temporary measure." He added: "I reserve to myself the decision concerning the times and the means by which the ghetto and with it the city of Lodz will be cleansed of Jews. The final aim *(Endziel)* must in any case bring about the total cauterization of this plague spot."[59]

Übelhör's plan became the model for the creation of subsequent ghettos in other parts of occupied Poland. On February 8, 1940, *SS-Brigadeführer* Johannes Schäfer (1903–1993), the *Polizeipräsident* (chief of police) in Łódź, announced the opening of the ghetto, followed by orders for Jews from other parts of the city to move there. By the end of April

Mordechai Rumkowski, chairman of the Jewish council in the Łódź ghetto with Hans Biebow, head of German ghetto administration. USHMM Photo No. 29112, courtesy of Al Moss.

1940, from 162,000 to 164,000 Jews were crowded into the 1.54-square-mile ghetto, an area suitable for only 23,000. During the next two years, the Germans deported another 38,000 Jews into the Łódź ghetto from the Wartheland, Germany, Austria, Czechoslovakia, and Luxembourg. At its peak of operations in 1942, the Łódź ghetto had a Jewish population of 204,800. Twenty-one percent would die of typhus and other diseases associated with crowded living conditions and malnutrition.

Since the Germans saw the Łódź ghetto as a temporary measure designed to force the city's Jews to use all their resources to buy food, they made no preparations to supply it with basic foodstuffs. Once it became apparent that the ghetto would be permanent, German officials began to discuss how to finance the ghetto's operation. Rumkowksi suggested opening ghetto factories, the revenues of which could be used to help feed poor Jews. The Germans initially resisted Rumkowski's idea, thinking that income from forced labor would prevent Jews from using their own resources to survive. But by the end of the summer of 1940, two thirds of the ghetto's Jews had nothing left to purchase or barter for food. The fact that Greiser was stealing part of the wages earned by Jews working in the ghetto only made matters worse.

On September 18, Übelhör appointed Hans Biebow (1902–1947) the ghetto's manager and ordered him to make it economically self-sustaining. Rumkowski quickly presented Biebow with a list of 15,000 skilled Jewish laborers and the goods they could produce. By 1942, Rumkowski and the Ältestenrat had opened seventy-four factories employing almost 69,000 Jewish workers. A year later, more than 78,000 workers, most of them producing textiles, were laboring in ninety-six factories. But despite the "work to live" mindset that kept the Łódź ghetto open until it was liquidated in the summer of 1944, deportations became a mainstay of ghetto life during the first two years of its existence. This was particularly the case once the Germans opened the Chełmno death camp in early December 1942 to murder the Jews in Łódź and the Wartheland. Between January and May, 1942, the Germans, as part of the early stages of the Final Solution, deported 55,000 Jews and 5,000 Roma from the ghetto to Chełmno. They deported another 20,000 Jews to the death camp in September. These were the last major deportations until the summer of 1944.

Yet Rumkowski did more than just help create a slave labor factory system for the Germans. Since hunger and malnutrition were a constant problem, he also did everything possible to increase food supplies in the ghetto. Jozef Zelkowicz wrote in his diary about "the hunger psychosis" in Łódź and the "fear of dying from starvation."[60] A January 20, 1944, entry in The Chronicle of the Łódź Ghetto, 1941–1941 noted that the food situation had become so bad that "people [were] faced with the catastrophe of inevitable starvation."[61]

In the midst of this growing horror, Rumkowski and the Ältestenrat tried to create some semblance of normal life in the ghetto. They opened forty-five schools that had been previously closed and also set up soup kitchens in many of the schools to insure that the children had food to eat. In 1940, a complex of orphanages (Kolonia) was set up, as well as a number of children's summer camps. Groups such as the Zionists, the Jewish Bund, and Agudat Israel were active in children's affairs. Unfortunately, children and the elderly were often the first selected for deportation to Chełmno because the Germans did not think them suitable factory workers. By the time the Germans had decided to close the ghetto, few children or elderly lived there.

In the winter of 1940–1941, ghetto leaders also opened a cultural center that sponsored concerts, plays, and choral performances; it also presented art exhibits and readings by ghetto writers. An underground intellectual movement also thrived during the early years of the ghetto. Dawid Sierakowiak, who died in the summer of 1943 of tuberculosis, wrote on June 14, 1941, that he had "attended a great lecture by Comrade Ziula Krengiel on dialectics." It was, he added, "an excellent scientific formulation and explanation." That afternoon, Dawid, a gifted young linguist, tutored his first student, who was, he wrote, "a total blockhead."[62]

The Germans also opened a small Roma compound in the larger ghetto in the fall of 1941. Several years earlier, Reinhard Heydrich informed Einsatzgruppen leaders that Hitler planned to deport all the Greater Reich's 30,000 Roma to occupied Poland during the

Entrance to Roma ghetto in Łódź. USHMM Photo No. 38093, courtesy of Muzeum Sztuki w Łódź.

next year. He followed this up by ordering the police to prohibit local Roma from leaving their homes; they also asked policemen to count the number of Roma and Roma *Mischlinge* in their districts. The police also had to determine whether or not their local Roma had been steadily employed for five years, lived in permanent residences, and were married to Aryans. Policemen were to arrest Roma they considered flight risks or itinerants and put them in "special collection camps."[63]

The Germans planned to send hundreds of Austrian Roma to Nisko. When this plan failed, several officials in the Nazi Party's *Rassenpolitisches Amt* (Racial Policy Office) proposed the expulsion of 100,000 Roma and "other alien elements," along with 800,000 Jews, to the General Government. The Germans did deport about 2,500 Roma to the General Government in the spring of 1940, though it was not until the fall of 1941 that the first major shipment of Roma arrived in Łódź. Greiser and Übelhör objected and told Himmler that the Roma presented a health risk

to the rest of the ghetto's residents. Rumkowski concurred; he told the *Ältestenrat* that he was being forced to take 5,000 Roma into the ghetto. He said that he had argued with Übelhör about this: "[W]e cannot live together with them. Gypsies are the sort of people who can do anything. First they rob and then they set fire and soon everything is in flames, including your factories and materials."[64]

The Germans shipped 4,996 Roma, more than half of them children, to Łódź in November 1941.[65] Übelhör put the Roma in a separate fenced-off area of the ghetto away from the Jews. They were given two unfurnished rundown houses. The sanitary conditions in the Roma compound were "catastrophic."[66] The *Ältestenrat*, which was responsible for the Roma, set up several soup kitchens to feed them. Jewish physicians provided medical care; they reported that 213 Roma had died several days after their arrival in the camp. Typhus, dysentery, and other diseases had plagued ghetto residents since its opening and they swept through the Roma compound soon after it opened. By the end of 1941, more than 600 Roma had died from typhus. The Germans, paranoid about the spread of the disease, decided to close the Roma compound and shipped its remaining inmates to Chełmno, where they were murdered in its gas vans in early 1942.

The leadership of the Łódź ghetto, particularly Rumkowski, came to symbolize the difficulty, morally and practically, that Jewish leaders faced as they tried to balance German demands with the survival of their ghetto communities. Rumkowski ruled the ghetto with an iron hand, particularly after a series of riots in 1941 and 1942 over inadequate food supplies. Isaiah Trunk considered Rumkowski and his *Ältestenrat* corrupt, and Dawid Sierakowiak called him a "sadist-moron."[67] In fact, Trunk concluded that "in no other ghetto did the Nazi *Führerprinzip* or authoritarian principle adapted to ghetto conditions take on such proportions as in Łódź." He added: "Nowhere else was the Jewish Council, as a collective representative body of the ghetto population, so degraded to such a miserable role of servile figureheads as in the Łódź Ghetto."[68]

Rumkowski used public speeches to rally public support for his decisions and to announce new German policies. Dawid Sierakowiak described them as "the demagoguery of a megalomaniac." The most infamous took place on September 4, 1942, when Rumkowski informed ghetto parents that the Germans had ordered him to ship 20,000 Jews out of the ghetto. However, Übelhör had told Rumkowski that if he was unable to obey this order, there was an alternative: "We will do it!" Rumkowski told the crowd that the Germans initially wanted to deport 24,000, but that he had convinced them to reduce the number to 20,000, though only on the condition that part of the group be made up of children younger than ten. The rest would be chosen from among the elderly and the sick. Rumkowski said that this was the most diffi-

cult decision he ever had to make and described himself as a "broken Jew" with the "heart of a bandit." His sole duty, he exclaimed, was "to preserve the Jews who remain[ed]."[69]

Yet there were other choices, at least individually. Adam Czerniaków (1882–1942), the head of the Warsaw ghetto's *Judenrat*, committed suicide when ordered to send the ghetto's children to the nearby Treblinka death camp. Janusz Korczak (1878/1879–1942; pen name of Henryk Goldszmit) chose to accompany the children in his Warsaw ghetto orphanage to Treblinka, even though Christian friends had offered to hide him. In the end, of course, none of these gestures saved any lives because the Germans mass murdered most of the Jews in Łódź. But there were ethical choices to be made, and some withstand the judgement of history better than others.

Warsaw

The largest ghetto in occupied Poland was in Warsaw, which had a prewar Jewish population of 368,000 (out of 1.26 million). Initial efforts to open a ghetto in Warsaw met with strong Jewish resistance, though the Wehrmacht ordered a quarantine zone in the Żoliborz district of the city, which was home to many Jews. On September 12, 1940, Hans Frank ordered that the Warsaw ghetto be created to prevent the spread of disease into the general Polish population. During the next few months, the Germans forced 113,000 Poles out of the future ghetto area to make room for more Jews. By early 1941, 445,000 Jews, some from the Warsaw district, were crammed into 2.4 percent of the city's living space.

But unlike Łódź, where the ghetto was initially seen as a temporary measure, German authorities saw the Warsaw ghetto as a way to isolate the region's large Jewish population from the surrounding Poles and Germans, and only belatedly struggled with how to pay for its upkeep. Mordechai Rumkowski visited Warsaw in September 1940 to advise German

Adam Czerniakow (center) with girl (right center) he freed from execution for stealing bread. USHMM Photo No. 15964, courtesy of Zydowski Instytut Historyczny Instytut Naukowo-Badawczy.

and ghetto leaders about how to create a viable ghetto economy. Later that year, the Germans created the *Transferstelle* (German Transfer Authority), which controlled goods coming in and out of the ghetto. The *Transferstelle*, under Waldemar Schön, tended to stifle economic activity in the ghetto, preferring instead to adopt policies designed slowly to starve the Jews there to death. Schön's office, though, had little control over the extensive black market, which dominated Warsaw's economy both inside and outside the ghetto.

Hans Frank eventually realized that the activities of the *Transferstelle* hindered the Warsaw ghetto's economic productivity. He was particularly concerned about the growing threat of epidemics caused by Schön's harsh "slow death" policies, and in the spring of 1941 appointed Max Bischof to replace Schön as head of the transfer office. Bischof's job was to make the ghetto's economy economically self-sufficient. This included organizing Jewish workshops that could receive orders directly from Polish and German businesses. Bischof also agreed to allow Warsaw's Jews to have some say in the running of these businesses in an effort to make them more productive. These changes worked. In June 1941, the Warsaw's ghetto's legal factories produced 333,000 złótys ($93,750) worth of goods, a figure that rose to 500,000 złótys ($156,250) by early fall. During the same period, the ghetto's underground factories produced about 10 million złótys ($3,125,000) worth of goods. Ghetto leaders used these funds to buy food for the malnourished and sick ghetto residents.

Adam Czerniaków, the head of the ghetto's *Judenrat*, did everything possible to maintain some semblance of civilized life in the Warsaw ghetto. Initially, the Germans banned religious services and education, though they allowed synagogues to reopen in the spring of 1941. Later that year, Czerniaków convinced the Germans to allow him to restart a public school system. The most dynamic life in the ghetto, though, centered around the illegal cultural, intellectual, and political organizations and activities that thrived in the Warsaw ghetto. All of prewar Poland's most important political organizations were active in the ghetto and the Jewish underground.

But what most diarists in the Warsaw ghetto talked about were the difficulties of ghetto life, disease, and death. Emmanuel Ringelblum (1900–1944), a prominent historian and ghetto archivist, wrote about the growing indifference to death in the midst of fear of hunger and disease. He considered ghetto officials "hyenas of the worst sort."[70] Yet despite their indifference to the death around them, those who were able to survive for any length of time feared the roundups, first for forced labor and later for shipment to the nearby Treblinka death camp. Henryk Bryskier noted after the war that people spent a lot of time finding a hiding place. People would pool their resources to insure that hiding places provided adequate water, electricity, and other necessities. Groups often avoided letting families with small children into their hiding places; if they did, they often anesthetized them.[71]

Kraków (Cracow)

At a distance, Kraków, with its prewar Jewish population of 64,348, would not seem to be particularly important when compared to Warsaw and Łódź. However, given that it was the capital of the General Government and the center of the Germans' "racial laboratory" and killing center, the ghetto in Kraków merits some discussion. In miniature, it suffered from the same horrors and deprivations as the ghettos in Warsaw and Łódź. And it was here in Kraków that Oskar Schindler underwent a transformation that, using Jewish workers first from the ghetto and later from Płaszów, the city's concentration camp, saw him save the lives of almost 1,100 Jews, many of them from Kraków and its environs.

After the Germans invaded Poland, about 5,000 Kraków Jews fled eastward. Those who

remained quickly became impoverished when they lost most of their legal and property rights.[72] In the spring of 1940, Hans Frank decided to move as many Jews as possible out of the city after several Wehrmacht generals complained that they had to live in homes where the only other tenants were Jews. Frank told a group of his officials that if the Germans wanted to maintain their authority in the General Government, something had to be done to insure that German officials did not meet Jews when they entered or left their homes since they might "be subjected to the risk of falling victims to epidemics." He thought "it was absolutely intolerable that thousands and thousands of Jews should slink about and have dwellings in a town which the Führer had done the greatest honour of making the seat of a high Reich authority." Frank added that he intended to make Kraków "the town freest of Jews in the General Government."[73]

But he thought that 5,000 to 10,000 Jews would have to remain in Kraków because of their handicraft, trade, and business skills. He later expanded this number to 15,000. On May 18, 1940, German authorities announced that Kraków's Jews had three months to leave the city for another town in the General Government. Those who chose to leave by August 15, 1940, could choose their new place of settlement and take all their personal possessions with them. Those who chose not to leave voluntarily would be expelled forcibly after this date and would be allowed to take only 25 kilos (55 pounds) of baggage per person with them.[74] The *Judenrat* under Dr. Marek Bieberstein was responsible for making sure that all the city's Jews complied with the May 18 decree. Initially, the *Judenrat* asked Jews who had come to Kraków from other parts of Poland to consider voluntary resettlement. When this appeal did not work, the *Judenrat* reminded the city's Jews of the August 15 deadline. On July 25, Dr. Bieberstein published a notice in the city's new Jewish news-

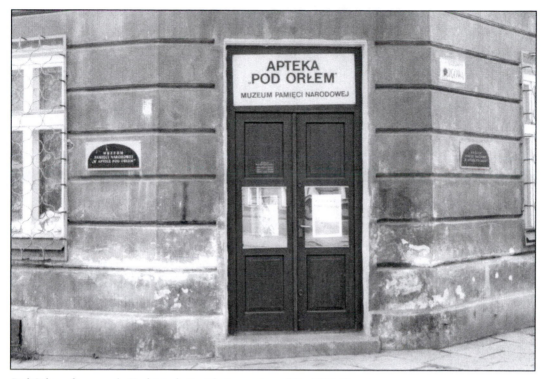

Pod Orłem pharmacy in Kraków ghetto. Photo courtesy of David M. Crowe.

paper, the *Gazeta Żydowska* (Jewish Gazette) reminding Jews of the resettlement regulations.[75] Bieberstein asked

> all Jews of Cracow to change the place of residence voluntarily and immediately irrespective of the fact if the order to move has been delivered or not. The permits to travel by train, identity documents and all sort of information concerning the possible reductions can be obtained from the Migration Committee of the Jewish Community in Cracow, in Brzozowa 5.[76]

Though many Jews did leave Kraków during this period, some returned to the city because they could not find places to live in other parts of the General Government. By August 15, there were still too many Jews in the city. In response, the Germans created a joint German-Jewish eviction committee that issued special residency permits, the *Ausweis*, for Jews permitted to stay in Kraków. The committee, though, issued too many permits; they were used to help fellow Jews or were sold on the black market.[77]

Frustrated, *SS- Brigadeführer* Otto Wächter (1901–1949), the Kraków district's governor, issued a new decree on November 25, 1940, that forbade any Jews to enter Kraków in order "to cleanse Cracow of its Jews and leave in it only those Jews whose professions are still needed." Only Jews with the *Ausweis* (*dokument odroczenia*) could remain in the city. They had to carry this document with them at all times; those without it would be expelled. Wächter warned that he intended to enforce the new decree and warned that anyone who failed to abide by it would be "severely punished."[78]

Several months later, Wächter decided to issue a new document for the city's Jews, the *Kennkarte,* to replace the *Ausweis.* But to receive it, Jews would have to turn in the old

Stella Müller-Madej (right) and Konstancja Szymura. Photo courtesy of David M. Crowe.

Ausweis and prove that they had steady work. Only Jews with the *Kennkarte* could remain in Kraków; all others had to leave.[79] On March 3, 1941, he announced that for security and health reasons a *Judischer Wohnbezirk* (Jewish Living Quarter), or ghetto, would be opened in the suburb of Podgórze.[80]

The *Judenrat* was responsible for making sure that the move into the ghetto went smoothly. Though the Germans forced 3,500 Poles to leave their homes in Podgórze to make room for the Jews, they allowed major factories and businesses producing goods for the Wehrmacht to remain. They also allowed Tadeusz Pankiewicz, who owned the pharmacy, *Pod Orłem* (Under the Eagle; today, Museum of National Remembrance), to continue operating his business in the ghetto, though he and his staff lived elsewhere. Pankiewicz, whom Yad Vashem later named a Righteous Among the Nations, stated in his wartime memoirs that the pharmacy, situated as it was on one of the ghetto's main squares, enabled him to become a "witness to the in-human deportations, monstrous crimes and the constant degradation of human dignity and self-respect of the occupants." One ghetto resident, Stella Müller-Madej, described Pankiewicz as "a wonderful human being."[81]

Fifteen thousand Jews began to make their way across the Vistula to the ghetto several days after Wächter had issued his ghetto decree. What was once a normal, though run-down, suburb of Kraków now became a crowded Jewish ghetto where disease and hunger were constant threats to human life. Stella Müller-Madej described the traumatic forced march into the ghetto:

A lot of people were heading for the Ghetto, big groups and small. Some were carrying only bundles, and others had all their possessions loaded on horse carts. Daddy was pushing a nondescript wagon that he had borrowed from the janitor.

It was a beautiful sunny day, but no one was smiling about the splendid weather. The whole crowd around us was grey, gloomy and sad. I felt bad because we must have looked the same in such company. To cheer things up, I said to Daddy, who was pushing the cart with a vacant expression on his face, "Let's pretend it's our car, and we'll step on the gas and run from the bridge here down to Zgoda Square, OK?"[82]

Stella excitedly jumped up on the cart, only to see the family's bundles tumble to the ground. Her father helped her put them back on the cart and began cheerfully to push it along the street; then, "skipping and letting out Indian whoops," Stella and her brother Adam followed along: "Mummy and my brother picked up the parcels that fell along the way. Some people looked at us indignantly, while others laughed at the sight. I heard somebody say, '*Quite right. We shouldn't let it get us down. It's not as though we were going to our death.*'"[83]

Stella and her family were given an apartment on Czarnieckiego Street. In reality, it was just a single room with a kitchen and a common toilet in the building's courtyard. It was also dirty and crawling with roaches. Stella's mother, Tusia, declared that she would "rather not live at all than vegetate for even a week in such conditions."[84]

A vivid photographic collection in the *Archiwum Pañstwowe* in Kraków paints a graphic picture of the forced Jewish exodus into the ghetto. The Germans forced Jews to walk or take trains or boats across the Vistula to reach the ghetto. After they had loaded their household goods onto decrepit horse-drawn wagons, men, women, and children carried whatever personal goods they could manage. German guards were everywhere and they constantly checked and rechecked identity cards. The stress of the transfer showed darkly on the face of every victim.[85]

The forced move into the ghetto came just before one of Judaism's most important religious festivals, Passover (Pesach). In fact, the Germans often chose a period around a spe-cial Jewish religious festival such as Passover or Rosh Hashana to begin a major transfer or roundup. The idea was to catch their victims off guard. When Passover ended, bricklayers began to construct the 3-meter (9.8-foot) wall around the ghetto. The Germans had workers finish off the walls with what appeared to be the tops of Jewish gravestones. They placed a large blue Star of David above the ghetto's main entrance. Below it was a phrase in Yiddish—*Jidischer wojnbecirk* (Jewish housing estate). All signs and other public inscriptions in Polish had to be redone in Hebrew throughout the ghetto. The only exception was the Polish sign over the entranceway to Tadeusz Pankiewicz's pharmacy.[86]

Rule, Life, and Work in the Kraków Ghetto

Polish "blue" police (they wore navy blue uniforms) guarded the three entrances into the ghetto. Though circumstances varied from ghetto to ghetto, particularly in the General Government, the Polish police had authority over the *Jüdischer Ordnungsdienst* (OD; Jewish Security Police) in Kraków. The offices of the *Judenrat* and the German police were near the main entrance on Podgórze Square. Only Jewish workers with a *Blauschein* issued by the *Arbeitsamte* (Labor Office) could work outside the ghetto. People would leave for their jobs as forced laborers through the Podgórze Square gate and return that evening through the one at Plac Zgody.[87]

The population in the ghetto changed frequently. Soon after the ghetto opened in the spring of 1941, the Germans shipped Jews there from surrounding villages. That fall, authorities deported 2,000 Jews from the ghetto who did not have proper identification. Though the Germans planned the roundups and deportations, the OD helped them gather Jews for the transports.[88] In Kraków, OD candidates usually had to have completed some military service, meet certain weight and height requirements, have an unblemished past, and be nominated by several reputable individuals. Theoretically, the *Judenrat* was to have final say over the appointment of OD members, though the Germans had their favorites, such as Symcha Spira, the head of the ghetto OD. Before the war, Spira was a devout, bearded Orthodox Jew. Now clean shaven, he wore a tailored uniform adorned with many official looking insignias. The *Judenrat* always approved German nominees like Spira.[89]

The Kraków ghetto OD had two sections, the *Zivilabteilung* (Civil Division) and the "uniformed" regular OD. Members of the *Zivilabteilung* wore neckties and blue coats; the regular OD wore coats buttoned to the neck. Members of both OD units wore armbands on their right sleeves with *Ordnungsdienst* in Hebrew. The Gestapo had direct contact with members of the Civil Division, but members of the regular OD received their orders from the *Judenrat*. The OD served both as ghetto civilian police and prison guards and could exact punishment without fear of the consequences. But what people most remembered about the OD was their help during roundups and deportations. In time, the OD became one of the most despised symbols of Nazi oppression throughout the ghetto system. Many OD policemen fell prey to the rampant corruption that plagued German rule in the General Government, a situation that aggravated Jewish hatred of these units.[90]

The Jewish OD were only part of a complex network of *Judenrat* organizations and facilities created to deal with the complexities of life and society in the Kraków ghetto. One of the most important was the *Jüdische Soziale Selbsthilfe* (JSS; Jewish Self-Help Society; *Żydowska Samopomoc Społeczna*). Headed by Dr. Michał Weichert, the JSS, a General Government–wide organization, was created in the spring of 1940 at the instigation of the AJJDC, which was searching for a Jewish-run organization in German-occupied Poland to distribute welfare aid to Polish Jews. The Germans insisted, though, that the JSS become part of a Nazi-run *Naczelna Rada Opiekuncza* (NRO; Main Welfare Council), which also had Polish and Ukrainian delegates. The NRO first came under the jurisdiction of the Nazi Party's *Nationalistiche Volkswohlfahrt* (NSV; National Socialist Volk Welfare Agency), and later Hans Frank's *Bevölkerungswesen und Fürsorge* (BuF; Population and Welfare Agency), created in April 1940. The Germans insisted that the German Red Cross, which was part of the NSV, act as the JSS liaison with the AJJDC. The JSS and the AJJDC had offices in Warsaw and Kraków.[91]

After Germany declared war on the United States on December 11, 1941, the Germans closed the AJJDC office in Warsaw, though it continued to operate illegally. Weichert still ran the JSS office in Kraków, first in the ghetto and later in Płaszów. Initially, Weichert tried to help Jews throughout the General Government, though once the SS took over control of all Jewish matters in the summer of 1942, it permitted him to help Kraków's Jews only. It also closed the NRO, but permitted Weichert to take over a new organization, the *Jüdische Unterstützungsstelle* (JUS; Jewish Aid Center), which was responsible for providing Jews in slave-labor camps with whatever aid arrived for them from abroad. The JUS continued to operate for about six months after the SS closed the Kraków ghetto in the spring of 1943. Weichert continued to work for the Polish relief organization, the *Rada Głowna Opiekuncza* (Chief Aid Committee), and somehow managed to continue sending goods into the slave labor camps. In early 1944, the SS allowed him to start JUS again, but soon closed it. Weichert then went into hiding and survived the Holocaust. After the war, he was tried several times in Poland for collaboration with the Germans, but was found innocent each time. He ultimately settled in Israel.[92]

There were three hospitals in the Kraków ghetto, as well as an orphanage, a post office, and a public bath, that had facilities for delousing and disinfection. Though it is unclear whether this was a *mikvah,* or Jewish ritual bath, one ghetto survivor, Sol Urbach, said that people in the ghetto found ways to maintain their own personal hygiene. He never was deloused or disinfected, and he never had to carry an *Entlausungsschein* (delousing certificate), a document required elsewhere that indicated that a Jew had been deloused and disinfected.[93]

Religion and Jewish education flourished in the ghetto, though the latter was officially outlawed.[94] Religious education continued illegally, and three synagogues served the residents' spiritual needs. Tadeusz Pankiewicz said that people continued to observe Shabbat and the Jewish holidays, though their suffering was always evident on their faces during worship. On Shabbat, Orthodox men and women often stood outside the makeshift synagogue, near the rear of his pharmacy, and recited their prayers. He added that the *Kaddish,* the prayers for the dead, were frequently recited in almost every Jewish ghetto home.[95]

Yet any hint of normalcy in the Kraków ghetto was a façade. The threat of violence and death was constant. Stella Müller-Madej's family lived in constant fear for their personal safety. Stella was eleven years old when the ghetto opened, and her brother Adam was fifteen. Adam and his parents left Stella alone every day to go to work. Her parents gave Stella a number of do's and don'ts, such as avoiding the ghetto wall area, strangers, and "quarrels with children." Stella said she would "kick around the Ghetto streets as if [she] were in a bewitched world." As the child of secular Jewish parents, she found the "little rabbis," the Orthodox Jewish children with their hair locks and conservative dress, "especially irritating." But what really frightened her was the random violence. On one occasion before the ghetto wall was completed, a gang of Polish children began to pick on her. When a Polish worker helping to build the wall intervened, his colleague admonished him to "let the kids have

Kraków ghetto wall. Photo courtesy of David M. Crowe.

fun with the little Jew." He added, "Hey, Sarah, here's an apple for you." He then threw the apple in Stella's face, bloodying her nose. The kind Polish worker angrily shouted at his coworker, "You son of a bitch, I'll show you! Aren't they putting them through enough hell without us?" He then wiped Stella's face and warned her that it would be best if she did not return to the construction site "because something really bad might happen." He then wanted to know her name. Ashamed of the behavior of his coworker, he told Stella that his name was Antoni. In fact, he added, it would be okay if she came back to the construction site. If she did, he would bring her a toy.[96]

Though Stella's parents forbade her to return to the wall or to speak to Antoni, she did so surreptitiously. On one occasion, Antoni

Jews signing up for work permits, Kraków ghetto. Photo courtesy of Archiwum Państwowe w Krakowie.

gave her a black puppy, whom Stella named Blackie. The puppy became Stella's constant companion in the ghetto. Although Stella's parents had originally been opposed to her keeping Blackie, they later agreed that the dog was a good companion for Stella in those dangerous times. Once the Germans had completed the ghetto walls, the atmosphere grew more deadly. Random acts of violence became more widespread and people no longer walked normally from place to place. In fear, they scurried about quickly to avoid being shot or beaten by Germans or Poles. Oftentimes, the rumors of such mistreatment and death was as frightening as the actual deeds. Stella constantly heard stories about German soldiers who drove around in cars killing Jews "like birds on a roof," or about children being tossed off of a hill overlooking the ghetto by the "Blacks," or the *Baudienst* (Baudinists), Poles drafted initially by the Germans for construction work and occasionally used in some Jewish roundups. But what frightened Stella

most were the stories she heard her father, an OD man, whisper secretly to her mother about Auschwitz and mass murder.[97]

Yet it was not education, religion, or even the fear of indiscriminate violence that concerned most ghetto residents—it was work. A job and the precious *Blauschein* was the key to life for Kraków's Jews. Both of Stella's parents and her teenaged brother, Adam, had jobs. Her father, Zygmunt, worked long hours in a quarry before he became an OD man. Adam was employed outside the ghetto in a nail factory, and her mother, Tusia, ran the office of an Austrian button factory. The wife of the factory owner, Frau Holzinger, became friendly with Tusia and gave her extra food to smuggle back into the ghetto. According to Stella, none of the Germans who met Tusia in the Holzinger office believed she was a Jew. On one occasion, Mrs. Holzinger invited Tusia to a reception in her home. Tusia hesitated, but Mrs. Holzinger insisted and promised to drive her back to the ghetto when the party was over. Everything went well until

Tusia's Jewish armband fell out of her purse in front of some of the German guests, including a few members of the SS. Mrs. Holzinger tried to explain away the incident as a joke, but Tusia feared it would cost her job. It did not.[98]

In the spring of 1941, the Germans allowed the *Judenrat* to open bakeries, dairies, and restaurants. There was even a restaurant with a night club that featured an orchestra with two musicians made famous in *Schindler's List*—Henry Rosner, a violinist; and his brother, Leopold Rosner, an accordionist. The restaurant and bar was owned by Alexander Förster, an SD agent who often entertained guests from the Gestapo there. The Rosners could provide the entertainment at such functions, but they could never be a part of them. With the exception of a few well-placed Jews such as Förster and Spira Symcha, few Jews could afford such luxuries, nor had they the energy for them. Jews fortunate enough to have a job worked long, hard hours, and they usually came home exhausted, not only from the work but from the stress of living as forced laborers and prisoners of the Germans.[99]

Forced Labor and Food

Hitler's economic planning for World War II was weak, and he chose, much to the chagrin of some of his generals, to go to war without regard for his nation's inability to fight a sustained conflict. This meant that the Third Reich would have to rely heavily on foreign sources for military production. Moreover, Hitler's unwillingness to put Germany, at least economically, on a full war footing was in part driven by his memories of the suffering of the German people during World War I. Hitler hoped that using blitzkrieg tactics would rapidly enable Germany to take over a country's economy.

The Nazis' terror campaign against Polish civilians was followed by efforts to rob Poland of its natural and human resources. Germany was heavily dependent on foreign sources for

many of its basic raw materials and, by the fall of 1939, had few financial resources to purchase such desperately needed items. Consequently, the theft of Polish and Jewish personal property, factories, and other vital economic sources was part of the greater German scheme to use conquered nations to make up for the Third Reich's economic shortfalls.

Another problem was the vast growing demands for soldiers in the Wehrmacht, particularly after the second phase of World War II began with the conquest of much of Western Europe in the spring and early summer of 1940. This, coupled with Hitler's hesitancy to allow German women to work in factories, meant that Germany's growing industrial and agricultural sectors would have to look for factory and farm labor elsewhere. Actually, the German use of *Fremdarbeiter* (foreign workers) began after the takeover of Austria in 1938. Eventually, 100,000 Austrians were sent to Germany to work, and they were later joined by 70,000 Czech and Slovak workers. After the outbreak of war, the Germans also began to use POWs as forced laborers.

The German army had begun to force Jews into forced or slave-labor situations within days after the beginning of the invasion of Poland. On October 26, 1939, Hans Frank ordered that all male Jews from fourteen to sixty years old had to perform forced labor, which would be overseen by the SS. The regulations were later extended to Jewish women and children who were from twelve to fourteen years old, and was to include Jews from other parts of former Poland. On December 12, 1939, a Second Implementation Order was issued by Friedrich Krüger (1894–1945), the *HSSPF* in the General Government; this one ordered Jews to serve two years as forced laborers, though the term could be extended if the "educational" value of the forced labor was not realized.

A month later, Hans Frank ordered the *Judenräte* in the General Government to register all eligible Jewish laborers and divide them into six categories based on trade or profession. The

Jewish slave laborers at Siemens factory in Bobrek, 1944. USHMM Photo No. 95270, courtesy of Henry Schwarzbaum.

Germans initially set up two types of labor camps for Jewish and other forced laborers. The SS created the first as part of bigger concentration camps; the second type, the *Einsatzlager*, were run by Robert Ley's (1890–1945) *Deutsches Arbeitsfront* (German Labor Front).

In the interim between the creation of the ghetto system in the General Government in 1939–1940 and the decision to implement the Final Solution in the summer of 1941, the Germans increasingly used Jewish and Polish forced workers throughout their empire. By the end of 1940, there were about 700,000 forced laborers in Poland. This figure does not include the vast Jewish population in Łódź, Warsaw, and other Jewish concentration areas where the inmates were forced to work or face starvation.

German labor policies for Jews varied throughout the General Government and changed as the Nazis developed new confinement and death policies for them. In the summer of 1940, *SS- Obersturmbannführer* Dr.

Max Frauendorfer (1909–1989), the head of Hans Frank's *Hauptabteilung Arbeit* (Labor Division), issued regulations that laid out general guidelines for the use and payment of Jewish workers in the General Government. The police were to deal with questions regarding Jewish labor, though in reality it was overseen by Frauendorfer's labor offices. Frauendorfer argued that it was necessary to use Jewish labor because so many Poles were being sent to Germany to work. He added that many Polish Jews were skilled laborers and were to be used as part of the normal labor pool throughout the General Government. Since the *Judenräte* and the *Ältestenrate* had limited resources, Frauendorfer decreed that Jews used in the normal labor market were to be paid salaries equal to 80 percent of that paid Polish workers. These guidelines did not apply to Jews used in forced-labor situations.[100]

In reality, Frauendorfer's policies were ineffective: Polish and German businessmen were unwilling to pay Jews anything near Frauen-dorfer's rates. If they were paid anything, it was usually in foodstuffs bought on the Aryan side. In all likelihood, the food "given" to Tusia Müller by her employer, Mrs. Holzinger, was probably her "salary." The situation worsened with the opening of the ghettos, which limited the ability of many Jews to continue working openly in the free Polish or German side of the economy outside the ghetto; and it was particularly true after the Germans had begun to think seriously about the "Final Solution of the Jewish Question" in the fall of 1941. Their plan would involve closing most ghettos, though questions remained about the use of Jews in slave-labor situations, particularly after the experiment with Soviet POW slave labor had failed.[101]

Work was essential to survival in the ghettos. When the war broke out, the Germans initiated a Reich-wide rationing system based on "race." Hitler was determined that the German people would not suffer the economic hardships they had endured during World War I, so the real burden of rationing fell on the occupied peoples. The Germans distributed ration books to Poland's Jews, though the food they acquired through official channels was never enough to sustain life, particularly when they were forced to work twelve hour days as forced laborers.[102]

In Łódź, for example, authorities decreed in 1939 that Jews were supposed to receive 25 percent of the city's food allocations. In reality, Jews got much less because of problems with food distribution and deliberate German efforts to starve them. During the month of November 1940, Warsaw's Jews were allotted only 3,250 grams of bread apiece, while the city's Aryans received 6,100 grams of bread during the same period. Warsaw's Jews got no sugar, flour, meat, eggs, or potatoes; these were reserved for non-Jews. The Polish historian Eugeniusz Duraczyński estimated that the average daily food allotment for residents in Warsaw in 1941 was 2,613 calories for Germans, 669 calo-

ries for Poles, and 184 calories for Jews. Because of the underground economy, some Poles were able to buy food to increase their daily caloric intake by 1,000 to 1,500 calories.[103]

Such underground activity was much more difficult for the General Government's impoverished Jewish population, particularly after the ghetto system was in place because it severely restricted their ability to buy food on the black market. And even if Jews could buy food or medicines on the black market, which dominated the General Government's economy, they were now so impoverished by the theft of their property that they had little to sell to Polish and German black marketeers. In desperation, *Judenräte* and *Ältestenrate* throughout the General Government set up food acquisition, production, and distribution systems that were able barely to raise Jewish daily caloric intake slightly above the 1,000 calories deemed necessary to sustain life over a long period. The situation worsened after Hans Frank decided in the fall of 1942 no longer to supply food to the 1.2 million Jews in the General Government not involved in jobs considered vital to the German economy. Starvation had now become an active German tool of mass death for Jews.[104]

Conclusion

The first two years of World War II was the intermediary stage of the Holocaust when the Germans intensified their campaign against the Jews, the Roma, the handicapped, and other minorities. For the handicapped in the Greater Reich, this phase of the Holocaust saw the implementation of the Nazis' first mass murder campaign—the "euthanasia" programs. The skills and techniques developed during the "euthanasia" campaigns would later be used on a much larger scale during the Final Solution of the "Jewish question" from 1941 to 1945.

Hitler's conquest of part of Poland in the fall of 1939 presented Reich officials with problems much more complex than they had ever before faced in Germany. The sheer size of the Jewish population in Poland made planning much more difficult. Moreover, the Germans had to deal not only with Poland's large Jewish population but also with a Polish population that was deemed racially inferior. The brutalization of the Polish elite was part of the German effort slowly to destroy the fabric of Polish society, which would gradually be transformed into a slave society. Yet the Polish Jewish question remained central to German thinking, and something much more dramatic had to be developed to deal with Poland's large Jewish population. What the Germans finally came up with was a massive ghetto system within the confines of what eventually became the German dumping ground for Jews and other minorities from throughout Europe— the General Government. Later, the General Government would become home to the major killing centers of the Final Solution.

The concept of the ghetto, though ageless, was to isolate Jews and Roma from the fabric of German and Polish society. The ghettos were designed to be totally self-supporting centers of slow death. Though ghettos such as Łódź and Warsaw became important manufacturing centers for the German war effort, which used extensive forced or slave Jewish labor, they ultimately became gathering points for the factories of death that dotted the Polish countryside. The Kraków ghetto, created as it was in the capital of the General Government, provides us with an intimate look not only into the intricacies of running a ghetto but also into the lives of Jews forced to live in these islands of horror.

SOURCES FOR FURTHER STUDY AND RESEARCH

Primary Sources

Adelson, Alan, and Robert Lapides, eds. *Łódź Ghetto: Inside a Community Under Siege.* New York: Viking, 1968.

Apenszlak, Jacob, Jacob Kenner, Isaac Lewin, and Moses Polakiewicz, eds. *The Black Book of Pol-* *ish Jewry: An Account of the Martyrdom of Polish Jewry Under the Nazi Occupation.* New York: American Federation for Polish Jews, 1943.

Arad, Yitzhak, Yisrael Gutman, and Abraham Margaliot, eds. *Documents on the Holocaust.* Jerusalem: Yad Vashem, 1981.

Bieberstein, Aleksander. *Zagłada Żydów w Krakowie.* Kraków: Wydawnictwo Literackie, 1985.

Dobroszycki, Lucjan, ed. *The Chronicle of the Łódź Ghetto.* Translated by Richard Lorrie et al. New Haven: Yale University Press, 1984.

Domarus, Max. *Hitler: Speeches and Proclamations, 1932–1945: The Chronicle of a Dictatorship.* Vol. 4, *1941–1945.* Wauconda, IL: Bolchazy-Carducci, 2004.

Du Prel, Max Freiherr. *Das General-Gouvernement.* Würzburg: Konrad Triltsch Verlag, 1942.

Goebbels, Joseph. *The Joseph Goebbels Diaries, 1942–1943.* Edited and translated by Louis P. Luchner. Garden City, NY: Doubleday, 1948.

Graf, Malvina. *The Kraków Ghetto and the Płaszów Camp.* Tallahassee: Florida State University Press, 1989.

"Groyczko, Dr. Roland to Handlowego przy Sądzie Okręgowym w Krakowie." September 11, 1941, SOKC 2023: III U 5/39, p. 2.

Grynberg, Michael, ed. *Worlds to Outlive Us: Eyewitness Accounts from the Warsaw Ghetto.* New York: Henry Holt, 2002.

Haney, Wolfgang. *Spuren aus dem Getto Łódź, 1940–1944: Dokumente der Sammlung.* Berlin: Haus der Wannsee-Konferenz, 2000.

Lukas, Richard C. *Forgotten Holocaust: The Poles Under German Occupation, 1939–1944.* New York: Hippocrene Books, 1990.

Mendes-Flohr, Paul, and Jehuda Reinharz, eds. *The Jew in the Modern World: A Documentary History.* 2nd ed. New York: Oxford University Press, 1995.

Müller-Madej, Stella. *A Girl from Schindler's List.* Translated by William R. Brand. London: Polish Cultural Foundation, 1997.

_____. Interview. August 9, 2000. Kraków, Poland.

Noakes, Jeremy, and Geoffrey Pridham, eds. *Foreign Policy, War and Racial Extermination.* Vol. 2 of *Nazism, 1919–1945: A History in Documents and Eyewitness Accounts.* New York: Schocken Books, 1988.

Pankiewicz, Tadeusz. *Apteka w Getcie Krakowskim.* Kraków: Wydawnictwo Literackie, 1995.

_____. *The Cracow Ghetto Pharmacy.* Translated by Henry Tilles. Washington, DC: United States Holocaust Memorial Museum, 2000.

Piłsudski, Joseph. *The Memories of a Polish Revolutionary and Soldier.* Edited and translated by D. R. Gillie. London: Faber & Faber, 1931.

Piotrowski, Stanislaw, ed. *Dziennik Hansa Frank.* Warsaw: Wydawnicto Prawnicze, 1956.

_____, ed. *Hans Frank's Diary.* Warsaw: Pañstwowe Wydawnictwo Naukowe, 1961.

The Polish Ministry of Information. *The Black Book of Poland.* New York: G. P. Putnam's Sons, 1942.

Ringelblum, Emmanuel. *Notes from the Warsaw Ghetto: The Journal of Emmanuel Ringelblum.* Edited and translated by Jacob Sloan. New York: ibooks, 2006.

Rosner, Manci. Interview. March 21, 2000. Miami, Florida.

Sierakowiak, Dawid. *The Diary of Dawid Sierakowiak.* Edited by Alan Adelson. Translated by Kamil Turowski. New York: Oxford University Press, 1996.

Snyder, Louis L., ed. *Hitler's Third Reich: A Documentary History.* Chicago: Nelson-Hall, 1981.

Trials of the War Criminals Before the Nuernberg Military Tribunals Under Control Council Law No. 10. Vol. 1, *The Medical Case.* Washington, DC: United States Government Printing Office, 1950.

Trunk, Isaiah. *Łódź Ghetto: A History.* Edited and translated by Robert Moses Shapiro. Bloomington: Indiana University Press, 2006.

The Warsaw Diary of Adam Czerniakow: Prelude to Doom. Edited by Raul Hilberg, Stanislaw Staron, and Josef Kermisz. Translated by Stanislaw Staron and the staff of Yad Vashem. New York: Stein and Day, 1979.

"Zbioru fotografii z 'akcji zydowskiej' w Krakowie/ eksmisje, wysiedlenia rejestracje, getto." Starosty Miasta Krakowa/Der Stadthauptmann der Stadt Krakau/ z lat 1939–1945. SMKr 211. Krakow: Archiwum Pañstwowe w Krakowie.

Secondary Sources

Bauer, Yehuda. *American Jewry and the Holocaust: The American Jewish Joint Distribution Committee, 1939–1945.* Detroit: Wayne State University Press, 1981.

Bauminger, Arieh L. *The Fighters of the Cracow Ghetto.* Jerusalem: Keter Press Enterprises, 1986.

Boroziej, Włodzimierz. *Terror und Politik: Die Deutsche Polizei und die Polnische Widerstandsbewegung im Generalgouvernement, 1919–1944.* Mainz: Verlag Philipp von Zabern, 1999.

Breitman, Richard. *The Architect of Genocide: Himmler and the Final Solution.* New York: Alfred A. Knopf, 1991.

Browning, Christopher R. *Nazi Policy, Jewish Workers, German Killers.* Cambridge: Cambridge University Press, 2000.

_____. *The Origins of the Final Solution: The Evolution of Nazi Jewish Policy, September 1939–March 1942.* Lincoln and Jerusalem: University of Nebraska Press and Yad Vashem, 2004.

Burleigh, Michael. *Death and Deliverance: "Euthanasia" in Germany 1900–1945.* Cambridge: Cambridge University Press, 1994.

Cookson, Clive. "Hunger, Horror and Heroism." *Financial Times.* July 28/29, 2001.

Crowe, David M. *Oskar Schindler: The Untold Account of His Life, Wartime Activities, and the True Story Behind "The List."* Boulder: Westview Press, 2004.

Davies, Norman. *God's Playground: A History of Poland.* Vol. 2, *1795 to the Present.* New York: Columbia University Press, 1982.

Dawidowicz, Lucy S., ed. *The Golden Tradition: Jewish Life and Thought in Eastern Europe.* New York: Schocken Books, 1984.

Duda, Eugeniusz. *The Jews of Cracow.* Translated by Ewa Basiura. Kraków: Wydawnictwo "Hagada" and Argona-Jarden Bookshop, 2000.

Duranczyński, Eugeniusz. *Wojna I Okupacja: Wrzesień 1939–Kwiecień 1943.* Warsaw: Wieza Powszechna, 1974.

Dziewanowski, M. K. *Joseph Piłsudski: A European Federalist, 1918–1922.* Stanford: Stanford University Press, 1969.

Favez, Jean-Claude. *The Red Cross and the Holocaust.* Edited and translated by John and Beryl Fletcher. Cambridge: Cambridge University Press, 1999.

Friedlander, Henry. *The Origins of Nazi Genocide: From Euthanasia to the Final Solution.* Chapel Hill: University of North Carolina Press, 1995.

Gross, Jan. *Fear: Anti-Semitism in Poland After Auschwitz.* New York: Random House, 2006.

_____. *Neighbors: The Destruction of the Jewish Community in Jedwabne, Poland.* Princeton: Princeton University Press, 2001.

_____. *Polish Society Under German Occupation: The Generalgouvernement, 1939–1944.* Princeton: Princeton University Press, 1979.

Gumkowski, Janusz, and Kazimierz Leszczyński. *Poland Under German Nazi Occupation.* Translated by Edward Rothert. Warsaw: Polonia, 1961.

Gutman, Yisrael, and Shmuel Krakowski. *Unequal Victims: Poles and Jews During World War II.* New York: Holocaust Library, 1986.

Hamburg Institute for Social Research. *The German Army and Genocide.* Translated by Scott Abbott. New York: New Press, 1999.

Herbert, Ulrich. *Hitler's Foreign Workers: Enforced Foreign Labor in Germany Under the Third Reich.* Translated by William Templer. Cambridge: Cambridge University Press, 1997.

Heller, Celia S. *On the Edge of Destruction: Jews of Poland Between the Two World Wars.* New York: Columbia University Press, 1977.

Hilberg, Raul. *The Destruction of the European Jews.* Rev. and definitive ed. 3 vols. New York: Holmes & Meier, 1985.

Hitler's Army: The Evolution and Structure of German Armed Forces. Edited by *Command* magazine. Conshohocken, PA: Combined Publishing, 1995.

Höhne, Heinz. *Canaris.* Translated by J. Maxwell Brownjohn. New York: Doubleday, 1979.

_____. *The Order of the Death's Head: The Story of Hitler's SS.* Translated by Richard Barry. London: Penguin, 2000.

Holc, Janine. "Working Through Jan Gross's *Neighbors.*" *Slavic Review* 61, no. 3 (Fall 2002): 453–459.

Kenrick, Donald, and Grattan Puxon. *The Destiny of Europe's Gypsies.* New York: Basic Books, 1972.

Kershaw, Ian. *Hitler, Nemesis, 1936–1945.* New York: W. W. Norton, 2000.

Kohl, Robert L. *RKFDV: German Resettlement and Population Policy, 1939–1945.* Cambridge, MA: Harvard University Press, 1957.

Lucas, Richard C. *Forgotten Holocaust: The Poles Under German Occupation, 1939–1944.* New York: Hippocrene Books, 1990.

Kroener, Bernhard R., Rolf-Dieter Müller, and Hans Umbreit, eds. *Germany and the Second World War.* Vol. 5, *Organization and Mobilization of the German Sphere of Power,* pt. 1, *Wartime Administration, Economy, and Manpower Resources, 1939–1941.* Translated by John Brownjohn, Patricia Crampton, Ewald Osers, and Louise Willmot. Oxford: Clarendon Press, 2000.

Madajzyk, Czesław. *Polityka III Rzeszy w Okupowanej Polsce.* 2 vols. Warsaw: Pañstwowe Wydawnictco Naukowe, 1970.

McKale, Donald M. *The Swastika Outside of Germany.* Kent, OH: Kent State University Press, 1977.

Meirtchak, Benjamin. *Jewish Military Casualties in the Polish Armies in World War II.* Jerusalem: Association of Jewish War Veterans of the Polish Armies in Israel, 1994.

_____. *Jews—Officers in the Polish Armed Forces, 1939–1945.* Bergen, NJ: Avotaynu, 2004.

Mendelsohn, Ezra. *The Jews of East Central Europe Between the World Wars.* Bloomington: Indiana University Press, 1983.

O'Brien, Darcy. *The Hidden Pope: The Untold Story of a Lifelong Friendship That Is Changing the Relationship Between Catholics and Jews: The Personal Journey of John Paul II and Jerzy Kluger.* New York: Daybreak Books, 1998.

Overy, R. J. *War and the Economy in the Third Reich.* Oxford: Clarendon Press, 1994.

Peck, Abraham J. "Poles and Jews." *Sarmatian Review* 18, no. 2 (April 1998): 1–3. http://www.ruf.rice.edu/~sarmatia/498/peck.html.

Pióro, Anna, and Wiesława Kraliñska. *Krakowskie Getto.* Kraków: Muzeum Pamiêci Narodowej "Apteka pod Orłem," 1995.

Rossino, Alexander B. *Hitler Strikes Poland: Blitzkrieg, Ideology, and Atrocity.* Lawrence: University of Kansas Press, 2003.

Roszkowski, Wojciech. "After *Neighbors:* Seeking Universal Standards." *Slavic Review* 61, no. 3 (Fall 2002): 460–465.

Rothschild, Joseph. *East Central Europe Between the Two World Wars.* Seattle: University of Washington Press, 1977.

Taylor, Telford. *Sword and Swastika: Generals and Nazis in the Third Reich.* New York: Barnes and Noble, 1952.

Thurner, Erika. *National Socialism and Gypsies in Austria.* Edited and translated by Gilya Gerda Schmidt. Tuscaloosa: University of Alabama Press, 1998.

Trunk, Isaiah. *Judenrat: The Jewish Councils in Eastern Europe Under Nazi Occupation.* New York: Scarborough Books, 1977.

United States Holocaust Memorial Museum. *Deadly Medicine: Creating the Master Race.* Washington, DC: United States Holocaust Memorial Museum, 2004.

_____. *Historical Atlas of the Holocaust.* New York: Macmillan, 1996.

_____. *Poles.* Washington, DC: United States Holocaust Memorial Museum, 1998.

Weigel, George. *Witness to Hope: The Biography of Pope John Paul II.* New York: Cliff Street Books, 2001.

Weinberg, Gerhard L. *Foreign Policy of Hitler's Germany, 1937–1939: Starting World War II.* Chicago: University of Chicago Press, 1980.

Zimmermann, Michael. *Rassenutopie und Genozid: Die nationalsozialistische "Lösung der Zigeunerfrage."* Hamburg: Hans Christians Verlag, 1996.

CHAPTER 6

The Invasion of the Soviet Union and the Path to the "Final Solution"

CHRONOLOGY

—**1940** *(June 15–17)*: Soviet Union conquers Baltic States (Estonia, Latvia, Lithuania)

—**1940** *(July 29–August 31)*: Jan Zwartebdijk and Sempo Sugihara issue visas for thousands of Jews fleeing Soviet territory

—**1940** *(August 1–6)*: Baltic States forced to become Fourteenth, Fifteenth, and Sixteenth Soviet Socialist Republics

—**1940** *(December 18)*: Adolf Hitler issues Operation Barbarossa directive

—**1941** *(March 13)*: Führer Directive gives Himmler and the SS responsibility for political administration in occupied parts of Soviet Union

—**1941** *(March 26)*: SS and Wehrmacht establish special relationship for operations in Soviet Union

—**1941** *(March 30)*: Hitler calls invasion of Soviet Union "war of extermination"

—**1941** *(April)*: German army issues its "Guidelines for the Conduct of the Army in Russia"

—**1941** *(April 28)*: Wehrmacht issues directive for Sipo and SD units in Soviet Union

—**1941** *(May)*: *Einsatzgruppen* units begin training at *Grenzpolizei* school in Pretsch

—**1941** *(May 19)*: OKW directive calls for "ruthless and energetic action" against Bolsheviks, Jews, saboteurs, and others

—**1941** *(June 6)*: Commissar Order issued

—**1941** *(June 17)*: Reinhard Heydrich meets with *Einsatzgruppen* commanders; orders them to kill Jews, Roma, and communist activists

—**1941** *(June 22)*: Germany invades the Soviet Union

—**1941** *(June 22–March 1942)*: Germans murder from 110,000 to 140,000 handicapped patients and others at Kiev Pathological Institute

—**1941** *(July 2)*: Heydrich reminds his SS and police leaders to be ruthless in their "political pacification" efforts

—**1941** *(July 1–September 3)*: Germans murder 13,000 Jews at Ponary

—**1941** *(July 3)*: Stalin calls for partisan activities behind German lines

—**1941** *(July 10)*: Jedwabne massacre

—**1941** *(July 17)*: *Reichsministerium für die besetzen Ostgebiete* (*Ostministerium*) created; subdivided into *Reichskommissariat Ostland* and *Reichskommisariat Ukraine*

—**1941** *(August 18)*: OKW issues *Führer* Directive "Instructions for the Intensified Fight Against Banditry in the East"

—**1941** *(mid-September)*: Arthur Nebe kills handicapped patients with dynamite and carbon monoxide in Minsk and Mogilev

—**1941** *(September 29–30)*: Germans and Ukrainians kill 33,771 Jews at Babi Yar
—**1941** *(October)*: Romanian army murders 25,000 Jews in Odessa
—**1941** *(November 21)*: Army Group Center orders halt in arrest of sedentary Roma in rear areas
—**1941**: Hinrich Lohse issues Roma decree for *Ostland*
—**1941** *(December 14)*: OKW issues directive that calls for "no holds barred" against partisans
—**1942** *(January)*: Order Police told to arrest only nomadic Roma in Latvia
—**1943** *(July)*: Alfred Rosenberg issues draft directive *The Treatment of the Gypsies in the Occupied Eastern Territories*
—**1943** *(November 15)*: Rosenberg issues Roma decree that orders that nomadic Roma and *Zigeunermischlinge* be treated like Jews

It is often forgotten that Europe was terrorized by two horrible dictatorships in the 1930s and 1940s—Nazi Germany and Stalinist Russia. During the early years of World War II, both countries were allies. As seen in earlier chapters, anti-Semitism had a long history in Russia, and it no doubt played a role in Soviet efforts to stamp out Jewish religious and cultural autonomy in those areas of Eastern Europe acquired during the Nazi-Soviet honeymoon between 1939 and 1941.

And though Soviet Jews suffered from ongoing policies of russification in the early years of this relationship, nothing prepared them for the German "war of annihilation" that began on June 22, 1941. Though Jews and communist activists were the principal targets of the well-planned German assault, the Nazi reign of terror soon began to envelope other groups such as the Roma, the handicapped, Soviet POWs, and others deemed enemies not only of the German state but of the Aryan race.

Traditionally, this phase of the Holocaust was viewed as the work of Heinrich Himmler and his specially trained killing squads—the *Einsatzgruppen*. But recent scholarship has expanded the list of perpetrators to include the Order Police, the Wehrmacht, and collaborators from throughout western Soviet Russia. The coordinated actions of these various military and paramilitary groups was deadly, but it took a heavy toll psychologically on the killing units and on the limited materiél re-

sources available in some sectors of recently conquered Soviet territory. Undeterred by these problems, Germany's leaders looked for more efficient ways to continue their mass murder campaign against their racial and biological enemies in the Soviet Union. In the fall of 1941, they began to experiment with new methods of extermination that would ultimately lead to the most horrendous phase of the Holocaust—the Final Solution—the program to murder all of the Jews in Europe.

Jews in Soviet-Conquered Territory

Once Stalin moved into Poland, he took a little more than half of the country. Of the 3.3 to 3.5 million Jews who lived in Poland before the outbreak of the World War II, 2.35 million were now trapped in the German sector, and from 1.3 to 1.15 million were in the Soviet zone. Another 300,000 to 350,000 Jews fled into Russian territory from German Poland during the early months of the war. Between the fall of 1939 and the summer of 1940, Russia's prewar Jewish population grew from 3.02 million to more than 5 million with the acquisition of parts of Poland, the Baltic States, Bessarabia, and northern Bukovina.[1]

Initially, many of the Jews who fled or found themselves in Soviet territory thought they were now safe from the harsh anti-Semitism of the Germans. They soon discovered, though, that Stalinist Russia was almost as anti-

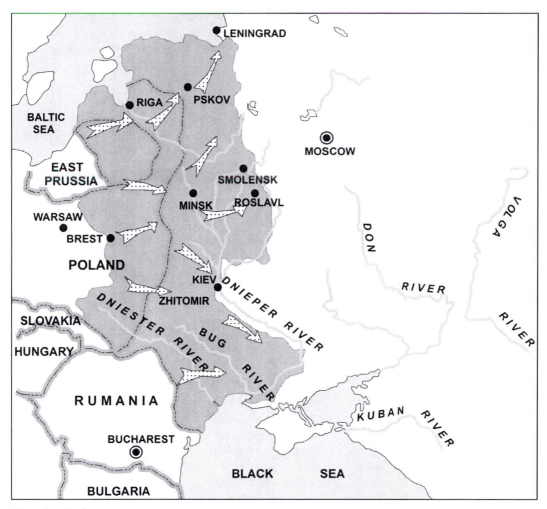

Operation Barbarossa.

Semitic as Nazi Germany. Stalin had severely persecuted the Soviet Union's Jews during the Purges in the 1930s and during the final weeks of the fighting in Poland ordered his border guards to stop Jews from trying to enter Soviet territory.

This was only a hint of other, more complex difficulties faced by Jews trapped in Soviet territory in the first year of the war. As foreigners, they quickly came under the watchful eye of Stalin's secret police, the NKVD (*Narodnyi Kommissariat Vnutrennikh Del*; People's Commissariat of Internal Affairs), who were suspicious of all refugees. By the end of 1939, Stalin integrated Soviet parts of Poland into the USSR, and its residents formally became Soviet citizens. Refugees had the choice of accepting Soviet citizenship or returning to the General Government. In the spring of 1940, the NKVD did a special "Reparation Census" to determine how many Jewish refugees lived in the USSR; the goal was to force Jewish exiles to accept Soviet citizenship. If they refused, they faced expulsion from Soviet territory. Nora Levin estimates that 250,000 or more Polish Jews were exiled to Siberia or Kazakstan because they refused to accept these terms.[2]

Most of the Jewish refugees had no jobs or homes and quickly became impoverished. The only available work was often in distant mining or industrial towns in the Urals or the Donbas, a rich mining area in the southeastern part of the country. Economically desperate and often separated from their families, some opted to return to the General Government. Stories abounded of widespread hunger and disease among those Jews who chose to remain in Russian territory. In the spring of 1940, the *New York Times* reported widespread hunger among Jewish refugees in Lvov, and a French report estimated that 200,000 hungry Jews were desperately looking for food in Galicia.[3] Stalin's decision to close or shut down some Jewish synagogues, temples, schools, and Jewish aid organizations, traditional anchors of the Jewish community, further exacerbated this situation.

To make matters worse, the NKVD often harassed Jewish intellectuals and forced some into internal exile. Jewish youths were forced to join atheistic communist organizations such as the Young Pioneers. Officials also closed Yiddish newspapers in Poland and replaced them with new, censored Soviet-Yiddish publications. They also opened new branches of the Soviet Writers' Union in Polish cities. Traditional Jewish schools were closed, replaced by new ones that were nothing more than mere instruments for Stalin's ongoing program of Sovietization. Ukrainian, Lithuanian, and Belorussian now replaced Yiddish as the language of instruction. Religious Jews suffered from a barrage of atheistic Soviet propaganda, and synagogues that remained open were often defaced with portraits of Lenin, Stalin, and other Soviet leaders.

Zwartendijk and Sugihara: Righteous Gentiles in Vilnius

Just days after Soviet troops moved into eastern Poland, Stalin consolidated control of his newly acquired sphere of influence in the Baltic States and Finland. By early October, the Kremlin had forced the three Baltic countries to accept mutual assistance pacts, arrangements that allowed the Soviet Union to establish small military bases in each country. Finland rejected Stalin's demands and quickly found itself at war with the Soviet Union. Though the Finns enjoyed some initial victories in what became known as the Winter War, they were unable to withstand the Soviet assault for very long; they capitulated in March 1940. Finland lost Karelia but retained its independence. The Baltic States were not so fortunate.

Stalin returned Vilnius (Vilna; Wilno), which had been under Polish control since 1922, to Lithuania in the fall of 1939. Lithuania's medieval capital, which some Jews lovingly referred to as the "Jerusalem of the North," was an important Jewish cultural and educational center as well as the home of the renowned Yivo Institute (*Yiddisher Visenshaftlikher Institut;* Yiddish Scientific Institute), today located in New York. Polish Jews flocked to Vilnius and Lithuania in the early months of the war.[4] When Stalin conquered the Baltic States in June 1940, Lithuania's 260,000 Jews faced a new wave of anti-Semitic persecution. Trapped as they were between the Soviet Union and Nazi Germany, many sought refuge elsewhere.

The Soviet takeover of the Baltic States in June 1940 was fast and brutal, and by early August Moscow declared the three nations the Fourteenth (Lithuania), Fifteenth (Latvia), and Sixteenth (Estonia) Soviet Socialist Republics. Vyacheslav Molotov (1890–1986), the Soviet foreign minister, ordered all foreign embassies and legations closed in each country by the end of the month. Soon after the Soviet takeover, Jewish refugees in Lithuania seeking exit visas to Palestine or the United States began flooding foreign legations. But given the chaotic situation in Kaunas, the British and the Americans were able to issue only about 755 visas. A

Chiune Sugihara. USHMM Photo No. 07624, courtesy of Hiroki Sugihara.

breakthrough came when L.P.J. de Decker (?–1948), the Dutch ambassador to the Baltic States, authorized his acting consul in Lithuania, Jan Zwartendijk (1899–1979), to issue visas to Curaçao, in the Dutch West Indies. In late July and early August 1941, Zwartendijk issued almost 2,400 visas to Jewish refugees before the Soviets forced him to close his office.

But the only way out of Soviet territory was eastward to Japan. Zwartendijk, working in league with Chiune Sugihara (1900–1986), the Japanese vice consul in Kaunas, issued Japanese transit visas for Jews holding Dutch visas to the Curaçao. But unlike Zwartendijk, who had the full support of his superiors, Sugihara had only limited authority to issue such documents, which required applicants to show adequate financial resources as well as a visa to a country other than Japan. Sugihara chose to ignore these regulations; he issued thousands of visas to Jews and others from July 29 to August 31, 1940, the date the Soviets ordered the Japanese consulate closed.

Though the visas permitted their holders to remain in Japan only for twelve days, Japanese authorities allowed many to stay much longer while they searched for alternative destinations. About half of those holding Dutch and Japanese visas were able to travel on to the United States, Palestine, and elsewhere; others went to Shanghai, home of Asia's largest Jewish community. According to Chinese sources, almost 30,000 Jews fled Europe through Shanghai during the war. In 1943, the Japanese army, which controlled Shanghai, required the city's remaining 18,000 Jews to move into a 2-square-mile area in the Hong Kou section of the city. All survived the Holocaust.[5] In 1985, Yad Vashem declared Sempo Sugihara Righteous Among the Nations (Righteous Gentile) for his heroic deeds. Twelve years later, it afforded Jan Zwartendijk the same honor. Little did those helped by Zwartendijk and Sugihara realize the horror that was about to befall those Jews unfortunate enough to be trapped in the Soviet Union in the summer of 1941.

Operation Barbarossa and Plans for Mass Murder

The German attack on the Soviet Union on June 22, 1941, began the most horrible phase of World War II and the Holocaust. From the Nazi perspective, Stalin's Russia was an "evil empire" because it was the center of world communism and was populated by large concentrations of Jews and Slavs. It is no accident that the Germans attacked the Soviet Union with a ferocity unparalleled in modern European warfare. As German air, land, and sea forces ravaged the Soviet Union and its unprepared people in the summer of 1941, specially trained killing squads, the *Einsatzgruppen,* aided by Order Police units, the Waffen-SS (Armed SS), the Wehrmacht, and willing native collaborators, began the mass murder of Jews, Roma, the handicapped, communists, and Soviet POWs. As the complexities of such mass executions began to weigh on a German political and military system used to quick blitzkrieg victories, the German leadership searched for a more efficient way of murdering their racial and biological enemies. Aided by the technological successes of the T-4 program, German leaders now planned an industry of death and slave labor that would murder millions of Jews, Roma, and others in an orgiastic blood bath driven by the best of German industry, science, and technology.

According to Franz Halder, Hitler had been thinking seriously about an invasion of the Soviet Union since the summer of 1940.[6] Initially, the invasion was scheduled for the spring of 1941. The goal was "to crush Soviet Russia in a quick campaign" and create "a cover against Asiatic Russia from the general line Volga–Archangel."[7] Beyond ideological considerations, Hitler saw great economic and strategic advantages in such an attack; he also thought, given Germany's earlier military successes, that the Reich could easily defeat Russia, particularly in light of Stalin's recent purges of the military.[8]

Preliminary military planning for the invasion of the Soviet Union began in the summer of 1940; by late October, the Wehrmacht had detailed plans for the invasion, which Hitler extensively reworked for his December 18, 1940, Operation Barbarossa directive: It envisioned a three-pronged attack led by Army Group Center under *Generalfeldmarschall* Fedor von Bock (1880–1945), which would move first against Minsk and Smolensk in a drive to take Moscow. Army Group South, under *Generalfeldmarschall* Gerd von Runstedt (1875–1953), was to move towards Kiev; Army Group North, under *Generalfeldmarschall* Wilhelm Ritter von Leeb (1876–1956), would try to take Leningrad. The Wehrmacht planned to destroy the Red Army without delay and then capture the Soviet Union's main industrial and agricultural centers. It hoped these quick victories would neutralize Soviet air threats to German territory and allow Hermann Göring's *Luftwaffe* to seize Soviet airbases; Göring would then use the bases to destroy Stalin's industrial centers deep inside Russia.

The same day that he issued the Operation Barbarossa directive, Hitler spoke to 5,000 military cadets, all future Wehrmacht and Waffen-SS officers, and reminded them of their duties to the military and to the *Volk.* He told them a biblical story in which a city was destroyed because "in the end, no one there deserved that it should any longer exist." Hitler added that the cadets were the "living banner" of the Greater German Reich "fighting for its destiny."[9] That evening, Hitler met with Himmler, and though we have no minutes of the meeting, Richard Breitman speculates that Himmler raised the subject of the SS's role in the invasion.[10]

In a meeting with his senior military commanders on March 30, 1941, Hitler told the generals that the coming attack on the Soviet Union, which was later postponed because of Germany's dual invasions of Greece and Yugoslavia, would be a "war of extermination."

He explained: "If we do not regard it as such, we may defeat the enemy, but in thirty years we will again be confronted by the communist enemy. We are not fighting a war in order to conserve the enemy."[11]

He expected army leaders to take the lead in this struggle against *"der bolschewistischen Kommissare und der kommunistische Intelligenz* [Bolshevik commissars and the Communist intelligentsia]" and told them that they "must make the sacrifice of overcoming their scruples."[12]

The forthcoming campaign [Hitler went on] would be no ordinary conflict, but a life and death struggle between two races and two ideologies; between German and Slav; between National Socialism and the criminal code of Jewish Bolshevism, which constituted the greatest threat to the future of civilization. In this struggle the German soldier was not to be bound by laws of war, nor was there any room for chivalry or out-of-date concepts about comradeship between soldiers. The ultimate objective of this war was not only the destruction of the Red Army in the field but the final elimination of the Russian-Bolshevik menace.[13]

Seven weeks later (May 19, 1941), OKW (*Oberkommando der Wehrmacht*; Armed Forces Supreme Command) issued a directive that told commanders that

1. Bolshevism is the deadly enemy of the National Socialist German people. Germany's struggle is directed against this subversive ideology and its functionaries.
2. This struggle requires ruthless and energetic action against Bolshevik agitators, guerillas, saboteurs, and Jews, and the total elimination of all active or passive resistance.[14]

This was followed by the June 6, 1941, Commissar Order, which was designed to as-

suage OKW fears about waging war against civilians. Instead, German forces could now wage war against Soviet political watchdogs assigned to Red Army units. From the German perspective, Soviet military political commissars were the driving spirit, ideologically speaking, behind Red Army units on the front lines.

COMMISSAR ORDER (JUNE 6, 1941)

In the fight against Bolshevism it is not to be expected that the enemy will act in accordance with the principles of humanity or international law. In particular, the political commissars of all kinds, who are the real bearers of resistance, can be expected to mete out treatment to our prisoners that is full of hate, cruel and inhuman.

The army must be aware of the following:

1. In this battle it would be mistaken to show mercy or respect for international law towards such elements. They constitute a danger to our own security and to the rapid pacification of the occupied territories.
2. The barbaric, Asiatic fighting methods are originated by the political commissars. Action must therefore be taken against them immediately, without further consideration, and with all severity. Therefore, when they [political commissars] are picked up in battle or resistance, they are, as a matter of principle, to be finished immediately with a weapon.[15]

From the German perspective, the Commissar Order freed German soldiers of legal responsibility for their actions against important communist operatives; other orders on June 6 said that German troops should deal ruthlessly with "restiveness" among Soviet POWs. In fairness, some German commanders, appalled by the June 6 decrees, refused to issue them to their troops. Several generals, including *Generalleutnant* Henning von Treschow (1901–1944), who later committed suicide to avoid arrest after the July 20, 1944, attempt on Hitler's life, was one of the few officers who formally protested the Commissar Order.

The Wehrmacht also established a special relationship with Himmler's SS. Earlier in the year, Reinhard Heydrich had told administrators in RSHA to plan for major police actions in the future. Simultaneously, he discussed the presence of Sipo units alongside regular army units with *Generalfeldmarschall* Walther von Brauchitsch (1881–1941), the head of the army. On March 13, OKW issued a Führer Directive that gave Himmler and the SS "*special tasks* for the preparation of the *political administration,* tasks which derive[d] from the decisive struggle that [would] have to be carried out between the two opposing political systems" in the military's areas of operations. Himmler would be acting "independently and on his own responsibility."[16] Thirteen days later, Heydrich and Quartermaster General *Generalleutnant* Eduard Wagner (1896–1944), an active participant in the plot to assassinate Hitler in 1944, worked out the details of this relationship, which Brauchitsch issued as a directive on April 28 outlining the role of Sipo and SD units in Russia. Heydrich's special commandos were to operate in army rear areas and ferret out anti-German activists. Though they remained under Heydrich's command, the Sipo and SD units had to coordinate their activities with the army to insure they did not interfere with military operations.[17] And though Brauchtisch's directive did not mention specific target groups, it was no secret who the victims would be because of the "*Flubereinigung* (clearing the field)" work of Himmler's forces in Poland and Hitler's March 30 directive to his generals, which made that clear. Such groups, though, were mentioned in the army's April 1941 "Guidelines for the Conduct of the Army in Russia," which ordered its commanders to deal ruth-

lessly and energetically with Jews, Bolshevik troublemakers, guerillas, and saboteurs.[18]

The *Einsatzgruppen*

The *Einsatzgruppen* were to be the vanguard of Nazi Germany's war against its racial, biological, and political enemies in Soviet Russia. Jürgen Matthäus estimates that by the end of 1941, from 500,000 to 800,000 Jews had been murdered in Russia, many of them by these units.[19] Planning for such murders began in March 1941, when Heydrich and his chief of personnel, *SS- Gruppenführer* Bruno Streckenbach (1902–1977), began consultations with Himmler about the selection of their top *Einsatzgruppen* officers. Once word got out that Heydrich was forming these elite units, many junior officers lobbied to join them to further their careers. The officers and men selected for the *Einsatzgruppen* were drawn from the SS, the SD, Kripo, the Order Police, and the Waffen-SS, the armed wing of the SS. Quite a few of them were attorneys.

Initially, Heydrich wanted to create three *Einsatzgruppen* units, but later added a fourth for the Romanian front. In May, those selected to serve in the units began three weeks of training at the *Grenzpolizei* (Border Police) school in Pretsch and surrounding towns. Heydrich had one final meeting with his *Einsatzgruppen* commanders just five days before the June 22, 1941, attack on the Soviet Union. *SS- Brigadeführer* Dr. Otto Ohlendorf (1907–1951), an attorney and the commander of *Einsatzgruppe* D, testified during the *Einsatzgruppen* trial in 1948 that Heydrich gave them orders "to protect the rear guard of the troops by killing the Jews, Gypsies, Communist functionaries, active communists, and all persons who would endanger the security." And though it has since been proven that Ohlendorf, in league with other trial defendants, gave false testimony to try to convince the court that they had been given specific orders on this matter, there is no question that the *Einsatzgruppen* entered the Soviet Union with a clear idea about who specifically to kill.[20] But if there were any doubts about their "tasks" in the field, Heydrich cleared them up quickly in a memo to his *Einstazgruppen* commanders a week after the invasion began. He reminded them of his orders two weeks earlier about the importance of supporting the *Selbstreinigungsbestrebungen* (self-cleansing efforts) of "anticommunist and anti-Jewish circles." On July 2, Heydrich sent a memo to his HSSPF in the east underlining the importance of encouraging such groups' activities "without leaving any trace or involvement or obligation."[21] Such orders provided the basis, for example, for the terrible massacre of Jews in the Polish town of Jedwabne by their Polish neighbors on July 10, 1941, while German police and other units remained in the background.[22]

Heydrich also told his officers that their primary goal was the "political pacification" of the areas under their control, which in turn would lead to the "economic pacification" of Soviet Russia. They were to carry out their work with "*rücksichtsloser Schärfe* (ruthless severity)."[23] Their victims were to be

Officials of the Comintern (together with professional Communist politicians in general).

Top- and medium-level officials and radical lower-level officials of the party. Central Committee and district and subdistrict committees:

People's Commissars; Jews in Party and State employment, and other radical elements (saboteurs, propagandists, snipers, assassins, inciters, etc.) insofar as they are, in any particular case, no longer required to supply information on political or economic matters which are of special importance for the further operations of the Security Police, or for the economic reconstruction of the Occupied Territories.[24]

At the end of his communiqué, Heydrich again reminded his officers that their units were to do everything possible to encourage local citizens to initiate actions against Jews and communists.[25]

These units would eventually be assisted by twenty-one battalions of *Ordnungspolizei* (Orpo; Order Police), totaling 11,000 men and some disparate *Waffen-SS* brigades, under a newly created *Kommandostab Reichsführer-SS* (Command Staff of the *Reichsführer-SS*), totaling 25,000 men. Himmler, who appointed three (later a fourth) HSSPF to oversee these units, reached an accord with the Wehrmacht on May 21, 1941, that gave him full authority over their activities in the field. Five years earlier, Himmler had reorganized the national police into two branches. The first, under Reinhard Heydrich, was the *Sicherheitspolizei* (Sipo or security police), which included the Gestapo and Kripo. The second branch, the *Ordnungspolizei*, under Kurt Daluege (1897–1946), included the *Schutzpolizei* (Schupo; urban police), the *Gendarmerie* (rural police), and the *Gemeindepolizei* (small-town police).

Initially, many Order Police recruits joined these units because it meant they could avoid serving in the Wehrmacht. However, when World War II broke out, 16,000 of the Order Police's 131,000 men were put into a police division under army control. Between 1939 and 1941, there was a growing need for troops to maintain control over those areas recently conquered by the Wehrmacht. Some Order Police units were integrated into the army's *Feldgendarmerie* (military police) units. The Order Police had the right to draft men, and by the summer of 1940 almost 250,000 men served in these units. As Christopher Browning has noted in his classic study, *Ordinary Men,* "The Order Police were quickly becoming an essential source of manpower for holding down German-occupied Europe." In the summer of 1941, there were 500 Order

The *Einsatzgruppen* in the Soviet Union[26]

Einsatzgruppez A (1941–1944; Army Group North; headquarters, Danzig; areas of operation, Estonia, Latvia, Lithuania, Leningrad district; 1,000 troops initially)

Sonderkommando 1a (1941–1944)

Sonderkommando 1b (1941–1943)

Einsatzkommando 2 (1941)

Einsatzkommando 3 (1941–1945)

COMMANDERS: *Einsatzgruppe* A's first commander was *SS- Standartenführer* Dr. Walter Stahlecker (1900–1942), a lawyer with close ties to Adolf Eichmann. Stahlecker once headed the SD in Vienna and had also served as HSSPF in the Protectorate of Bohemia and Moravia and Norway. After Stahlecker's death in a firefight with guerillas in 1942, *Einsatzgruppe* A was led by Heinz Host (1942), *SS- Oberführer* Dr. Humbert Achamer-Pifrader (lawyer; 1942–1943; 1901–1994), and *SS- Oberführer* Dr. Friedrich Panzinger (lawyer; 1943–1944; 1903–1959).

Einsatzgruppe B (1941–1944; Army Group Center; headquarters, Smolensk; areas of operation, Belorussia, Smolensk district; 655 troops initially)

Sonderkommando 7a (1941–1944)

Sonderkommando 7b (1942–1944)

Sonderkommando 7c (also *Vorkommando Moscau;* 1941–1943)

Einsatzkommando 8 (1942–1943)

Einsatzkommando 9 (1941–1943)

Teilkommando Trupp Smolensk (part of *Einsatzkommando* 9)

COMMANDERS: *SS- Obergruppenführer* Arthur Nebe (1894–1945), its first commander, studied law at the University of Berlin and later headed Kripo (*Kriminalpolizei;* criminal police under the SD). Nebe had no stomach for the mass murders in the field and returned to Berlin as head of Kripo in 1942. He was implicated in the July 20, 1944, assassination attempt against Hitler and executed in the spring of 1945. Himmler replaced him with *SS- Gruppenführer* Erich Naumann (1941–1943; 1905–1951) and, later, *SS- Oberführer* Dr. Horst Böhme (lawyer; 1943 and 1944; 1909–1945) and *SS- Standartenführer* Dr. Heinz Seetzen (lawyer; 1944; 1906–1945).

Einsatzgruppe C (1941–1944; Army Group South; headquarters, Kiev; areas of operation, southern and central Ukraine; 750 commandos initially)

Sonderkommando 4a (1942–1943)

Sonderkommando 4b (1941–1944)

Einsatzkommando 5 (1941–1942)

Einsatzkommando 6 (1941–1943)

COMMANDERS: *SS- Brigadeführer* Dr. Emil Otto Rasch (1891–1948), formerly a lawyer in Dresden, was the unit's first leader. He joined the Nazi Party in 1931 and rose quickly through the ranks of the SD and Sipo. *Einsatzgruppe* C's bloodiest action took place on September 29–30, 1941, when it murdered 33,771 Jews at Babi Yar in Kiev. Rasch, certainly one of the SS's most effective commanders, was soon ordered back to Berlin after running afoul of Himmler and Erich Koch (1896–1986), the *Reichskommissar* of the Ukraine, in the fall of 1941. He soon became head of *Kontinental Öl* (Continental Oil), which the Germans had created to exploit the petroleum resources in the east. Himmler replaced Rasch with *SS- Gruppenführer* Dr. Max Thomas (physician; 1941–1943; 1891–1945) and later Dr. Horst Böhme.

Einsatzgruppe D (1942–1943; Eleventh Army; headquarters, Piatra-Neamt, Romania; areas of operation, southern Ukraine, Crimea, Ciscaucasia; 600 troops initially)

Sonderkommando 10a (1942–1943)

Sonderkommando 10b (1943)

Einsatzkommando 11a (1942)

Einsatzkommando 11b (1941–1943)

Einsatzkommando 12 (1942–1943)

COMMANDERS: Dr. Otto Ohlendorf (1907–1951), a lawyer, commanded *Einsatzgruppe* D. He also headed the SD from 1939 to 1945. Himmler promoted him to *SS -Brigadeführer* and *Generalmajor der Polizei* after he returned to Berlin in the summer of 1942. Ohlendorf continued as head of the SD and in 1943 became Second Secretary of the Ministry of Economics. Himmler replaced him with *SS- Brigadeführer und Generalmajor der Polizei* Dr. Walther Bierkamp (lawyer; 1901–1945).

Police in the *Einsatzgruppen;* but as the murder campaign intensified, Himmler sent another 5,500 to work with Einsatzgruppen units during the early months of the German invasion.[27]

Yet these "ordinary men" were often reservists who were not infused with Himmler's brand of Nazi racial fanaticism. In the weeks before the invasion, the *Reichsführer-SS* tried to address this failing by having officers deliver propaganda lectures—designed to remind the Order Police of their responsibilities as police "soldiers"—and circulating articles and circulars on "Jews and criminality," the "blood community of the German *Volk*," and the "Greater German Reich."[28] These efforts did little, though, to clarify the confusing orders given to each Order Police battalion just before the invasion of the Soviet Union. Some received orders that specifically identified Jews as their principal enemies; others received vaguer orders, meaning they "would come to these tasks more gradually."[29] And eventually they did. Daniel Goldhagen has estimated that ultimately thirty-eight Order Police battalions with 19,000 men murdered more than 800,000 Jews between the summer of 1941 and the fall of 1943.[30]

The Wehrmacht

But there was also another group—the Wehrmacht—involved in the early mass murders in the Soviet Union. Until recently, not much had been said about the role of the Wehrmacht in the Holocaust. After the war, the Wehrmacht "became every man's bill to a clean conscience" because a myth had developed in Germany about the "clean army": "[T]he *Wehrmacht* was the millions of good people as opposed to the bad hundreds of thousands in the SS that acknowledged the burden of the German past." According to this interpretation, the Wehrmacht and its soldiers kept their distance from the Nazi regime and Hitler and fulfilled their military duties with decency and dignity.[31]

In other words, it was the Nazi Party that committed the atrocities during the Holocaust, not the good German people. This myth was shattered in Germany in 1995 with the appearance of the controversial exhibit *Vernichtungskrieg. Verbrechen der Wehrmacht 1941 bis 1944* (War of Annihilation. Crimes of the Wehrmacht 1941–1944), which clearly showed that German soldiers played a "direct and massive" role in the "implementation of the Final Solution."[32]

Efforts in the 1980s to cast some blame on the military for its role in the Holocaust centered around charges against senior field commanders. At most, it was argued, although the German army certainly helped create the conditions militarily that helped make the Final Solution possible, the average German soldier knew little about the atrocities committed by Himmler's forces in Russia and elsewhere. He was too busy fighting and surviving.

More recent studies, particularly by Wolfram Wette, Hannes Heer, Klaus Naumann, Christian Streit, and Omer Bartov have suggested a more active role for the Wehrmacht in the Final Solution. By August 1941, Professor Streit added, the Wehrmacht had become an active supporter of the mass killings by the *Einsatzgruppen* and the Order Police. Professor Bartov added that the average German soldier, a product of years of Nazi racial indoctrination, was particularly susceptible to the ideological underpinnings of the mass murders. For many German soldiers, Goebbels's stereotypical images of Jews, Slavs, and political commissars seemed to come to life in the unimaginable horror of the Russian battlefields. Reality was now turned inside out, and whatever moral valves they took into battle was soon cast aside. Countless letters from German soldiers to their families talked again and again about dirty, evil Jews and Soviets, often lumping the two groups together into a particularly threatening Bolshevik horde.[33]

Yet the "active support" of such "actions" does not directly implicate the Wehrmacht in the murders themselves; the Operational Situation Reports prepared by Heydrich's staff from *Einsatzgruppen* field reports for distribution to high-ranking party, military, and business leaders do. One, for example, noted the involvement of a Wehrmacht unit in a "pacification action" in the Vitebsk area that resulted in the deaths of nineteen Jews in early September, and a similar report from *Einsatzgruppen* B stated that the 10th Company of the 354th Infantry Regiment helped "liquidate" 118 partisans, most of them "Jewish activists." In Smolensk, the intelligence officer from Second Army headquarters asked *Sonderkommando* 7b to help it in its "fight against the partisans." More often than not, the so-called partisans were usually captured Jews.

Operational Situation Report No. 58 of August 20, 1941, applauded the special ties between the army and the *Einsatzgruppen:*

> The relationship with the German Army is as cordial as it was previously. In particular, Army circles show a steadily growing interest in and understanding of tasks and matter concerning the work of the Security Police. This could be observed particularly during the executions. On the other hand, the Army itself endeavors to further the tasks relating to the Security Police. Thus, all the offices of the Einsatzgruppe are continually receiving reports from the Army concerning arrested communists officials and Jews. It even happens at times that the Security Police is the last resort of the Army. Thus, for example, on August 5 [19]41, the local military commander of Radomyshl called for help of the Einsatzkommando 4a requesting support, since

he was unable to cope with the prevailing conditions.[34]

Other *Einsatzgruppen* reports document similar levels of cooperation with the Wehrmacht.

Equally damning, of course, is the excessively high death rate of Soviet POWs, who were initially captured and interned by the Wehrmacht. Soviet POWs are not often seen as Holocaust victims, though they suffered horribly at the hand of the Wehrmacht and Himmler's killing squads. *General* G. F. Krivosheev has estimated that more than half of the 4.5 million Soviet POWs died in captivity compared to 37.5 percent of German POWs in Soviet camps and 3.6 percent of the Anglo-American POWs in German camps. Those who died were shot by the Wehrmacht or SS units, murdered in death or concentration camps, or slowly starved to death in Wehrmacht camps. Increasingly, the line between Jews, political commissars, and other Soviet citizens was slowly blurred in the Nazis' brutal war against the Soviet Union.[35]

The German Invasion of the Soviet Union

The German invasion of the Soviet Union began during the early morning hours of June 22, 1941. Despite ample warning of Hitler's plans, the attack surprised Stalin and other Soviet leaders. Months earlier, Hitler had made a prediction to his generals: "[W]hen Barbarossa commences the world will hold its breath and make no comment."[36] Several hours after the attack began, Joseph Goebbels went on German radio and read Hitler's lengthy proclamation announcing the invasion. It was a conflict aimed at opposing "the conspiracy of the Jewish-Anglo-Saxon warmongers and likewise the Jewish ruling powers in the Bolshevik control state at Moscow." According to Hitler, this was no longer a war to protect individual countries. Instead, it involved "the securing of Europe and the salvation of all." Finally, he reminded his soldiers that he was placing "the fate and future of the German Reich and our *Volk*" in their hands. "May the Lord Almighty help us especially in this battle."[37]

Within days, the Soviet press and various propaganda outlets were referring to the conflict as the *Velikaya Otechestvennaya Voina Sovetskogo Naroda* (Great Patriotic War of the Soviet People), putting it on the same historical plateau as the Patriotic War of survival in 1812 against Napoleon Bonaparte. The Russo-German conflict was a war that would, according to the most recent scholarship, result in the deaths of from 25 to 27 million Soviet citizens. Almost two thirds of those who died were civilians, the rest military. Between 1 and 1.5 million Jewish civilians died in the Soviet Union between 1941 and 1945, most of them genocidal victims of the Germans. Another 200,000 Jews died serving in the Red Army. About 30,000 to 35,000 Roma died during this conflict out of a 1941 population of 207,000. More than a million German soldiers died in the Russo-German conflict, a third of total German losses in World War II.[38] Such high casualties, of course, show that this was no ordinary war; instead, it was a "war of annihilation."[39] A 1985 Soviet account of the 1941–1945 war, *Velikaya Otechestvennaya Voina* (Great Patriotic War), best captures Russian attitudes towards the "Fascists" and the atrocities they committed during this conflict. According to *Marshal* Vasily Chuikov (1900–1982), Twice Hero of the Soviet Union: "The Nazi rulers absolved their officers and soldiers in advance from any responsibility for the crimes committed on Soviet soil, having trained a multimillion army of robbers, rapists, sadists and murderers. The army acted as it had been trained. The Nazis exterminated 10 million Soviet people on temporarily occupied territory. Those cutthroats killed everyone within their reach—children, old men and women."[40]

The Germans were initially surprised by the weak resistance they encountered as they swept into Soviet territory: "[M]ilitary developments in the East are excellent beyond all our expectations," Joseph Goebbels noted in his diary on June 24. "Our new weapons are carrying all before them. The Russians are emerging from their bunkers trembling, unfit for interrogation for a day afterwards."[41] Such observations, both in the field and in Germany, strengthened general attitudes about Slavic racial inferiority. As German victories mounted, even some of Hitler's skeptical generals began to sense that victory was in sight and that little was left to do but to mop up pockets of Soviet resistance. The Germans captured more than 600,000 Soviet POWs in the first six weeks of fighting; by early October 1941, the Red Army had suffered more than 2 million casualties.[42] German losses were considerably smaller. The Germans now controlled a vast swath of western Soviet territory that ran from Estonia on the Baltic Sea through Moldavia in the south. On July 14, seemingly assured of victory, Hitler issued guidelines to reduce the size of the army: "[M]ilitary domination of the European area after the defeat of Russia allows us to reduce the size of the army accordingly," he noted.[43] He then ordered a shift in arms production away from field weapons to U-boats and airplanes.

Yet in the midst of this euphoria, there were hints of trouble. As the Germans moved deeper into Russian territory, they met stronger Soviet resistance. German casualties also began to mount; by the end of September Soviet forces had killed, wounded, or captured more than half a million German soldiers. Most who survived were exhausted, and few reserves were on hand to replace them. German intelligence had miscalculated Red Army reserves and by the fall of 1941, the Soviets began to strengthen their resistance to the German assault, an indication that in the early months of fighting Hitler had failed to achieve his principal military goal: the destruction of the Red Army.

Despite these losses, the Germans forged ahead with administrative plans to govern some of the more secure areas of western Russia. On July 17, Hitler laid out the guidelines for the administration of the newly conquered eastern lands. Those areas not integrated directly into Reich, Romanian, or Finnish territory were to be placed under the *Reichsministerium für die besetzen Ostgebiete* (RmfdbO; *Ostministerium*; Omi; Reich Ministry for the Occupied Eastern Territories) under Alfred Rosenberg. This area was later subdivided into two *Reichskommissariate*, the *Reichskommissariat Ostland* (Baltic States and Belorussia) under Hinrich Lohse (1896–1964) and the *Reichskommissariat Ukraine* under Erich Koch. Eastern Galicia became part of the General Government, and Bialystok was integrated into East Prussia. Romania, which had committed most of its military forces to the attack on the Soviet Union, was rewarded with Transnistria.

Early German Killing Operations in the Soviet Union

As the Wehrmacht swept into the Soviet Union, Himmler's killing units quickly began their operations, hindered only by the rapid move of German forces into Russian territory. The activities of these units can be divided into two major phases—June through December 1941, and January 1942 to the summer of 1943. The actions of Himmler's troops in the first phase of mass killing was determined by the speed of German conquests, the problems associated with numerous victims, and the large number of Soviet POWs. With the exception of *Einsatzgruppe* A, which operated in the Baltic States, the rest of the *Einsatzgruppen* moved so quickly through other parts of Russia that they often left large Jewish and other targeted populations behind. The second phase of the mass

killing operations was much more clinical and designed to "cleanse" the recently conquered areas of all unwanted Jews, Roma, and the handicapped. This second wave of mass killings would involve far more troops and would also include clearing the ghettos in Poland and the occupied parts of the Soviet Union.

Heydrich's Operational Reports underscored the breadth of the initial massacres and the rationales used to justify them. Almost from the outset, they depicted Jews as saboteurs and partisans who were a constant threat to the safety of German troops. A report dated July 6, 1941, noted, for example, that *Einsatzgruppe* A had shot 201 Jews in Garsden for helping Soviet border guards who were "repulsing the German attacks." In a separate report, the unit informed Berlin that Latvian auxiliary police had arrested 1,125 Jews and executed most of them. *Einsatzgruppe* B reported that it had "liquidated" a number of Jews in Minsk for burning down their own homes, and *Einsatzgruppe* D's *Kommando* 10a reported in early August that it had shot 97 Jews and taken another 1,756 hostages because of "riots and attacks" against the German army in Yambol, in southern Ukraine. The Jewish prisoners were to be "executed on the slightest pretext." Elsewhere in Ukraine, *Einsatzgruppe* C informed Berlin in mid-July that Sipo units had killed 7,000 Jews for "inhuman atrocities."[44]

The threat of partisan activity was real, though not in the early stages of the German invasion. On July 3, 1941, Stalin called for anti-German actions behind enemy lines, though such activities would not have an impact on the German war effort for some time. But by early 1942, anti-German partisan activity was such that Joseph Goebbels warned Wehrmacht forces in Belorussia and Ukraine to be on their guard against such units. On August 18, 1942, OKW issued Führer Directive No. 46, "Instructions for the Intensified Fight Against Banditry in the East," which ordered Himmler and the military to do everything possible to "substantially exterminate" the "intolerable banditry in the East" by the winter of 1942–1943. Himmler was to be in charge of such efforts in the *Ostministerium,* and *Generalleutnant* Franz Halder (1884–1972), chief of the *Oberkommando des Heeres* (OKH; Army High Command), was responsible for such activities in areas under military control.[45]

Himmler's units intensified their efforts against what the *Reichsführer SS* insisted were nothing more than "bandits." He also appointed a Plenipotentiary for Combating Bandits who was to coordinate SS efforts against guerillas in Soviet territory. The Wehrmacht did the same. On November 11, 1942, OKW issued its "Combat Directive for Anti-Bandit Warfare in the East." Partisans and anyone who helped them were to be executed, preferably by hanging. The directive stated that troops should avoid "sentimental considerations" when dealing with "bandits," and it added a new category of victims—women.[46]

Hitler discussed the growing problems with partisans in a meeting with some of his top military leaders at his *Wolfsschanze* (Wolf's Lair) headquarters in East Prussia on December 1. The "essential thing" in the war against guerillas, he thought, was that "whatever succeed[ed]" was right. The purpose of the German campaign against partisans was "to exterminate the guerillas and re-establish order." Anything, he went on, that "assist[ed] in the annihilation of the guerillas [would] be considered right" and anything that did not help the campaign would be wrong. And if the partisans, he added, chose to use women and children as covers, then the "officer or NCO must be authorized, if necessary, to shoot them down ruthlessly." All that mattered in such a situation was that he "wipe out the gang."[47]

Two weeks later, Wilhelm Keitel, who attended this meeting as head of OKW, issued a new directive that noted the current battle

against partisans had "nothing to do with soldierly chivalry or with the agreements of the Geneva Convention." It was a "war with no holds barred," meaning that troops were authorized to use "every means, even against women and children" to achieve victory. Furthermore, "no German involved in the war against the bandits [would] be subject to disciplinary action or a courtmartial for his behavior in the war against the bandits and their accomplices."[48]

Collaboration in Latvia, Lithuania, and Ukraine

The August 18 OKW directive also encouraged Himmler and Halder actively to use reliable "native units" against partisans. They operated in support of the *Einsatzgruppen* in Ukraine, Lithuania, Poland, and elsewhere, and sometimes independently of Himmler's special killing squads. Many of these units had already proven their loyalty and reliability in the early days of the German invasion, particularly when it came to dealing with Jews. The Jews in Kaunas, Lithuania's capital, suffered horribly at the hands of the *Einsatzkommandos* and local collaborators. On June 23, 1941, *SS- Obersturmbannführer* Dr. Erich Ehrlinger (1910–?), an attorney who was commander of *Einsatzkommando* 1b, asked local nationalist groups for help in dealing with the city's Jews.[49] In his diary, Avraham Tory described what happened next:

Like a pack of bloodthirsty dogs the Lithuanian partisans prowled the streets and courtyards, seizing panic-stricken Jews who had managed to find various hiding places. These Jews were dragged away in groups to unknown destinations.

Through holes in roofs and apertures in window shutters, other Jews watched the spectacle taking place on the streets; Jews, lined up in long columns, were being beaten with truncheons on every part of their bodies;

the Lithuanians were spitting in their faces. Sick people were being carried by their relatives, since they were too weak to stand on their feet after the treatment accorded to them by the Lithuanians. Other Lithuanians stood on the sides of the street and mocked the Jewish tragedy.

Gangs of Lithuanian partisans would surround one of two houses; some of them guarded the entrance while the rest raided the apartments. At gunpoint they would drive the occupants outside, take what was worth taking, and depart, issuing threats about the impending destruction of the Jews. Many Jews were murdered inside their apartments. Robbery and looting followed. There were cases where women were raped at the very moment when looting and murder were in progress. One house was suddenly full of partisans. Curses and screams: "You damned Zhids, we've been shot at from this house; admit it, or we'll kill you." One partisan fires his revolver and pandemonium breaks out. They start looking for men. "Where did all the men disappear to, you damned Bolsheviks! We'll find them before long." They start dragging pieces of furniture, beds and tables; closets are being emptied of their contents. Amid the turmoil the partisans grab the valuables and vanish. They move from house to house in this fashion leaving destruction and death in their wake. In Slobodka [Vilijampolé; Jewish settlement across the Niemen River from Kaunas that became the site of Kaunas ghetto] the murder had been going on for two days. Pogrom! They shave off the beards of rabbis and yeshiva students; heads are bashed, arms are twisted.[50]

The Germans transformed the local units into five companies of auxiliary police. Two were attached to *Einsatzgruppe* A. One of the Lithuanian companies worked as guards at the VII Fort, one of the concentration centers for Jews in Kaunas. Every day, the Lithuanian guards would round up groups of Jewish women and children and torture or rape them before executing them. The Lithuanians referred to the atrocities as "going to peel potatoes." The Germans and their Lithuanian auxiliary troops murdered 10,000 Jews in Kaunas during the first six weeks of the German occupation, many of them at the VII Fort.[51]

Fifty-seven thousand Jews were trapped in Vilnius when German forces occupied the city on June 24. By early July, *Einsatzkommando* 9, aided by 150 Lithuanian auxiliary troops, began to ship Jewish males to the site of a former Soviet fuel dump outside of the city at Ponary, where they were murdered and dumped into pits. The Germans and their collaborators murdered 5,000 Jews at Ponary in July, and another 8,000 between August 31 and September 3, 1941. A teacher, Sima Katz, described one of the later massacres:

We were imprisoned there until Thursday [September 11, 1941]. At 2 a.m. the courtyard of the prison was suddenly flooded with lights. We were loaded onto trucks, each of which had 50–60 people and several armed Lithuanians with rifles. We were thus driven in the direction of Ponar. We reached a wooded spot . . . lay down, tired. . . . Not far away we heard volleys of rifle fire. The Lithuanians began marshaling us into groups of ten, and led the tens into the hillocks from which the firing was heard. Suddenly it became clear to us what this was all about. The women began pleading with the Lithuanians . . . to no avail . . . when their turn came, they rose up, quiet and despairing, without protests or pleas. . . . Thus family after family proceeded on their final journey. Our turn came at about 5:30. I set my face for the walk, my daughters with me . . . we were lined up and I felt how my elder daughter slipped out of my hand.[52]

During the next three years, the Germans and the Lithuanians would murder between 70,000 and 100,000 Jews at Ponary.

Execution of Jewish women at Liepaja, Latvia, 1941. USHMM Photo No. 19124, photographer: Carl Stout; courtesy of Zentrale Stelle der Landesjustizverwaltungen.

The Germans and their collaborators committed similar atrocities in Latvia. In early July, Ehrlinger's unit moved northward to Daugavpils, Latvia, where he was dismayed to discover that Latvian nationalists had murdered only "a few thousand Jews." With the help of local Latvian auxiliary police, Ehrlinger and his subordinate, *SS- Obersturmbannführer* Joachim Hamann (1913–1945), oversaw the butchery of more than 9,000 Jews by the third week of August. Some of the worst killings took place on July 9–10, 1941, when *Einsatzkommando* 1b, in league with Latvian police units, murdered 1,000 Jews. The Latvian press explained that the Jews were killed because they had been trying to destroy the Latvian nation and its cultural traditions.[53] Andrew Ezergailis thought that local Latvians were initially indifferent towards Daugavpils's Jews, and had to be "tricked" by Ehrlinger to kill them. One of his favorite "tricks" was to make local auxiliary police round up Jews and use them to dig up the graves of Latvians murdered or executed earlier by the communists. Ezergailis explained that this was a way of "associating the Jews with communism, most specifically with the killings that the Soviets carried out in Latvia" after they took over the country in the summer of 1940.[54]

Similar acts of collaboration and mass murder took place in Ukraine. Two factions of the *Orhanizatsiya Ukrainskykh Natsionalistiv* (OUN; Organization of Ukrainian Nationalists), a revolutionary group that advocated Ukrainian independence, sought German support for their nationalistic aspirations. One, under Stefan Bandera (1909–1959), played a prominent role in creating two Ukrainian battalions, *Nachtigall* (Nightingale) and *Roland*, which were attached to the Wehrmacht on the eve of the Soviet invasion. The *Nachtigall* battalion wore Wehrmacht *feldgrau* (field gray), and *Roland* troops wore uniforms similar to those worn by members of the Galician wing of

Execution of Ukrainian Jews at Vinnitsa, Ukraine. USHMM
Photo No. 64407, courtesy of Libray of Congress.

of a defensive struggle, we have suffered bloody sacrifices, and we suffer especially at present through the frightful slaughter of so many of our compatriots. We request that we be allowed to march shoulder to shoulder with the legions of Europe and with our liberator, the German Wehrmacht, and therefore we ask to be permitted to create a Ukrainian military formation."[56]

After the war, the *Nachtigall* battalion was accused of taking part in the mass murder of 4,000 Jews in Lvov in early July 1941. This charge has entered the literature as a fact, though Alfred M. DeZayas has noted in his study on the Wehrmacht's War Crimes Bureau that the persecution and murder of Jews in Lvov by German and Ukrainian forces must not be confused with the murder of 4,000 imprisoned Ukrainian nationalists by the Soviet NKVD on the eve of the German occupation of the city in the summer of 1941. And it was 7,000 Jews, not 4,000, that the Germans executed in Lvov in the early days of the occupation.[57]

The Germans disbanded the OUN units at the end of 1941 because of their political unreliability; they integrated some of their troops into the *Ukrainische Hilfspolizei Schutzmannschaft* (UAP; Ukrainian Auxiliary Police Constabulary), which served under the German police. UAP units took part in roundups in the Kraków ghetto in the fall of 1942 and the brutal closing of the ghetto on March 14, 1943. One of the Jewish inmates in Kraków's Płaszów concentration camp, Jack Mintz, described the Ukrainian guards there, who wore the black uniforms of the *Allgemeine* (general) SS, as "the best killers."[58] In 1943, the SS created the 14. *Waffen-Grenadier-Division der SS (ukrainische Nr. 1)* (14th Waffen Grenadier division of the SS Galizien (1st Ukrainian). Its 80,000 troops were drawn from Poland's large Ukrainian community and it was unique among Waffen-SS units because its oath of loyalty to

the Ukrainian army several decades earlier.[55] In late June, Bandera declared a new Ukrainian state. The Germans responded by arresting Bandera and sending him, along with some of his lieutenants, to Berlin for interrogation. Bandera's movement was quickly suppressed and he was sent to the Sachsenhausen concentration camp, outside Berlin.

OUN's other faction, under Andry Melnyk (1890–1964), tried to take advantage of Bandera's misfortunes, but soon ran afoul of the Wehrmacht because of its own political ambitions. But before this happened, Melnyk, in league with other prominent Ukrainian nationalist leaders, sent an appeal to Hitler on July 6, 1941, requesting "the honor of taking part in the crusade against Bolshevik barbarism." He continued: "In twenty-one years

Hitler was based on the fight against Bolshevism. It also had Ukrainian Byzantine Catholic and Ukrainian Orthodox chaplains in the division, a rarity in the Waffen-SS at this time. It was commanded by German and Ukrainian officers. After the war, this division was also accused of war crimes.

Though these charges remain controversial, there is no question that UAP units committed horrible atrocities during the war, particularly at Babi Yar, outside Kiev. The Germans occupied Kiev on September 19, 1941; a week later, it was decided to massacre the city's remaining 60,000–70,000 Jews in retaliation for attacks against Wehrmacht units. *Sonderkommando* 4a under *SS-Standartenführer* Paul Blobel (1894–1951), was given responsibility for the executions, aided by Waffen-SS, Order Police, and UAP troops. On September 27–29, crude signs appeared throughout the Jewish parts of Kiev: "Kikes of the city of Kiev and surroundings! On Monday, September 29, you are to appear by 7 a.m. with your possessions, money, documents, valuables, and warm clothing at Dorogozhitskaya Street, next to the Jewish cemetery. Failure to appear is punishable by death. Hiding Kikes is punishable by death. Occupying Kike apartments is punishable by death."

One Jewish family, fearful of the roundup, tried to escape:

> The mother decided to take her two children and leave for the countryside. Drunken Germans stopped them at Galitsky Market and murdered them all cruelly. Before the mother's eyes, they decapitated one child and then killed the second. Insane with grief, the woman clasped the two dead children to her body and began to dance. When they had sated themselves with this spectacle, the Germans killed her as well. At this point the father of the family arrived on the spot where his family had just perished. He shared their fate.[59]

Once Kiev's Jews reached the roundup point, they were marched to Babi Yar in the northwest part of the city. *The Black Book*, a collection of eyewitness testimony, describes what happened next.

> Streams of people flowed into the endless human current on Lvov Street, while German patrols stood on the sidewalks. So enormous was the mass of people moving along the pavement from early morning until late at night that it was difficult to cross from one side of the street to the other. This procession of death continued for three days and three nights. People walked, stopping once in a while, embraced each other without words, said goodbye, and prayed.
>
> An entire office operation with desks had been set up in an open area. The crowd waiting at the barriers erected by the Germans at the end of the street could not see the desks. Thirty to forty persons at a time were separated from the crowd and led under armed guard for "registration." Documents and valuables were taken away. The documents were immediately thrown to the ground, and witnesses have testified that the square was covered with a thick layer of discarded papers, torn passports, and union identification cards. Then the Germans forced everyone to strip naked: girls, women, children, old men. No exceptions were made. Their clothing was gathered and carefully folded. Rings were ripped from the fingers of the naked men and women, and these doomed people were forced to stand at the edge of a deep ravine, where the executioners shot them at point-blank range. The bodies fell over the cliff, and small children were thrown in alive. Many went insane when they reached the place of execution.[60]

On the last two days of September 1941, the Germans and their collaborators executed 33,771 Jews at Babi Yar. But this was only the beginning. Babi Yar now became a favored

German killing site, and during the next two years, 70,000 Jews, Roma, and Soviet POWs were murdered there.

Efforts after World War II to memorialize the horrible deaths at Babi Yar met strong Soviet resistance. Though driven by Stalin's anti-Semitism and the desire to hide the true number of Soviet deaths during the war, Soviet officials explained that it was official policy not to differentiate between various groups murdered by the Fascists during the Great Fatherland War. Yevgeni Yevtushchenko (1933–) broke this taboo in 1961 when he published his poem "Babi Yar" to protest official Soviet plans to build a soccer field and park at the execution site. The following year, Dmitri Shostakovich (1906–1975) used Yevtushchenko's poem as the basis for his new Thirteenth Symphony. In 1966, Anatoly Kuznetsov (1929–1975), who lived through the German occupation of Kiev, published a "documentary" novel, *Babi Yar,* that dealt with the occupation and the massacres at Babi Yar. He said at the end of the novel that he had suffered from nightmares for years after completing *Babi Yar,* yet he felt that "we dare not forget these cries [of victims], both because such things are unforgettable and because these problems of the Babi Yars hang over mankind like a black cloud."[61]

In 1966, Soviet authorities permitted a small monument to be placed at the killing site, though it mentioned only "victims of fascism." They erected a more striking monument there in 1974, though nothing was said about the Jews who died there. In fact, nothing was done to memorialize the Jewish dead there until 1991, when a large stone Menorah was placed at the memorial site.

Babi Yar
by Yevgeny Yevtushchenko

No monument stands over Babi Yar.
A drop sheer as a crude gravestone.
I am afraid.
    Today I am as old in years
as all the Jewish people . . .

Now I seem to be
    a Jew.
I seem to be
    Dreyfus . . .
I am behind bars.
    Beset on every side.
Hounded,
    spat on,
        slandered.
I seem to be then
    a young boy in Byelostok.
Blood runs, spilling over the floors.
The bar-room rabble-rousers
give off a stench of vodka and onion.
A boot kicks me aside, helpless.
In vain I plead with these pogrom bullies.
while they jeer and shout,
    "Beat the Yids, Save Russia!"
some grain-marketeer beats up my mother.
O my Russian people!
How vile these anti-Semites—
    without a qualm
they pompously called themselves
"The Union of the Russian People"!
I seem to be
    Anne Frank
transparent
    as a branch in April . . .
The wild grasses rustle over Babi Yar.
The trees look ominous,
    like judges.
Here all things scream silently,
    and, baring my head,
slowly I feel myself
    turning gray.
And I myself
    am one massive, soundless scream
above the thousand thousand buried here.
I am
    each old man
        here shot dead.
I am
    every child
        here shot dead.
Nothing in me
    shall ever forget!

The "Internationale," let it
    thunder
when the last anti-Semite on earth
is buried forever.
In my blood here is no Jewish blood.
In their callous rage, all anti-Semites
must hate me now as a Jew.
For that reason
    I am a true Russian![62]

Hungarian and Romanian Collaboration

These special Ukrainian, Latvian, and Lithuanian units were not the only forces that collaborated with the Germans during this phase of the Holocaust. Large numbers of Hungarian and Romanian troops also took part in the invasion of the Soviet Union, and they soon joined in the murderous activities sweeping western Russia. In July 1941, the Hungarian government of Regent Miklós Horthy (1868–1957) and his prime minister, László Bárdossy (1890–1946), agreed, in a gesture of solidarity with Nazi Germany, to round up 30,000 to 35,000 "alien" Jews. They sent about half this group to Kamenets-Podolski in Ukraine, where they were murdered by the SS on August 27 and 28, 1941. And although there is no clear evidence that Hungarian troops participated in the massacre, reports do exist of Ukrainian involvement.

Romanian forces operating in Soviet territory in the summer of 1941 also played a role in the massacre of Jews. *Einsatzkommando* 10 reported that Romanian forces had committed "considerable excesses" against Jews in the Belzy area. On July 10, this German unit reported that the Romanians had rounded up four hundred Jews "of all ages" and were going to execute them for attacks against Romanian soldiers. *Generalleutnant* Walter Wittke (1888–?), the commander of the German army's 170th Infantry Division, convinced the Romanians to execute only fifteen.[63] Later that day, an *Einsatzkommando* unit found the

fifteen Jews in the Belzy ghetto and shot those who were still alive. In Chernovtsy, *Einsatzkommando* 1b reported that Romanian troops, which considered northern Bukovina to be Romanian territory, were "inclined to exterminate the upper echelon of Ukrainian leadership" to insure full "spiritual" control over the region. The Germans also encouraged the Romanians "to take measures concerning the Jewish question" in the area.[64] On August 3, 1941, *Einsatzgruppe* D reported that "in cooperation with the Romanian police in Chernovtsy 682 of the approximately 1,200 Jews arrested were killed." Romanian soldiers in other parts of their zone of operation also looted and terrorized local populations.[65]

The worst Romanian atrocities, though, took place in Odessa and Transnistria. The Black Sea port of Odessa had a prewar Jewish population of 180,000, though almost half had fled before the city fell to the Fourth Romanian Army on October 16, 1941. Almost immediately after taking Odessa, Romanian intelligence units and *Einsatzkommando* 11b murdered 8,000 Odessans, most of them Jews. A week later, new massacres took place after partisans blew up Romanian army headquarters in Odessa. In response, the Romanian dictator, Marshal Ion Antonescu (1882–1946), ordered the city's commandant, *General de brigadă* Constantin Trestioreanu (1891–1983), to take retaliatory measures against Jews and communists in the city. Romanian troops hanged 5,000 Jews throughout the city and marched 20,000 more to Soviet antitank ditches at Dalnik, where they were murdered. Troubled with the slow speed of the executions, Trestioreanu ordered his soldiers to force the remaining Jews into warehouses along the harbor and machine gun them to death through holes cut into the side of the warehouse walls. Alexa Neacsu, an officer who witnessed the massacres, testified during Antonescu's war crimes trial in 1946:

Marshal Ion Antonescu and Adolf Hitler. USHMM Photo No. 80527, courtesy of National Archives and Records Administration, College Park.

saw weapons leveled at them, they would disappear for a moment from the window, only to reappear after a few seconds, making the same signals to the soldiers and turning their backs so as not to see for a moment when they were fired at. The operation lasted into the night, when even more gruesome scenes were visible by the light of the flames. Those who appeared were naked, because they had torn off their clothes, which had caught fire. Some of the women threw children out of the windows. I remember one scene when a boy four or five years old who had been thrown out of a window wandered for five to ten minutes with his hands up among the corpses, because the Romanians soldiers did not want to fire on him.[66]

Dr. Wilhelm Filderman (1882–1963), the respected leader of the *Unicenea Evreilor Romani* (UER; Union of Romanian Jews), sent Antonescu a letter protesting the massacre. Antonescu's response:

Observing that by machine gun fire alone they could not succeed in killing all those who were inside, those who were in charge of this operation and who were visibly worn out and worried went into another conference and resorted to spattering the warehouses with kerosene for lighting and gasoline and setting them afire. When the fire broke out, some of those who were still inside the warehouses and who were only slightly wounded or unscathed tried to escape by jumping out the windows or to get out over the roof. The soldiers had a general order to the effect that [if] anyone should come out [they] should be shot. Some who were inside, as if to escape from the fire, appeared at the windows and made signs to shoot them, pointing with their hands to their heads or hearts; but when they

In two successive petitions you have written me about the "enormous tragedy" and have "implored" me in emotional words mentioning "conscience" and "humaneness.". . . In order to inject yourself as an intervening tragedian you emphasize that this measure [transfers to Transnistria] "is death, death, death without guilt, without any guilt other than that of being a Jew.". . . I understand your pain, but [you] especially must understand, once for all, that my [concern] was for a whole nation. Will you think, have you thought about what happened in our souls last year when Bessarabia was evacuated? [At Hitler's request, Romania ceded Bessarabia and northern Bukovina to Stalin on June 28, 1940.] The hatred with which the people of your religion treated us during the retreat from Bessarabia, how they receive[d] us when we returned. In direct response to the generosity with which you have been accepted into our society and treated, you Jews, joining the Soviet commissars, by terror without equal, witnessed by the Russian prisoners, pushed the Soviet troops in the region of Odessa to a useless massacre, only in order to cause us new losses. . . . Do you ask yourself about such hatred on the part of some Russian Jews with whom I have never had anything to share? But this hatred of theirs belongs to all of you. It is your hatred.[67]

Like Hitler, Antonescu blamed the Jews for the horrors that they now faced.

The Roma and the Handicapped

The Roma

Though Jews and communist leaders were the Germans' principal victims in the early stages of their onslaught against the Soviet Union, the Roma and the handicapped were soon caught up in the genocidal war sweeping the country. Comparatively speaking, the Roma in the Soviet Union enjoyed a modicum of acceptance relative to the status of the Roma in other parts of Central and Eastern Europe in the 1920s and 1930s. In the early years of Soviet power, the Roma, along with the country's other ethnic minorities, were given a modest amount of freedom to develop their own cultural and educational institutions in return for support of communist ideals and policies. This enabled Roma activists to address some of the deeper social, economic, and educational problems that had plagued the Roma before 1917.

Soviet leaders set aside land for Roma settlements to encourage an end to their nomadic lifestyle, though some Roma resisted such efforts. Between 1926 and 1928, almost 20 percent of the Soviet Union's 150,000 to 200,000 Roma settled in the Crimea, Ukraine, the northern Caucasus, and elsewhere. Collectively, these efforts stimulated a Roma cultural and educational awakening that saw the development of a Roma Cyrillic alphabet and the opening of several Romani (the language of the Roma) language schools. The most lasting cultural innovation during this period, though,

was the opening of the Gypsy Theater "Romen" in Moscow in 1931. The Theater "Romen," which still exists, was seen as a vehicle to help preserve Roma culture and help integrate the Roma more deeply into the fabric of Soviet society. Artists from the Moscow Jewish Theater played an important advisory role in the early years of Theater "Romen"'s operations, though Roma artists remained its driving spirit.

Unfortunately, the gains made by the Roma during this period were lost in the 1930s as Soviet minority policies began to emphasize *sliiane* (drawing together), which really meant russification. Authorities closed the Roma language schools, and nothing was published in Romani between 1937 and 1989. The Theater "Romen" somehow managed to survive this cultural purge, though thousands of Roma fell victim to Stalin's purges or were forced to settle on collective farms.

The Soviet Union's Roma population grew with the acquisition of eastern Poland, the Baltic States, Bessarabia, and northern Bukovina during the Soviet-German honeymoon between 1939 and 1941. By the summer of 1941, about 207,000 Roma lived in the Soviet Union. The Roma in the newly acquired parts of the USSR suffered principally from efforts to force them to adopt a new Soviet lifestyle, which caused the Roma in some parts of western Russia, particularly the Baltic States, to see the Germans as liberators. When war came, such attitudes changed quickly once the Roma realized that the Germans considered them racial enemies.

Though initial *Einsatzgruppen* reports concentrated primarily on Jewish and communist victims, by the fall of 1941 they had begun to discuss the murder of Roma. Although there are no documents indicating specific instructions for the murder of Roma in the Soviet Union, *Einsatzgruppen* commanders were well versed in Nazi attitudes towards this "asocial" group and had no difficulty encouraging their troops to kill Roma as part of the broader campaign against an individual or group consid-

ered a threat to the Nazi state or to military security. Otto Ohlendorf, the commander of *Einsatzgruppe* D, testified at his trial that he saw no
difference between Jews and Roma, whom he
considered dire threats to Wehrmacht security
in Russia. The Roma, he went on, had a history
of involvement in "espionage organizations
during [military] campaigns." As such, they
were "notorious bearers of intelligence."[68] *SS-
Obersturmbannführer* Dr. Otto Bradfisch
(1903–1994), an attorney who commanded
Einsatzkommando 8, thought that the May 19,
1941, OKW directive and the June 6, 1941,
Commissar Order "provided for the liquidation
of Jews and 'other racially inferior elements.'"[69]

In early August, *Einsatzkommando* 8 reported that it was involved in "actions . . . to
render harmless . . . criminals, asocial elements
and Asiatics with contagious diseases." According to Wolfram Wette, "criminal" was a "cam-
ouflage" word used by military commanders
to describe Roma.[70] At the end of August, one
unit informed Berlin that it had shot six Roma
for looting, and on September 23, *Einsatzkommando* 8 reported that it had given "special
treatment" to twenty-three Roma for theft and
"terrorizing the population of the countryside."[71] During the same period, *Sonderkommando* 4b reported that it had "liquidated" six
Roma asocials, and *Sonderkommando* 4a noted
that it had stopped thirty-two Roma in mid-
September and searched their wagons, where
they found pieces of German equipment.
Since the Roma did not have adequate identification papers, and could not explain where
they had got the German goods, they were
shot.[72] Such an approach was becoming the
norm among various *Einsatzgruppen* units:
At a meeting of military police officials and
army officers in November 1941, Otto Bradfisch argued that if males of military age who
were stopped at checkpoints could not produce identification papers and "had been
itinerating since the beginning of the war,"
they should be considered partisans and
"liquidated as asocials and a threat to public

safety."[73] Though the *Einsatzgruppen* were involved in most of the killings of Roma during
this period, at least one Wehrmacht commander in Byelorussia issued orders to kill all
captured Roma "on the spot."[74]

In the Crimea, *Einsatzgruppe* D wrote that
its "work with Jews [was] rendered much
more difficult because of the Karaite/Krim-
chaks [two Jewish sects in the Crimea] and
Gypsy problem."[75] Consequently, the unit intensified its executions of Roma and between
November 16 and December 15, 1941, and informed Berlin that it had "liquidated" 824
Roma. By early January 1942, Ohlendorf reported that his unit had completely "solved"
the Roma problem in the Crimean city of
Simferopol; he also noted that the local population had "generally welcomed" the action.
Yet he continued to report the executions of
"asocials" in the city through the end of January.[76] He mentioned public support again
in his report about the deportations of
12,000 to 13,000 Jews, Roma, and Krimchaks
in the Crimea in December and the first few
weeks of January 1942. The deportations
frightened the local residents, who did everything possible to show their support of the
Germans.[77]

Einsatzgruppe D continued its roundup
and executions of Roma well into the spring
of 1942. It executed 421 Roma and asocials in
the last two weeks of February and another
"810 asocial elements, Gypsies, mentally ill
and saboteurs" in the first half of March. It
shot another 261 asocials, including Roma,
later that month. By April 8, Ohlendorf was
proud to report that the northern Crimea was
now free of "Jews, Krimchaks, and Gypsies."[78]

The roundup and murder of the Roma
was just as horrible in Ukraine. Anatoly
Kuznetsov painted a vivid picture of German
brutalization of the Roma in *Babi Yar.*

The fascists hunted the Gypsies as if they
were game. I have never come across anything official concerning this, yet in the

Ukraine the Gypsies were subject to the same immediate extermination as the Jews.

Passports had decisive importance. They were checked in the streets and during house searches. Next in importance was appearance. Persons with dark hair and eyes and long noses were better off not showing themselves in the streets. Whole tribes of Gypsies were taken to Babi Yar, and they did not seem to know what was happening to them until the last minute.

According to Kuznetsov, there was a popular but dark saying in Kiev at the time: "Jews *kaputt*, Gypsies too; and the Ukrainians, and then you."[79]

Similar murders of Roma took place in other parts of western Russia. At the end of 1942, *SS- Brigadeführer* Kurt von Gottberg (1896–1945), who soon became the *SS- und Polizeiführer* (SSPF; SS and Police Chief) for Belorussia, led a special antipartisan unit formed to hunt down and "destroy . . . every bandit, Jew, Gypsy and suspected partisan" in the region as enemies of the Reich. In its first sweep of the region, Gottberg's unit murdered 2,658 Jews and thirty Roma. During a second operation, it murdered another 1,265 Jews and twenty-four Roma, though Guenter Lewy noted that "undoubtedly many more Gypsies were killed than documented."[80]

All these massacres were brutal. But those perpetrated by *Sonderkommando* 7a, commanded by *SS- Obersturmbannführer* Dr. Albert Rapp (1908–?), an attorney, were particularly barbaric. At his war crimes trial in 1965, Rapp testified that he considered Jews and Roma "depraved and asocial people, dirty and infested with disease, who had to be exterminated." In scenes reminiscent of Babi Yar, Rapp oversaw the massacre of numerous Roma women and children in the Smolensk area in the early spring of 1942.

Despite the cold weather, the victims had to take off their outer garments before being shot. Mothers had to carry their babies to the ditch prepared as a mass grave. There the executioners snatched them from the arms of their mothers, held them at arm's length, shot them in the neck, and then tossed them into the ditch. According to many witnesses, the shooting was carried out with such haste that many victims fell or were thrown into the ditch while they were still alive. "The tangled pile of bodies kept on moving and rose and fell."[81]

During the *Einsatzgruppen* trial, one of the prosecution team's attorneys, James E. Heath, asked Otto Ohlendorf why his unit had executed innocent Jewish and Roma children. What threat, Heath wanted to know, did a child constitute to the "security of the Wehrmacht"? Though Ohlendorf claimed he never saw children killed by his units, he did think that it was easy to explain the murders from the perspective of "permanent security," meaning that "because the children would grow up and surely, being the children of parents who had been killed . . . would constitute a danger no smaller than that of the parents." Furthermore, he added, his orders had included the execution of children.[82]

The *Einsatzgruppen* were not the only units involved in these mass murders. Himmler also had at his disposal various battalions of his *Ordnungspolizei* and units from his *Kommandostab Reichsführer-SS*. Beyond this, the Wehrmacht became increasingly involved in the mass executions of Jews, Roma, and others. The Wehrmacht had two special units, the *Feldpolizei* (military police) and the *Geheime Feldpolizei* (secret field police), that were directly involved in what Bernd Boll, Hannes Heer, and Walter Manuschek called "campaigns of annihilation."[83] During the war in Russia, these units, as well as regular Wehrmacht units, became involved in the devastating genocidal campaign in the Soviet Union. In what Omer Bartov has called the "perversion of discipline," some in the Wehrmacht began to condone "'official' and 'organized' acts of murder against enemy civilians, POWs, and property," which led to "'wild' requisitions and indiscriminate shootings explicitly forbidden by their commanders."[84]

Initially, the Wehrmacht simply rounded up Roma, Jews, and others and turned them over to Himmler's killing squads for "follow up."[85] In one instance, a Wehrmacht officer tried to protect sedentary Roma. On November 21, 1941, *General der Infantrie* Max von Schenckendorff (1875–1943), the commander of the Rear Area, Army Group Center, ordered that Roma who had an established residence for two years and "were not suspected of any political or criminal wrongdoing" were to be exempt from execution.[86] It is doubtful whether this order originated with Schenckendorff, who had earlier established a training course on antipartisan warfare for units in his area. Several members of the *Einsatzgruppen* later mentioned the order in their war crimes trial testimony after the war and said they thought it had originated with Himmler, who was fascinated with certain groups of German Roma.

In reality, such orders did little to protect the Roma in any battle area. Three days after Schenckendorf had issued his order about sedentary Roma, a separate Wehrmacht directive in Belorussia discussed the fate of Jews and Roma. Jews were to "disappear from the countryside" and "Gypsies had to be annihilated."[87] And after the Wehrmacht investigated the execution of 128 Roma by Army Group North's 281st Security Division in the spring of 1942, it did little to punish the unit. The 281st Division had been ordered to treat all Roma as partisans. Once the investigation was concluded, the commander of the division was told that the Roma partisans order conflicted with Schenckendorff's November 21 order. The unit's commander understood this, but thought that its actions were justifiable. The Roma, he explained, were "in almost all cases connected with partisans and such a link had to be assumed in this case as well" even though he had no proof that the Roma in question were partisans. But what really justified the killings, he

added, was the absence of partisan attacks after his division had executed this particular group of Roma.[88] In the end, "security" needs took precedence over orders from above, meaning that field units continued to murder any Roma they deemed a threat to Wehrmacht security. This was the thrust of a report sent to the heads of the Wehrmacht's *Feldpolizei* in the Soviet Union on August 25, 1942:

> The appearance of Gypsy bands is a major threat to the pacification of the territory as their members are roaming the country as beggars and render many services to the partisans, providing them with supplies, etc. If only part of these Gypsies who are suspected or convicted of being partisan supporters were punished, the attitude of the remainder would be even more hostile towards the German forces and support the partisans even more than before. It is necessary to exterminate these bands ruthlessly.[89]

The Roma fared no better in those portions of Soviet territory now under German civilian control. This was particularly true in the Ostland, which included the Baltic States, parts of Belorussia, and the *Reichskommissariat Ukraine*. Though Alfred Rosenberg administered these areas, Himmler's various units operated freely and usually independently of Rosenberg's authority. In late December 1941, *SS- Gruppenführer und Generalleutnant der Polizei* Georg Jedicke (1887–1969), the head of the Order Police in the Ostland, convinced Hinrich Lohse, the *Reichskommissar* for the Ostland, to write and back-date a decree that would help justify the murder of Roma in the Ostland, particularly Latvia. Lohse's December 4 decree stated:

> Gypsies who wander about the countryside represent a twofold danger:
>
> 1. as carriers of contagious diseases, especially typhus

2. as unreliable elements who neither obey the regulations issued by German authorities nor are willing to do useful work

There exists well-founded suspicion that they provide intelligence to the enemy and thus damage the German cause. I therefore order that they are to be treated like the Jews.[90]

Though Jedicke's forces were supposed to do no more than arrest Roma and turn them over to the Security Police, Lohse's decree provided his units with the cover they needed to murder Roma throughout the Ostland. Jedicke's units, though, did not differentiate between settled and nomadic Roma and turned them all over to Sipo units for execution.

This led *SS- Standartenführer* Karl Friedrich Knecht, the head of the Order Police in Latvia, to issue a directive in January 1942 that ordered his units to arrest only nomadic Roma. Knecht's order stated that settled, regularly employed Roma who presented no criminal or political threat to their communities were exempt from arrest and property seizure. On April 3, he reminded his officers that only *vagabundierende Zigeuner* (wandering Gypsies) were to be arrested.

Knecht's directive did little to halt the widespread arrest and murder of Roma in Latvia and other parts of the Ostland. In March 1942, a group of sedentary Roma in Frauenburg asked Ostland officials in Riga for work and noted that they were responsible citizens who owned their own homes and sent their children to local schools. Unfortunately, they told members of Ostland's Political Department they were not able to haul wood, their principal occupation, because their horses had been taken. The Political Department asked the HSSPF office how they should respond. They were told that a special personal arrangement had been reached between Lohse and *SS- Gruppenführer und General* Friedrich Jeckeln (1895–1946), the HSSPF in the Ostland, on the "Gypsy ques-

tion," which would be resolved by the police. When the Political Department asked Lohse's office for specifics, it sent them a copy of his December 4, 1941, decree.

Ostland officials faced similar problems on June 11, 1942, when Otto Bräutigam (1895–1992), deputy chief of the political section of the *Ostministerium,* told Lohse that Alfred Rosenberg intended to deal more firmly with the Roma question in the occupied eastern territories. Bräutigam asked Lohse whether the Roma should now be treated as Jews. He also wanted to know how many settled and nomadic Roma lived in the Ostland, their occupations, and the number of *Zigeunermischlinge* there. Bräutigam sent a similar request to the *Kommissariat Ukraine.* Lohse responded on July 2, though he did not say anything about treating the Roma like Jews. He did talk about the continual problems his men faced with nomadic Roma, particularly in Latvia, and mentioned his own decree of December 4. He considered nomadic Roma "specialists in horse stealing" and argued that currently "the removal of the Gypsies [was] irrevocably linked to police measures against typhus." Lohse's response became the basis of a draft decree, *The Treatment of the Gypsies in the Occupied Eastern Territories,* which Rosenberg hoped would develop into a new set of regulations dealing with the Roma. It proposed that "Gypsies who have their residence or regular stopping place in the Occupied Eastern Territories are to be treated as Jews, unless they possess foreign nationality. No distinction is to be made between settled and nomadic Gypsies. Gypsies of mixed race are as a rule to be treated as Jews, particularly when they live in a Gypsy fashion or are not socially integrated."[91]

Ultimately, the discussion in the *Ostministerium* seemed to coincide with Himmler's thinking about the plight of sedentary German Sinti in the Greater Reich. By 1943, Rosenberg's ministry decided against equating Roma with Jews and instead proposed that all

Roma be rounded up and placed under armed guard in "special camps and settlements."[92]

There was general agreement on these regulations throughout the Ostland, and, on June 11, the *Generalkommissar Lettlund* (Latvia), Otto-Heinrich Drechsler (1895–1945), informed his superiors that to "put all Gypsies into work camps [could] only be welcomed, especially since the Gypsies in Latvia [were] not only work-shy but also a criminal and politically tainted element."[93] Jeckeln obliquely criticized Drechsler for his reply and reminded him that Sipo was responsible for dealing with the Roma in Latvia. That fall, Jeckeln told Lohse that Himmler had decided that settled Roma and Roma *mischlinge* were to be treated like everyone else in the Ostland and that nomadic Roma and nomadic *Zigeunermischlinge* were to be treated like Jews and sent to concentration camps. On November 15, 1943, Rosenberg's office finally issued a decree based on Himmler's earlier policies for dealing with the Roma: "Gypsies and Zigeuner-Mischlinge who reside or have their usual abode in the occupied eastern territories and are sedentary are to be treated like regular inhabitants. All itinerating Gypsies and Zigeuner-Mischlinge in the occupied eastern territories are to be assigned the same status as the Jews [*sind den Juden gleichzustellen*] and are to be put into concentration camps."[94]

As will be seen in the next chapter, these policies were linked to Himmler's decision in late 1942 to send all but a select group of German Sinti to Auschwitz.

The Handicapped

Little has been written about the mass murder of the handicapped during the German invasion of the Soviet Union. Yet by the fall of 1941, references to such actions increasingly appear in *Einsatzgruppen* reports, underlining the totality of the racial and biological war being waged by the Germans in Russian territory. Early references to the execution of the handicapped center around what the Ger-

mans termed "asocials," meaning hardened criminals and Roma, who by German law could be put in mental hospitals. Once the Germans did begin to execute Soviet citizens confined to mental institutions, they justified these actions by accusing the "communists" of arming retarded and mentally ill patients and somehow training them as saboteurs.

Einsatzkommando 5a reported that it had executed twenty-two mentally retarded people in the Ukrainian villages of Ulianov and Uledovka. These mental patients, the *Kommando*'s report went on, had been trained by local NKVD operatives as saboteurs to blow up bridges and railway tracks. *Einsatzkommando* 5a claimed that these individuals, despite their mental challenges, had "enough energy for their criminal activities."[95] *Einsatzkommando* 3 noted that it, along with a detachment of Latvian auxiliary police, had executed 544 "insane persons" at the Aglona mental hospital on August 22, 1941. The unit, after consultation with the hospital's director, agreed to release ten "partially cured" inmates after they had been sterilized.[96]

To justify their actions, the *Einsatzgruppen* also accused mentally challenged individuals of armed resistance. *Sonderkommando* 1b executed 87 "insane persons" who had "armed themselves and roamed the countryside looting." Their efforts were "incited" by communist partisans.[97] *Sonderkommando* 7b reported that the Red Army had armed all the inmates in Chernigov's Asylum for the Insane. When it entered the city, it discovered that the inmates were "marching down the streets marauding." The German unit killed twenty-one former inmates immediately; then, with the help of local citizens, they began to capture others and return them to the mental hospital, where they would be "treated according to the usual procedure," meaning execution. About three weeks later, *Sonderkommando* 4a reported that the asylum's director had requested that it "liquidate" 270 inmates, which it did promptly. Other *Einsatzgruppe* B units reported the execution of 632 "mentally deficient" individuals in Minsk and 836 in Mogilev.[98]

Occasionally, some of the inmates in these asylums were Jews. *Einsatzkommando* 5 reported that it had "liquidated" three hundred Jews at an institution in Kiev, an action, its report noted, that "represented a particularly heavy psychological burden" on the commandos involved in the executions. Regardless, the unit continued to murder the city's handicapped patients. Between January 10 and February 6, 1942, *Einsatzkommando* 5 murdered 400 inmates at the city's Igrin mental hospital and another 320 at the Vasilkovska mental institution.[99]

As the war in Russia progressed, the Wehrmacht also began to play a role in the murder of the handicapped. In the fall of 1941, the headquarters of the Sixth Army under *Generalleutnant* Walther von Reichenau (1884–1942), approved *Sonderkommando* 4b's request to murder some of the inmates in Poltava's mental institution. Reichenau, a virulent anti-Semite who not only approved of the *Einsatzgruppen's* actions but encouraged his units to do everything possible to support them, needed the food produced by the asylum's farm for the area's three military field hospitals. Problems arose when the director of the asylum explained that such executions would stir up the local population. *SS- Sturmbannführer* Fritz Braune, the commander of *Sonderkommando* 4b, worked out a solution: Families would be told that 565 of the asylum's "incurables" were to be transferred to a better institution in Kharkov; instead, this group was taken outside the city and shot. The assumption was that remaining inmates would be "released shortly." In the meantime, the Sixth Army took over the asylum and its farmlands. The Wehrmacht forced the two hundred people who remained incarcerated to work in the institution's food processing plant. It distributed the clothing and other personal items of the dead inmates to the army's three field hospitals. Elsewhere in the region, Himmler's units murdered another 1,500 handicapped patients in various mental institutions.[100]

The Germans also used some handicapped patients from Minsk and Mogilev in one of the Third Reich's first mass death experiments in the fall of 1941. Himmler, who had witnessed an execution in Minsk in mid-August, asked Arthur Nebe (1894–1945), the head of Kripo and the commander of *Einsatzgruppe* B, to see how effective dynamite was in killing a large group of people. In early August, Nebe ordered *SS- Obersturmführer* Dr. Albert Widman (1912–?), a T-4 support specialist who had long advocated the use of carbon monoxide as a killing agent, and the head of the *Referat Chemie* (Chemical Analysis Department) at Sipo's *Kriminaltechnisches Institut* (KTI; Technical Institute for the Detection of Crime), to come to Smolensk and conduct the experiments. Widman, aided by his assistant, Hans Schmidt (1892–1975), also brought an explosives expert with him. Nebe, who insisted on using handicapped patients from the Novinki mental hospital in Minsk in the dynamite trial, wanted civilians to conduct the "experiment" because "he could not ask his troops to shoot these incurably insane people."[101]

The first experiment took place in mid-September. Widman and Schmidt locked a group of asylum inmates in a pill box and blew it up with dynamite. It took two charges to blow up the pill box and kill everyone inside. The explosions were so powerful that they scattered body parts everywhere, and even obliterated the surrounding trees. The next day, Nebe decided to change tactics and, following Widman's advice, locked inmates from an asylum in Mogilev into a sealed room, where they were asphyxiated with carbon monoxide fumes piped in from a car and truck parked just outside. As will be seen in the next chapter, asphyxiation was quickly becoming a favored Nazi method of mass death.

The handicapped, along with Jews, Roma, and other Soviet minorities, were also murdered at the Pathological Institute in Kiev from the summer of 1941 until March 1942. Dr. Wilhelm Gustav Schueppe (1910–?) headed a special unit of ten physicians and ten SD operatives dressed as medics at the Institute. Schueppe told his U.S. Army interrogator in the spring of 1945 that the goal of his unit was the "liquidation of the 'life unworthy of life people.'" He added that he was absolutely "convinced of the righteousness of destroying" such individuals, though he did not believe in destroying the lives of "the upper classes of those inferior races, especially Jews."[102] Later in his statement, he added: "I believe in this system. It is comparable to pruning the tree, thereby removing the old undesirable branches in order to produce the highest yield. In a nation this system must be carried out to prevent decadence."[103]

According to Schueppe, his unit used morphine injections to "liquidate" from 110,000 to 140,000 individuals deemed "life unworthy of life." Their bodies were then trucked to a crematory outside of the city.

Conclusion

The German decision to initiate its mass murder campaign against Jews and others in the Soviet Union grew out of policies dating back to the early years of the Nazi state that had persecuted, isolated, sterilized, "euthanized," and murdered various groups deemed unfit to live in an expanding Nazi empire. As they did in Poland, Germany's leaders sought to use war to mask the genocidal nature of the campaign of death in Russia. They reminded their invading forces of the special nature of the new war of survival, a conflict that pitted the superior Aryan Germans against an atheistic, inferior race of Slavic peoples led by an atheistic, Jewish-dominated Bolshevik dictator. Everyone, soldiers and civilians alike, were their enemies. And to rationalize what would become a flood of death that swept the Soviet Union in the early months of the attack, the German leadership instilled deep fear of partisan attacks in the minds of their invading troops. This fear became the justification used by many soldiers and their commanders, whether they be *Einsatzgruppen* or Wehrmacht, to murder select groups at will once they entered Russia.

But it was not just Germans who entered the Soviet Union with such passions. Two of Germany's allies, Hungary and Romania, also played an important role in the invasion. And while there are serious questions about the role of the Hungarians in the mass murders, there are none about the Romanians, who contributed most of their army to the invasion and were more than willing to kill Jews and others at will in their areas of control. The Germans also found some Latvians, Lithuanians, and Ukrainians who shared the Germans' hatred of the Jews, Roma, and the handicapped. Such collaboration only deepened Germany's commitment to eliminate those deemed unfit to live in Hitler's growing eastern empire.

These efforts were frighteningly successful. And though Jews and communist activists were the principal targets of the Germans in the early months of the invasion, other groups such as the Roma and the handicapped soon were caught up in the web of genocidal murder enveloping Russia. In the midst of these "successes," the German leadership became troubled by the psychological and matériel costs of these "actions" on units in the field. Within months after invading the Soviet Union, Himmler and others began to explore new ways of eliminating a Jewish presence in Russia. The next chapter will look at Nazi efforts to find an economical and more efficient way to murder the Jews, first in Russia and Poland and later in all of Europe. The new machinery of death that they developed would enable German leaders to plan a Final Solution of the "Jewish problem" in Europe. Eventually, other minorities were also caught up in this broader campaign of murder enveloping Europe, though Jews would remain the Germans' principal victims.

SOURCES FOR FURTHER STUDY AND RESEARCH

Primary Sources

Arad, Yitzhak, Israel Gutman, and Abraham Margaliot, eds. *Documents on the Holocaust.* Translated by Lea Ben Dor. Lincoln and Jerusalem: University of Nebraska Press and Yad Vashem, 1999.

"Directive No. 46: Instructions for Intensified Action Against Banditry in the East." Fuehrer Headquarters. August 18, 1942. http://www.geocities.com/Pentagon/1084/hitler_directives/dir46.htm?200623.

Domarus, Max, ed. *1939–1940.* Vol. 3 of *Hitler: Speeches and Proclamations, 1932–1945: The Chronicle of a Dictatorship.* Translated by Chris Wilcox. Wauconda, IL: Bolchazy-Carducci, 1997.

_____. *1941–1945 with Indices.* Vol. 4 of *Hitler: Speeches and Proclamations, 1932–1945: The Chronicle of a Dictatorship.* Translated by Chris Wilcox. Wauconda, IL: Bolchaazy-Carducci, 2004.

Dorian, Emil. *The Quality of Witness: A Romanian Diary, 1937–1944.* Edited by Marguerite Dorian. Translated by Mara Soceanu Vamos. Philadelphia: Jewish Publication Society, 1982.

Ehrenburg, Ilya, and Vasily Grossman. *The Black Book: The Ruthless Murder of Jews by the German-Fascist Invaders Throughout the Temporarily-Occupied Regions of the Soviet Union and in the Death Camps of Poland during the War, 1941–1945.* Translated by John Glad and James S. Levine. New York: Holocaust Library, 1981.

The Einsatzgruppen Reports. Edited by Yitzhak Arad, Shmuel Krakowski, and Shmuel Spector. New York: Holocaust Library, 1989.

The Goebbels Diaries, 1939–1941. Translated and edited by Fred Taylor. New York: G. P. Putnam's Sons, 1983.

Halder, Generaloberst [Franz]. *Kriegstagebuch: Bearbeitet Hans-Adolf Jacobsen.* 3 vols. Stuttgart: W. Kohlhammer Verlag, 1962–1964.

The Memoirs of Field-Marshal Wilhelm Keitel, Chief of the German High Command, 1938–1945. Edited by Walter Gorlitz. New York: Cooper Square Press, 2000.

Noakes, Jeremy, and Geoffrey Pridham, eds. *Foreign Policy, War and Racial Extermination.* Vol. 2. *Nazism 1919–1945: A History in Documents and Eyewitness Accounts.* New York: Schocken Books, 1988.

Nuremberg Trial Proceedings. Monday, 10 December, 1945, 338. The Avalon Project at Yale Law School. http://www.yale.edu/lawweb/avalon/int/proc/12–10–45.htm.

Rosenberg, Alfred. *Memoirs of Alfred Rosenberg.* Translated by Eric Posselt. Chicago: Ziff-Davis, 1949.

Testimony of Schueppe, Dr. Wilhelm Gustav. April 14, 1945. http://library.lawschool.cornell.edu/donovan/show.asp?id=481.

Thomas, Georg. *Geschichte der deutschen Wehr- und Rüstungswirtschaft (1918–1943/45).* 2 vols. Boppard am Rhein: Harald Boldt Verlag, 1966.

Tory, Avraham. *Surviving the Holocaust: The Kovno Ghetto Diary.* Edited by Martin Gilbert. Translated by Jerzy Michalowicz. Cambridge, MA: Harvard University Press, 1990.

Trials of War Criminals before the Nuernberg Military Tribunals Under Control Council Law No. 10, vol. 4, *Nuernberg, October 1946–1949.* Washington, DC: United States Government Printing Office, 1950.

Warlimont, Walter. *Inside Hitler's Headquarters, 1939–1945.* Translated by R. H. Barry. Novato, CA: Presidio Press, 1964.

Secondary Sources

Altshuler, Modechai. *Soviet Jewry Since the Second World War: Population and Social Structure.* New York: Greenwood Press, 1987.

Arad, Yitzhak. *Ghetto in Flames: The Struggle and Destruction of the Jews in Vilna in the Holocaust.* New York: Holocaust Library, 1982.

Armstrong, John. *Ukrainian Nationalism.* New York: Columbia University Press, 1963.

Bartov, Omer. *Hitler's Army: Soldiers, Nazis, and War in the Third Reich.* New York: Oxford University Press, 1991.

Breitman, Richard. *The Architect of Genocide: Himmler and the Final Solution.* New York: Alfred A. Knopf, 1991.

Browning, Christopher R. *Ordinary Men: Reserve Police Battalion 101 and the Final Solution in Poland.* New York: HarperCollins, 1992.

_____. *The Origins of the Final Solution: The Evolution of Nazi Jewish Policy, September 1939–March 1942.* Lincoln and Jerusalem: University of Nebraska Press and Yad Vashem, 2004.

Butunaru, I. C. *The Silent Holocaust: Romania and Its Jews.* New York: Greenwood Press, 1992.

Cesarani, David. *The Final Solution: Origins and Implementation.* London: Routledge, 1996.

Chodakiewicz, Marek Jan. *The Massacre in Jedwabne, July 10, 1941: Before, During, After.* New York: Columbia University Press, 2005.

Chuikov, V. I., and V. S. Ryabov. *Velikaya Otechestvennaya*. Moscow: Izdatel'stvo "planeta," 1985.

Conquest, Robert. *The Great Terror: A Reassessment*. New York: Oxford University Press, 1991.

Cooper, Matthew. *The Nazi War Against Soviet Partisans, 1941–1944*. New York: Stein and Day, 1979.

Cowell, Alan. "The Past Erupts in Munich as War Guilt Is Put on Display. *New York Times,* March 3, 1997.

Crowe, David M. *The Baltic States & the Great Powers: Foreign Relations, 1938–1940*. Boulder: Westview Press, 1993.

_____. *Oskar Schindler: The Untold Account of His Life, Wartime Activities, and the True Story Behind the List*. Boulder: Westview Press, 2004.

Dallin, Alexander. *German Rule in Russia, 1941–1945: A Study of Occupation Policies*. 2nd ed. London: Macmillan, 1981.

Deletant, Dennis. *Hitler's Forgotten Ally: Ion Antonescu and His Regime, Romania 1940–1944*. New York: Palgrave Macmillan, 2006.

DeZayas, Alfred M. *The Wehrmacht War Crimes Bureau, 1939–1945*. Lincoln: University of Nebraska Press, 1979.

Dupuy, Trevor N. *A Genius for War: The German Army and General Staff, 1807–1945*. Garden City, NY: Military Book Club, 2002.

Ellman, Michael. "Soviet Deaths in the Great Patriotic War: A Note—World War II." *Europe-Asia Studies* (July 1994): 1–8. http://www.findarticles.com/p/articles/mi_m3955/is_n4_v46/ai_15664726/print.

Ezergailis, Andrew. *The Holocaust in Latvia, 1941–1944*. Riga and Washington, DC: The Historical Institute of Latvia and the United States Holocaust Memorial Museum, 1996.

Friedlander, Henry. *The Origins of Nazi Genocide: From Euthanasia to the Final Solution*. Chapel Hill: University of North Carolina Press, 1995.

Goldhagen, Daniel. *Hitler's Willing Executioners: Ordinary Germans and the Holocaust*. New York: Alfred A. Knopf, 1996.

Gross, Jan. *Neighbors: The Destruction of the Jewish Community in Jedwabne, Poland*. Princeton, NJ: Princeton University Press, 2001.

Gutman, Israel, ed. *Encyclopedia of the Holocaust*. 4 vols. New York: Macmillan, 1990.

Hamburg Institute for Social Research. *Crimes of the German Wehrmacht: Dimensions of a War of Annihilation, 1941–1944*. Hamburg: Hamburg Institute for Social Research, 2004.

_____. *The German Army and Genocide*. Translated by Scott Abbott. New York: New Press, 1999.

_____. *Vernichtungskrieg. Verbrechen der Wehrmacht 1941 bis 1944*. Hamburg: HIS Verlag, 1996.

Harrison, Mark. "Counting Soviet Deaths in the Great Patriotic War: Comment." *Europe-Asia Studies* 55, no. 6 (2003): 939–944.

Hayes, Michael. "Counting Soviet Deaths in the Great Patriotic War: A Note." *Europe-Asia Studies* 55, no. 2 (2003): 303–309.

Heer, Hannes. "Killing Fields: The Wehrmacht and the Holocaust in Belorussia, 1941–1942." Translated by Carol Scherer. *Holocaust and Genocide Studies* 11, no. 1 (Spring 1997): 79–101.

Heer, Hannes, and Klaus Naumann, eds. *War of Extermination: The German Military in World War II, 1941–1944*. New York: Berghan Books, 2004.

Hitchins, Keith. *Rumania, 1866–1947*. Oxford: Oxford University Press, 1994.

Howell, Edgar M. *The Soviet Partisan Movement, 1941–1944*. Washington, DC: Department of the Army, 1956.

Ioanid, Radu. *The Holocaust in Romania: The Destruction of Jews and Gypsies Under the Antonescu Regime, 1940–1944*. Chicago: Ivan R. Dee, 2000.

Kenrick, Donald, and Grattan Puxon. *The Destiny of Europe's Gypsies*. New York: Basic Books, 1972.

Kenrick, Donald, ed. *In the Shadow of the Swastika: The Gypsies During the Second World War*. Hatfield, UK: University of Hertfordshire Press, 1999.

Kershaw, Ian. *Hitler: 1936–1945: Nemesis*. New York: W. W. Norton, 2000.

Krivosheev, G. F., ed. *Soviet Casualties and Combat Losses in the Twentieth Century*. London: Greenhill Books, 1997.

Kuznetsov, Anatoly. *Babi Yar: A Documentary Novel*. Translated by Jacob Guralsky. New York: Dell, 1967.

Levin, Nora. *The Jews in the Soviet Union Since 1917: Paradox of Survival*. 2 vols. New York: New York University Press, 1988.

Levine, Hillel. *In Search of Sugihara*. New York: Free Press, 1996.

Lewy, Guenter. *The Nazi Persecution of the Gypsies*. Oxford: Oxford University Press, 2000.

MacLean, French L. *The Field Men: The SS Officers Who Led the Einsatzkommandos: The Nazi Mobile Killing Units*. Atglen, PA: Schiffer Military History, 1999.

Matthäus, Jürgen. "What About the 'Ordinary Men?' The German Order Police and the Holocaust in the Occupied Soviet Union." *Holocaust and Genocide Studies* 10, no. 2 (Fall 1996): 134–150.

Medoff, Rafael. "Chairman Mao, Holocaust Rescuer? Not Quite," 1–2. http://www.wymaninstitute.org/articles/2003–120-mao.php.

Mitcham, Samuel W., Jr., and Gene Mueller. *Hitler's Commanders: Officers of the Wehrmacht, the Luftwaffe, the Kriegsmarine, and the Waffen-SS.* New York: Cooper Square Press, 2000.

Paldiel, Mordechai. *Diplomat Heroes of the Holocaust.* Jerusalem: KTAV, 2007.

"Poland-Jewish Plight." *New York Times,* March 15, 1940, 10.

Polonsky, Antony, and Joanna B. Michlic, eds. *The Neighbors Respond: The Controversy Over the Jedwabne Massacre in Poland.* Princeton: Princeton University Press, 2003.

Rhodes, Richard. *Masters of Death: The SS-Einsatzgruppen and the Invention of the Holocaust.* New York: Alfred A. Knopf, 2002.

Rich, Norman. *Hitler's War Aims: Ideology, the Nazi State, and the Course of Expansion.* New York: W. W. Norton, 1973

Shanghai Municipal Tourism Administration Commission. *Forever Nostalgia: The Jews in Shanghai.* Translated by Deng Xinyu. Shanghai Municipal Tourism Administration Commission, 2000.

Stokes, Lawrence D. "From Law Student to Einsatzgruppen Commander: The Career of a Gestapo Officer." *Canadian Journal of History* (April 2002): 1–24. http://findarticles.com/p/articles/mi_qa3686/is_20024/ai_n9027171/print.

Stola, Dariusz. "Jedwabne: Revisiting the Evidence and Nature of the Crime." *Holocaust and Genocide Studies* 17, no. 1 (Spring 2003): 139–152.

Swain, Geoffrey. *Between Stalin and Hitler: Class War and Race War on the Dvina, 1940–1946.* London: Routledge, 2004.

Werth, Alexander. *Russia at War, 1941–1945.* New York: E. Dutton, 1964.

Westermann, Edward B. *Hitler's Police Battalions: Enforcing Racial War in the East.* Lawrence: University of Kansas Press, 2005.

Wette, Wolfram. *The Wehrmacht: History, Myth, Reality.* Translated by Deborah Lucas Schneider. Cambridge, MA: Harvard University Press, 2006.

Wixman, Ronald. *The Peoples of the USSR: An Ethnographic Handbook.* Armonk, NY: M. E. Sharpe, 1988.

CHAPTER 7

The "Final Solution," 1941–1944

Death Camps and Experiments with Mass Murder

CHRONOLOGY

- **1940** *(August 27)*: Heinrich Himmler orders creation of Auschwitz concentration camp
- **1941** *(March)*: Himmler orders building of Auschwitz II-Birkenau camp
- **1941** *(June 22)*: Germany invades Soviet Union
- **1941** *(July 1941)*: Himmler orders the opening of the Minsk ghetto
- **1941**: Himmler visits SS killing sites in Auschwitz, Lublin, Kovno, Riga, and Minsk
- **1941** *(July 20)*: Himmler discusses plans for Final Solution with Odilo Globocnik
- **1941** *(July 31)*: Hermann Göring gives Reinhard Heydrich authority to plan Final Solution
- **1941** *(August)*: Himmler orders creation of Riga ghetto
- **1941** *(August)*: Kovno ghetto opened
- **1941** *(September 1–3)*: First gassing experiments at Auschwitz I using Zyklon B
- **1941** *(September 3–5)*: Vilna ghettos I and II opened
- **1941** *(September 18)*: Himmler tells Arthur Greiser that Reich Jews will soon be deported
- **1941** *(October)*: First prisoners arrive at Majdanek
- **1941** *(October 10)*: Himmler and Adolf Eichmann decide to open Theresienstadt ghetto
- **1941** *(November 1)*: Construction begins on Bełżec, *Aktion Reinhard* death camp
- **1941** *(November 1–2)*: Herbert Lange uses gas van to murder from 70–80 Jews near Chełmno
- **1941** *(December 8)*: Lange begins gassing operations at Chełmno
- **1942** *(January 20)*: Wannsee Conference
- **1942** *(February)*: First experimental gassings at Bełżec
- **1942** *(March)*: Construction begins on Sobibór, *Aktion Reinhard* death camp; opens in May
- **1942** *(March 2)*: Minsk *Judenrat* refuses SS order to supply 5,000 Jews for deportation
- **1942** *(July 23)*: First gassings at Treblinka II, *Aktion Reinhard* death camp
- **1942** *(November 1)*: Riga ghetto reorganized in response to underground escape attempts
- **1942** *(December 16)*: Himmler orders Reich *Zigeunermischlinge* deported to East
- **1943** *(January 29)*: Reich Criminal Police issue detailed directive to deport *Zigeunermischlinge*
- **1943** *(April 19–May 16)*: Warsaw Ghetto uprising

—**1943** *(August 2)*: Treblinka uprising

—**1943** *(August 19)*: SS begins to close Treblinka

—**1943** *(September 1)*: Jewish underground in Vilna ghetto attacks German forces

—**1943** *(September 23–24)*: Vilna ghetto liquidated

—**1943** *(October 14)*: Sobibór uprising; Himmler orders camp closed

—**1943** *(October 21)*: Minsk ghetto closed

—**1943** *(November 1)*: Riga ghetto reorganized in response to underground escape attempts; closed
     later in month

—**1943** *(November 3)*: *Erntefest* massacres in Lublin area

—**1944** *(May 16)*: Roma stop SS from closing Gypsy Family Camp in Auschwitz II-Birkenau

—**1944** *(June 23–August 30)*: Most of Łódź's Jews deported to Auschwitz and Chełmno

—**1944** *(July 8)*: Kovno concentration camp (formerly ghetto) closed

—**1944** *(August 3–4)*: *Zigeunernacht*; SS liquidates Gypsy Family Camp at Auschwitz II

—**1944** *(October 7)*: Jewish *Sonderkommandos* blow up crematoria IV at Auschwitz II; Himmler
     orders destruction of all crematoria-gas chambers at Auschwitz

As the Germans' flood of death and destruction swept through western Russia from the Baltic to the Black Sea in the summer and fall of 1941, the Third Reich's leadership now looked for a more efficient means to kill and dispose of the bodies of Jews cut down in this horrific, bloody, genocidal tide. At a distance, the decision to eliminate Jews totally from the face of Europe would seem to flow from what was already going on in the Soviet Union. Until this point, the Germans had tried to rationalize these murders as consequences of war. Great efforts were made in the *Einsatzgruppen* reports to depict the Jews, the Roma, and even the handicapped as physical threats to German personnel in the field. But what was about to happen—the development of equipment and the opening of camps designed solely to mass murder Jews—could not be explained away as acts of war. Yet what makes this particular phase of the Holocaust so heinous is that the best of German science, technology, industry, and medicine was used to create an unimaginable killing program designed to mass murder one group: the Jews.

The SS rounded up those Jews not murdered by the *Einsatzgruppen* and other units and forced them into major ghettos in the Soviet Union. In 1942, the Germans began sending the Jews in the ghettos in Poland and Russia to the six new death camps in occupied Poland—Auschwitz, Bełżec, Chełmno, Majdanek, Sobibór, and Treblinka. In the midst of this growing mass murder program, Jews began to resist Nazi brutality, mostly through spiritual resistance; but as the Final Solution spread, acts of bold, heroic physical resistance stunned the Nazi leadership.

Planning for the Final Solution

No single document points to Hitler's decision to eliminate the Jews from the face of Europe. It is obvious, though, that Hitler and the senior Nazi leadership had already planned to murder as many Jews, Roma, handicapped, Soviet POWs, communist activists, and others as they could once they entered Soviet territory. What pushed the German leadership to the next plateau of mass murder—the development of a vast industry of genocidal death—was a blend of Hitlerian arrogance and military invincibility that sought, in the midst of what seemed to be the greatest military victory in German history, to fulfill the Nazi dream of eliminating its greatest racial enemy, the Jews.

The seed for this new genocidal experiment came partially out of a five-hour meeting called by Hitler on July 16, 1941. Several days earlier, Himmler met with *SS- Hauptsturmführer* Rudolf Höss (1900–1947), the commandant of the Auschwitz concentration camp in the General Government. Himmler told Höss that Hitler had recently ordered the "Final Solution of the Jewish question." Auschwitz, Himmler went on, would be the site of this new "campaign" because of its isolation and excellent transportation network. Himmler felt that Höss was just the person to carry out this new assignment. *SS- Sturmbannführer* Adolf Eichmann, the *Reichsführer SS* noted, would soon contact Höss about developing plans for the "projected installations." Himmler expected these plans on his desk in a month. Himmler ended his meeting with Höss with an announcement: "The Jews are the eternal enemies of the German people and must be exterminated. All the Jews within our reach must be annihilated during this war. If we do not succeed in destroying the biological foundation of Jewry now, then one day the Jews will destroy the German people."[1]

It was this spirit that permeated that portion of the July 16 meeting in the Reich Chancellery dealing with the Jews. In attendance were Hermann Göring, Alfred Rosenberg, Martin Bormann, Hans Heinrich Lammers, and Field Marshal Keitel. Himmler was not there but received a copy of the minutes. Because he felt that Russia was about to be defeated, Hitler was in a celebratory mood. He talked initially about insignificant military problems. Most of the time, though, was spent planning the post-victory administration of conquered Soviet territory. Hitler told the group that he planned to turn Russia into a "Garden of Eden" and that all "necessary measures," including "shootings, resettlements, etc.," had to be used to create this new German paradise. Stalin's recent call for a Soviet partisan uprising against the Wehrmacht played right into their hands, Hitler explained, since it gave the Germans the "opportunity to exterminate anyone who [is] hostile to us."[2]

Adolf Eichmann, 1940. USHMM Photo No. 74907.

Himmler, who was seldom in Berlin during the summer of 1941, fully understood the spirit of Hitler's remarks and quickly sent over 12,000 troops from his *Kommandstab* to Russia to help with the killing operations there. He also visited various *Einsatzgruppen* units in the Soviet Union during the next month. On July 20, he met with *SS- Brigadeführer* Odilo Globocnik (1904–1945), the HSSPF in the Lublin district. Himmler approved Globocnik's plans to make Lublin a special SS city and to open the Majdanek concentration camp in the suburbs. Richard Breitman and Joseph Poprzeczny both think that they also discussed Globocnik's role in the Final Solution.[3]

After the war, at least one Order Police officer testified that he was told on July 21 that Himmler had ordered the destruction of all of the Jews in Europe. The same day, Hitler, who insisted on being kept up-to-date on the actions of the *Einsatzgruppen,* told Field Marshal Slavko Kvaternik (1878–1947), the head of the armed forces in the new, pro-Nazi Independent State of Croatia, that no nation in Europe should tolerate the presence of even one Jewish family since it could "become the bacillus source for a new decomposition [of society]." The Führer added that if there "were no more Jews in Europe, then the unity of European states would be no longer destroyed."[4]

On July 31, Hermann Göring, who was still technically in charge of Jewish affairs, signed a decree that gave Heydrich the authority to begin planning the Final Solution:

> To supplement the task that was assigned to you on 24 January 1939 [creation of Reich Central Office for Jewish Emigration], which dealt with the solution of the Jewish problem by emigration and evacuation in the most suitable way, I hereby charge you with making all necessary preparations with regard to organizational, technical and material matters for bringing about a complete solution of the Jewish question [*Gesamtlösung der Judenfrage*] within the German sphere of influence in Europe.
>
> Wherever other governmental agencies are involved, these are to cooperate with you.
>
> I request you further to send me, in the near future, an overall plan covering the organizational, technical and material measures necessary for the accomplishment of the final solution of the Jewish question [*Endlösung der Judenfrage*] which we desire.[5]

Though scholars differ on the significance of this document and its relationship to the development of the Final Solution, it does mark an important turning point in the German move towards a terminal solution to its "Jewish problem."[6]

There was a dramatic increase in the number of Jews murdered on all Russian fronts during the next month, and *Einsatzgruppen* commanders proudly reported the statistics to Berlin. One element new in these reports was the shooting of women and children.

This deadly, symbolic shift indicates that Germany's leadership was slowly moving towards a new solution to its "Jewish problem." All that remained was to find an organized mechanism for the campaign.

And although historians disagree on the exact timetable and planning for the Final Solution, there is no question that by the early fall of 1941, as German forces seemed on the verge of victory in the Soviet Union, Hitler and the SS were developing plans to murder not only the Jews in the East but throughout Europe.

In mid-August, Heydrich and Goebbels began to pressure Hitler to approve a plan to deport Jews in the Greater Reich (Germany, Austria, and Bohemia-Moravia) to the East. On August 18, Goebbels met with Hitler and told him how disgusting it must be for soldiers returning from the front to see Jews roaming the streets of Berlin and living off the hard work of native Berliners. Something, Goebbels argued, must be done to rid Germany of its Jews. Hitler promised his propaganda minister that when the war with the Soviet Union was over, the Jews of Berlin would be deported to the East, where they would "*dort werden sie dann unter einem härteren Klima in die Mache genommen*" (get what they deserved in the harsh climate)." He reminded Goebbels of his comments before the Reichstag on January 21, 1939. If world Jewry plunged the world into war, it would end with the extermination of the Jewish race.[7]

On September 1, 1941, the RSHA issued a police decree that required all German Jews older than six to begin wearing in public a palm-sized yellow Star of David inscribed with the word "*Jude*" in the middle of the star. When Jews were in public, they had to wear the star on the left front chest of their outer garments. The decree also forbade Jews from leaving their districts without police approval, or the wearing of decorations on their clothing except the star. These regulations did not apply to Jews in mixed marriages where the children were not Jewish or to a Jewish wife in a childless marriage.[8]

Though Hitler had initially decided to put off the deportation of Reich Jews until the end of the Russian campaign, by mid-September he had begun to change his mind, in large part because of what appeared to be new German successes on the eastern front. On September 18, Himmler wrote Arthur Greiser, the *Statthalter* (governor) in the Wartheland, that Hitler had now decided that "the Altreich [old Reich] and the Protectorate [of Bohemia and Moravia] should be emptied and liberated from the Jews from west to east as soon as possible."[9]

The Transfers from the Greater Reich

Initially, Himmler wanted to send about 80 percent of the 75,000 deportees (70,000 Jews and 5,000 Roma) to Łódź. However, after *SS-Brigadeführer* Friedrich Übelhör (1893–1945), the *Regierungspräsident* in the Kalisz-Łódź district, and Werner Ventzki (1906–?), the *Oberburgermeister* (mayor) of Łódź, voiced strong objections, Himmler reduced the number to 20,000 Jews and 5,000 Roma. He chose Riga, Minsk, and Kovno as alternative sites despite similar protests from Nazi leaders there. Between October 15, 1941, and February 21, 1942, Himmler deported 53,000 Jews and 5,000 Roma to Łódź, Riga, Minsk, and Kovno from cities throughout the Greater Reich. These transports marked the formal beginning of the Final Solution even though Reich leaders were still experimenting with the most efficient means of mass murder. This first experiment in mass deportation, with all its associated problems, proved most useful to the Nazi leadership as they struggled to develop and build the complex mechanism for murdering the Jews of Europe.

Theresienstadt

The Jews in the Protectorate of Bohemia and Moravia presented Reich leaders with special challenges. Reinhard Heydrich, the recently appointed *Reichsprotektor in Bohmen und Mähren* (Reich Protector in Bohemia and Moravia), wanted to use the handling of the Jewish question in the Protectorate as a model for the Greater Reich. In early October 1941, Heydrich and Adolf Eichmann decided to send some Czech Jews to a new camp north of Prague in Terezín (Theresienstadt). Though initially a ghetto for elderly and privileged Reich Jews, Eichmann later transformed it into a special "show" camp to dispel rumors about the Final Solution. In reality, Theresienstadt was a transit camp for Jews on their way to death camps and ghettos in the East.

Theresienstadt was Eichmann's pet project and he kept an office there. In the spring of 1942, he told a group of Gestapo agents that the ghetto would "save face with the outside world."[10] To maintain this façade, Eichman allowed the ghetto's large community of scholars, writers, musicians, and artists a certain amount of creative freedom to study, write, and compose. The ghetto even had a 60,000-volume library complete with a strong Judaica collection. And in 1944, Joseph Goebbels began production on a propaganda film, *Theresienstadt: Ein Dokumentarfilm aus dem jüdischen Siedlungsgebiet* (Documentary Film of the Jewish Resettlement), that was shown to a visiting Red Cross delegation in April 1945.[11] By then, only 17,472 Jews remained in the ghetto out of the 157,126 sent there between 1941 and 1945. More than 33,000 Jews died in Theresienstadt, and over 87,000 were sent to death camps. Only from 3,000 to 4,000 of those sent to the East survived the Holocaust.[12]

Fifteen thousand children passed through Theresienstadt during the war. Only their toys, poetry, and artwork survived. Some of their art and poems were subsequently collected and published in . . . *I Never Saw Another Butterfly* . . . . This touching volume, certainly one of the most poignant examples of spiritual resistance during the Holocaust, captures the

Entrance to Theresienstadt. Photo courtesy of David M. Crowe.

pain and horror of the *Shoah* through the eyes of its youthful victims. "Teddy" wrote: "[H]ere in Terezin, life is hell"; and fifteen-year-old Petr Fischl, who was murdered at Auschwitz, described getting "accustomed to seeing people die in their own excrement, to seeing piled-up coffins full of corpses, to seeing the sick amidst dust and filth."[13]

Yet in the midst of this pain and suffering, Miroslav Košek was able to write that "Terezín is full of beauty," though he predicted that the justice of death would finally entrap those "who wear their noses in the air." Hanuš Hackenburg dreamed of a new day when he would "wake up a child again, and start to laugh and play."[14] But perhaps the most touching poem was written by Pavel Friedman, who wrote "The Butterfly" in the summer of 1942:

> The last, the very last,
> So richly, brightly, dazzlingly yellow.
> Perhaps if the sun's tears would sing
> Against a white stone . . .
> Such, a yellow

> is carried lightly way up high.
> It went away I'm sure because it wished to
> kiss the world goodbye.
> For seven weeks I've lived in here,
> Penned up inside this ghetto
> But I have found my people here.
> The dandelions call to me
> And the white chestnut candles in the court.
> Only I never saw another butterfly.
> That butterfly was the last one.
> Butterflies don't live here,
> In the ghetto.[15]

These poems reflect the vibrant cultural life in Theresienstadt. Perhaps no person achieved more in this deadly environment than Rafael Schächter (1905–1944), a gifted young Czech conductor who became obsessed with performing Verdi's *Requiem* in the ghetto. Like Verdi, Schächter poured his heart and soul into his work on the *Requiem*. Though Schächter conducted many works in Theresienstadt, Verdi's *Requiem* was his passion. He insisted, for example, on a large orchestra and a chorus of 150 voices, no small feat given that

Karel Ancerl directs Theresienstadt Orchestra; still photograph from Goebbels' film *Theresienstadt*. USHMM Photo No. 59558, courtesy of Ivan Vojtech Fric, photographer.

scores and instruments had to be smuggled into the ghetto. In addition, there was no rehearsal space large enough for the entire group, and Schächter had to rehearse small sections of the orchestra and chorus separately. His work was further complicated by the fact that by the summer of 1944, when the *Requiem* was first performed, the Germans had begun to empty out the ghetto, sending soloists and some members of the orchestra and chorus eastward to their deaths.

Yet Schächter persisted and conducted the first of sixteen performances of the *Requiem* at Theresienstadt between the summer and fall of 1944. After the first concert, audience members sat in stunned silence, but then jumped up and gave a long, standing ovation. Yet Schächter, who saw the performance as a form of defiant spiritual resistance, was not satisfied. Before the next performance, he

rewrote the music of the *Requiem*'s "Libera me" so that its final words were carried along by Ludwig von Beethoven's victory code with three short notes and a long one. On June 23, 1944, Schächter conducted the *Requiem* for a visiting delegation from the International Red Cross. In the audience was Adolf Eichmann, who applauded modestly afterwards, unaware of the new secret code in the "Libera me."[16]

It takes little imagination to understand the power of the words of the *Requiem*'s "Dies irae" ("This day of wrath, shall consume the world in ashes"); the "Confutatis" ("Consigned to the searing flames"); or the "Libera me" ("Deliver me, O Lord, from eternal death in that awful day") to Jewish musicians about to be sent to their deaths in the gas chambers of Auschwitz.[17] These words were particularly meaningful during the last performance because many of the musicians had just learned they were about to be deported eastward. With grace, dignity, and courage, they performed brilliantly. To the last moment of their creative lives they chose to defy death by giving their all to their music and heritage.

Experiments with the Machinery of Death

The problem with transporting large numbers of Jews to the East was only one aspect of the German search for a more efficient, secretive solution to the "Jewish question." Since shooting was too problematic, the SS had to find alternative methods of mass murder. Furthermore, where would the executions take place? And what was to be done with the bodies of the dead Jews? The German search for answers shows how the Final Solution was developed in the latter part of 1941 and early 1942.

First, Himmler had to select killing sites. In July and August 1941, he visited Auschwitz, Lublin, Kovno, Riga, and Minsk. He was sickened by the execution of one hundred partisans in Minsk, but he was also concerned about the impact the executions had on the *Einsatzgruppe* killing squad. During this period, Adolf Eichmann also visited Auschwitz and had discussions with the commandant, Rudolf Höss, about the possibility of using gas vans. The SS had used gas vans, often disguised with a *Kaisers Kaffee Geschäft* logo on the side, in 1940 to kill the handicapped in the Wartheland and East Prussia. A special T-4 unit commanded by *SS- Sturmbannführer* Herbert Lange (1909–1945) oversaw this operation. Once Lange's unit had loaded the inmates from an asylum into the special gas van, the driver pumped pure carbon monoxide into the back as he drove away. During a ghastly nineteen-day period in the late spring of 1940, the Lange *Kommando* murdered 1,559 German and from 250 to 300 Polish mental patients in East Prussia.

Eichmann, though, was troubled by shortages of bottled carbon monoxide used in the vans and told Höss that he wanted to find a more readily available gas that did not require a special installation to use it. Höss and Eichmann then drove around the Auschwitz area looking for a suitable killing site and found an abandoned farmhouse near the Polish village of Brzezinka (Birkenau) that would be useful for gassing. According to Höss, the initial idea was to gas victims in the farmhouse and bury their bodies in nearby pits. They later decided that cremation was the best way to dispose of the bodies. Höss claimed in his memoirs that several days later he sent detailed plans for this operation to Himmler, who approved them.[18] In his trial in Israel in 1961, Eichmann denied that he had been given such authority.[19]

The first experimental gassing took place at Auschwitz on September 1, 1941. Höss was away, and his vice commandant, *SS- Hauptsturmführer* Karl Fritsch (1903–1945), decided to use Zyklon B, a rodent and insect poison used around the camp, on a handful of Soviet POWs who had been brought to Auschwitz for "liquidation." Two days later, Höss oversaw the gassing of 600 Soviet POWs and 250 Polish inmates from the camp's infirmary in the basement of Block 11. After SS guards put the 850 men in the basement, they covered its windows with dirt. SS guards wearing gas masks then dumped Zyklon B pellets into the room and closed the doors. The next day, the SS opened the doors and discovered that some of the victims were still alive. They threw more Zyklon B into the room and resealed it. Twenty-four hours later, twenty prisoners equipped with gas masks entered Block 11's basement and began to take the bodies upstairs to the courtyard between the barracks. This included the bodies of those gassed on September 1, who were still wearing their military uniforms. In what would become common practice in the death camps and ghettos, inmate dentists, supervised by the SS, began to remove the gold fillings and crowns from the prisoners' mouths. The bodies were then taken to the nearby crematory.[20]

Chełmno gas van. Source: Yad Vashem.

Höss, frustrated because it took two days to air out the basement of Block 11, decided to use the morgue at the Auschwitz crematory for future gassings until the Birkenau site was ready.

Gassing, though, was not the only method of execution used at Auschwitz and other concentration camps and ghettos. Auschwitz records show that a growing number of inmates were shot or injected with phenol; many died from beatings, malnutrition, and exhaustion. Later, some were murdered in gruesome "medical" experiments. But it was gassing, Himmler and his "experts" decided, that was the most efficient way to kill what would become a flood of Jewish victims between 1942 and 1944. In anticipation, Höss built more crematoria at the camp. The SS had been using crematoria in their camps since 1937 because the local crematory no longer had the capacity to handle SS needs. In 1937, the SS contracted with J. A. Topf and Sons in Erfurt to build a crematorium at Dachau. When World War II began, the SS asked J. A. Topf to build new crematoria for the Buchenwald, Auschwitz, and Flossenburg concentration camps. By early 1942, two crematoria were operating at Auschwitz I; more were opened near the newly designated killing center at the Auschwitz II-Birkenau camp farm house.

Other gassing experiments took place at Chełmno (German, Kulmhof) about 40 miles west of Łódź. Himmler sent its first commandant, Herbert Lange, to the area in the fall of 1941 to find a death-camp site for the Jews in the Łódź ghetto and the Wartheland. Lange chose the small Polish village of Chełmno because of its isolation. On November 1–2, Lange's team, enroute from Poznan to Chełmno, decided to test their gas van on a group of Jews from the village of Kazimierz

Biskupi. The van, which had been used in earlier "euthanasia" operations, was equipped with carbon monoxide canisters. Later that month, men from Lange's unit drove the gas van to the village of Kozminek, where they murdered from seventy to eighty Jews. Once the victims were loaded into what appeared to be a large moving van, the driver activated the carbon monoxide canisters and drove away from the loading area. Lange continued his gassing experiments through the end of November. Seven hundred Jews, including many children, died during these experimental gassings. The first formal killing operations began in Chełmno on December 8, 1941.

In Lublin, Odilo Globocnik, who was trying to transform the region into a special SS economic and racial paradise, was one of the early proponents of gassing. In the fall of 1941, Phillipe Bouhler and Victor Brack, who had been in charge of Hitler's "euthanasia" program in Germany, met with Globocnik in Lublin to discuss the transfer to Lublin of some of the specialists in their disbanded program. Later, Heydrich sent Eichmann to Lublin to talk with Globocnik about the mass killing network he was setting up throughout occupied Poland. Globocnik asked *SS- Sturmbannführer* Hermann Julius Höfle (1911–1962), who was in charge of Globocnik's killing operations, to show Eichmann the site of what was probably to become the Bełżec death camp near Lublin. Höfle showed Eichmann the specially sealed buildings that would be used in the gassing operation. Höfle planned to use a captured Soviet submarine engine to pump carbon monoxide into the gassing chambers.

Globocnik also had another visitor that fall, *SS- Obersturmführer* Christian Wirth (1885–1944), who had run several T-4 "euthanasia" centers in Germany. Wirth, who would soon become commandant at Bełżec, and later served as *Inspekteur der SS- Sonderkommando, Aktion Reinhard,* gave Globocnik more insight into the running of the planned death camps. At the time, most of the specialists of the old

"euthanasia" and T-4 units were working as medical support staff behind the German lines in Russia. Globocnik, desperate for experts, now had many of them transferred to Poland, where he used them to help develop the last phases of the Final Solution. Consequently, by the end of 1941 and the beginning of 1942, most of the basic planning for the Final Solution was well in place. The infamous meeting at Wannsee on January 20, 1942, which brought together representatives from all elements of the Nazi Party and German government to discuss broad-scale coordination for the Final Solution, was, as Richard Breitman has pointed out, designed "to give an official stamp of approval to a prior policy."[21] The Wannsee Conference would also come to symbolize the cold, machine-like approach the Germans took as they planned the murder of millions of innocent Jews, Roma, and others in the network of death camps and other killing facilities opening up in the General Government and elsewhere.

The Wannsee Conference

Reinhard Heydrich had originally planned to hold the Wannsee Conference, named for the site of an SS villa in the suburbs of Berlin, on December 9, 1941; but the Japanese attack on Pearl Harbor on December 7, and Hitler's decision to declare war on the United States four days later, prompted Heydrich to delay the meeting until the third week of January 1942. Heydrich had bought the villa a year earlier for the Nordhav SS Foundation, which he had set up to construct and maintain vacation homes for the SD. Sitting as it did on a tranquil lake in a community of elegant homes miles from the center of Berlin, Wannsee was a perfect setting for Heydrich's personal and official needs.

The Wannsee Conference had little to do with the planning of the major phases of the Final Solution, which had been well underway since the late summer and early fall of 1941. Instead, the conference was more informational

Wannsee villa. Photo courtesy of David M. Crowe.

and was called to share with most of the major organs of the state and Nazi Party the planning already underway to deal with the mass murder of Jews throughout Europe. This idea of informing the Nazi bureaucracy of certain aspects of Final Solution planning began on October 30, 1941, when *SS- Gruppenführer* Heinrich Müller, the head of the Gestapo, sent Joachim von Ribbentrop, the German foreign minister, the first of five reports about the activities of the *Einsatzgruppen* in the Soviet Union. The reports carefully detailed the large-scale massacres of Jews and "Bolshevik" activists, actions that were justified, Müller's reports noted, because of threats to Wehrmacht security.

Müller's reports quickly spread throughout the upper echelons of the German government and, by December 1941, the mass murder of the Jews in the East was common knowledge to most top-ranking government and party leaders. On November 18, Alfred Rosenberg told a group of reporters in confidence that the Reich had to solve the "Jewish question." The only

way to do this, he went on, was "in a biological eradication of the entire Jewish people." This could be solved only when there were no Jews in Germany or Europe "up to the Urals." Jews, he concluded, had to be expelled beyond the Urals or "eradicat[ed] . . . in some other way."[22]

In late November, Heydrich decided it was time to meet with representatives from government and party offices that would be important to the success of the Final Solution. When he sent out invitations for the December 9 meeting, he included a copy of Göring's July 31 document authorizing Heydrich to oversee planning for the "final solution of the Jewish question."[23] Three days after the cancelled meeting was supposed to have taken place, Hitler met with important party leaders to discuss the war. When it turned to the conflict in the East, Hitler brought up the "Jewish question." He reminded everyone present of his comments to the Reichstag on January 21, 1939, when he had prophesied that if the Jews caused a world war, it would

Reinhard Heydrich. USHMM Photo No. 79522, courtesy of KZ Gedenkstaette Dachau.

lead to "*ihre Vernichtung erleben würden* (their destruction)." Europe was now at war, Hitler went on, and "*die Vernichtung des Judentums muss die notwendige Folge sein* (the destruction of the Jews is inevitable)." One hundred and sixty thousand German soldiers had died in Europe's "Jewish war," and the Jews had to pay for these losses "*mit ihrem Leben bezahlen müssen* (with their lives)."[24]

Several days later, Hans Frank met with a group of party leaders in the General Government and repeated Hitler's remarks about the fate of the Jews. They had to "disappear." Frank's plan was to deport them to the East, where they would be liquidated. It was essential, he reminded his subordinates, that they show no compassion for the Jews, who had to be destroyed to protect Germany.[25]

Several weeks later, Heydrich sent out new invitations for the January 20 meeting at Wannsee. In one sense, the bucolic setting would seem out of place for a gathering that was to discuss the coordination of party and government efforts to murder the Jews of Europe. But in another way, it was perfect because the lunch-time meeting and its peaceful environment were perfect symbols of the boardroom type approach taken by the Germans to the planning of the Final Solution. For every killer in a death camp, ghetto, or concentration camp, there were scores of "desk murderers" planning the greatest mass murder in history. Some sat around the table at Wannsee on January 20, 1942. And according to Adolf Eichmann, each delegate attending the Wannsee Conference was fully aware of the mass killings going on in the East.[26]

The Wannsee Conference began at noon on a cold, snowy day. Adolf Eichmann, who prepared the background material used by Heydrich during his presentation, was also responsible for the male stenographer who sat beside him taking down the minutes of the conference. Eichmann, who evidently had done quite a bit of work well before the conference, barely made it back to Berlin from Theresienstadt the evening before the meeting. He described the atmosphere of the meeting as relaxed, in large part because orderlies kept serving the delegates cognac. Heydrich opened the conference by reminding everyone that Hermann Göring had made him the "delegate" for developing plans for the Final Solution of the "Jewish question" in Europe. Heydrich explained that he had called the January 20 meeting to clarify "fundamental questions" about the Final Solution. He added that he and Heinrich Himmler were officially responsible for all "central handling of the final solution" throughout Europe. This meeting, Heydrich declared, was essential to insure "an initial common action of all central offices immediately concerned" with various aspects of the Final Solution. From Heydrich's prespective, it was very important that the various agencies represented at the Wannsee meeting accept SS supremacy over the "Jewish question," particularly in the East.[27]

───────── **Wannsee Conference Participants** ─────────

Reinhard Heydrich (1904–1942; assassinated). Dishonored naval officer. *SS- Obergruppenführer.* Head of RSHA. Deputy Reich Protector of Bohemia and Moravia. Architect of the Final Solution. Assassinated by Czech partisans, May 27, 1942.

Adolf Eichmann (1906–1962; executed). Traveling salesman. *SS- Obersturmbannführer.* RSHA "Jewish 'expert'" who organized transports of more than 3 million Jews to death camps. Kidnapped by Israelis in Argentina in 1960. Tried, convicted of war crimes in Israel. Executed May 31, 1962.

Dr. Josef Bühler (1904–1948; executed). Lawyer. *Staatssekretär. Stellvertreter* (Deputy) to Hans Frank. General Government. Extradited to Poland. Tried, executed 1948.

Dr. Roland Freisler (1893–1945). Lawyer. *Staatssekretär.* Reich Ministry of Justice. President of People's Court. Died during Allied bombing of Berlin.

Otto Hofmann (1896–1982). Wine merchant. *SS- Obergruppenführer und Generalleutnant der Polizei.* Head of the SS Race and Settlement Office. Dismissed by Himmler in 1943. Became HSSPF South-West (Stuttgart). Sentenced to twenty-five years in prison, 1948. Released in 1954.

Dr. Gerhard Klopfer (1905–1987). Lawyer. *SS- Oberführer. Ministerialdirektor* Nazi Party Chancellery. Assistant to Martin Bormann. Interned 1945–1949. Released after investigation determined he was "minimally incriminated." Returned to law practice in 1956. Died in Fairfax, Virginia.

Dr. Friedrich Wilhelm Kritzinger (1890–1947). Lawyer. Judge. *Ministerialdirektor.* Vice head of Reich Chancellery. Arrested; released for ill health.

Dr. Rudolf Erwin Lange (1910–1945). Lawyer. *SS- Standartenführer.* Commanded *Einsatzkommando* A. Headed Sipo-SD in Latvia. Expert on use of gas vans. Committed suicide, February 1945.

Dr. Georg Leibbrandt (1899–1982). Lawyer. *Reichsamleiter. Ministerialdirektor.* Reich Ministry for Occupied Eastern Territories. Arrested and interned in 1945. War crimes investigation called off in 1950.

Martin Luther (1895–1945). Furniture shipping agent. *SA- Brigadeführer. Unterstaatssekretär* German foreign office. Expert on "Jewish question." Foreign office liaison to Himmler and Eichmann. Imprisoned in Sachsenhausen in 1943 for attempt to overthrow Foreign Minister Ribbentrop. Freed by Red Army at end of war, died one month later.

Dr. Alfred Meyer (1891–1945). PhD. Political Science. *SA- Obergruppenführer. Staatssekretär.* Reich Ministry for Occupied Eastern Territories in Berlin. Deputy to Alfred Rosenberg. Committed suicide, May 1945.

Heinrich Müller (1900–?). Policeman. *SS- Gruppenführer und Generalleutnant der Polizei.* Head of the Gestapo. Disappeared May 1945.

Dr. Erich Neumann (1892–1948). Lawyer. *SS- Oberführer. Staatssekretär.* Office of the Plenipotentiary for the Four Year Plan. Hermann Göring's personal representative at the Wannsee meeting. Deputy chairman, Continental Petroleum Association. General manager German Potassium Syndicate. In prison 1945–1948. Released for health reasons.

Dr. Karl Eberhard Schöngarth (1903–1946). Lawyer. *SS- Brigadeführer und Generalmajor der Polizei.* Commander of Security Police and SD in General Government and later in the Netherlands (1944–1945). Commanded three special killing *kommandos* in Poland and Belorussia in summer of 1941. Tried and executed by the British.

Dr. Wilhem Stuckart (1902–1953). Lawyer. *SS- Obergruppenführer. Staatssekretär.* Reich Ministry of the Interior. Tried, sentenced to three years, ten months prison. Fined 50,000 DM as "fellow traveler" in 1953. Killed in car accident.

Heydrich then went over the rationale, history, and difficulties Germany faced trying to force Jews to leave Reich territory. But by the fall of 1941, he boasted, 537,000 Jews had been forced to leave Germany. Furthermore, they had paid for their own emigration. The war, though, had prevented further emigration efforts, meaning that Reich leaders had to search for new solutions to the "Jewish problem." And that solution was "evacuation of the Jews to the East."[28]

Heydrich noted that there were 11 million Jews in Europe. Once they were sent eastward, they would be separated by gender and put into forced-labor situations, where "a large portion [would] be eliminated by natural causes." Those who survived would be "treated accordingly," since, if they were released, they would be "the seed of a new Jewish revival." The German plan, presuming Hitler gave his approval, was to ship all European Jews to the East. They would first be sent to "transit ghettos" and then on to the East. The SS would send elderly Jews and decorated Jewish war veterans to Theresienstadt. The foreign office and various RSHA officials assigned to German diplomatic missions abroad would deal with deportations in countries occupied by Germany or in Nazi-allied states such as Italy. Martin Luther of the foreign office said he felt there would be "no great difficulties" moving Jews out of these countries to the East.[29]

Heydrich explained that he planned to use the Nuremberg Laws to determine who was a Jew subject to deportation. Given that some Jews were married to Aryan Germans and had *mischlinge* children, this was a delicate matter. Jewish *mischlinge* of the first degree, meaning that they had two Jewish grandparents and practiced Judaism or were married to Jews, would be considered Jews. *Mischlinge* who were married to Germans but had only one Jewish grandparent were considered Germans. There could be exemptions, but they would be made on a case-by-case basis. Jews who received such exemptions would be sterilized; those with bad police or political records would be deported to the East.

SS- Obergruppenführer Hofmann, one of the few men present who had considerable experience with mass murder techniques, said that sterilization would have to be widely used since some *mischlinge* would choose this over "evacuation." Dr. Stuckart complained that trying to determine who was and who was not a Jew would cause his office considerable administrative work. Dr. Neumann insisted that efforts should be made to protect Jews working in industries vital to the war economy. Dr. Bühler added that officials in the General Government would like the Final Solution to begin there since the Jews there were not only "epidemic carriers[s]" but also "causing permanent chaos in the economic structure through continued black market dealings." Furthermore, he added, most of the 2.5 million Jews in the General Government were "unfit for work." He fully supported Heydrich's plans and asked only that he "solve the Jewish question" in the General Government as "quickly as possible."[30]

After everyone had left, Heydrich, Müller, and Eichmann sat down to discuss the meeting over brandy and cigarettes while they waited for the stenographer to type up the minutes. When the stenographer had finished his work, Heydrich carefully read and edited the notes. Thirty copies were later prepared for distribution to appropriate party and government officials. According to Eichmann, much of what had been discussed at the conference was left out of the official minutes:

These gentlemen stood together and sat together, and in very blunt words they referred to the matter [the Final Solution] without putting it down in writing. . . . Look at Stuckart, who was always considered to be a very precise and very particular stickler for the law, and here the whole tone and all manner of speech were totally out of keeping with legal language.[31]

The Final Solution

What followed was a mass murder program that centered around the movement of large Jewish populations from the ghettos, camps, and other restricted areas of Europe to the new death camps and ghettos of occupied Poland and the Soviet Union. Adolf Eichmann, aided by his staff in the Gestapo's IVB4 office in Berlin, became what David Cesarani has called "the managing director of the greatest single genocide in history."[32] His role was to implement policies decided by others. Eichmann, an extremely efficient manager, oversaw a staff of experts who planned the mass movements of Jews and others to the camps and ghettos in the East. His efficiency and dedication was such that he was able to overcome the constantly changing regulations and the "kaleidoscope of institutions, agencies, personalities and priorities" that were "constantly shifting for political or military reasons."[33] During the next three years, Eichmann oversaw a program that murdered from 3 to 3.5 million Jews and hundreds of thousands of Roma, handicapped, and others. And though there were thousands upon thousands of perpetrators involved in this unimaginable horror, Adolf Eichmann correctly remains the symbol of Nazi Germany's plan to rid Europe of its Jews and other "objectionable" minorities.

Most of these victims, particularly in the General Government, were sent to the six new death camps set up principally to murder the Jews of Europe. Three—Bełżec, Sobibór, and Treblinka—were part of *Aktion Reinhard,* a program run by Odilo Globocnik to murder the Jews in the General Government. The other major death camps in occupied Poland—Auschwitz, Chełmno, and Majdanek—were used to kill Jews and others throughout Europe. About 3.5 million Jews and tens of thousands of Roma and others would die in these killing centers. The Germans and their collaborators would murder millions more in ghettos, in occupied communities, in forced- or slave-labor facilities, or in transit to the East.

Chełmno

Chełmno (German, Kulmhof) was the first fully operational death camp in the Third Reich. Himmler opened it in late 1941 to murder Jews and Roma in the Łódź ghetto and the Wartheland district of Greater Germany. Chełmno, located almost 50 miles northwest of Łódź, was divided into two parts. The central camp was located in an old castle in the village of Chełmno, where the SS gassed the victims. The bodies were then taken about 2.5 miles to the *Waldlager* (forest camp) for burial and later, cremation. Himmler took great interest in his first death camp and provided its first commander, Herbert Lange, with a *Sonderkommando* staff of from 10 to 15 SS men and a contingent of eighty Order Police, who served as guards. Each staff member received a daily bonus for their work at the death camp. The first gassings took place on December 8, 1941. The first Jewish victims were brought to the castle from nearby communities and were told by one of the SS men that they were about to be sent to work camps in Germany and needed to be disinfected. After they had undressed and made lists of their valuables, they walked down to the basement and up a ramp to the camp's gas van. Once they had entered the specially sealed gassing compartment through the rear of the van, the door was closed. The driver then started the engine and crawled under the van to connect the exhaust pipe to a pipe that ran into the sealed compartment. He then revved up the engine, slowly asphyxiating with carbon monoxide the fifty to seventy Jews inside. Adolf Eichmann, who witnessed one of the first experimental gassings at Chełmno in the fall of 1941, described the screams that came from the van once the gassing began to his police interrogator in Israel in 1960. They shook him up so much that

Jews awaiting gassing at Chełmno. USHMM Photo No. 33399, courtesy of Sheva Zilberberg.

he refused to look inside through a glass peephole. Eichmann then followed the van in his private car to the *Waldlager:*

> There I saw the most horrible sight I had seen in all my life. It [the gas van] drove up to a fairly long trench. The doors were opened and corpses were thrown out. The limbs were as supple as if they'd been alive. Just thrown in. I can still see a civilian with pliers pulling out teeth. And then I beat it. I got into my car and drove off. I didn't say another word. I sat there for hours without saying a word to my driver. I'd had enough. I was through.[34]

But, professional that he was, he dutifully reported what he saw to Müller, "who didn't get much out of it."[35] Eichmann then prepared to implement the rest of the Final Solution.

Initially, the bodies were buried in large pits. But after complaints from local residents about the smell, the SS began to burn the bodies on large wooden pyres. In January 1942, Himmler sent two new gas vans to Chełmno. One of the inmates, Walter Podchlewnik, testified at Eichmann's trial that SS guards stood outside the gas vans poised to beat people who hesitated to enter them. Afterwards, small work teams of Jewish inmates sorted the clothing and other personal items, which were ultimately given to ethnic Germans recently settled in the Wartheland. On one occasion, Podchlewik was sent to the *Waldlager;* there, he saw the bodies of his wife and two children being placed in a mass grave: "I lay down by my wife and the two children and wanted them to shoot me. Then an SS man came up to me and said 'You still have strength enough, you can yet work.' He hit me twice with his stick and dragged me away to continue working."[36]

The mass murders at Chełmno took place in several phases. The first was between December 1941 and March 1943. At that point, the SS had murdered all the Jews in the

Wartheland except those in the Łódź ghetto whose work was deemed valuable to the war effort. Himmler ordered the castle and the *Waldlager* crematory destroyed. The camp was reopened in the summer of 1944 to kill the remaining Jews in Łódź. That fall, a special *Aktion* 1005 unit was sent to the *Waldlager* to disinter and burn the bodies still buried there. Himmler had created the *Aktion* 1005 program in the summer of 1942 to deal with the growing number of corpses in the death camps and later to eliminate all traces of the Final Solution. Headed by *SS- Standartenführer* Paul Blobel (1894–1951), the *Aktion* 1005 *Sonderkommando* units initially worked at the Chełmno, Bełżec, Treblinka, and Sobibór death camps burning corpses. Blobel, an engineer, developed a special system for burning bodies, crushing bones, and disposing of the ashes. In the summer of 1943, Himmler ordered Blobel to "cleanse" the death camps and other sites of their mass graves. This work was done almost exclusively by Jewish slave laborers supervised by Blobel *Sonderkommandos*. Once an *Aktion* 1005 unit had "cleansed" a site, they would often "reclaim" it by planting young trees and shrubs. Chełmno was one of the last death camp sites "cleansed" by a Blobel unit. The Red Army liberated Chełmno on January 17, 1945. The Germans murdered 147,000 Jews and 5,000 Roma at Chełmno from 1941 to 1944.

The Aktion Reinhard Death Camps: Bełżec, Sobibór, and Treblinka

Several months before the Wannsee Conference, Himmler asked Odilo Globocnik to develop *Aktion Reinhard,* an SS program designed to murder the 2.3 million Jews in the General Government in three death camps— Bełżec, Sobibór, and Treblinka. Hermann Höfle, whom Joseph Poprzeczny described as "the most sinister and powerful of Globocnik's 'court of killers,'" served as his chief-of-staff.[37] Globocnik drew heavily from the staff

Odilo Globocnik. USHMM Photo No. 45251, courtesy of Geoffrey Giles.

of Germany's "euthanasia" program to develop *Aktion Reinhard's* killing centers. Himmler had never intended the *Aktion Reinhard* death camps to be permanent and decided in March 1943 to close them once the SS had murdered all the Jews in the General Government.

Bełżec

Bełżec, which is 85 miles southeast of Lublin, was chosen, like the rest of the *Aktion Reinhard* death camp sites, for its remoteness, its access to rail lines, and its close proximity to Jewish populations in the General Government and the occupied parts of the Soviet Union. In early 1940, the Germans built a small forced labor camp for Jews in Bełżec, but closed it that fall. Construction of the death camp began on November 1, 1941, and

Jewish slave laborers at Bełżec. USHMM Photo No. 51528, courtesy of Muzeum Regionalne w Tomaszow Lubelski.

opened the following month. It was, like the rest of the *Aktion Reinhard* camps, small and utilitarian. Bełżec's commandant, Christian Wirth, was familiar with the gas vans being used at Chełmno and decided to construct permanent gas chambers at Bełżec. Wirth, like Eichmann, did not like bottled carbon monoxide gas and used diesel engines in his gas chambers. He built three gas chambers, 13 feet by 26 feet, in a barracks and lined the floors and walls with tin. A narrow, sand-filled barrier separated each chamber.

The first gassing experiments took place at the end of February 1942. Mieczylaw Kudyba, a Pole who lived in the nearby village, described the first gassing:

The Germans took out a group of Jews from Lubycze-Krolweska and brought them by car to the Belzec camp. One Jew from that group told me that he had been in the camp some time cutting pine trees. One day all the Jews were driven into a barrack. This Jew was able to hide and later to escape. While in hiding, he heard long screams from the barrack in which the Jews had been locked and then si-

lence. This was the first experimental killing in Belzec.[38]

During the next few days, Wirth gassed several hundred Jews. Wirth, and his adjutant, *SS- Obersturmführer* Josef Oberhauser (1915–1979), developed methods of transport, gassing, and burial at Bełżec that would later be used at Sobibór and Treblinka. Wirth thought that it was important to delude the arriving victims into thinking that they were being sent to a forced labor camp in Germany. Everything in the camp was designed to create this illusion. *SS- Obersturmführer* Kurt Gerstein (1905–1945), who visited Bełżec in the summer of 1942, reported what he saw in his controversial *Der Gerstein-Bericht* (Gerstein Report):

Near the small railway station, there was a large hut marked "Cloakroom" with a wicket marked "Valuables." There was also a room with a hundred barber chairs, and then a passage a hundred and fifty metres long in the open, fenced with barbed wire on both sides, with signs "To the Showers and Inhalation Establishments." We come to a house, the bathhouse, which is flanked at the right and left by large concrete flower pots with geraniums and other flowers. After going up some steps, we come to three rooms to our right and three to our left, like garages, 5×4 metres in area, 1.90 high. At the back, not visible, there are piles of wood. A brass Star of David is on the roof. At the front of the building there was a sign which read "The Heckenholt Foundation."[39]

Once the victims arrived at Bełżec, they were herded into the castle. Gerstein described what happened next:

[After being brutally forced off of the train cars by Ukrainian guards] orders are given over a large loudspeaker. They must undress completely in the open, some also in a hut, and also remove artificial limbs and spectacles. Shoes are to be tied together with a small piece of string, handed to them by a Jewish boy of four. All valuable objects must be handed in at the "Valuables" counter. No confirmations or receipts are given in exchange. Later, the women and young girls must go the barber's, where their hair is cut off in two or three strokes. The hair disappears into large potato sacks "to be used for something special, for submarines as insulation, etc."[40]

All this took place quickly because Wirth counted on the confusion and shock of arrival to deter outbursts and protests. In the midst of this organized chaos, an SS man tried to reassure everyone that there was nothing to worry about. "[N]othing will happen to you" an SS man kept reassuring the group as it was being moved towards the "showers." "All you have to do [in the showers] is to breathe deeply. This inhalation is necessary because of infectious diseases. It is a good disinfectant." If someone asked what was going to happen to them, the SS men present would reply: "[O]f course, the men will have to work, to build roads and houses, but the women do not have to work. At most, if they wish, they may help around

the house or in the kitchen." But Gerstein concluded that most of the victims were aware of what was about to happen to them because the "smell carrie[d] the tidings of their fate."[41]

Wirth picked a small group of healthy Jews to sort through and organize the victims' clothing and other valuables and also to clear out the gas chambers. Gerstein described what he saw after one of the chambers had been opened after a gassing:

The dead stand erect like basalt columns, for there is no room to fall or to collapse. Even in death, one can recognize the families, holding hands. It is only with difficulty that they can be separated to make room in the chambers for the next transport.

The bodies, blue, drenched in sweat and urine, the legs covered with dirt and menstrual blood, are thrown outside; amongst them babies, the bodies of children. Two dozen labourers check the mouths, which they open with the aid of iron tongs. "Gold to the left, without gold to the right!" Others examine sexual organs and the anus in search of money or diamonds, gold, etc. Dentists extract gold teeth, the crowns and the bridges, with tongs and hammers.[42]

Wirth, who was with Gerstein during his visit, proudly showed him the gold and other valuables that he had collected from Jewish victims. He picked up a jar full of gold teeth and asked Gerstein to "lift it up and estimate for yourself the weight of the gold!"[43]

The Jews forced to do this work lived only a few days before they were shot and replaced by a new Jewish work force. There was also a small group the Germans nicknamed the *Hofjuden* (court Jews), skilled craftsmen who worked for the German and Ukrainian guards. Bełżec had a staff of from 20 to 30 SS men and from 90 to 120 Ukrainian guards drafted from Lublin's Trawniki POW camp. It normally took from twenty to thirty minutes to kill everyone in the gas chambers. After the chambers were cleared of carbon monoxide, the bodies were put into mass graves; the burial pits were then covered with small layers of dirt. *SS- Hauptsturmführer* Franz Stangl (1898–1971), who was the commandant at Sobibór and, later, Treblinka, described the problems with the mass graves during a visit in the spring of 1942:

> Wirth was not in his office, they said he was up at the camp. . . . I asked what was the matter. The man I was talking to said that one of the pits had overflowed. They had put too many corpses in it and putrefaction had progressed too fast so that the liquid underneath had pushed the bodies on top up and over, and the corpses had rolled down the hill. I saw them—oh God, it was awful.[44]

Wirth and his staff had been overwhelmed by the death process since the camp had opened, and they closed it in the spring of 1942 to build larger gas chambers. By the end of December 1942, the Germans had killed most of the Jews in the General Government and had ordered Bełżec closed. Six hundred thousand Jews died in Bełżec between February and December 1942. After Himmler closed the camp, an *Aktion* 1005 unit was sent to Bełżec to open the mass graves and burn the corpses. The camp was demolished and converted into a farm to prevent the villagers from plundering the area. The farm was given to one of the camp's former Ukrainian guards.

Sobibór

Sobibór, which was located about 65 miles northeast of Lublin, was built and operated along the same lines as *SS* Bełżec. The Germans began constructing Sobibór in March 1942 and opened it the following month. Franz Stangl was its first commandant. Sobibór was divided into four small camps and had an SS staff of from twenty to thirty men and from 90 to 120 Ukrainian guards. Sobibór III was the site of the gas chambers,

mass graves, and barracks for the Jewish slave laborers. Stangl, like Wirth, strongly believed that delusion and speed were the key to the camp's success. There were three carbon monoxide asphyxiation chambers at Sobibór. The first experimental gassing took place in April 1942, and Wirth was on hand to offer advice. By early May, Sobibór was ready to receive its first transport of Jews.

The gassings at Sobibór took place in stages. From May to July 1942, Stangl and his staff murdered from 90,000 to 100,000 Jews from Poland, Slovakia, and the Greater Reich. He stopped the gassings in August and September because of problems with rail transport into the camp and used the time to build three new gas chambers. Himmler transferred Stangl to the Treblinka death camp during this period and replaced him with *SS- Hauptsturmführer* Franz Reichleitner (1906–1944). The gassings resumed in October and continued until the summer of 1943, at which time Himmler decided to transform Sobibór into a concentration camp. Between April 1942 and September 1943, the Germans murdered 250,000 Jews in Sobibór.

The Sobibór Uprising and the "Erntefest" Massacres

Resistance is one of the most sensitive topics in Holocaust studies. Raul Hilberg says that there was almost no Jewish resistance during the Holocaust, at least in the traditional sense; but Yad Vashem and the United States Holocaust Memorial Museum take a much more nuanced approach to this subject: They point out the significance not only of armed resistance but also of "spiritual" resistance, meaning "attempts by individuals to maintain their humanity and integrity in the face of Nazi attempts to dehumanize and degrade them."[45]

Józef Marszalek best describes the breadth of Holocaust resistance activity:

> [The] instinct to live, the will for survival, the striving to make public what was happening

within the wire fence of the camp caused the prisoner to begin fighting against the order imposed upon him. This struggle assumed various forms, from the simplest and spontaneous, to the more cautious and better organized. Every action aimed at saving the lives of fellow inmates, their physical and mental health, was a form of resistance. Thus, resistance included inmates' self-help, cultural life, religious life, contact with the outside world, political activity, sabotage and escapes. In a word, "everything could constitute resistance since everything was forbidden," according to the Italian researcher on the questions of psychology in concentration camps, Andrea Devoto.[46]

Thomas Toivi Blatt, a Sobibór survivor, said that "preserving Jewish identity . . . was a powerful, subversive way of resistance. Jews prayed for the dead and, despite the danger, celebrated Jewish holidays." Even suicide, Blatt felt, which some Jews considered a "grave sin," was an act of "protest" since it deprived the Germans of determining "the precise time and place of a Jew's death."[47] According to Rabbi Joseph Telushkin, rabbis have traditionally tried to "search for any rationale" to avoid declaring a person's death a suicide because of the stigma attached to it for the family. But Jewish tradition does "justify" suicide in situations where an individual "would be forced to live a shameful existence."[48]

There were many acts of physical and spiritual resistance during the Holocaust. One of the most famous took place at Sobibór on October 14, 1943. Such acts were common at Sobibór, although it took news of the Warsaw ghetto uprising to stimulate camp leaders to begin thinking of more organized forms of resistance. Leon Feldhendler, the former head of the *Judenrat* in Żołkiew, organized a small, secretive underground group that began to develop an escape plan in the spring of 1943. Esther Raab explained why: "You felt like you [were] doing something, you [are] planning

something. You['re] trying something. If you'll [sic] succeed it would be wonderful. If not, you'll get a bullet in the back—it's better than going to the gas chambers. I promised myself I'll never go the gas chambers."[49] Their initial plans involved poisoning the camp's guards, seizing their weapons, and escaping. These plans fell through when the SS discovered the poison and shot five Jews in retaliation. Feldhendler's group also thought of setting the camp on fire and escaping while the guards put it out. What complicated everything was the SS's decision in the summer of 1943 to place mines on the camp's perimeter. The only safe way out of Sobibór now was through the camp's main gate.

In September 1943, the Germans discovered an escape tunnel in Sobibór III and executed 150 prisoners in retaliation. Later that month, a group of Soviet POWs arrived from Minsk. One of the soldiers in this transport was *Leitenant* Alexander Pechersky (1909–1990), a veteran Red Army officer who soon became head of Feldhendler's group. Pechersky revived the idea of an escape tunnel, though he later abandoned it because of flooding problems. Pechersky, assisted by Feldhendler, developed a new plan that involved killing the camp's principal SS personnel, seizing the arms in the camp's arsenal, and fighting their way out through the main gate. They decided to act after the SS had murdered a large number of prisoners on October 11–12.

Pechersky described what happened on October 11: "A new transport had arrived. When the people were already undressed, they realized where they were being taken and began to run, naked. But where were they to run? . . . So they ran toward the barbed wire fence. There they were met by a hail of bullets from the automatic rifles. Many fell dead on the spot. The rest were led away to the gas chambers."[50]

The following day, the SS killed eighteen of the camp's sick Jewish workers. Pechersky and Feldhendler's group decided it was time to act, since they could be next.

Jewish participants in the Sobibór uprising. USHMM Photo No. 10625, courtesy of Misha Lev.

The plan was simple. At 3:30 P.M. on October 14, a small group of inmates would kill four important SS men. Thirty minutes later, others would cut the camp's telephone lines. Simultaneously, other SS men would be invited individually to the camp's workshops; there, they would be killed. At 4:30 P.M., some of the Soviet POWs would seize control of Sobibór's arsenal as the camp's 550 Jewish workers lined up for roll call. Once they had arms, the Soviet POWs would join the column of workers moving towards the main gate. The idea was to give the guards at the gate the impression that the workers were lined up for a special work assignment. If the group met resistance, they would fight back. If the SS or the Ukrainian guards cut off the escape route through the main gate, the workers would cut holes in the fence and use wood and bricks to clear a path through the mine field.

At first, everything went according to plan. Chaim Engel (1916–?), who was assigned to kill *SS- Unterscharführer* Walter Ryba, described the attack: "I stabbed our overseer [Ryba] to death. With each jab I cried, 'This is for my father, for my mother, for all the Jews you killed.' The knife slipped, cutting me, covering me with blood."[51] Elsewhere in the camp, one of the Ukrainian guards discovered the body of an SS man. The surviving Germans, backed by the Ukrainian guards, opened fire on the Jewish workers as they moved towards the main gate. The escapees then climbed the fence or cut holes through it, and tried to open a path through the minefield. Thomas Blatt noted that 320 Jews made it out of the camp, but 80 were killed during the initial phase of the escape. The Germans, stunned by the revolt and the escape, mounted a major manhunt for the escapees and captured 170 of them. Ninety escapees who joined the partisans died in battle or were killed by local Poles. Sixty-two Sobibór Jews survived the Holocaust, nine of them earlier escapees. The Germans executed everyone else as well as those who had not made it out of the camp. Himmler, shocked and angered by the revolt and escape, ordered Sobibór closed and turned into a farm that, like Bełżec, was given to a former Ukrainian guard.

Himmler also decided, in response to earlier revolts in Warsaw, Treblinka, and elsewhere, to murder all the Jews still alive in the Lublin district. He named this two-day campaign Operation *Erntefest* (Harvest Festival). On November 3, 1943, *SS- Obergruppenführer und General der Polizei* Friedrich Wilhelm Krüger (1894–1945), the HSSPF in the General Government, oversaw a mass murder program in three forced-labor camps—Trawniki, Poniatowa, and Majdanek. *SS- Gruppenführer und Generalleutnant der Polizei* Jakob Sporrenberg (1902–1951), the HSSPF in the Lublin district, used several thousand Waffen SS and Order Police to carry out a highly secret rapid extermination campaign that killed from 42,000 to 45,000 Jews in forty-eight hours in these three camps. Most of the Jews were shot, though one group of rebellious Jews was burned alive in a barracks in Poniatowa. The SS used several hundred Jews to clean up the camps after the massacres and then shot them.

Treblinka

Only one other death camp, Auschwitz, claimed as many lives as Treblinka. From July 23, 1942, until August 2, 1943, the date of the Treblinka uprising, the Germans murdered 874,000 Jews and several thousand Roma at Treblinka. The site was chosen because it was remote and surrounded by forests. Treblinka I opened in the summer of 1941 as a forced-labor camp for Poles and Jews from the Warsaw district. It was divided into two camps. The forced laborers at Treblinka I worked principally in a gravel pit near the Malkinia railway station and in an irrigation area in the Bug River valley. Treblinka I was small and never had more than 100 to 2,000 workers at any given time. Of the 20,000 inmates who worked at Treblinka I between 1941 and 1944, half perished; they died either by execution or from exhaustion or mistreatment.

Globocnik opened Treblinka II, the death camp, in July 1942. Soon after it began operations, Himmler replaced its first commandant, *SS- Untersturmführer* Imfried Eberl (1910–1948) with Stangl because he wanted someone experienced to operate what would become Germany's second deadliest mass murder facility. Globocnik used Treblinka, which is 65 miles northeast of Warsaw, first to murder the remaining 366,000 Jews in the Warsaw district, then 337,000 Jews from Radom, 35,000 from Lublin, and 107,000 from Białystok. Another 29,000 Jews from other parts of Europe also died at Treblinka.

Treblinka's operations were very similar to Sobibór's, though Stangl, dissatisfied with the amount of time it took to unload victims and gas them, wanted to improve the efficiency of Treblinka's killing operations. He not only cut in half the time it took to unload train cars but also added ten new gas chambers to the three already operating when he arrived. It now took only about fifteen minutes to kill several hundred Jews in one of his asphyxiation chambers. Stangl was proud of his ability to unload a transport of twenty cars and gas its victims in no more than two or three hours. He insisted that women and children be gassed first after the former had been shorn of their hair. To him, the Jews and Roma at Treblinka were nothing more than "cargo." He remembered standing with Wirth over the large pits filled with Jewish dead and thinking that they were not human beings; instead, they were "a mass of rotting flesh." He felt the same way about those he saw in the gas chambers just before they perished.[52]

Like Wirth, Stangl thought it was important to disguise the entrance of the death camp to hide its real purpose from arriving victims:

A sham station was erected on the platform of the siding in the camp. The nearby blocks of the camp had signs on the walls indicating a waiting room, buffet, ticket office, etc.

Memorial railway entrance to Treblinka. Photo courtesy of David M. Crowe.

Bogus indicators showed the platform for changing to Białystok, etc. The final stroke of cynicism was a "hospital" situated in the administrative block in a small compound surrounded by a high, impenetrable fence. The entrance was through a small wooden hut with a Red Cross flag over it. Beyond this was a small building called the "waiting room" in which stood a number of plush sofas. Just past the "waiting room" in the courtyard, a pit had been dug beside which a[n] SS man from the camp shot the victims in the back of the head with a small-calibre pistol. The "hospital" was used to liquidate those who were incapable of moving fast enough from the ramp to the gas chamber, in other words, the sick, the crippled, unattended children, the elderly.[53]

The testimony of Jewish Holocaust survivors often provides us with some of the best information we have about the fate of the Roma. This was certainly the case in Treblinka. One Jewish worker, Jakob Wiernik, described

what happened after the arrival of one group of Roma:

One day, while I was working near the gate, I noticed the Germans and Ukrainians making special preparations. The *Stabsscharführer* [staff sergeant], a short, squat man of about fifty, with a face of a murderer, left the camp several times in a car. Meanwhile the gate opened, and about 1,000 Gypsies were brought in (this was the third transport of Gypsies). About 200 of them were men, and the rest women and children. All their belongings were piled up with them on the wagons—filthy rags, torn bedding, and other beggar's belongings. They arrived with nearly no security escort; they were brought in by two Ukrainians in German uniform who themselves did not know the entire truth. The latter asked to take care of the formalities and get a receipt for delivering the transport. They weren't even allowed into the camp. Their request was honored with a sarcastic smile. As this procedure was being carried out, they learned from the Ukrainians in the camp that they had brought victims to an extermination camp. They paled, didn't believe what they had been told, and made an attempt to enter the camp. Then the *Stabsscharführer* came out and gave them a sealed envelope. They left. All the Gypsies were taken to the gas chambers and then burned.

Another Jewish worker, Shimon Goldberg, described the gassing of the Roma at Treblinka:

> While I was there, they killed about 2,000 Gypsies. The Gypsies went wild, screamed awfully and wanted to break down the chambers. They climbed up the walls toward the apertures at the top and even tried to break the barred window. The Germans climbed onto the roof, fired inside, sealed off the apertures and asphyxiated everyone.[54]

The Treblinka Uprising

Attempted escapes and small acts of resistance were a constant problem at Treblinka. Some of the more significant efforts were led by Jewish leaders such as Dr. Julian Chorazycki (1883–1943), the controversial Benjamin Rakowski (?–1943), and Marceli Galewski (1889–1943). Dr. Chorazycki, a Jewish convert to Christianity forced to work in the camp's SS clinic, played a prominent role developing the first major escape plan in Treblinka II in the spring of 1943. Chorazycki, who worked with the small and secretive Organizing Committee, was responsible for buying weapons from the Ukrainian guards, who were willing to smuggle arms into the camp for large bribes. Dr. Chorazycki got his funds from the "gold Jews" who were forced to sort through Jewish clothing after the gassings. They gave most of what they found to the SS, but also kept small amounts to give to Dr. Chorazycki. He was caught with some of the money by Stangl's vice commandant,

SS-*Untersturmführer* Kurt Franz (1914–1998). Chorazycki attacked Franz with a surgical knife and then swallowed poison. Franz, furious over the assault, viciously beat Chorazycki even though he was already dead.

Other members of Treblinka's underground continued Chorazycki's work. In April 1943, the Treblinka rebels used young *putzers*, boys who cleaned the SS's uniforms and boots, to steal hand grenades (the boys accomplished this feat by using a spare key made by a Jewish locksmith). Once armed, the rebels intended to attack camp guards and escape. Unfortunately, they discovered that the boys had stolen grenades without detonators and quickly returned them to the arsenal. Benjamin Rakowski, who replaced Chorazycki as camp "elder," helped develop new escape plans but was executed at the *Lazarett* (German, military hospital) when the SS discovered the money he had hidden to buy arms. *Lazarett* was the name given to the pits in Treblinka II where the SS shot inmates or buried those who had died on the transports.

Rakowski's successor, Marceli Galewski (1889–1943), was stimulated by the news of the Warsaw Ghetto Uprising. He brought new life to the Organizing Committee and developed several uprising and escape plans. The second plan involved stealing weapons from the arsenal between 2:30 and 4:30 P.M., followed immediately by attacks on camp headquarters and the SS. The rebels would also cut the camp's telephone lines and set fire to all the buildings. Once they had destroyed the camp and the gas chambers, they would flee into the surrounding forests. After some delays, Galewski and the Organizing Committee chose the late afternoon of Monday, August 2, for the uprising.

Earlier in the day, one of the Jewish workers responsible for spraying disinfectant around the camp filled his can with gasoline and spread it around the base of the camp's wooden buildings. Several *putzers* stole some weapons and grenades, meaning that some of

Memorial to those murdered at Treblinka. Photo courtesy of David M. Crowe.

the Treblinka rebels had arms when the rebellion began. Their detailed plans fell apart when *SS- Oberscharführer* Kurt Küttner found a large sum of money on one of the young rebels. Fearing discovery, another rebel shot Küttner on the spot. This act signaled the beginning of the rebellion.

What followed was sheer chaos. As the sounds of gunshots and explosions echoed throughout the camp, about 740 out of the camp's 840 to 850 inmates began climbing the fences in their efforts to escape. Many were shot on the fences, though several hundred were able to make it into the forest. Kalman Tiegman was one of those lucky enough to escape from the camp: "The Germans chased us on horses and also in cars. Some of those who escaped had arms. I also ran with a group that

possessed a rifle and revolvers. The people returned the Germans' fire, and the Germans withdrew. In this way we managed to reach the forest which was near this camp."[55]

During the next few days, the Germans captured about a hundred of the remaining escapees. Another one hundred remained free somewhere in Poland, and about seventy of the Treblinka escapees survived the Holocaust.

The rebels destroyed part of the camp during the uprising, though the brick gas chambers remained intact. This allowed Globocnik to continue sending transports to Treblinka until August 19, when he began to close it. Stangl, who was certain that Globocnik would punish him for the uprising, was sent instead to Trieste, where he would join Globocnik, Christian Wirth, and Franz Reich-

Entrance to Auschwitz I. 'Work Makes You Free.' Photo courtesy of David M. Crowe.

leitner in fighting partisans. Kurt Franz, who later joined Stangl in Trieste, was given command of Treblinka and ordered to erase all physical evidence of the crimes committed there. He used a hundred Jewish prisoners for this work and later sent thirty of them to help demolish Sobibór. Franz had all his Jewish workers shot once they had finished their work at Treblinka II. Ukrainian guards then burned their bodies. The site was turned over to a former Ukrainian guard, Strebel, to farm. He used the bricks from the former gas chambers to build his farm house.

By the fall of 1943, the SS had murdered almost 1.8 million Jews during *Aktion Reinhard* and the *Erntefest* massacres. But these death camps were only part of the various death facilities operated by the SS, which would continue its campaign against the Jews until the final hours of World War II. And as horrible as these deaths were in the *Aktion Reinhard* camps, the Germans and their collaborators committed equally unbelievable atrocities in two other death camps in the General Government: Auschwitz and Majdanek.

Auschwitz

Like Eichmann, Auschwitz has come to represent the collective horrors of the Shoah. Between 1940 and 1945, the Germans deported 1.1 million Jews, 140,000 to 150,000 Poles, 23,000 Roma, and 15,000 Soviet POWs to Auschwitz, and they murdered almost all of them. More than two thirds of the Jewish victims were from Hungary (438,000) and Poland (300,000). The Roma were from Greater Germany. But Auschwitz is also known for something else—unimaginable medical experiments and its vast slave-labor factory complex.[56]

Though all the death camps were divided into sections, Auschwitz was unique both for its size and sense of permanency. In addition to its three major camps, Auschwitz I, II, and

Crematory and gas chamber at Auschwitz I. Photo courtesy of David M. Crowe.

III, Auschwitz had a network of twenty-eight agricultural and industrial *Nebenlager* (subcamps) that, by 1944, housed 41,500 prisoners. Auschwitz I was the *Stammlager* (main camp), or concentration camp. Auschwitz II-Birkenau was the death camp, and Auschwitz III-Buna/Monowitz was the I. G. Farben complex that used camp labor to manufacture synthetic rubber. Unlike some of the smallish *Aktion Reinhard* camps, Auschwitz was a sprawling prison and death camp complex covering 25 square miles. And although the Germans deported more than 1.3 million people to Auschwitz between 1940 and 1944, only 120,000 to 150,000 people were incarcerated there at any given time.

From the outset, Auschwitz had a horrible reputation for brutality and cruelty. Most of these crimes were committed by members of the camp's large SS sentry staff, which by January 1945 had grown to 4,480 male SS guards and seventy-one female *Aufseherinnen*.[57] They were assisted by a large contingent of inmate leaders who served as *Kapos* (prisoner trustees; Italian, *capo*; French, *caporal*), *Block-*

älteste (block or barracks elders), and *Vorarbeiter* (workers' foreman). In Auschwitz II-Birkenau, inmate *Sonderkommandos* were responsible for removing the bodies from the gas chambers and burning them in the crematoria. Höss vividly described the work of the *Sonderkommandos:*

> They dragged the bodies from the gas chambers, removed the gold teeth, cut off the hair, then dragged the bodies to the pits [used when crematoria were backed up] or to the ovens. On top of that, they had to maintain the fires in the pits, pour off the accumulated fat, and poke holes into the burning mountains of bodies, so that more oxygen could enter.[58]

Stella Müller-Madej, one of three hundred Schindler women sent to Auschwitz for three weeks before being sent on to Oskar Schindler's new factory in Brünnlitz in the fall of 1944, described the capricious cruelty of the female guards: Prisoners would be forced to crawl over crushed brick if they had failed to sew their camp numbers on their

Dr. Josef Mengele (left), Rudolf Höss (center), and Josef Kramer (second from right) at Auschwitz Solahutte retreat. USHMM Photo No. 34755, courtesy of Anonymous Donor.

uniforms properly. Stella also remembered a *Blockälteste* throwing marmalade in her face because she had made the mistake of putting out a piece of bread instead of her hand when in line for the marmalade. Beatings were also a part of the daily routine.[59] Sim Kessel was beaten for what he described as his "worthiest endeavor," reconditioning only two ammunition crates in two months. As punishment, he received the "*Fünfundzwanzig auf Arsch,*" twenty-five lashes on his back side:

> My chastiser's whip cut into muscles and skin that barely covered the unprotected bone. Each blow made my knees buckle. . . . When I tried to straighten up again, my behind running with blood, I thought my lower back was paralyzed. For at least a week, I was unable either to sit down or to stand erect and could only attain the minimum of comfort lying on my stomach. Going to the latrine was indescribable torture, worse than the beating itself.[60]

The SS also tortured prisoners in Block 11's basement and used the "Black Wall" just outside to execute thousands more. Next door was Block 10, where SS physicians conducted horrible medical experiments on inmates.

Those who were not tortured to death or executed often died in inhumane slave-labor conditions. Above the entrance way to Auschwitz I was the "greeting" *Arbeit Macht Frei* (work makes you free). The reality, of course, was much different since the life expectancy in Auschwitz's slave labor units was usually no more than a few months because of the harsh conditions and brutal mistreatment of prisoners. Those who survived much longer were often no more than walking skeletons. Rudolf Vrba (1924–2006) described the struggle for life among Auschwitz's inmates:

> Again I saw the columns trudging towards the gates in rows of five and blocks of a hundred. Fries [*SS- Oberscharführer* Jakob], the

indefatigable, monumental Fries, was there as usual, weeding out the weak and the sick with blows from his huge club, cursing and kicking occasionally at the kapos.

I watched the rejected lope back into the camp in a pathetic attempt at haste, for now they knew they had only one hope. These were the living dead, known for some strange reason as *Muselmanns*, Moslems, the men whose eyes were empty, whose flesh had fled, whose blood was near to water. Off they straggled to the timber yard, where some decent kapo might let them work for their lives, for they knew the alternative was hospitalization which meant a dose of phenol in the heart and death.[61]

The work was unimaginably difficult. Primo Levi (1919–1987) described the almost impossible task of malnourished workers trying to unload a large 2-ton iron cylinder from a wagon and trying to move it to a nearby factory on "wooden sleepers."

But the wooden sleepers are mortized in the ground and weigh about 175 pounds; they are more or less the limits of our strength. The more robust of us, working in pairs, are able to carry sleepers for a few hours; for me it is a torture, the load maims my shoulder-bone. After the first journey I am deaf and almost blind from the effort, and I would stoop to any baseness to avoid the second journey.[62]

Rena Kornreich Gelissen spoke of the pain and fear that swept over her as she worked with other inmates moving a pile of bricks. The *Aufseherin* ordered the young women to form a line and toss the bricks one to another, constantly yelling *"Schnell! Schnell!"* Soon, "blood begins to ooze from my hands," she recalled. "The rough edges of the baked clay slice into our palms, repeating the injuries over and over."[63]

Otto Rosenberg, a Roma prisoner, described most of what he did as a slave laborer at Auschwitz as "senseless work." He "carried sand and stone from there to there and from there to here" with a shovel, and also loaded cement and stones from a wagon. "If you did not move quickly enough when carrying 100 kilo [220 pounds] bags of cement, they would put another one on your shoulders."[64]

Hunger and thirst were a constant for all Auschwitz prisoners since they were given only a portion of the rations they were supposed to receive. Otto Rosenberg recalled: "We were only allowed to drink tea. Drinking water was forbidden. Whoever got water and drank and was caught at it was beaten to death, because the water was infected with typhoid. They wanted to prevent the typhoid from spreading."

Regardless, he searched constantly for water even though camp officials kept the water shut off to prevent prisoners from drinking it. But Rosenberg kept a red cup hidden in his coat and would try to draw water from one of the closed taps when no one was looking. "You had to open the tap and suck on it and as soon as you felt the water, to block the pipe with your tongue. Then I held the cup underneath. Some water always dripped out. What I had sucked out and held in my mouth I also spat into the cup."[65]

Corruption was rampant among the camp's staff, and they often kept the best food for themselves to eat or to trade. The bread was often made of sawdust and dough, and the soup was a mixture of camp grasses, dead mice, human hair, and other things. The average Auschwitz slave laborer subsisted on 750 to 1,500 calories a day. According to Charlotte Delbo, a French political prisoner, the female inmates got ersatz coffee for breakfast, watery soup for lunch, and bread for dinner. There was also occasionally early morning tea in the winter:

To drink tea means triumphing in a wild tug-of-war, a melee of club blows, elbowings, fisticuffs, screams. Consumed by thirst and fever, we whirl and swirl in the melee. We drink our tea standing, jostled by those who

Entrance to Auschwitz II-Birkenau. Photo courtesy of David M. Crowe.

fear not being served and those who want to exit, because they must do so at once, as soon as they're up. A last blow of the whistle. Alles raus [everyone move quickly].[66]

Pelagia Lewinska, a Polish prisoner, remembered the terrible thirst:

Thirst tormented us all from the first moment, the first spoonful of soup tasting of saltpeter. The coffee or infusion granted us each evening was insufficient to desalt us. In many of the blocks, particularly those of Jewesses, there was nothing to drink at all in the evening. The unfortunate women surrounded the other sheds and clung to us on the paths, pleading to buy a little water to drink at no matter what the price. They would give up all their food for that little water.[67]

The Factory of Death: Auschwitz II-Birkenau

Auschwitz II-Birkenau was located 2 miles away from the *Stammlager*. Höss converted an old farm house into the first gas chamber. Over time, he built four large crematoria-gas chambers (II, III, IV, V) and made plans for a fifth (VI). There was also a crematorium (I) at Auschwitz I. Birkenau was made up of three camps (BI, BII, BIII), which were subdivided into nine sections (BIa-b, BIIa-BIIf, and BIII). BIIb, for example, was the Theresienstadt Family Camp and BIIe was the Gypsy Family Camp. Once the deportation trains arrived at Birkenau, Höss used methods similar to those developed for the *Aktion Reinhard* camps for disembarkation, gassing, and body disposal. Once off the trains, the victims were divided along gender lines and forced to give up their personal belongings. As they began to march in columns towards the hidden gas chambers about a quarter of a mile away, they passed through a small line of SS physicians, who, with a gesture to the left or right, decided who would be gassed or who would live briefly as slave laborers. Once they reached the entrance to one of the gas chambers, they walked downstairs where signs directed them: *"zu den Bädern* (to the baths)" and *"zur Desinfektion* (to Disinfection)." Once in the disrobing area, SS officers and *Sonderkommandos* assured the victims that they would be sent to a labor camp after they had showered and received clean clothing. If there was a backlog of victims, some were taken behind the death chambers and shot. After the gassings, SS physicians selected some of the bodies for dissection.

Höss, who seldom watched a gassing, described in his memoirs what happened when the victims were in the gas chamber:

> The door would now be quickly screwed up and the gas discharged by the waiting disinfectors through vents in the ceilings of the gas chambers, down a shaft that led to the floor. This insured the rapid distribution of the gas. It could be observed through the peephole in the door that those who were standing nearest to the induction vents were killed at once. It can be said that about one third died straightaway. The remainder staggered about and began to scream and struggle for air. The screaming, however, soon changed to the death rattle and in a few minutes all lay still. . . . The door was opened half an hour after the induction of the gas and the ventilation switched on . . . the special detachment now set about removing the gold teeth and cutting the hair from the women. After this, the bodies were taken up by elevator and laid in front of the ovens, which had meanwhile been stoked up. Depending on the size of the bodies, up to three corpses could be put into one oven at the same time. The time required for cremation . . . took twenty minutes.[68]

After the chambers were aired out, *Sonderkommandos* entered the chambers, looking for gold and other hidden items. They burned items of no value in special incinerators. They then carried the bodies upstairs for cremation. They combed through the ashes to separate bone and other remains. The ashes were dumped in the Vistula River or in local streams or ponds, and other remains were crushed and buried in nearby pits.

Inmates sorted and stored the victims' food, clothing, and other personal items. The stolen goods of Jewish and other victims were then stored in several dozen barracks that the inmates nicknamed Kanada (Canada), a name they associated with prosperity. Most of the usable goods were either used by the SS or sent to ethnic German colonists in Poland or Ukraine. In February 1943, Höss shipped 824 train cars of goods from Auschwitz and Majdanek for use elsewhere in the Reich. When the Soviets entered Auschwitz in January 1945, they found 350,000 mens' suits, more than 800,000 women's dresses and other personal items, a lot of children's clothing, and almost seven tons of human hair.

The Gypsy Family Camp

On December 16, 1942, Himmler ordered that all Greater Reich *Zigeunermischlinge* be sent to Auschwitz. Himmler, who was fascinated by the mystery of Aryan origins, created the *Ahnenerbe Forshcungs -und Lehrgemeinschaft* (Ancestral Heritage Research and Teaching Society) to investigate the roots of Aryanism. He was convinced that pure Roma groups, such as the Sinti and the Lalleri, provided a key to this mystery because of their Indo-Germanic/Aryan origins. Consequently, as he developed plans for the expulsion of the Roma from the Greater Reich, he wanted to exclude pure-blooded Sinti and Lalleri for further study. Martin Bormann, Hitler's personal secretary, wrote Himmler a letter on December 3, 1942, opposing these exemptions:

> I consider this view of your expert [Dr. Georg Wagner, *Ahnenerbe*'s Roma expert] as overblown. Such a special treatment for the racially pure Gypsies would represent a fundamental departure from presently applied measures for fighting the Gypsy plague and would not be understood by the population

"Canada" warehouses in Auschwitz II-Birkenau. USHMM Photo No. 50788, photographer: Stanislaw Luczko; courtesy of Instytut Pamieci Narodowej.

and the lower ranks of the party leadership. The Führer too would not approve of it if a segment of the Gypsies is given back their old freedoms.[69]

Himmler met personally with Hitler and Bormann on the matter and ultimately convinced the Führer to side with him. His December 16 decree simply mentioned the transport of *Zigeunermischlinge* to Auschwitz. More specific details were outlined in a memo issued by the *Reichskriminalpolizeiamt* (RKPA; Reich Criminal Police Office) on January 29, 1943, which stated that *Zigeunermischlinge* and other Roma groups from the Greater Reich and the Balkans were to be rounded up and sent to a Gypsy Family Camp at Auschwitz. Excluded were Roma married to non-Roma, assimilated Roma, those in the military, skilled Roma workers, foreign Roma, and the children and spouses of Roma in the above categories. In reality,

these exemptions meant little since RKPA gave Kripo officers a lot of authority to decide who was and who was not to be excluded from deportation. Furthermore, Kripo wanted Roma who were allowed to stay in the Reich to be sterilized. The first roundups began in February, and by the end of 1943 Kripo had shipped almost 18,000 Roma to Auschwitz. By the spring of 1944, 23,000 Roma were incarcerated in Auschwitz. Almost all would die there.

Life in the Gypsy Family Camp was harsh and disease was rampant. According to Hermann Langbein (1912–1955), an Auschwitz underground leader and secretary for *SS-Sturmbannführer* Dr. Eduard Wirths (1909–1945), the chief SS physician at Auschwitz:

The Gypsies were all undernourished. I controlled and tasted the food in the kitchen. It was sort of grain soup, no, rather it was water soup with a few grains swimming in it. The imprisoned Gypsies were often shrunken to skeletons. I went to the kitchen and found that the food did not contain the prescribed 1,680 calories. I wrote a memo immediately but Hartjenstein [SS- *Obersturmbannführer* Friedrich, 1904–1954; commandant of Auschwitz II-Birkenau] said "Oh, they are only Gypsies after all."

The Roma, particularly children, were susceptible to a terrible disease known as *noma* [dry gangrene of the face]. "The children were all skin and bone. The thin skin rubbed on the bones and became infected. The sick children would drink the washing-up water as there was often no other water. Sometimes the children's blankets (in the sick barracks) were washed and put back still wet on the beds." *Noma* reminded Langbein of leprosy: "[T]heir little bodies wasted away with gaping holes in the cheeks big enough for one to see through, a slow putrefaction of the living body."[70]

Himmler decided to close the Gypsy Family Camp in the spring of 1944. At this time, there were about 6,000 Roma in Birkenau and 1,500 in Auschwitz I. At 7:00 P.M. on May 16, 1944, SS units surrounded the Roma camp in Birkenau. The day before, *SS-Hauptscharführer* Georg Bonigut, the commandant of the Gypsy Family Camp, told one of the Roma who worked for him about the plans to liquidate the Family Camp. Once the SS was in place, Roma armed with crude weapons came out of the barracks prepared to fight the SS to the death. The SS soon withdrew, fearing a violent confrontation that could possibly spill over into other camps just beyond the barbed wire fence surrounding the Roma compound. During the next three months, the Germans slowly reduced the size of the Gypsy Family Camp by sending about two thirds of its inmates to labor camps in the Reich. On August 2, the SS shipped the Roma in Auschwitz I to Buchenwald. The following evening (*Zigeunernacht*; the night of

the Roma), the SS rounded up Birkenau's remaining 2,897 Roma and gassed them.

We were within easy ear shot of the terrible final scenes as German criminal prisoners using clubs and dogs were let loose in the camp against the women, children, and old men. A desperate cry from a young Czech-speaking lad suddenly rent the air. "Please Mr. SS man, let me live." Blows with a club were the only answer. Eventually, all inmates were crammed into lorries and driven away to the crematorium. Again they tried to offer resistance, many protesting that they were Germans.

Terrible scenes took place. Women and children were on their knees in front of Mengele and Boger [SS- *Scharführer* Wilhelm; 1906–?] crying, "Take pity, take pity on us." Nothing helped. They were beaten down brutally, trampled on and pushed on to the trucks. It was a terrible gruesome sight. Some persons lay lifeless after being beaten and were also thrown on to the lorries.[71]

Before Birkenau's remaining Roma had been sent to the gas chambers, Dr. Josef Mengele, the Gypsy camp physician, marked a Z.S. on the chests of twelve sets of Roma twins. Mengele, who had a laboratory in the Gypsy Family Camp, wanted to keep their bodies for further medical experiments.[72]

Medical Experiments in Auschwitz I and II

Some of the Nazis' most inhumane experiments took place at Auschwitz. The Germans set up seventy-five medical experiment programs in Europe between 1939 and 1945. Two hundred physicians and their staffs conducted gruesome experiments on more than 7,000 victims. Two medical experiment programs were conducted at Auschwitz; one was run by *SS- Sturmbannführer* Dr. Carl Clauberg (1898–1957), a former professor of gynecology at the University of Königsberg. Clauberg joined the Nazi Party in 1933 and rapidly rose through the ranks of the SS because of his enthusiastic support for the Nazi movement. Clauberg specialized in the treatment of infertility. In 1940, he met with Himmler and told him of plans to set up a special institute to treat infertility and find cheap, quick, nonmedical ways to sterilize patients. Himmler, interested only in the sterilization part of Clauberg's research, agreed to fund his work. In 1941, Himmler suggested that Clauberg move his research program to Ravensbrück women's camp, located outside of Berlin. Instead, Clauberg convinced Himmler to let him set up his new laboratories at Auschwitz because it was closer to Clauberg's clinic in Königsberg.

Clauberg experimented on more than seven hundred victims, many of them Jewish and Roma women in Auschwitz I's medical lab in Block 10. According to one of Clauberg's Jewish victims:

> Dr. Clauberg ordered me to lie down on the gynecological table. I was able to observe Sylvia Friedman [a prison orderly] preparing an injection syringe with a long needle. Dr. Clauberg used this needle to give me an injection [of formalin] in my womb. I felt that my belly would burst with the pain. I began to scream so that I could be heard throughout the entire block. Dr. Clauberg told me roughly to stop screaming immediately, otherwise I'd be returned at once to the camp, to Birkenau [i.e., the gas chamber]. . . . After this experiment I had an inflammation of the ovaries.[73]

Clauberg was assisted by Dr. Johannes Göbel (1891–1952), a former chief chemist who had helped develop formalin (a blend of formaldehyde, water, and methyl alcohol) while working for Schering, the German pharmaceutical company. Formalin proved to be an ineffective sterilization drug, though Clauberg continued to use it in his experi-

ments despite growing criticism from other physicians at Auschwitz. In late 1944, he fled to Ravensbrück, taking some of his patients with him. He was captured by the Red Army, tried, and sentenced to twenty-five years in prison by a Soviet court for his crimes. After his release in 1955, he returned unrepentantly to West Germany, where he bragged of his work. He was soon imprisoned and died mysteriously in 1957.

SS- Sturmbannführer and *Luftwaffe Oberleutnant* Dr. Horst Schumann (1906–1983) also worked in Block 10. He sterilized 1,000 Jews and Poles with powerful x-rays. Most of his "patients" died during the procedure. He removed the ovaries of the women who survived and castrated his male victims. He left Auschwitz in early 1945 and joined Clauberg in Ravensbrück, where he experimented on Roma women. Dr. Eduard Wirths and his brother, Dr. Helmut Wirths, conducted research on cervical cancer in Block 10. This block was also home to a small branch of the SS's *Hygienischen Institutes der Waffen SS* (Hygienic Institute of the Waffen SS); the institute's head physician, *SS- Hauptsturmführer* Dr. Bruno Weber (1915–1956), conducted painful blood and bacteria experiments on patients.

But *SS- Hauptsturmführer* Dr. Josef Mengele (1911–1979), who held a PhD from the University of Munich and an MD from Frankfurt University, conducted the most notorious medical experiments at Auschwitz. A gifted medical researcher, Mengele specialized in the relationship between heredity and physical characteristics. When the war cut short his research, he served with various Waffen-SS units until he was wounded in action in Russia. Afterwards, he requested a transfer to a concentration camp; in the spring of 1943, he was sent to Auschwitz. Wirths, a great admirer of Mengele's, made him chief physician at the Gypsy Family Camp. Mengele was particularly interested in twins and Roma children afflicted with *noma,*

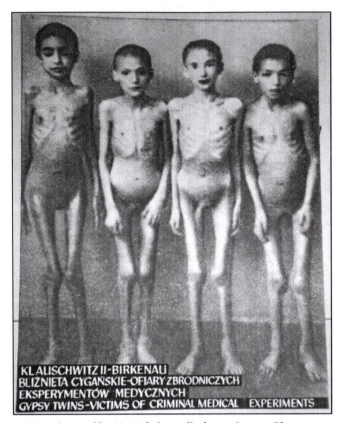

KL.AUSCHWITZ II-BIRKENAU
BLIŹNIĘTA CYGAŃSKIE-OFIARY ZBRODNICZYCH
EKSPERYMENTÓW MEDYCZNYCH
GYPSY TWINS-VICTIMS OF CRIMINAL MEDICAL EXPERIMENTS

Roma twins used by Mengele in medical experiments. Photo courtesy of David M. Crowe and Auschwitz State Museum.

though he also experimented on dwarfs.[74] He hoped his research would lead to "a biological and medical clean-up of society and its preventive hygiene."[75]

His former mentor at Frankfurt University, Otmar Freiherr von Verschur (1896–1969), who was now head of the prestigious *Kaiser–Wilhelm–Institut für Anthropologie, Menschliche Erblehre und Eugenik* (Kaiser Wilhelm Institute for Anthropology, Human Genetics, and Eugenics) in Berlin, helped Mengele secure a government grant to do his research in Auschwitz on twins. Mengele also served as Verschur's assistant at the Kaiser Wilhelm Institute during his time at Auschwitz and supplied him with data on the bodies of Roma, twins, human heads, eyeballs, and organs for further "research." After the war, the West German government fined Verschur 600 marks for his

wartime activities. In 1951, he became the chair in human genetics at the University of Münster, a position he held until his death in 1969.

To strengthen his research team, Mengele ordered the transfer of Dr. Bertold Epstein, a world-famous Jewish pediatrician, to Auschwitz II to treat Roma children suffering from *noma*. Epstein's assistant, Dr. Rudolf Vitek-Weisskopf, described *noma*: "A blister appeared on the mucous membrane inside the mouth and quickly spread until it covered the skin of the whole face. The tissue wasted away so quickly that the oral cavity was exposed. The process of decay also frequently spread with rapidity to the cheekbones and could destroy half of the face, if death did not occur first."[76]

When the SS closed the Gypsy Family Camp, Mengele shifted his interests to the Jews in the Theresienstadt Family Camp, where he was assisted by Dr. Miklos Nyiszli (1901–1956), a Jewish physician from Hungary. After *Zigeunernacht*, Mengele ordered Nyiszli to do a pathological study of the twelve sets of Roma twins he had saved from cremation. Nyiszli's memoirs, *Auschwitz: A Doctor's Eyewitness Account*, deals with his work with Mengele and the lives of the Jewish *Sonderkommandos* who worked in the gas chambers and crematoria. His memoirs provided the basis for the 2001 film *The Grey Zone*. Mengele, who also joined other SS physicians in the *Selektion* of new arrivals at Birkenau, seemed to be one of the few who enjoyed this life-or-death selection process.

Mengele opened a kindergarten for the children he was studying at the Gypsy Family Camp. He supplied his young charges with good food, toys, and even a playground; they, in turn, called him "Uncle Pepi." In reality, the kindergarten was a showpiece for SS leadership visits. Though it difficult to determine

Heinrich Himmler (center left) visits Auschwitz III-Buna/Monowitz. USHMM Photo No. 50777, courtesy of Instytut Pamieci Narodowej.

the number of twins that Mengele experimented on in 1943–1944, Dr. Nyiszli said there were several hundred to choose from throughout Auschwitz.

Mengele took detailed measurements of the twins he worked on. They often died after he had collected their blood or given them blood transfusions. On one occasion, Mengele had two Gypsy twins sewn together. Vera Alexander, a Jewish nurse, described the gruesome operation:

One day Mengele brought chocolate and special clothes. The next day an SS man, on Mengele's instructions, took away two children, who happened to be my two favorites: Guido and Nino, aged about four. Two, perhaps three days later the SS man brought them back in a frightening condition. They had been sewn together like Siamese twins. The hunchbacked child was tied to the second one on the back

and wrists. Mengele had sewn their veins together. Their wounds were filthy and they festered. There was a powerful stench of gangrene. The children screamed all night long. Somehow their mother managed to get hold of morphine and put an end to their suffering.[77]

Auschwitz III-Buna/Monowitz

Almost immediately after they arrived in Auschwitz, inmates were selected for quarantine or death:

Those happy few who survived the selection on the ramp were marched off to the quarantine barracks, where they were initiated into a series of rituals designed to destroy their identity and their personality and thus their capacity for resistance. First they were taken to the yard between Blocks 15 and 16 and ordered to strip off all their clothes. All their hair was shaved off. Then they had to run to a nearby bathhouse and take a cold shower. Then they had to run to another yard where they were provided with ill-fitting blue and white stripped prison uniforms and wooden clogs. Their uniforms bore triangles of different colors, according to the categories of prisoners— green for professional criminals, red for political opposition, black for prostitutes and other "asocials," pink for homosexuals, purple for fundamentalist "exponents of the Bible." (Jews who fitted any of these categories had their yellow triangle superimposed on their other triangle to form a Star of David.) Finally, the prisoners were tattooed on the left forearm with their prison number. Henceforth, they were told, they were to be known only by this number, not by name.[78]

If an inmate survived quarantine, he or she was sent to a forced-labor unit in Auschwitz I, Auschwitz II-Birkenau, or to the Auschwitz III-Buna/Monowitz complex or one of its subsidiary camps; a few inmates were chosen for medical experiments. There were different types of subsidiary camps, most of them using Jewish slave laborers; many of the subsidiary camps were located some distance from Auschwitz, where inmates worked in the factories, mines, and other facilities of major German companies such as I. G. Farben, Krupp, Siemens-Schuckert, and Hermann Göring Werke. About two thirds of the subsidiary camps did work for the German armament industry. These factories hired the workers (about two thirds of them were Jews) from the SS for Zł 5 ($1.56) a day for males and Zł 4 ($1.25) for females. The factories were allowed to deduct up to Zł 1.60 ($0.50) for "maintenance."[79]

Resistance in Auschwitz

Auschwitz's large slave-labor population dictated the breadth of underground activity. This involved not only acts of physical rebellion, escape planning, and attempts but also efforts to save people from death. In 1943, inmates formed a multinational *Kampfgruppe Auschwitz* (Battle Group Auschwitz) in all three camps. Young Czech Zionists formed a separate resistance group in the Theresienstadt Family Camp. The group's plans for revolt collapsed after the suicide of one of its leaders, Freddy Hirsch (?–1943). Individuals and groups within the camp established contacts with prisoners who had access to food and medical supplies. The underground would use these goods to bribe sympathetic guards and establish links to the outside world. The Auschwitz underground was also able to keep some inmates informed about the course of the war and to send reports through the Polish underground to the British government in London about what was happening in Auschwitz.

But some of the most daring acts of resistance were unplanned. On October 23, 1943, a transport of 1,800 Polish Jews arrived in Auschwitz. Unaware of their fate, the men and women were separated, with the women sent to Crematorium II and the men to Crematorium III. It was not until they began to undress that the women realized they were about to be sent to their deaths. After undressing, one woman threw her clothes at *SS-Unterscharführer* Joseph Schillinger and seized his pistol. She shot him three times and wounded another guard, Wilhelm Emmerich. Jerzy Tabeau, a Polish survivor, described what happened next: "The other women fell on the SS with their bare hands; one received a bite wound on the nose, another's face was scratched. . . . Some of the women were shot down, the rest were led to the gas chambers and killed. Schillinger died on the way to the hospital. Emmerich eventually recovered his health; his leg, however, was lamed."[80]

The most dramatic rebellion in Auschwitz took place on October 7, 1944, when three

Ruins of Crematorium II at Auschwitz II-Birkenau. Photo courtesy of David M. Crowe.

hundred *Sonderkommandos*, who had just learned of Himmler's plans to close Auschwitz, blew up crematorium IV and fought the SS with hammers and axes. The SS killed 451 Jews during the uprising and executed others involved in the plot.

Himmler ordered the crematoria at Auschwitz I and II destroyed after the October 7 rebellion; he sent the salvageable equipment to the Groß-Rosen concentration camp. He then ordered special work units to remove all traces of the mass murders that took place at Birkenau and to reclaim the site by planting trees over the ash pits. On January 17, 1945, the Germans began to force march Auschwitz's remaining 58,000 prisoners westward. Many of them died during this death march. Ten days later, the Red Army liberated Auschwitz. All that remained of its once vast prisoner population were 7,000 sick or dying inmates.

Majdanek

Like Auschwitz, Majdanek was a sprawling (676 acres) death and forced-labor camp. In the summer of 1941, Himmler ordered Globocnik to open a labor camp in the suburbs of Lublin that would house from 25,000 to 50,000 forced laborers. Globocnik would then use Majdanek's prisoners to build an SS center in the Lublin region that would become, among other things, an SS base of operations for activities in the Soviet Union. It opened as the *Kreigsgefangenenlager der Waffen SS in Lublin* (*KGL Lublin*; Waffen-SS POW Camp Lublin). In 1943, it became the *Konzentrationslager der Waffen SS Lublin* (*KL Lublin*; Waffen-SS Concentration Camp Lublin). More than a half million prisoners passed through Majdanek during its three-year existence. Of this number, 360,000 of them would die there, 60 percent from harsh labor conditions, malnutrition, or

Crematory at Majdanek. Photo courtesy of David M. Crowe.

disease. One hundred thousand of the victims were Poles, 80,000 were Jews, and 50,000 Soviet POWs.[81] Those who did not die from harsh camp conditions either were executed on the camp's gallows or guillotine or were gassed in one of Majdanek's four gas chambers. Two were outfitted to use carbon monoxide and Zyklon B, and two used Zyklon B exclusively. Oddly enough, most of the Lublin ghetto's Jews died in Bełżec, though several thousand were murdered in Majdanek before the ghetto's closing in the summer of 1944.

Majdanek had various forced-labor satellite camps throughout the region, including one in Warsaw. The main camp was run by two hundred SS men and a staff of from 900–1,200 guards. Most of them were Lithuanians or *Volksdeutsche* from Croatia and Romania. The first commandant was *SS- Standartenführer* Karl Otto Koch (1897–1945), the former commandant at Buchenwald. Himmler, who was fond of Koch, sent him and his wife, Ilse Koch (1906–1967), "*Die Hexe von Buchen-*

wald (the Witch of Buchenwald)," to Majdanek despite charges of corruption and brutality at Buchenwald. The Kochs soon ran afoul of the SS, which again charged them with the same crimes at Majdanek. The SS arrested both of them and executed Karl Koch for his crimes in April 1945. Himmler released Ilse Koch, who was tried by the United States for war crimes after the war and sentenced to life imprisonment. General Lucius D. Clay (1897–1978), the commander of the U.S. Zone in Germany, pardoned her, but public protests led to her arrest again in 1951. She committed suicide while in prison in 1967.

Koch was succeeded by *SS- Obersturmführer* Max Koegel (1895–1947), the former commandant at the Ravensbrück women's camp. Himmler replaced him with *SS- Standartenführer* Hermann Florstedt (1895–1945), Koch's former adjutant. Florstedt continued his mentor's campaign of terror and mass murder and was often present at the *Selektion* of recently arrived prisoners.

Slave laborers at Majdanek. USHMM Photo No. 50496, courtesy of Instytut Pamieci Narodowej.

After a Jewish transport had arrived, it was isolated in an empty yard surrounded with barbed wire, next to the bath and the gas chamber situated in the same building. . . . There the Jews would spend the first night in the open air. In the morning, Florstedt, assisted by [SS- Obersturmführer Anton; 1912–1946] Thumann (head of the prisoner division) and the crematorium's chief, Muhstedt [SS- Oberscharführer Muhsfeldt, Erich; 1913–1947], started the selection of prisoners. The healthy and the young ones were sent to the bath. The old and weak and the children were directed to the other room, seemingly furnished like a bath, which actually was a gas chamber. . . .

The prisoners from smaller transports, who had not been gassed for various reasons, were assembled in a shed next to the old crematorium, in the so-called Zwischenfeld between Compounds 1 and 2. After the evening roll call, when the traffic in the camp sub-

sided, the door to the adjoining room would open and the prisoners were summoned one by one. Two hoodlums holding metal bars were standing behind the door and struck the incomers on the head. This continued until all were done away with.[82]

Florstedt was as corrupt as the Kochs, and an SS court indicted him for failing to send the property of dead prisoners to Berlin. Himmler replaced him with SS- Obersturmbannführer Martin Weiss (1905–1946). Majdanek's last commandant, Arthur Liebehenschel (1901–1948), served only for a few months before the Red Army liberated the camp on July 23, 1944.

Though life was harsh in all of Germany's concentration camps, Majdanek gained a special reputation for brutality. At first, most prisoners were shot, though by the fall of 1942, the SS began to gas most of its victims. Mass shootings resumed the following September.

The worst massacre took place on November 3, 1943, as part of the *Erntefest* campaign. Several days before, prisoners dug three large ditches behind the crematorium. Globocnik transferred a hundred SS men and Order Policemen to Majdanek from Auschwitz, Kraków, Warsaw, and elsewhere for the executions. In twenty-four hours, they shot 10,000 Jews from Majdanek and its satellite camps.

A Polish prisoner, Feliks Siejwa, described the executions:

> When the first columns came level with the pool, the Germans started forming columns of a hundred each, and led them towards the gate. Following the first, second, third, and forth [*sic*] hundred, there were more, till not a single miserable Jew [was left].
>
> The first machine-gun shots were heard, immediately drowned out by the sound of an army parade march, flowing from the tens of loudspeakers placed up on poles to that purpose erected during the night. From that moment till 2 pm a loud orchestra went on and on, playing marches, tangos, sentimental waltzes. This infernal concert went on, nonstop, for eight hours; for eight hours death was beating the gruesome staccato.[83]

Another prisoner who survived the massacres, Ida Mazower, talked about her fears:

> [W]e were still not certain what our fate was going to be. Most were sure that they would leave us alone only for a while to wait for our turn to come, and them would appear to fetch us too. An S. S. from the Revier approached us and said, "Do you know what they did to your inmates? Soon they'll do the same to you," and broke into tears. Immediately afterwards, a supervisor came to tell us to fall into line by fives. The S. S. from the Revier brought fifteen more women, his acquaintances. He took us to field I [Field I was one of five barracks' complexes and farthest from the execution site], into a block where there were bowls of still warm soup dished up for those who had just been murdered.[84]

What sustained other prisoners like Feliks Siewja and Ida Mazower were their own acts of spiritual resistance in Majdanek. Polish female prisoners formed camp "families," though one Majdanek survivor, Gizella Abramson, said she was afraid to make new friends after losing someone close to her in the camp. When that happened, the survivor tended to turn inward, fearful of the pain of losing someone else. Slovak Jews secretly sang songs in Hebrew in the evening. There were also secret compositions, such as the *Judenlied des K. G. L. Lublin* (The Jewish Song of Concentration Camp Lublin) and *O Yoy Majdanek unsere Leben und Tod* (Majdanek Our Life and Death). There were also acts of physical resistance; for example, Gizella Abramson, who cleaned SS offices, stole blank copies of SS forms and letterheads. She smuggled them out of the camp to the Polish underground, which used them for false documents and orders. There were numerous escape attempts and some successful escapes.

Liquidation of the Major Ghettos

Himmler used six ghettos in Warsaw, Vilna, Minsk, Riga, Kovno, and Łódź as major concentration centers for Jews in occupied Poland and the Soviet Union. Himmler never intended these ghettos to be permanent, and once they had outlived their usefulness as concentration or labor camps and/or transit points, he ordered them closed. His efforts to liquidate the Reich's largest ghetto in Warsaw triggered the most dramatic Jewish uprising of the Holocaust.

The Warsaw Ghetto Uprising: April 19–May 16, 1943

The SS began deporting Jews from the Warsaw ghetto in the summer of 1942. On July 22, *SS- Sturmbannführer* Hermann Höfle met

Memorial to 1943 Warsaw ghetto uprising, Warsaw. Photo courtesy of David M. Crowe.

with Adam Czerniaków, the head of the ghetto's *Judenrat,* and told him that "all the Jews irrespective of sex and age, with certain exceptions, [would] be deported to the East." Höfle ordered Czerniaków to "provide" 6,000 people for deportation by 4:00 P.M. that afternoon, the minimum number of people to be deported each day.[85]

That afternoon, Höfle told Czerniaków that his wife would not be subject to deportation. However, if Czerniaków interfered with the deportations in any way, she would be "the first one shot as a hostage." The next day, Czerniaków committed suicide rather than supply Höfle with more Jewish victims. "[S]o far 4,000 are ready to go," he noted in his last diary entry at 3:00 P.M. on July 23. "The orders," he wrote, "are there must be 9,000 by 4 o'clock."[86] Before he bit into the cyanide tablet that ended his life, Czerniaków wrote to his wife, Dr. Felicja (Niunia) Czerniaków, and told her that Höfle's order for the 23rd included children. He simply could not send children to their deaths. Felicja somehow managed to escape from the ghetto after her husband's death and was hidden by Polish

friends. She was able to smuggle her husband's diary out of the ghetto, which she published after the war.

Janusz Korczak (1878–1942) took a similar stand for the children of his orphanage in the ghetto. Korczak, the pen name of the famous Polish children's writer and pediatrician, Dr. Henryk Goldszmit, had opened the Dom Sierot orphanage for Jewish children in Warsaw in 1912. For the next thirty years, he was assisted by Stefania Wilczyńska (1886–1942) in his work with Warsaw's Jewish orphans. Korczak, who served in the Russian army during the Russo-Japanese War (1904–1906) and World War I, tried to enlist in the Polish army when the Germans invaded in 1939. He was rejected because of his age. He refused to acknowledge the German occupation of Poland and would not wear the Star of David, an act of resistance that landed him in prison. After his release, he moved the orphanage into the ghetto and dedicated himself to the wellbeing of his beloved children. Polish friends tried to convince Korczak to leave the ghetto, but he refused. On August 6, 1942, the SS raided the orphanage and escorted its 192 children and ten

Statute to Jan Korczak, Warsaw Jewish cemetery. Photo courtesy of David M. Crowe.

instructors, including Korczak and Wilczyńska, to the ghetto's dreaded *Umschlagplatz* for transport to Treblinka. They were joined by 4,000 other children and their instructors. SS troops, Ukrainian volunteers, and Jewish policemen lined the way.

Marek Edelman (1922–?), one of the leaders of the Warsaw Ghetto Uprising, described the horror of the *Umschlagplatz:*

No words of any human language are strong enough to describe the "Umschlag" now, when no help from anywhere or anybody can be expected. The sick, the adults as well as children,

previously brought here from the hospital, lie deserted in the cold halls. They relieve themselves right where they lie, and remain in the stinking slime of excrement and urine. Nurses search the crowd for their fathers and mothers and, having found them, inject longed for deathly morphine into their veins, their own eyes gleaming wildly. One doctor compassionately pours a cyanide solution into the feverish mouths of strange, sick children. To offer one's cyanide to somebody else is a really heroic sacrifice, for cyanide is now the most precious, the most irreplaceable thing. It brings a quiet, peaceful death, it saves from the horror of the cars.[87]

Korczak, ever the disciplinarian, did everything possible to calm his children. At the *Umschlagplatz,* Korzcak learned that influential Polish friends had intervened on his behalf and that he could return to the orphanage, but without his children. Korzcak refused.

As Korczak led his children calmly toward the cattle cars, the Jewish police cordoning off a path for them saluted instinctively. Remba [Nahum Remba; a *Judenrat* official] burst into tears when the Germans asked who that man was. A wail went up from those still left on the square. Korczak walked, head held high, holding a child by each hand, his eyes straight ahead with his characteristic gaze, as if seeing something far away.[88]

When World War II ended, Korczak became an international martyr because of his legendary courage; he is a national hero in Israel and has won respect in Poland for his writings and work with children. A statue of Korczak stands to the right of the entranceway to the sprawling Jewish cemetery in Warsaw. In 1978, UNESCO (United Nations Educational, Scientific, and Cultural Organization) declared 1978–1979 the year of Korczak in league with the Year of the Child.

As the deportations mounted, an equally brave group of Jewish activists decided to resist further deportations. The *Judenrat* and the *Żydowskie Towarzystwo Opieki Spolecznej* (ŻTOS; Jewish Mutual Aid Society) agreed to work with the Jewish underground movement in the ghetto. In late July 1942, several organizations created the *Żydowska Organizacja Bojowa* (ŻOB; Jewish Defense Organization). Desperate for arms, the ŻOB contacted the Polish underground *Armija Krajowa* (AK; Home Army), which sent it a small number of weapons. Why, Israel Gutman asked, was AK so unwilling to help the Jews in the Warsaw ghetto? First of all,

> the officers of the AK did not consider the Jews capable of preparing themselves for armed resistance. Another reason was the suspicious attitude that Jews were potential Communists, and still another reason was the fact that the AK's political and strategic aims were mainly directed toward activating the Polish forces at the end of the war, and not towards stirring up the atmosphere in Warsaw or encouraging the creation of another focus of fighting in the city.[89]

Evidently the leadership of the AK was unaware of the fact that almost 200,000 Jews had served in the Polish armed forces at the beginning of World War II.

The Jews who remained in the Warsaw ghetto after the first wave of deportations were now more willing to support underground organizations such as ŻOB and *Żydowski Zwiazek Wojskowy* (ZZW; Jewish Military Union). Consequently, when the Germans began the second wave of deportations on January 18, 1943, several underground groups fought back. More and more Jews refused to report to the *Umschlagplatz* and instead found hiding places in the ghetto. The SS responded with raids to keep up deportation numbers. The Germans began their final sweep of the Warsaw ghetto on

April 19, 1943, the eve of Passover. Himmler sent a force of 868 men under the Warsaw district's SSPF, *SS- Oberführer* Ferdinand von Sammern-Frankenegg (1897–1944), to round up all Jews still there. Frankenegg's forces met with such strong resistance that Himmler relieved him of his command and replaced him immediately with *SS- Gruppenführer und Generalleutnant der Waffen-SS* Jürgen Stroop (1895–1952). Stroop met equally strong resistance during his units' forays into the ghetto.

Mordecai Anielewicz (1919–1943), the ŻOB commander, wrote to Yitzhak Zuckerman (1915–1981), a fellow resistance leader:

> Something has happened which is beyond our wildest dreams. The German have fled twice from the Ghetto. . . . From this evening we move over to partisan methods of operation. Three of our squads go out tonight, with two objectives: to get food and to secure weapons. . . . I cannot describe the conditions under which the Jews are living. Very few will hold out. Sooner or later the rest will perish. The die is cast. In all the bunkers where our comrades are hiding, it is impossible to light a candle at night for lack of air. . . . Keep well, dear friend. Perhaps we shall meet again. The main thing is—the dream of my life has come true. I have lived to see a Jewish defence force in the Ghetto in all its greatness and glory.[90]

For the next twenty-three days, a ragtag army of 750 Jews equipped with few weapons held off more than 2,000 German troops. When forced to surface by scorching fires, gas, poison, or police dogs, the rebels fought to the death. Marek Edelman described the scene:

> The flames cling to our clothes which now start smouldering. The pavement melts under our feet into a black, gooey substance. Broken glass, littering every inch of the streets, is transformed into a sticky liquid in which our feet are caught. Our soles begin to

Underground survivors of the Warsaw ghetto uprising atop ruins of bunker at Mila 18. USHMM Photo No. 17920, courtesy of Leah Hammerstein Silverstein.

burn from the heat on the stone pavement. One after another we stagger through the conflagration. From house to house, from courtyard to courtyard, with no air to breathe, with a hundred hammers clanging in our heads, with burning rafters continuously falling over us, we finally reach the end of the area on fire. We felt lucky just to stand here, to be out of the inferno.[91]

Once in the central part of the ghetto, Edelman and the other Jewish guerillas continued their fight against the Germans until May 10, when, Edelman noted, "the history of the Warsaw Jews came to an end."[92]

Six days later, Stroop sent a report to *SS-Obergruppenführer und General der Polizei* Friedrich-Wilhelm Krüger, the HSSPF in the General Government, claiming "180 Jews, bandits, and subhumans destroyed." He added: "The Jewish quarter of Warsaw is no more! The grand operation terminated at 2015 hours when the Warsaw synagogue was blown up. The total number of Jews apprehended and destroyed, according to record, is 56,065."[93]

In a final report on May 24, Stroop told Krüger that the Germans had killed 7,000 Jews in the fighting and had sent another 6,929 to Treblinka. Stroop, who was later tried and executed in Poland for war crimes, wrote that in addition to the 65,065 Jews his troops executed, another 5,000 to 6,000 Jews were killed in explosions. Stroop's forces captured nine rifles and fifty-nine pistols. The Jewish fighters, Stroop claimed, had killed only sixteen Germans and had wounded eighty-five. His earlier reports contradict these figures. Moreover, Stroop does not account for the several hundred Jews who remained hidden in the ghetto's bunkers, and the 20,000 who had fled to the Polish side in the months before the Jewish uprising. Edelman, for example, re-

SS arrests members of the Jewish underground, Warsaw ghetto uprising, 1943. USHMM Photo No. 46193, courtesy of National Archives and Records Administration, College Park.

ported that at least two ŻOB battle groups survived the German onslaught and remained in the ghetto until June.[94] Some of the Jews who survived the 1943 uprising would fight in the Polish Warsaw uprising, which took place from August 1 to October 2, 1944.

Vilna

Vilna (Vilnius), the "Jerusalem of the North," had a prewar Jewish population of 200,000. When the Germans occupied the city on June 24, 1941, only 57,000 to 59,000 Jews remained in Vilna. Within weeks after the German occupation of Vilna on June 24, 1941, the SS began a campaign of mass murder at a former Soviet fuel depot at Ponary. In the next two months, they murdered 13,000 Jews. That fall, Hans Christian Hingst, the *Gebeitskommissar* (district commissioner) in Vilna, and his Jewish expert, Franz Murer (1917–1963), the "Butcher of Wilna," opened two ghettos in the

city.[95] Jews without a *schiene* (work permit) were sent to Ghetto 2; those with proper work papers went to Ghetto 1. In the first three weeks of October, the Germans liquidated Ghetto 2, sending from 9,000 to 11, 000 residents to Ponary and death. Since from 27,000 to 28,000 Jews remained in the Vilna ghetto, Hingst planned to reduce this number to 12,000 by limiting the number of "yellow *scheine*" given to ghetto residents. The SS conducted several sweeps through the ghetto that ultimately reduced its population to 12,000. Another 8,000 Jews were in hiding.

Some members of the *He-Halutz* (the Pioneer) Jewish youth movement, which prepared young people for settlement in Palestine, issued a call for a campaign against the Germans in response to the ongoing massacres. On January 1, 1942, *He-Halutz* issued a manifesto in Yiddish and Hebrew written by Abba Kovner (1918–1988). It read:

Abba Kovner in Vilna, 1944. USHMM Photo No. 24561, courtesy of Vitka Kempner Kovner.

illusion. Your children, your wives, and husbands are no more. Ponar is no concentration camp. All were shot dead there. Hitler conspires to kill all the Jews of Europe, and the Jews of Lithuania have been picked at the first line. Let us not be led as sheep to the slaughter!

True, we are weak and defenceless. But the only answer to the murderer is: To rise up with arms!

Brethren! Better fall as free fighters than to live at the mercy of murderers. Rise up! Rise up until your last breath.[96]

Oddly enough, a period of calm settled over the ghetto once Hingst had reduced its population. Jacob Gens (1905–1943), who became head of the *Judenrat* in the summer of 1942, encouraged the development of an extensive community welfare system and some semblance of cultural life in the ghetto. Gens, a former hospital administrator and head of the ghetto police, became disillusioned with the activities of the *Fareynegte Partizaner Organizatsye* (FPO; United Partisan Organization), fearing they would bring harsh reprisals from the Germans. Herman Kruk discussed this conflict in his diary:

Jewish youth!

Do not place your trust in those who deceive you. Of 80,000 Jews in "Yerushalayim de Lita [Jerusalem of Lithuania]," only 20,000 are left. Our parents, brothers, and sisters were torn from us before our eyes. Where are the hundreds of men who were seized for labor?

Where are the naked women and the children seized from us on the night of fear? Where are the Jews sent on the Day of Atonement? [Yom Kippur, Judaism's most holy day]

And where are our brethren of the second ghetto? No one returned of those marched through the gates of the ghetto. All the roads of the Gestapo lead to Ponar. And Ponar means death. Those who waver, put aside all

1. The behavior of the police is a logical consequence of involving it in the activity of the ghetto cadre. The police now feel the org. [FPO] is a hostile political force and want to paralyze its activity.

2. Every kind of armed resistance against the Jewish police is a provocation for the "outside" [Germans] and can lead to complete liquidation of the ghetto.

3. Our participation in the org. [FPO] means taking on the martyr's role of being able to die like men. An armed struggle with the ghetto authorities means bringing about the downfall of the ghetto.

4. We must try to influence the ghetto police. But by no means to allow social and historical crime of exploding the ghetto.[97]

This conflict worsened after the Wittenberg incident in mid-July. The Germans demanded that Gens arrest Itsak Wittenberg, an FPO leader, or risk the liquidation of the ghetto. When the arrest attempt failed, Hingst warned Gens that if Wittenberg was not taken into custody, the SS would close the ghetto. The general sense in the ghetto was that Wittenberg had to surrender. Wittenberg agreed, and he turned himself in to Sipo on July 16. The following day, he was found dead in his cell. Gens had given him a cyanide tablet the evening before. Ghetto residents now regarded Wittenberg as a hero because of his sacrifice.

In August and September 1943, the SS deported more than 7,000 ghetto Jews to a concentration camp in Estonia. During a German *Aktion* on September 1, FPO forces attacked German units in the ghetto. Before the assault, FPO leaders issued the following manifesto:

Jews! Defend yourselves with arms! The German and Lithuanian hangmen have arrived at the gates of the ghetto. They have come to murder us! Within a short while, they will lead us group after group through the gate. Thus they led us out on the Day of Atonement [Yom Kippur]! Thus they led us out on the night of the White, the Yellow and the Pink Passes. Thus they led our brethren and sisters, our mothers and fathers, our children. Thus were tens of thousands taken out to their death! But we shall not go! We shall not stretch out our necks like sheep for the slaughter! Jews! Defend yourselves with arms! Do not believe the reassuring prevarications of the murderers. Do not believe the statements of the traitors. Anyone who does go out of the ghetto gate has only one route—to Ponar. And Ponar means death! Jews! We have nothing to lose, death will snatch us up in any event. And who still believes he will remain alive when the assassin is obliterating us with systematic consistency.

The hand of the hangman will fall upon every person. Flight and cowardice will not save life! Only armed resistance can save our lives and honor. Brothers! Better to fall in battle in the ghetto than to be led as sheep to Ponar. And know ye: There is an organized Jewish force within the walls of the ghetto that will rise up with arms. Lend a hand to the revolt! Do not cower in hideouts and *malines*. Your end will be to die as rats in the grips of the murderers.

Jewish masses! Go out into the street! Whoever has no weapons, take up a hatchet; and whoever has no hatchet, take steel and cudgel and stick! For our fathers. For our murdered children! To revenge Ponar, hit the murderers! In every street, in every courtyard, in every room. Inside the ghetto and outside it. Hit as the dogs! Jews! We have nothing to lose! We shall save our lives only if we wipe out our murderers. Long live freedom! Long live armed defense, Death to the murderers!

September 1, 1943, Vilna Ghetto
The Command of the F.P.O.[98]

Gens convinced the Germans to withdraw from the ghetto by promising them that he would round up the Jews they needed for transport. There were still from 11,000 to 12,000 Jews living in the ghetto. During the lull, several hundred FPO members escaped into the forests and joined the partisans. Two weeks later, Gens was summoned to local Gestapo headquarters and shot. He was warned beforehand that the Germans were planning to execute him. He decided that if he tried to flee, the Germans would "bring calamity on the entire ghetto."[97]

The Germans liquidated the ghetto on September 23 and 24, 1943. They sent 3,700 Jews to concentration camps in Latvia and Estonia, and shipped more than 4,000 children, women, and elderly men to Sobibór and death. Several hundred more were murdered at Ponary. Twenty-five hundred Jews continued to live

Jewish men publically humiliated in Minsk, 1941. USHMM Photo No. 22064, courtesy of Zydowski Instytut Historyczny Instytut Naukowo-Badawczy.

and work as slave laborers in several German armaments factories. Another 80 Jews worked for an *Aktion* 1005 unit cleaning up the Ponary killing site; when they had completed their work, the SS executed them. There were only a few hundred Jews left in Vilna when the Red Army liberated it on July 13, 1944. Of the 57,000 to 59,000 Jews in Vilna when the Germans occupied the city in the summer of 1941, only 2,000 to 3,000 survived the Holocaust.

Minsk

The Jewish population of Minsk, the capital of Belorussia (today, Belarus), numbered from 75,000 to 80,000 on the eve of the German invasion of the Soviet Union. The Germans occupied Minsk on June 28 and ordered the opening of a ghetto three weeks later with an initial population of 100,000. The SS resorted to periodic *Aktion* slowly to reduce the size of the ghetto's population and make room for Jews from the Greater Reich.

Between August and November 1941, the Germans murdered 24,000 Russian Jews in the ghetto; the next year, they were replaced by 35,000 Jews from the Reich.

These atrocities helped bring about an active resistance movement, led by Hersh Smolar (1905–) and others, in the ghetto. The Minsk Jewish underground movement had strong ties to the Soviet partisan movement, and it bought illegal arms with funds supplied by the *Judenrat*. Its first major action took place in response to a German demand on March 2, 1942, that the Minsk *Judenrat* turn over 5,000 Jews for "transport." The *Judenrat*, acting in league with the Jewish underground, refused. The Germans responded by attacking a Jewish labor column, killing more than 5,000 people, some of them from a children's orphanage:

The column of children of all ages from the smallest to 13–14 years of age presented a terrible sight. It was led by the director of the orphanage. The children shouted: "Why? Our people will come and take vengeance for our blood and the blood of our fathers and mothers!" They were whipped on the heads and went on, covered with bruises, their faces swollen from beatings, their clothes in rags. If a child fell behind, he was shot. The entire street was littered with the bodies of children.[100]

A second set of massacres took place between July 28 and July 31, 1942, when the Germans murdered 30,000 German and Soviet Jews from the Minsk ghetto. Vasily Grossman described the killings:

The Fascists exceeded all boundaries of human imagination. Before the eyes of the mothers, who were either fainting or losing their wits, the drunken Germans and policemen shamelessly raped the girls before each other and others. They cut out the sexual organs with daggers, forced living and dead bodies to asssume the most disgusting poses, cut off noses, breasts, and ears.

Mothers rushed at the Fascists in a rage and fell dead with crushed skulls.[101]

Thousands more were sent to Sobibór that summer. On October 21, 1943, the Germans killed the remaining 4,000 Jews in the Minsk ghetto and closed it. Hersh Smolar described the German *Aktion*:

At dawn on October 21st, it began. What was left of the ghetto was surrounded on all sides. To the accompaniment of their usual bellowing—Raus! Raus!—the Nazis drove people from their homes half-undressed. The advance unit consisted of Epstein, Rosenblatt and the rest of that gang, shouting "Jews, there's no use hiding, we'll find you anyway!" People they found hiding were often shot on the spot. The dead lay in the streets. The barking of dogs smothered the groans of the

wounded. The ghetto of the hundred thousand Jews of Minsk no longer existed.[102]

German brutality in Belorussia triggered some of the most significant Jewish partisan activities of the Holocaust. The most successful of these movements was led by Tuvia Bielski (1906–1987), whose units reigned terror on the Germans and their Belorussian collaborators. Yet the Bielski partisans did more than fight Germans: They also developed an extensive Jewish family camp in the dense Belorussian forests; there, the Bielski Jews were able to keep alive the rudiments of Jewish culture and religion. Similar camps were opened by Jewish partisan groups throughout Belorussia and western Ukraine during the Holocaust.

Riga

According to the 1935 census, there were 93,479 Jews in Latvia. About half of them lived in Riga. German forces captured Riga on July 1, 1941. The first killings in the city were instigated by a Latvian *Sonderkommando* unit led by Viktors Arājs (1910–1988), which was made up of volunteers from the *Pērkoņkrusts* (Thunder Cross), a Latvian fascist movement. Over the next six months, the Germans and their Latvian collaborators would murder 60,000 Latvian Jews. Those who survived the initial wave of mass killings were forced into the Riga ghetto, which Franz Stahlecker, the Commander of *Einsatzgruppe* A, opened in the fall of 1941. It had an initial population of 29,000 to 32,000 Jews. On November 19, 1941, the Germans forced Jews healthy enough to work into a special compound at the edge of the ghetto. Eleven days later, they began to murder everyone else. Most of the killings took place on November 30 and December 8 in the Rumbula forest 10 miles outside of Riga. Estimates are that German and Latvian forces under Ostland HSSPF Friedrich Jeckeln (1895–1946) murdered from 25,000 to 28,000 Riga Jews during this period. Frida Michelson, who survived the Rumbula massacre, described the roundup on November 30:

I went to the window to see what was going on.

It was already beginning to get light. An unending column of people, guarded by armed policemen, was passing by. Young women, women with infants in their arms, old women, handicapped, helped by their neighbors, young boys and girls—all marching, marching. Suddenly, in front of our window, a German SS man started firing with an automatic gun point blank into the crowd. People were mowed down by the shots, and fell on the cobblestones. There was confusion in the column. People were trampling over those who had fallen, they were pushing forward, away from the wildly shooting SS man. Some were throwing away their packs so they could run faster. The Latvian policemen were shouting "Faster! Faster!" and lashing whips over the heads of the crowd.[103]

Now only 4,000 Jews were left in the Riga ghetto, which was divided into two sections—one for new Jewish arrivals from the Greater Reich and one for Latvian Jews. Each was run by its own *Ältestenrat*. In the next few months, the Germans transported 16,000 Reich Jews to Riga.

In 1942, the SS began to "clear" both ghettos of elderly Jews, who were taken away and shot. The worst of the killings took place on March 15, 1942, when the SS shot almost 2,000 Riga Jews, along with 1,840 Jews from the Jungfernhof (Jumpravmuiza) concentration camp, in the nearby Bikernieki forest. Others were sent to work building the Salaspils concentration camp just outside of Riga. The Germans would construct two concentration camps in the Salaspils area. More than a 100,000 people died in both camps during the war.

On November 1, 1942, the Germans reorganized the ghetto in retaliation for an underground—led Jewish escape attempt sev-

eral days earlier. They closed the Latvian ghetto and created two sections in the Greater Reich ghetto—one for Latvians and one for Jews from the Reich. During the escape, some members of the underground got into a firefight with an SD unit outside the ghetto. The Germans discovered afterwards that some of the ghetto's most important leaders, including some members of the ghetto police, had helped plan the escape. They rounded up a large number of hostages, including some elderly men and about thirty-nine ghetto policemen, and shot them.

What happened there was told by German Jews who witnessed the massacres from the upper windows:

A short distance before entering the Blechplatz (Tin Place; square in German section of ghetto), Anatoly Nathan [head of the ghetto police] shouted out in Latvian, "Boys run, save your lives!" The Jewish ghetto policemen lunged with their clenched fists towards their German guards, who opened machine gun fire. Seligson, Nathan's assistant, screamed out to Krause, "You bloody dog!" Some of the boys managed to run into the adjoining streets but the Nazi bullets caught them there too.

Genkin, heavily injured in his leg, ran into a basement apartment of the German ghetto. Several men did renovation work there. The Gestapo asked the German Jews whether they saw anyone hiding there. When they answered that they had not seen anyone, the Gestapo shot one of them in front of his children. Shortly after that, Genkin was found and they killed him on the spot.

Only two, Damsky [Meilach] and Israelowitz [Sasha], managed somehow to survive this carnage [they were later caught and executed by the Gestapo].

Thus, 41 gallant men of the Latvian Jewish ghetto police were massacred in this bloodbath. The coats and boots which were later taken off the victims were punctured by bullets like a sieve. One Gestapo man was killed by a stray bullet from his own men.[104]

The SS continued to reduce the size of the population in the ghetto during the spring and summer of 1943, sending almost 8,000 Jews to the newly constructed Kaiserwald concentration camp outside of Riga. In November, the SS sent the ghettos' remaining Jews to Auschwitz. The following month, the ghetto site was returned to the city of Riga.

Kovno

The SS opened the Kovno (Kaunas) ghetto in August 1941. During the next few months, the Germans slowly reduced the size of the ghetto's population (29,760) by a third with executions at the IX Fort, one of a series of nineteenth-century forts surrounding the city. On October 28, 1941, the SS executed 9,000 Jews there. Avraham Tory (1909–2002), a prominent Jewish guerilla leader, described the murders:

> In the fort, the wretched people were immediately set upon by the Lithuanian killers, who stripped them of every valuable article—gold rings, earrings, bracelets. They forced them to strip naked, pushed them into pits which had been prepared in advance, and fired into each pit with machines guns which had been positioned there in advance. The murderers did not have time to shoot everybody in one batch before the next batch of Jews arrived. They were accorded the same treatment as those who had preceded them. They were pushed into the pit on top of the dead, the dying, and those still alive from the previous group. So it continued, batch after batch, until the 10,000 men, women, and children had been butchered.[105]

Those who remained in the ghetto worked in German arms factories outside the ghetto. In early 1942, the Germans issued regulations that outlawed the ownership of books or any other written material. That summer, they closed Jewish schools and synagogues. The ghetto's *Ältestenrat,* headed by Dr. Elhanan Elkes (1879–1944) and a Zionist leader, Leib Garfunkel (1876–?), encouraged the development of various illegal religious, political, and cultural activities. Some of the *Ältestenrat's* Zionist members helped create *Matsok* (Hebrew acronym for Zionist Center Vilijampole, Kovno) that worked with other ghetto underground groups. A six-hundred-member *Yidishe Algemenye Kamfs* (YAK; Jewish Fighting Organization) helped Jews escape and join Soviet partisan units. The ghetto police helped train some YAK members to use weapons before their escape. The most daring YAK escape took place at the end of 1943, when 170 YAK members fled into the forests. Nearby, in the IX Fort, a Soviet POW, Captain Kolya Vassilenko, helped sixty-four Jewish prisoners escape on December 25.

There were more than 350 escape attempts in the Kovno ghetto; almost two thirds of them were successful. On March 27, 1944, *SA General* Hans Kramer, Kovno's city administrator, ordered 1,800 elderly Jews and children executed in retaliation for these escapes. The Germans also executed forty Jewish policemen who had helped train some of the escapees. Kramer then abolished the *Ältestenrat* and reorganized the Jewish police force.

In the fall of 1943, Himmler transformed the Kovno ghetto into a concentration camp and shipped 4,000 Kovno Jews to satellite camps outside the city. Another 2,800 Jews were sent to labor camps in Estonia. On July 8, 1944, the Germans began to liquidate the Kovno ghetto as the Red Army moved closer to the city. Their plan was to ship remaining ghetto residents to concentration camps elsewhere. Many of the ghetto's Jews went into hiding when they learned of the plan to close it. Kramer sent 4,000 Kovno Jews to the Kaufering and Stutthof concentration camps. Several thousand ghetto Jews, though, tried to escape the Nazi roundup by hiding in specially

Jewish children wait in deportation line, Łódź, 1942. USHMM Photo No. 50328, courtesy of Instytut Pamieci Narodowej.

prepared underground bunkers. Kramer sent troops into the ghetto who used bloodhounds, smoke grenades, and other weapons to drive these Jews into the open. Only ninety of them survived the Nazi onslaught. Two thousand Kovno Jews survived the Holocaust out of a pre-1941 population of 30,000.

Łódź

Though originally opened as a stopgap measure, the Łódź ghetto became a model for other ghettos in occupied Poland. Its *Ältestenrat*, led by the controversial Mordechai Rumkowski, concluded that the only way to save lives was to make the ghetto self-sustainable and valuable to the Germans as a large factory complex producing goods for the war effort. When the ghetto first opened, it had a Jewish population of 164,000; during the next eighteen months, its population grew to 204,800

through transports of Jews from other parts of the Reich. The Germans dramatically reduced the size of the ghetto in 1942 with a series of transports to Chełmno—the last major deportations until the summer of 1944. Twenty-one percent of the ghetto's population would die of disease and other causes from 1940 to 1944. By January 1943, the ghetto had ninety-six factories employing 78,946 Jewish workers. Himmler decided to close the Łódź ghetto in the summer of 1944. Between June 23 and August 30, 1944, the SS, aided by the *Ältestenrat*, which helped organize the transports, shipped 90 percent of the ghetto's 77,000 Jews to Auschwitz. Most of the rest died in Chełmno. The SS sent 600 Łódź Jews to forced labor camps in Germany and put 830 in an *Aufräumungskommando* (cleanup unit) camp to collect the goods of the ghetto's residents in preparation for shipment to Germany. Somehow, this group managed to flee the last German roundup and were still alive when the Red Army liberated Łódź on January 19, 1945. After the war, many Jewish survivors returned to Łódź, which had a Jewish population of 38,000 by the end of 1945. It became the center of Jewish life in postwar Poland and was home to the *Centralna Żydowska Komisija Historyczna* (Central Jewish Historical Commission). An array of Jewish schools, theaters, and newspapers thrived there in the early years after the war. Unfortunately, the communization of Poland and a resurgence of traditional anti-Semitism saw most of Łódź's Jews leave the city during the next two decades.

Conclusion

The Final Solution, the systematic German program to murder all of the Jews in Europe, is one of the most horrible genocidal crimes in history. Although the seeds for the Final Solution can be found in earlier German efforts to drive Jews from Germany or to isolate them from mainstream society in Poland, its true origins lie in the complexities of mass murdering Jews as German armed forces swept into the Soviet Union in the summer of 1941. Driven by the unparalleled successes of the Wehrmacht in the early months of the Soviet invasion as well as the growing problems associated with the *Einsatzgruppen*'s efforts to kill Jews in the towns and villages of Western Russia, Hitler, Himmler, and other Nazi leaders began to explore more efficient and secretive ways to murder Jews. The Germans had already developed a highly successful "euthanasia" program for dealing with the handicapped in the Greater Reich; now the "euthanasia" experts were asked to help develop a much more efficient mechanism—the death camps—to murder first the Jews in occupied Poland and the Soviet Union and then the Jews in other parts of German-occupied Europe. By the time Heydrich and Eichmann

met with representatives of all the major branches of government involved in the Final Solution in Wannsee on January 20, 1942, the first killings of the Final Solution were already under way. By the summer of 1942, the Germans had opened six death camps—Auschwitz, Bełżec, Chełmno, Majdanek, Sobibór, and Treblinka—where, in the next two and a half years, they would murder more than 3,000,000 Jews and tens of thousands of Roma.

The Germans went to great lengths to delude Jews into thinking they were being sent to forced-labor situations where conditions would be better than in the crowded ghettos of Poland and the Soviet Union. Though Jews had always found ways to stand up to Nazi efforts to break their spirit through illegal acts of spiritual resistance, they became bolder when they learned their true fate. Acts of physical resistance intensified as some Jews decided to do everything possible to resist German efforts to kill them. The major uprisings in three of the six death camps stunned the Nazi leadership. And although Jews could do little to thwart the power of the SS and the Wehrmacht, these acts of physical resistance showed the Nazi leadership that Jews were not willing to go "like sheep to slaughter."

SOURCES FOR FURTHER STUDY AND RESEARCH
Primary Sources
Blatt, Thomas (Toivi). *Sobibor: The Forgotten Revolt.* Issaquah, WA: Thomas Blatt, 2004.

Bor, Josef. *The Terezín Requiem.* Translated by Edith Pargeter. New York: Alfred A. Knopf, 1963.

Czech, Danuta. *Auschwitz Chronicle, 1939–1945.* New York: Henry Holt, 1990.

Delbo, Charlotte. *Auschwitz and After.* Translated by Rosette C. Lamont. New Haven: Yale University Press, 1995.

Der Führer Schent der Juden ein stadt. Berlin: Reichsministerium für Volksaufklärung und Propaganda, 1944.

Der Gerstein-Bericht, in *NS-Archiv: Dokumente zum Nationalsozialismus.* http//www.ns-archiv.de/verfolgung/gerstein/gerstein-bericht.php.

Eichmann Interrogated: Transcripts from the Archives of the Israeli Police. Edited by Jochen von Lang in collaboration with Claus Sibyll. Translated by Ralph Manheim. New York: Farrar, Straus & Giroux.

Ehrenburg, Ilya, and Vasily Grossman, eds. *The Black Book.* New York: Holocaust Library, 1981.

Friesová, Jana Renée. *Fortress of My Youth: Memoir of a Terezín Survivor.* Translated by Elinor Morrisby and Ladislav Rosendorf. Madison: University of Wisconsin Press, 2002.

Gelissen, Rena Kornreich. *Rena's Promise: A Story of Sisters in Auschwitz.* With Heather Dune Macadam. Boston: Beacon Press, 1995.

Goebbels, Joseph. *Die Tagebücher von Joseph Goebbels.* Edited by Elke Fröhlich. Pt. 2, *Diktate 1941–1945,* vol. 1, *Juli–September 1941.* Munich: K. G. Saur, 1996.

———. Edited by Elke Fröhlich. *Die Tagebücher von Joseph Goebbels.* Pt. 2, *Diktate 1941–1945,* vol. 2, *Oktober–Dezember 1941.* Munich: K. G. Saur, 1996.

Höss, Rudolf. *Death Dealer: The Memoirs of the SS Kommandant at Auschwitz.* Edited by Steven Paskuly. New York: Da Capo Press, 1996.

. . . I Never Saw Another Butterfly . . . : Children's Drawings and Poems from Terezín Concentration Camp, 1942–1944. New York: Schocken Books, 1978.

Kessel, Sim. *Hanged at Auschwitz: An Extraordinary Memoir of Survival.* New York: Cooper Square Press, 2001.

Korczak, Janusz. *Ghetto Diary.* New Haven: Yale University Press, 2003.

Krall, Hanna. *Shielding the Flame: An Intimate Conversation with Dr. Mark Edelman, the Last Surviving Leader of the Warsaw Ghetto Uprising.* Translated by Joanna Stasinska and Lawrence Weschler. New York: Henry Holt, 1986.

Kruk, Herman. *The Last Days of the Jerusalem of Lithuania: Chronicles from the Vilna Ghetto and the Camps, 1939–1944.* Translated by Barbara Harshav. New Haven: Yale University Press, 2002.

Langbein, Hermann. *People in Auschwitz.* Translated by Harry Zohn. Chapel Hill: University of North Carolina Press, 2004.

Lengyel, Olga. *Five Chimneys: The Story of Auschwitz.* Chicago: Ziff-Davis, 1947.

Levi, Primo. *Survival in Auschwitz* and *The Awakening: Two Memoirs.* Translated by Stuart Woolf. New York: Summit Books, 1986.

Michelson, Frida. *I Survived Rumbuli.* New York: Holocaust Library, 1979.

Minutes of the Wannsee Conference, January 20, 1942. http://prorev.com/wannsee.htm.

Müller-Madej, Stella. *A Girl from Schindler's List.* London: Polish Cultural Foundation, 1997.

Noakes, Jeremy, and Geoffrey Pridham, eds. *Foreign Policy, War and Racial Extermination.* Vol. 2 of *Nazism 1919–1945: A History in Documents and Eyewitness Accounts.* New York: Schocken Books, 1988.

Nyiszli, Dr. Miklos. *Auschwitz: A Doctor's Eyewitness Account.* Translated by Tibère Kremere and Richard Seaver. New York: Frederick Fell, 1960.

Rittner, Carol, and John K. Roth, eds. *Different Voices: Women and the Holocaust.* New York: Paragon House, 1993.

Rosenberg, Otto. *A Gypsy in Auschwitz.* Translated by Helmut Bögler. London: London House, 1999.

Schneider, Gertrude, ed. *Muted Voices: Jewish Survivors of Latvia Remember.* New York: Philosophical Library, 1987.

Smolar, Hersh. *The Minsk Ghetto: Soviet-Jewish Partisans Against the Nazis.* New York: Holocaust Library, 1989.

State of Israel, Ministry of Justice. *The Trial of Adolf Eichmann: Record of Proceedings in the District Court of Jerusalem.* Vol. 5. Jerusalem: Israel State Archives and Yad Vashem, 1994.

The Stroop Report. Translated by Sybil Milton. New York: Pantheon, 1979.

Suhl, Yuri, ed. *They Fought Back: The Story of the Jewish Resistance in Nazi Europe.* New York: Schocken Books, 1975.

Testimony of Chaim Engel. United States Holocaust Memorial Museum. http://www.org/outreach/id1184.htm.

Testimony of Esther Raab. United States Holocaust Memorial Museum. http://www.ushmm.org/outreach/erp0620f.htm.

Tory, Avraham. *Surviving the Holocaust: The Kovno Ghetto Diary.* Cambridge, MA: Harvard University Press, 1990.

Verdi, Giuseppe. *Requiem in Full Score.* Mineola, NY: Dover, 1998.

Vrba, Rudolf. *I Escaped from Auschwitz.* Fort Lee, NJ: Barricade Books, 2002.

The Warsaw Diary of Adam Czerniaków: Prelude to Doom. Edited by Raul Hilberg, Stanislaw Staron, and Josef Kermisz. Translated by Stanislaw Staron and the staff of Yad Vashem. New York: Stein and Day, 1979.

We Are Children Just the Same: Vedem, the Secret Magazine of the Boys of Terezín. Edited by

Marie Rút Køíková, Kurt Jiøí Kotouè, and Zdenìk Ornest. Philadelphia: Jewish Publication Society, 1995.

Wiesenthal, Simon. *The Murderers Among Us: The Simon Wiesenthal Memoirs.* New York: Bantam Books, 1968.

Secondary Sources

Aly, Götz. *"Final Solution": Nazi Population Policy and the Murder of the European Jews.* Translated by Belinda Cooper and Allison Brown. London: Arnold, 1999.

Ancel, Jean. "The German-Romanian Relationship and the Final Solution." *Holocaust and Genocide Studies* 19, no. 2 (Fall 2005): 252–275.

Arad, Yitzhak. *Belzec, Sobibor, Treblinka: The Operation Reinhard Death Camps.* Bloomington: Indiana University Press, 1987.

_____. *Ghetto in Flames: The Struggle and Destruction of the Jews in Vilna in the Holocaust.* New York: Holocaust Library, 1982.

Bankier, David. *The Germans and the Final Solution: Public Opinion under Nazism.* Oxford: Blackwell, 1996.

Browning, Christoper R. *Fateful Months: Essays on the Emergence of the Final Solution.* Rev. ed. New York: Homes & Meier, 1991.

_____. *The Origins of the Final Solution: The Evolution of Nazi Jewish Policy, September 1939–March 1942.* Lincoln and Jerusalem: University of Nebraska Press and Yad Vashem, 2004.

Breitman, Richard. *The Architect of Genocide: Himmler and the Final Solution.* New York: Alfred A. Knopf, 1991.

Cesarani, David. *Becoming Eichmann: Rethinking the Life, Crimes, and Trial of a "Desk Murderer."* New York: Da Capo Press, 2004.

_____, ed. *The Final Solution: Origins and Implementation.* London: Routledge, 1996.

Chládková, Ludmilla. *The Terezín Ghetto.* Translated by Vlasta Basetlíková. Prague: Naåe vojsko, 1995.

Crowe, David M. *Oskar Schindler: The Untold Account of His Life, Wartime Activities, and the True Story Behind the List.* Boulder: Westview Press, 2004.

Fleming, Gerald. *Hitler and the Final Solution.* Berkeley: University of California Press, 1982.

Friedlander, Saul. *Kurt Gerstein: The Ambiguity of Good.* Translated by Charles Fullman. New York: Alfred A. Knopf, 1969.

Friedrich, Otto. *The Kingdom of Auschwitz.* New York: Harper Perennial, 1994.

Gryñ, Edward, and Zofia Murawska-Gryñ. *Majdanek.* Lublin: Pañstwowe Muzeum na Majdanku, 1984.

Gumkowski, Janusz, and Kazimierz Leszcyñski. *Poland Under Nazi Occupation.* Warsaw: Polonia, 1961.

Gutman, Israel. *Resistance: The Warsaw Ghetto Uprising.* Boston: Houghton Mifflin, 1994.

Gutman, Yisrael, and Michael Berenbaum. *Anatomy of the Auschwitz Death Camp.* Bloomington: Indiana University Press, 1994.

Herbert, Ulrich, ed. *National Socialist Extermination Policies: Contemporary German Perspectives and Controversies.* New York: Berghan Books, 2000.

Hilberg, Raul. *The Destruction of the European Jews.* Vol. 3. 3rd. ed. New Haven: Yale University Press, 2003.

Iwaszko, Tadeusz, Helena Kubica, Franciszek Piper, Irena Strzelecka, and Andrzej Strzeleck, eds. *Auschwitz, 1940–1945.* Vol. 2, *The Prisoners: Their Life and Work.* Oświęcim: Auschwitz-Birkenau State Museum, 2000.

Karas, Joa. *Music in Terezín.* New York: Beaufort Books, 1985.

Kenrick, Donald, and Grattan Puxon. *The Destiny of Europe's Gypsies.* New York: Basic Books, 1972.

Kogon, Eugen, Hermann Langbein, and Adalbert Rückerl, eds. *Nazi Mass Murder: A Documentary History of the Use of Poison Gas.* New Haven: Yale University Press, 1993.

Lasik, Aleksander, Franciszek Piper, Piotr Setkiewicz, and Irena Strzelecka, eds. *Auschwitz, 1940–1945: Central Issues in the History of the Camp.* Vol. 1, *The Establishment and Organization of the Camp.* Oświęcim: Auschwitz-Birkenau State Museum, 2000.

Lewy, Guenter. *The Nazi Persecution of the Gypsies.* Oxford: Oxford University Press, 2000.

Lifton, Betty Jean. *The King of the Children: A Biography of Janusz Korczak.* New York: Schocken Books, 1988

Lifton, Robert Jay. *The Nazi Doctors: Medical Killing and the Psychology of Genocide.* New York: Basic Books, 1986.

Marszalek, Józef. *Majdanek: The Concentration Camp in Lublin.* Warsaw: Interpress, 1986.

Piper, Franciszek. *Auschwitz: How Many Perished: Jews, Poles, Gypsies . . . .* Kraków: Poligrafia, 1991.

Poprzeczny, Joseph. *Odilo Globocnik: Hitler's Man in the East.* Jefferson, NC: McFarland, 2004.

Pucher, Siegfried J. *". . . in der Bewegung führend tätig": Odilo Globocnik—Kämpfer für den "Anschluß" Vollstrecker des Holocaust.* Klagenfurt: Drava Verlag, 1997.

Rajca, Czeslaw, and Anna Wisniewska. *Majdanek Concentration Camp.* Lublin: Pañstwowe Muzeum na Majdanku, 1983.

Rein, Leonid. "Local Collaboration in the Execution of the 'Final Solution' in Nazi-Occupied Belorussia." *Holocaust and Genocide Studies* 20, no. 3 (Winter 2006): 381–409.

Richie, Alexandra. *Faust's Metropolis: A History of Berlin.* New York: Carroll & Graf, 1998.

Roseman, Mark. *The Wannsee Conference and the Final Solution.* New York: Metropolitan Books, 2002.

Rosen, David. *Verdi: Requiem.* Cambridge: Cambridge University Press, 1985.

Rovit, Rebecca, and Alvin Goldfarb, eds. *Theatrical Performance During the Holocaust.* Baltimore: Johns Hopkins University Press, 1999.

Sereny, Gitta. *Into That Darkness: An Examination of Conscience.* New York: Vintage Books, 1974.

Sofsky, Wolfgang. *The Order of Terror: The Concentration Camp.* Translated by William Templer. Princeton: Princeton University Press, 1997.

Telushkin, Rabbi Joseph. *Jewish Wisdom: Ethical, Spiritual, and Historical Lessons from the Great Works and Thinkers.* New York: William Morrow, 1994.

Totten, Samuel, William S. Parsons, and Israel W. Charny. *Century of Genocide: Critical Essays and Eyewitness Accounts.* 2nd ed. New York: Routledge, 2004.

United States Holocaust Memorial Museum. *Resistance During the Holocaust.* Washington, DC: United States Holocaust Memorial Museum, n.d.

The Wannsee Conference and the Genocide of the European Jews: Guide and Reader to the Permanent Exhibit in the House of the Wannsee Conference. Berlin: Gedenkstätte Haus der Wannsee-Konferenz, 2002.

The Warsaw Ghetto: The 45th Anniversary of the Uprising. Warsaw: Interpress, 1988.

Zimmermann, Michael. "The National Socialist 'Solution of the Gypsy Question': Central Decisions, Local Initiatives, and Their Interrelation." *Holocaust and Genocide Studies* 14, no. 3 (Winter 2001): 412–427.

_____. *Rassenutopie und Genozid: Die nationalsozialistische "Lösung der Zigeunerfrage."* Hamburg: Hans Christians Verlag, 1996.

CHAPTER 8

The Final Solution in Western Europe and the Nazi-Allied States

CHRONOLOGY

—**1938** *(May 28)*: First Jewish Law, Hungary

—**1938** *(September 2–November 17)*: Italy issues anti-Semitic race laws

—**1939** *(May 4)*: Second Jewish Law, Hungary

—**1940** *(April 9)*: Germany invades Norway and Denmark

—**1940** *(May 10)*: Germany invades Belgium, Luxembourg, and the Netherlands

—**1940** *(June 29)*: Romanian army massacres Jews as it retreats from Bessarabia and Bukovina

—**1940** *(September 5)*: Ion Antonescu becomes dictator of Romania

—**1940** *(October 3)*: *Status des Juifs* adopted for both zones in France

—**1940** *(October 28)*: Italy invades Greece

—**1940** *(November 15)*: Bulgarian church leaders protest draft *Law for the Protection of the Nation*

—**1941** *(February 25)*: National strike in Netherlands to protest Jewish roundups

—**1941** *(April 6)*: Germany invades Greece and Yugoslavia

—**1941** *(May 13)*: Creation of Independent State of Croatia (NDH)

—**1941** *(June 22)*: Germany invades Soviet Union

—**1941** *(June 28)*: Iași pogroms in Romania

—**1941** *(July 16–17)*: Roundups of Jews begin in Vichy France

—**1941** *(August 2)*: Third Jewish Law, Hungary

—**1941** *(August 30)*: Transnistria created

—**1942**: Lety and Hodonín transformed into Roma concentration camps in Protectorate

—**1942** *(Spring)*: Jewish Working Group formed in Slovakia to save Jews

—**1942** *(March–October)*: Slovaks deport Jews to Auschwitz; Roma census in Romania

—**1942** *(July 5)*: Margot Frank ordered to register for deportation; family hides in Secret Annex

—**1942** *(August 29)*: SS- *Gruppenführer* Harald Turner declares Serbia free of Jews and Roma

—**1942** *(November 10)*: Lutheran bishops in Norway protest Jewish roundups; read in churches

—**1943** *(January 31)*: Germans surrender at Stalingrad

—**1943** *(March 4)*: Roundup of Jews in Bulgarian-controlled Thrace and Macedonia

—**1943** *(March 9–April 15)*: Bulgarian Politicians and church leaders protest Jewish roundups

—**1943** *(July 24–25)*: Mussolini deposed; later declares Italian Social Republic in north

—**1943** *(September 8)*: Italy signs armistice with Allies

—**1943** *(August 29)*: Martial law declared in Denmark

—**1943** *(October 2)*: Sweden will accept all Danish Jewish refugees; Danes save 7,220 Jews

—**1943** *(October 16)*: Roundups begin of Jews in German-dominated Italian Social Republic
—**1944** *(March 19)*: Germany occupies Hungary
—**1944** *(April 25)*: Joel Brand has first of three meetings with Adolf Eichmann
—**1944** *(May 15–July 7)*: Eichmann deports Hungarian Jews to General Government
—**1944** *(July 9)*: Raoul Wallenberg arrives in Budapest
—**1944** *(August 4)*: Arrest of Anne Frank and others in Secret Annex
—**1944** *(August 29–October 27)*: Slovak National Uprising
—**1944** *(November 7)*: Hannah Szenes executed in Budapest as British military spy
—**1945** *(January 13)*: Raoul Wallenberg arrested by Soviets as American spy
—**1945** *(February–March)*: Anne Frank and sister Margot die in Bergen-Belsen

Soon after they had conquered much of Western Europe in the spring and early summer of 1940, the Germans began to isolate and persecute Jews, Roma, and others Aryan enemies. Later, Jews in each of these countries were included in planning for the Final Solution. This was also true for Jews in the Nazi-allied states in Central and Eastern Europe. The Germans quickly learned, though, that it was going to be difficult to round up and transport Jews, and later Roma, to the concentration camps and death centers of the East. Their successes, to a great extent, were going to depend on the active support of collaborators as well as the sympathy, or lack thereof, of local populations. Although efforts to round up Jews were sometimes met with opposition, the Germans found that they could usually depend on the active support of local officials, the police, and various paramilitary organizations that were more than willing to do the Germans' murderous dirty work. This was true in almost every country conquered by the Germans or part of their alliance network, but there were exceptions.

Timing would also be a factor. By 1943, defeats at Stalingrad and elsewhere convinced some of Nazi Germany's erstwhile allies that Hitler could not win the war. Leaders in some of the German satellite states began to look for ways to signal to the Allies their growing lack of sympathy with the Nazi cause. Although such changes in attitudes would affect, in some instances, domestic policies towards the Jews, this had more to do with diplomacy than with moral qualms about German efforts to force leaders in each country to cooperate in the rounding up and deportation of Jews to concentration and death camps in the East. In this environment some of the most heroic efforts to save Jews took place during the Holocaust.

The Holocaust in Western Europe

Belgium and Luxembourg

Though estimates vary, from 55,000 to 70,000 Jews lived in Belgium in 1940, most of them refugees. Belgium was run by the Wehrmacht under *General der Infanterie* Alexander von Falkenhausen (1878–1966) and his civilian administrator, Eggert Reeder (1894–1959). Belgium's king, Leopold III (1901–1983), remained in power and tried to work with Falkenhausen, though many of his former cabinet ministers formed a government-in-exile in London. Although Falkenhausen's general policies were designed to win Belgian support for Germany's war effort, his policies towards the Jews were similar to those in other parts of Nazi-occupied Europe. His first Jewish decrees were designed to do two things—define Jewishness and remove the Jews from the socioeconomic fabric of Belgian society. In August 1941, Falkenhausen enacted a Jewish curfew; later that year, he ordered all Jews to

Europe in 1941.

join the *Association des Juifs en Belgique* (AJB; Association of Jews in Belgium), which was created to oversee Jewish education and welfare.[1]

There was constant friction between Falkenhausen and *SS-Sturmbannführer* Ernst Ehlers (1909–1980), Himmler's SS representative in Belgium. In the spring of 1942, Ehlers decreed that all Jews must register for labor service and begin wearing a yellow Star of David. There was a strong public outcry against this measure; Brussels city leaders told Falkenhausen that they would not let him use city offices to distribute the yellow badges. One underground newspaper, *La Libre Belgique*, appealed to its readers: "Citizens, out of hate for Nazism

and through loyalty to yourselves, do what you haven't been doing: Greet the Jews."[2]

Not all Belgians were so sympathetic. Pro-Nazi Belgian groups such as Stal de Clerq's (1884–1942) *Vlaasch National Verbond* (National Flemish Union) and *Rexists*, led by future Waffen-*SS-Obersturmbannführer* Léon Joseph Marie Degrelle (1906–1994), actively supported the Germans' anti-Semitic policies. For the most part, though, the Belgian population opposed them and hid 25,000 Jews during the war. On July 25, 1942, Ehlers told the AJB that 10,000 Jews had to report to the newly opened Mechelen transit camp for "labor mobilization." By early September, only 3,900 Jews had complied with the AJB order. In the interim, the SS raided Jewish homes to meet their quota. On August 18, the first deportees were sent to Auschwitz, almost a third of them children. The raids continued until mid-September. During the next two years, Ehlers rounded up 25,257 Belgian Jews and sent them to the General Government via Mechelen, principally Auschwitz. Several Roma transports were also sent to Auschwitz from Mechelen in 1943 and 1944. The Germans murdered 29,902 Belgian Jews during the Holocaust.

The Germans considered the Grand Duchy of Luxembourg an ethnic German area, though it was never formally integrated into the Third Reich. Its civilian administrator, *Gauleiter* Gustav Simon (1900–1945), did what he could to destroy the duchy's French culture and language and fully Germanize it. Luxembourg had a prewar Jewish population of 3,800, most of them German refugees, but on the eve of the German invasion in 1940 only 2,000 remained. Over the next year, the Germans encouraged as many Jews as possible to leave Luxembourg.

Simon introduced the Nuremberg Laws in the fall of 1940 and slowly stripped the remaining Jews of their rights, jobs, and possessions. In August 1941, he forced the 750 Jews still in Luxembourg to move into the Fünf-brunnen Monastery camp. In September, they had to begin wearing a yellow Star of David. On October 16, 1941, the SS began to deport the Jews in Fünfbrunnen to Łódź and other camps in Poland and the Protectorate of Bohemia and Moravia. The Germans murdered almost 2,000 of Luxembourg's Jews during the *Shoah*. This number includes many who fled the duchy in the early years of the war.

Denmark

There were about 7,500 Jews in Denmark in 1940, approximately 1,500 of them refugees. Initially, the Germans left the Jews alone because the Danes, unlike some of their neighbors, not only had not resisted the German invasion but had appeared willing to cooperate with the Nazis. During the first few years of the German occupation, life went on much as it had before the war. The Danish government and military continued to function, and the Reich's prewar ambassador, Cecil von Renthe-Fink (1885–1964), kept his post in Copenhagen. Early on, Danish authorities let the Germans know that the "Jewish question" was off limits for discussion, though German officials continually pestered the Danes about this matter. In a cable to the *Auswärtiges Amt* (Foreign Ministry) on January 7, 1942, Renthe-Fink told his superiors about a widely publicized article by Professor Hal Koch (1904–1963), a prominent professor of church history at Copenhagen University. Koch wrote that since Denmark had signed Hitler's Anti-Comintern Pact (1937; renewed 1941), as had other German allies, it was assumed that the government would now adopt an "active anti-Jewish policy." Danes should reject this idea, Koch argued, because to do so would "deliver a blow to Danish political activity that would shake it to its foundations." Koch added: "It is as much an issue of truth and justice in the Jewish matter as of truth and justice with respect to the lives of the entire Danish people." Renthe-Fink noted that Koch's article had touched off an "internal political dispute" in Denmark; he warned Berlin not to get involved in it because it would "bring the Jewish problem to the Danish public consciousness more intensively than ever before."[3]

Renthe-Fink went on to say that it was Germany's policy to "eradicate Jewish influence at every opportunity," meaning the Reich should do everything possible to "oust the Jews altogether." German officials, he concluded, "should also take future action to inspire greater understanding of the Jewish problem."[4] German attitudes began to change after Hitler replaced Renthe-Fink with *SS-Standartenführer* Dr. Werner Best (1903–1989). Though Best wanted to maintain the most cordial relations possible with the Danish government, this became increasingly difficult given the rise of Danish resistance efforts against Nazi rule. National elections in March 1943, combined with a growing sense that Germany was going to lose the war, sparked a wave of strikes and other civil outbursts against the occupation that spring and summer.

On August 28, 1943, the German government demanded that Danish officials outlaw public gatherings and strikes, introduce a curfew, and begin censoring the press. Berlin also insisted that the Danish government allow Reich authorities to set up military courts that could impose the death penalty for acts of sabotage. Danish authorities refused to accept these demands; the following day, *General der Infantrie* Hermann von Hanneken (1890–1981), the Wehrmacht's military commander in Denmark, dissolved the government and declared martial law. He now imposed all the demands in the August 28 ultimatum.

Best, whose reputation was tarnished by the unrest in Denmark, thought it was a good time to revisit the Jewish question. Hitler concurred, and the SS began to gather lists of Jewish addresses. On September 11, Best told Georg Ferdinand Duckwitz (1904–1973), an attaché at the German legation in Copenhagen, that the German *Aktion* would take place on the night of October 1–2. In late September, Duckwitz flew to Stockholm on business and asked Swedish authorities whether they would accept Denmark's Jews. When he returned to Copenhagen, Duckwitz told Hans Hedtoft (1903–1955), a prominent politician and staunch critic of the Nazis, about the German plans. Hedtoft quickly informed resistance leaders of Best's scheme. Duckwitz also told Jewish leaders about the planned deportation. Individual Danes now stepped forward and began to hide Jewish friends and acquaintances.

In the meantime, Sven Grafström (1902–1955), the press secretary for the Swedish foreign office, told the press on the evening of Saturday, October 2, that his government was ready "to receive all the Danish Jews in Swe-

den."[5] The following day, a letter from all the Lutheran bishops in Denmark was read in churches throughout the country. It said that the German mistreatment of Jews went against teachings in the New Testament and promised that Danish Christians would "struggle for the right of our Jewish brothers and sisters to preserve the same liberty that we prize more highly than life itself."[6]

The legendary King Christian X (r. 1912–1947) also voiced his opposition to the German *Aktion*. Over time, a legend developed about the king, an important symbol of Danish spiritual resistance: He was reputed to have threatened to wear a yellow Star of David if the Germans forced the Jews to wear one; another story said that during his 8:00 A.M. public horseback rides he wore a Star of David to support the Jews. In reality, the Germans never forced Danish Jews to wear the Star of David because they were afraid of the Danish reaction to such a decree.

What began as a disorganized attempt by Danes to save Jews became a highly organized effort throughout the country during the next three weeks, first to hide Jews and then to send them by boat across the Danish straits to Sweden. Though some fishermen initially tried to charge Jews for passage, the underground stepped in and stopped such practices. In the end, wealthy Danes contributed most of the money to help pay the rescue costs. The Gestapo did what it could to halt the deportations, but being undermanned, it was able to capture and arrest only about 461 Danish Jews, who were then sent to Theresienstadt. The Danes were able to send 7,220 Jews to Sweden and safety. Afterwards, Adolf Eichmann, whose office helped plan the deportations, was sent to Copenhagen to see what went wrong. He learned that it was essential to convince local officials to play a key role in future deportations. Yad Vashem would later name Denmark Righteous Among the Nations, the only country ever to receive this honor. In 1971, Yad

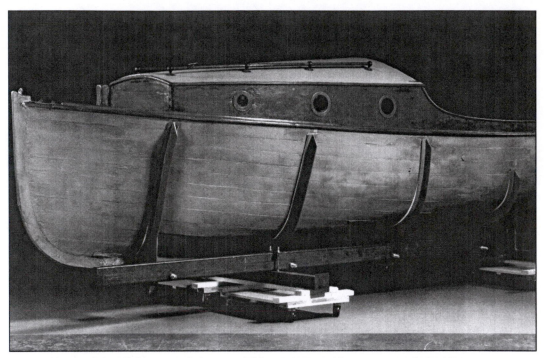

Boat used in Danish Jewish rescue mission on exhibit at USHMM. Photo courtesy of USHMM.
Photographer: Arnold Kramer.

Vashem declared Georg Ferdinand Duckwitz a Righteous Gentile.

France

The rapid and humiliating German conquest of France in the late spring and early summer of 1940 was a crushing blow to one of Europe's most important countries. France had never recovered fully from the devastation of World War I; the crippling effect of that war not only had hurt every aspect of French society but had played a role in the gradual revival of the anti-Semitic passions of the Dreyfus era. Anti-Semitism had waned in the years before the outbreak of World War I, though it rested just below the surface. It reemerged during the Depression, exacerbated by the fact that, per capita, France had become the largest immigrant nation in the world. Michael Marrus and Robert Braxton have argued that French xenophobia and anti-Semitism centered around three themes—the threat to jobs, the dilution of the quality of

French culture, and concern that France's large immigrant population might somehow involve France in unwanted international conflicts.[7]

The election of Leon Blum (1872–1950), the country's first Jewish premier, in the summer of 1936, inflamed French rightists, who termed Blum's new government the "Talmudic cabinet." The collapse of Blum's government two years later did little to assuage extremists who claimed that France's large Jewish population would somehow plunge France into war. The German march into Austria, the Spanish Civil War, the Sudeten crisis, and the murder of Ernst vom Rath in Paris on November 7, 1938, exacerbated these fears. As one French newspaper proclaimed several days after *Kristallnacht:* "Today synagogues burn; tomorrow it will be our churches." Not all Frenchmen shared these views; there were considerable outcries against the rising surge of anti-Semitism, and much of the French press expressed horror at the excesses of *Kristallnacht.*[8]

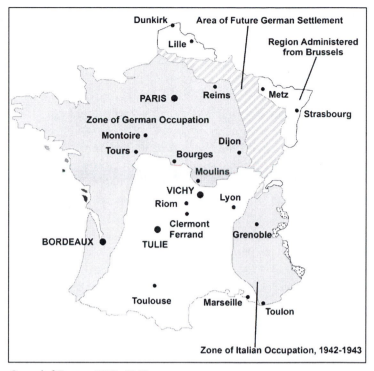

Occupied France, 1940–1943.

These factors, though, did nothing to temper the growing wave of anti-foreign sentiment sweeping France throughout the 1930s. In the spring of 1939, the government of Edouard Daladier (1884–1970) set up internment camps along the Spanish frontier. New legislation gave French authorities the ability to control immigrant organizations and seize foreign publications. *Le Temps* argued that French security was more important than traditional liberties.

France, like much of the rest of Europe, was ill-prepared for the German invasion in 1940. The government of Paul Reynaud (1878–1966) and his vice premier, Marshal Philippe Pétain (1856–1951), declared Paris an "open city" on June 13. Nine days later, a new government under Marshal Pétain concluded an armistice with Germany and, on June 24, with Italy. The armistice agreement divided France into two zones. The northern and western three-fifths of the country, including Paris, came under direct German military control; Alsace and Lorraine

were treated as special provinces and integrated into the Third Reich. What remained of France was run by a collaborationist government, its capital in Vichy, led by Pétain and his new vice premier, Pierre Laval (1883–1945). Pétain, a World War I hero, felt he could somehow work with the Germans and improve the lot of his countrymen. Laval was more sympathetic to the policies of the Reich and wanted a place for his country in Hitler's new European empire.

Initially, most of France's 330,000 to 340,000 Jews lived in what became the German-occupied zone. During the early days of the German invasion, thousands of French Jews had fled southward; for this reason, by the time the French National Assembly created the Vichy state on July 10, about 150,000 to 195,000 Jews were living in what became Vichy France. Several months later, the Vichy government enacted its most significant piece of Holocaust legislation, the *Status des Juifs* (Jewish Statute), which went into force in both zones of France on October 3, 1940. The statute defined Jewishness along German racial lines and deprived Jews of most of their civil and professional rights. A new law the following day ordered local French prefects to begin interning foreign Jews in special facilities or to place them under the watchful eye of the police in isolated rural villages. On October 7, a third Vichy law deprived Algerian Jews of French citizenship. Later that month, French authorities ordered Jewish businesses, which they soon Aryanized, to register with local authorities.

The architects of Jewish policy in France were *SS- Hauptsturmführer* Theodor Dannecker (1913–1945), one of Eichmann's trusted subordinates and head of the RSHA's *Judenreferat* in Paris, and Xavier Vallat (1891–1972), a deeply religious Roman Catholic and anti-German nationalist known for his strong anti-Semitic views. In early 1941, Dannecker and two of Germany's top officials in France, *Generaloberst* Otto von Stülpnagel (1878–1948), the *Militärbefehlshaber in Frankreich* (MBF; Military Commander in France), and Dr. Werner Best, the head of the civilian administration in the German zone, began to pressure Pétain to adopt more aggressive policies towards the Jews. The result was the law of March 29, 1941, that created the *Commissariat General aux Questions Juives* (CGQJ; General Commissariat for Jewish Affairs), under Vallat. Soon after his appointment as head of the CGQJ, Vallat told a group of soon-to-be civil servants that "[t]he Jew is not only an unassimilable foreigner, whose implantation tends to form a state within the state; he is also, by temperament, a foreigner who wants to dominate and who tends to create, with his kin, a super state within the state."[9]

The policies he developed eliminated French Jews from all but a number of government, business, and professional roles in Vichy society and later helped the Germans locate Jews for deportation to the East. Vallat considered his policies pro-French and hesitated to do anything that helped the Reich, actions that later caused his downfall.

Vallat, prodded by Dannecker, created the *Union Génerale des Israélites de France* (UGIF; General Union for Israelites in France) for both zones at the end of 1941. All French Jews now had to pay dues to UGIF, which quickly took control of the assets of all Jewish relief organizations. Though Dannecker promised autonomy for both branches of the UGIF, he soon demanded it pay a 1-billion-franc ($2.28 million) fine for German soldiers killed by the French resistance. Best and Stülpnagel were critical of Vallat and thought he lacked the killer instinct necessary to implement the next phase of German Jewish policy in France—the Final Solution. On the other hand, some officials in Petain's government were uncomfortable with Vallat's extreme anti-Jewish policies, even though Marshal Pétain thought his government had to do more against the Jews. In early 1942, Best had Vallat fired, explaining that he wanted only to be the "Commissioner for the Protection of the Jews." On the other hand, Dannecker thought that Vallat had done a good job in promoting and implementing Germany's anti-Jewish policies in France.

Pétain replaced Vallat with Darquier de Pellepoix (1897–1980), who was more than willing to embrace Germany's deadly anti-Semitic policies. Vallat's dismissal was part of a larger administrative shakeup in France that saw *Generalleutnant* Karl Heinrich von Stülpnagel (1886–1944) replace his cousin, Otto von Stülpnagel, as military commander in France. Heinrich Himmler took control of all police operations in France and placed them under HSSPF *SS- Oberführer* Carl Albert Oberg (1897–1962). Dannecker was transferred to Bulgaria; he was replaced by *SS-Obersturmführer* Heinz Röthke. René Bousquet (1909–1952) became head of the French national police, and Pierre Laval (1883–1945) became the effective head of state. Planning for the first deportation of native French Jews began in the spring of 1942. Several months later, the Germans rounded up and shot thousands of foreign Jews in the military zone as part of their campaign to execute from fifty to one hundred Frenchmen for every German killed by the French resistance. In June 1942, Himmler told his subordinates that he wanted 100,000 French Jews sent East for "labor service," half of them to come from the Vichy zone. On June 17, German authorities required all the Jews in the German military zone older than six to begin wearing a Star of David on the left side of their outer garments. Although the Vichy government refused to require its Jews to wear the Star of David, it did force Jews to have their important identity cards stamped with *Juif* or *Juive*.

The first major roundup of Jews in Vichy France took place in Paris on July 16–17, 1942. The plan was to arrest 28,000 Jews and put them in the Vélodrome d'Hiver sports center in preparation for shipment eastward. Several days earlier, many French Jews had learned of the roundup and went into hiding; consequently, the police were able to arrest only about 9,000 Jews. These unfortunates were taken to the Drancy transit camp in the northern suburbs of Paris. During the next two years, almost all the 75,000 French Jews deported to the East and death left on trains from Drancy. About 70,000 died in Auschwitz.

Undeterred, the Germans pushed forward with the roundups; by the end of 1942, they had deported 42,500 Jews to the East, a third of them from Vichy. Hitler strengthened Dannecker's hand at the end of 1942 when he ordered the Wehrmacht to occupy Vichy France to shore up the Reich's southern military flank. Italy was now given control of eight Vichy *départements* in southeastern France. One of the problems Dannecker faced was the hesitancy of Vichy officials to deport French Jews, though they had no qualms with similar plans for foreign Jews. In fact, according to Richard Cobb, German officials "would have been largely ineffective [in rounding up Jews] had [they] been deprived of the willing ser-

vices of . . . *le Gestapo français.*"[10] This had more to do with the changing tide of war for Nazi Germany than with any deep sympathy for the Jews. Regardless, by late 1942 and early 1943, some Roman Catholic leaders, disenchanted with Vichy extremism, broke with Laval and Pétain's government and began openly to criticize the Jewish roundups.

The strongest opposition came from France's small Protestant community, which itself had been persecuted in the past. From 1941 to 1944, Huguenots in the Vichy hamlet of Le Chambon-sur-Lignon hid from 3,000 to 5,000 Jews. Le Chambon's religious leader, Pastor André Trocmé (1901–1971), worked closely with the Protestant underground rescue group, the *Comité intermouvements auprès des évacués* (CIMADE), which helped send Jews to the Huguenot village. In a sermon to his parishioners in the summer of 1942, Trocmé said, in a reference to the Vélodrome d'Hiver roundups, that "the Christian Church should drop to its knees and beg the pardon of God for its present incapacity and cowardice." When Vichy authorities insisted he stop his activities, he replied: "[T]he people came here for help and for shelter. I am their shepherd. A shepherd does not forsake his flock . . . I do not know what a Jew is. I know only human beings."[11] Yad Vashem later declared thirty-five residents of this village as "Righteous Among the Nations."

Pastor Marc Donadille, who saved about 80 Jews in Alsace and sent another 100 to Le Chambon, said that he first learned of the Final Solution in a meeting with other Protestant ministers in the fall of 1942. Fifty years later, he explained his reaction to the news and how it affected his relations with the Jews he was hiding:

You have to understand our situation. The people who informed us were people we trusted. . . . Now, why didn't we talk a lot about it after that? First of all, it is not very wise to say to the Jewish friends we are hiding,

**Jewish children in La Guespy children's home, Le Chambon-sur-Lignon, 1941. USHMM Photo No. 03686,
courtesy of Hanne Liebmann.**

who are living in our homes: "Later, they will
kill all of you, be careful." We had other
things to do than to analyze "Hitler wants to
kill them all."

What haunted us was the fate of these Jewish friends under our roofs. We didn't see beyond that, you must understand, and that
was enough to keep us busy! When they were
well hidden, when they were secure, when we
all ate together—in these moments we were
content, we were happy together, and we
sang! You have to put yourself in this atmosphere. We didn't spend every day assessing
and reflecting theoretically on all these problems, as we now do as the good intellectuals
we have become! We were not journalists! We
lived from day to day, saying to each other:
"In the end, those we save now, will be saved,
and one beautiful day, Hitler will fall." So that

explains a little why, knowing, we acted as if
we had forgotten.

We had not forgotten, but it was urgent
to live. And one cannot always live, being
haunted by the apocalypse.[12]

French Quakers, the YMCA, and the American Jewish Joint Distribution Committee
(AJJDC) also played active roles in saving
French Jews. In 1941, several Quakers wrote a
letter to Vallat:

It is unjust and easy to throw on Jews alone,
like on capitalists and Governments, all the
responsibilities of war: we are indeed *all responsible*, and Christians, by the mere fact of
calling themselves so, more than all others.

Besides, does such a crime exist which can
justify condemnation without defense or ap-

peal? What crime, for instance, can oblige a government to condemn children yet unborn? All violence brings with it violence, and we know by experience that such measures raise hatred and violence, which we would like to avoid.

And then we cannot and do not wish to forget that Jesus Christ, of whom we are disciples, belonged to the Jewish people.

That is to say, French Quakers, wishing rather to work than to criticize, have solicited from you, Your Excellency, an interview, not only to confirm their attitude, but also to offer you their voluntary services and they promise to fulfil [sic] loyally all work you wish to submit to them with the purpose of humanising, at least, the measures taken against Jews.

Vallat, who refused to meet with the Quakers, replied: "I limit myself to retain the feeling of Christian charity which has inspired you, and to confirm to you that I shall gladly accept your offer of voluntary services to help particular distresses endured by unhappy Jewish families."[13]

Elsewhere, Varian Fry (1907–1967), a journalist working with the American Emergency Rescue Committee, helped smuggle more than 2,000 refugees out of Marseilles before he was arrested and deported by the Vichy government in the fall of 1941. These efforts, unfortunately, did little to protect the 75,000 French Jews from France who died during the Holocaust. About a third were French citizens.

Greece

Like other countries in southeastern Europe, Greece struggled to create a viable democracy after World War I. A series of military coups in the 1920s and early 1930s weakened Greece's democratic institutions, and in 1936, King George II (r. 1922–1925, 1935–1947) appointed General Ioannis Metaxas (1871–1941) prime minister. Metaxas, fearing growing labor unrest and a communist uprising, quickly dissolved parliament and declared a

state of emergency throughout the country. Backed by the king and the military, Metaxas, who was also the minister of foreign affairs and minister of education, gradually transformed Greece into an Italian-style Fascist dictatorship. When war came in 1939, Greece declared itself neutral. In the summer of 1940, Benito Mussolini, who wanted to conquer Greece and make it part of a greater Italian Mediterranean empire, tried to draw Metaxas into war by sinking the Greek cruiser *Elli*. Metaxas refused to take the bait and reasserted Greece's neutrality. That fall, Mussolini, jealous over Hitler's recent western victories and his own humiliation in France, decided to invade Greece. On October 28, 1940, Italian forces, expecting a quick *Blitzkrieg* victory, moved into Greece.

The Greeks stopped the Italians in their tracks and pushed them back into Albania, which Mussolini had conquered in 1939. The Greek move into Albania presented the Allies with a new potential front against the Axis. In early 1941, George II accepted a British offer to move 100,000 troops and supplies into Greece to aid in the war against Italy. Hitler, fearful of Allied moves in southeastern Europe, responded with a simultaneous invasion of Greece and Yugoslavia on April 6, 1941, a move that delayed his plans for the campaign against the Soviet Union. The Wehrmacht conquered Greece in less than two weeks, a victory that forced the king and most of the British Expeditionary Force to flee to Crete.

The Germans divided Greece into three spheres of influence. The Italians took over most of central and southern Greece, including Athens, and the Bulgarians got Thrace in the northwest. Germany occupied parts of Macedonia and eastern Thrace. At this time, 77,000 Jews lived in Greece, 50,000 of them in German-occupied Salonika (Thessaloniki). In February 1943, Eichmann sent *SS- Hauptsturmführer* Dieter Wisliceny (1912–1948) and *SS- Haupsturmführer* Alois Brunner (1912–?),

"Eichmann's best tool," to Salonika to begin planning the Final Solution in the German sector.[14] During the next seven months, Wisliceny and Brunner oversaw the roundup and transport of 48,000 Saloniki Jews to Auschwitz. Two-thirds were immediately gassed. More than 4,000 Jews from other parts of Greece were also sent to Auschwitz and Bergen-Belsen during this period.

The deportations drew sharp criticism from Greek politicians and churchmen, though they had little impact on the Bulgarians and the Germans. Bulgarian authorities deported almost all the 4,300 Jews in their zone of Greece to Treblinka in the spring of 1943, but the Jews in Italian Greece were initially spared the harsh treatment suffered by those in other parts of the country. This all changed that summer with the collapse of Mussolini's government. The Wehrmacht marched into central and southern Greece, and in the spring of 1944, Wisliceny, aided initially by *SS- Gruppenführer* Jürgen Stroop, began the roundup and deportation of more than 8,000 Jews to Auschwitz. Estimates are that about 60,000 Greek Jews died during the Holocaust, almost 80 percent of them from the German zone.

The Netherlands

The Jewish community in the Netherlands was one of the most assimilated in Europe, and by 1930, 41 percent of Dutch Jews had married Gentiles. Most Dutch Jews lived in the country's largest cities, particularly Amsterdam, which had a Jewish population of almost 69,000 by 1920. Jewish refugees from Germany and Austria flocked to the Netherlands in the 1930s, and by 1940 there were 140,000 Jews in the Netherlands. The Dutch Jewish community set up the *Comité voor Bijzondere Joodse Belanger* (Committee for Special Jewish Interests) to help the new refugees. In 1939, the Dutch government opened an internment camp for illegal immigrants at Westerbork and then forced the country's Jewish community

to bear the costs of running it. In 1942, the Germans took over the camp and transformed it into the *Durchganglager Westerbork* (Transit Camp Westerbork); it now became the principal concentration and transfer camp for Dutch Jews.

The dramatic German invasion and conquest of the Netherlands in May 1940 caught the Dutch by surprise. Initially, German officials seemed disinterested in the Jewish question, though Arthur Seyss-Inquart, Hitler's *Reichskommissar füf die besetzten Niederland* (Reichscommissar for the Occupied Netherlands), considered the country's Jews enemies of the state. In the fall of 1940, Seyss-Inquart adopted a series of anti-Jewish regulations that banned all publications except the *Het Joodse Weekblad* (The Jewish Weekly Newspaper). Dutch civil servants also had to fill out a form asking whether they were Jewish or were married to a Jew. On November 4, Seyss-Inquart fired all Jewish government workers and teachers and cited the Nuremberg Laws as the justification for his actions. Several weeks earlier, Seyss-Inquart ordered Dr. Hans Fischböck (1895–1967), his finance minister, to register all businesses fully or partially owned by Jews. He used this information to close about 20,000 Jewish firms. The 3,000 that were allowed to remain open were carefully watched by the Germans. In response, the Netherlands' Jewish communities formed the *Joodse Coördinatiecommissie* (JCC; Jewish Coordinating Committee) to oversee Jewish affairs throughout the country.

Dutch Nazis hoped to play an important role in governing the Netherlands during the German occupation. Members of Adrian Mussert's (1894–1946) *National Socialist Beweging* (NSB; National Socialist Movement) proved willing allies of the Germans during the early days of the occupation. His SS-modeled *Weer-afdelingen* (WA; Defense Division), which had a strong following among the Dutch police, hoped to make the Netherlands *verjudet* (Jewish free). By the end of 1940, WA

Deportation of Jews from Westerbork, 1943–1944. USHMM Photo No. 05198A.

units were roaming city streets and harassing Jews and non-Jews alike. In response, Jews and Christians organized defense units to protect Amsterdam's Jewish quarter. On February 11, 1941, a Dutch Nazi died in a street fight between the WA and a Jewish defense group in Amsterdam. Seyss-Inquart ordered the Jewish quarter transformed into a ghetto and sealed. He also created a *Joodse Raad* (Jewish Council) to coordinate Jewish affairs with his administration. On February 22–23, HSSPF *SS-Brigadeführer* Hans Albin Rauter (1895–1945) ordered the arrest and deportation of 389 young Jewish males to Buchenwald and Mauthausen; two days later, a national strike of protest broke out. Seyss-Inquart quickly suppressed it and imposed heavy fines on the cities of Amsterdam, Hilversum, and Zaadan. He also adopted harsher anti-Jewish policies and opened a *Zentralstelle für jüdische Auswanderung* (Central Office for Jewish Emi-

gration), which, as a branch of Eichmann's RSHA IVB4 office, would oversee the arrest and deportation of Dutch Jews to the East. At the end of 1941, Rauter informed the *Joodse Raad* that it had to supply Jewish workers for recently opened forced-labor camps near Westerbork and Vught. By the spring of 1942, Rauter had deported 15,000 Dutch Jews to these camps.

Seyss-Inquart also forbade Jews from living anywhere but Amsterdam, Westerbork, or Vught. On May 3, 1942, he ordered all Jews to wear a yellow Star of David; those who refused to comply were told they would be deported to Mauthausen. The badges were an ominous sign of things to come: On June 26, Ferdinand aus der Fünten (1909–1989), the German head of the *Zentralstelle*, told Dr. David Cohen (1882–1967), the vice chair of the *Joodsche Raad,* that individuals and families were to be rounded up and sent to forced-labor camps in Germany. The first to be deported would be young healthy Jews. First they would receive a deportation notice and then they would have to register with the *Joodse Raad*. One of those who received a notice was Margot Frank (1926–1945), the older sister of Anne Frank. Few Jews registered for the deportations, and Rauter responded with a manhunt in mid-July, arresting 740 Jews. Cohen was told that if he did not immediately supply the *Zenstralstelle* with 4,000 Jews, the 740 hostages would be sent to Mauthausen.

Dutch Protestant and Roman Catholic leaders sent Seyss-Inquart and Rauter a telegram voicing their opposition to the roundups and ordered the telegram read during church services. Seyss-Inquart warned them that if the telegram was read in the churches, he would deport "all non-Aryan Christians." Protestant leaders decided not to read the telegram to their congregations because they did not want to be responsible for the deaths of fellow Christians. But Johannes de Jong (1885–1955), the archbishop of Utrecht and Roman Catholic Primate of the Netherlands, insisted that the telegram be read in all Roman Catholic churches. In retaliation, the Germans deported 201 Dutch Jewish converts to Roman Catholicism to Auschwitz.[15]

If anything, the church protests strengthened Seyss-Inquart's determination to make the Netherlands *judenfrei*. On October 2, 1942, the SS, assisted by the NSB and Dutch volunteers from the *Grüne Polizei* ("Green," or Border, Police), began to round up all Jewish males in labor camps throughout the country and transfer them to Westerbork. The Germans deported from 105,000 to 107,000 Dutch Jews to the East in eleven months. About 60,000 Dutch Jews were sent to Auschwitz and 34,000 to Sobibór. Others were sent to Theresienstadt and Bergen-Belsen. Only 5,200 survived the Holocaust.

About 25,000 Dutch Jews went into hiding after the roundups began in the summer of 1942. The Germans, aided by a Dutch police

Jewish registration list, hunted down the Jews in hiding. With the help of Dutch informers, the Germans found about a third of those in hiding and sent them to death and concentration camps. One of the groups discovered and deported in the summer of 1944 were the Jews in Anne Frank's Secret Annex.

Anne Frank

It's really a wonder that I haven't dropped all my ideals, because they seem so absurd and impossible to carry out. Yet I keep them, because in spite of everything I still believe that people are really good at heart. I simply can't build up my hopes on a foundation consisting of confusion, misery, and death. I see the world gradually being turned into a wilderness, I hear the ever approaching thunder, which will destroy us too, I can feel the sufferings of millions and yet, if I look up into the heavens, I think that it will all come right, that this cruelty too will end, and that peace and tranquility will return again.

In the meantime, I must uphold my ideals, for perhaps the time will come when I shall be able to carry them out.[16]

For many people, the story of Anne Frank is synonymous with the tragedies of the Holocaust. Others find her Holocaust experiences to be incomplete, particularly if all they know about her comes from reading her famous diary. Anne Frank was born on June 12, 1929, in Frankfurt, Germany. In 1933, Anne's father, Otto Frank (1889–1980), moved his family to Amsterdam, where he set up two businesses that made food preparation products. In 1938, Otto tried to obtain visas so that his family could move to the United States, but he was unsuccessful. In the spring of 1941, he wrote to Nathan Straus Jr. (1889–1961), an old friend from their days at Heidelberg University and the owner of Macy's department store in New York, about the prospects for immigration to the United States. Frank told Straus that he felt that the

Anne Frank (left) and Margot Frank (second from right) play with friends in Amsterdam, 1934. USHMM Photo No. 63541, courtesy of Penny Boyer.

United States was the only country that would accept his family and that he was doing this for his two daughters, Anne and Margot. Mr. Straus agreed to help his old friend and wrote affidavits of support, as did Otto's two brothers-in-law, Julius and Walter Hollander, who lived in Boston. But nothing came of the Franks' application, which ran afoul of deteriorating American-German relations and the highly restrictive and, at times, anti-Semitic immigration policies of the United States.[17]

On July 5, 1942, the Frank's oldest daughter, Margot, received a notice to register for deportation. With the aid of his assistant, Miep Gies (1909–), Otto Frank and his family moved into the Secret Annex above Frank's business office at Prinsengracht 263 in Amsterdam. With them was the family of Herman van Pels (1898–1944), one of Frank's business partners. They were later joined by Fritz Pfef-

fer (1889–1944), a dentist. With the help of Miep Gies and several other Dutch friends, both families and Pfeffer successfully hid from the Germans for more than two years. But on August 4, 1944, the SD, operating on an anonymous phone tip, broke into the Secret Annex and arrested everyone. Two months later, they were all sent to Auschwitz. Only Otto, Margot, and Anne survived. Anne and Margot were sent to Bergen-Belsen in Germany. Margot, ill with typhus, fell from her bunk and died in early March 1945; Anne, malnourished and alone, died a few days later. Her body was thrown into a mass grave.

Miep Gies found Anne's diary in the ransacked Secret Annex and gave it to Otto after he returned from Auschwitz at the end of the war. In 1947, he published excerpts from it, and in 1952 it came out in English as *The Diary of Anne Frank*. Other excerpts from her diary include *The Works of Anne Frank* (1959;

1974), *Tales from the House Behind* (1966), and *Anne Frank's Tales from the Secret Annex* (1983). The play, titled *The Diary of Anne Frank*, won a Tony Award and a Pulitzer Prize for drama in 1955. In her introduction to the 1952 English edition of *The Diary of Anne Frank*, Eleanor Roosevelt (1884–1962) explained the reason for the success of Anne's work: "It is one of the wisest and most moving commentaries on war and its impact on human beings I have ever read."[18]

Yet there were those who claimed the diary was fabricated by Otto Frank. In 1986, the Netherlands State Institute for War Documentation published a definitive edition of Anne's diary to counter these charges, though it did not still the criticism of the diary. In an article in the *New Yorker* in 1997, "Who Owns Anne Frank," Cynthia Ozick argued that the misappropriation and distortion of the diary and its stories undermined its deeper significance. Such criticism has not blunted the universality of Anne's writings and message, which are memorialized in the Anne Frank House in Amsterdam, run by the international Anne Frank Foundation. Otto Frank insisted that the Anne Frank Foundation focus its resources on combating international anti-Semitism and racism.

Norway

There were about 1,700 to 1,800 Jews in Norway in 1940. The Germans did not begin to adopt harsh policies towards Norway's Jews until 1942, when they sent Jews in the northern part of the country to forced-labor camps and required that all Jews have a "J" stamped on their identity cards. Later that year, Vidkun Quisling (1887–1943), the head of the Norwegian Nazi Party (*Nasjonal Samling;* National Gathering), and Norway's puppet minister president, ordered a census of all Norwegian Jews. He used this information to arrest male Jews throughout the country in the fall of 1942. On October 26–27, the Norwegian police, aided by the SS and Norwe-

gian Nazis, arrested and interned 260 male Jews in Oslo. A month later, the police rounded up all Jews still in Oslo and sent them to Auschwitz. On November 10, Norway's seven Lutheran bishops, who played an important spiritual role in the Norwegian resistance and had earlier resigned their posts to protest Quisling's policies, sent him a letter protesting the roundups:

> The Church has God's call and full authority to proclaim God's law and God's gospel. Therefore, it cannot remain silent when God's commandments are being trampled underfoot, and now it is one of Christianity's basic values which is being violated, the commandment of God which is fundamental to all society. . . . . Stop the persecution of Jews, and stop the race hatred which, through the press, is being spread through the land.[19]

Churches throughout the country held special services to protest the arrest of Norway's Jews, and ministers read the bishops' letter to their congregations on December 6 and 13. The Germans ultimately interned the Church of Norway's bishops, and most of the clergy refused to have anything to do with the Quisling government. About 900 Norwegian Jews escaped to Sweden and others went into hiding. Quisling sent those unable to escape the German dragnet to death or labor camps. About 760 Norwegian Jews died during the Holocaust.

The Nazi-Allied States

A number of European countries were allies of the Germans during much of World War II, and they played an important role in the Holocaust. Several of the countries in Hitler's alliance network, among them Bulgaria, Hungary, Romania, and Slovakia, had some of Europe's largest Jewish and Roma communities. Others, such as Finland, Italy, Croatia, and Serbia, had smaller Jewish and Roma populations, but they played important roles in the concentration, murder, or salvation of Jews and Roma. They were often driven by traditional prejudices and the desire to prove themselves loyal Nazi allies. In some instances, though, the wishes of national leaders was weakened by public outcries over the fate of the Jews and, to a lesser degree, the Roma. Things began to change in 1943 when, after the German defeats at Stalingrad and North Africa, once-pliable allies began to look for ways to change sides. This would affect policies towards the Jews, Roma, and other minorities.

Bulgaria

On the eve of World War II, there were about 50,000 Jews and 150,000 Roma in Bulgaria. Most of them would survive the Holocaust. Bulgaria paid a considerable price for its support of Germany in World War I when it lost territory to Romania, Serbia, and Greece in the postwar settlements. Bulgaria became a politically unstable nation after World War I and saw the army and the king emerge in 1923 as the dominant political forces in the country. Jews enjoyed a modicum of economic and cultural success in interwar Bulgaria, and they played an important role in the country's urban economic life. The country's Roma were socially and economically marginalized, but they did enjoy a modest cultural awakening during this period. The country's Muslim Roma suffered from prejudice not only for their ethnicity but also for their faith, which linked them to the country's Turkish population.

A coup in 1935 created a monarchial dictatorship under King Boris III (r. 1918–1943) modeled along Italian Fascist lines. A number of anti-Semitic groups, such as the *Soyuz na B'lgarskite Natsionalni Legioni* (Union of Bulgarian National Legions), the *Ratnitsi Napreduka Bulgarshtinata* (Guardians of the Advancement of Bulgarian National Spirit), and the Nazi-inspired youth organization *Branik* (defense), flourished under the monarchial

dictatorship. Bulgaria was deeply affected by the rise of Nazism in Germany. As Europe moved closer to war in 1939, Bulgaria found itself drawn politically and economically into the German-Italian orbit, though Boris III declared neutrality when World War II broke out. In 1940, Hitler offered Bulgaria southern Dobrudja to counter a similar offer from Stalin. On March 1, 1941, Bulgaria joined the Axis and participated in the invasion of Yugoslavia and Greece. It received Macedonia and western Thrace as a reward for supporting the Germans. Now an active German ally, Bulgaria began an uncomfortable three-year relationship with Hitler's Reich.

Earlier that year, the Bulgarian parliament had passed the *Zakon za Zashtita na Natziata* (ZZN; Law for the Protection of the Nation). The ZZN was modeled on the Nuremberg Laws, though its definition of Jewishness was much less stringent, a sore point with the Germans. It forbade any international Jewish organizations to operate in Bulgaria, and said that Jews could no longer run for public office. It proposed that Jewish government workers be dismissed and imposed strict marital, educational, economic, and residency requirements on Jews. A broad coalition of prominent lawyers and physicians, along with the leadership of the Bulgarian Orthodox Church, criticized the ZZN when the government published it in draft form in October 1940. Metropolitan Stefan (1878–1957), the head of the church in Sofia, called a meeting of church leaders to discuss the ZZN. They released the following statement on November 15:

> The proposed law contains measures that cannot be considered as just or useful to the defence of the nation. If there are dangers facing our nation, then the steps that are taken to counter them must target actions, not nationalities or religious groups; the proposed law, however, seems to have as its goal the special treatment of a Bulgarian national minority. All men and all peoples must defend

their rights and protect themselves from danger, but this just aspiration must not serve as a pretext for injustice and violence towards others.[20]

The Metropolitans followed this up with two suggestions for the government. The first was that Jewish converts to Christianity be treated just like other Bulgarian Christians. They also challenged the government not to develop prejudicial policies towards the Jews. Instead, the government should "prepare satisfactory measures against any real dangers to the spiritual, economic, social and political life of the Bulgarian people, from whatever source these dangers might come."[21] These protests had little impact on the fate of the ZZN, which the *Subranie* (parliament) passed in early January 1941. Boris III signed the bill into law soon afterwards.

Five months earlier, the government had created the *Konisarstvo za Evreiskite Vuprosi* (KEV; Commissariat for Jewish Questions) to implement and oversee Jewish policies. The KEV was headed by Alexander Belev (?–1944), an attorney just returned from Germany, where he had studied the Nuremberg Laws to help write the ZZN. The KEV was funded by property stolen from Jews. Other anti-Jewish regulations limited the number of Jews who could work in certain professions, defined Jewishness along racial lines, laid the groundwork for the seizure of Jewish property, and proposed the deportation of the Jews in Sofia to the countryside. Jewish businesses also had to identify themselves as such. Jews were now required to wear the yellow Star of David.

Officials were hesitant about taking similar measures against the Roma, though German authorities pressured Boris III to apply the spirit of the ZZN to the Roma. In May 1942, the government decreed that Roma had to register for forced labor, and several months later the government outlawed marriages between Roma and Bulgarians. These policies prompted violent attacks against the Roma; these were spurred by press reports that criticized the government for spending too much money policing them.

At the end of 1942, Belev's office began to discuss the deportation of Bulgarian Jews to Poland. On February 22, 1943, Theodor Dannecker, Eichmann's representative in Bulgaria, reached an agreement with Belev for the transport of "20,000 Jews from the new Bulgarian lands [of] Thrace and Macedonia into the German eastern regions."[22] Gideon Hausner (1915–1990), the chief prosecutor at the Eichmann trial in Israel, later noted that Bulgaria was "the only country that signed a written contract 'to supply Jews to Germany,' undertook to pay for their transport, and stipulated that she would never and under no circumstances request their return."[23] On March 4, 1943, Bulgarian military and police units began the roundup of 11,500 Jews in the former Greek and Yugoslav provinces. They were first sent to transit camps in Bulgaria. Rosa Yakova, a nurse at one of the camps, reported: "We saw children, old people, mothers, all of them helpless, naked, and barefoot. It was dark. A strong wind was blowing. Mr. Ovcharov [the KEV delegate] started yelling: 'Get off right away and get into the small open cars!' He ordered the police officers and the soldiers: 'Beat them with your rifles, make them hurry. We are not going to wait all night.'"[24] At the end of March, almost all the Thracian and Macedonian Jews were sent to Treblinka and death.

Since he was still short of his quota, Belev decided in early March to fill it with Jews from Kyustendil, in western Bulgaria. Dimitar Peshev (1894–1973), the deputy speaker in parliament and minister of justice, learned of Belev's plans from Jewish leaders in Sofia. He called the deportations "a grave crime, both from a constitutional-political and from a moral, humane point of view," and was able to get forty-three members of parliament to sign a petition on March 9 protesting them. Such moves, the petition declared, were "unthinkable" and would "burden her [Bulgaria] morally, but also would

King Boris III and Adolf Hitler, 1940. USHMM Photo No. 80526, courtesy of National Archives and Records Administration, College Park.

void all her moral standing." Such an act, the petition went on, would affect all of Bulgaria: "The honor of Bulgaria and her people . . . is above all an element of her policy. It is a political asset of the greatest value, therefore nobody has the right to waste it without the approval of the entire nation."[25]

The Bulgarian Orthodox Church also reacted strongly against Belev's deportation scheme. On March 10, Belev ordered a roundup of Jews in Plovdiv. When the local metropolitan, Kiril (1901–1971), learned of the deportation plans, he sent a wire to King Boris and asked him to halt the transports. He then went to the local railroad station and told the police that if a train tried to leave with Jews, he would lie across the tracks to stop it. Yad Vashem later named Kiril, who became patriarch in 1953, a Righteous Among the Nations.

Similar actions took place elsewhere in Bulgaria, and the deportations were quickly called off. But this did not end the church protests. On April 2, church leaders met in Sofia to discuss the government's Jewish policies; they also drafted a letter of protest to the prime minister and king stating that people throughout the country had asked the Holy Church to help the Jews and demanded that the government do nothing to deprive Jews of their basic rights and the right to live in Bulgaria as normal human beings. The letter asked that the government ease its restrictions on the Jews and to stop making Jewish converts to Christianity wear both a cross and the Star of David; it also asked that converts not pay taxes to the KEV. It reminded the prime minister and king of the admonition in the book of Matthew: "With the measure you use, it will be measured back to you."[26]

Church leaders followed this up with a letter to Boris III asking for a private meeting. The king, furious and hurt, agreed to meet with a church delegation on April 15. He spent half an hour attacking the Jews, castigating them for centuries of "profiteering" that, he claimed, had greatly damaged "humanity for centuries." Jewish profiteering, he explained, had caused untold unrest and was the principal cause of the current war. He pointed to efforts by other nations in Europe to end Jewish influence in an effort to strengthen their "national feeling and patriotism." He concluded by saying that the government would look for ways to lessen Jewish suffering and do what it could to stop the mistreatment of Jewish converts to Christianity.[27]

The public outcry over the March deportations forced Boris III to change course. On May 21, the government approved a plan to force Sofia's Jews to move to the countryside. Metropolitan Stefan let it be known that the church would christen any Jews who sought its protection. The Ministry of Religions said it would refuse to recognize such christenings and would deport Jews who were christened that year. Stefan told ministry officials that he would inform all his parish priests of this decision. The Ministry of the Interior responded by ordering Stefan to close all the churches in Sofia. When he refused, the Interior Ministry ordered his arrest for "crimes" against the state. Belev stepped in and convinced Interior officials not to take action against the metropolitan, though this was not the end of the matter. On May 24, Belev ordered the expulsion of Jews from the capital to twenty towns and villages throughout the country. During the summer of 1943, more than 19,000 Jews left Sofia for the countryside.

The government also decided to force all Roma between the ages of seventeen and fifty to move to rural forced-labor camps; thousands were deported from the capital to the countryside during this period. In August 1943, the government ordered authorities throughout the country to restrict the movement of Roma on the pretext that they were spreading infectious diseases, particularly ty-

phus. One of the interesting offshoots of these transfers was the creation of a new subgroup of Roma, the Zuti. The Zuti were poor Roma and Jews who met in the forced-labor camps and intermarried. Since neither community would accept them, the Zuti created their own closed society.

In time, the Germans decided it would be unwise to press the Bulgarians on the deportation matter. *SA- Obergruppenführer* Adolph-Heinz Beckerle (1902–1976), the German ambassador to Bulgaria, told Joachim von Ribbentrop on June 7, 1943, that the reason for the Bulgarians' refusal to deport Jews to Poland was the lack of ideological strength in the Bulgarian mentality; in particular, the Bulgarians had no innate prejudice against the Jews, as did the people of northern Europe, because they had grown up with Armenians, Greeks, and Gypsies.[28]

The mysterious death of Boris III on August 28 caused a dramatic change in Bulgarian policy and its relationship with Nazi Germany. Two weeks earlier, the king had met with Hitler at his military headquarters in East Prussia and refused the Führer's demand that Bulgaria declare war on the Soviet Union. Boris III was succeeded by his son, Simeon II (r. 1943–1946), with a new government under Dobri Bozhilov (1884–1945). Though the government continued to support earlier anti-Semitic policies, it decided to end talk of deportations. In the spring of 1944, a new government under Ivan Bagrianov (1891–1945) implemented new policies towards the Jews. The idea was to restore their full rights, but, given the continued presence of the Wehrmacht in Bulgaria, to do so discreetly. Bagrianov dismissed Belev and that summer voided the ZZN and other restrictions against the Jews. The Soviet Union declared war on Bulgaria on September 5, 1944, and four days later put a pro-Soviet regime in power in Sofia.

After the war, Bulgarian Jews and Roma credited King Boris III with saving them from certain death during the Holocaust. Boris III was a popular monarch, and this romantic view of his role saving Jews and Roma is centered partly around his mysterious death. Some say he was poisoned by the Germans for refusing to ship Jews to Hitler's death camps. The reality is quite different. King Boris III, the dominant figure in Bulgarian politics in the decade before his death, was an anti-Semite who was more than willing to take any measures necessary against the Jews and Roma to underscore his allegiance to Nazi Germany. It should also be remembered that many of the legislators who voiced opposition to the deportation of Jews had voted for some of the country's early anti-Semitic legislation. One of the few institutions that consistently opposed restrictions against Jews was the Bulgarian Orthodox Church. Whatever the motivations, collective Bulgarian efforts saved most of the Jews and Roma from death during the Holocaust. Unfortunately, these same voices of restraint said little about the death of almost 11,500 Jews in Bulgarian-controlled Macedonia and Thrace.

Finland

Finland had a Jewish population of 2,000 when World War II began. Finland's Jews, who lived in Helsinki, Turku, and Viipuri, enjoyed a rich cultural and religious life. During the 1930s, right-wing groups published a lot of anti-Semitic material, much of it influenced by Nazi German writers and propagandists. Jewish soldiers served valiantly in the Finnish army during the Winter War (1939–1940) against Russia. In 1944, Marshal Carl Gustaf Emil Mannerheim (1867–1957), Finland's president, honored the country's Jews for their contributions to the war effort. Finland tried to maintain a delicate neutral balance between the region's two aggressive powers—the Soviet Union and Germany—but was drawn militarily into the German camp in the weeks before the attack on the Soviet Union in 1941.

The Finns joined the Reich in the war against the USSR principally to regain control of the Karelian territory lost to the Soviets in the Winter War. German troops massed in the northern part of Finland just days before the June 22 assault. Three days later, the Finnish parliament declared war on the Soviet Union after Red Air Force incursions over Finnish territory. On June 29, Finland invaded the Soviet Union and quickly regained Karelia. Finnish forces then halted their operations. After the German defeat at Stalingrad in early 1943, the Finnish government looked for ways to withdraw from the war. Efforts to reach an accord with Moscow failed in early 1944, and later that summer the Soviets invaded Finland. The Finns quickly accepted a German offer of military aid in return for an agreement not to seek a separate peace. Though German forces had little impact on the Soviet advance, their superior weapons helped the Finns stop the Red Army's advance in mid-July 1944. Stalin, who wanted to concentrate his efforts on the drive to Berlin, now agreed to talks, and on September 19, 1944, Marshal Mannerheim's government broke its promise to Berlin and signed a separate peace with the Kremlin. The terms were harsh, but Finland kept her independence. What followed was a third war for the Finns, who now fought with the Russians to drive the 200,000 German troops out of Lapland.

Though Finland escaped German occupation during the war, Reich officials considered Finnish Jews statistically part of Final Solution planning. During a visit to Finland in the summer of 1942, Heinrich Himmler asked Johann Wilhelm Rangell (1894–1982), the Finnish prime minister, about his country's Jews. Rangell told Himmler that the Jews were loyal Finns who were serving in the army like other Finns. In Finland, he added, "*Wir haben keine Judenfrage* (we have no Jewish question)."[29] Traditionally, it was thought that only eight Finnish Jews perished during the Holocaust. However, recent scholarship by Serah Beizer, a researcher at Yad Vashem's International School for Holocaust Studies, has challenged these statistics. Her work, supported by Finnish scholarship, indicates that possibly as many as 500 to 600 Jews were among the 3,000 Soviet POWs turned over to the Germans by the Finns during the war. Of this number, at least 70 were arrested by the Gestapo. In 2000, Prime Minister Paavo Lipponen (1941–) apologized to the country's Jews for these deportations. Finland's Evangelical Lutheran Church also apologized: "The church admits to having remained silent about the persecution of the Jews and wishes to apologize to the Jewish community for this. . . . The handover, even of one single Jew, was a sin. . . . More instruction on Judaism and the common roots of Judaism and Christianity should be given in the parishes." Finland's national church leaders also stated that Martin Luther's ideas about the Jews "should be reexamined."[30]

Hungary

There were 725,000 Jews in Hungary in 1941 as well as another 100,000 Jewish converts to Christianity who were legally considered Jewish. There were also 100,000 Roma in Hungary at the time. Jews had played an important role in the creation of the Hungarian state after the *Ausgleich* of 1867, and they received equal political and civil rights with Christians in return for their support of Hungarian national aspirations. Judaism, though, never gained equal status with Christianity. Anti-Semitism, fed by the growing prominence of Jews in the economy and certain professions during the next seventy-five years, remained just below the surface. Hungary paid dearly for its part in World War I: It lost 60 percent of its population in the Treaty of Trianon (1919), and 70 percent of its territory. Hungary now became an almost purely Magyar (the language of the Hungarians) state. Some Hungarians began to blame the

country's minorities, who now made up a little more than 10 percent of the population, for these difficulties. Such attitudes dashed all hope for significant gains in minority rights in the 1920s, particularly in light of an ongoing policy of Magyarization.

Hungary's rightward drift politically came earlier than some of its Central European neighbors. In 1932, Prime Minister Gyula Gömbös (1886–1936), an old ally of Admiral Miklós Horthy (r. 1920–1944; 1868–1957), Hungary's regent and chief of state, tried unsuccessfully to transform Hungary along Italian Fascist lines. After his party won control of parliament in 1935, Gömbös signed a personal agreement with Hermann Göring in Berlin stating that in two years he hoped to have in place "a system closely resembling that of the Third Reich."[31] Gömbös died the following year, and Horthy, hoping to halt the country's drift towards Germany and Italy, replaced him with Kálmán Darányi (1886–1939).

Unfortunately, Darányi also proved to have strong rightist tendencies and, in league with Ferenc Szálasi (1897–1945), the head of the recently outlawed *A Magyar Nemzeti Szocialista Part* (Hungarian National Socialist Party), pushed through parliament Hungary's First Jewish Law (Law No. XV) several months after Hitler's *Anschluß* with Austria. Though a broad spectrum of liberal intellectuals spoke out against the bill, it had the strong support of Hungary's Roman Catholic and Protestant churches. According to Randolph L. Braham, the support of the churches not only insured the passage of the First Jewish Law but also led to the "legitimization of anti-Semitism and of the many anti-Jewish movements."[32] The First Jewish Law stipulated that Jews could make up no more than 20 percent of those working in business and the professions; it also created "chambers" for the press and the entertainment industry. "Chambers" already existed for the legal, medical, and engineering professions, and anyone who wanted to work in these fields had to belong to one.

One of the reasons Darányi proposed the First Jewish law was to counter the growing political threat of right-wing groups, such as Szálasi's new party, the *Nyilaskeresztes Párt-Hungarista Mozgalon* (Arrow Cross Party-Hungarianist Movement), which was modeled on the German Nazi Party. Arrow Cross was extremely successful in national elections in the spring of 1939, garnering over 25 percent of the vote. Darányi's alliance with Szálasi and other extreme right-wing groups led to his downfall. His successor, Béla Imrédy (1891–1946), cracked down on these movements and had Szálasi imprisoned for his illegal activities. Yet Imrédy soon fell prey to the allure of Germany and Italy: Later that year he participated in the First Vienna Award negotiations, an agreement that gave Hungary parts of Slovakia. He thus partially fulfilled one of the cornerstones of Hungarian politics since 1919—the recovery of territory lost to other countries in the Treaty of Trianon. Afterwards, Imrédy let it be known that he intended to draw closer to the Reich. In the midst of preparations for new anti-Jewish legislation, his political enemies charged him with having Jewish ancestry. Horthy dismissed Imrédy, a devout Roman Catholic, in early 1939.

His successor, Pál Teleki (1879–1941), an avowed anti-Semite, supported the Second Jewish Law, which parliament approved on May 4, 1939. It stated that "a person belonging to the Jewish denomination is at the same time a member of the Jewish racial community and it is natural that the cessation of membership in the Jewish denomination does not result in any change in that person's association with the racial community."[33]

The Second Jewish Law also severely restricted Jewish political and civil rights and forbade Jews from holding government jobs. It also stated that Jews could make up no more than 6 percent of those working in education and the professions. New restrictions were also placed on Jewish business and economic activities.

Teleki strengthened Hungary's ties with Germany by joining the Tripartite Pact (Germany, Italy, and Japan) after acquiring northern Transylvania in the Nazi-brokered Second Vienna Award.[34] Germany now began to play a more influential role in Hungarian politics. The Nazis' hand was strengthened by the creation of a new, pro-German party, the *A Magyar Megújulás Pártja* (MMP; The Party of Hungarian Renewal), which Berlin thought was "the best assurance for stability and law and order in an envisioned Nazi-oriented Hungary."[35] The MMP was to be everything that Arrow Cross was not: disciplined, organized, and strongly oriented toward German Nazism. Teleki concluded afterwards that the only way he could curb Germany's new influence and growing right-wing extremism was to out-Nazi the Nazis.

In 1941, Teleki released Szálasi from prison and promised to enact more anti-Semitic legislation. Yet he committed suicide in the spring of 1941 after Horthy agreed to join Hitler in the invasion of Yugoslavia because he felt that Horthy's decision had violated a recently concluded treaty of friendship with Yugoslavia. László Bárdossy (1890–1946), Teleki's successor, followed through on Horthy's promise. Hungary received Yugoslavia's Délvidék region in compensation for it role in the assault on Yugoslavia. Hungary also joined the Reich in its invasion of the Soviet Union a few months later. Bowing to German pressure, Hungary's parliament enacted the Third Jewish Law later that year; this law resembled the Nuremberg Laws and defined Jewishness along racial lines. It also forbade marriage between Jews and non-Jews.

Horthy dismissed Teleki in the spring of 1942 because of his strong pro-German sentiments and his refusal to support the appointment of Horthy's son, Istvan, as deputy regent. Teleki's successor, Miklós Kállay (1887–1967), was initially a strong supporter of the alliance with Germany. But by 1943 Kállay and Horthy began to have doubts about a German victory. On the other hand, their fear of Soviet communism tempered efforts to weaken ties with the Reich. Instead, Kállay, initially with German support, explored the prospect of an agreement with the Allies. Over time, Germany became fearful that Hungary would withdraw from the war. On March 17, 1944, at Hitler's insistence, Horthy dismissed Kállay and, two days later, occupied Hungary. The new head of government, General Döme Sztójay (1883–1946), was a pro-Nazi who had earlier served as Hungary's ambassador to Germany. Sztójay's government was committed to keeping Hungary in the war and supported Adolf Eichmann's efforts to deport Hungary's Jews.

The Germans had first demanded that Hungary ship its Jews to concentration camps in the East in the spring of 1942. Kállay initially ignored Germany's demand and, in response to continued pressure to deport Hungary's Jews, explained that they were simply too important to the country's economy and the Axis war effort to deport them. This all changed with the German occupation of Hungary in the spring of 1944. Though Hungary's Jews had suffered considerably during the war, "they had been spared the ravages inflicted on the Jews in neighboring Poland and Slovakia."[36] But, as David Cesarani has noted, what followed was not an anti-Semitic campaign driven by sheer blood lust. The Germans saw Hungary's large Jewish community as a new source of slave labor and economic plunder.[37]

The central figure in all of this was Adolf Eichmann, who led a special commando unit that swept into Hungary on the heels of the Wehrmacht. Horthy had already agreed in a meeting with Hitler to deport 100,000 Jews to the Reich as slave laborers. By early April 1944, Eichmann, in league with Hungarian officials, developed a plan that would force the country's Jews into ghettos and seize their property and wealth. The deportations would begin on May 15. But most of the trains were not bound for the Reich; instead, most went to Auschwitz.

Once there, the SS selected about a third of the new arrivals for slave labor; the rest were quickly murdered in Birkenau's gas chambers. Between May 15 and July 8, the Germans and the Hungarians deported 437,403 Jews to the General Government. On July 7, Horthy, bowing to growing international and domestic pressure, ordered the deportations halted.

Rescue efforts began almost immediately. One of the most important rescue organizations in Hungary was Va'ada (*Va'adat ha-Ezra ve-ha-Hatsala be-Budapest;* Relief and Rescue Committee of Budapest), which was created in late 1941 to help the flow of Jewish refugees from neighboring parts of Europe. Two years later, Va'ada became an official part of the Jewish Agency of Palestine. By 1944, it had also established contact with the AJJDC and the recently created War Refugee Board (WRB), which President Franklin Roosevelt had created in early 1944 in response to mounting pressure to rescue victims of Nazi oppression, particularly Jews.

Soon after the Germans occupied Hungary, Joel Brand (1906–1964), a Va'ada leader, had three meetings with Eichmann to discuss the rescue of Hungarian Jews. A year earlier, Va'ada had been a conduit for funds to members of Slovakia's Jewish Working Group, which had established contact with Dieter Wisliceny, Himmler's representative in Slovakia. Though Wisliceny collected only $169,000 from the Working Group, Eichmann was intrigued by the idea of using Jewish resources to help strengthen the hand of the SS.

According to the testimony Brand gave during the Eichmann trial, and later in his own memoirs, *Desperate Mission,* Eichmann was willing to sell him 1 million Jews in a "goods for blood" deal. Eichmann told Brand that he wanted 10,000 new trucks as well as several tons of tea, coffee, and soap in return for the Jews. The trucks, Eichmann assured Brand, would be used on the eastern front against the Soviets. When Brand asked how he should pay for the goods, Eichmann told him he should

Geza Lajtbs (forefront) and other Hungarian Jews at selection in Auschwitz II-Birkenau. USHMM Photo No. 77236, photographer: Bernhardt Walter/Ernst Hofmann; courtesy of Yad Vashem.

get the funds from the Allies. Brand was free to choose any Jews he wanted for the exchange. During their last meeting, Eichmann told Brand that he would "close Auschwitz and bring ten percent of the promised million to the frontier." He added: "You can take one hundred thousand Jews away, and afterward bring one thousand trucks. We'll go on like that. A thousand trucks for every hundred thousand Jews. You can't ask for anything more reasonable than that."[38] Eichmann gave Brand two weeks to conclude his talks with the Allies in Istanbul and kept Brand's family as hostages during the negotiations.

Brand left Budapest on May 17; he was accompanied by Bandi Grosz, a spy who used Brand's talks as a cover to set up a meeting between high ranking SD officials and Allied officials about a separate peace agreement. Grosz told Brand that the Nazis knew they had lost the war: "They know that peace can-

not be reached with Hitler. Himmler wants to use all possible contacts to get down to negotiations with the Allies. Your Jewish affair was only an auxiliary question."[39]

Brand, undeterred, was determined to fulfill his mission. His meetings with representatives of the JA, first in Istanbul and later in Aleppo, were less than fruitful. Though the JA agreed in principle to the deal, little came of it after the British arrested Brand in Aleppo.

News of Eichmann's offer, though, reached London and Washington. The British government rejected the offer because lawmakers feared the trucks would strengthen the Wehrmacht and prolong the war. They also feared the deal could drive a wedge between the Allies and the Soviets and hinder military operations in Europe, a situation that Himmler wanted all along. On July 19, the *New York Herald Tribune* called the negotiations a "Gestapo plot," and the *Times* of London

Hannah Szenes and brother Giora in Palestine, 1944.
USHMM Photo No. 60133, courtesy of Beit Hannah
Senesh.

responded by pressuring Admiral Horthy to halt the deportations, which he did on July 7. Unfortunately, their efforts could not save the Jews already murdered at Auschwitz and elsewhere. The situation worsened in the fall of 1944 after the Germans, frustrated by Horthy's drift towards the West, forced him to resign; they replaced him with Szálasi as prime minister and head of state. What followed was a reign of terror that lasted until Hungary was liberated on April 4, 1945.

It was in the midst of this German-Arrow Cross anti-Semitic blood purge that the Hungarians brutally tortured and executed Hannah Szenes (1921–1944), a Hungarian-born, British-trained commando who had parachuted into Yugoslavia to help rescue Hungarian Jews. Hannah, who was born in Budapest, made *aliyah* (ascent or going up) to British Palestine in 1939. She lived for several years in Kibutz Sdot Yam before joining *Palmach* (*Plugot Mahatz;* strike companies), the small, elite strike force of *Haganah* (the Defense), the underground Jewish self-defense force in Palestine. Her assignment, after joining the British army as a commissioned officer, was to parachute into Hungary to help organize partisan activities against the Germans and rescue Jews. After the German occupation of Hungary, the British decided to have Hannah's small group of Jewish commandos dropped into Yugoslavia. After three frustrating months working with partisans in Yugoslavia, Hannah entered Hungary, where she was quickly arrested. She was brutally tortured by the Hungarian police and then turned over to the Gestapo. Interrogated almost daily, she refused to reveal the details of her mission. On the other hand, she regaled her German interrogators with tales about Palestine and warned them of the price they would pay for their crimes when the war ended. She was ultimately convicted as a British military spy and executed on November 7, 1944. In 1950, her remains were brought to Israel; she was interred in the military cemetery on Mount

termed it one of the "most loathsome" stories of the war. A BBC report on July 21 called the Eichmann offer "humanitarian blackmail."[40] Brand remained in British custody until that fall; fearful that the SS would murder him if he returned to Hungary, he went to Palestine.

By the time the deportations began, the *Auschwitz Protocols,* a thirty-two-page document written by two Auschwitz escapees, Rudolf Vrba (1924–2006) and Alfréd Wetzler (1918–1988), were widely circulated throughout Europe and government circles in the United States. In three reports on German killing operations at Birkenau, the BBC broadcast information from the *Protocols* on June 15; a *New York Times* article appeared five days later. President Franklin Roosevelt, Pope Pius XII, and King Gustav V of Sweden

Herzl. In 1993, her family in Israel learned that a Hungarian military court had exonerated her for the charges of treason.

Hannah Szenes entered Hungary just as the major transports of Jews were leaving for Auschwitz. Her singular efforts were matched by those of Budapest's diplomatic community. Va'ada, working with the Swiss diplomat Carl Lutz (1895–1975) of the Swiss Legation, the *Papal Nuncio* Angelo Rotta (1872–1965), the Italian diplomat Giorgio Perlasca (1910–1992), and the Swiss International Red Cross representative Friedrich Born (1903–1993), was able to save thousands of Jews from deportation. But the most storied efforts were those of the Swedish diplomats Per Anger (1913–2003), Carl Ivan Danielsson (1880–1963), the head of the Swedish Legation, and Raoul Wallenberg (1912–1947). Yad Vashem later named all these diplomats Righteous Among the Nations.

Several days after the deportations ended in July, Raoul Gustav Wallenberg arrived in Budapest as first secretary of the Swedish legation. Wallenberg, working closely with Danielsson, Anger, and other members of Budapest's diplomatic community, used funds from the AJJDC, filtered through the American War Refugee Board, to issue special *Schutzbriefe* or *Schutzpässe* (protection passes) to Hungarian Jews, which identified the holders as Swedish subjects awaiting repatriation. Though the documents were fake, they were official-looking enough to convince most German and Hungarian officials that they were valid. Wallenberg and Anger also used the WRB funds to rent thirty buildings in Budapest to house "Swedish" Jews awaiting transfer, declaring the buildings inviolable Swedish territory. Wallenberg and Anger housed almost 10,000 Jews in these buildings. Wallenberg risked his life time and again to save as many Jews as possible. John Bierman described one occasion:

> He climbed up on the roof of the train and began handing in protective passes through

Per Anger in front of a photo of Raoul Wallenberg, Stockholm, 1985. USHMM Photo No. 00018, courtesy of Per and Ellena Anger.

> the doors which were not yet sealed. He ignored orders from the Germans for him to get down, then the Arrow Cross men began shooting and shouting at him to go away. He ignored them and calmly continued handing out passports to the hands that were reaching out for them. I believe the Arrow Cross men deliberately aimed over his head, as not one shot hit him, which would have been impossible otherwise. I think this is what they did because they were so impressed by his courage. After Wallenberg had handed over the last of the passports he ordered all those who had one to leave the train and walk to the caravan of cars parked nearby, all marked in Swedish colours. I don't remember exactly how many, but he saved dozens off that train, and the Germans and Arrow Cross were so dumbfounded they let him get away with it.[41]

When the Soviets arrived in Budapest in January 1945, there were still some 97,000 Jews in the city's two ghettos. On January 13, Wallenberg requested a meeting with Soviet authorities. Four days later, he left for Debrecen, in eastern Hungary, to meet with Soviet military officials; then he disappeared. In 1957, the Soviets, who considered him an American spy, claimed that he had died in Moscow's infamous Lubyanka prison a decade earlier, though reports of Wallenberg sightings persisted in the Soviet prison camp system years later. Yad Vashem named Wallenberg a Righteous Among the Nations, and in 1981 the United States made him an honorary citizen. Despite these valiant efforts, about two-thirds of Hungary's Jews died during the Holocaust.

The Roma.   Hungary's Roma fared much better. There were about 100,000 Roma in Hungary in 1941. The government began a severe crackdown on the Roma in the summer of that year, even though many served in military units on the Russian front. Officials also began to open Roma ghettos in various parts of the country. Rightist groups pledged: "After the Jews the Gypsies"; and the Hungarian press, which claimed there were 300,000 Roma in the country, criticized the large sums being spent by the government to keep an eye on the Roma. Some Hungarian officials expressed concern about the intermarriage of Roma and Hungarians, fearing this would create a new group of "half castes" in the country. In the summer of 1942, the Budapest Chamber of Agriculture asked the government to begin sterilizing all Roma males, and the semi-official *Esti Ujság* (Evening News) suggested the opening of labor camps to solve the "Gypsy problem."[42]

Some Hungarian Roma were deported to Auschwitz during this period as part of a larger shipment of Austrian Roma. But a major drive against the Roma did not start until the fall of 1944, when Arrow Cross units, aided by Hungarian gendarmes, began to round them up and send them to special internment or transport camps. Many were sent to a camp in Komáron. One Roma survivor described a roundup and conditions in Komáron:

The police came early in the morning and took us. They said we would never return home again. They took the young men out, all of them. We never saw them again. We didn't see my father again either. I was taken over to the group, my mother saw me from the bunker, made a sign with her eyes, "run, my little child, come back." I ran back to her fast. Mother wrapped a scarf round my head and there was a little baby, so she pressed it into my hands, so they didn't take me to Germany. . . . There were so many Roma that they couldn't all fit into the camp. There were so many, like ants. There was a Romania woman, she had a bent stick which she beat us with. She was made a Kapo, and when anyone made a noise or caused problems she would hit us. And she did really hit us. May God punish her. She was bad. The guards were bad but she was worse.

We were in the bunker the whole day, and watched by armed guards. If anyone was caught outside the soldiers beat them, if anyone made a noise, they shot them. We are in dirt all day. Mud. And if anyone went out to the rubbish heap [to look for food] if they were caught they were killed. There was a poor girl who was buried alive in the rubbish. She pulled herself out and ran into the cellar. She smelled, she stank. "Where were you?" I asked. "I was buried." I was sorry for her. She was blond and fat. She ran off all the time. She was captured again and buried in the heap of rubbish. I never saw her again. What happened to her? Dead? I don't know.[43]

Recent scholarship indicates that the government deported from 30,000 to 31,000

Roma during this period, most of them to Auschwitz. According to the Hungarian War Victims Association, only 3,000 returned after the war. Katalin Katz estimates that 50,000 Hungarian Roma were murdered during the Holocaust.[44]

Italy

Of the 42,500 Jews in Italy in 1940, about 85 percent would survive the Holocaust. In the early years after World War I, Italian Jews enjoyed the fruits of emancipation won in the latter part of the nineteenth century, and they played an active role in Italian political and professional life. Little changed after Benito Mussolini's accession to power on October 30, 1922. There were some Jews in Mussolini's *Partito Nazionale Fascista* (PNF; Fascist National Party), and some rose to positions of importance. In fact, according to Susan Zuccotti, the PNF was relatively free of anti-Semitism, which she feels reflected the general lack of anti-Semitism in Italian society.[45] But R.J.B. Bosworth has noted that although most Italians accepted Jews as part of the Italian nation-state, "anti-Semitism lurked in a number of Italian minds."[46]

Regardless, there were some prominent Jews in Mussolini's government. Aldo Finzi (1891–1944) was an undersecretary in the Ministry of the Interior. He was later expelled from the PNF and executed during the Fosse Ardeatine massacre on March 24, 1944. Guido Jung (1876–1949) served as Mussolini's minister of finance from 1932 to 1935. Maurizio Rava was vice governor of Italian Somalia and governor of Libya. He was also a general in the *squadristi*, or Blackshirts, Mussolini's Fascist militia. Margherita Sarfatti (1880–1961), Mussolini's long-time mistress, was also Jewish. Mussolini broke with her in 1938 in the midst of his anti-Semitic crusade.

Initially, Mussolini seemed to reject many of the Nazis' views on race. He told German biographer Emil Ludwig (1881–1948) in 1932 that

Of course there are no pure races left; not even the Jews have kept their blood unmingled. Successful crossing have often promoted the energy and beauty of a nation. Race! It is a feeling, not a reality; ninety-five percent, at least, is a feeling. Nothing will ever make me believe that biologically pure races can be shown to exist today. Amusingly enough, not one of those who have proclaimed the "nobility" of the Teutonic race was himself a Teuton. . . . National pride had no need of the delirium of race.

He added:

Anti-Semitism does not exist in Italy. Italians of Jewish birth have shown themselves good citizens, and they fought bravely in the war. Many of them occupy leading positions in the universities, in the army, in the banks. Quite a number of them are generals; Modena [Gen. Angelo], the commandant of Sardinia, is a general of artillery.

Why then, Ludwig asked, were there no Jews in the Italian Royal Academy? Mussolini replied: "The accusation is absurd. Since my day, there has been no Jew suitable for admission. Now Della Seta is a candidate; a man of great learning, the leading authority on prehistoric Italy."

Ludwig then asked:

If you are falsely accused in this matter, you suffer in good company. In Germany there is a preposterous fable that Bismarck and Goethe were prejudiced against Jews. Without any justification, the French speak of a certain anomaly as "*le vice allemand* [flaw of the Germans]." The term might be more reasonably applied to anti-Semitism.

Mussolini asked Ludwig to explain this: "Whenever things go awry in Germany, the Jews are blamed for it. Just now we are in an exceptionally bad case!" "Ah, yes," Mussolini replied, "the scapegoat!"[47]

Mussolini's remarks came at a time when Italy was becoming more aggressive internationally and developing uncertain ties with Hitler's Germany. Mussolini invaded Ethiopia in 1935 and became increasingly involved in the Spanish Civil War (1936–1939). Italy now found itself allied with Germany in a conflict that pitted Fascists and Nazis against the hated communists. An Italian anti-Zionist campaign soon morphed into an anti-Semitic crusade that culminated in the 1938 race laws. These laws had little to do with Nazi efforts to force Italy to adopt Nuremberg-style race laws, which they never did. Instead, they were the product of a rising tide of anti-Bolshevik sentiments that surfaced during the Spanish Civil War. Giorgio Almirante (1914–1988), a minor figure in the PNF and a prominent neo-Fascist leader after World War II, explained that anti-Semitism in the late 1930s was a way of "clarifying ourselves to ourselves." He claimed that Mussolini's anti-Semitic campaign was "the biggest and most courageous recognition of itself that Italy had ever attempted."[48]

And it was Benito Mussolini, not Adolf Hitler, who was at the center of this campaign. This did not mean, though, that Nazi racial ideas did not influence Mussolini's anti-Semitic crusade. Dr. Guido Lander, the author of the controversial July 14, 1938, *Manifesto degli Scientziati razzisti* (Manifesto of the Racial Scientists), was deeply affected by the teachings of Dr. Eugen Fischer (1847–1967), the director of the Kaiser Wilhelm Institute of Anthropology at the University of Berlin. According to Aaron Gillette, the *Manifesto* was Mussolini's introduction to "a massive campaign of racial propaganda and discrimination."[49]

These were the main points of the *Manifesto*:

• The concept of race is purely biological
• The population of Italy today is of Aryan origin and its civilization is Aryan
• There exists today a pure "Italian race"
• It is time for the Italians to proclaim themselves openly racists
• The Jews do not belong to the Italian race[50]

Public criticism of the *Manifesto* was "swift, and largely unfavorable." One Jesuit priest noted that "German racism, which is purely materialistic, cannot be applied to the whole human being, without lowering a reasonable creature to the level of animals." Pope Pius XI (r. 1922–1939), like most Italians, agreed with this assessment and was ashamed that Mussolini's government had adopted policies based on "German neo-barbarism." Aaron Gillette noted that criticism of the *Manifesto* was so harsh that it threw "the entire program of racial propaganda into disarray for the remainder of the regime's existence."[51]

Such criticism did not deter Mussolini from implementing anti-Semitic race laws in the fall of 1938. They forbade the marriage of Jews and non-Jews and would not allow Jews to own businesses linked to military production or that used more than one hundred Italian workers. The government now limited the amount of land that Jews could own; it also decreed that Jews could no longer belong to the PNF or the military. Jewish professors and teachers were also forbidden to attend the country's universities and public schools. Finally, foreign Jews and Jews who became Italian citizens after 1918 had to leave Italy by mid-March 1939. Exemptions were made for war veterans and older members of the PNF.

The race laws had a devastating social and economic impact on Italy's Jews. They also further weakened and divided a society that was ill-prepared for the growing international crises that would plunge Europe into war. Mussolini, aware of his country's problems, declared neutrality when war broke out in 1939. This all changed the following spring when he joined Hitler in the invasion of

France on June 10, 1940. Italy did so badly against the French that Mussolini had to ask the Wehrmacht for help to conquer his small portion of southeastern France, which he soon abandoned. A humiliated Mussolini now sought new adventures to prove his military prowess. Not satisfied with his 1939 conquest of Albania, he invaded Greece in the fall of 1940. When the Greeks quickly drove the Italians back into Albania, Hitler was forced to delay his invasion of the Soviet Union to conquer Greece and secure this important military flank.

Mussolini's military misadventures left Italy's economy in shambles. This, coupled with growing losses in North Africa and the successful Allied invasion of Sicily in the summer of 1943, led to his dismissal by the *Gran Consiglio del Fascismo* (Fascist Grand Council) on July 24–25, 1943. The king appointed *Marescialla d' Italia* (Marshal) Pietro Badoglio (1871–1956) head of the new government. Though Bagdolio declared Italy's continued loyalty to Germany, he was secretly doing everything possible to take it out of the war. On September 8, five days after Allied forces landed in southern Italy, Badoglio signed an armistice with the Western powers. On September 12, German paratroopers rescued Mussolini from prison and flew him to Bavaria, where he announced on September 18 the creation of a new "puppet" state in northern Italy, the *Repubblica Sociale Italiana* (RSI; Italian Social Republic), its capital in Salò. During the next few weeks, the Germans occupied Italy from Rome northward. The Badoglio government, now in Brindisi, declared war against the Axis on October 13. Most of Italy's Jews were now trapped in the German zone.

Things were relatively quiet in the first weeks of the German occupation of central and northern Italy. But behind the scenes, Himmler was making plans to deport Italy's Jews. On September 12, his office informed *SS- Obersturmbannführer* Herbert Kappler

(1907–1978), the head of the German Security Police in Rome, of the deportation plans. Two weeks later, Kappler was told that all Jews in German-occupied Italy were to be "transferred to Germany and liquidated."[52] On September 26, Kappler met with Dante Almansi (?–1949), the president of the *Unione delle Comunità Ebraiche Italiane* (Union of Italian Jewish Communities) and Ugo Foà, the president of the *Comunità Israelitica di Roma* (Israeli Community of Rome). He told them that they had thirty-six hours to collect 50 kilograms (110 pounds) of gold. The gold, he explained, would be used to buy arms for the Wehrmacht, which now had 300,000 troops in Italy. If they failed to come up with the gold, Kappler warned, he would deport two hundred Jews to Germany. Kappler explained in his written testimony for the Eichmann trial in Israel that he came up with the idea of a "ransom" to prevent the roundup and deportation of Italian Jews. Susan Zuccotti contested this: Kappler, she explained, was not about to disobey an order of this magnitude even if he disagreed with it. From her perspective, he probably thought the "ransom" would give the Jews a false sense of security while he made plans for their later deportation.[53]

As word spread throughout the Jewish community about the ransom, Jews and some Christians rallied to help. At some point, Pope Pius XII (r. 1939–1958) offered to loan the Jewish community whatever gold it could not raise. In the end, the papal loan was unnecessary, and at 4:00 P.M. on September 28, Jewish representatives delivered 50 kilograms of gold to Gestapo headquarters on Via Tasso in Rome. Kappler's efforts to lull Rome's Jews into a sense of false security did not last long. The following day, the SS raided the offices of the *Comunità* and seized millions of Italian lire and valuable Jewish community records. This prompted many well-connected Jews to go into hiding; they were aided by the Roman Catholic Church and innumerable brave non-Jews.

Kappler began his *Aktion* in Rome on October 16 and sent 1,259 Jews to Auschwitz. Italian *Carabinieri* (gendarmerie and military police of Italy) played an increasingly active role in the roundups, which continued until the Allies liberated Rome on June 4, 1944. Overall, the Germans deported from 7,500 to 10,000 Italian and foreign Jews to Auschwitz. Two thirds of them died there. Another 5,000 to 6,000 Italian Jews fled to Switzerland, and from 2,000 to 3,000 joined the Italian resistance.

Several weeks before Kappler began his *Aktion*, Odilo Globocnik arrived in Trieste with his special squad of trained killers to take charge of SS affairs in what Berlin called the *Adriatisches Küstland* (Adriatic Coastal Land Zone). According to Joseph Poprzeczny, Globocnik's arrival in Trieste could best be "viewed as a re-run of the entry of the *Einsatzgruppen* into Poland in September 1939, and the Soviet Union in 1941." The only difference, of course, was that Globocnik's men now had "many years of experience in mass murder and policing." Globocnik quickly transformed a prison camp, La Risiera di San Sabba, into a death camp, aided by *SS- Hauptscharführer* Lorenz Hackenholt (1914–1954), a gassing expert who had worked at Bełżec, Treblinka, and Sobibór. La Risiera had a fully operational crematoria and estimates are that from 3,000 to 4,500 people died there, most of them partisans. About 50 Jews were also executed at Globocnik's Trieste camp. It also served as a major transit point for deportation trains to Auschwitz between October 1943 and November 1944. About 1,100 Jews were sent to Auschwitz from La Risiera during this period. Only about 15 percent of Italy's 42,500 Jews would die during the Holocaust.

Protectorate of Bohemia-Moravia and Slovakia

On March 15, 1939, Germany invaded what remained of the Czech provinces of Bohemia and Moravia and integrated them into the Third Reich as the *Reichsprotektorat Böhmen und Mähren* (Reich Protectorate of Bohemia and Moravia). Slovakia survived as a Nazi puppet state. Between November 2, 1938, and March 1939, Hungary annexed portions of eastern Slovakia, which had a Jewish population of almost 70,000. Before the annexations, there were more than 92,000 Jews in the Protectorate and almost 136,000 Jews in Slovakia. About 26,000 Slovak Jews managed to emigrate during the next two years. The Protectorate had a Roma population of only 6,540, though there were 60,000 Roma in Slovakia. During the next four years, 40,000 Roma refugees made their way to Slovakia, and by the end of the war Slovakia had a Roma population of 100,000.

German rule was initially moderate in the Protectorate, but this changed dramatically after public unrest swept the Czech lands in the fall of 1939. This, and the fact that the Protectorate was a part of the Greater Reich, meant that Jews and Roma were dealt with like their kinsmen in other parts of the Nazi kingdom. Konstantin von Neurath, Bohemia and Moravia's first *Reichsprotektor,* seemed unable to curb the Protectorate's Czech resistance movement. In the fall of 1941, Himmler replaced him with Reinhard Heydrich, who ordered the opening of a new concentration camp for Protectorate Jews north of Prague in Terezín (Theresienstadt). During the next three years, the Germans deported more than 73,000 Czech Jews to Theresienstadt. Another 8,700 were sent to camps in occupied Poland. The Germans murdered 71,000 Protectorate Jews in various concentration and death camps during the Holocaust, and another 7,000 died in the Protectorate itself.

The Roma in the Protectorate

Despite their low numbers, the Roma were subjected to equally harsh policies. In the summer and late fall of 1940, the Germans opened two forced-labor camps in the Protectorate, Lety and Hodonín, that were later transformed into camps just for Roma. In 1940, authorities decreed that the Roma could no longer travel freely. Two years later, Richard Bienert (1881–1949), the Protectorate's Czech interior minister, ordered a Roma census. Using this information, *SS- Obersturmführer und Oberstleutnant der Polizei* Horst Böhme (1909–1945), the head of the Protectorate's Security Police, deported all Czech Roma to Lety and Hodonín. Both camps were run by Czech police. A typhoid epidemic broke out in Lety at the end of 1942 and ravaged the camp, forcing the Czechs to close it the following spring. The Germans and Czechs also used Lety as a deportation center for Czech Roma, whom they sent to Auschwitz. They sent 511 Roma to Auschwitz between December 1942 and May 1943. They then closed the camp, sending its remaining Roma to Hodonín. About a third of the 1,300 Czech Roma sent to Lety died there. Czech officials transformed Hodonín into a Roma camp in the fall of 1941, and sent 1,229 Roma there during its first months of operation. Transports to Auschwitz began on December 2, 1942. A typhoid epidemic broke out during this period and ravaged the camp. By May 1943, more than 90 percent of the Roma in Hodonín had contracted the disease. New transports to Auschwitz began in the fall of 1943 and continued until Hodonín was closed the following year. The Czechs deported 863 Hodonín Roma to Auschwitz, and 207 died in the Czech camp. Another 67 escaped.

Hlinka guards watch Jews awaiting deportation in Bratislava. USHMM Photo No. 33005, courtesy of Ehud Nahir.

Slovakia

Wartime Slovakia was run by a triumvirate of anti-Semitic leaders who supported most of Nazi Germany's racial policies. Father Jozef Tiso (1887–1947), a Roman Catholic priest, was the country's president. Vojtech Tuka (1880–1946), the prime minister and foreign minister, was also head of the *Nástupists,* the radical wing of the *Hlinkova slovenská ľudová strana* (HSLS; Hlinka Slovak People's Party). Alexander Mach (1902–1980), Slovakia's propaganda minister, headed the *Hlinka garda* (Hlinka Guards), the armed Nazi-Fascist wing of the HSLS. This triumvirate gradually transformed Slovakia into a Fascist state. Himmler sent Dieter Wisliceny to Bratislava to advise the government on Jewish affairs. In 1941, the Hlinka Guards and the *Freiwillige Schutzsstaffel* (FS; Volunteer SS), which was made up of Slovak ethnic Germans, were reorganized along SS lines. These groups became the paramilitary vanguard of the government's anti-Jewish policies.

Greta Vrbová lived in Trnava and vividly remembered the Nazi-like atmosphere that enveloped Slovakia after the war began. Her family business was Aryanized and constantly harassed by Hlinka Guards. Greta was forced to quit school because she was Jewish; when she walked by her former friends, they would shout: "Jews out, Czechs out." On one occasion, she and several of her Jewish friends decided to get even with their former classmates by letting the air out of their bicycle tires and wedging pebbles between the tires and the rims. On another occasion, Greta and her friends, angered by attacks from three members of the *Hlinka mládež* (Hlinka Youth), decided to retaliate again:

> We smeared our faces with soot and used all sorts of camouflage, then waited for our victims. We did succeed in ambushing those three and beating them up, but none of us really got any satisfaction out of this and we were in fact embarrassed about our behaviour. Yet in a strange way it helped us to feel better. It made us feel that we were not just lying down and accepting all the humiliation, but were trying to preserve our dignity.[54]

The Tiso government eventually stripped the Jews of their rights and property. A Central Economic Office was set up to handle the "aryanization" of Jewish property, while a *Ústredna Židov* (Jewish Center), or *Judenrat*, was created in the fall of 1940 to act as a liaison between the government and the Jewish community. Anti–Jewish policies hardened in the summer of 1941; the government now required all Jews to wear a yellow Star of David armband. On September 10, 1941, the government issued the Nuremberg-styled *Židovskü Kodex* (Jewish Code), which included the various anti-Jewish laws and decrees issued since 1939. The following day, the government explained that the Jews were historically the sources of the country's problems; it invoked the name of the founder of the HSLS, Father Andrej Hlinka (1864–1938) and his ideas as justification for its policies. His successor, Father Tiso, had "expressed himself similarly and clearly, in the new situation [about the Jews]."[55] By the end of the

year, severe anti-Jewish residency and curfew regulations were implemented throughout the country.

Slovakia supported Hitler's invasion of the Soviet Union. That fall, Tuka and Mach met privately with Hitler and agreed to begin deporting Slovak Jews to Poland. The Slovak government also agreed to pay Germany a "bounty of 500 Reichsmarks for every 'resettled' Jew."[56] Between March and October 1942, the Slovak police, assisted by the Hlinka Guards and the FS, rounded up from 56,000 to 60,000 Jews and sent them to forced-labor and concentration camps throughout Slovakia. From there they were transported to the border and turned over to German authorities, who deported them to Auschwitz, Majdanek, Sobibór, and other camps in the General Government. Tiso's government also agreed to send 120,000 Slovaks to Germany for forced labor. Aliza Barak-Rewssler described one of the roundups in Michalovce:

> The [Slovak] troops were vicious and had lost every trace of humanity. They spared neither the very old, nor the very young, and behaved like animals. The deportees were taken to the local high school and spent three days in the schoolyard before being packed on a freight train and transported to the Lublin area in eastern Poland. Not long afterwards, the first postcards arrived from them, containing clear hints about killing and starvation.[57]

Jewish leaders learned of the deportations in the spring of 1942 and formed the *Pracovná Skupina* (Working Group), led by Gisi Fleischmann (1897–1944) and Rabbi Michael Dov Weissmandel (1903–1956), to do what they could to save as many Jews as possible. After their efforts at legal rescue failed, the Working Group decided to try to bribe Wisliceny to stop the transports. Though estimates vary, the Working Group paid Wisliceny between $40,000 and $50,000 to end the depor-

Jews await deportation in Zilina, Slovakia, 1942. USHMM Photo No. 80643, courtesy of Lydia Chagoll.

tations. After the war, Wisliceny claimed he was responsible for halting the transports. Livia Rothkirchen says that pressure from the Vatican and growing protests from the Slovak population, particularly after the German defeat at Stalingrad, were other reasons the transports finally came to an end. Jörg Hoensch noted, though, that this did not end German efforts to convince the Slovak government to resume the deportations. Tuka and Mach sided with the Germans. Father Tiso, who supported the initial deportation plan, now refused to revisit the issue.[58]

Encouraged by their seeming success, Slovak Jewish leaders developed a new scheme, the Europa Plan, which involved paying Wisliceny between 2 and 3 million dollars to save Jews elsewhere. Wisliceny, acting on instructions from Himmler, deluded the Working Group into thinking that further payments could also help save the Jews of Greece and Hungary. In reality, these tactics were smokescreens to hide the greater horrors of the Final Solution and to see how

much world Jewry was willing to pay to save the Jews of Europe. Himmler ordered an end to the talks with the Working Group in August 1943.

By the summer of 1944, the Working Group possessed detailed information about the murderous operations at Auschwitz; it sent this information to the Allies with a request that the Western powers bomb the rail lines into Birkenau. The JA in Palestine made similar proposals to the British government, but Prime Minister Winston Churchill (1874–1965) and his government paid little attention to the request, arguing "technical difficulties" with such attacks. The United States War Department rejected similar requests, which included bombing the gas chambers at Birkenau, from the World Jewish Congress (WJC) and other groups, saying that it would take a considerable diversion of air power to achieve success. In reality, the War Department had decided after President Roosevelt created the War Refugee Board in early 1944 to adopt a passive role in civilian rescue efforts.

Roma school children in prewar Užhorod, Slovakia. Source: *Gypsies: Their Life and Customs*, Martin Friedrich Block. AMS Press Inc., 1939.

The Slovak National Uprising of August 29–October 27, 1944, severely compromised the efforts of the Working Group. Jewish partisans were actively involved in this uprising against Tiso's government, which led to the German occupation of Slovakia. About 40 percent of the 4,000 to 5,000 Jews serving in partisan units died in the fighting, including Palestinian Jewish parachutists dropped in to help Jewish partisan units against the Germans and their Slovak allies. Once the rebellion ended, *Einsatzgruppe* H rounded up 12,000 Jews and sent them to Auschwitz and Theresienstadt. About 100,000 Slovak Jews died during the Holocaust. Overall, the Germans murdered 203,000 Czechoslovakian Jews during the *Shoah*, including those in Hungary.

The Roma

There were 80,000 Roma in Slovakia in 1940. Seventy-nine thousand survived the Holocaust. This did not mean, though, that the Slovak government left its Roma population at peace. Within months after the creation of

the Slovak puppet state in 1939, the government ordered a halt to Roma nomadism. To retain Slovak citizenship, Roma later had to prove that they

lived an orderly way of life; had a steady place of residence and employment; and were honorable citizens as reflected in their education, their moral and political trustworthiness, and their activity in their community, only then could they be included in the Slovak national community. If they did not fulfill the aforementioned conditions, or if they fulfilled them only partially—if they worked only occasionally, if they spoke the Gypsy language among themselves, if their moral and political trustworthiness was doubtful, etc.—they could not be considered members of the Slovak national community. In other words, wandering Gypsies did not qualify for citizenship.[59]

Since so many Roma considered themselves Slovaks, the government issued Law

No. 130/1940 of June 18, 1940, which defined a Roma either as a person who had two Roma parents and lived as a nomad or as a sedentary person who avoided work. In 1941, the government began to send Roma to seasonal labor camps. Conditions in these camps were horrible, and on one occasion they prompted a protest from a member of the country's national legislature.

The government also placed severe travel restrictions on all Roma and required them to obtain special permission to leave their local communities. They were also required to move if their residences were located on a public road. One Roma song captured the frustration with these travel restrictions:

Two two two twenty two
I won't go I won't go to town
In town they could rob me
Cut off my lovely hair
All the whores in Prešov would cry[60]

The situation worsened for Slovakia's Roma in the summer of 1944. In June, officials accused Roma of spreading typhoid and decreed that to ride on trains they had to possess special passes and medical documents certifying that they were free of typhoid. The following month, the Interior Ministry ordered the Roma to vacate Slovakia's roadways and said that those who refused to do so would be executed. At the same time, the government began working on plans to force Roma into permanent forced-labor camps.

The plight of the Roma deteriorated further after the Slovak National Uprising. The Germans cracked down on the Roma because they had played an active role in the insurrection. Hlinka Guards executed one Roma rebel unit in front of their families and then murdered the bystanders. Another Hlinka Guard unit burned sixty-five Roma to death in their huts in Èierny Balog and forced other Roma to dig graves for their comrades. One observer reported that "women and children were burned alive in wooden hovels, men shot in the valley of Vydrovo."[61] Hlinka Guards massacred the entire Roma community in Ilija (Banská Štravnica) in late November 1944, and committed similar atrocities at Slatina and Neresnice, where only two Roma families survived.

Romania

The substantial territory that Romania gained after World War I saw its population increase from 7.2 million to more than 16 million. There were more than 756,000 Jews in Romania in 1930 and 262,501 Roma, though some scholars suggest that as many as 400,000 Roma lived in Romania when World War II broke out.[62] Postwar Romania suffered from a political malaise throughout the 1920s that saw the country drift between political normalcy and martial law. In 1930, Prince Carol, who had renounced his right to the throne in 1925 after a marital scandal, overthrew his son, Mihai (Michael), and began a disastrous reign as Carol II (r. 1930–1940). One source of continued instability was Corneliu Zelea Codreanu's (1899–1938) pro-Nazi *Legiunea Arhanghelul Mihail* (League of the Archangel Michael) and its paramilitary wing, the *Garda de Fier* (Iron Guard). The Legionaires, as they were commonly known, operated much like the German Nazi Party's SA in the 1920s and early 1930s. After the government banned it and other paramilitary groups in 1933, Codreanu transformed the league into a viable political party that garnered almost 16 percent of the popular vote in 1937 elections as part of the rightist coalition *Totul Pentru Ţară* (Everything for the Fatherland). Carol II responded to this rightist threat by outlawing the Iron Guard and executing Codreanu and other Iron Guard leaders. The king, despite his own rightist feelings, tried in the coming years to remain out of the growing conflict between Europe's major powers. But by 1940, Romania found itself being drawn more closely into the German-Italian orbit.

In the summer of 1940, Carol II acceded, with Hitler's approval, to Soviet demands for Bessarabia and northern Bukovina. This was quickly followed by Hungarian and Bulgarian demands for Romanian territory. With the loss of northern Transylvania to Hungary and Southern Dobrudja to Bulgaria, there were now only 328,968 Jews in Romania. On September 5, 1940, Carol II's newly appointed prime minister, Ion Victor Antonescu (1882–1946), forced the king to abdicate and replaced him with his son, Mihai I (r. 1927–1930, 1940–1947). Antonescu declared himself *Conducător* (leader) and became Romania's new dictator. After the country's other political parties refused to join his government, Antonescu turned to the Iron Guard as political allies.

Romania's large Jewish community suffered from inadequate minority rights and protections throughout the interwar period. Things worsened in the 1930s, and the country's Jews became the principal target of the Iron Guard and other right-wing groups. In 1938, Prime Minister Octavian Goga (1881–1938) and Carol II issued a decree that called for a "review" of the citizenship of all Romanian Jews. Both leaders claimed that a large percentage of the country's Jews were not citizens. Goga proposed sending half a million Romanian Jews to Madagascar. Another law that year distinguished Romanians "by race" and "by residence."[63] Two years later, the government issued several Nuremberg-style laws that defined Jewishness using much stricter guidelines than its German model. Other laws isolated and impoverished the Jews. On December 5, 1940, the government announced that Jews would serve in forced-labor units.

The first Romanian massacres of Jews began in the summer of 1940 as Romanian troops retreated from Bessarabia and Bukovina. That fall, the Iron Guard mounted pogroms throughout the country that were so violent and destructive that they began to affect the economy. Adolf Hitler, concerned about the impact of the pogroms on Romania's oil industry, which was essential to the Reich, reminded Antonescu in a meeting on January 14, 1941, of the importance of getting rid of "fanatical militants who think that, by destroying everything, they are doing their duty."[64] A week later, the Iron Guard unleashed new pogroms as part of an attempt to overthrow Antonescu. Emil Dorian (1893–1956), a prominent Romanian Jewish writer, described one of the massacres:

> On the road to Jilava [a Bucharest suburb] dozens of corpses have been found, their identification papers scattered about. Before the victims were killed, their noses were smashed, their limbs broken, their tongues cut out, their eyes gouged. The two sons of an old rabbi were shot in his arms. Jewish corpses were hung from hooks in the city slaughterhouse or simply dumped in the street. One of my patients who lives in that neighborhood saw them. Some were chewed up by dogs. . . . They are still lined up like slaughtered lambs lying under the falling snow in the yard of the morgue. The sidewalk in front of the morgue is black with waiting relatives. The list of the beaten and tortured people is endless, and the crimes cover the complete range of a demented imagination—Jews forced to drink gasoline with Epsom salts—crosses cut on the skin of their back—torture and killing—on and on.[65]

Antonescu committed fifteen divisions to the German invasion of the Soviet Union. Romanian troops moved quickly into Bessarabia, Bukovina, and the southern Ukraine, where they became involved in a number of massacres. About six days after the invasion began, Romanian and German forces initiated a pogrom in Iaşi and brutally murdered from 3,200 to 13,266 Jews. They murdered another 10,000 Jews in pogroms in Bukovina and Bessarabia. Many who survived were deported to transit camps and ghettos. From there the

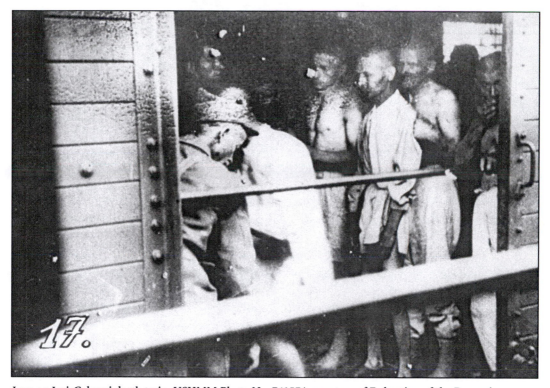

Jews on Iaşi-Calarasi death train. USHMM Photo No. 74157A, courtesy of Federation of the Romanian Jewish Communities.

Romanians deported many to Transnistria, a new racial reserve on the Romanian-Soviet border. Estimates are that in the summer of 1941 as many as 27,000 Jews died in these camps and in Transnistria. Overall, the Romanians and the Germans murdered 217,000 Jews in Transnistria. The Germans were directly responsible for 50,000 Jewish deaths; the rest were murdered by Romanians. Another 33,000 Jews died from malnutrition, disease, and exposure, bringing the total number of Jews who died in Transnistria to 250,000. Elsewhere, Romanian troops, acting on orders from Antonescu, were involved in the massacre of from 95,000 to 96,000 Jews in Odessa, Bogdanovka, Acmecetka, and Dumanovca.

Antonescu learned of German plans to ship all of Europe's Jews to Poland on the eve of the invasion of the Soviet Union. Several months earlier, Adolf Eichmann sent *SS- Hauptsturmführer* Gustav Richter (1912–?) to serve as An-

tonescu's adviser on Jewish affairs; he also worked closely with Antoneuscu's Jewish specialist, Radu Lecca (1902–1980). In August 1942, Mihai Antonescu (1907–1946), the *Conducător*'s closest adviser, agreed to a German-sponsored plan to deport Romania's Jews to Bełżec. Dr. Wilhelm Filderman, the respected leader of Romania's Jewish community, as well as other Jewish leaders, continued to protest the deportations. Several intellectuals sent a letter of protest to the king, and Filderman asked important politicians, diplomats, and Orthodox churchmen to protest Antonescu's plans. *Papal Nuncio* Archibishop Andrea Cassulo (1869–1952) spoke with Antonescu several times about this matter. These developments, and the changing fortunes of war, now came into play to help save the remaining 300,000 Jews in Romania. In November 1942, Filderman was told that the government planned to repatriate the 50,741 Romanian

Jews still alive in Transnistria. Officials allowed about 10,800 Jews to return to Romania before they halted the repatriation program.

In the meantime, Antonescu tried to draw closer to the Allies because he hoped to sign a separate peace treaty that would keep the Red Army from occupying Romania. Western diplomats told him that Romania would have to change sides to join their coalition. On August 23, 1944, King Mihai had Antonescu arrested; he then set up a coalition government under General Constantin Sanatescu (1885–1947). The new government quickly found itself caught in a trap between a recalcitrant German army of occupation and Soviet forces about to move into the country. The king offered the Allies what remained of Romania's battered armed forces, and they joined with the Red Army in driving the Germans out of the country. In the fall of 1944, Mihai I installed a new government under General Nicolae Rădescu (1874–1953), which did away with Antonescu's anti-Jewish and anti-Roma legislation. On February 6, 1945, the Rădescu government issued its Statute for National Minorities; the new law "gave complete equality to all Romanian citizens, without prejudice towards nationality, language, or religion."

The 2004 International Commission on the Holocaust in Romania (ICHR) estimated that between 280,000 and 380,000 Romanian and Ukrainian Jews were murdered or died during the Holocaust in Romania and the territories under its control. An additional 135,000 Romanian Jews living under Hungarian control in northern Transylvania also perished in the Holocaust, as did some 5,000 Romanian Jews in other countries. Referring to Romania, Raul Hilberg concluded that "no country, besides Germany, was involved in massacres of Jews on such a scale."[66]

The Roma

Romania, the traditional homeland of many of Europe's Roma, was also the place of their greatest suffering, given their long status as slaves, or *robi*, in Romania's historic provinces, Wallachia and Moldavia. Though some Roma fled Romania after emancipation in the 1850s, many remained, often tied to the land and the owners of their previous enslavement. Emancipation did little to improve the lot of Romania's Roma, and most remained deeply impoverished and illiterate well into the twentieth century. Things worsened for the Roma in the late 1930s. In a speech on July 8, 1941, Antonescu talked about the importance of eliminating minorities from national life in Romania. During his war crimes trial in 1946, he explained that his government had rounded up Roma because of public complaints that they were breaking into homes and stealing. Police investigations, Antonescu claimed, found that heavily armed Roma were responsible for the burglaries.[67] In 1991, the exiled King Mihai I said that Antonescu's government viewed nomadic and semi-nomadic Roma as "antisocial." They were particularly prey to mistreatment because their papers and documents were inadequate and they had no one outside the country to defend them.[68]

Initial discussions about the deportation of the Roma began in early 1941 and centered around the idea of forcing the Roma in Bucharest to settle in the Romanian countryside. In the spring of 1942, Antonescu personally decided to deport "problem" Roma to Transnistria, aided by a May 25, 1942, national census of this group. The census identified 40,909 Roma who lived as nomads, had criminal records, or had no steady employment. Most of the 25,000 Roma deported to Transnistria in 1942 and 1943 were drawn from this list.

According to one survivor, Petre Radita, the Roma were shipped

> from Bucharest in cattle trucks, the journey took some weeks and because of the cold nights, lack of blankets and inadequate food supply, many died of hunger and exposure before arriving at the River Bug in the

Ukraine. Those that had survived were lodged in huts and made to work digging trenches. Those found with gold teeth had them pulled out. Two children caught carrying messages to the partisans were executed in front of their parents.[69]

Some German officials feared that the Roma might now try to across the Bug River into Ukraine. In August 1942, Erich Koch, the *Reichskommissar Ukraine,* wrote to Alfred Rosenberg, the Reich minister for the Ostland, complaining about this potential problem. The following month, Rosenberg sent a letter to Joachim von Ribbentrop, the German foreign minister, pointing out this danger. Rosenberg noted that this part of Ukraine was populated by ethnic Germans and asked Ribbentrop to do what he could to discourage the Antonescu government from sending Roma there in the future. "Tens of thousands of defenseless Gypsies were herded together in Transnistria," the Romanian War Crimes Commission reported. "Over half of them were struck by the typhus epidemics. The gendarmerie practiced unprecedented terror; everybody's life was uncertain; tortures were cruel; the commanders lived in debauchery with beautiful Gypsy women and maintained personal harems."[70]

Soon after Rosenberg had sent his letter to Ribbentrop, Constantin Bratianu (1866–1951), an important pre– and post–World War II Romanian political leader, sent a letter to Antonescu questioning the transport of Roma to Transnistria:

[The Roma are] Orthodox and have an important role in the economy, being good handicraftsmen, such as farriers, blacksmiths, brick layers, farmers, and unskilled day laborers. Many are small merchants, small landowners, milkmen, etc. Almost all fiddlers in our country are Gypsies, and there is no holiday where people can enjoy themselves without their music.[71]

Constantin Bratianu. USHMM Photo No. 61927, courtesy of Dennis Deletant.

Now, Bratianu argued, Roma were being forced to leave Romania, a "country for which they shed their blood (due to army enrollment)." Winter was approaching, he went on, which would be particularly hard on the elderly, on women, and on children. Bratianu also wondered whether Romania could afford to sacrifice citizens who were skilled craftsmen and workers. He felt that the transfers were being initiated without Antonescu's knowledge; he asked that the persecution and deportation of Roma be stopped since such actions "would take us a few centuries back in world history."[72]

Official circles, though, felt quite differently about the Roma. In October 1942, the Romanian newspaper *Eroica* (Heroic) argued that the "Gypsy problem" was as important as the Jewish issue, and it criticized those who believed Roma were Romanians. Romania, the article went on, was burdened by 600,000

Roma children in music school in prewar Bucharest. Source: *Gypsies: Their Life and Customs*, Martin Friedrich Block. AMS Press Inc, 1939.

Roma "half-castes" who were the products of mixed marriages. It also proposed the outlawing of marriages between Roma "half-castes" and Romanian women, and said that Roma should be prevented from participating in Romanian society. One solution to the problem was to send all Roma nomads to forced-labor camps.

By the time this article appeared, though, the government had decided to halt the major deportations of Roma to Transnistria, though some Roma continued to be sent there through the end of 1943. The halt in deportations had less to do with moral qualms and more to do with complaints from the army about the impact of the transfers on military operations in the area. At the end of 1942, a Romanian intelligence agent filed this report:

During the time that they have spent in the barracks in Aleksandrodar, the Gypsies have lived in indescribable misery. They weren't sufficiently fed. They were given 400 grams of bread for the ones that were capable of working and 200 grams each for the elderly and the children. They were also given few potatoes and, very rarely, salty fish, and all these in very small quantities.

Due to the malnutrition, some of the Gypsies—and these make up the majority—have lost so much weight that they have turned into skeletons. On a daily basis—especially in the last period—ten to fifteen Gypsies died. They were full of parasites. They were no longer paid any medical visits and they did not have any medicine. They were naked . . . and they didn't have any underwear or clothing. There were women whose bodies . . . were [completely] naked in the true sense of the word. They had not been given any soap since arriving; this is why they haven't washed themselves or the single shirt they own.

In general, the situation of the Gypsies is terrible and almost inconceivable. Due to the misery, they have turned into shadows and are almost savage. This condition is due to the bad accommodations and nutrition as well as the cold. Because of the hunger . . . they have scared the Ukrainians with their thefts. If there had been some Gyspies in the county who were stealing . . . not of mere habit, here even a Gypsy who used to be honest would begin stealing, because the hunger led him to commit this shameful act.[73]

More than 300 Roma died at Aleksandrodar by the end of the year.

In Landau county, almost 5,000 Roma died of a typhus outbreak in the winter of 1942–1943. In response to these deaths, authorities closed the Roma settlements and moved the Roma into local villages. They also intensified efforts to find work for Roma laborers. "The Jews are not given food for months; the same is true of the Gypsies, and prisoners in the Golta [Roma] camp, where 40 individuals are imprisoned," wrote one official in Golta county. "All of them work and are forced to work until they are exhausted from hunger. Please advise."[74]

Local officials continued to complain about conditions in Golta: "During the day we work in the Kolkhoz [collective farm], but at night we patrol the precinct," Ion Stancu, the Roma leader in Kamina Balka, reported in the fall of 1943. "[T]hey give us very little food: 300 grams of [corn] flour, 500 grams of potatoes and 10 grams of salt per person, without any other kind of food; we haven't been given oil for 8 months."[75]

Given these conditions, it is not surprising that 11,000 of the 25,000 Roma sent to Transnistria died there during the Holocaust.

Yugoslavia (Croatia and Serbia)

The Kingdom of the Serbs, Croats, and Slovenes was created at the end of World War I as a confederation of six southern Slavic ethnic groups: Bosnians, Croats, Macedonians, Mongtenegrans, Serbs, and Slovenes. This new state was dominated by the Serbian Karadjordjeviæ dynasty, a source of continual fric-

tion during the interwar period, particularly between the Croats and the Serbs. In 1929, King Alexander (r. 1921–1934) dissolved the parliament and created a royal Serb dictatorship, renaming the country Yugoslavia.

The 1930s was a time of great instability in Yugoslavia. In 1934, Croatian and Macedonian separatists with ties to Hungary and Italy assassinated King Alexander and the French foreign minister, Louis Barthou (1862–1934), in Marseilles. The new king, Peter II (r. 1934–1945), was dominated by his cousin and regent, Prince Paul (regency, 1934–1941), who struggled to keep the country together and tried to resolve the growing friction between the Serbs and the Croats who were demanding greater autonomy within the Yugoslav confederation.

Yugoslavia declared neutrality when World War II broke out. At the time, there were about 82,242 Jews in Yugoslavia and 79,500 Roma. About 60 percent of the Jews were Ashkenazic, the rest Sephardim. About half the Roma were Muslims. In 1940, the country adopted a series of anti-Jewish laws that limited the number of Jews who could attend public schools and universities, and also restricted Jewish involvement in certain areas of business and commerce. Though initially sympathetic to the Allied side, Paul ultimately succumbed to German pressure to join Hitler's Tripartite Pact on March 25, 1941. Two days later, army officers opposed to this agreement overthrew Paul and restored Peter II to the throne. On April 6, Germany, Italy, Bulgaria, Hungary, and Romania invaded Yugoslavia and occupied different parts of the country. The Germans created two Nazi-puppet states, the *Nezavism Drzava Hrvatska* (NDH; Independent State of Croatia), which included Bosnia and Herzegovina, and Serbia, which was occupied by the Wehrmacht.

The NDH (Croatia)

The NDH was run by Ante Pavelić (1889–1959), who headed the *Ustaše* (the insurgents)

Ante Pavelić and Adolf Hitler, 1941. USHMM Photo No. 85432, courtesy of Muzej Revolucije Narodnosti Jugoslavije.

movement. There were 2 million Serbs in the NDH as well as 700,000 Bosnian Muslims (Bosniaks), 40,000 Jews, and 28,500 Roma. Officials in the NDH considered Serbs, Jews, and Roma "outside the law." In the spring of 1941, Marshal Slavko Kvaternik (1878–1947), the head of the NDH's armed forces, declared that members of these groups could not serve in the military.[76] Two laws, the April 17, 1941, Law Decree on the Defense of the People and the State, and the April 30 Law Decree on Citizenship provided the "legal" basis for the NHD's policies towards Serbs, Jews, Roma and unpatriotic Croatians. The April 17 law gave Pavelić the authority to execute anyone who "acted against the honor and vital interests of the Croatian People" or threatened the NDH; the April 30 law stated that "a citizen is a resident of the state of Aryan origin." This, when coupled with the Nuremberg-style Law Decree on Racial Belonging (April 30) and the Law Decree on the Protection of Aryan Blood and Honor of

the Croatian People (April 30), placed Jews and Roma outside the pale of Croatian society and forbade sexual relations between Croatian Aryans and non-Aryans.[77] Jews and Serbs soon had to register their property, which was gradually taken from them. The NDH also required them to wear armbands that indicated they were *Židov* (Jews) or *Pravoslavac* (Orthodox; the Serbs were predominantly Orthodox, the Croats Roman Catholic). Finally, at least according to Pavelić's June 26, 1941, Extraordinary Law Decree and Command:

Since Jews spread false reports in order to cause unrest among the people and since by their speculation they hinder and increase the difficulty of supplying the population, they are considered collectively responsible. Therefore the authorities will act against them and beyond criminal legal responsibility, they will be confined in assembly camps under the open sky.[78]

Ustaše guards execute prisoners at Jasenovac. USHMM Photo No. 78512, courtesy of Jewish Historical Museum, Belgrade.

The government also ordered a census of the Roma and deported those who had fled to what later became the NDH after the outbreak of the war. According to Èedonil Huber, NDH policies towards Jews and Roma were similar to those in Nazi Germany. On the other hand, the treatment of the Serbs was "the product of a 'domestic racism' unique to Croatia."[79]

Pavelić began to open the first concentration camps in the summer of 1941 to deal with the NDH's many racial and political enemies, particularly the Serbs. Initially, Pavelić thought he could rid the NDH of Serbs by deporting them to neighboring Serbia. Public outcries over the treatment of the NDH's minorities as well as Nazi objections quickly convinced him that the only way to be rid of this large minority, which made up almost a third of the NDH's population, was to murder them. The public reaction to these killings was so strong that NDH leaders decided to change policy and put their enemies in concentration camps. Though there were a number of concentration camps in the NDH, Jasenovac, which was opened in the summer of 1941, was the largest and the most deadly. Estimates vary widely and remain a subject of controversy, particularly between Croats and Serbs, but the latest scholarship suggests that the Croats murdered 48,000 Serbs, 13,000 Jews, 10,000–20,000 Roma, and 12,000 Croats and Muslims at Jasenovac during the Holocaust.

Jasenovac quickly gained a reputation for brutality and cruelty. This was particularly true when it came to the camp's Serbian inmates. Božo Švarc described one horrible scene:

One day, when the weather was nice, like today, the Ustashe had a competition in cruelty. They brought the children outside from the prison. The children were shivering like branches of a tree in the wind. Then I saw the Ustashe grab small children and whirl them in the air above their heads so fast until they ripped their arms off, leaving the Ustashe holding only the arm. The other Ustashe would try to catch the flying bodies of the children on their bayonets.[80]

On another occasion, Sadik Darron described what happened to one infant after a mother fought with a guard who had taken her child from her:

> The child was crying in his hands, and he [the guard] started to take off the baby's swaddling clothes, swearing all the time. When the baby was naked, he took hold of the small feet with three fingers and started to whirl the child in the air. He whirled him faster and faster and then suddenly thumped the child to the ground next to the mother's head [the mother had been knocked down during the struggle]. The small skull smashed like a ripe pumpkin and blood and brains spattered the terrified mother's face. The woman screamed in despair and then lost consciousness. I saw them take her away by the legs and drag her away.[81]

The *Ustaše* guards also used other methods to murder children at Jasenovac. Darron saw one guard with a group of 200–250 Bosnian Serb children:

> "Come with me, you are going to your mother, grandmother, father." About twenty children, naively believing his words, were following him closely. When they approached the pit, a number of the Ustashe came closer and surrounded them. They stood in line and passed the children in a chain closer to the pit. The last Ustashe in the chain was holding an ordinary joiner's hammer. He took one child after another, hit them on the back of their heads with the hammer, and threw them in the pit. Then there was a spell of silence.[82]

Serbs were not the only inmates singled out for such brutal treatment. The Croats viewed the Roma prisoners as a lawless group and usually killed Roma children and women as soon as they arrived in the camp. Roma men were put in Jasenovac's Camp IIIc, where working conditions were particularly harsh. They were given little or no food and forced to work on heavy construction projects or burial details. Occasionally, Croatian guards forced the Roma males to execute fellow Roma prisoners. All the Roma males in Camp IIIc died there.

Serbia

There were only about 16,000 Jews in German-occupied Serbia in 1941 and about 40,000 Roma. About two-thirds of Serbia's Jews lived in Belgrade. The Wehrmacht treated occupied Serbia like German territory and sent most of the Jews, and some Roma, to concentration and death camps in Serbia. On May 31, 1941, German military authorities decreed that Roma were to be treated like Jews and required both groups to wear armbands identifying them as *Juden* or *Zigeuner*. However, in July, officials decreed that Serbian Roma who could prove that their families had been settled since the mid-nineteenth century and were an integral part of Serbian life were not subject to these restrictions. Jews and Roma who were not exempt from these regulations soon lost their jobs and were required to register for forced labor. Both groups were forbidden to enter public places and had to observe a daily curfew from 8:00 P.M. to 6:00 A.M. In late October 1941, authorities opened the Sajmište concentration camp. In early December, they told Belgrade's Jews to turn in their house keys and report to the Security Police. They were then rounded up and transported to Sajmište. Conditions in the camp were appalling, and many of the camp's Jews froze or starved to death. The camp's males were shot by German units; the women and children were murdered in a special gas van in the spring of 1942. Estimates are that 100,000 Serbs were also sent to

Serbian guard escorts Roma about to be executed. USHMM Photo No. 85181, courtesy of Muzej Revolucije Narodnosti Jugoslavije.

Sajmište. About 40,000 Serbs and 7,500 Jews died there.

Part of the rationale for opening Sajmište was to deal with the growing problems with partisans. The Wehrmacht frequently took Roma as hostages and executed them in reprisal for guerilla attacks against military units. *SS-Gruppenführer* Harald Turner (1891–1947), the *Chef der Deutschen Militärverwaltung* (Chief of German Military Administration) in Belgrade, made reference to this practice in a memo to local Wehrmacht commanders on October 26, 1941:

> The Gypsy cannot, by reason of his inner and outer makeup [*Konstruktion*] be a useful member of international society [*Völkerge-meinschaft*]. . . . As a matter of principle it must be said that the Jews and Gypsies repre-sent an element of insecurity and thus a dan-

> ger to public order and safety . . . that is why it is a matter of principle in each case to put all Jewish men and all male Gypsies at the disposal of troops as hostages.[83]

The Wehrmacht also used the Roma as slave laborers to build camps such as Sajmište, which was near one of Belgrade's Roma quarters. The Roma in these camps suffered from physical mistreatment, disease, and malnutrition. From Turner's perspective, the Wehrmacht's campaign against the Roma and the Jews was such that on August 29, 1942, he claimed: "[I]n the interests of pacifi-cation, the Gypsy Question has been fully liq-uidated. Serbia is the only country in which the Jewish Question and the Gypsy Question have been solved."[84]

This was not true, though, when it came to the Roma. In reality, German authorities had woefully overestimated the number of Roma in Serbia and Belgrade. And even though they had succeeded in murdering most of Serbia's Jews by this time, many of the country's Roma were still alive. German officials initially calculated that there were 150,000 Roma in Serbia and expected to send 16,000 Jews and Roma to Sajmište when it opened. Many of Belgrade's Roma had escaped the German dragnet by going into hiding or slipping into Bulgarian or Italian territory. Others joined the resistance, but were often unwelcome. Estimates are that the Germans murdered 95 percent of Serbia's Jews during the Holocaust and about 20 percent of its Roma.

Overall, almost 82 percent of Yugoslavia's Jews were murdered during the Holocaust. The highest losses were in Croatia, which during the war included Bosnia and Herzegovina as well as parts of Slovenia and Serbia. Roma losses are more difficult to determine. After the war, the Yugoslav government claimed that the *Ustaše* murdered 40,000 Roma in Jasenovac. Since there were probably only about 25,000 Roma in the NDH at the time, these figures are suspect, though it is logical to presume that most of the Roma in Croatia and Bosnia and Herzegovina were murdered during the Holocaust. On the other hand, survival rates in Serbia, Kosovo, and Macedonia, which traditionally had large Roma populations, were much higher.

Conclusion

The German conquest of much of Western Europe dramatically broadened the scope of the Holocaust. The Germans discovered, though, that it was going to be difficult to deal with the Jews in this part of Hitler's expanding empire. The same was true among the Nazi-allied states in Central and Eastern Europe. But the one thing that the Germans could count on in most of these countries was the active support of national leaders and/or local collaborators. Given the later problems with

the war on the eastern front, Reich officials initially came to rely more and more on these collaborators to implement the Final Solution.

Foreign Jews were much more vulnerable to persecution and arrest during the early days of the German occupation; in fact, when it came to public support and sympathy, a distinct line was initially drawn between Jews who were foreign-born and those who were citizens. This line would begin to blur as the Germans or their allies throughout Europe began to adopt Nazi-style racial laws. Leaders in Vichy France actively supported the deportation of foreign Jews, and they played an important role in helping the Germans round up and send this group to death centers in the East. Even in the Netherlands, where opposition to the roundups and the occupation was widespread, the Germans found willingness, particularly among the police and Dutch Nazis, to help send more than two-thirds of the Jewish population eastward to their deaths. Many of those deported were not Dutch citizens.

But in the midst of such collaboration, there were also bold efforts to save Jews in the countries under German control in Western Europe. The most famous example, of course, is Denmark, where the nation rose collectively to save the country's small Jewish community from transport to the East and death by sending them to Sweden. There were also brave efforts to rescue Jews in the Netherlands and France. The Dutch paid dearly for their efforts and were unable, in the face of determined German efforts, to save many of their Jews. On the other hand, despite widespread collaboration among French officials, particularly in Vichy France, a handful of Protestant leaders, Jewish relief organizations, and scattered individuals worked actively to save as many Jews as possible; this, as well as the peculiar administrative structure of France during the war, helped save more than three-quarters of France's Jewish population.

The story was just as complex in the German-allied states in Central and Eastern Europe. National leaders in Bulgaria, Croatia, Hungary, and Romania were quite supportive of German plans to deport Jews to the General Government. Ante Pavelić, Croatia's dictator, and his counterpart in Romania, Ion Antonescu, seemed determined to out-Nazi the Nazis and prove their loyalty to Hitler by brutalizing each country's minorities. In Hungary, the government adopted an on-again, off-again campaign against the Jews and Roma that isolated and persecuted both groups. What little quality of life remained changed with the German occupation of Hungary in the spring of 1944. Adolf Eichmann, eager to apply his considerable expertise in Final Solution roundups and transport, was able, with the help of the Hungarian government, Arrow Cross, and police, to round up, deport, and murder two-thirds of the Jews in Central Europe's last major Jewish community.

Bulgaria, with its large Roma and smaller Jewish communities, proved to be the exception to the racial blood lust that swept Central and Eastern Europe during the Holocaust. Although national leaders were more than willing to do Germany's bidding when it came to the idea of deporting Jews to Poland, a coalition of religious, political, and intellectual leaders rose up successfully to protest and stop efforts to turn Jews over to the Germans. But it should also be remembered that these same voices said little about the persecution and murder of Jews and Roma in those parts of Europe occupied by Bulgaria as an active German ally during the war. And, as in other parts of Central and Eastern Europe, the change in national attitudes towards the persecution and murder of Jews and Roma was at least partially driven by the changing fortunes of war. Would the supposed moral outrage that helped temper Bulgarian, French, Hungarian, and Romanian policies towards the Jews and Roma have been any different if Germany had won at Stalingrad?

SOURCES FOR FURTHER STUDY AND RESEARCH

Primary

Affidavit of Dieter Wisliceny. *Nazi Conspiracy and Aggression.* Vol. 8. Washington, DC: United States Government Printing Office, 1946, 606–619.

Alpern, Joil. *No One Awaiting Me: Two Brothers Defy Death During the Holocaust in Romania.* Calgary, AB: University of Calgary Press, 2001.

Ancel, Jean, ed. *Documents Concerning the Fate of Romanian Jewry During the Holocaust.* 12 vols. New York: Beate Klarsfeld Foundation, 1985.

_____. *Transnistria, 1941–1942: The Romanian Mass Murder Campaigns.* Translated by Rachel Garfinkel and Garen Gold. 3 vols. Tel Aviv: Goldstein-Goren Diaspora Research Center, Tel Aviv University, 2003.

Anger, Per. *With Raoul Wallenberg in Budapest: Memories of the War Years in Hungary.* Translated by David Mel Paul and Margareta Paul. New York: Holocaust Library, 1981.

Barak-Ressler, Aliza. *Cry Little Girl: A Tale of the Survival of a Family in Slovakia.* Jerusalem: Yad Vashem, 2003.

Barnouw, David, and Gerrold van der Stroom, eds. *The Diary of Anne Frank: The Critical Edition.* Translated by Arnold J. Pomerans and B. M. Mooyaart-Doubleday. New York: Doubleday, 1989.

Belpoliti, Marco, and Robert Gordon, eds. *The Voice of Memory. Primo Levi: Interviews, 1961–1987.* Translated by Robert Gordon. New York: The New Press, 2001.

Bluglass, Kerry. *Hidden from the Holocaust: Stories of Resilient Children Who Survived and Thrived.* Westport, CT: Praeger, 2003.

Bolle, Kees W., ed. *Ben's Story: Holocaust Letters with Selection from the Dutch Underground Press.* Carbondale, IL: Southern Illinois University Press, 2001.

Cahan, Maier. *Between My Father and the Old Fool: A Holocaust Memoir.* Adapted into English by Yosef Neumark. Brooklyn, NY: Menorah Publications, 2004.

Carmelly, Felicia Steigman. *Shattered! 50 Years of Silence: History and Voices of the Tragedy in Romania and Transnistria.* Scarborough, Canada: Abbeyfield, 1997.

Carp, Matatias. *Holocaust in Romania: Facts and Documents on the Annihilation of Rumania's Jews, 1940–1944.* Translated by Sean Murphy. Budapest: Primor, 1994.

Cecil von Renthe-Fink to German Foreign Ministry, Berlin, January 7, 1942, 1–3. http://www.jewish virtual libary.org/jsource/Holocaust/Denmarkdis .html.

Danon, Braco, and I. Cadik. *The Smell of Human Flesh: A Witness of the Holocaust—Memories of Jasenovac.* Translated by Nadežda Obradović. Beograd: Slobodan Mašić, 2002.

"Decree for the Establishment of the Association of the Jews in Belgium (November 25, 1941)," 102. http://www.jewishvirtuallibrary.org/jsource/ Holocaust/decreesjb.html.

Dedijer, Vladimir, ed. *The Yugoslav Auschwitz and the Vatican: The Croatian Massacre of the Serbs During World War II: Selected Documents.* Translated by Harvey L. Kendall. Buffalo, NY: Prometheus Books, 1992.

"Defining the Legal Position of the Jews in Slovakia," September 11, 1941. http://www.jewishvirtual library.org/source/Holocaust/definingjewbud .html.

Dorian, Emil. *The Quality of Witness: A Romanian Diary, 1937–1944.* Edited by Marguerite Dorian. Translated by Mara Soceanu Vamos. Philadelphia: Jewish Publication Society of America, 1982.

Dunai, Eleanor C. *Surviving in Silence. A Deaf Boy in the Holocaust: The Harry I. Dunai Story.* Washington, DC: Gallaudet University Press, 2002.

Feldman, Alfred. *One Step Ahead: A Jewish Fugitive in Hitler's Europe.* Carbondale: Southern Illinois University Press, 2001.

Frank, Anne. *Anne Frank's Tales from the Secret Annex.* Translated by Michel Mok. New York: Pocket Books, 1983.

———. *The Diary of a Young Girl.* Translated by B. M. Mooyaart-Doubleday. New York: Pocket Books, 1952.

———. *Works from the House Behind.* London: Pan Books, 1971.

———. *The Works of Anne Frank.* Westport, CT: Greenwood Press, 1974.

Friedlander, Henry, and Sybil Milton, eds. *Archives of the Holocaust.* 22 vols. New York: Garland, 1989–1995.

Friedländer, Saul. *When Memory Comes.* Translated by Helen R. Lane. New York: Farrar, Straus and Giroux, 1979.

Gies, Miep, and Allison Gold. *Anne Frank Remembered: The Story of the Woman Who Helped to Hide the Frank Family.* New York: Simon & Schuster, 1987.

Goldberg, Michel. *Namesake.* New Haven: Yale University Press, 1982.

Gross, Elly. *Storm Against the Innocents: Holocaust Memories and Other Stories.* New York: E. Gross, 2000.

Haas, Albert. *The Doctor and the Damned.* New York: St. Martin's Press, 1984.

Halivni, David Weiss. *The Book and the Sword: A Life of Learning in the Shadow of Destruction.* Boulder: Westview Press, 1998.

Hannah Senesh: Her Life and Diary. Translated by Marta Cohn. New York: Schocken Books, 1972.

Hausner, Gideon. *Justice In Jerusalem.* New York: Holocaust Library, 1968.

Herskovic, Patricia. *Escape to Life: A Journey Through the Holocaust: The Memories of Maria and William Herskovic.* Jerusalem: Yad Vashem, 2002.

Jagendorf, Siegfried. *Jagendorf's Foundry: Memoirs of the Romanian Holocaust, 1941–1944.* New York: HarperCollins, 1991.

Joffo, Joseph. *A Bag of Marbles.* Translated by Martin Sokolinsky. Chicago: University of Chicago Press, 2000.

"Julius Hollander to Nathan Straus," June 3, 1941, YIVO Institute for Jewish Research. http://www .npr.org/templates/story.php?storyId=7400998 #7401663.

Kahn, Annette. *Why My Father Died: A Daughter Confronts Her Family's Past at the Trial of Klaus Barbie.* Translated by Anna Cancogni. New York: Summit Books, 1991.

Kalmanovits, Sarah. *An Orphan of the Transnistria Concentration Camp.* Jerusalem: Sarah Kalmanovits, 2005.

Koller, Mark. *Surviving Transnistria: An Autobiographical Account.* S. I. Mark Koller, 2001.

Kroh, Aleksandra. *Lucien's Story.* Translated by Austryn Wainhouse. Evanston, IL: Marlboro Press/ Northwestern, 1996.

Levi, Primo. *Survival in Auschwitz* and *The Reawakening: Two Memoirs.* Translated by Stuart Woolf. New York: Summit Books, 1966.

Lindwer, Willy. *The Last Seven Months of Anne Frank.* Translated by Alison Meersschaert. New York: Random House, 1991.

Lituchy, Barry M. *Jasenovac and the Holocaust in Yugoslavia: Analyses and Survivor Testimonies.* New York: Jasenovac Research Institute, 2006.

Loy, Rosetta. *First Words: A Childhood in Fascist Italy.* Translated by Gregory Cohn. New York: Henry Holt, 2000.

Lubac, Henri de. *Christian Resistance to Anti-Semitism: Memories from 1940–1944.* Translated by Sister Elizabeth Englund. San Francisco: Ignatius Press, 1990.

Ludwig, Emil. *Talks with Mussolini.* Translated by Eden and Cedar Paul. Boston: Little, Brown, 1933.

Micheels, Louis J. *Doctor #117641: A Holocaust Memoir.* New Haven: Yale University Press, 1989.

Nossiter, Adam. *The Algeria Hotel: France, Memory, and the Second World War.* Boston: Houghton Mifflin, 2001.

Ofer, Dalia, and Lenore J. Weitzman, eds. *Women in the Holocaust.* New Haven: Yale University Press, 1998.

"Otto Frank to Nathan Straus," April 30, 1941, YIVO Institute for Jewish Research. http://www .npr.org/templates/story.php?storyId=7400998 #7401663.

Raoul Wallenberg: Dossierdokumentation från Beskickningen I Budapest och Utrikesdepartementet, 1944–1957. Stockholm: Utrikesdepartementet, 1980–1982.

Rittner, Carol, and Sondra Myers, eds. *The Courage to Care: Rescuers of Jews During the Holocaust.* New York: New York University Press, 1986.

Rosengarten, Israel J. *Survival: The Story of a Sixteen-Year-Old Jewish Boy.* Syracuse, NY: Syracuse University Press, 1999.

Samuel, Vivette. *Rescuing the Children: A Holocaust Memoir.* Translated by Charles B. Paul. Madison: University of Wisconsin Press, 2002.

Sebstian, Mihail. *Journal, 1935–1944.* Chicago: Ivan R. Dee in association with the United States Holocaust Memorial Museum, 2000.

Seel, Pierre. *Liberation Was for Others: Memoirs of a Gay Survivor of the Nazi Holocaust.* Translated by Joachim Neugroschel. New York: DaCapo Press, 1997.

Sonnino, Piera. *This Has Happened: An Italian Family in Auschwitz.* Translated by Ann Goldstein. New York: Palgrave Macmillan, 2006.

State of Israel Ministry of Justice. *The Trial of Adolf Eichmann: Record of Proceedings in the District Court of Jerusalem.* 9 vols. Jerusalem: Israel State Archives and Yad Vashem, 1993–1995.

Stein, André. *Quiet Heroes: True Stories of the Rescue of Jews by Christians in Nazi-Occupied Holland.* New York: New York University Press, 1988.

Steinberg, Paul. *Speak You Also.* Translated by Linda Coverdale with Bill Ford. New York: Henry Holt, 2000.

Stivelman, Michael. *The Death March.* Translated by Peter Lewnny. Rio de Janiero: Imago Editora, 1997.

Świebocki, Henryk, ed. *London Has Been Informed: Report by Auschwitz Escapees.* Oświęcim: The Auschwitz-Birkenau State Museum, 1997.

Tamler, Gisela. *Before and After: Surviving the Romanian Holocaust in Transnistria.* Montreal: G. Tamler, 2002.

Todorov, Tzvetan, ed. *The Fragility of Goodness: Why Bulgaria's Jews Survived the Holocaust: A Collection of Texts with Commentary by Tzvetan Todorov.* Translated by Arthur Denner. Princeton: Princeton University Press, 2001.

Transylvanian World Federation. *Genocide and Ethnocide of the Jews and Hungarians in Rumania: Testimony Submitted by the Transylvanian World Federation to the International Conference on the Holocaust and Genocide, Tel Aviv, Israel, 1982.* Tel Aviv: n.p., 1982.

Valensi, Lucette, and Nathan Wachtel, eds. *Jewish Memories.* Translated by Barbara Harshav. Berkeley: University of California Press, 1990.

Vegh, Claudine. *I Didn't Say Goodbye.* Translated by Ros Schwartz. New York: E. P. Dutton, 1984.

Velmans, Edith. *Edith's Book.* London: Penguin Books, 1999.

Vrba, Rudolf. *I Escaped from Auschwitz.* Fort Lee, NJ: Barricade Books, 2002.

Vrbová, Gerta. *Trust and Deceit: A Tale of Survival in Slovakia and Hungary, 1939–1945.* London: Vallentine Mitchell, 2006.

Wallenberg, Raoul. *Letters and Dispatches, 1924–1944.* Translated by Kjersti Board. New York: Arcade, 1995.

Weissberg, Alex. *Desperate Mission: Joel Brand's Story.* Translated by Constantine FitzGibbon and Andrew Foster-Melliar. New York: Criterion Books, 1958.

Wilson, Cara. *Love, Otto: The Legacy of Anne Frank.* Kansas City, KS: Andrews and McMeel, 1995.

Wolf, Jacqueline. *"Take Care of Josette": A Memoir in Defense of Occupied France.* New York: Franklin Watts, 1981.

Secondary Sources

Abrahamsen, Samuel. *Norway's Response to the Holocaust.* New York: Holocaust Library, 1991.

Achim, Viorel. *The Roma in Romanian History.* Translated by Richard Davies. Budapest: Central European University Press, 2004.

Ackovíc, Dragoljub. *Roma Genocide in Jasenovac Camp.* Translated by Ljubomir Vukosavljević and Vesna Ajnšpiler. Belgrade: Museum of the Victims of Genocide, 1997.

Adeli, Lisa. "From Jasenovac to Yugoslavism: Ethnic Persecution in Croatia During World War II." PhD diss., University of Arizona, 2004.

Adler, Franklin Hugh. "Why Mussolini Turned on the Jews." *Patterns of Prejudice* 39, no. 3 (September 2005): 285–300.

Adler, Jacques. *The Jews of Paris and the Final Solution: Communal Response and Internal Conflicts, 1940–1944.* New York: Oxford University Press, 1987.

Angier, Carole. *The Double Bond: Primo Levi—A Biography.* New York: Farrar, Straus & Giroux, 2002.

Anissimov, Myrian. *Primo Levi: Tragedy of an Optimist.* Translated by Steve Cox. Woodstock, NY: Overlook Press, 2000.

Anne Frank Stichting. *Anne Frank in the World.* Amsterdam: Anne Frank Stichting, 1985.

Bar-Zohar, Michael. *Beyond Hitler's Grasp: The Heroic Rescue of Bulgaria's Jews.* Avon, MA: Adams Media Corporation, 1998.

Bauer, Yehuda. *Jews for Sale: Nazi-Jewish Negotiations, 1933–1935.* New Haven: Yale University Press, 1994.

_____. *Rethinking the Holocaust.* New Haven: Yale University Press, 2001.

Beker, Avi, ed. *The Plunder of Jewish Property During the Holocaust: Confronting European History.* New York: New York University Press, 2001.

Bierman, John. *Righteous Gentile: The Story of Raoul Wallenberg, Missing Hero of the Holocaust.* New York: Viking Press, 1981.

Bijlsma, Frans. *Raoul Wallenberg: 1912–1947?* Soersterberg, The Netherlands: Aspekt, 2005.

Bosworth, R. J. B. *Mussolini's Italy: Life Under the Fascist Dictatorship, 1915–1945.* New York: Penguin Books, 2006.

Boyens, Armin F. C. "The Ecumenical Community and the Holocaust." *The Annals of the American Academy of Political and Social Science,* no. 450 (July 1980): 140–152.

Braham, Randolph L., ed. *The Destruction of Romanian and Ukrainian Jews During the Antonescu Era.* New York and Boulder: Social Science Monographs and Columbia University Press, 1997.

_____. *The Politics of Genocide: The Holocaust in Hungary.* 2 vols. New York: Columbia University Press, 1994.

_____. *Genocide and Retribution: The Holocaust in Hungarian-Ruled Northern Transylvania.* Boston: Kluwer-Nijhoff, 1983.

Braham, Randolph L., and Scott Miller, eds. *The Nazis' Last Victims: The Holocaust in Hungary.* Detroit: Wayne State University Press in association with the United States Holocaust Memorial Museum.

Breitman, Richard. "New Sources on the Holocaust in Italy." *Holocaust and Genocide Studies* 16, no. 3 (2003): 401–414.

Bryant, Chad. *Prague in Black: Nazi Rule and Czech Nationalism.* Cambridge, MA: Harvard University Press, 2007.

Buckser, Andrew. *After the Rescue: Jewish Identity and Community in Contemporary Denmark.* New York: Palgrave Macmillan, 2003.

_____. "Group Identities and the Construction of the 1943 Rescue of Danish Jews. *Ethnology* 37, no. 3 (1998): 209–226.

Bulajić, Milan. *Tudjman's "Janesovac Myth": Genocide Against Serbs, Jews, and Gypsies.* Translated by Miroslava Janković and Ann Pešić. Belgrade: Struèna knj, 1996.

_____. *Ustashi Genocide in the Independent State of Croatia (NDH) from 1941–1945.* Translated by Vida Jankovic and Svetlana Raicevic. Belgrade: Ministry of Information of the Republic of Serbia, 1992.

Burleigh, Michael. *The Third Reich: A New History.* New York: Hill and Wang, 2000.

Butnaru, I. C. *The Silent Holocaust: Romania and Its Jews.* New York: Greenwood Press, 1992.

Bútorová, Zora, and Martin Bútorá. *Attitudes Toward Jews and the Holocaust in Independent Slovakia.* New York: American Jewish Committee, 1995.

Campion, Joan. *In the Lion's Mouth: Gisi Fleischmann & the Jewish Fight for Survival.* Lanham, MD: University Press of America, 1987.

Caracciolo, Nicola. *Uncertain Refuge: Italy and the Jews During the Holocaust.* Translated and edited by Florette Rechnitz Koffler and Richard Koffler. Urbana: University of Illinois Press, 1995.

Carpi, Daniel. *Between Mussolini and Hitler: The Jews and the Italian Authorities in France and Tunisia.* Hanover, NH: Brandeis University Press and University Press of New England, 1994.

Cesarani, David. *Becoming Eichmann: Rethinking the Life, Crimes, and Trial of a "Desk Murderer."* Cambridge, MA: Da Capo Press, 2004.

Chary, Frederick B. *The Bulgarian Jews and the Final Solution, 1940–1944.* Pittsburgh: University of Pittsburgh Press, 1972.

Cobb, Richard. *French and Germans, Germans and French: A Personal Interpretation of France Under Two Occupations, 1914–1918/1940–1944.* Cambridge, MA: Brandeis University Press, 1983.

Cohen, Richard I. *The Burden of Conscience: French Jewish Leadership During the Holocaust.* Bloomington: Indiana University Press, 1987.

Constantinesco, Nicholas. *Romania in Harm's Way, 1939–1941.* Boulder and New York: East European Monographs and Columbia University Press, 2004.

Courtine-Denamy, Sylvie. *The House of Jacob.* Translated by William Sayers. Ithaca: Cornell University Press, 2003.

Crowe, David M. *A History of the Gypsies of Eastern Europe and Russia.* 2nd ed. Updated and rev. ed. New York: Palgrave Macmillan, 2007.

Crowe, David M., and John Kolsti, eds. *The Gypsies of Eastern Europe.* Armonk, NY: M. E. Sharpe, 1991.

Dallinn, Alexander. *Odessa, 1941–1944: A Case Study of Soviet Territory Under Foreign Rule.* Iaşi and Portland, OR: Center for Romanian Studies, 1998.

De Costa, Denise. *Anne Frank and Etty Hillesum: Inscribing Spirituality and Sexuality.* Translated by Mischa F. C. Hoyinck and Robert E. Chesal. New Brunswick, NJ: Rutgers University Press, 1998.

De Felice, Benzo. *The Jews in Fascist Italy: A History.* Translated by Robert L. Miller. New York: Enigma Books, 2001.

De Jong, Louis. *The Netherlands and Nazi Germany.* Cambridge, MA: Harvard University Press, 1990.

Długoborski, Wacław, ed. *The Tragedy of the Jews of Slovakia, 1938–1945: Slovakia and the "Final Solution of the Jewish Question."* Oświęcim: Auschwitz-Birkenau State Museum, 2002.

Dobroszycki, Lucjan, and Jeffrey S. Gurock, eds. *The Holocaust in the Soviet Union: Studies and Sources on the Destruction of the Jews in the Nazi-Occupied Territories of the USSR.* Armonk, NY: M. E. Sharpe, 1993.

Fatram, Gila, and Naftali Greenwood. "The 'Working Group.'" *Holocaust and Genocide Studies* 8, no. 2 (1944): 164–201.

Feinstein, Wiley. *The Civilization of the Holocaust in Italy: Poets, Artists, Saints, Anti-Semites.* Madison, WI: Fairleigh Dickinson University Press, 2003.

Final Report of the International Commission on the Holocaust in Romania, Bucharest, Romania, November 11, 2004. http://www.yad.vashem.org.il/about_yad/what_new/data_whats_new/report1/html and http://www.ushmm.org/research/center/presentation/details/2005–03–10/pdf/english/executive-summary.pdf.

Fings, Karola, Herbert Heuss, and Frank Sparing, eds. *From "Race Science" to the Camps.* Vol. 1, *The Gypsies During the Second World War.* Translated by Donald Kenrick. Hatfield, UK: University of Hertfordshire Press, 1997.

Finkielkraut, Alain. *Remembering in Vain: The Klaus Barbie Trial and Crimes Against Humanity.* Trans-

lated by Roxanne Lapidus with Sima Godfrey. New York: Columbia University Press, 1992.

"Finland's Tarnished Holocaust Record: An Interview with Serah Beizer." Jerusalem Center for Public Affairs, March 1, 2007, 1–7. http://www.jcpa.org/JCPA/Templates/ShowPage.asp?DBID=1&LNG.

Fisher, Julius S. *Transnistria: The Forgotten Cemetery.* South Brunswick, NJ: T. Yoseloff, 1969.

Flender, Harold. *Rescue in Denmark.* New York: Waldon Press, 1963.

Freidenreich, Harriet Pass. *The Jews of Yugoslavia: A Quest for Community.* Philadelphia: Jewish Publication Society of America, 1979.

Friedländer, Saul. *The Years of Extermination: Nazi Germany and the Jews, 1939–1945.* New York: HarperCollins, 2007.

Fuchs, Abraham. *The Unheeded Cry: The Gripping Story of Rabbi Weissmandl, the Valiant Holocaust Leader Who Battled Both Allied Indifference and Nazi Hatred.* Brooklyn, NY: Mesorah, 1984.

Geller, Jay Howard. "The Role of Military Administration in German-Occupied Belgium, 1940–1944." *Journal of Military History* 63, no. 1 (January 1999): 99–125.

Gerlach, Christian, and Götz Aly. *Das letzte Kapitel: realpolitik, Ideologie und der Mord an der ungarischen Juden 1944–1945.* Stuttgart: Deutsches Verlags-Anstalt, 2002.

Gersten, Alan. *A Conspiracy of Indifference: The Raoul Wallenberg Story.* Philadelphia: Xlibris, 2001.

Gilbert, Martin. *Auschwitz and the Allies.* London: M. Joseph/Rainbird, 1981.

Gillette, Aaron. "The Origins of the 'Manifesto of Racial Scientists.'" *Journal of Modern Italian Studies* 6, no. 3 (2001): 305–323.

Goldstein, Slavko. *Jews in Jasenovac.* Translated by Nikolina Jovanović. Jasenovac, Croatia: Jasenova Memorial Area, 2003.

Goslan, Richard J., ed. *Memory, the Holocaust, and French Justice: The Bousquet and Touvier Affairs.* Translations by Lucy B. Goslan and Richard J. Goslan. Hanover, MA: University Press of New England, 1996.

———. *The Papon Affair: Memory and Justice on Trial.* Translations by Lucy B. Goslan and Richard J. Goslan. New York: Routledge, 2000.

Gur, David. *Brothers for Resistance and Rescue: The Underground Zionist Youth Movement in Hungary During World War II.* Edited by Eli Netzer. Translated by Pamela Segev and Avri Fischer. Jerusalem: Gefen, 2004.

Hanebrink, Paul A. *In Defense of Christian Hungary: Religion, Nationalism, and Antisemitism, 1890–1944.* Ithaca: Cornell University Press, 2006.

Hay, Peter. *Ordinary Heroes: The Life and Death of Chana Szenes, Israel's National Heroine.* New York: Paragon House, 1989.

Hewins, Ralph. *Count Folke Bernadotte: His Life and Work.* Minneapolis: T. S. Denison, 1950.

Hilberg, Raul. *The Destruction of the European Jews.* 3 vols. New York: Holmes & Meier, 1985.

_____. *The Destruction of the European Jews.* 3rd ed. 3 vols. New Haven: Yale University Press, 2003.

Homer, Frederic D. *Primo Levi and the Politics of Survival.* Columbia: University of Missouri Press, 2001.

Hondius, Dienke. *Return: Holocaust Survivors and Dutch Anti-Semitism.* Translated by David Colmer. Westport, CT: Praeger, 2003.

Hyman, Paula E. *The Jews of Modern France.* Berkeley: University of California Press, 1998.

Institute for Political Studies of Defense and Military History. *The Holocaust and Romania: History and Contemporary Significance.* Tel Aviv: Goldstein Goren Diaspora Research Center, 2003.

Ioanid, Radu. *The Holocaust in Romania: The Iasi Pogrom of June 1941.* Translated by Maria Vamos Soceanu. Cambridge: Cambridge University Press, 1993.

_____. *The Holocaust in Romania: The Destruction of Jews and Gypsies Under the Antonescu Regime, 1940–1944.* Chicago: Ivan Dee, 2000.

Jensen, Mette Basthold, and Steven L. B. Jensen, eds. *Denmark and the Holocaust.* Copenhagen: Institute for International Studies and Department for Holocaust and Genocide Studies, 2003.

Kárnü, Miroslav, ed. *Terezinska pametni kniha.* 2 vols. Prague: Melantrich, 1995.

Kayfetz, Victor, trans. *Raoul Wallenberg.* Stockholm: Swedish Institute, 1988.

Kenrick, Donald, ed. *The Final Chapter.* Vol. 3 of *The Gypsies During the Second World War.* Hatfield, UK: University of Hertfordshire Press, 2006.

_____, ed. *In the Shadow of the Swastika.* Vol. 2 of *The Gypsies During the Second World War.* Hatfield, UK: University of Hertfordshire Press, 1999.

Kenrick, Donald, and Grattan Puxon. *The Destiny of Europe's Gypsies.* New York: Basic Books, 1972.

Kertzer, David I. *The Popes Against the Jews: The Vatican's Role in the Rise of Modern Anti-Semitism.* New York: Alfred A. Knopf, 2001.

Kitchens, James H. *The Bombing of Auschwitz Re-Examined.* Lexington, VA: Society of Military History by the George C. Marshall Foundation and the Virginia Military Institute, 1994.

Kljakić, Slobodan. *A Conspiracy of Silence: Genocide in the Independent State of Croatia and Concentration Camp Jasenovac.* Belgrade: Ministry of Information of the Republic of Serbia, 1991.

Korey, William. *The Last Word on Wallenberg? New Investigations, New Questions.* New York: American Jewish Committee, 2001.

Kostić, Lazo M. *The Holocaust in the "Independent State of Croatia": An Account based on German, Italian, and the Other Sources.* Chicago: L. M. Kostich Fund, 1981.

Kranzler, David. *The Man Who Stopped the Trains to Auschwitz: George Mantello, El Salvador, and Switzerland's Finest Hour.* Syracuse, NY: Syracuse University Press, 2000.

Kritzman, Lawrence D., ed. *Auschwitz and After: Race, Culture, and "the Jewish Question" in France.* New York: Routledge, 1995.

Larsen, Anita. *Raoul Wallenberg: Missing Diplomat.* New York: Crestwood House, 1992.

Larsen, Jan. *Raoul Wallenberg.* Translated by Victor Kayfetz, 1995. Uppsala, Sweden: Swedish Institute, 1995.

Last, Dick Van Galen, and Rolf Wolfswinkel. *Anne Frank and After: Dutch Holocaust Literature in Historical Perspective.* Amsterdam: Amsterdam University Press, 1996.

Latour, Anny. *The Jewish Resistance in France (1940–1944).* New York: Holocaust Library, 1981.

Lazare, Lucien. *Rescue as Resistance: How Jewish Organizations Fought the Holocaust in France.* New York: Columbia University Press, 1996.

"Le Chambon." Jewish Virtual Library. http://www .jewishvirtuallibrary.org/jsource/Holocaust/ Chambon/html.

Lee, Carol Ann. *The Hidden Life of Otto Frank.* New York: HarperCollins, 2003.

Lester, Elenore. *Wallenberg: The Man in the Iron Web.* Englewood Cliffs, NJ: Prentice-Hall, 1982.

Linnéa, Sharon. *Raoul Wallenberg: The Man Who Stopped Death.* Philadelphia: Jewish Publication Society, 1993.

Mamatey, Victor S., and Radomír Luža, eds. *A History of the Czechoslovak Republic, 1918–1948.* Princeton: Princeton University Press, 1973.

Mandel, Maud S. *In the Aftermath of Genocide: Armenians and Jews in Twentieth-Century France.* Durham, NC: Duke University Press, 2003.

Manoschek, Walter. *"Serbien ist judenfrei": militärische Besatzungpolitik und Judenvernichtung in Serbian 1941/42.* Munich: R. Oldenbourg, 1993.

Marino, Andy. *A Quiet American: The Secret War of Varian Fry.* New York: St. Martin's Press, 1999.

Marrus, Michael R., and Robert O. Paxton. *Vichy France and the Jews.* Stanford: Stanford University Press, 1995.

Marton, Kati. *Wallenberg.* New York: Random House, 1982.

Mason, Henry L. "Testing Human Bonds Within Nations: Jews in the Occupied Netherlands." *Political Science Quarterly.* 99, no. 2 (Summer 1984): 315–343.

Matsas, Michael. *The Illusion of Safety: The Story of the Greek Jews During the Second World War.* New York: Pella, 1997.

McArthur, Debra. *Raoul Wallenberg: Rescuing Thousands from the Nazis' Grasp.* Berkeley Heights, NJ: Enslow, 2005.

Mendelsohn, John. *Relief in Hungary and the Failure of the Joel Brand Mission.* New York: Garland, 1982.

Michlic, Joanna Beata. *Poland's Threatening Other: The Image of the Jews from 1880 to the Present.* Lincoln: University of Nebraska Press, 2006.

Milton, Sybil. "The Context of the Holocaust." *German Studies Review* 13, no. 2 (May 1990): 269–283.

Moore, Bob. *Victims & Survivors: The Nazi Persecution of the Jews in the Netherlands, 1940–1945.* London: Arnold, 1997.

Moyn, Samuel. *A Holocaust Controversy: The Treblinka Affair in Postwar France.* Waltham, MA: Brandeis University Press, 2005.

Müller, Melissa. *Anne Frank: The Biography.* Translated by Rita Kimber and Robert Kimber. New York: Henry Holt, 1998.

Neufeld, Michael J., and Michael Berenbaum, eds. *The Bombing of Auschwitz: Should the Allies Have Attempted It?* Lawrence: University of Kansas Press in association with the United States Holocaust Memorial Museum, 2003.

"Newly Discovered File Documents Efforts of Anne Frank's Father to Escape from Nazi-Occupied Holland." YIVO Institute for Jewish Research, February 14, 2007. http://www.yivoinstitute.org/events/index.php.

Ozick, Cynthia. "Who Owns Anne Frank?" *New Yorker* (October 6, 1997): 76–87.

Palmklint, Ingrid, and Daniel Larsson, eds. *Raoul Wallenberg: Report of the Swedish-Russian Working Group.* Stockholm: Ministry for Foreign Affairs, Department for Central and Eastern Europe, 2000.

Petrow, Richard. *The Bitter Years: The Invasion and Occupation of Denmark and Norway: April 1940–May 1945.* New York: William Morrow, 1974.

Poznanski, Renée. *Jews in France During World War II.* Translated by Nathan Bracher. Hanover, NH: Brandeis University Press in Association with the United States Holocaust Memorial Museum 2001.

Presser, J. *Ashes in the Wind: The Destruction of Dutch Jewry.* Translated by Arnold Pomerans. Detroit: Wayne State University Press, 1988.

Ranki, Vera. *The Politics of Inclusion and Exclusion: Jews and Nationalism in Hungary.* New York: Holmes & Meier, 1999.

Rautkallio, Hannu. *Finland and the Holocaust: The Rescue of Finland's Jews.* Washington, DC: United States Holocaust Memorial Museum, 1988.

Rayski, Adam. *The Choice of the Jews Under Vichy: Between Submission and Resistance.* Translated by François Bédarida. Notre Dame, IN: University of Notre Dame Press, 2005.

"Reactions to the Trap." Joods Museum van Deportatie en Verzet-Judaico. http:www.cicb.be/eng/shoah/jewishlifebefore.html.

"The Righteous Among the Nations: France." http://www.yadvashem.org/righteous/bycountry/france/andre_trocme.

Rittner, Carol, ed. *Anne Frank in the World: Essays and Reflections.* Armonk, NY: M. E. Sharpe, 1998.

Robbins, Christopher. *Test of Courage: The Michel Thomas Story.* New York: Free Press, 2000.

Rosenfeld, Harvey. *Raoul Wallenberg: Angel of Rescue: Heroism and Torment in the Gulag.* Buffalo, NY: Prometheus Books, 1982.

Rothkirchen, Livia. "The Slovak Enigma: A Reassessment of the Halt to the Deportations." *East Central Europe* 10, nos. 1–2 (1983): 3–13.

――――. *The Jews of Bohemia and Moravia: Facing the Holocaust.* Lincoln: University of Nebraska Press, 2005.

Rozen, Marcu. *The Holocaust under the Antonescu Government: Historical and Statistical Data About Jews in Romania, 1940–1944.* Bucharest: A.R.J.V.H., 2004.

Schwab, Gerald. *The Day the Holocaust Began: The Odyssey of Herschel Grynszpan.* New York: Praeger, 1990.

Shachan, Avigdor. *Burning Ice: The Ghettos of Transnistria.* Translated by Shmuel Himelstein. Boulder and New York: East European Monographs and Columbia University Press, 1996.

Shelach, Menachem. "Sajmište: An Extermination Camp in Serbia." *Holocaust and Genocide Studies* 2, no. 2 (1987): 243–260.

Skoglund, Elizabeth R. *A Quiet Courage: Per Anger, Wallenberg's Co-Liberator of Hungarian Jews.* Grand Rapids, MI: Baker Books, 1997.

Smith, Danny. *Lost Hero: Raoul Wallenberg's Dramatic Quest to Save the Jews of Hungary.* London: HarperCollins, 2001.

Steinberg, Jonathan. *All or Nothing: The Axis and the Holocaust, 1941–1943.* London: Routledge, 1990.

Stille, Alexander. *Benevolence and Betrayal: Five Italian Jewish Families Under Fascism.* New York: Summit Books, 1991.

Stræde, Therkel. *October 1943: The Rescue of the Danish Jews from Annihilation.* Copenhagen: Royal Danish Ministry of Foreign Affairs, 1993.

Streissguth, Thomas. *Raoul Wallenberg: Swedish Diplomat and Humanitarian.* New York: The Rosen Publishing Group, 2001.

Švob, Melita. *Jews in Croatia: Holocaust Victims and Survivors.* Zagreb: Jewish Community Zagreb, Research and Documentation Center of the Holocaust Victims and Survivors in Croatia, 2000.

Szabolics, Szita. *Trading Lives: Operations of the Jewish Relief and Rescue Committee in Budapest, 1944–1945.* Budapest: Central European University, 2005.

Szita, Szabolcs. *Trading in Lives? Operations of the Jewish Relief and Rescue Committee in Budapest, 1944–1945.* Translated by Sean Lambert. Budapest: Central European University Press, 2005.

Thomas, John Oram. *The Giant-Killers: The Story of the Danish Resistance Movement, 1940–1945.* London: Michael Joseph, Ltd. 1975.

Tomasevich, Jozo. *War and Revolution in Yugoslavia, 1941–1945: Occupation and Collaboration.* Stanford: Stanford University Press, 2001.

_____. *War and Revolution in Yugoslavia, 1941–1945: The Chetniks.* Stanford: Stanford University Press, 1975.

Touw, H. C. "The Resistance of the Netherlands Churches." *ANNALS of the American Academy of Political and Social Science* 245 (May 1946): 149–161.

Tschuy, Theo. *Dangerous Diplomacy: The Story of Carl Lutz, Rescuer of 62,000 Hungarian Jews.* Grand Rapids, MI: William B. Eerdmans, 2000.

United States Holocaust Memorial Museum. *Hungary and the Holocaust: Confrontation with the Past.* Washington, DC: Center for Advanced Holocaust Studies, 2001.

_____. *Roma and Sinti: Under-Studied Victims of Nazism.* Washington, DC: Center for Advanced Holocaust Studies, 2002.

Vickers, Miranda. *The Albanians: A Modern History.* London: I. B. Taurus, 1997.

Vinen, Richard. *The Unfree French: Life Under the Occupation.* New Haven: Yale University Press, 2006.

Webster, Paul. *Pétain's Crime: The Full Story of French Collaboration in the Holocaust.* Chicago: Ivan R. Dee, 1991.

Weisberg, Richard H. *Vichy Law and the Holocaust in France.* New York: New York University Press, 1996.

Werbell, Frederick E. and Thurston Clarke. *Lost Hero: The Mystery of Raoul Wallenberg.* New York: McGraw-Hill, 1982.

Werner, Emmy E. *A Conspiracy of Decency: The Rescue of the Danish Jews during World War II.* Boulder: Westview Press, 2002.

Wolf, Diane L. *Beyond Anne Frank: Hidden Children and Postwar Families in Holland.* Berkeley: University of California Press, 2007.

Wolf, Joan B. *Harnessing the Holocaust: The Politics of Memory in France.* Stanford: Stanford University Press, 2004.

Wyman, David S. *The Abandonment of the Jews: America and the Holocaust, 1941–1945.* New York: Pantheon Books, 1984.

Yahil, Leni. *The Rescue of Danish Jewry: Test of a Democracy.* Philadelphia: The Jewish Publication Society of America, 1969.

Zasloff, Tela. *A Rescuer's Story: Pastor Pierre-Charles Toureille in Vichy France.* Madison: The University of Wisconsin Press, 2003.

Zuccotti, Susan. *The Holocaust, the French, and the Jews.* Lincoln: University of Nebraska Press, 1999.

_____. *The Italians and the Holocaust: Persecution, Rescue, and Survival.* Lincoln: University of Nebraska Press, 1988.

CHAPTER 9

The Holocaust and the Role of Europe's Neutrals

Then and Now

CHRONOLOGY

—**1922–1939:** Reign of Pope Pius XI

—**1929** *(February 11)*: *Lateran Accords* signed between Vatican and Italy

—**1933** *(July 20)*: *Concordat* signed between Vatican and Germany

—**1936–1939:** Spanish Civil War

—**1937:** Pius XI issues *Mit brennender Sorge*

—**1938:** Germany begins to stamp passports of all German Jews with red "J"

—**1939–1958:** Reign of Pope Pius XII

—**1939** *(October 19)*: Turkey signs mutual support treaty with Britain and France

—**1939** *(October 19)*: Swiss order all illegal refugees deported

—**1941** *(June 18)*: Turkey signs friendship treaty with Germany

—**1942:** Żegota founded in Warsaw to help Jews

—**1942** *(August 4)*: Swiss police order all illegal refugees, mainly Jews, to leave Switzerland

—**1942** *(November 25)*: Polish government releases Jan Karksi's report about Final Solution

—**1942** *(December 3)*: Swedish government says it will accept all Danish Jews

—**1943:** Allies issue "Gold Warning" to neutrals and German allies

—**1943** *(March 31)*: Deadline for repatriation of Jews from neutral and German allied countries

—**1944:** Allies announce "Operation Safehaven" to monitor economic activities of Switzerland

—**1945** *(March 9–April 15)*: "White Bus" operation saves 5,000–11,000 Jews and many others

—**1946** *(May 25)*: Washington Agreement between Allies and Switzerland

—**1962–1965:** Second Vatican Ecumenical Council in Rome

—**1963:** Rolf Hochhuth's play, *The Deputy*, performed in Berlin

—**1979:** Pope John Paul II visits Auschwitz

—**1986:** Pope John Paul II visits Synagogue of Rome

—**1993:** Vatican establishes diplomatic relations with Israel

—**1994:** World Jewish Congress begins investigation into missing Jewish assets in Swiss banks

—**1996:** U.S. Congressional investigations into Swiss gold matter

—**1996:** Volcker Commission begins meetings with Swiss banks

—**1996:** Swiss parliament appoints International Commission of Experts to look at Switzerland's role in World War II; extensive report published in 2002

—**1997** *(January)*: Christoph Meili discovers Holocaust era documents about to be destroyed in Zürich

—**1997** *(January)*: Swiss government and banks create special fund for Holocaust victims

—**1998:** Vatican releases *We Remember: A Reflection on the Shoah*

—**1998** *(August 18)*: Swiss banks and World Jewish Congress announce $1.25 billion Holocaust settlement

—**1999:** Vatican releases *Memory and Reconciliation*

—**2000:** John Paul II visits Yad Vashem

—**2002:** Special Master appointed by Brooklyn Federal Court to develop plan for distribution of $1.25 billion Swiss gold funds

—**2002:** Vatican releases *The Jewish People and Their Sacred Scriptures in the Christian Bible*

—**2005:** Benedict XVI becomes pope

Europe's Neutrals

Neutrality in twentieth-century warfare seemed to be a status that existed totally at the mercy of the belligerent. In that century's two world wars, Europe's neutrals often compromised their national integrity to maintain their nonbelligerent status. Such was the case in World War II.

Almost all of Europe's neutrals in World War II—Portugal, Spain, Switzerland, Sweden, and Turkey—supported the German war effort to varying degrees, either through the direct supply of essential raw materials or as financial conduits for German gold and other liquid assets, some gruesomely taken from Holocaust victims. And many question whether the neutral Vatican, certainly Europe's most important spiritual and moral force, did everything it could to save the Jews, Roma, and others during the Holocaust. On the other hand, Europe's neutrals also played varying roles in helping save Jews and others during the Shoah. It is because of these contradictions that the role of Europe's neutrals during the Holocaust remains a source of debate and controversy.

Portugal

Prewar Portugal had a Jewish population of no more than 1,000. Portugal's greatest failing

during the Holocaust was its role as a conduit for laundered German funds, some of which were stolen from Holocaust victims. Portugal was also a principal supplier of tungsten to the German war effort, though it also sold tungsten to the Allies. Portugal was also an important center for Holocaust rescue efforts. Like many other nations in Europe at this time, Portugal was ruled by a Fascist dictator, António de Oliveira Salazar (1889–1970), who assumed power in 1932 and ruled Portugal until 1968.

According to Gerhard Weinberg, the Portuguese felt vulnerable to a German attack and hesitated to take any actions during the war that might prompt an invasion.[1] However, spurred by its historically close ally, Brazil, the Portuguese government agreed to allow the British to use Portuguese air bases in the Azores in their campaign against German submarines. Portugal's tilt towards the Allies enabled groups such as the American Jewish Joint Distribution Committee (AJJDC) and the War Refugee Board to use Portugal as a base of operations for some of its European rescue efforts. Portugal was particularly important as a transit point out of Europe. Jews wanting to escape to Latin America had first to acquire a visa for Portugal, which would then allow them to apply for transit visas through Spain. A local Portuguese organization, the *Commisão Portugesa de Assistencia aos Judeos Refugiados* (CPAJR; Portugese Commission for Helping Jewish Refugees), headed by Dr. Augusto d'Esaguy, began working with the AJJDC soon after World War II broke out. According to Yehuda Bauer, between the summer of 1940 and early 1942, when the CPAJR was disbanded, 40,000 Jews entered Spain via Portugal. Once the CPAJR closed, the AJJDC worked closely with the Jewish Agency (JA) in Lisbon to help Jewish refugees in Portugal.[2] And as Heinrich Himmler and Adolf Eichmann played out their charade with Joel Brand and Va'ada in the spring and summer of 1944, the Germans suggested that they meet in Lisbon to discuss the "blood for trucks" deal.

This image of Portugal as a caring country willing to accept Jewish refugees is somewhat clouded by the story of Aristides de Sousa Mendes (1885–1954). Sousa Mendes was the son of a Portuguese supreme court justice and a descendant of *marranos*. Sousa Mendes was the consul general at Portugal's consulate in Bordeaux, France, when Germany invaded that country in the spring of 1940. His consulate was deluged by refugees requesting visas to escape the Nazi onslaught. According to Avraham Milgram, Portugal's policy towards Jewish refugees at that time was quite simple: They could be granted thirty-day tourist visas but would not be allowed to settle in the country.[3] But Jews were also placed on a list of undesirable foreigners who were to be denied entry to Portugal. Yet, despite such regulations, thousands of Jews did make their way into Portugal, with the help of individuals such as Sousa Mendes and organizations such as the AJJDC and CPAJR.

Sousa Mendes' decision to help Bordeaux's refugees came in the midst of discussions with a Belgian rabbi, Haim Kruger, who sought visas for himself and his family. At the

same time, he begged Sousa Mendes to help the Jewish refugees of Bordeaux, many of whom had gathered outside the consulate. Moved by the sight of these terrified Jews, Sousa Mendes agreed to issue visas to anyone who wanted them. He told his staff, who disagreed with his decision, that

> My government has denied all applications for visas for any refugees. But I cannot allow these people to die. Many are Jews and our constitution says that the religion, or politics, of a foreigner shall not be used to deny him refuge in Portugal. I have decided to follow this principle. I am going to issue a visa to anyone who asks for it—regardless of whether or not he can pay. I know that Mrs. de Sousa Mendes agrees with me. Even if I am dismissed, I can only act as a Christian, as my conscience tells me.[4]

Word of Sousa Mendes' decision quickly spread among Bordeaux's refugee community and he was flooded with requests for visas. He opened his home and the consulate to them. His nephew, Cesar Mendes Jr., described the scene at the consulate:

> Since May 10, 1940 until the occupation of the city, the dining-room, the drawing-room and the consul's offices were at the disposal of the refugees, dozens of them of both sexes, all ages, and mainly old and sick people. They were coming and going, there were pregnant women who did not feel well, there were people who had seen, powerless to defend themselves, their relatives die on the highways, killed by machines guns firing from planes. They slept on chairs, on the floor, on the rugs, there could never be any control again. Even the consul's offices were crowded with dozens of refugees who were exhausted, dead tired because they had waited for days and nights on the street, on the stairways and finally in the offices. They could not satisfy their needs, they did not eat nor drink for fear of losing

their places in the lines, what happened nevertheless caused some disturbances. Consequently, the refugees looked bad, they did not wash themselves, they did not shave. Most of them had nothing but the clothes they were wearing. The incidents took such proportions that it was imperative to ask the [French] army to preserve the order. In each room and in each office there was a soldier.... The sidewalks, the front door, the large stairways that led to the chancellery were crowded with hundreds of refugees who remained there night and day waiting their turn.... In the chancellery they worked all day long and part of the night. My uncle got ill, exhausted, and he had to lie down. He considered the pros and cons and decided to give all the facilities without distinction of nationalities, races or religion and bear all the consequences. He gets up impelled by a "divine power" (these were his own words) and gives orders to grant visas freely to everybody.[5]

The Portuguese foreign office was furious with Sousa Mendes and ordered his immediate return to Lisbon. It had already warned him earlier in the year about issuing visas to two Jewish refugee families. He was told that if he continued to disobey the foreign office's orders, he would face disciplinary action. In other words, Sousa Mendes knew before he began to issue visas to large numbers of Jewish refugees that his actions could end his career. To insure that he returned home promptly, the foreign office sent two "emissaries" to escort him back to Portugal. On the way, they stopped in Bayonne, France. Sousa Mendes asked his subordinate, the vice consul in Bayonne, what he was doing about the Jewish refugee problem. He said he was following government orders and doing nothing. Sousa Mendes reminded him that he was still his superior and began to issue visas to the refugees outside the Bayonne consular office. He spent the rest of the day issuing visas that carried these words: "The Portuguese government requests the Spanish government the courtesy of allowing the bearer to pass freely through Spain. He is a refugee from the European conflict en route to Portugal."[6]

The next day, Sousa Mendes and his party arrived in the Spanish town of Biarritz, where he discovered that Spanish border guards, acting on information from the Portuguese government, were not permitting refugees carrying visas issued by the Bordeaux consulate to cross the border. Though stories vary, Sousa Mendes convinced the Spanish border guards to let the Jewish refugees pass through the Spanish checkpoint.

When Sousa Mendes returned to Lisbon, the Portuguese foreign office dismissed him and deprived him of all of his government benefits. His appeal to the Salazar government fell on deaf ears; with no job or career, he now faced the prospect of caring for a wife and thirteen children. To survive, he sold his family estate. The U.S.-based Hebrew Sheltering and Immigrant Aid Society provided him with some support and helped two of his children emigrate to the United States. His wife died in 1948; six years later, Aristides de Sousa Mendes died, "forgotten, heartbroken, and impoverished."[7] In 1966, Yad Vashem declared him a Righteous Among the Nations. Twenty-two years later, Portugal rehabilitated his name and reputation. He regained his consular ranking in 1996, and later that year the government decided to "indemnify" his family.[8] After the war, he told Rabbi Kluger what had motivated him: "If thousands of Jews can suffer because of one Catholic [i.e., Hitler], surely it is permitted for one Catholic to suffer for so many Jews. I could not have acted otherwise, and I therefore accept all that has befallen me with love." On another occasion, Sousa Mendes said: "My desire is to be with God against man, rather that with man against God."[9]

Spain

Medieval Spain was home to one of Europe's most vibrant Jewish communities. This all began to change in the fourteenth and fifteenth centuries as a growing wave of anti-Semitic violence forced many Jews to convert to Christianity or leave Spain to survive. Some suggest there were as many as 300,000 *conversos* in Spain by the end of the fifteenth century. In 1492, Ferdinand and Isabella ordered all nonconverted Jews out of the country. Those who remained were forced to convert to Roman Catholicism. What remained was a community of *conversos*, Jewish converts to Roman Catholicism, who were derisively known as *marranos*. Some, by pain of death, tried to remain true to their faith, though the vast majority of Jews still in Spain either embraced Roman Catholicism or found haven in the growing number of Sephardic (Hebrew, *Sepharad*; Spain) Jewish communities in Europe and the Ottoman Empire.

Spain did not officially repeal the 1492 expulsion edict until 1968. The Spanish constitution of 1868 offered some protections for religious diversity, and, by the end of the nineteenth century, Jews began returning to Spain, though they were not allowed to develop an organized community. By the early 1930s, there were about 2,000 Jews in Spain, most of them refugees from the Balkan Wars of 1912–1913.[10] Spain lost most of its empire by the end of the nineteenth century and was neutral in World War I. Spain enjoyed something of a renaissance under King Alfonso XIII (r. 1886–1931), though the country was politically unstable. In 1923, *Capitaine Géneral* Miguel Primo de Rivera (1870–1930) overthrew the parliamentary government and created a military dictatorship. During the next seven years, Rivera transformed Spain along Italian Fascist lines. In 1924, the government issued a decree that gave Sephardic Jews living abroad the right to claim Spanish citizenship and live in Spain. The plight of the Sephardic Jews abroad became an important issue for the Spanish government during the Holocaust.

Rivera was driven from power in 1930, replaced by *Général* Dámaso Berenguer (1873–

1953). Berenguer was overthrown the following year, replaced by a democratic Second Republic under President Niceto Alcalá Zamora (1877–1949). Zamora instituted numerous reforms, including equal rights guarantees for non–Roman Catholics. The next few years saw Spain open its door to 4,000 Jews, many of them refugees from Nazi Germany. The republican experiment, though, fell prey to the hardships of the Depression and ensuing political conflicts with Spain's conservatives, and Zamora inability to institute land reform. In national elections in February 1936, the left-liberal *Frente Popular* (Popular Front), which barely won control of parliament, defeated the conservative National Front. That summer, General Francisco Franco (1892–1975), the army chief of staff, led a military uprising against the government of President Manuel Azaña (1880–1940). What followed was the Spanish Civil War (1936–1939), a tragic conflict complicated by the decisions of Hitler, Mussolini, and Stalin to use Spain as a battleground for their own ideological and military purposes.

The Republican forces, who backed Azaña's legally elected government, drew their support from democratic and leftist groups, as well as the navy; Franco's *Nacionales* (Nationalists) were backed by important army leaders, most of the Roman Catholic Church, monarchists, and the *Falange*, a Fascist organization founded and led by José Antonio Primo de Rivera (1903–1936), the son of Miguel Primo de Rivera. Germany and Italy actively supported the Nationalists under Franco, and Stalin gave modest support to the Loyalists.

Estimates are that from about 6,500 to 8,000 Jews were among the 35,000 foreign volunteers who joined the Republicans' International Brigades. For them, the civil war in Spain was an opportunity to fight against the Nationalists, who, with their strong ties to Italy and Germany, represented the anti-democratic, anti-Semitic spirit so prevalent in Central and Eastern Europe at the time. Almost 2,000 Spanish Jews fought for the Republicans, and another two hundred were murdered by Franco's forces. Though estimates vary considerably, between 500,000 and 1 million Spaniards died during the Spanish Civil War. Afterwards, Franco, who had thousands of Republicans executed in a post–civil war blood purge, outlawed all Jewish organizations in Spain.

The Spanish Civil War devastated Spain and affected Spanish policy throughout World War II. Franco declared neutrality when the war broke out in 1939 but remained loyal to the Nazi-Fascist cause and permitted the Germans to use Spain as an important center for intelligence operations. German submarines used Spanish ports for refueling and repair throughout the war. Spain was also a conduit for laundered German funds, some of it taken from Holocaust victims. The German conquests in the spring and summer of 1940 saw a new wave of refugees attempt to enter Spain. Though Spanish officials tried to stop the flood of refugees by tightening entry regulations, they allowed Jews with entry visas to Portugal to travel through Spain.

Between 1940 and 1942, 30,000 Jews entered Spain as temporary emigrants en route to other countries. This all changed in the fall of 1942, when the Vichy government, pressured by Germany, refused to grant travel visas for Jews trying to enter Spain. After the Wehrmacht occupied Vichy as the end of the year, a new wave of Jewish refugees began to enter Spain illegally. The Spanish government set up internment camps for those they did not send immediately back to France. Franco agreed not to turn the 7,000 to 7,500 Jews in these camps over to the Germans after the personal intervention of Winston Churchill and other Allied leaders. Franco decided to allow the interned Jews to remain temporarily in Spain as long as the Allies paid for their support. Spanish authorities allowed several

relief agencies to oversee the care of the Jewish refugees. Dr. Samuel Sequerra, who posed as a representative of the Portuguese Red Cross, worked distributing funds provided by the American Jewish Joint Distribution Committee. David Blickenstaff, a representative of the Quakers' American Friends Service Committee, worked in Spain as a representative of the International Red Cross because the Spanish government did not consider the Quakers a legitimate religious group. Blickenstaff also acquired most of his funds from the AJJDC. The Germans were extremely critical of Blickenstaff. In December 1944, the *Hamburger Fremdenblatt* published an article claiming that Blickenstaff's real name was Hirschfeld and that he helped send communist spies to the United States and North Africa.[11]

About 4,000 Sephardic Jews living in German–occupied Europe had special Spanish diplomatic protection. Some even had Spanish passports. In early 1943, the German foreign office told the Franco government that it had to repatriate these Jews by March 31. Madrid had until June 15 to repatriate the Sephardic Jews in Greece. Franco stipulated that he would allow only small groups of Sephardic Jews to enter Spain at a time and that they would be able to use Spain only as a transit point of departure to another country. Since this meant that entering Jews had to have visas to another country, only about a fifth of those eligible actually made it into Spain. Those who entered Spain were quickly transferred to United Nations Relief and Rehabilitation Administration (UNRRA) camps in Casablanca and Palestine. Franco made it particularly difficult for the 600 Sephardic Jews in Salonika to enter Spain despite initial promises to help them. When it became apparent to the Germans that Franco could not make up his mind what to do about this community, they transported those still left in Salonika to Bergen-Belsen to await his decision. Only 367 ultimately made it to Spain in early 1944. A key player in Spanish efforts to save Greece's Sephardic community was Sebastian de Romero Radigales, the Spanish consul general in Athens. He played an important role in saving hundreds of Jews.

Spanish diplomats were also involved in saving Hungarian Jews. In 1943, the Spanish government agreed to issue visas for five hundred Hungarian Jewish children and from fifty to seventy adults. Though the visas were never issued, Ángel Sanz-Briz (1910–1980), the head of the Spanish legation in Budapest, worked closely with Carl Lutz in issuing *Schutz* passes to Jews in the summer of 1944. He also set up eight Spanish safe houses for Jews in the Hungarian capital. He asked Giorgio Perlasca (1910–1992), an Italian who had recently become a Spanish citizen because he had fought with the Nationalists in the Spanish Civil War, to watch over the Spanish safe houses. On November 29, 1944, Sanz-Briz decided to leave Budapest because he was being pressured by the Szálasi government about Spain's refusal to grant it *de jure* recognition. He told Perlasca that if he left Budapest openly, the Hungarians would consider relations with Spain "officially interrupted" and would close the legation. He added that he had a German visa for Perlasca and could use it to enter Switzerland in a few days. "What," Perlasca wanted to know, "am I supposed to do now?"

The next day, Perlasca found out that the Szálasi government had learned of Sanz-Briz's departure and ordered raids on all Spanish safe houses. As Perlasca ran from house to house trying to stop the Arrow Cross roundups, he shouted an appeal to one Arrow Cross commander:

Hold everything! You're making a mistake. Sanz Briz has not fled, he has simply gone to Bern in order to communicate more easily

Schutzpass issued to Lili Katx in Budapest. USHMM Photo No. 71944, courtesy of Lena Kurtz Deutsch.

with Madrid, seeing as it is no longer possible to communicate from here. You're making a very serious mistake. Go ask the Ministry of Foreign Affairs! Sanz Briz informed two officials there of his departure. His trip involves a most important diplomatic mission!

Then, almost without noticing what he was saying, he exclaimed, with the utmost self-confidence, "Please inform yourselves at the Ministry of Foreign Affairs! Sanz Briz left a specific note naming me as his replacement during his absence! You are speaking with the official representative of Spain!" A few minutes later, the Arrow Cross commander, who had gone to call the ministry, returned, and said that the raids on the Spanish safe house "[were] to be suspended 'for a few days.'"[12]

For the next six weeks, Perlasca was able to convince the Hungarians and the Germans that he was Spain's new chargé d'affaires, even though he had no official diplomatic status or credentials. One morning after he had assumed his new "post," he went to Budapest's Jozsefvaros train station to search for two boys taken from one of the Spanish safe houses. He found the children waiting in the deportation line and hurried them to his black Buick, which flew a Spanish flag. As Perlasca pushed them into the back seat, a German soldier challenged him and ordered him to return the boys to the line. He told the soldier that his car was "foreign territory" and that if he touched the boys he would be violating "international law." The guard then tried to push his way past Perlasca to grab the boys. While they scuffled, an SS officer walked over and told the soldier to leave the boys alone. He then told Perlasca, "Go ahead and take them. Their time will come." Raoul Wallenburg, who was at the station and knew Perlasca, walked over to the Spanish "diplomat" and asked, "You realize who that was, don't you?" "No," Perlasca responded, "who was it?" "That," Wallenberg told him, "was Adolf Eichmann."[13]

This was not Perlasca's only run-in with armed troops. One day, an Arrow Cross unit broke into one of the Spanish safe houses and seized a group of Jews. They began marching them towards the Danube, where each would be shot in the back of the head and pushed in the river. Suddenly, Perlasca appeared and warned the unit's commander that he would wire his government in Madrid about this particular "violation of Spanish rights." Such a violation, Perlasca warned, could hurt Hungarian-Spanish relations as well as the officer's career. Hesitatingly, the commander turned over all the Jews to Perlasca, who returned them to the safe house.[14] Yad Vashem would later declare Giorgio Perlasco, Ángel Sanz-Briz, and Sebastian de Romero Radigales Righteous Among the Nations.

Sweden

There were from 6,000 to 7,000 Jews in Sweden prior to World War II, and they were well-integrated into Swedish society. Paul A. Levine wrote:

> While on the whole few Swedes responded sympathetically to Nazi persecution of Jews in the 1930s, significant sectors of Swedish society at least shared (again, similar to other liberal democracies) many of the Nazi movement's definitions and prejudices. Although Swedish "Nazi" parties remained small and relatively politically unimportant on the national level, they did manage to influence the overall debate and climate towards Jewish immigration.
>
> Although Swedish Nazism tended to be located in marginal and lower socio-economic groups, there is no question that many of the prejudices and negative attitudes towards Jews which made up Nazism's political program were shared on a cultural and ideological level by many in the socio-economic groups from which government officials, policy-makers and other elites were drawn.[15]

Sweden adopted a policy of neutrality in the mid-nineteenth century and continues to embrace it today. Sweden reaffirmed its neutrality when World War II broke out, but adopted a policy towards Germany that "was rather pro German."[16]

The Reich was extremely dependent on Swedish iron ore to help fuel its war economy. By 1940, Germany imported more than half its iron ore, 83 percent of it from Sweden. In fact, according to Adam Tooze, if Sweden had stopped shipping iron ore to the Reich when World War II broke out, it would have had a dramatic long-range impact on German arms production.[17] But Germany never had to worry about Sweden cutting off supplies; in April 1939, the Swedish prime minister, Per Hansson (1886–1946) assured Berlin that his country would continue to supply the Reich with all the iron ore it needed. In fairness to Hansson, his policies towards Germany were driven more by a desire to keep Sweden out of war at any cost rather than sympathy for Germany's wartime goals and policies.

Regardless, Hansson compromised Sweden's neutrality by selling valuable war materiél to the Reich. He also permitted the Wehrmacht to use the Swedish railway network to transport more than 2 million soldiers, many of them on leave from duty in Norway, to and from Germany. But the Wehrmacht used Sweden's railway network for more than transporting soldiers on leave; the Reich also used it to reinforce combat units in Norway and to supply German forces in the campaign against the Soviet Union. Klaus Wittman has concluded that "Sweden's support to the German war effort meant a considerable relief but was not of crucial importance."[18]

Sweden's willingness to open its markets and railways to Germany convinced Reich officials of the importance of drawing Sweden more closely into the Nazi orbit. Some German organizations, including Alfred Rosenberg's *Nordische Gesellschaft* (Nordic Society) and the *Auslandsorganisation der NSDAP* (Overseas Organization of the NSDAP) tried to influence public opinion and draw Sweden into a *Grossgermanien* (Greater Germany). Although the propaganda offensive had some impact on Swedish public opinion during the first two years of the war, it began to decline after 1942. In addition to trying to mold Swedish public opinion, Reich officials also tried to convince Swedish firms to adopt German Aryanization policies. By this time, the Swedish economy was closely tied to the German economy. German firms operating in Sweden Aryanized themselves and used spies to find out whether Jews worked for these firms. To protect themselves from the Aryanization policies, Jewish owners of firms that did business with Germany set up phony companies to hide their Jewish identity. The Germans intensified their Aryanization efforts after the conquest of Norway and Denmark, though it is difficult to determine how successful they were. There were also some major exceptions to these policies. In 1941, the German chamber of commerce asked officials in Berlin to permit the Stockholm department store, *NK (Nordiska Kompaniet)*, which was partly owned by Jews, to take part in a special furniture exhibit because of its solid reputation in Sweden and its strong economic ties to the Reich.

Swedish policies began to change in 1941 as Swedish officials became more and more concerned about Holocaust victims with ties to Sweden. News about the German atrocities in the Soviet Union were widely covered in the Swedish press. What specifically triggered this shift was news that Germany was about to deport Norwegian Jews to death camps in Poland. On December 3, 1942, Prime Minister Hansson asked Arvid Richert (1887–1981), the Swedish ambassador to Berlin, to inform the German foreign office that Sweden was "prepared to accept all remaining Jews in Norway should they be subject to removal."[19] Over the next month, Swedish officials met with their German counterparts to explore ways to save those Jews still in Norway.

In early 1943, Berlin informed Sweden and other Allied countries that they had until March 31 to repatriate their Jewish citizens. On January 26, Gösta Engzell, the head of the Swedish foreign office's legal department and the architect of its prewar immigration policies, said that all efforts should be made to help former Swedish citizens and their families who wanted to immigrate to Sweden. Stockholm later warned Berlin that if Germany harmed Swedish citizens, particularly after the March 31 deadline, such actions would seriously affect Swedish-German relations. This

Danish Jewish refugees flee to Sweden. USHMM Photo No. 62191, courtesy of Frihedsmuseet.

change in policy helped open the doors to nine hundred Norwegian Jews and, later that year, to the Jews in Denmark. After all the Danish Jews were safely in Sweden, Rabbi Stephen Wise (1874–1949), a prominent American Jewish leader, wired the Swedish Foreign Ministry that Sweden's dramatic efforts to save Denmark's Jews was not only a "victory for humanity" but marked a "turning point in [the] struggle for reestablishing immemorial spiritual values for common humanity." Sweden's help, he went on, was an act of "moral grandeur" that would insure Sweden an "honored place among [the] most cherished memories of eternal people."[20]

And though Sweden was certainly deserving of Wise's praise, it should also be remembered that before the war, Sweden had some of the most restrictive immigration policies in Europe, particularly when it came to Jews. In 1938, the Swedish government asked the German foreign office to find a way to identify German Jewish immigrants. Berlin hesitated to find a solution because it did not

want to stop the flow of Jews out of Germany. After considerable discussion, the German foreign office agreed to stamp all Jewish passports with a bold red J for *Juden*. By the time World War II broke out, only 2,000 Jewish refugees remained in Sweden out of a total population of 6 million. Swedish policy was driven by xenophobia and fears that refugees would take Swedish jobs. In 1938, officials in the *Socialstyrelsen* (National Board of Health and Welfare) asked whether "Swedish citizens who invited 'non-Aryans' as guests were in fact acting disloyally to their country."[21] And although there is no doubt that anti-Semitism played a role in Sweden's Jewish refugee policies before the war, it is difficult to gauge how deeply it affected such policies.

This all changed in late 1942 and, as the work of Swedish diplomats in Hungary would later show, Sweden's grandest moment during the Holocaust was still to come. Swedish officials in Budapest watched with horror as Adolf Eichmann began the mass deportation of Hungary's Jews in the spring of 1944. On

June 28 and 29, the Swedish legation in Budapest sent two appeals to King Gustav V (r. 1907–1950) asking him to do what he could to stop the deportations. The king immediately responded and asked Admiral Horthy to "take measures to save those who remain of that unfortunate people [the Jews]."[22] Horthy told Carl Ivan Danielsson, the head of the Swedish legation in Budapest, and Per Anger, his chargé d'affaires, that the Germans were responsible for the deportations and there was little he could do about them. But about a week later, Horthy ordered a halt to the transports, an action that set the stage for Raoul Wallenberg's mission to Hungary.

Sweden still had strong ties to Germany economically, but the Allies wanted to change that. The United States was particularly adamant, despite Swedish claims that its neutrality benefited the Allies. The United States government put it bluntly: If Sweden did not change its economic relations with Germany, shipments of oil to Sweden would be cut off. From the American perspective, Stockholm's continued ties with Germany "symbolized Sweden's mercenary attitude towards the war."[23] In the fall of 1943, Sweden signed a special agreement with the Allies stipulating that it would grant no further economic credits to Germany and its allies and would reduce its exports to Axis countries in return for the continued shipment of "basic rations" from the United States and Britain. Stockholm also pledged to halt the export of arms and iron ore to Germany and promised that anything it received from the Allies would not fall into German hands. Unfortunately, the Swedes found loopholes in these agreements and continued to ship war materiél to Germany, though certainly not on the same scale as it had through 1942.

This seemingly changed atmosphere led Salomon Adler-Rudel (1894–1975), a representative of the Jewish Agency, to approach the Swedish government about the prospect of saving more Jews in Europe. Though Adler Rudel proposed that Sweden help rescue 20,000 Jewish children, nothing ever came of this proposal. In fact, there is nothing to indicate that the Swedish government ever seriously considered it. On the other hand, in early 1945, the Swedish government did support a plan to rescue Scandinavian citizens, including Jews, still in camps in Greater Germany.

The idea was initially proposed by Niels Christian Ditleff (1881–1956), the Norwegian government-in-exile's representative in Stockholm. In late 1944, he presented the Swedish government with a draft proposal for such an undertaking, and suggested that Sweden should send a Red Cross delegation to Berlin to negotiate such a deal. Part of his plan included the rescue of Scandinavian Jews. In February 1945, the Swedish government asked the vice chairman of the Swedish Red Cross, Count Folke Bernadotte (1895–1948) (who had close ties to the Swedish royal family), to go to Berlin and talk with the Germans about such an operation. Bernadotte had his first meetings with *SS- Obergruppenfhrer und General der Polizei* Ernst Kaltenbrunner (1903–1946), the head of the SD, and *SS- Brigadefhrer* Walter Schellenberg (1910–1952), the head of RSHA's counterintelligence office. He later met with Foreign Minister Ribbentrop and, finally, with Heinrich Himmler. Hitler learned second-hand of the meetings and said that "one cannot accomplish anything with this sort of nonsense in a total war."[24] When Sweden agreed to cover the operation's expenses, Himmler hesitatingly approved the rescue proposal. He also agreed to transfer all Scandinavian prisoners to the Neuengamme concentration camp, outside Hamburg, which would facilitate the easy transfer of the prisoners to Sweden via Denmark.

The Swedish government approved the rescue plan on March 2 and a week later sent the "White Bus" team to Germany, where it set up operations at Friedrichsruh Castle, near Hamburg. The Swedish expedition was

Count Folke Bernadotte. USHMM Photo No. 80532, courtesy of National Archives and Records Administration, College Park.

made up of 250 Swedish army personnel who had removed their military patches and replaced them with Red Cross insignias. It had seventy-five vehicles, which included thirty-six ambulances, and enough supplies to sustain the team indefinitely while it was in Germany. At any given time it would be able to handle all the needs, medical and otherwise, of from 1,000 to 1,200 prisoners. The ambulances were painted white and prominently displayed red crosses. Since the White Bus team was entering an active and dangerous military area, all its vehicles prominently displayed Swedish flags.

Himmler never fulfilled his promise to concentrate all the Scandinavian prisoners in Neuengamme, which meant that the Swedish team had to pick up prisoners in camps throughout the Reich. The Swedish expedition, split in half, drove to Sachsenhausen and Theresienstadt for prisoners. By early April, most of the Scandinavian prisoners,

including 400 Jews, were in Neuengamme awaiting transfer to Sweden. At this point, half the Swedish rescue team returned home, replaced by Danes. Bernadotte now negotiated a new round of transfers with Himmler, which involved the evacuation of female prisoners from Ravensbrück.

After the war, Hugh Trevor-Roper, in the introduction to the memoirs of Felix Kersten, Himmler's masseur, claimed that Bernadotte had refused to agree to rescue Jews and did so only after being forced into a corner on the issue during a meeting with Himmler, Kersten, and Norbert Masur, a representative of the World Jewish Congress.[25] The reality was different. According to Masur, Bernadotte never attended the meeting with Himmler.[26] Sune Persson added that Bernadotte was sensitive to the plight of the Jews and was in contact with Jewish leaders in Stockholm as well as with Hillel Storch (1910–?), the Swedish representative of the World Jewish Congress. Storch said after the war that he thought Bernadotte was sensitive to the plight of the Jews in Germany and called him the driving force behind the White Bus operation. Bernadotte brought up the question of Jewish prisoners during his first meeting with Kaltenbrenner, who agreed to transfer 800 Jews to Neuengamme. When he failed to keep his promise, Bernadotte angrily demanded that the Swedish embassy in Berlin press Ribbentrop on the matter. The Swedish government suggested that Bernadotte address the matter during his meetings with Himmler in April.[27]

In fact, the principal reason that a White Bus team went to Theresienstadt in mid-April was to save Jews. They brought back 423 Jews from the Protectorate's concentration camp. Several days after the Theresienstadt team returned to Neuengamme, Bernadotte told Storch, who had been pressing him about Jews in Bergen-Belsen, that Himmler had recently promised him "not to evacuate the internment camps at the approach of the Allied armies, but to surrender them in good order—espe-

Ravensbrück prisoners liberated by Swedish White Bus team. USHMM Photo No. 10859, courtesy of Sigmund Baum.

cially Bergen Belsen, Buchenwald, and Theresienstadt, and the camps in southern Germany."[28] After Theresienstadt, the White Bus teams concentrated on Ravensbrück, where they dramatically saved 7,000 women, half of them Jews. Though estimates vary widely, Bernadotte's White Bus operation saved between 20,000 and 31,000 Scandinavians and others, including from 5,000 to 11,000 Jews. In a sad footnote to this remarkable effort, Count Bernadotte was assassinated in Jerusalem on September 17, 1948, by members of a radical Zionist group, the Stern Gang. He was in Jerusalem serving as the United Nations mediator for the Israeli-Palestinian conflict.

Switzerland

Switzerland, home to the International Committee of the Red Cross, the League of Nations, and, today, certain branches of the United Nations, has been a country traditionally associated with international peace and justice, an image that would be shattered during World War II. Switzerland has been neutral internationally since the end of the Napoleonic Wars. It reaffirmed this status at the beginning of World War I and World War II. Traditionally, the Swiss saw their country as a refuge for victims of political oppression from other parts of Europe. In 1943, one Roman Catholic newspaper proclaimed that Switzerland was the "European post of good Samaritans," a "great European sick bay," and a "world refuge for children."[29]

Yet Switzerland was not a secure haven for its 19,000 Jews, who were regarded by many Swiss as "alien to the nature of Switzerland." According to Jacques Picard, "the Swiss variety of hostility to the Jews blinded people to the dangers of racial antisemitism; even members of the elite and the authorities held this view covertly."[30] Such attitudes deeply affected Swiss immigration policy towards Jews in the 1930s. Swiss authorities searched for ways during this period to stem the tide of Jewish immigration into Switzerland. When the Germans suggested a red *J* on German passports, the Swiss hesitated, concerned about the impact of such a designation on Swiss Jews living in Germany. Even Heinrich Rothmund (1881–1961), the head of the Swiss national police and the architect of Swiss immigration policy in the late 1930s, was concerned about the legality of such a move. The Swiss finally agreed to the proposal in the fall of 1938. At the same time, they asked German border officials to do what they could to keep all Jews with the red *J* on their passports away from the Swiss border.

The Swiss government followed up on this decision with a decree on October 19, 1939, that ordered the expulsion of all refugees who entered Switzerland illegally. Some officials rigidly enforced these regulations, but others, in Basle-Land, Basle-Stadt, Neuchâtel, Schaffhausen, and Graubünden cantons, did a lot to help illegal refugees. But punishment could be severe for anyone who violated immigration regulations. In the spring of 1939,

Captain Paul Grüninger (1891–1972), the police chief in St. Gall (Sankt Gallen), was fired for altering the visas of more than 3,600 Jews to insure that they could stay in Switzerland. Despite warnings to stop his illegal activities, Grüninger continued and finally caught the eye the Gestapo, which reported his activities to the Swiss police in Bern. Grüninger lost his government benefits and spent the rest of his life in obscurity. In 1971, though, Yad Vashem declared him a Righteous Among the Nations. "My natural inclination to help had its roots in my deep Christian beliefs and in my concepts of the world," Grüninger explained during the ceremony in Jerusalem naming him a Righteous Gentile. "Although I got myself in difficulties in many cases, there was always a way to get through. I felt God's help in a powerful and abundant way."[31]

Swiss willingness to work with the Germans on the Jewish immigration matter was driven partly by fear of a German invasion. In the summer of 1940, the Wehrmacht did develop a plan for the invasion of Switzerland, *Operation Tannenbaum* (Operation Christmas Tree). Hitler never approved it, preferring to concentrate his energies first on Great Britain and later the Soviet Union. In reality, Germany did not need to conquer Switzerland to gain access to its resources and important rail links because the Swiss were so willing to sell them to the Reich. As a result, the Swiss franc became the common international currency for the Axis. And after the fall of France, the Reich hoped to use Switzerland, now surrounded by the Axis, as its "extended workbench." The Nazis' goal was to integrate "Switzerland's economic potential into Germany's own efforts to arm itself."[32] For the next two years, the Wehrmacht "was able to obtain large quantities of Swiss armaments at will and without difficulty."[33] However, Swiss arms imports to the Reich never amounted to more than 1 percent of German total arms production. In other areas, though, the Swiss provided the Germans from 3 to 10 percent of their total industrial output. Some of this was vital to the German war effort since 10 percent of the time fuses and their components for air defense weapons came from Switzerland. In turn, the Axis supplied Switzerland with coal, textiles, pig iron, non-ferrous metals, and machine parts.

Equally important, Swiss banks acted as an important conduit for gold reserves stolen from the various countries occupied by the Germans, and, presumably, gold stolen from Holocaust victims. In fact, almost four-fifths of Germany's shipments of gold went through Swiss banks. Between 1940 and 1945, the Reichsbank sold Swiss commercial banks 101.2 million francs ($23,226,367) of gold and 1,231 million francs ($283,011,490) to the Swiss National Bank (SNB). Estimates are that the Germans stole more than $620 million in gold during the war, not including that of victims. More than half this stolen gold was deposited in secret Swiss bank accounts. According to a U.S. Army intelligence report, "Switzerland constituted the principal foreign market for the large quantities of gold which Germany spent in financing her war effort."[34]

Switzerland's refugee policy changed with the ebb and flow of the war, though the Swiss consistently tried to restrict the inflow of Jews. On August 4, 1942, Dortmund issued a new directive that was driven by concern about a new influx of refugees entering the country. It stated that refugees entering Switzerland, "mainly Jews of various nationalities," must be sent back across the border for security and economic reasons. The only exceptions would be political refugees, who would not be sent back; otherwise, "persons who [had] fled purely on racial grounds, for example Jews, [could] not be considered political refugees." Yet during a meeting of police officials in Bern later that month, most agreed that Jews were political refugees; but for diplomatic and political reasons, they were to be treated as non-political refugees.[35] At another meeting in Zürich that month, Eduard von Steiger, the head of the Federal Department of Justice and Police, explained that his office had adopted this policy because "there was no [more] room in the Swiss 'lifeboat.'"[36] Later that year, after the Wehrmacht had occupied Vichy France, the Swiss tightened entry regulations for all refugees. About 295,000 refugees passed through Switzerland during World War II. Of this number, 51,129 were civilians without entry visas. More than 21,000 were Jews; all total, 30,000 Jews found refuge in Switzerland during the Holocaust.

Jews who made it to Switzerland and were allowed to settle there were cared for by private organizations such as the *Schweizerischer Israilitischer Gemendebund* (Swiss Federation of Jewish Communities), the *Verband Schweizerischer Jüdischer Fürsorgen* (Association of Swiss-Jewish Welfare Organizations), the *Schweigerische Flüchtlingshilfe* (Swiss Refugee Aid Joint Committee), the AJJDC, and the HICEM (acronym for the three Jewish aid organizations that joined together to make up HICEM-HIAS, Hebrew Immigrant Aid Society; JCA, Jewish Colonization Association; Emdirect). The Swiss government did little financially to help Jewish refugees. The AJJDC and the World Jewish Congress kept offices in Geneva and were able to obtain detailed information about the mass murders in Eastern Europe. On July 30, 1942, Eduard Schulte (1891–1966), a German businessman with close ties to prominent Nazi officials, met with Isidor Koppelman, an Austrian-born Swiss banker and an Allied spy. Schulte told Koppelman that he had just learned details about German plans to mass murder all the Jews of Europe. Koppelman shared this information with Dr. Gerhart Riegner (1911–2001), the WJC representative in Geneva, who passed it on to Sidney Silverman (1898–1968), a member of Britain's House of Commons.

Riegner also tried to convince Leland Harrison, the American minister to Switzerland,

Gerhart Moritz Riegner. USHMM Photo No. 17309, photographer: J. Kernen, courtesy of Linda Mittel.

to send this information on to Rabbi Stephen Wise via the State Department in Washington. Harrison, who considered the report "a wild rumor inspired by Jewish fears," passed it on to officials in Washington.[37] In the meantime, Silverman sent it separately to Wise. It read:

Received alarming report that in Führer's headquarters plan discussed and under consideration according to which all Jews in countries occupied or controlled Germany numbering 3 1/2–4 million should after deportation and concentration in east be exterminated at one blow to resolve once and for all the Jewish question in Europe. Action reported planned for autumn; methods under discussion including prussic acid [Zyklon B]. We transmit information with all necessary reservation as exactitude cannot be confirmed. Informant stated to have close con-

nections with highest German authorities and his reports generally speaking reliable.[38]

When Wise received the telegram, he arranged a meeting with Under Secretary of State Sumner Welles (1892–1961), who asked that Wise not make the contents public until the information could be confirmed.

One of the sources of confirmation was a report written by Jan Karski (1914–2000), a Polish diplomat sent by the Polish government-in-exile to Poland in the fall of 1942 to report on conditions there. But before he left, he met with Jewish leaders in London; they asked him to give them an update on the fate of the Jews. Karski visited what remained of the Warsaw ghetto twice and also Bełżec. After he returned to London in November, he met with Foreign Secretary Anthony Eden (1897–1977), Sydney Silverman, and other prominent government and Jewish leaders. Later, in Washington, he met with President Franklin Roosevelt, Secretary of State Cordell Hull (1871–1955), Supreme Court Justice Felix Frankfurter (1882–1965), and Rabbi Stephen Wise. His detailed report, which was published in 1944 as the *Story of a Secret State,* provided specific details about the Final Solution. At the beginning of their meeting, Justice Frankfurter asked Karksi whether he knew he was Jewish. After listening to graphic details about Karski's visit to Poland, Frankfurter told him, "I am unable to believe you." Offended, Jan Ciechanowski (1887–?), Poland's ambassador to the United States, said angrily that Karski had the full backing of his government and was telling the truth. Frankfurter replied, "I did not say this young man is lying. I said I am unable to believe him. There is a difference."[39] On November 25, the Polish government-in-exile gave a copy of Karski's report to A. L. Easterman, the political secretary of the WJC. The following day, Easterman and Silverman met with Richard Law (1901–1980), the British under secretary of state for foreign affairs, to discuss the report. Four days later, Stephen Wise held news conferences in New York and Washington. The press reaction was mixed. The headline for the *New York Herald Tribune* read: "Wise Says Hitler Has Ordered 4,000,000 Jews Slain in 1942."[40] Other newspapers discounted Wise's warnings, claiming they were nothing more than another example of Jewish hysteria. The *Christian Century* said the information was "unpleasantly reminiscent of the 'cadaver factory' lie which was one of the propaganda triumphs of the First World War."[41]

Public opinion in Switzerland, though, was much more easily swayed by growing reports of Nazi atrocities and it played an important role in forcing a change in the country's refugee policy, particularly after Rothmund issued his August 4 decree. What followed was an orchestrated public outcry against government refugee policies led by religious leaders, labor unions, various liberal and leftist groups, and relief organizations. Gradually, the government began to ease its refugee policies; by the end of 1943, 30,000 new civilian and military refugees had entered Switzerland. Some Jews were also given asylum, though some were still turned back at the border. But it was not until July 12, 1944, that the Swiss government decided to permit those facing physical harm to enter the country.

This change in Swiss refugee policy allowed Swiss diplomats to make efforts to help save the Jews in Hungary in 1944. The Swiss government had been involved in Jewish refugee issues in Hungary since 1941, when it agreed to represent British interests through the Swiss legation in Budapest. In the summer of 1944, for example, the Swiss government agreed to sponsor 7,000 Jews who had received British approval to emigrate to Palestine. This more liberal approach to refugee issues was driven in part by a Swiss press campaign orchestrated by George Mantello (1901–1992), a Transylvanian-born Jewish diplomat working with the Salvadorian con-

sulate in Geneva. The driving force behind Swiss action in Budapest in the late spring and early summer of 1944 was Carl Lutz, the head of the foreign interests section of the Swiss legation. Lutz worked with Moshe Krausz, the Jewish Agency representative in the Hungarian capital, and other diplomats. Together, they were able to secure thousands of collective passports for Hungarian Jews. Lutz opened some Swiss safe houses to protect these Jews while they awaited Hungarian emigration approval.

Switzerland's belated shift on refugee matters coincided with similar changes in its economic ties with the Reich. As a neutral, Switzerland maintained diplomatic and economic ties with the Allies and the Axis; after the conquest of France in 1940 and Italy's subsequent entrance into the war, however, its ties with the Western powers were considerably reduced. This changed with the Allied conquest of southern Italy in 1943. Earlier that year, the American and British governments had issued the first of their "Gold Warnings" to remind neutral and belligerents not to buy gold from Germany because much of it was stolen. The Allies intensified their efforts to convince Switzerland to reduce its economic ties with Germany in an attempt to force it to join with "freedom loving countries" in the war against the Reich.[42]

In 1944, the British and the Americans created Operation Safehaven to monitor the economic activities of neutrals, particularly Switzerland. An American intelligence report concluded that Swiss "aid to the enemy in the banking field was clearly beyond the obligations under which a neutral must continue to trade with a belligerent, aid solely dictated by the profit motive of the Swiss banks."[43] But it was not until early 1945 that the Americans convinced the Swiss to freeze German assets, stop the German use of its railroads, and reduce Swiss trade with the Third Reich. Paul B. Miller noted that "the Allies' goal was to ensure that Switzerland would not become a

Swiss Red Cross workers feed Jews liberated from Theresienstadt, 1945. USHMM Photo No. 98439, photographer: Walter Scheiwiller; courtesy of Stadtarchiv (Vadiana) St. Gallen.

'financial hideout' (in the words of Henry Morgenthau, Jr., the U.S. treasury secretary) for the next generation of Nazi warriors."[44]

And it was this, Switzerland's financial ties to the Reich, that has so tarnished the country's reputation. According to Jacques Picard, the view of Switzerland as "a threatened companion in misfortune, determined to resist and support humanitarian relief, has been tempered by a growing understanding that Switzerland, a small country, deeply entwined in Europe, benefited from the business possibilities of war."[45]

After the war, the question of the unclaimed assets of Holocaust victims in secret Swiss bank accounts, insurance policies, and holdings in Swiss businesses became an important issue for survivors, their children,

and Jewish organizations. There was also the question of stolen Jewish assets and gold, some of it extracted from the mouths of gassed victims. In 1946, the United States and Switzerland signed the Washington Agreement, which required Switzerland to put 250 million Swiss francs ($58.1 million) in an Allied "gold pool" in compensation for looted German gold in Swiss banks. These funds would be used to reimburse countries whose treasuries had been looted by the Germans. The Allies suspected at the time that from $1.8 to $3.5 billion in Nazi gold was still in Swiss banks. Switzerland was also required to liquidate German assets in Switzerland and split them with the Allies. In return, the Allies agreed to unfreeze Swiss assets and to take Switzerland off the Allied trade blacklist.

Given the vast sums that Switzerland made during the war from its economic ties with Germany, its total contribution to the Allied rebuilding effort in Europe was $86 million. Why did Switzerland get off so easily? In addition to worrying about the use of Swiss funds to revive a Nazi movement in Europe, the Western powers were concerned about keeping Switzerland in the Allied camp during the early stages of the cold war. Switzerland was viewed as a key player in rebuilding Europe, and the Allies did not want Switzerland, which was already doing a lot of business with the Soviet Union, to strengthen its economic ties with the Kremlin.[46]

In the 1950s and 1960s, Swiss banks signed secret accords with Hungary and Poland that compensated them modestly for the unidentified accounts of Hungarians and Poles who had died during the war. Some of the funds used to make these payments came from "dormant accounts of presumed Holocaust victims."[47] This pattern of deceit and trickery was also used when it came to considering claims of Holocaust victims or their families. The powerful and secretive Swiss Bankers Association (SBA) used delusion and questions about adequate documentation to reject Holocaust-era claims. In the end, the Swiss banks paid few of the thousands of claims filed by Holocaust victims and their families. Until the mid-1990s, the banks claimed they were able to locate only about $2.5 million in stolen assets.

This began to change in 1994 when Rabbi Israel Singer, the secretary general of the World Jewish Congress (WJC), read *The Swiss Account,* a novel by Paul Erdman (1932–2007). Rabbi Singer decided it was time to revisit the issue of Holocaust assets in Swiss banks and started an investigation into what had happened to funds deposited by Jews in Swiss accounts between 1933–1945. In 1995, Edgar Bronfman (1929–), the president of the WJC, went to Switzerland to discuss this question with prominent Swiss bankers. Later that year, the JA in Israel demanded that the Swiss return all the Holocaust-era funds to survivors and their families. Within a month, Swiss bankers claimed they had suddenly found $34 million in assets from the war, some of it possibly from accounts of Holocaust victims.

In 1996, Senator Alfonse D'Amato (1937–) initiated a congressional investigation into the Swiss "gold" questions. The same year, a special committee chaired by the former U.S. Federal Reserve chairman Paul Volcker (1927–) and representatives of the SBA, the World Jewish Restitutions Association, and the WJC met to resolve the mystery of Jewish assets in Swiss banks. In late 1996, the Swiss parliament created a special Independent Commission of Experts Switzerland–Second World War (ICE) to look into all of Switzerland's dealings with the Germans during the Holocaust.

In the midst of these developments, Carlo Jagmetti, the Swiss ambassador to the United States, warned the Swiss government in a cable that the discussions with Jewish groups was "a war which Switzerland must conduct on the foreign and domestic front, and must win." He added, "If you thought that Jewish circles and Senator D'Amato could be quickly satisfied, and you want to do a deal to get this solved, that is one way of looking at it."

Ambassador Jagmetti warned, though, that the matter of Jewish Holocaust funds in Swiss banks was "going to be a long affair" that would "trigger difficult soul-searching."[48]

Yet even before Jagmetti's comments became public, the president of the Swiss Federation, Pascal Delamuraz (1936–1998), claimed that the WJC was using "extortion and blackmail" in its talks with the SBA. Delamuraz said that a recent report by Thomas Borer (1957–), the Swiss representative in the WJC-SBA talks, indicated "a formidable political will to destabilize and compromise Switzerland" and a desire in Washington and London to "demolish the Swiss financial center."[49]

In reality, at least according to the WJC, the Volcker commission discussions had been cordial, particularly after the Swiss suggested the creation of a special Holocaust fund (from $230 to $300 million) to compensate Holocaust victims and their families for lost Swiss funds. Delamuraz's comments stunned American Jewish leaders, who threatened a boycott of Swiss banks. Ambassador Jagmetti quickly apologized and resigned his post. President Delamuraz, who was about to end his term in office, did likewise, and then became Switzerland's economics minister.

In early January 1997, Christoph Meili (1968–), a night watchman at the Union Bank of Switzerland (UBS) in Zürich, discovered two cartloads of ledgers and documents about to be shredded. Some of the files appeared to be Holocaust-related. Meili gave them to the Israeli Cultural Center (ICC) in Zürich, who turned them over to the police. Once the story of Meili's discovery broke in the press, Swiss officials began a preliminary investigation into Meili's possible violation of Switzerland's laws on banking secrecy. Meili lost his job and, fearing prosecution, fled to the United States, which granted him and his family political asylum. UBS later admitted that the documents might have had some ties to Jewish Holocaust claims against Swiss banks.

In late January 1997, the Swiss government and the SBA agreed to set up a special fund for Holocaust victims in keeping with "the humanitarian traditions of Switzerland." Initially, the fund was to be worth $70 million, though it was later increased to $192 million. The United States, Great Britain, and France responded by announcing that they would freeze the remaining $68 million (1997 value: $4 billion) in gold bars looted by the Germans and being held in the Federal Reserve Bank in New York and in the Bank of England—funds that possibly could have been used to compensate Holocaust victims for assets stolen during the war. Within a month, the Swiss government announced that it would set up a $4.7 billion Swiss Foundation for Solidarity to aid victims of the Holocaust and other genocides. Yet the fund, which would come from a reevaluation and sale of Swiss gold reserves, had to be approved by the Swiss parliament and put to a vote in a public referendum. Though approved by parliament, the referendum was narrowly defeated at the polls on September 22, 2002.

Several months before the Swiss banks announced the creation of its special fund for Holocaust victims, Stuart E. Eizenstat (1943–), the U.S. undersecretary of commerce, issued a report prepared by a special commission appointed by President Bill Clinton (1946–) to look into the question of assets stolen by the Germans during World War II. The Eizenstat report strongly criticized the Truman administration, and particularly the State Department, for unfreezing Swiss assets after World War II. This, the report claimed, prevented the United States government from forcing the Swiss to be more forthcoming about their Nazi gold and other assets. It added that the Swiss knew the gold Germany deposited in their banks during the war was stolen from other countries, though they were probably not aware that some of it was taken directly from Holocaust victims. The U.S. report estimated that there was about $5 billion in looted German gold in Swiss banks. It was equally critical, though less exacting, of Portugal, Spain, Sweden, and Turkey, and their relations with Nazi Germany.

On August 13, 1998, Switzerland's Credit Suisse and UBS announced that they had reached a settlement of $1.25 billion with the WJC and attorneys involved in a class-action suit against Swiss banks. But three years after this settlement was reached, survivors had received nothing from the settlement. In 1999, 100,000 Holocaust survivors had received single payments of $500 to $1,200 from a separate Swiss humanitarian fund. The question of distribution of the $1.25 billion would be decided in a Brooklyn, New York, federal court, which was handling the class-action suit against the Swiss banks. Judge Edward R. Korman (1942–), the chief judge of the United States District Court for the Eastern District of New York, would oversee what was to become a controversial legal struggle for the distribution of these assets.

In 2000, Judge Korman appointed Judah Gribetz (1929–), a prominent New York attorney and Jewish community leader, special master to develop a plan for distribution of the Swiss "gold" settlement. Gribetz recommended that $800 million be set aside for individuals and their families who held Holocaust-era deposits in Swiss banks. He estimated that there were from 832,000 to 960,000 Jewish Holocaust survivors still alive as well as large numbers of non-Jewish victims. The remaining $450 million would be set aside for four other classes of Holocaust victims. The Looted Assets Class would receive $100 million, though Gribetz qualified this by stating that payments would be based on proof of need. Another $90 million would be distributed to Jewish Holocaust survivors, and $10 million to other victims of Nazi persecution such as Roma, Jehovah's Witnesses, the handicapped, and homosexuals. In addition, Gribetz recommended that two classes of slave laborers receive payments from the Swiss gold fund. Those in Slave Labor Class I who were compensated by the German *Stiftung Erinnerung Verantwortung und Zukunft* (Foundation Remembrance, Responsibility and the Future) would be given $1,000.[50] Slave Labor Class II included individuals who had worked as slave laborers for a "Swiss entity." Their payments would range from $500 to $1,000.

Finally, the special master recommended that some funds be made available to a Refugee Class of individuals who either had been allowed to settle in Switzerland and were mistreated or had been turned away at the border. Gribetz referred to the Independent Commission of Experts' 1999 report, *Switzerland and Refugees in the Nazi Era*, which stated that 50,000 civilian refugees had been allowed to settle in Switzerland during the war. Another 4,000 had been expelled or forbidden to enter the country.[51]

Judge Korman quickly approved Gribetz's plan. He had earlier created a Claims Resolution Tribunal (CRT) to deal with the claims under the Swiss Gold Settlement. The CRT initially thought that it would receive 85,000 claims. However, by August 2001, only 30,000 individuals had filed claims. Of this number, only 5,000 were directly linked to the 21,000 Holocaust-era accounts published earlier by the Swiss banks. By 2002, the court had paid $10 million to a small number of claimants. Though there were still thousands of claims to adjudicate, it was probable that hundreds of millions of dollars would be left over in the Swiss gold account. In 2004, the special master filed a report recommending that 75 percent of the surplus funds go to needy Jews in the former Soviet Union. The State of Israel quickly filed a complaint with the court about Gribetz's recommendations, as did a number of Holocaust survivor groups, who thought that the surplus funds should be more evenly distributed. By 2007, the CRT had paid out $382.9 million for those with claims to the funds in Holocaust-era Swiss bank accounts. In addition, over 170,000 slave laborers had received payments of $1,450 each. The court paid out $10 million to claimants in the Refugee Class and another $205 million to needy survivors, mainly in the former Soviet Union and its Eastern Bloc countries.[52]

In the midst of these developments, the Independent Commission of Experts in Switzerland released its final report about Switzerland's role in World War II. It explained that Switzerland survived by maintaining close ties with the Axis, surrounded as it was by Germany, Italy, and France. Although this detailed and scholarly study expressed some understanding of Switzerland's vulnerable position, it did question whether the country had crossed a line "between unavoidable concessions and international cooperation" in its ties with the Reich. After the war, the Swiss, with their economy strong and central to European reconstruction, chose to view their role from this same positive perspective. The report was most critical of wartime Switzerland's refugee policies, particularly when it came to Jews and Roma; these policies were in "stark contrast to the image of Switzerland as a humanitarian and open country," the report noted. "Foreign money, of course, protected by the principle of client protection and banking secrecy, was very welcome; desperate people attempting to flee from the threat of deprivation and persecution by the Nazi regime were often refused entry."

When it came to refugees, the report went on, "neutral Switzerland not only failed to live up to its own standards, but also violated fundamental humanitarian principles."[53] The ICE's study was also critical of Switzerland's ties to the German economy and the willingness of Swiss firms to adapt to Germany's racial and political standards. Swiss banks, the report went on, were more concerned about the deposit of Axis funds in their banks than the origins of some of these assets. The report concluded that Switzerland "often hid behind its neutrality and this same neutrality was improperly invoked to justify not only decisions made in all kinds of spheres, but also inaction on the part of the state." In the end, Switzerland was able to keep out of the war primarily because of the "determined fighting by the Allies and good fortune."[54]

Turkey

Turkey arose from the ashes of the Ottoman Empire at the end of World War I. Jews enjoyed a tolerable life in the Ottoman Empire; some even supported the Young Turks during the 1908 revolution leading to the founding of modern Turkey. Sadly, before and during World War I, a story persisted, particularly in

some British circles, that the 1908 revolution had really been a Jewish-Masonic plot against the sultan. With the breakup of the Ottoman Empire at the end of World War I, Kemal Atatürk (1881–1938), the father of modern Turkey, worked to transform his new country into a secular state free of the complexities of a traditionally rigid Muslim state. Jews and Christians were to have equal rights with Muslims, though Atatürk's restrictions against religious education hurt the Jews severely. As a result, Jewish cultural life declined significantly during the interwar period. More than 81,000 Jews lived in Turkey in 1927, though this figure declined to about 77,000 by the end of World War II.

In the fall of 1939, Turkey signed a treaty of mutual support with Britain and France that granted Turkey military credits and a loan of £16 million ($3.45 million). In return, Turkey was to "collaborate effectively" with both countries, but was not required to become involved in a war with the Soviet Union. The conquest of France in 1940 changed the dynamics of Turkey's ties with the Allies and in 1941 it signed a friendship treaty with Germany. Turkish leaders, though, were determined to do everything they could to keep Turkey out of the war. Allied and Axis pressure on Turkey to join one side or the other intensified in 1943. President Ismet İnönü (1884–1973), fearful of the Soviet Union, broke diplomatic ties with Germany in August 1944 and declared war on the Reich the following February.[55]

Turkey became a center for various Jewish groups trying to save Jews, particularly from the Balkans. The most important organization was the Jewish Agency (JA), which operated out of Istanbul, Ankara, Izmir, and Edirne. By 1942, Istanbul became the "center of all the Jewish Agency operations in Europe" and the "Bridge to Palestine" for some of Europe's Jews.[56] A year later, the JA set up its Joint Rescue Committee (JRC) in Turkey. Its operations, unfortunately, were handicapped because the

Turks refused to recognize it legally, which meant that the JRC could not transfer foreign currency in and out of the country. Regardless, the JRC was able to act as a funnel for funds and information to Jewish communities in Eastern Europe; it also provided escape routes to Palestine. From March to December 1944, the JRC was legally able to send 5,250 Jewish refugees to Palestine. Estimates are that the JRC helped more than 10,000 Jewish refugees escape from Europe during the Holocaust.

According to Stanford Shaw, 16,474 Jews used Turkey as their entrance way to Palestine, and another 75,000 "unofficial" refugees also passed through Turkey during the war. The JA in Turkey was able to send £523,547 ($129,912) in aid to Jews in Europe. American relief organizations such as the AJJDC distributed another $215,000 in aid to Jewish refugees. One of the people actively involved in the distribution of these funds in Poland was Oskar Schindler. By late 1942, Schindler had already gained a reputation as someone who treated his Jewish workers well. This prompted Va'ada (Relief and Rescue Committee, Budapest) and the JA to try to recruit him to smuggle letters and money into the Kraków ghetto and later the Płaszów concentration camp to help buy needed food, medicine, and other goods on the black market for Jews. Schindler's initial contact with the JA was Dr. Rudi Sedlacek, a Viennese dentist and Abwehr agent.[57] According to Joel Brand, Sedlacek "was an intellectual and was ashamed of the colleagues [in Abwehr] with whom he worked. He wished to appear better than they, and in conversation with our people he always stressed the contempt he felt for the other Abwehr agents."[58]

By the fall of 1942, Va'ada was dealing with a flood of Jews from Poland, and it desperately needed funds to help them. Bandi Grosz helped establish contact with Zionist organizations in Istanbul, particularly the JA, which decided to create a "courier service" to work with its Joint Rescue Committee.[59] Grosz helped the JRC establish important contacts with Abwehr in Budapest. According to Brand, "these people [Abwehr] not only restored our contacts with the neutral countries, but also established channels of communication with the Jewish communities in Poland, in Czechoslovakia, in Germany proper, and in the other German-occupied territories."[60]

Such contacts were an integral part of the Jewish Agency's efforts in Turkey to do whatever it could to help the Jews in Nazi-occupied Europe.[61] One of the JRC's principal goals was to maintain contact with the Jewish communities of Central and Eastern Europe. Moshe Sharett (1894–1965), a future foreign minister and prime minister of Israel who had spent some time during the war observing JRC operations, called its operations in Istanbul "a peep hole to the other side."[62] Soon after the JRC had opened its office in Istanbul, its office staff began to write hundreds of letters to Jews in occupied Eastern Europe asking them about conditions there and what it could do to help them. Initially, these letters went through the regular Turkish postal system, though later the JRC used couriers to carry them into Nazi-held territory. Often the couriers were Turkish truck drivers and businessmen, though some were diplomats; even representatives of the papal legate to Ankara (the Turkish capital), Angela Roncalli, the future Pope John XXIII (r. 1958–1963), worked with the JRC. When the JRC learned of the mass murders in the Nazi concentration and death camps, the JRC's staff sent letters of condolence to those who survived in hopes they would continue to supply the JRC with information about conditions there. They supplied this information to the British government in hopes that London would lower its restrictions on the number of Jews permitted to enter Palestine. But couriers such as Schindler did more than carry letters in and out of Nazi territory; they also brought food, clothing, and money with them, which the JRC hoped would be used to help purchase more food and clothing or to bribe German officials to help Jews.[63]

Oskar Schindler with his Jewish workers at Emalia in Kraków. Photo: USHMM.

The JRC was particularly interested in recruiting German and Hungarian spies as couriers in hopes that these double agents could provide aid to Jews in Germany. And one of the spies they tried to recruit was Oskar Schindler.[64] It did not take Dr. Sedlacek long to size up Schindler and determine that he would be a willing courier for Va'ada and later the JRC. To test him, Schindler was given 50,000 RM ($11,905) as well as some letters and other messages to distribute to JRC representatives in Kraków. When Schindler did exactly as he was told, the JRC knew they could trust him.[65]

During the next year, Sedlacek made six or seven trips to Kraków to meet with Schindler. Sedlacek brought money to help Jews in Kraków's Płaszów concentration camp as well as personal letters for them from Palestine. Dr. Resző Kasztner stated in his 1946 *Der Bericht des Jüdischen Rettungskomitees aus Budapest, 1942–1945* (A Report on the Jewish Rescue Committee in Budapest, 1942–1945) that Sedlacek brought Schindler "several hundred thousand Reichsmarks" during his three trips to Kraków."[66] Schindler, in turn, gave the money to Dr. Chaim Hilfstein, a Jewish physician at Schindler's Kraków subcamp, Emalia. Dr. Hilfstein later told Brand "that this money was always punctually delivered" by Schindler to Jewish representatives in the concentration camp.[67]

Once the JRC had determined that Schindler was honest and trustworthy, they invited him to Budapest to give them information on the plight of the Jews in occupied Poland. The JRC's leadership saw Schindler as a leading German industrialist in Kraków and an important contact person.[68] He met with "Schmuel" (Shmuel Springmann) and "Israel" (Resző Kasztner) of the JRC in November 1943 in the Hotel Hungaria in Budapest. Afterwards, Springmann and Kasztner prepared a detailed report of this meeting, *Bekenntnisse des Herrn X* (The Confessions of Mr. X). Oskar Schindler was Mr. X. The authors stated that they had met with Schindler to try "to discover the truth." They said they tried to write down the conversation exactly as it had taken place and added no editorial comments. They described "Mr. X" as a "tall, blond man with broad shoulders" who was forty to fifty years old. What they wanted from Schindler, who came "from the other side," was details about what was really happening to Jews in the General Government. "What does this terrible world look like behind the walls, viewed by one who at best could only be called an 'objective' spectator?" There was a third person in the room, a *Schaliach* (Hebrew, emissary or courier), who gave Schindler a large package that contained "clothing, special brands of cigarettes and toiletry items." According to Kasztner and Springmann, these items were to be handed over to the SS leader [Amon Göth (1908–1946), the monstrous, corrupt commandant of Płaszów] on "whose good will the lives of 20,000 Jews currently depend[ed]."[69]

Schindler began the meeting by handing Springmann and Kasztner several letters from inmates in his camp for friends and relatives in Palestine. After a brief discussion about the difficulty of getting goods to Jewish prisoners in Poland, they asked Schindler about conditions there. Schindler was quite open about "the magnitude of the tragedy," which he described as a "chapter of the political mistakes the Germans committed in Europe." He added that "crushing the skulls of infants with a boot is not proper military behavior."[70]

The JRC representatives then wanted to know how many Jews were still in Poland. He replied that there were about seventeen camps in Poland containing between 220,000 and 250,000 Jews. In addition, he said that there were just as many Jews in hiding, living on Aryan papers, or working for the partisans. Springmann and Kasztner then wanted to know whether there was a universal order to annihilate Jews. If that was so, why were so many still alive? On the other hand, if there was no such order, why had the Germans already killed so many Jews? Schindler replied that he did not think such an order existed: "I rather assume that each SS leader wanted to outperform the others with annihilation numbers. None of these wanted to risk his career."[71] But, Schindler added, these SS men did not act on their own. "A higher authority most likely gave them the order to destroy dangerous or useless Jews. They executed this order with the brutality they had already been used to at home."[72] Schindler then described these SS leaders as "primitive people with bestial instincts" who had served previously in internment camps such as Dachau, where they had become "dull, bestialized."[73]

Springmann and Kasztner had difficulty believing that mid-level SS leaders could initiate such crimes without orders from above. Schindler said that probably someone from above had "ordered the annihilation," though he doubted that the goal was "total annihilation."[74] If this were so, the two JRC representatives wondered, did the Jews still alive in Poland have a chance to survive the war? Schindler told them that he was sure that those still alive would survive the war; he mentioned Himmler's decision several weeks earlier to halt the murderous assault against Jewish workers in forced-labor situations throughout occupied Poland. The "tendency is obvious" Schindler noted. "One wants to preserve the Jewish work force." He said that during the past few months, the "smaller camps were liquidated and able Jewish workers from the province were concentrated around industrial centers."[75]

Kastzner and Springmann were skeptical, and wanted to know whether Himmler's new order would be respected. Schindler replied: "[S]omewhat." He went on to explain that some SS leaders had difficulty breaking the habit of shooting from ten to one hundred Jews each day. He said that the situation regarding the Jews who worked in military factories was somewhat different from that of Jews in the ghettos since they, to a certain degree, were protected by the military inspectors of each factory.[76]

How many Jews, they asked, had been killed since the outbreak of the war? Schindler said this was difficult to answer and the only figure he could give them was one that he got from the SS—from 4 to 4.5 million. Schindler stated that he thought these figures were exaggerated because the SS seemed to take pride in these numbers.[77] Given all this, Springmann and Kasztner wondered what could be done to help the Jews still alive in German-occupied territory. Schindler said that there were three possibilities: "to make money available, [to] send packages with food and medicine, and try to influence the S.S. leaders."[78]

Schindler noted that little of the money sent by Istanbul through Budapest ever reached Kraków. He assured both men that he did not mean to imply that people in Kraków were unappreciative of the Jewish Agency's funds; it was, in fact, "a great blessing for the people." They had bought flour with the money and on several occasions from 3,000 to 4,000 extra loaves of bread. This not only meant more food rations for the inmates but also forced the black market price of bread to drop from 130 złotys ($40.65) to 40 or 50 złotys ($12.50 to $15.62) a loaf. Schindler and others were also able to buy eighty pairs of shoes on the black market for barefoot workers.[79]

Springmann and Kasztner also wanted to know whether any children were still alive in the General Government: "Only a very few," Schindler said. "They have indeed been exterminated."[80] He estimated that about 90 percent of the children up to fourteen years had been "shot or gassed." Some children, though, were still alive "by accident." Others had survived because they had received "special protection" or were "the children of the police or the Jewish OD men [jüdischer Ordungsdienst]."[81] He knew, for example, of one Jew "who was the protege of an inspector" in Płaszów's business office who was able to save his two children because their father was an OD man. "Thus only the children who belong to the Jewish police are in the Jewish camps."[82]

Schindler said that the fate of the elderly was the same as that for children, particularly those older than fifty. Older inmates did everything they could to look younger, including dying their hair and wearing makeup. But most of those still alive in the camps were between ages fourteen and fifty.[83] Schindler was sensitive about the question of age and survival. He said after the war began that he had hired the elderly parents of some of his workers "even though many of them were not able to work."[84] In 1942 and 1943, he employed from two hundred to three hundred

"new workers" even though he had no work for them. He paid the SS 5 złotys ($1.56) a day for these workers because he "had to maintain the reputation that my firm did not have enough laborers." He estimated that it cost him 720,000 złotys ($225,000) to maintain this group of unemployable workers throughout the course of the war.[85]

Kasztner and Springmann then wanted to know the location of those Jews still alive in Poland. Schindler said they were mainly in Auschwitz. He estimated that there were about 80,000 Jews in Auschwitz, but did not know how many of the hundreds of thousands who had been deported there were still alive. His figures were remarkably accurate. Auschwitz records indicate that on December 31, 1943, there were 85,298 (55,785 men and 29,513 women) prisoners in Auschwitz I, II (Birkenau), and III (Buna-Monowitz). Springmann and Kasztner told Schindler that they had heard that Auschwitz was an "extermination camp." Schindler said that was possible, particularly for the "elderly and children." He added that he had also heard that Jews were "gassed and burned there." The Germans, he thought, had "perfected a scientific system there in order to avoid more Katyns," a reference to the Soviet murder and burial of 15,000 Polish officers in Katyn forest in the spring of 1940.[86]

Both men also wanted to know the prospect of escapes. Schindler said this would be very difficult since the camps were "very strictly guarded." He explained that the Jewish OD did not want "to endanger their own positions" and, to prevent escapes, called roll two or three times a day to make sure every inmate was accounted for. A more serious problem was the Jewish "Konfidenten," or informers, who were the "most dangerous." Schindler noted that he had to deal with five levels of police authority in the General Government, the Gestapo, the German police, the Polish police, the Ukrainian militia, and the Jewish OD men, and that they could not all be bribed.[87] He explained that the only Jews able to escape from Poland were those living outside the camps. He knew, for example, of one instance in which eighteen extremely wealthy Jews bribed the driver of a *Deutsche Arbeitsfront* (German Labor Front) truck to take them to the Slovak border. The driver hid them inside the double floor of the truck; but when the vehicle was stopped at the border and searched, the Jews were discovered and detained. Sixteen were executed on the spot and two others were returned to Poland. Schindler said that the two Jews who survived were informers. And he knew of hundreds of similar cases of escape attempts.[88]

He added that you could rescue some people, but only individuals or groups of two or three, and then only after a great deal of preparation. If this was so, the two JRC representatives asked, did the Jews in the General Government have any money they could use to help themselves or could they "help themselves in other ways?" Schindler explained that some Jews had hidden a lot of money. He noted, for example, that during a recent body search at Emalia, which was made under threat of death, the SS discovered "6 large laundry baskets with gold, dollars, diamonds, gold watches, zloty, etc."[89] These goods were seized without receipts and taken to Göth's house, where a third of it "turned to dust," meaning it disappeared into Göth's pockets. The rest was turned over to the general SS camp fund. But Schindler admitted that only a few Jews possessed "hidden wealth," and it was often hidden in places now inaccessible to them. So it was important for the Jewish Agency to supply financial resources to help Jews in Płaszów and Emalia.[90] Springmann and Kasztner then wanted to know whether it was possible to influence SS leaders in Poland to help Jews. Schindler never really answered this question.

Kasztner and Springmann's ended their lengthy meeting with Schindler by asking him questions about the Warsaw ghetto uprising in 1943. He said that he had heard that a Jewish self-defense organization had been created that had "let wagons with cement derail, built themselves bunkers, bought guns from Italian and German soldiers, and executed suspicious Jews that might betray them."[91] He estimated that from 120,000 to 150,000 Jews were still living in the ghetto when the uprising took place. The uprising lasted from two to three weeks and was a "heroic chapter in [the history] of Polish Jewry," Schindler noted. "In their desperation they wanted to salvage the honor of the Polish Jews, when everything else already seemed hopeless."[92] He told Springmann and Kasztner that 50,000 Jews escaped from the ghetto along the canals of the Vistula River during the fighting. He did not know what happened to those who escaped. He had heard, though, that there were Jewish girls who had fired at tanks using 0.8-caliber revolvers. Tens of thousand of Jews died in the uprising, and the ghetto burned to the ground, along with "an immense amount of valuables." He noted that an international commission [Polish Red Cross] on its way to Katyn to investigate the Soviet massacre there reported that it could hear the shootings in the distance and see the fires from the ghetto.[93] Needless to say, Oskar's account of the uprising is not completely accurate, though it does show that he continued to have good contacts with the SS and the Wehrmacht.

At some point in the lengthy discussion about ways to help the Jews in Poland, Springmann and Kasztner asked Schindler about the prospect of going to Turkey to work with the Jewish Agency to help inform "prominent people about the situation of the Jews in Poland and the terrible consequences of the SS policies (liquidation of ghettos, opening of death camps) [on them]."[94] In particular, they mentioned a possible meeting with the American ambassador to Turkey, Lawrence Steinhardt (1892–1950).[95] Schindler never made it to Turkey.

Despite the importance of Turkey to Jewish rescue operations during the Holocaust, only one Turk, Selahâttin Ülkümen (1914–2003), was declared Righteous Among the Nations by Yad Vashem. Ülkümen was the Turkish consul on the Greek island of Rhodes, which the Germans occupied in the spring of 1941. In the summer of 1944, the Gestapo began to deport the island's 1,700 Jews to Auschwitz. Ülkümen went to the island's military commander, *Generalleutnant* Ulrich Kleeman (1892–1963), and asked him to free 15 Jews who were Turkish citizens and their families. When asked whether the family members were Turkish citizens, Ülkümen lied and said they were. When Kleeman resisted, Ülkümen told him that his refusal to free the Turkish Jews could cause an "international incident." He added that in Turkey people do not "differentiate between citizens who were Jewish, Christian, or Muslim."[96] Though Kleeman allowed the 15 Jews and their families to remain free on the island, they were constantly harassed. In addition, the Germans bombed the Turkish legation in retaliation, killing Ülkümen's pregnant wife, Mihrinissa, among others. In early January 1945, Kleeman released the Jews to Ülkümen on the eve of a visit by the International Red Cross. The Turkish Jews were taken in small boats for the short trip to Turkey and safety.

The Vatican

The role of the Vatican, and particularly of Pope Pius XII (r. 1939–1958), is one of the most controversial issues in Holocaust studies. In part, it centers on the relationship of the Roman Catholic Church and its ties with Benito Mussolini's Italy. In 1870, Pope Pius IX (r. 1846–1878) refused to recognize the Italian occupation of Rome and for the next fifty-nine years church officials considered themselves prisoners in the Vatican. This all changed in 1929 when Mussolini and Pope Pius XI (r. 1922–1939) signed the Lateran Accords, completing a decade-long trend of church-state reconciliation. Some conservative Roman Catholics had long been fascinated with Mussolini's blend of Italian nationalism and anticommunism, and they supported Mussolini's rise to power. Soon after Mussolini became premier in 1922, he made gestures that slowly restored a Roman Catholic presence in the public schools and enhanced the status of priests. The Lateran Accords resolved the lingering financial losses of the Roman Catholic Church and also recognized Vatican independence. Most important, it did away with much of prewar Italy's antichurch legislation and restored most of the pre-1860 (the initial year of Italian independence) power of the Roman Catholic Church throughout Italian society. According to R. A. Webster, the Lateran Accords made Fascist Italy "a confessional state unique among the great powers of contemporary Europe."[97]

Although the Roman Catholic Church in Italy gained a great deal from its new ties with Mussolini's government, it paid a moral price for this new status. A. C. Jemolo argued that, in many ways, the Roman Catholic Church came out of these agreements a loser, since its ties with Mussolini's Fascist government, with its militant tendencies and core anticlericalism, would in the future hinder the Vatican's abilities to speak out more firmly against the growing atrocities of the Holocaust.[98]

Yet the Vatican remained enough of a moral force within Italy to cause Mussolini some concern when he initiated his anti-Jewish campaigns in 1938. The responsibility for any moral stands taken by the Vatican and the Roman Catholic Church on the plight of Jews in predominantly Roman Catholic countries throughout Europe during the Holocaust rested on the shoulders of two men, Pope Pius XI and Pope Pius XII. Pius XI had voiced some concerns over rising anti-Semitism in Germany, and he spoke in general terms about this same trend in Europe. In 1937, Pius XI attacked German anti-Semitism in his encyclical *Mit brennender Sorge* (With Burning

Concern). *Mit brennender Sorge,* which was smuggled into Germany and read during Palm Sunday services that year, severely criticized Hitler's racist mythology and his paganistic attacks against the church. The Nazis severely criticized *Mit brennender Sorge,* calling it "a call to battle against the Reich."[99]

The following year, the pope condemned Mussolini's *Manifesto of the Racial Scientists* and called on Roman Catholics to "defy it." He told a group of young people that the church clearly understood "racism and exaggerated nationalism as creating barriers between men and men, people and people, populations and populations."[100] Just before his death in early 1939, Pius XI was preparing a new encyclical, *Humani Generis Unitas* (The Unity of the Human Race), attacking racism and anti-Semitism. Considered by many scholars to be weak and compromised by traditional Roman Catholic attitudes about the refusal of most Jews to convert to Christianity, it nevertheless would have been an important papal document condemning racism and anti-Semitism. It reached the elderly pope only weeks before his death. His successor, Pius XII, decided not to release it because he was trying to improve Vatican relations with Nazi Germany.

Pope Pius XII assumed the papal throne on March 2, 1939. He is without question the most controversial pope in modern church history. He served as *Papal Nuncio* to Weimar Germany from 1920–1929. He was appointed a cardinal in 1929 and soon became the Vatican's secretary of state, a position that gave him an important role in negotiating the Concordat with Nazi Germany. Yet, like the Italian Lateran Accords, the Concordat was a fateful compromise that would rob the Roman Catholic Church of its moral autonomy. According to Klaus Epstein, "[a]ll that remained of once mighty political Catholicism was a gaping vacuum—the natural consequence of a half—decade of impotence, opportunism, and insufficient devotion to democracy and parliamentary government."[101]

Yet it is important to put all this in some historical context. First of all, Pius XII was not an anti-Semite. He was, though, the eternal diplomat who was primarily concerned with the fate of the church in Europe. The future pope was also a product of the Anglo-French era of appeasement that ignored the evils of Nazism and instead chose to deal with Adolf Hitler as a reasonable statesman. He was also concerned about the impact of any stance on the status of the Vatican, first under Mussolini and later under the Germans. Another issue was communism. José M. Sánchez disagreed with Saul Friedländer's assertion that Pius XII's greatest fear was the "Bolshevization" of Europe and hoped that if Germany could ever repair its ties with the Allies, it could join them in a common stand against the atheistic Soviet Union.[102] The pope was also afraid to take a position that might alienate Roman Catholics in Europe or cause them harm. In a wartime interview with the Vatican's newspaper, *L'Osservatore Romano* (The Observer of Rome), Pius XII said in response to a question about whether he would protest the extermination of the Jews, "Dear friend, do not forget that millions of Catholics serve in the German armies. Shall I bring them into conflicts of conscience."[103]

Pope Pius XII's failure to exert his vast moral authority more aggressively throughout a Europe looking for just such a beacon compounded the Holocaust tragedy. In the end, Pius XII was morally neutralized by the desire to protect and preserve his church in the face of the strong anti-Christian tendencies at play throughout Nazi and Fascist Europe.

Given all this, would the voices of Pius XI and Pius XII have had any impact on the growing mistreatment of Jews and others during the Holocaust? Of course. A strong, consistent stance against Nazi and Fascist mistreatment of Jews, Roma, and other groups could have created a moral base for other leaders in the free world to speak out against these atrocities. Susan Zuccotti has noted that Pius XII was the leader of millions of Catholics, who had been taught to look to him above all others for spiritual and moral guidance. He was also esteemed throughout the world as a symbol and spokesman for ethical principles. His obligations during the Second World War to guide and instruct the masses exceeded those of politicians, statesmen, diplomats, soldiers, philanthropists, and lower-level Christian pastors and priests. As 6 million Jews were being torn from their homes, crammed into trains, deported to unknown destinations, and shot before open ditches or gassed and burned in factories of death, men and women of all faiths and persuasions looked to him for a word, a sign, an indication of how to respond. As some 6,746 Jews from Italy were being shipped north to share the fate of the others, the pope's own countrymen similarly looked to him for guidance. They found little or nothing.[104]

The Vatican's failure to mount a strong moral campaign against the mistreatment of Jews and other minorities in Greater Germany, Italy, and other parts of Nazi-controlled Europe did not mean that it did nothing to help Jews, nor did it try to keep individual Roman Catholics from rendering aid and moral support to Holocaust victims. Yet Pius XII seldom mentioned Jews specifically in his writings and speeches. Instead, he chose to deal with the mistreatment of Jews and others obliquely. To some, the only Jews the Vatican seemed interested in helping were those who had converted to Roman Catholicism.

On the other hand, the memoirs and personal testimonies of Holocaust survivors are replete with tales of aid by individual Roman Catholics, priests, and nuns. Ona Simiate (1899–1970), a librarian at the University of Vilnius, was so distressed by the mistreatment of Jews that she could not sleep: "I was ashamed not to be Jewish myself. I knew how dangerous it would be [to help Jews], but it didn't matter. A force stronger than myself was at work."[105] She got permission to enter the Vilna ghetto after explaining that she needed to recover books checked out by former Jewish students. In reality, once in the ghetto, she began to retrieve as many books as she could from the Yivo Institute, hiding them outside the ghetto. She also brought food, medicines, and other things to friends there. Ona also helped hide Jews who escaped from the ghetto. She hid ten-year-old Tanya Sterntal in her apartment, caring for her "like the mother of an unfortunate child."[106] The Germans, who had been watching Ona for some time, arrested her in 1944 and brutally tortured her, rupturing her spine. Friends at the university were able to bribe the police, which saved her from execution. She was sent to Dachau and then later to France. She refused to accept recognition for her work with Jews in Vilna, but she was eventually declared a Righteous Among the Nations by Yad Vashem. Tanya Sterntal said in her statement to Yad Vashem that Ona was one of those special individuals "who reach out to give but are incapable of taking." To Ona, the real heroes of the Holocaust were the Jews. Abba Kovner said that "if there are ten Righteous Among the Nations, Ona Simiate is certainly to be counted among them."[107]

In Lyon, France, Father Pierre Chaillet (1900–1972), a Jesuit priest, was actively involved in the resistance movement as the publisher of the underground newspaper *Cahiers du Témiognage Chrétien* (Letters of Christian Evidence). He also found time to wander the streets of Lyon looking for orphaned Jewish children. One day he found four Jewish children hiding in a cave, "half-dead and trembling with fear."[108] He took them to a local monastery where several hundred Jewish children were already in hiding. He rescued other Jewish children from police stations and the streets. He got them false identity papers and developed a network of families who agreed to hide them. In September 1942, the Vichy police demanded that Father Chaillet turn over 120 Jewish children for deportation. He refused and was arrested.

In the meantime, the children in question were hidden in the homes of local villagers. Father Chaillet's activities were supported by Pierre Marie Gerlier (1880–1965), the cardinal archbishop of Lyon, and his adviser on Jewish affairs, Abbé Alexandre Glasburg (1902–1981), a Ukrainian Jewish convert to Roman Catholicism. Abbé Glasburg was credited with, among other things, saving 180 children from deportation in the Vénissieux detention camp. After the Holocaust, he said in an interview, "I am not a hero. I accomplished no heroic deeds. The two thousand Jews I helped rescue . . . this was a drop in the ocean. Six million Jews were killed. We could have rescued many more if we'd had more money."[109]

In Poland today, they talk of a Polish Oskar Schindler. Her name is Irena Sendlerowa (1910–). Irena was a member of Żegota, the code name for the Polish underground organization, *Rada Pomocy Żydon* (Council for the Aid to Jews). Żegota drew its members from a number of Roman Catholic and Jewish organizations "who could not remain indifferent to the terrible barbarity of the treatment of the Jews, our fellow citizens."[110] Founded in 1942, Żegota helped save 4,000 Jews by providing them with phony identity papers and funds to help them live as Christian Poles in the General Government. The *Żydowski Komitet Narodowy* (Jewish National Committee), which worked closely with *ŻOB*, the Jewish Fighting Organization, protected another 5,600 Jews. The *Yidisher Arbeter Bund* (Jewish Labor Bund) hid another 1,500 Jews. Overall, these three organizations worked to care for more than a third of the 28,000 Jews in hiding outside of the ghetto in Warsaw, and another 1,000 elsewhere in the General Government. It was illegal for Poles to hide Jews, and if they were caught it meant the death penalty. It is estimated that 700 of the 200,000 Poles who helped to hide Jews during the Holocaust were caught and executed by the Germans.

Irena Sendlerowa was responsible for hiding Jewish children in Warsaw. She placed most of

Irena Sendlerowa. Photo by Mariusz Kubik.

them in foster homes or hid them in Roman Catholic convents and orphanages. She was working for the city of Warsaw's Social Welfare Department when war broke out. When she saw the atrocities, she was shocked. She used forged documents to care for impoverished Jews, and eventually had about 3,000 Jews under her care, most of whom were forced into the Warsaw ghetto when it opened in the fall of 1940. She worked closely with Julian Grobelny ("Trojan"; 1893–1944), the driving force behind Żegota. Riddled with tuberculosis and hunted by the Gestapo, "Trojan" was "always thinking of others, never of himself, particularly when it came to saving Jewish children."[111] Irena, who went by the code name "Jolanta," also worked closely with Irena Schutz, who obtained illegal documents from the city of Warsaw's Sanitary-Epidemiological Office, which gave both women daily access to the ghetto. "Yolanta" always wore a Star of David when she was in the ghetto, not only to blend in but also "to show solidarity with these people."[112]

One day, she stumbled upon Dr. Janusz Korczak leading his children from his orphanage to the ghetto's *Umschlagplatz*. She was deeply traumatized by what she saw: "I could hardly walk home and when I got there I was in such a state of nervous shock that my mother had to call the doctor."[113] Irena realized now that

Żegota had to do everything possible to save Jews. Children were smuggled out of the ghetto through underground tunnels. They were then taken briefly to special "safe" apartments, and then to Polish families, many of whom were "poor and crowded into small flats" with "children of their own." These families

> not only gave considerable assistance, devoting themselves selflessly and ardently to this work, but also gave their warm hearts to the children whose fate it was to live through hell on earth. And it was often in these crowded basements and attic rooms ... that a hounded child of the ghetto had its frozen heart thawed by the caresses of the work-worn hand of a working woman and its eyes, filled with horror on its arrival, began to look at the world differently.[114]

Żegota provided medical care for the hidden children and sometimes was able to provide the families who cared for them with funds to help pay for food and clothing. Most of the children required special medical care because they were malnourished, dirty, and sick. Some were in such bad shape that they had to be taken to special Roman Catholic shelters or convents such as the Family of St. Mary, where they received special care. Żegota also worked with ŻOB to save adults, particularly those involved in daily work details outside the ghetto. Żegota gave ŻOB the addresses of safe houses for adults who escaped from the ghetto. Once in the safe houses, the escapees were given forged Aryan papers and then integrated into the local Polish population.

Żegota was able to find work for some of the female escapees with Polish families. But they had to fit in perfectly and behave like good Catholics. Żegota taught them the Ten Commandments, Roman Catholic prayers, and gave them Roman Catholic *Missals* and medallions. One young Jewish woman was sent to work as a maid for a Polish policeman in Otwock. She looked "every inch an Aryan"

and did an excellent job for the family. They were very complimentary of her work but faulted her for going "to church too often." Irena got in touch with the young woman and advised her to be less "religious."

The Gestapo arrested Irena in the fall of 1943 and sent her to Pawiak, a tsarist-built prison used by the Gestapo, where she was severely beaten and interrogated. Julian Grobelny somehow managed to bribe the Gestapo officer in charge of her case, who released her. Later that day, notices appeared throughout Warsaw listing those just executed for treason. Irena's name was on the list. Once the Gestapo learned what had happened, they looked for her. Irena escaped the German dragnet and went into hiding. When her husband was put into a concentration camp, she "threw all of [her] energy into ... work for the Council of Aid to the Jews [Żegota]."[115]

Efforts by Roman Catholics such as Irena Sendlerowa and other Christians to save Jews during the Holocaust were not readily acknowledged after the war. On the other hand, Pope Pius XII was widely hailed for the "immense good and the incomparable charity that [his] Holiness extended generously to the Jews of Italy and especially the children, women and elderly of the communities of Rome."[116] The World Jewish Congress so appreciated his efforts that it donated $20,000 to papal charities. And when he died in 1958, Golda Meier (1898–1978), the Israeli foreign minister, sent the following message to the Vatican: "We share in the grief of humanity. . . . When fearful martyrdom came to our people in the decade of Nazi terror, the voice of the pope was raised for the victims. The life of our times was enriched by a voice speaking out on the great moral truths above the tumult of daily conflict. We mourn a great servant of peace."[117] And during a performance of the New York Philharmonic Orchestra soon after the pope's death, Leonard Bernstein asked "for a moment of silence for the passing of a very great man, Pope Pius XII."[118]

This glowing image of Pope Pius XII was tarnished in the early 1960s when Rolf Hochhuth's controversial play, *Der Stellvertreter: Ein christliches Trauerspiel* (The Deputy: A Christian Tragedy), criticized Pius XII's refusal to speak out during the Holocaust. Recently, Ion Mihai Pacepa, a former Romanian intelligence officer, has charged that *The Deputy* was actually part of a larger KGB plot to discredit Pius XII and the Roman Catholic Church.[119] Hochhuth (1931–) dedicated his play to Father Maximilian Kolbe (1894–1941) and Provost Bernhard Lichtenberg (1875–1943). Kolbe was a Franciscan priest from Łódź who operated a religious center near Warsaw. He was arrested on several occasions by the Germans for helping refugees. But most of Father Kolbe's fame came from his willingness to volunteer to die in place of another prisoner in Auschwitz. In 1971, questions were raised about his beatification after it was discovered that Kolbe was an anti-Semite who accepted the fictitious *Protocols of the Elders of Zion* as authentic. He wrote about the "perverse Jewish-Masonic press " and claimed that the *Talmud* "breathes hatred against Christ and Christians." He also thought that the Holocaust was God's punishment for Jewish sins.[120] In 1982, Pope John II canonized him as a "martyr of charity."

On the other hand, Bernhard Lichtenberg was truly a heroic figure whom Yad Vashem recently declared a Righteous Among the Nations. A staunch critic of the Nazis as rector and later provost of St. Hedwig's Cathedral in Berlin, Lichtenberg became involved in efforts to stop the persecution of Jews soon after Hitler took power. In 1933, Reinhard Heydrich tried unsuccessfully to bring charges against him. When Lichtenberg later protested the inhuman conditions for Jews in the Esterwegen concentration camp, Theodor Eicke, the SS inspector for the camp, demanded that Lichtenberg be placed in "protective detention." After *Kristallnacht*, Lichtenberg addressed his congregation: "[W]e know what happened yesterday. We do not know what tomorrow holds. However, we have experienced what happened today. Outside, the synagogue burns. That is also the house of God."[121]

He now began daily public prayers for Jews and Christians. In a debate with the Roman Catholic theologian Karl Adam (1876–1966) in 1940, Lichtenberg said that the "idea of the *Volksgemeinschaft* (people's community) was unchristian, and the 'Holy Spirit goes wherever it wishes, irrespective of the *Volk*.'"[122] A year later, the Gestapo arrested Lichtenberg and charged him with attacks against the state and the Nazi Party. When they searched Lichtenberg's apartment, Gestapo agents found a copy of a sermon he had planned to deliver. Among other things, it said that "National Socialist theology is incompatible with the teaching and commands of the Catholic Church."[123]

He was convicted and sentenced to two years in prison. His bishop, Konrad von Preysing (1880–1950), reported Lichtenberg's conviction to the Vatican, but Pius XII refused to intervene. The best Preysing could do was to convince the Gestapo to allow Lichtenberg to regain his freedoms after he had completed his sentence in return for a promise not to preach until the war was over. Lichtenberg refused. After his release, he was sent to a work camp, beaten, and then sent to Dachau. He died en route.

One of the principal characters in Hochhuth's work is *SS- Obersturmbannführer* Kurt Gerstein, who wrote an early report on the gassing operations at Bełżec. Evidently unaware of Gerstein's role in delivering Zyklon B gas to Auschwitz and other camps, Hochhuth intended Gerstein to be a moral counterpoint to Pius XII.

In her study of prominent men and women in the "dark times" of the first half of the twentieth century, Hannah Arendt tells a story she heard about Pope John XXIII (r. 1958–1963). After he had read Hochhuth's play, he was asked what could be done against it: "Whereupon he allegedly replied, 'Do against it? What can you do against the truth?'"[124] This story is presumably apocryphal, but it does provide a contrasting link between the roles of Pope Pius XII and Angelo Roncalli, the future Pope John XXIII during the Holocaust. Angelo Roncalli served as *Papal Nuncio* to Turkey and Greece from 1934 to 1944. There he played an active role in providing thousands of baptismal certificates for Jewish refugees. Soon after he assumed the papal throne in 1958, he began to look for ways to heal the terrible rift between the Roman Catholic Church and the Jews—a wound deepened by centuries of Christian anti-Semitism and charges of Roman Catholic Church inaction during the Holocaust.

On the Good Friday before he assumed the papal throne, Roncalli told Cardinal Augustin Bea (1881–1968) of Germany to delete the offensive phrase "*perfidia Judaica* (faithless Jews)" from the Tridentine Mass. The pope later asked Cardinal Bea, who was head of the Secretariat for Promoting Christian Unity, to prepare a Vatican II declaration that would condemn anti-Semitism and acknowledge the importance of Judaism to Christianity. John XXIII was supported by Germany's Roman Catholic bishops, who released a pastoral letter asking for atonement for the Holocaust on the eve of what would be one of the most revolutionary gatherings in the history of the Roman Catholic Church, the Second Ecumenical Council of the Vatican (1962–1965), or Vatican II. Once it became known that the question of the church's historic relations with the Jews would be discussed at Vatican II, some conservative Roman Catholic theologians and several Arab states voiced opposition to statements about Jews. The latter claimed it might "jeopardize the status of their Catholic subjects."[125] After numerous drafts and considerable debate, Vatican II approved *Nostra Aetate* (In Our Time), the *Declaration on the Relation of the Church to Non-Christian Religions* in 1965. Sadly, John XXIII died before it was finished. *Nostrae Aetate,* which was released by John XXIII's successor, Pope Paul VI (r.

1963–1978), acknowledged the special relationship between Christianity and Judaism, particularly the commonality of their spiritual beliefs. And although it acknowledged that the death of Jesus Christ could not be blamed on the Jews, it did say that the "Jewish authorities and those who followed their lead pressed for the death of Christ." It also decried "hatred, persecution, [and] displays of anti-Semitism, directed against Jews at any time or anyone."[126]

But it was John Paul II (r. 1978–2005) who did the most to improve Roman Catholic relations with the world's Jews. John Paul II "took a giant step in drastically changing the traditional church theology about Jews in the most direct way," noted Dr. Mordecai Paldiel, the head of the Righteous Gentile Department at Yad Vashem. "He displayed an unashamed fondness, if not more, for the Jewish people, and left a mark on the Catholic Church which his successors will find hard to disregard."[127] Born Karol Józef Wojtyła (1920–2005) in Wadowice, Poland, the future pope had several Jewish friends as a boy. One, Jerzy ("Jurek") Kluger, remembered an incident that underscored the future's pope's attitude towards Jews. He had just learned that he and "Lolek" (Karol) had successfully passed the entry exams for the Marcin Wadowska high school. Excited, he dashed over to St. Mary's Church, where "Lolek" was serving as a altar boy. As the service ended, one of the elderly parishioners asked "Jurek" whether he was the son of Wilhelm Kluger, the leader of the town's Jewish community. As the woman walked away in a huff, "Lolek" appeared and asked, "What's up?" Jurek told him what has just happened and said he thought the woman "was surprised to see a Jew in a church." "'Why?' Lolek laughed, 'aren't we all God's children?'"[128]

Karol Wojtła entered Kraków's Jagiellonian University in 1938, where he developed his passion for theater and music. He lived in Kraków throughout the war and was deeply affected by the horror he saw there.

In 1942, he began his theological studies at an underground seminary founded by his spiritual mentor, Archbishop Stefan Sapieha (1881–1951). A gifted scholar and educator, Karol rose quickly through the Polish church's ranks, becoming auxiliary bishop of Kraków in 1958 and cardinal eleven years later. Poland was controlled by a harsh communist dictatorship during this period, and Karol Wojtła was one of its quietest but harshest critics. During the early days of the Solidarity movement in 1979, he spoke out in support of the workers' movement.

From the moment he became pope, John Paul II began to build bridges of friendship and love with the world's Jews. In 1979, he visited Auschwitz, though this was not his first visit there. He kneeled and prayed at the Wall of Death outside Barracks 11, and at a mass later in the day called Auschwitz the "Golgotha of the contemporary world."[129] Seven years later, he was the first pope ever to visit a synagogue. His sermon at the Synagogue of Rome on April 13, 1986, underscored the deep religious and cultural bonds that tied Jews to Christians. Jews, he said, "had been called by God 'with an irrevocable calling'" and "Catholics could not think about their faith without thinking about Judaism." Jews, he went on, were not only "our dearly beloved brothers," but "our elder brothers." He reiterated the church's condemnation of anti-Semitism and charges that Jews were responsible for the death of Christ. He ended by reciting the 118th Psalm in Hebrew.[130]

Much of the goodwill from this visit disappeared after he received Kurt Waldheim (1918–2007), the president of Austria and former secretary general of the United Nations, in 1987. A year earlier, charges were made during Waldheim's election campaign for the Austrian presidency that he had lied about his role as a Wehrmacht intelligence officer in Yugoslavia during World War II, and that he had knowledge of war crimes. An international committee of scholars appointed by the Austrian government later confirmed these charges. John Paul later made Waldheim a knight in the Order of Pius IX. The pope was also criticized for beatifying Edith Stein (1891–1942), a Jewish convert to Roman Catholicism and a Carmelite nun who was murdered in Auschwitz because she had been born a Jew. The pope responded to this criticism in a sermon in Cologne in 1987. He celebrated Edith Stein as "a servant of God and a daughter of Israel." She was killed, he added, because she was a Jew and a Roman Catholic. He shared with the congregation Edith Stein's own words about her conversion. She had given up her faith when she was a young teenager but said that her "return to God made [her] feel Jewish again." She was, the pope concluded, "a great daughter of Israel."[131] She was canonized as Saint Teresa Benedicta of the Cross in 1998.

John Paul II continued efforts to heal the historic rift between the Roman Catholic Church and the Jews throughout the rest of his papacy. In 1993, the Vatican established diplomatic ties with Israel; in 1998, it released *We Remember: A Reflection on the Shoah,* which admonished Roman Catholics for their failure to speak out more forcefully during the Holocaust and criticized the church for its traditional anti-Semitism. *We Remember,* though, did not offer an apology for the church's inaction during the Holocaust. Despite these shortcomings, the spirit of *We Remember* was one of conciliation and deep regret, as evidenced by John Paul II's cover letter. *We Remember* would, he hoped, "help heal the wounds of past misunderstandings and injustices." He added: "May it enable memory to play its necessary part in the process of shaping a future in which the unspeakable iniquity of the Shoah will never again be possible."[132]

In perhaps his greatest gesture of reconciliation, Pope John Paul II visited Yad Vashem in 2000. Frail and suffering from the advanced stages of Parkinson disease, he listened as Prime Minister Yehud Barak welcomed him to

Israel and thanked him for a visit that "[would] be remembered forever as a magical moment of truth and a victory for justice and hope." He added that His Holiness had "done more than anyone else to bring about the historic change in the attitude of the Church towards the Jewish people."[133] John Paul responded by saying that what his heart most hoped for in this place of dark memory was silence. He still remembered his Jewish neighbors and friends and the horrors they had suffered during the Shoah. He wanted to assure the Jewish people that "the Catholic Church, motivated by the Gospel law of truth and love, and by no political considerations, is deeply saddened by the hatred, acts of persecution, and displays of anti-Semitism directed against the Jews by Christians at any time and at any place." He hoped that together, Christians and Jews could "build a new future in which there would be no more anti-Jewish feeling among Christians and anti-Christian feeling among Jews, but rather the mutual respect required of those who adore the one Creator and God, and look to Abraham as our common father in faith."[134] When John Paul II died on April 3, 2005, Silvan Shalom (1958–), the Israeli foreign minister, honored him with these words: "Israel, the Jewish people and the entire world, lost today a great champion of reconciliation and brotherhood between the faiths. This is a great loss, first and foremost for the Catholic Church and its hundreds of millions of believers, but also for humanity as a whole."[135]

The accession of the German-born Benedict XVI (r. 2005–) to the papal throne after John Paul II's death concerned some Jews because of his background as a member of the Hitler Youth and the Wehrmacht. But Benedict quickly explained that as a teenager in Germany he had no choice but to join the Hitler Youth and was drafted into the Wehrmacht, where he served in an artillery unit. Many Jewish leaders accepted his explanation and hoped that all this would make him particularly sensitive to the threat of anti-Semitism. They were

heartened because he had been actively involved in the preparation of the Vatican's 1999 *Memory and Reconciliation: The Church and the Faults of the Past,* which asked forgiveness for the failure of Christians to do more during the Shoah. It also asked whether traditional anti-Semitism had made Nazi persecution easier. As Joseph Cardinal Ratzinger (1927–), he released the 2002 publication *The Jewish People and Their Sacred Scriptures in the Christian Bible,* which acknowledged that both Jews and Christians shared a common belief in the Messiah. It also expressed sadness that certain parts of the Bible had been used to justify anti-Semitism and said that the Torah was important to Christians.

Yet Benedict XVI has also sent other signals that seem less conducive to maintaining a healthy relationship with Jews. He has expressed traditional Catholic views about wanting Jews to convert to Roman Catholicism and has permitted the return of the Tridentine Mass with it Good Friday prayers for the conversion of Judaism. Although John XXIII removed some of the more offensive language in this mass, the mere fact that this traditional Roman Catholic mass with its prayer for Jewish conversion was being revived was taken by some Jewish leaders as "a theological setback in the religious life of Catholics and a body blow to Catholic-Jewish relations." Other Jewish leaders took a wait-and-see attitude, suggesting that the issue of the phrases referring to Jews could possibly be eliminated and, if not, a topic of discussion with Roman Catholic leaders in future.[136]

Conclusion

Economics, politics, and geography played major roles in determining the success of the neutral stances of Portugal, Spain, Sweden, Switzerland, Turkey, and the Vatican during World War II. Each of these countries compromised traditional international codes of neutrality to maintain a semblance of autonomy.

Each played a delicate balancing act between the Axis and the Allies, though in most instances, particularly during the early years of the war, they tended to drift more towards Hitler and his partners. Geography and politics favored Spain and Portugal, both spiritually tied to the Fascist-Nazi camp. Portugal served as an important transit stop for Jews trying to flee Europe, though the government of António Salazar severely punished Aristides de Sousa Mendes for issuing illegal visas to Jews in Bordeaux. Spain was also a temporary safe haven for Jews, though it also remained a loyal ally of Italy and Germany through most of the war. Two Spanish diplomats, Ángel Sanz-Briz and Giorgio Perlasca, played important roles in helping save Jews in Hungary in 1944 and 1945.

Sweden occupied something of a middle ground as a neutral, providing Germany with major supplies of iron ore and serving as an important rail link between German-occupied Norway, Germany, and the Finnish-Soviet front. But Sweden also opened its doors readily to Scandinavian Jews fleeing Nazi persecution. Regardless, it was not until 1943 that Sweden, driven by the changing fortunes of war and Allied pressure, began to reduce its trade ties with the Reich. By 1944, Sweden had become much more aggressive in its efforts to help save Jews. It sponsored Raoul Wallenberg's mission to Budapest and was actively involved in Count Folke Bernadotte's "White Bus" mission to Germany the following year.

The roles of Switzerland and the Vatican as neutrals in World War II are much more problematic. Despite its long tradition as a haven for European refugees, Switzerland severely compromised its neutrality during World War II through its highly restrictive immigration policies and its role as one of Nazi Germany's most important industrial and economic partners. Swiss policies were driven by racism and economic opportunism. For decades after the war, Switzerland hid behind the façade of benign, kind neutrality. This was shattered in the 1990s when international investigations revealed not only the considerable violations of Swiss neutrality during the war but also the fact that its banks were hiding vast sums deposited by or stolen from Holocaust survivors.

A similar controversy has haunted the Vatican, particularly when it comes to the question of Pope Pius XII and his role as Europe's most important moral voice during the Holocaust. Pius XII was a diplomat who chose not to speak out forcefully against Nazi persecution of the Jews, Roma, and others for fear of the harm it might cause the Roman Catholic Church throughout German-dominated Europe. Surrounded as it was first by Italy and, later, by Germany, Pius XII was also concerned about the autonomy of the Vatican. This did not prevent individual Roman Catholic nuns, priests, and lay persons from bravely living their faith by risking their lives to help thousands upon thousands of Jews and others escape the ravages of Nazi persecution. Though hailed as a savior of the Jews after the war, Pius XII's image was tarnished after Rolf Hochhuth criticized his role in the war in *The Deputy*. The Roman Catholic Church responded with a staunch defense of Pius XII, and two popes, John XXIII and John Paul II, worked hard to heal the traditional rift between Jews and Roman Catholics. Only history will tell whether the German-born Benedict XVI will be able to continue this trend successfully.

SOURCES FOR FURTHER STUDY AND RESEARCH

Primary Sources

Adler, David, and Karen Ritz. *Hiding from the Nazis.* New York: Holiday House, 1997.

Adler-Rudel, Salomon. "A Chronicle of Rescue Efforts." *Leo Baeck Institute Yearbook.* Vol. 11. Leo Baeck Institute, 1966.

Alland, Bronislawa. *Memoirs of a Hidden Child During the Holocaust: My Life During the War.* Lewiston, ME: Edwin Mellen Press, 1992.

Bartoszewski, Władysław and Zofia Lewin, eds. *Righteous Among Nations: How Poles Helped the Jews, 1939–1945.* London: Earlscourt, 1969.

Die Bekenntnisse des Herrn X, Budapest. November 1943. Bundesarchiv (Koblenz). Nachlaß Oskar Schindler, 1908–1974. Bestand N 1493. No. 1. Band 18.

Bernadotte, Count Folke. *The Curtain Falls: Last Days of the Third Reich.* Translated by Count Eric Lewenhaupt. New York: Alfred A. Knopf, 1945.

———. *Instead of Arms: Autobiographical Notes.* Stockholm: Bonniers, 1948.

Bieberstein, Aleksander. *Zagłada Żydów w Krakowie.* Warsaw: Wydawnictwo Literackie, 1985.

Braitstein, Marcel. *Five to Ten: A Story of a Hidden Child.* Montreal: Concordia University Chair in Canadian Jewish Studies and the Montreal Institute for Genocide and Human Rights, 1999.

Buchignani, Walter. *Tell No One Who You Are: The Hidden Childhood of Regine Miller.* Montreal: Tundra Books, 1994.

Cahn, Eric, and Marilyn Saltzman. *Maybe Tomorrow: A Hidden Child of the Holocaust.* Arvada, CO: Casan, 1995.

Catholic Church. Commission for Religious Relations with the Jews. *We Remember: A Reflection on the Shoah.* Boston: Pauline Books & Media, 1998.

Ciechanowski, Jan. *Defeat In Victory.* London: Gollanz, 1948.

Cretzmeyer, Stacy. *Your Name Is Renée: Ruth's Story as a Hidden Child.* Brunswick, ME: Biddle, 1994.

Czech, Danuta. *Auschwitz Chronicle, 1939–1945.* New York: Henry Holt, 1990.

Eizenstat, Stuart. *Imperfect Justice: Looted Assets, Slave Labor, and the Unfinished Business of World War II.* New York: Public Affairs, 2003.

Epstein, Helen. *Children of the Holocaust: Conversation with Sons and Daughters of Survivors.* New York: Penguin Books, 1979.

Friedländer, Saul. *Pius XII and the Third Reich: A Documentation.* Translated by Charles Fullman. New York: Alfred A. Knopf, 1966.

Greenfeld, Howard. *The Hidden Children.* New York: Ticknor & Fields, 1993.

"Holocaust Victims Assets Litigation (Swiss Banks): Certified Awards Rendered by the CRT." 1 page. http://www.crt-ii.org/_awards/index.phtm.

"Holocaust Victim Assets Litigation (Swiss Banks) CV–96–4849." http://www.swissbankclaims.com/home_main.asp.

Independent Commission of Experts Switzerland—Second World War. *Switzerland, Nationalism and the Second World War: Final Report.* Zurich: Pendo Verlag, 2002.

International Theological Commission. *Memory and Reconciliation: The Church and the Faults of the Past.* December 1999. http://vatican.va/roman_curia/congregations/cfaith/cti_documents/rc_con_cfaith_doc_20000307-memory-recon-itc_en.html#Christians%20and20%Jews.

Jacobsen, Ruth. *Rescued Images: Memories of Childhood in Hiding.* New York: Mikaya Press, 2001.

Jeruchim, Simon. *Hidden in France: A Boy's Journey Under Nazi Occupation.* Santa Barbara, CA: Fithian Press, 2001.

Karski, Jan. *Story of a Secret State.* Boston: Houghton Mifflin, 1944.

Kasztner, Resző. *Der Bericht des Jüdischen Rettungskomittes aus Budapest.* Privately published, 1946.

Keller, Stefan. *Documents Relating to the Paul Grueninger Case.* Washington, DC: United States Holocaust Memorial Museum Archives.

Kersten, Felix. *The Kersten Memoirs, 1940–1945.* Translated by Constantine Fitzgibbon and James Oliver. London: Hutchinson, 1956.

Kessel, Barbara. *Suddenly Jewish: Jews Raised as Gentiles Discover Their Jewish Roots.* Hanover, NH: University Press of New England, 2000.

Krajewski, Stanisław. *Poland and the Jews: Reflections of a Polish Jew.* Warsaw: Wydawn. Austeria, 2005.

Kuper, Jack. *Child of the Holocaust.* New York: New American Library, 1987.

Kustanowitz, Esther. *The Hidden Children of the Holocaust: Teens Who Hid from the Nazis.* New York: Rosen, 1999.

Law-Related Resources on Nazi Gold and Other Holocaust Assets, Swiss Banks During World War II, and Dormant Accounts. http://www2.lib.uchicago.edu/~llou/nazigold.html.

"Letter of Pope John Paul II." *We Remember: A Reflection on the Shoah.* March 12, 1998. Commission for Religious Relations with the Jews. http://vatican.va/roman_curia/pontifical_councils/chrstuni/documents/rc_pc_chrstuni_doc_16031998_shoah_en.html.

Lubac, Heenri de. *Christian Resistance to Anti-Semitism: Memories from 1940–1944.* San Francisco: Ignatius Press, 1990.

Lukas, Richard C., ed. *Forgotten Survivors: Polish Christians Remember the Nazi Occupation.* Lawrence: University of Kansas Press, 2004.

Mann, Delbert. Papers. Vanderbilt University Special Collection Library.

Marchione, Margherita. *Yours Is a Precious Witness: Memoirs of Jews and Catholics in Wartime Italy.* New York: Paulist Press, 1997.

Marks, Jane. *The Hidden Children: The Secret Survivors of the Holocaust.* New York: Ballantine Books, 1993.

Mendelsohn, John, ed. *The Holocaust: Selected Documents in Eighteen Volumes.* Vol. 16, *Rescue to Switzerland: The Musy and Saly Mayer Affairs.* New York: Garland, 1982.

Moskovits, Sarah. *Love Despite Hate: Child Survivors of the Holocaust and Their Adult Lives.* New York: Schocken Books, 1983.

Noakes, Jeremy, and Geoffrey Pridham. *Nazism: A History in Documents and Eyewitness Accounts, 1919–1945.* 4 vols. New York: Schocken Books, 1988.

Nostra Aetate: Declaration on the Relation of the Church to Non–Christian Religions. Proclaimed by His Holiness, Paul VI on October 28, 1965. Boston: Pauline Books & Media, n.d.

"Oskar Schindler Financial Report 1945." July 1945. Yad Vashem Archives, 01/164.

Paul, John II. *John Paul II on the Holocaust.* Selected by Eugene J. Fisher. Washington, DC: National Conference of Catholic Bishops, 1988.

Plunder and Restitution: Presidential Advisory Commission on Holocaust Assets in the United States and Staff Report. December 2000. http://www.pcha.gov/PlunderRestitution.html/html/Home_Contents.html.

The Pontifical Biblical Commission. *The Jewish People and Their Sacred Scriptures in the Christian Bible* (2002). http://www.vatican.va/roman_curia/congregations/cfaith/pcb_document/rc-con-cfaith_doc_20020212_popolo-ebraico_en.html.

"Prime Minister Barak's Speech at Yad Vashem During Visit by Pope John Paul II (23/03/2000)." Yad Vashem. http://www.yadvashem.org/about_yad/what_new/data_pope/Barak.html.

Ratzinger, Joseph Cardinal. *Milestones: Memoirs, 1927–1977.* San Francisco: Ignatius Press, 1998.

_____. *Salt of the Earth: The Church at the End of the Millenium. An Interview with Peter Seewald.* San Francisco: Ignatius Press, 1997.

Richman, Sophia. *A Wolf in the Attic: The Legacy of a Hidden Child of the Holocaust.* New York: Haworth Press, 2002.

Rosenberg, Maxine B. *Hiding to Survive: Stories of Jewish Children Rescued from the Holocaust.* New York: Clarion Books, 1994.

Rudel, Shlomo Adler. *Jüdische Selbsthilfe unter dem Naziregime, 1933–1939: Im Spiegel der Berichte der Reichsvertretung der Juden in Deutschen.* Tübingen: J. C. Mohr, 1974.

Schellenberg, Walter. *The Labyrinth: Memoirs of Walter Schellenberg, Hitler's Chief of Counterintelligence.* Translated by Louis Hagen. New York: Da Capo Press, 2000.

Stein, Andre. *Hidden Children: Forgotten Survivors of the Holocaust.* Toronto: Penguin Books, 1994.

Stein, Edith. *Life in a Jewish Family.* Translated by Josephine Koeppel. Washington, DC: ICS, 1999.

_____. *Self-Portrait in Letters, 1916–1942.* Translated by Josephine Koeppel. Washington, DC: ICS, 1994.

Summary of Special Master's Plan of Allocation and Distribution of Settlement Fund. United States District Court, Eastern District of New York. Case No. CV96–4849 (ERK)(MDG).

Sutters, Jack. *American Friends Service Committee.* Vol. 2. *Archives of the Holocaust: An International Collection of Selected Documents.* Edited by Henry Friedlander and Sybil Milton. New York: Garland, 1989–1995.

"Text of Pope John Paul II's Speech at Yad Vashem (23/3/2000)." Yad Vashem. http://www.yadvashem.org/about_yad/waht_new/data_pope/speech.html.

Tittmann, Harold H. *Inside the Vatican of Pius XII: The Memoirs of an American Diplomat During World War II.* Edited by Harold H. Tittmann, III. New York: Image Books/Doubleday, 2004.

Tolly, Nelly S. *Behind the Secret Window: A Memoir of a Hidden Childhood During World War Two.* New York: Dial Books, 1993.

Trudi, Alexy. *The Mezuzah in the Madonna's Foot: Oral Histories Exploring Five Hundred Years in the Paradoxical Relations of Spain and the Jews.* New York: Simon & Schuster, 1993.

United States House of Representatives. *The Disposition of Assets Deposited in Swiss Banks by Missing Nazi Victims: Hearing Before the Committee on Banking and Financial Services, December 11, 1996.* Washington, DC: U.S. Government Printing Office, 1997.

United States Senate. *Current Developments in Holocaust Assets Restitution: Hearing Before the Committee on Banking, Housing, and Urban Affairs, July 22, 1998.* Washington, DC: U.S. Government Printing Office, 1999.

_____. *Swiss Banks and Attempts to Recover Assets Belonging to the Victims of the Holocaust: Hearing Before the Committee on Banking, Housing and Urban Affairs, May 15, 1997.* Washington, DC: U.S. Government Printing Office, 1997.

_____. *Swiss Banks and the Shredding of Holocaust Era Documents: Hearing Before the Committee on Banking, Housing, and Urban Affairs, May 6, 1997.* Washington, DC: United States Government Printing Office, 1997.

_____. *Swiss Banks and the Status of Assets of Holocaust Survivors or Heirs: Hearing Before the Committee on Banking, Housing, and Urban Affairs, April 23, 1996.* Washington, DC: U.S. Government Printing Office, 1996.

Weinstein, Frida Scheps. *A Hidden Childhood, 1942–1945.* New York: Hill and Wang, 1985.

Weissberg, Alex. *Desperate Mission: Joel Brand's Story as Told by Alex Weissberg.* Translated by Constantine FitzGibbon and Andrew Foster-Melliar. New York: Criterion Books, 1958.

Winter, Miriam. *Trains: A Memoir of a Hidden Childhood During and After World War II.* Jackson, MI: Kelton Press, 1997.

Secondary

Aalders, Gerard, and Cees Wiebes. *The Art of Cloaking Ownership: The Secret Collaboration and Protection of the German War Industry by the Neutrals: The Case of Sweden.* Amsterdam: Amsterdam University Press, 1996.

Ahnborg, Bertil. *Commission on Jewish Assets in Sweden at the Time of the Second World War: Progress Report.* Stockholm: Ministry of Foreign Affairs, 1998.

Alvarez, David. "No Immunity: Signals Intelligence and the European Neutrals, 1939–1945." *Intelligence and National Security* 12, no. 2 (April 1977): 22–43.

_____. *Spies in the Vatican: Espionage & Intrigue from Napoleon to the Holocaust.* Lawrence: University of Kansas Press, 2002.

Angst, Kenneth, ed. *Der Zweite Weltkrieg und die Schweiz.* Zürich: Neue Züricher Zeitung, 1997.

Arendt, Hannah. *Men in Dark Times.* New York: Harcourt, Brace & World, 1968.

Banki, Judith H., and John T. Pawlikowski, eds. *Ethics in the Shadow of the Holocaust: Christian and Jewish Perspectives.* Franklin, WI: Sheed & Ward, 2001.

Bartoszewski, Władysław. *The Convent at Auschwitz.* New York: G. Braziller, 1991.

Bartov, Omer. *Hitler's Army: Soldiers, Nazis, and War in the Third Reich.* New York: Oxford University Press, 1991.

Bauer, Yehuda. *American Jewry and the Holocaust: The American Jewish Joint Distribution Committee, 1939–1945.* Detroit: Wayne State University Press, 1981.

_____. *Jews for Sale? Nazi-Jewish Negotiations, 1933–1945.* New Haven: Yale University Press, 1994.

Bauminger, Arieh L. *The Righteous Among the Nations.* Jerusalem: Yad Vashem, 1990.

Bazyler, Michael J., and Roger P. Alford, eds. *Holocaust Restitution: Perspectives on the Litigation and Its Legacy.* New York: New York University Press, 2006.

Bazyler, Michael J. "Suing Hitler's Willing Business Partners: American Justice and Holocaust Morality." *Jewish Political Studies Review* 16, nos. 3–4 (Fall 2004): 1–27. http://www.jcpa.org/phas-bazyler-f04.htm.

Beevor, Antony. *The Battle for Spain: The Spanish Civil War, 1936–1939.* Rev. ed. London: Penguin, 2006.

Beker, Avi, ed. *The Plunder of Jewish Property During the Holocaust.* New York: New York University Press, 2001.

Berger, Alan L., Harry Cargas, and Susan E. Nowak. *The Continuing Agony: From the Carmelite Convent to the Crosses at Auschwitz.* Binghamton, NY: Global Publications, 2002.

Bernstein, Carl, and Marco Politi. *His Holiness: John Paul II and the History of Our Time.* New York: Penguin, 1996.

Bosworth, R.J.B. *Mussolini's Italy: Life Under the Fascist Dictatorship, 1915–1945.* New York: Penguin, 2006.

Bottum, Joseph, and David G. Dalin, eds. *The Pius War: Responses to the Critics of Pius XII.* Lanham, MD: Lexington Books, 2004.

Bower, Tom. *Nazi Gold: The Full Story of the Fifty-Year Swiss-Nazi Conspiracy to Steal Billions from Europe's Jews and Holocaust Survivors.* New York: HarperCollins, 1997.

Bradsher, Greg, and Stuart E. Eizenstat. *Appendix: U.S. and Allied Efforts to Recover and Restore Gold and Other Assets Stolen or Hidden by Germany During World War II: Finding Aid to Records at the National Archives at College Park.* Washington, DC: Department of State, 1997.

Braham, Randolph L., ed. *The Vatican and the Holocaust: The Catholic Church and the Jews During the Nazi Era.* New York: Rosenthal Institute for Holocaust Studies, Graduate Center/City University of New York, 2000.

Braillard, Phillipe. *Switzerland and the Crisis of Dormant Assets and Nazi Gold.* Translated by Denys Crapon de Caprona and André Lötter. London: Kegan Paul International, 2000.

Breitman, Richard. "American Rescue Activities in Sweden." *Holocaust and Genocide Studies* 7, no. 2 (1993): 202–215.

_____. *Official Secrets: What the Nazis Planned, What the British and the Americans Knew.* New York: Hill and Wang, 1998.

Brown-Fleming, Suzanne. *The Holocaust and Catholic Conscience: Cardinal Aloisius Muench and the Guilt Question in Germany, 1946–1959.* South Bend, IN: University of Notre Dame Press, 2006.

Bugnion, Francois. "ICRC Action During the Second World War." *International Review of the Red Cross,* no. 317 (March 1, 1997): 156–177.

Burns, Margie. "Turkey Served as Safe Haven for Jews during the Holocaust." Raoul Wallenberg International Foundation. January 18, 2005. http://www.raoulwallenberg.net/?en/saviors/diplomats/turkey-served-safe-havenjews.2110.htm.

Cargas, Harry James, ed. *Holocaust Scholars Write to the Vatican.* Westport, CT: Greenwood Press, 1998.

Carigren, W. M. *Swedish Foreign Policy During the Second World War.* Translated by Arthur Spencer. New York: St. Martin's Press, 1977.

Carroll, James. *Constantine's Sword: The Church and the Jews.* Boston: Houghton Mifflin, 2001.

Cassels, Alan. *Fascist Italy.* 2nd ed. Arlington Heights, IL: Harlan Davidson, 1985.

Catholic Church. National Conference of Catholic Bishops: Secretariat for Ecumenical and Interreligious Affairs. *Catholic Teaching on the Shoah: Implementing the Holy See's We Remember.* Washington, DC: United States Catholic Conference, 2001.

Cesarani, David, and Paul A. Levine, eds. *"Bystanders" to the Holocaust: A Re-Evaluation.* London: Frank Cass, 2002.

Conti, Gregory. "A Most Unlikely Hero: A Fascist Who Saved Jews—Giorgio Perlasca." *Commonweal* (December 3, 1999): 1–3. http://findarticles.com/p/articles/mi_m1252/is_21_126/ai_58675361.

Coppa, Frank J. *The Papacy, the Jews, and the Holocaust.* Washington, DC: Catholic University of America Press, 2006.

Cornwell, John. *Hitler's Pope: The Secret History of Pius XII.* New York: Viking, 1999.

Cowell, Alan. "How Swiss Strategy on Holocaust Fund Unraveled." *New York Times,* January 26, 1997, 6.

Dalin, David G. *The Myth of Hitler's Pope: How Pope Pius XII Rescued Jews from the Nazis.* Washington, DC: Regnery, 2005.

Deaglio, Enrico. *The Banaltiy of Goodness: The Story of Giorgio Perlasca.* Translated by Gregory Conti.

Notre Dame, IN: University of Notre Dame Press, 1998.

Doobov, Arieh. *The Vatican and the Shoah: Purified Memory or Reincarnated Responsibility?* Jerusalem: Institute of the World Jewish Congress, 1998.

Dulles, Avery Robert. *The Holocaust, Never to Be Forgotten: Reflections on the Holy See's Document "We Remember."* New York: Paulist Press, 2001.

Eizenstat, Stuart E., and William Z. Slany. *U.S. and Allied Efforts to Recover and Restore Gold and Other Assets Stolen or Hidden by Germany During World War II: Preliminary Study.* Washington, DC: Department of State, 1997.

_____. *U.S. and Allied Wartime and Postwar Relations and Negotiations with Argentina, Portugal, Spain, Sweden, and Turkey on Looted Gold and German External Assets and U.S. Concerns About the Fate of the Wartime Ustasha Treasury.* Washington, DC: Department of State, 1998.

Ekman, Stig, Klas Åmark, and John Toler. *Sweden's Relations with Nazism, Nazi Germany, and the Holocaust: A Survey of Research.* Stockholm: Universitet Stockholms, 2003.

Engel, David. "The Western Allies and the Holocaust." *Holocaust and Genocide Studies* 5, no. 4, pp. 363–380.

Erdman, Paul. *The Swiss Account.* New York: Tor Books, 1993.

Favez, Jean-Claude. *The Red Cross and the Holocaust.* Edited and translated by John and Beryl Fletcher. Cambridge: Cambridge University Press, 1999.

Felice, Renzo de. *The Jews in Fascist Italy: A History.* Translated by Robert L. Miller. New York: Enigma Books, 2001.

Fischer, Klaus P. *Nazi Germany: A New History.* New York: Continuum, 1995.

Fox, Frank. "A Jew Talks with Himmler." *Liberty* 17, nos. 9–10 (September-October 2003): 1–10. http://www.libertyunbound.com/archive/2003_10/fox-himmler.html.

Fralon, José Alain. *A Good Man in Evil Times: The Story of Aristides de Sousa Mendes.* Translated by Peter Graham. New York: Carroll & Graf, 2001.

Friedenson, Joseph, and David Kranzler. *Heroine of Rescue: The Incredible Story of Recha Sternbuch Who Saved Thousands from the Holocaust.* Brooklyn, NY: Menorah Publications, 1984.

Friedländer, Saul. *The Years of Extermination: Nazi Policy and the Jews, 1939–1945.* New York: HarperCollins, 2007.

Friedman, Philip. *Their Brothers' Keepers.* New York: Holocaust Library, 1978.

Gallo, Patrick J. *Pius XII, the Holocaust, and the Revisionists.* Jefferson, NC: McFarland, 2006.

Gaon, Solomon, and M. Mitchell Serels, eds. *Sephardim and the Holocaust.* New York: J. E. Safra Institute of Sephardic Studies, Yeshiva University, 1987.

Garlinski, Josef. *The Swiss Corridor: Espionage Networks in Switzerland During World War II.* London: J. M. Dent & Sons, 1981.

Gilbert, Martin. *Auschwitz and the Allies.* New York: Holt, Rinehart and Winston, 1981.

_____. *The Righteous: The Unsung Heroes of the Holocaust.* New York: Henry Holt, 2003.

Goldhagen, Daniel Jonah. *A Moral Reckoning: The Role of the Catholic Church in the Holocaust and Its Unfulfilled Duty of Repair.* New York: Alfred A. Knopf, 2002.

Halbrook, Stephen. *The Swiss and the Nazis: How the Alpine Republic Survived in the Shadow of the Third Reich.* Drexel Hill, PA: Casemate, 2006.

_____. *Target Switzerland: Swiss Armed Neutrality During World War II.* Rockville Centre, NY: Sarpedon, 1998.

Hartmann, Frederick H. *Swiss Press and Foreign Affairs in World War II.* Gainesville: University of Florida Press, 1960.

Häsler, Alfred. *The Lifeboat Is Full: Switzerland and the Refugees, 1933–1945.* Translated by Charles Lam Markmann. New York: Funk & Wagnalls, 1969.

The Heart Feels an Extreme Need for Silence: The Visit of Pope John Paul II to Yad Vashem, Jerusalem, March 23, 2000. Jerusalem: Yad Vashem, 2000.

Hedin, Sven Fredrik. *Sweden and the Shoah: The Untold Chapters.* Jerusalem: Institute of the World Jewish Congress, 1997.

Hewins, Ralph. *Count Folke Bernadotte: His Life and Work.* Minneapolis: T. S. Denison, 1950.

Hilberg, Raul. *The Destruction of the European Jews.* 3rd ed. 3 vols. New Haven: Yale University Press, 2003.

Hochhuth, Rolf. *The Deputy.* Translated by Richard and Clara Winston. New York: Grove Press, 1964.

Huonker, Thomas, and Regula Ludi. *Roma, Sinti und Jenische: Schweizerische Zigeunerpolitik zur Zeit des Nationalsozialismus.* Zurich: Chronos Verlag, 2001.

Katz, Robert. *Fatal Silence: The Pope, the Resistance and the German Occupation of Rome.* London: Weidenfeld & Nicolson, 2003.

Keller, Stefan. *Grüningers Fall: Geschichten von Flucht und Hilfe.* Zürich: Rotpunktverlag, 1993.

Kertzer, David I. *The Popes Against the Jews: The Vatican's Role in the Rise of Modern Anti-Semitism.* New York: Alfred A. Knopf, 2001.

Kessell, Joseph. *The Man with the Miraculous Hands: Himmler's Private Doctor.* Translated by Helen Weaver and Leo Raditsa. New York: Dell, 1961.

Kestenberg, Judith S., and Ira Brenner. *The Last Survivor: The Child Survivor of the Holocaust.* Washington, DC: American Psychiatric Press, 1996.

Koblik, Steven. *The Stones Cry Out: Sweden's Response to the Persecution of the Jews, 1933–1945.* Translated by David Mel Paul and Margareta Paul. New York: Holocaust Library, 1988.

Kranzler, David. *The Man Who Stopped the Trains to Auschwitz: George Mantello, El Salvador, and Switzerland's Finest Hour.* Syracuse, NY: Syracuse University Press, 2000.

Kurek, Ewa. *Your Life Is Worth Mine: How Polish Nuns Saved Hundreds of Jewish Children in German-Occupied Poland, 1939–1945.* New York: Hippocrene Books, 1997.

Laquer, Walter. *The Terrible Secret: Suppression of the Truth About Hitler's "Final Solution."* Harmondsworth, UK: Penguin, 1980.

Laquer, Walter, and Richard Breitman. *Breaking the Silence.* New York: Simon & Schuster, 1986.

Lawler, Justus George. *Popes and Politics: Reform, Resentment, and the Holocaust.* New York: Continuum, 2002.

LeBor, Adam. *Hitler's Secret Bankers: The Myth of Swiss Neutrality During the Holocaust.* Secaucus, NJ: Carol Publishing Group, 1997.

Levin, Itamar. *The Last Deposit: Swiss Banks and Holocaust Victims' Accounts.* Translated by Natasha Dornberg. Westport, CT: Praeger, 1999.

Levine, Paul A. *From Indifference to Activism: Swedish Diplomacy and the Holocaust, 1938–1944.* Uppsala, Sweden: Almqvist & Wiksell International, 1996.

Lewy, Guenter. *The Catholic Church and Nazi Germany.* New York: McGraw-Hill, 1964.

Lipschitz, Chaim U. *Franco, Spain, the Jews, and the Holocaust.* Edited by Ira Axelrod. Hoboken, NJ: KTAV Publishing House, 1984.

Lipstadt, Deborah. *Beyond Belief: The American Press & the Coming of the Holocaust, 1933–1945.* New York: Free Press, 1986.

Littell, Franklin, and Hubert G. Locke, eds. *The German Church Struggle and the Holocaust.* Detroit, MI: Wayne State University Press, 1974.

Luckas, Richard C. *Did the Children Cry? Hitler's War Against Jewish and Polish Children, 1939–1945.* New York: Hippocrene Books, 2001.

——, ed. *Out of the Inferno: Poles Remember the Holocaust.* Lexington: The University of Kentucky Press, 1989.

Ludwig, Carl. *Die Flüchtlingspolitik der Schweiz seit 1933 bis zur Gegenwart: Beilage zum Bericht des Bundesrates an die Bundesversammlung über die Flüchtlingspolitik der Schweiz seit 1933 bis zur Gegenwart.* Bern: Bundesrat, 1957.

Manhattan, Avro. *The Vatican's Holocaust: The Sensational Account of the Most Horrifying Religious Massacre of the 20th Century.* Springfield, MO: Ozark Books, 1986.

Mattioli, Aram, ed. *Antisemitismus in der Schweiz, 1848–1960.* Zürich: Orell Füssli, 1998.

McInery, Ralph M. *The Defamation of Pius XII.* South Bend, IN: St. Augustine's Press, 2001.

Meier, Heinz K. *Friendship Under Stress: U.S.-Swiss Relations, 1900–1950.* Bern: Herbert Lang, 1970.

Milgram, Avraham. "Portugal, the Consuls, and the Jewish Refugees, 1938–1941." Shoah Resource Center, The International School for Holocaust Studies, Yad Vashem, 2004, 1–31.

Miller, Paul B. "Europe's Gold: Nazis, Neutrals and the Holocaust." *Dimensions: A Journal of Holocaust Studies* 11, no. 1 (1997): 11–13.

Morley, John F. *Vatican Diplomacy and the Jews During the Holocaust, 1939–1943.* Hoboken, NJ: KTAV Publishing House, 1980.

O'Brien, Darcy. *The Hidden Pope: The Personal Journey of John Paul II and Jerzy Kluger.* New York: Doubleday, 1998.

Pacepa, Ion Mihai. "Moscow's Assault on the Vatican." *National Review* (January 27, 2007): 1–5. http://article.nationalreview.com/?q=YTUzYmJhMGQ5Y2UxOWUzNDUyMWUwODJiOTEzYjY4NzI=.

Padfield, Peter. *Himmler.* New York: Henry Holt, 1990.

Paldiel, Mordecai. *Churches and the Holocaust: Unholy Teaching, Good Samaritans, and Reconciliation.* Hoboken, NJ: KTAV Publishing House, 2006.

——. "Fear and Comfort: The Plight of Hidden Children in Wartime Poland." *Holocaust and Genocide Studies* 6, no. 4 (1992): 397–413.

——. *The Path of the Righteous; Gentile Rescuers of Jews During the Holocaust.* Hoboken, NJ, and New York: KTAV Publishing house in association

with The Jewish Foundation for Christian Rescuers/ADL, 1993.

Palmer, Raymond. "Felix Kersten and Count Bernadotte: A Question of Rescue." *Journal of Contemporary History* 29, no. 1 (January 1994): 39–51.

Paul, Allen. *Katyn: The Untold Story of Stalin's Polish Massacre.* New York: Charles Scriber's Sons, 1991.

Perry, Marvin, and Frederick M. Schweitzer, eds. *Jewish-Christian Encounters Over the Centuries.* New York: Peter Lang, 1994.

Phayer, Michael. *The Catholic Church and the Holocaust, 1930–1964.* Bloomington: Indiana University Press, 2000.

Picard, Jacques. *On the Ambivalence of Being Neutral: Switzerland and Swiss Jewry Facing the Rise and Fall of the Nazi State.* Washington, DC: United States Holocaust Memorial Museum, 1998.

Pike, David Wingeate. *Spaniards in the Holocaust: Mauthausen, the Horror on the Danube.* London: Routledge, 2000.

Pius XII and the Holocaust: A Reader. Milwaukee, WI: Catholic League for Religious and Civil Rights, 1988.

Popper, Nathaniel. "Israel Criticizes Report on Swiss Holocaust Funds." *Forward.com* (April 30, 2004): 1. http://www.forward.com/articles/israel-criticizes-report-on-swiss-holocaust-funds/.

Rader, John S., and Kateryna Fedopryka. *The Pope and the Holocaust.* Alexandria, SD: Family Apostolate, 1994.

Ramati, Alexander. *The Assisi Underground: The Priests Who Rescued Jews.* New York: Stein and Day, 1978.

——. *While the Pope Kept Silent: Assisi and the Nazi Occupation.* London: Boston: Allen & Unwin, 1978.

Rein, Raanan. *In the Shadow of the Holocaust and the Inquisition. Israel's Relations with Francoist Spain.* Translated by Martha Grenzeback. London: Frank Cass, 1997.

Reisman, Arnold. *Turkey's Modernization: Refugees from Nazism and Ataturk's Vision.* Washington, DC: New Academia, 2006.

Rogow, Sally M. *They Must Not Be Forgotten: Heroic Priests and Nuns Who Saved People from the Holocaust.* Martinsburg, WV: Holy Fire, 2005.

Rychlak, Ronald J. *Righteous Gentiles: How Pius XII and the Catholic Church Saved Half a Million Jews from the Nazis.* Dallas, TX: Spence, 2005.

Rittner, Carol, and John K. Roth, eds. *Memory Offended: The Auschwitz Convent Controversy.* New York: Praeger, 1991.

———. *Pope Pius XII and the Holocaust.* London: Leicester University Press, 2002.

Sachar, Howard. *A History of the Jews in the Modern World.* New York: Alfred A. Knopf, 2005.

Sánchez, José M. *Pius XII and the Holocaust: Understanding the Controversy.* Washington, DC: Catholic University of America, 2002.

Sanger, David E. "Swiss Envoy to U.S. Resigns: He Urged 'War' Over Holocaust-Fund Dispute." *New York Times,* January 28, 1997.

Schmitt, Hans A. *Quaker & Nazis: Inner Light and Outer Darkness.* Columbia: University of Missouri Press, 1997.

Scholder, Klaus. *The Churches and the Third Reich.* Translated by John Bowden. Philadelphia: Fortress Press, 1988.

Schwarz, Ted. *Walking with the Damned: The Shocking Murder of the Man Who Freed 30,000 Prisoners.* New York: Paragon House, 1992.

Shaw, Stanford J. *The Jews of the Ottoman Empire and the Turkish Republic.* New York: New York University Press, 1991.

———. *Turkey and the Holocaust: Turkey's Role in Rescuing Turkish and European Jewry from Nazi Persecution, 1933–1945.* New York: New York University Press, 1993.

Steinberg, Jonathan. *Why Switzerland?* 2nd ed. Cambridge: Cambridge University Press, 1996.

Szulc, Tad. *Pope Paul II: The Biography.* New York: Scribner, 1995.

Tenembaum, Baruch. "The Example of Grüninger." International Raoul Wallenberg Foundation. http://www.raoulwallenberg.net/?en/saviors/others/example-gr-uuml-n.

Thavis, John. "Pope Relaxes Restrictions on use of Tridentine Mass." *Catholic News Service,* July 9, 2007, 1–5. http://www.catholicnews.com/data/stories/cns/0703892.htm.

Tomaszewski, Irene, and Tecia Werbowski. *Zegota: The Rescue of Jews in Wartime Poland.* Montreal: Price-Patterson, 1994.

Tooze, Adam. *The Wages of Destruction: The Making and Breaking of the Nazi Economy.* New York: Viking, 2006.

United States Holocaust Memorial Museum. *Children and the Holocaust: Symposium Presentation.* Washington, DC: Center for Advanced Holocaust Studies, 2004.

———. *Confiscation of Jewish Property in Europe, 1933–1945: New Sources and Perspectives.* Washington, DC: Center for Advanced Holocaust Studies, 2003.

Vincent, Isabel. *Hitler's Silent Partners: Swiss Banks, Nazi Gold, and the Pursuit of Justice.* New York: William Morrow, 1997.

Wagner, Meir, Andreas C. Fischer, and Graham Buik, eds. *The Righteous of Switzerland: Heroes of the Holocaust.* Hoboken, NJ: KTAV Publishing House, 2001.

Waller, John H. *The Devil's Doctor: Felix Kersten and the Secret Plot to Turn Himmler Against Hitler.* New York: John Wiley, 2002.

Waters, Donald Arthur. *Hitler's Secret Ally, Switzerland.* Le Mesa, CA: Pertinent, 1994.

Weigel, George. *Witness to Hope: The Biography of Pope John Paul II.* New York: Cliff Street Books, 2001.

Weinberg, Gerhard. *A World at Arms: A Global History of World War II.* Cambridge: Cambridge University Press, 1994.

Weisbord, Robert G. *The Chief Rabbi, the Pope, and the Holocaust: An Era in Vatican-Jewish Relations.* New Brunswick, NJ: Transaction, 1992.

Wood, E. Thomas, and Stanisław M. Jankowski. *Karski: How One Man Tried to Stop the Holocaust.* New York: John Wiley, 1994.

Wooden, Cindy. "ADL Head Calls Pope's Tridentine Mass Letter a 'Theological Setback.'" *Catholic News Service,* July 9, 2007, 1–3. http://www.catholicnews.com/data/stories/cns/0703900.htm.

"World Reaction to Death of Pope." BBC News. April 3, 2005. http://news.bbc.co.uk/2/hi/europe/4404971.stm.

Ziegler, Jean. *The Swiss, the Gold, and the Dead: How Swiss Bankers Helped Finance the Nazi War Machine.* Translated by John Brownjohn. New York: Harcourt Brace, 1998.

Zimmerman, Joshua D., ed. *Contested Memories: Poles and Jews During the Holocaust and Its Aftermath.* New Brunswick, NJ: Rutgers University Press, 2003.

Zohar, Zion. *Sephardic and Mizrahi Jewry: From the Golden Age of Spain to Modern Times.* New York: New York University Press, 2005.

Zuccotti, Susan. *Under His Very Windows: The Vatican and the Holocaust.* New Haven: Yale University Press, 2000.

Züricher, Erik J. *Turkey: A Modern History.* London: I. B. Taurus, 1997.

CHAPTER 10

Liberation, DPs, and the Search for Justice

War Crimes Investigations and Trials in Europe, the United States, and Israel

CHRONOLOGY

—**1917** *(November 2)*: Balfour Declaration promises Jewish homeland in Palestine
—**1939**: A British White Paper reneges on Balfour Declaration promise
—**1941**: Allies created United Nations War Crimes Commission; Stalin refuses to join
—**1943** *(July 14–17)*: Krasnodar trial in Soviet Union
—**1943** *(November 1)*: Churchill, Roosevelt, Stalin warn Germany and Japan about war crimes
—**1943** *(December 15–18)*: Kharkov trial in Soviet Union
—**1944** *(November 22)*: Majdanek trial in Lublin begins
—**1945** *(May 7–May 9)*: World War II ends in Europe
—**1945** *(July 17–August 2)*: Potsdam Conference
—**1945** *(August 8)*: London Agreement and Charter of International Military Tribunal (IMT)
—**1945** *(August 14)*: World War II ends in Asia
—**1945** *(September 17–November 17)*: Bergen-Belsen trial
—**1945** *(October 18–October 1, 1946)*: IMT trial in Nuremberg
—**1945–1946**: French "show trials" of Pierre Laval, Charles Maurras, Jospeh Darnard, Marshal Pétain
—**1946** *(January 10)*: László Bárdossy executed for war crimes in Hungary
—**1946** *(February 28)*: Béla Imredy executed for war crimes in Hungary
—**1946** *(March 29–April 12)*: Hungarian "deportation trio" executed
—**1946** *(May 3–November 12, 1948)*: IMT Tokyo trial
—**1946** *(July 4)*: Kielce pogrom in Poland
—**1946** *(July 30–August 2)*: "Show trial" of Andrei Vlasov in Moscow
—**1946** *(August 22–September 5)*: Trial of Amon Göth in Kraków
—**1946** *(October 25–August 20, 1947)*: Doctors' trial
—**1946** *(December 5–February 3, 1947)*: Ravensbrück trials
—**1947** *(March 11–29)*: Trial of Rudolf Höss in Poland

—1947 *(April 8–November 3)*: WVHA/Pohl trial

—1947 *(July 11)*: *Exodus* departs Marseilles for Palestine

—1947 *(July 3–April 10, 1948)*: *Einsatzgruppen* trial

—1947 *(August 27–July 31, 1948)*: I. G. Farben trial

—1947 *(November 29)*: UN approves Resolution 181 creating separate Jewish, Arab states

—1947 *(December 8–July 31, 1948)*: Krupp trial

—1948 *(May 14)*: Israel declares independence

—1948 *(June 24–May 11, 1949)*: Berlin blockade

—1950 *(April–June)*: Waldheim trials in German Democratic Republic (East Germany)

—1952–1954: French sentence Klaus Barbie to death in absentia for war crimes

—1953 *(May 18)*: Yad Vashem Law

—1960 *(May 11)*: Israeli Mossad agents kidnap Adolf Eichmann in Buenos Aires

—1961 *(April 11–August 14)*: Adolf Eichman trial; Eichman executed May 31/June 1, 1962

—1977–2007: United States begins thirty-year extradition case against John Demjanjuk

—1979 *(February 7)*: Josef Mengele dies in Brazil

—1983–2002: French pursue war crimes case against Maurice Papon

—1987 *(May 11–July 4)*: Trial of Klaus Barbie in Lyon

As Allied armies drove into German territory in the fall of 1944 and early 1945, they encountered horrors unimaginable even to seasoned war veterans. Though the Germans had not succeeded in making Europe *Judenfrei,* they had continued their mass murder campaign until the very end of the war. There is no way fully to comprehend the genocidal murder of 6 million Jews, hundreds of thousands of Roma, and from 200,000 to 250,000 handicapped victims. And although these figures pale in comparison to the total World War II losses of 50 to 60 million, the genocidal victims of World War II in Europe stand uniquely alone in the course of modern history as symbols of supposedly civilized societies gone mad.

The liberation of what remained of the concentration and death camps, and the flood of displaced persons at war's end, taxed the resources of military forces trained for war, not for its chaotic aftermath. Tragically, the groups who suffered most from Nazi excesses during World War II now faced hard times as stateless persons forced to live in Allied-run camps that initially offered them little hope of a return to normalcy. Those Jews and

Roma who did return home, particularly in Eastern Europe, faced renewed prejudice and mistreatment. The handicapped were merely ignored. Eventually, Jews were able to gain some reparations and property restitution from West Germany and other European countries. Such payments, of course, could never come close to compensating them for their tremendous losses and pain. Initially, the Roma and the handicapped had no common voice or defenders, and they failed in their efforts to gain recognition in the courts for their suffering.

As Holocaust survivors struggled to rebuild their lives at the end of the war, the legal mechanisms designed to deal with this incomprehensible tragedy fell into place. What followed were numerous war crimes trials in Allied- and Soviet-occupied territory that were designed to punish those responsible for the various crimes of the Nazi era. Western trials tended to follow established legalistic traditions of innocence until proven guilty, but courts in Central and Eastern Europe were often less concerned with such legal niceties than they were with revenge. Once the major war crimes trials

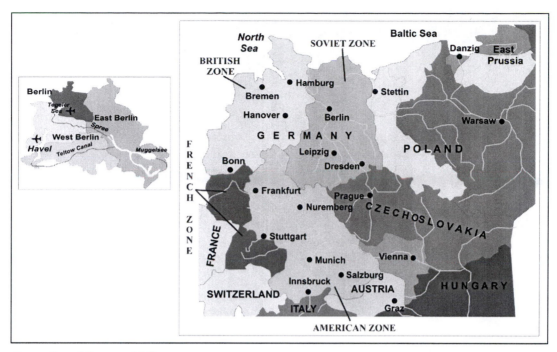

Occupation of Germany, 1945.

ended in the early years after the war, the question of war crimes followed different paths in a Europe increasingly divided along democratic–communist lines. Individual countries in Western Europe continued to conduct war crimes investigations, though these became less and less frequent as time went on. In the Soviet bloc, war crimes investigations tended to serve the ideological needs of the Stalinistic system. Soviet jurists were much more concerned about punishments for crimes against Soviet citizens who died in the war (from 26 to 28 million) than about the fate of the Holocaust's genocidal victims.

Liberation of the Camps

On July 23, 1944, the Soviets liberated the first major concentration camp, Majdanek. *General-Feldmarshal* Georgy Zhukov (1896– 1974) ordered his men to tour the camp; they forced German POWs to walk through a crowd of angry Poles and Jews who shouted "*Kindermörder! Kindermörder!* (Child murderers)." Zhukov also ordered a detailed investigation into the German crimes at Majdanek. Roman Kamen, one of the first reporters allowed into the camp, wrote that he had "never seen a more abominable sight than Majdanek." He reported that only 1,000 "living corpses" had survived the horror there and that he found it "difficult to believe" the "world's largest crematorium." *New York Times* reporter H. W. Lawrence also toured Majdanek and called it "the most horrible place on the face of the earth." A later report in the *Illustrated London News* said that Majdanek was "a grim reminder of that streak of utter inhumanity which is found in every German."[1]

As Soviet forces continued their sweep into eastern Poland, Hitler decided that none of the concentration camp inmates would be liberated. That fall, Himmler ordered a halt to the mass murder of Jews and Roma, though this

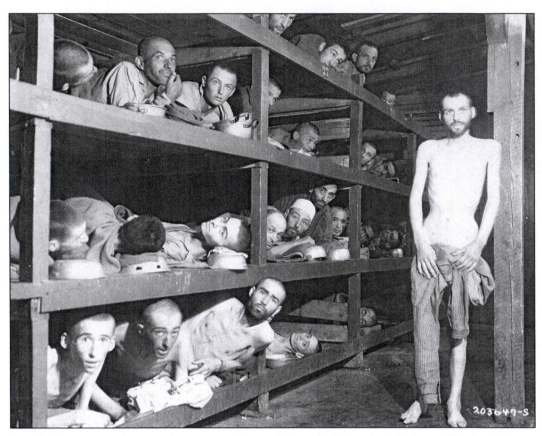

Liberated prisoners at Buchenwald. Elie Wiesel is seventh from the left on the second row of bunks. USHMM Photo No. 74607, courtesy of National Archives and Records Administration, College Park.

did not prevent the continued death of victims through forced marches and other acts of violence. When the Red Army entered Auschwitz on January 27, 1945, only 7,000 inmates were still there; another 58,000 were in its satellite camps. Overall, there were 714,211 prisoners (511,537 men; 202,674 women) in German concentration camps in the last months of the war.[2]

By early 1945, there were still eleven major concentration camps under German control. As the Allies moved deeper into German territory, the SS force-marched inmates from these camps to the interior of Germany. SS guards shot those too weak to go on, and others died from freezing temperatures, hunger, and disease. It is estimated that more than 25 percent of the 60,000 inmates

evacuated from Auschwitz died on "death marches."

Given the "iron curtain" of silence that began to separate the Soviet Union and its Allies at the end of the war, far less is known about the camps liberated by the Red Army. The Soviets did not give Auschwitz the attention they gave Majdanek. In February 1945, the British asked the Kremlin about what it had found in Auschwitz. Two months later, the Soviets reported that the Germans had murdered 4 million Europeans at Auschwitz and its satellite camps. The Red Army also liberated Sachsenhausen, Ravensbrück, and several other small camps during the last months of the war. In the West, it was not Majdanek or Auschwitz that got the most attention; instead, it was Bergen-

Belsen, which the British liberated on April 12, 1945.

Bergen-Belsen was one of the few camps that the Wehrmacht surrendered full of prisoners—dead and alive. The sight of thousands of dead, skeletal bodies and diseased, ragged inmates stunned the outside world. Brigadier R. B. T. Daniell (1901–1996), of the South Nottinghamshire Hussars, described what he saw soon after his unit arrived in the camp:

Inside [one of the huts] a sight revealed itself that daunted even a battle-experienced man like myself. Inside there were tiers of bunks containing one and sometimes even three completely naked human beings, the stench was appalling. It was a truly terrible sight, quite obviously they had received no food or medical attention for some time, yet outside were lusty young SS soldiers, fit and well, milling around. I had had enough. Never will I forget what I had seen that day and never will I forgive the race that produced men capable of [causing] such cold blooded misery and death to the thousands who were driven into Belsen camp.[3]

Liberation, though, did not mean survival. More than a third of the inmates in Bergen-Belsen died from disease and malnourishment in the months after they were freed, despite valiant British medical efforts to save them. According to Lieutenant Colonel M. W. Conin of the Royal Medical Corps,

Those who died of illness usually died in the huts, when starvation was the cause of death they died in the open for it is an odd characteristic of starvation that its victims seemed compelled to go on wandering until they fall down and die. Once they have fallen they die almost at once and it took a little time to get used to seeing men, women, and children collapse as you walked by them and to restrain oneself from going to their assistance.

One had to get used early to the idea that the individual just did not count. One knew that 500 a day were dying and that 500 a day were going to go on dying before anything we could do would have the slightest effect. It was, however, not easy to watch a child choking to death from diphtheria when you knew a tracheotomy and nursing would save it.[4]

The Americans discovered similar scenes when they liberated Dachau, Buchenwald, and Mauthausen. Dr. Douglas Kelling later described what he saw at Dachau:

The camp was filthy, full of diseases, and literally lousy with body and others types of lice and vermin. Prisoners were dirty; their clothes were dirty, old, and tattered. The prisoners were starving, a forced starvation; many were sick. Their faces were depressed in a fixed stare; their appearance was one of resigned hopelessness. Their gait was listless, slow, and I am sure many at times wished that they were dead instead of being confined in such a cruel, unbelievable place.

Many of these prisoners weighed 70 to 80 pounds. I was told an average of 270 cases a day were dying from typhus fever, and many were dying from tuberculosis which was rampant, from other diseases, and from the forced starvation. The prisoners were fed a sloppy type of food and bread which was made from small portions of wheat flour and a major portion of ersatz flour, which was powdered sawdust.[5]

Many of the victims in these camps were Jewish. In 1939, Europe had a Jewish population of 9.5 million. In 1945, there were only 3.3 million Jews still alive. Ninety percent of Poland's prewar Jewish population were dead. Only 230,000 Polish Jews survived the death camps. Most who tried to return home left quickly in the aftermath of anti-Semitic pogroms that swept Central and Eastern Europe and left hundreds dead. The worst

Burial of the Kielce pogrom Jewish victims. USHMM Photo No. 14393, courtesy of Leah Lahav.

violence took place in Kielce, Poland, once home to 20,000 Jews. The Kielce pogrom, which took place on July 4, 1946, was fueled by rumors that Jews had either kidnapped a Polish boy (who was later found unharmed) or were killing Polish children in the building of the former Jewish community center at No. 7 Planty Avenue. At this time, there were about 200 Jews in Kielce, most of them Holocaust survivors; many lived in the community center building because they were homeless. As the rumors spread, police, soldiers, and townspeople stormed the building, killing several Jews. Outside, a mob attacked the Jews forced from the building, killing many more. Others were attacked on their way to the hospital. By the end of the day, from 37 to 42 Jews were dead and another 50 to 82 seriously injured. News of the pogrom triggered a massive migration of Jews out of Poland. A hasty trial sentenced nine supposed perpetrators to death, and some top police officials who had participated in the pogrom were acquitted. Jan T. Gross argued in his *Fear: Anti-*

Semitism in Poland after Auschwitz that the rumors had little to do with the pogrom. What really drove the Poles, he maintained, was the fact that "Jews were perceived as a threat to the material status quo, security, and peaceful conscience of their Christian fellow citizens after the war because they had been plundered and because what remained of Jewish property, as were Jews' social roles, had been assumed by Polish neighbors in tacit and often directly opportunistic complicity with Nazi-instigated institutional mass murder."[6]

According to Cardinal August Hlond (1881–1948), the leading Roman Catholic official in Poland at the time, "The fact that this condition is deteriorating is to a great degree due to the Jews who today occupy leading positions in Poland's (Communist-dominated) government, and who endeavor to introduce a governmental structure which the majority of the people do not desire."[7]

This became the standard Polish explanation for the cause of the Kielce pogrom. By the end of 1947, two-thirds of Poland's surviving Jews had fled the country; even more left the next year. The periodic anti-Semitic outbursts that occurred for the next four decades had reduced Poland's official Jewish population to 3,600 by 1992. Today, there are no more than 10,000 Jews in Poland.

Jewish refugees suffered similar abuse in Bulgaria, Czechoslovakia, and Romania. From about 270,00 to 290,000 Hungarian Jews survived the Holocaust. Many of them were living in Budapest at the end of the war, then home to the largest Jewish population in Eastern Europe. Momentarily, Jews played a prominent role in postwar Hungarian politics, though this honeymoon soon ended. Between 1946 and 1956, 50,000 Jews left Hungary, many for Palestine and Israel. Those who remained found themselves trapped in a country whose government placed severe restrictions on Jewish religious and cultural life. Outward migration continued for the next four decades; by 1992, there were officially only 56,000 Jews in Hungary.

Perhaps most tragic was the fate of Bulgaria's Jews, most of whom had survived the Holocaust. Few were able to regain the property they had lost during the Holocaust, and by 1948 most Bulgarian Jews were impoverished. The new communist government severely clamped down on Jewish religious and cultural organizations, and in 1948–1949, 90 percent of postwar Bulgaria's Jewish population migrated to Israel.

Displaced Persons: Jews and Roma

The Jews

Jews who were not able or willing to return home were often put in Displaced Persons (DP) camps. Mark Wyman has estimated that there were "7 million civilians on the move in western Europe during the early summer of 1945" and a similar number in those parts of Central and Eastern Europe under Soviet control. The Allies also had 7.8 million German soldiers under their control

at the end of the year. There were another 2 million German POWs in the Soviet Union. Although most refugees made their way home within months after the war, by the fall of 1945 there remained 1.8 million displaced persons in Europe.[8] Initially, the Allies did what they could for the flood of refugees they encountered; but when it became apparent that there remained a large number who would not or could not return home, they asked the United Nations Relief and Rehabilitation Administration (UNRRA) to care for permanently displaced refugees. Created in 1943, UNRRA was charged with helping refugees and displaced persons under Allied jurisdiction at the end of World War II.

The Allied occupation forces initially rebuffed efforts by Jewish relief organizations to get into the DP camps, where Jews and non-Jewish displaced persons were mixed together. Jewish chaplains were able to do some relief work, but the military in general either was not inclined to provide the care needed by Holocaust survivors or was incapable of doing so. At first, the soldiers who guarded the DPs were sympathetic towards the plight of the Jews, Roma, and others because they had seen the horrors of the concentration camps; however, they were gradually replaced by recruits who had not fought in the war. This new group had little sympathy for the DPs and began to spread rumors that Jews were behind the budding black market in the DP camps.

The reality was quite different. Since the Allies seemed initially unwilling to provide the survivors with the care they needed to recover and rehabilitate, the Jews, Roma, and other DPs took matters into their own hands. In the British-run Belsen DP camp, built on the site of the former concentration camp, a Central Jewish Committee (CJC) was formed under Josef Rosensaft to help care for survivors. Though the CJC continually ran afoul of the British, it successfully created a network of health, cultural, religious, and educational

Jewish protesters at the Belsen DP camp, 1945–1946. USHMM Photo No. 32382, courtesy of Hilde Jacobsthal Goldberg.

fences, in camps of several descriptions (built by the Germans for slave-laborers and Jews), including some of the most notorious of the concentration camps, amidst crowded, frequently unsanitary and generally grim conditions, in complete idleness."[9] With the exception of the work of Jewish chaplains and the AJJDC, little had been done to help Jews, particularly when it came to locating family members.

Thus far, Harrison wrote, the Allies had failed to recognize the special needs of Jews and the problems caused by the Nazis' "barbaric persecution" of them. Most of the Jewish DPs wanted to leave Germany as soon as possible and go to Palestine. He realized that "evacuation from Germany" was the best solution to the Jewish DP problem; but, given Britain's strict immigration policies, he also knew how difficult it would be for the DPs to make it to Palestine. He urged the United States to do what it could to convince the British government to make it possible for a "reasonable" number of Jews to settle in Palestine. If humane solutions were not found to the Jewish refugee problem, the United States would "appear to be treating Jews as the Nazis treated them except that we do not exterminate them. They are in concentration camps in large numbers under our military guard instead of the S.S. troops. One is led to wonder whether the German people, seeing this, are not supposing that we are following or at least condoning Nazi policy."[10]

If immediate resettlement in Palestine or another country was not possible, Harrison suggested, the United States should create separate DP camps for Jews to avoid charges of "preferential" treatment and "discrimination" by other DPs. This was not a matter of giving a certain group "special privileges." Instead, it was "a matter of raising to a more normal level the position of a group which [had] been depressed to the lowest depths conceivable by years of organized and inhu-

programs designed to help restore the inmates' sense of humanity and dignity.

Reports of these problems reached the White House; Franklin Roosevelt's successor, Harry S. Truman (1884–1972), sent Earl G. Harrison (1899–1955), dean of the University of Pennsylvania's law school, to Germany in June 1945 to look into the problems in the DP camps. Harrison's report was instrumental in transforming U.S. policy towards DPs. During his tour of the DP camps, Harrison was joined by Dr. Joseph J. Schwartz, the European director of the AJJDC, and representatives of the War Refugee Board. Harrison's report described horrible scenes of pathetically malnourished and discouraged Jews "living under guard behind barbed-wire man oppression."[11] Harrison suggested that these camps be turned over to UNRRA as quickly as possible. He also advised that the United States move forward with plans to create a tracing service to help displaced Jews find missing relatives. Harrison noted that the "civilized world owe[d] it to this handful of survivors to provide them with a home where they [could] again settle down and begin to live like human beings."[12]

On August 31, President Truman sent General Dwight David Eisenhower (1890–1969), the supreme commander of Allied forces in Europe, a copy of Harrison's report, which emphasized the urgency of the crisis facing Jewish refugees. In his cover letter, he quoted the phrase "treating the Jews as the Nazis treated them," a reference to the United States and its actions. He emphasized the need for the military to develop a more humane plan for dealing with Jewish DPs. He added that he was in contact with the British government about opening the doors of Palestine to Jewish refugees.[13]

Though Henry Friedlander considered Harrison's assessment of the military's role in handling Jewish DPs somewhat unfair, his report did force the military to rethink its dealings with DPs. Living conditions improved substantially. And when UNRRA took over the camps, Jewish relief organizations found it much easier to work with the Jewish DPs.[14]

In 1944, the Supreme Headquarters Allied Expeditionary Forces (SHAEF) set up a tracing service, which was taken over by the International Relief Organization (IRO) three years later. It was renamed the International Tracing Service (ITS) in 1948 and placed under the Allied High Commission for Germany in 1951. Three years later, it was taken over by the International Committee of the Red Cross. Located in Bad Arolsen, Germany, the ITS, which is run by an eleven-member International Commission (IC), compiled millions of records, principally on inmates, in more than fifty Nazi camps and prisons. In 2006, the ITS opened its archives to researchers and a year later agreed to share copies of its files with Yad Vashem, the United States Holocaust Memorial Museum in Washington, DC, and archives in other IC member states. In 1990, the American Red Cross opened its Holocaust and War Victims Tracing Center in Baltimore, Maryland.

Although the Harrison report had a dramatic impact on forcing the military to improve conditions in the DP camps, it only suggested a solution to the Jewish DP's greatest worry—emigration. Unfortunately, few practical options existed for emigration. According to statistics gathered by the AJJDC in the camps, 62 percent of the survivors wanted to go to Palestine, and 18 percent wanted to go to the United States. Harrison said that the number of Jews who would like to emigrate to the United States was small, and he suggested that "reasonable numbers" of Jews with family ties now be allowed into the United States. President Truman did ease some immigration quotas from 1946 to 1948, but not enough to help the tens of thousands of Jewish and non-Jewish DPs who wanted to emigrate to the United States. What really made a difference was the Displaced Persons Act of 1948 and its 1950 revision, which together allowed 400,000 DPs to enter the United States from 1945 to 1952, about 80,000 of them Jews.

The Harrison report also recommended that the British revise its infamous White Paper of 1939 and allow 100,000 Jews to enter Palestine.[15] The whole question of a Jewish presence in the British Mandate in Palestine went back to World War I: In 1917, Great Britain released the Balfour Declaration, which stated:

His Majesty's Government view with favour the establishment in Palestine of a national home for the Jewish people and will use their best endeavors to facilitate the achievement of this object, it being clearly understood that nothing shall be done which may prejudice the civil and religious rights of existing non-Jewish communities in Palestine, or the rights and political status enjoyed by Jews in any other country.[16]

Twenty-two years later, the British, bowing to Arab pressure, reneged on this promise in its White Paper. It said the 450,000 Jews now in Palestine met the obligations of the Balfour Declaration. It called for the creation of an independent Palestine in ten years, a state to be governed by the Arabs and the Jews. Jewish emigration to Palestine would be limited to 75,000 during the next five years. An increase after this would be allowed only if "the Arabs of Palestine [were] prepared to acquiesce in it."[17] Arab leaders argued that no more Jews be allowed in Palestine since they already made up a third of the population. They added that they had no interest in sharing power with Jews. Arab leaders also urged British officials to reject the idea of a Jewish homeland in Palestine.

In late 1945, the Anglo-American Committee on Palestine failed to reach a decision on Harrison's proposals about Jewish emigration to Palestine. This did little to stop the flow of illegal Jewish immigrants into the British enclave there. There had, of course, always been a Jewish presence in Palestine. After the outbreak of pogroms in Russia in 1882, an increasing number of Russian Jews made *aliyah* (immigration) to Palestine (Hebrew *Pelishtim*, or Philistine). Between 1882 and 1929, 157,000 Jews emigrated to Palestine; another 250,000 Jews arrived there in the 1930s. The British, alarmed by these numbers, placed severe limits on Jewish immigration. In response, Mossad, today Israel's CIA, and Irgun, a Zionist paramilitary organization, began to organize *aliyah bet* (secondary immigration) to Palestine. From 1933 to 1948, *aliyah bet* brought 110,000 Jews into Palestine. The most famous *aliyah bet* operation involved the *Exodus*, a refitted American

ship chosen specifically to draw world attention to the plight of the Jewish refugees while the United Nations Special Committee on Palestine (UNSCP) was deciding what to do about the British protectorate.

The *Exodus* left Marseilles on July 11, 1947. A week later, British destroyers intercepted the *Exodus* in international waters and forced it to dock in Haifa. The British forcibly removed the ship's passengers, killing three and injuring more in the struggle. They put the *Exodus*'s Holocaust survivors on three British prison ships and returned them to Marsailles, where the French government offered them asylum. But the *Exodus* refugees refused to disembark. Efraim Menaker, who was on the *Exodus,* explained: "[A]fter Auschwitz and all those things we went through [we didn't want] to go to another place where the same thing would happen. We said we would get out only in Israel." Determined to rid themselves of the *Exodus* survivors, the British ordered the three prisons ships to Hamburg, Germany, where they forcibly removed all the passengers. "There," Menaker went on, "we were put in camps surrounded by barbed wire so they couldn't again try to go to Palestine." During the next two years, most of the *Exodus*'s passengers found ways to get into Israel.[18]

The British mishandling of the *Exodus* crisis had a dramatic impact on the future of Palestine. Several members of the UNSCP had watched in horror as the British forced the Holocaust survivors off of the *Exodus* in Haifa. This action would influence their input on the report the UNSCP presented to the United Nations several months later that recommended an end to the British Mandate in Palestine and the creation of a Jewish homeland in Palestine.

On November 29, 1947, the United Nations General Assembly approved Resolution 181, which proposed the creation of "independent Arab and Jewish states in Palestine" with Jerusalem governed as a "corpus separatum" administered by the United Nations.

Exodus arrives in Haifa harbor. USHMM Photo No. 64286, courtesy of Avi Livney.

In a vote of 33 to 13 with 10 abstentions, the General Assembly approved the resolution. The day after the UN's historic vote, the League of Arab States (Arab League) announced that it refused to accept the UN's decision and would go to war to stop the creation of a Jewish state in Palestine.[19] Israel declared statehood on May 14, 1948. What followed was its War of Independence against a coalition of Arab states that invaded Israel within weeks after its declaration of independence.

The Roma

Like the Jews, and to a lesser extent the handicapped, the Roma were treated as "homeless" or "stateless" displaced persons by the Allied occupying powers at the end of World War II. One British soldier, Frederick Wood, described the sight of Roma survivors in Bergen-Belsen: "We faced something terrible. Heaps of unburied bodies and unbearable stench. When I saw the surviving Romanies [Gypsies], with small children among them, I was shaken. Then I went over to the ovens and found on one of the steel stretchers the half-charred body of a girl and I understood in one awful minute what had been going on there."[20]

Weakened by malnutrition and disease, the Roma who survived the death and concentration camps were often too weak to leave them; many died in the days after liberation. According to Donald Kenrick and Grattan Puxon, those who had survived outside the camps

had lived for the most part in appalling conditions deprived of normal human contact. They had been denied every basic right, outlawed and isolated in remote areas. This isolation caused a breakdown and reversal of the process of *natural* integration, producing a generation further handicapped by war-weary parents. Thus the holocaust had touched everyone, killing many, blighting all. Many

[Gypsies] suffered mental breakdown as a result and some committed suicide.[21]

Life in the Displaced Persons camps was also difficult and painful. The Roma were often housed together with former SS members and other ethnic groups, which created a great deal of tension. Roma who had been interned by the Germans before World War II in the Düsseldorf-Lierenfeld holding camp were sent back there by the Allies after the war ended. Efforts by Allied officials to gather information from the Roma about their families were met with deep suspicion caused by centuries of discrimination. The Roma had learned that most official information gathered on them would later be used against them. This deeply ingrained distrust of non-Roma (gadje) made it difficult for Allied relief agencies to gain detailed facts from the Roma about their own experiences or the fate of their families.[22]

Roma orphans and single survivors were hit hard by the complexity of national or UNRRA regulations, particularly if they had lost their identity cards or were found to have served a prison sentence before or during the Holocaust. In such circumstances, the Roma could be denied proper identification papers, which meant they could be picked up by the police and imprisoned. In Germany, there were instances in which local officials seized Roma identity papers issued by the Allies identifying them as victims of Nazi persecution. Many Roma also lacked documentation proving their German nationality, which made them stateless. Yet such documentation was readily available to local or state officials. Local police records also had copies of prewar Roma identity cards proving their German citizenship. This was especially true for Roma who could not find a country that would allow them permanent settlement. In 1972, Donald Kenrick and Grattan Puxon estimated that there were 30,000 "stateless" Roma throughout Europe who were caught in this legalistic vise.[23]

Though it is difficult to estimate the number of Roma survivors in Europe, fewer than 5,000 survived the Holocaust in Germany. Of this number, 2,000 had survived concentration or death camps; the rest had somehow survived in hiding. The Nazis had seized all their possessions, which made it difficult for nomadic Roma to resume their previous lifestyles. Given the importance of family to Roma, their first task after the Holocaust was to find family members who had survived the war. Impoverished, and often illiterate, most Roma and Sinti found it difficult to find jobs, though some were able to return to traditional prewar occupations of selling horses or small wares. Most Roma and Sinti were so poor that they were forced to turn to petty crime to feed their families. Otto Pankok (1912–1966), a prominent German printmaker and sculptor who befriended, painted, and photographed the Roma in Düsseldorf in the 1930s, said that "it is as clear as daylight that among people in distress, criminal offenses, begging money, stealing food, etc. are more frequent than among officials who earn good salaries or citizens who are well established."[24]

The one constant in all this was the continued hatred of the Roma. It did not take long after the war for the prejudices and hatred that had haunted the Roma before and during the Nazi era to reappear. As the Roma returned to various towns and villages in Germany, the old stereotypical accusations against them resurfaced. Otto Pankok observed: "Hitler has sunk, but the racial hatred has remained unchanged; to those who do not believe this, I recommend a walk, accompanied by a Gypsy, in the streets of a city."[25]

Police throughout Germany began to revive prewar Roma offices, renaming them the Landfahrerpolizeistellen (Vagrancy Police Offices). They used the vast collection of information on Roma and Sinti gathered before and during the Nazi era to harass Roma. According to Wolfgang Wippermann, the police also used this Nazi-era network, which assumed "Mafia-like" proportions, to deny small business licenses to Roma and Sinti, and to refuse their requests for "repatriation and the restoration of their German citizenship."[26]

There were exceptions to this growing trend of postwar German abuse of the Roma and Sinti. Those fortunate enough to obtain a membership card in the *Vereinigung der Verfolgten des Naziregimes* (VVN; Union of the Persecuted by the Nazi Regime) found that officials in some parts of Germany were hesitant to mistreat them because the cards identified them as victims of Nazi persecution. Though founded in 1945 "to coordinate the efforts toward restitution in all of Germany," the VVN ultimately became a tool of East Germany's governing *Sozialistische Einheitspartei Deutschlands* (SED; Socialist Unity Party).

The question of citizenship and status as a persecuted survivor was important to Roma and Sinti because if they could document that they were victims of persecution, regardless of citizenship, they would legally fall under the jurisdiction of the Allied occupying powers in Germany, not the jurisdiction of the Germans. The Roma were also plagued by questions of nationality. The Roma and Sinti claimed that they were part of the friendly "united nations" who had defeated Nazi Germany, meaning they were subject not to German governments but to the jurisdiction of the military governments in occupied Germany. The Office of Military Government, United States (OMGUS), decided in 1947 that since there was no international recognition of the Roma as an "independent nation," their "nationality would be determined according to the rules to the establishment of citizenship." In reality, even though they acknowledged that the Roma and Sinti had been "victims of [Nazi] racial persecution," the Allied occupying powers in Germany had no interest in them. In fact, from 1945 to 1949, the Allies made no attempt "to deal with the Gypsies' unique problems or to formulate an overall plan for their rehabilitation and integration into German society."[27]

This seeming disinterest in the fate of the Roma during and after the Holocaust stems in part from the failure of the Allies to consider the Roma one of the core victim groups during their postwar trials in Germany. In fact, according to Drexel A. Sprecher (1914–2006), an assistant prosecutor at the IMT trial in Nuremberg, "the failure to make a separate submission to the Tribunal on the persecution and murder of the Gypsies" was one of the Nuremberg trial's significant failings.[28] Although the Roma are certainly mentioned again and again in many of these trials, it was almost as an afterthought as an "other" victim group with little depth or explanation. As a result, no significant body of testimony or other historical evidence came to the surface after World War II to help build a collection of documentation that Roma victims could later use in their modest efforts to try to gain justice and compensation for their considerable losses. Moreover, at least in some compensation cases in the Federal Republic of Germany (West Germany), judges again and again turned down Roma claims of Holocaust victimization, arguing that they were not victims of Nazi racial discrimination. Instead, they were simply common criminals prosecuted by the Nazis because of their asocial behavior. Though some German courts did begin to accept that the Roma were racial victims of the Nazis, this fact was not universally accepted in the Federal Republic until the *Bundesgerichthof* (Federal Supreme Court) finally ruled in 1963 that, from 1938 on, the Roma had been racial victims of the Nazis. Although this opened the door for claims and more documented testimony on Roma Holocaust victims in West Germany, it did little to help the largest group of Roma Holocaust victims: those who lived in communist societies in Central and Eastern Europe, where governments refused, for the most part, to recognize individual or ethnic suffering during the Holocaust.

The Trials of the Major War Criminals

In addition to dealing with the complex problems of the Jewish and Roma DPs, the Allies also faced the daunting task of denazifying Germany and placing important Reich leaders on trial for war crimes. Though there was ample legal precedent going back to the American Lieber Code of 1863 governing the behavior of soldiers during time of war, particularly when it came to the treatment of civilians, there were few legal precedents or guidelines for dealing with the types of crimes committed during the Holocaust. Efforts by the Allies to punish German war criminals after World War I had failed. According to Telford Taylor, the chief American prosecutor at the Nuremberg trials, the best that could be said of Allied efforts to prosecute war criminals after World War I was that "the mountain labored and brought forth a mouse."[29]

During the interwar period, the Allies tried to strengthen international provisions regarding instigation of war and responsibility for it, particularly when it came to aerial warfare, the use of gas, and submarines. The League of Nations' Committee for the Progressive Codification of International Law failed in its efforts to clarify such responsibilities and right of trial and punishment. Theoretically, the 1928 Kellogg-Briand Pact, signed by fifteen countries and later accepted by forty-four other nations, made these issues moot because each of the signatory powers had denounced war as a means of resolving international differences and now pledged to use peaceful means to resolve conflicts.

Yet the failure of the League of Nations, or more precisely of its great power members, to stand up to aggression severely crippled international efforts to make the Kellogg-Briand Pact anything more than an empty gesture. This, along with the angry walkout of Germany, Italy, and Japan from the League, its expulsion of the Soviet Union, and the refusal of the United States to join the League, added to this problem.

When World War II broke out, the world was not adequately prepared, legally or otherwise, to deal with massive genocidal deaths in Europe and Asia. As early as the fall of 1941, Winston Churchill and Franklin Roosevelt warned the Axis that one of the principal tasks of the Allies at war's end would be the prosecution of war criminals. Germany declared war on the United States four days after the Japanese attack on Pearl Harbor on December 7, 1941. A month later, the Allies created the Inter-Allied Commission on the Punishment of War Crimes and issued the Declaration of St. James, which stated that the Allied powers opposed retribution "by acts of vengeance on the part of the general public" and stated that "the sense of justice of the civilized world required that the signatory powers place among their principal war aims the punishment, through the channel of organized justice, of those guilty of or responsible for these crimes, whether they have ordered them, perpetuated them or participated in them."[30]

Later that year, in response to growing evidence of German atrocities, the Allies created the United Nations' War Crimes Commission (UNWCC). Fearing Allied involvement in Soviet internal affairs, Stalin refused to join the UNWCC and instead created the *Chrezvychainaia gosudarstvennaia komissiia* (ChGK; Extraordinary State Commission for Ascertaining and Investigating Atrocities Perpetrated by the German Fascist Invaders and their Accomplices) to investigate war crimes in Soviet territory. On December 17, 1942, the United Nations, a term coined by President Roosevelt, issued a statement accusing the Germans of the "bestial extermination of the Jewish people in Europe." Such actions could "only strengthen the resolve of all freedom-loving people to overthrow the barbarous Hitlerite tyranny," the statement went on. "They reaffirm their solemn resolution to ensure that those responsible for these crimes shall not escape retribution."[31]

It took a year for the UNWCC, which was politically weak, to organize itself. It had few resources and staff even though it was supposed to investigate and collect evidence on war crimes. In reality, it could do nothing more than record charges of war crimes. By the spring of 1944, the UNWCC had received reports on six cases of atrocities, none of them dealing with the Final Solution. In the meantime, on November 1, 1943, Churchill, Roosevelt, and Stalin issued a further warning to the Germans and the Japanese about war crimes: "Let those who have hitherto not imbued their hands with innocent blood beware lest they join the ranks of the guilty, for most assuredly, the Three Allied Powers will pursue them to the uttermost end of the earth and deliver them to their accusers in order that justice may be done."[32]

This meant that the crimes of the major war criminals would be decided by the major Allied powers, not by the UNWCC. On March 24, 1944, President Roosevelt appealed to the German people to distance themselves from those committing inhuman war crimes in their name.

The International Military Tribunal

The war in Europe officially ended on May 8, 1945, with the unconditional surrender of Germany; Japan agreed to similar terms on August 14, 1945. Six days earlier, the United States, Great Britain, France, and the Soviet Union put the final touches to the charter for the International Military Tribunal (IMT) as part of the London Agreement, which would oversee the prosecution and punishment of Nazi Germany's major war criminals. Initially, Churchill opposed this idea and wanted instead to shoot the most important German leaders. The charter gave the IMT the right to try individuals for three crimes and for conspiracy to commit such crimes:

1. CRIMES AGAINST PEACE: namely, planing, preparation, initiation, or waging of war of aggression, or a war in violation of international treaties, agreements or assurances, or participation in a common plan or conspiracy for the accomplishment of any of the foregoing.

2. WAR CRIMES: namely, violations of the laws or customs of war. Such violations shall include, but not be limited to, murder, ill-treatment or deportation to slave labor or for any other purpose of civilian population of or in occupied territory, murder of or ill-treatment of prisoners of war or persons on the seas, killing of hostages, plunder of public or private property, wanton destruction of cities, towns or villages, or devastation not justified by military necessity;

3. CRIMES AGAINST HUMANITY: namely, murder, extermination, enslavement, deportation, and other inhumane acts committed against any civilian population, before or during the war; or persecution on political, racial or religious grounds in execution of or in connection with any crime within the jurisdiction of the Tribunal, whether or not in violation of domestic law of the country where perpetrated.

Leaders, organizers, instigators and accomplices participating in the formulation or execution of a common plan or conspiracy to commit any of the foregoing crimes are responsible for all acts performed by any persons in execution of such plan.[33]

The charter guaranteed that all the defendants would get a fair trial based on rules agreed upon before the IMT trial began.

International Military Tribunal Nuremberg Trial

The IMT trial began on October 18, 1945, in Nuremberg, Germany, with the indictment of twenty-four Nazi war criminals. The Allies chose Nuremberg for the trial because of its

International Military Tribunal trial in Nuremberg, 1945–1946. USHMM Photo No. 65508, courtesy of Albert Rose.

historical importance to the Nazi movement and because it had a relatively intact courthouse large enough to handle the proceedings. The first session was held in Berlin, but was soon moved to Nuremberg. The IMT court was headed by Colonel Sir Geoffrey Lawrence (1880–1971), of Great Britain. The other judges were Professor Henri Donnedieu de Vabres (1880–1952) of France; *General-Maior* Ion T. Nikitchenko (1895–1967) of the Soviet Union; and Francis Biddle (1886–1968) of the United States. Each nation also provided alternate judges. Each of the four IMF charter states appointed chief prosecutors to oversee the investigations and trial: Robert H. Jackson (1892–1952), United States; Sir Hartley Shawcross (1902–2003), United Kingdom; *General-Leitnant* Roman A. Rudenko (1907–1981), USSR; François de Menthon (1900–1984), France.

When the trial began, there were only twenty-two defendants in the dock. Martin Bormann was to be tried in absentia, and Gustav Krupp was not tried because of ill health. The defendants were allowed to pick their own defense lawyers. Legal expenses were paid by IMT, which was able to find German attorneys untainted with a Nazi past. There was also simultaneous interpretation at the trial, and each of the defendants was given a copy of the indictment in German. Justice Jackson, an important figure in the trial, said in the spring of 1945 that "you must put no man on trial before anything that is called a court . . . under the forms of judicial proceedings if you are not willing to see him freed if not proven guilty."[34] The accused were indicted for one or more of the crimes in the IMF charter. Count one was the "common plan for conspiracy," meaning membership in organizations or groups

---

Nuremberg IMT Trial Defendants

Hermann Göring (1893–1946). *Reichsmarschall.* Headed Luftwaffe; Four Year Plan. *Death.* Committed suicide before execution.

Fritz Sauckel (1894–1946). General Plenipotentiary for Labor Deployment. *Death.*

Alfred Jodl (1890–1946). Chief of the Wehrmacht Command Staff. *Death.*

Joachim von Ribbentrop (1893–1946). Foreign Minister. *Death.*

Wilhelm Keitel (1882–1946). Head of OKW (Wehrmacht High Command). *Death.*

Ernst Kaltenbrunner (1903–1946). Headed RSHA, Security Police, SD. *Death.*

Alfred Rosenberg (1893–1946). Head Party Foreign Office; Reichminister Ostland. *Death.*

Hans Frank (1900–1946). Governor General, General Government. *Death.*

Wilhelm Frick (1877–1946). Headed Interior Ministry. Reich Protector Bohemia and Moravia. *Death.*

Julius Streicher (1885–1946). *Gauleiter* of Franconia. Editor, *Der Stürmer. Death.*

Arthur Seyss-Inquart (1892–1946). Reich Governor, Austria. Reich Commissioner, Netherlands. *Death.*

Martin Bormann (1900–1945). Headed Reich Chancellery. Tried in absentia. *Death.*

Rudolf Hess (1894–1987). Hitler's private secretary (before 1933); Deputy Führer. *Life.*

Walther Funk (1890–1960). Reich Economics Minister. *Life.*

Erich Raeder (1876–1960). Supreme Navy Commander to 1943. *Life.*

Baldur von Schirach (1907–1974). Youth Führer. *Gauleiter* and Reich Governor, Vienna. *Twenty years.*

Albert Speer (1905–1981). Reich Minister, Armaments and Munitions. *Twenty years.*

Konstantin von Neurath (1873–1956). Foreign Minister to 1938. *Fifteen years.*

Karl Dönitz (1891–1980). Supreme Navy Commander. President of Germany, 1945. *Ten years.*

Franz von Papen (1879–1969). Vice Chancellor. Ambassador to Austria, Turkey. *Acquitted.*

Hjalmar Schacht (1877–1970). Headed Reichsbank. Economics Minister. Plenipotentiary for War Economy. *Acquitted.*

Hans Fritsche (1900–1953). Headed Radio division, Propaganda Ministry. *Acquitted.*

Robert Ley (1890–1945). Head of German Labor Front. *Committed suicide.*

Gustav Krupp (1870–1950). Military Economy Führer. *Not tried because of health.*

---

deemed criminal by the court, namely, the SA (*Sturmabteilung*; Storm Detachment), the Reich Cabinet, the leadership of the Nazi Party, the SS, the SD, the Gestapo, and the General Staff and High Command of the Wehrmacht. The charge of crimes against humanity was the most innovative of the charges and the one most directly related to Holocaust deaths. Almost all the IMF defendants were accused of this crime, and only two were acquitted of it.

In his opening statement to the court, Judge Jackson said that

> The privilege of opening the first trial in history for crimes against the peace of the world imposes a grave responsibility. The wrongs we seek to condemn and punish have been so calculated, so malignant and so devastating, that civilization cannot tolerate their being ignored because it cannot survive their being repeated. That four great nations, flushed with victory and stung by injury stay the hand of vengeance and voluntarily submit their captive enemies to the judgement of the law is one of the most significant tributes that Power ever has paid to Reason.[35]

All the defendants pleaded not guilty at the beginning of the trial. For the next eleven and a half months, the court heard and accepted two hundred witnesses, 300,000 affidavits, and 3,000 documents, producing a trial record of 15,000 pages. The trial ended with

Hermann Göring testifies at the IMT trial. USHMM Photo No. 96334, courtesy of Gerald (Gerd) Schwab.

closing remarks by each of the prosecuting attorneys. *General* Rudenko ended his statement with these words:

> [I]n the name of the sincere love of mankind which inspires the peoples who consented to the greatest sacrifices in order to save the world, freedom, and culture, in memory of the millions of innocent human beings slaughtered by a gang of murderers who are now before the Court of a progressive mankind, in the name of the happiness and the peaceful labor of future generations, I appeal to the Tribunal to sentence all the defendants, without exception, to the supreme penalty. Such a verdict will be greeted with satisfaction by all of progressive mankind.[36]

The following day, each defendant was given the opportunity to make a brief statement. Hermann Göring denied he had any knowledge of the Holocaust; he declared:

"The only motive which guided me was my ardent love for my people, its fortunes, its freedom, and its life. And for this I call on the Almighty and my German people as a witness."[37] Out of the courtroom, an angry von Papen told Göring, "Who in the world is responsible for all this destruction if not you? You haven't taken the responsibility for anything! All you do is make bombastic speeches. It is disgraceful."[38] Though Göring merely laughed off von Papen's remarks, Hans Frank, who had converted to Roman Catholicism during the trial, said the crimes presented before the court had been committed because the German people had turned "away from God." Frank added: "I beg of our people not to continue in this direction be it even a single space, because Hitler's road was the way without God, the way of turning from Christ, and, in the last analysis, the way of political foolishness, the way of disaster, the way of death."[39]

A defiant Julius Streicher addressed the mass murder of Jews most directly:

> The prosecution had asserted that mass killings [of Jews] would not have been possible without Streicher and his "Stuermer." The prosecution neither offered nor submitted proof of this assertion.
>
> These actions of the leader of the State against the Jews can be explained by his attitude upon the Jewish question, which thoroughly differs from mine. Hitler wanted to punish Jewry because he held them responsible for the unleashing of the war and for the bombs dropped on the German civilian population.
>
> The executed mass killings I reject in the same way as they are being rejected by every decent German.
>
> Gentlemen of Tribunal.
>
> Neither in my capacity as Gauleiter nor as political author have I committed a crime, and I therefore look forward to your judgement with a good conscience.
>
> I have no request to make of myself. I only have a request for the people from whom I originate. Gentlemen of the Tribunal, fate has given you the power to pronounce every judgement. Do not pronounce a judgement which would imprint the stamp of dishonor upon the forehead of an entire nation.[40]

Hans Frank in his cell at Nuremberg. USHMM Photo No. 74835, courtesy of National Archives and Records Administration, College Park.

Albert Speer, who played a major role in war planning and use of forced and slave labor, talked of the danger of modern technology. Though Speer had accepted general responsibility for the crimes of the Nazi regime and admitted to using tens of thousands of Jews as slave laborers in underground aircraft factories, he still maintained that he was not guilty of crimes against humanity and of conspiracy to commit such crimes. He also claimed he knew nothing about the Final Solution. After his release from prison in 1966, Speer wrote a series of best-selling books on the Nazi era, and he expressed deep sadness for the crimes against the Jews; yet he still refused to accept responsibility for being anything more than a German technocrat. In her study of Speer's life, *Albert Speer: His Battle with Truth* (1996), Gitta Sereny called Speer's claim that he knew nothing about the Final Solution his *Lebenslüge*, the "lie of his life."[41]

The trial was over at the end of August. On September 30, 1946, the court reconvened and for the next two days the judges took turns reading the judgement. It began by describing the history of the court, the origins and rise of Nazism, and the evolution of the Holocaust. The judgement discussed the charges against various Nazi organizations and went into detail about the charges against the defendants. On the afternoon of

Albert Speer testifies at the IMT trial. USHMM Photo
No. 10375, photographer: Charles Alexander; courtesy of
Harry S. Truman Library.

October 1, the court announced its sentences. Nikitchenko cast the only dissenting
vote: He wanted to condemn all the defendants to death and find all Nazi German organizations criminal. In the end, the court
found only four of the indicted organizations and groups to be criminal—the SS, the
SD, the Gestapo, and the Nazi Party leadership. This meant that it was a crime to belong to any of these groups and that such
membership could result in future prosecution. Exceptions were made for anyone
below the rank of *Ortsgruppenleiter* (local
group leader), staff members who were not
office chiefs, and those who were not members of the Nazi Party leadership after the
outbreak of World War II. Hermann Göring
committed suicide before his sentence could
be carried out.

A world away, General Douglas McArthur
(1880–1964) created a separate International
Military Tribunal for the Far East to try
Japanese war criminals for crimes against
peace, war crimes, and crimes against humanity. The Tokyo IMT court was made up
of eleven judges drawn from various countries invaded by Japan. The court tried
twenty-eight major Japanese civilian and
military leaders. The IMT Tokyo trials lasted
from May 3, 1946, to November 12, 1948.
The court sentenced seven of the defendants
to death and sixteen others to life imprisonment. The remaining defendants received
lesser terms.

Allied Nuremberg Trials

The IMT proceedings at Nuremberg were the
first and, legally speaking, most important of
a series of war crimes trials at Nuremberg
and elsewhere in Europe that continued for
years after the war. The trials in three of the
occupation zones in Germany were part of
the overall effort by the Americans, the
British, and the French to denazify Germany
and prepare it for a return to democracy. The
legal basis for these trials was Allied Control
Council Law No. 10, which gave the occupying powers the right to investigate and try individuals "suspected of having committed a
crime, including those charged with a crime by
one of the United Nations."[42] Each of the occupying powers in turn reconfirmed the four
basic IMT charges, and added that the charge
of "crimes against humanity" could be used
even if the crime was committed before the
outbreak of World War II. Overall, the Americans, British, and French convicted more
than 5,000 Germans of war crimes between
1945 and 1949. More than 800 were given the
death penalty, though only about 500 were
actually executed.

Dick de Mildt estimates that "the grand
total of Germans and Austrians called to account for their involvement in Nazi crimes
before the various courts of the formerly occupied European countries as well as those of
the 4 main Allies, amounted to 60,000 persons." The "larger part" of those convicted

were in Eastern Europe and the USSR. In the Soviet occupation zone in Germany alone, "Russian military tribunals sentenced nearly 18,000 persons in *secret* proceedings during the immediate postwar years."[43] Between 1946 and 1947, U.S. Army courts tried 1,672 individuals in the American zone for violations of the laws of war.

Telford Taylor was the chief prosecutor at the twelve American Nuremberg trials, which involved some of Nazi Germany's most important organizations and individuals. Though all the trials and defendants could be linked directly or indirectly to the Holocaust, some were far more significant in bringing Nazi criminals to light than others. The *Einsatzgruppen* trial (*U.S.A. vs. Otto Ohlendorf, et al*; July 3, 1947–April 10, 1948) indicted twenty-four of the *Einsatzgruppen*'s most important leaders on charges of crimes against humanity, war crimes, and membership in a criminal organization. All the defendants pleaded not guilty to all the charges. The principal defendant, Otto Ohlendorf, who commanded *Einsatzgruppe D* and had earlier testified at the IMT trial, argued that he considered almost all the 90,000 Jews his unit murdered to be security threats to the Wehrmacht. What about Roma? "There was no difference between Gypsies and Jews," Ohlendorf replied.[44] Later, the prosecutor James Heath asked Ohlendorf about the murder of Jewish and Roma children. They were killed, he explained, because they would "grow up, and surely, being the children of parents who had been killed, they would constitute a danger no smaller than that of their parents." Then, he added, "I have seen very many children killed in this war through air attacks for the security of other nations."[45] Estimates are that as many as 1.5 million Jewish children died in the Holocaust.

Paul Blobel, who commanded *Einsatzgruppe* C's SK4a and later Himmler's *Aktion* 1005 units, made this statement to the court: "I did my duty as a soldier towards my Fatherland

Otto Ohlendorf, *Einsatzgruppen* trial mug shot. USHMM Photo No. 09929, courtesy of Benjamin Ferencz.

according to the orders given me by Richenau [*Generalleutnant* Walther von, 1884–1942]. I did not commit war crimes and crimes against humanity . . . I can face my wife and children with a clear conscience, and I can look into their eyes. I am not guilty before God and my conscience."[46]

The court found all the defendants guilty of all charges except *SS- Hauptsturmführer* Felix Rühl (1910–) and *SS- Untersturmführer* Mathias Graf, who were only found guilty of two of the three charges. Fourteen of the *Einsatzgruppen* leaders were sentenced to death by hanging; the rest received prison sentences ranging from ten years to life. *SS- Brigadeführer* Otto Rasch (1891–1948), commander of *Einsatzgruppe* C, was excused from the trial for health reasons, and *SS- Sturmbannführer* Emil Haussmann (1910–1947), who headed *Einsatzgruppe* D's EK12, committed suicide before the trial began. Only four of the defendants were executed—Blobel, *SS-Obersturmbannführer* Dr. Werner Braune

Paul Blobel pleads not guilty at *Einsatzgruppen* trial. USHMM Photo No. 09948, courtesy of Benjamin Ferencz.

(1909–1951), who commanded *Einsatzgruppe* D's EK 11b, *SS- Gruppenführer* Erich Naumann (1905–1951), who headed *Einsatzgruppe* B from 1941–1943, and Ohlendorf. The others—*SS- Sturmbannführer* Ernst Biberstein (1899–1986), *SS- Standartenführer* Dr. Walter Blume (1906–1974), *SS- Obersturmbannführer* Dr. Walter Hänsch, *SS- Sturmbannführer* Waldemar Klingelhöfer (1900–?), *SS- Obersturmbannführer* Adolf Ott (1904–1977), *SS- Standartenführer* Dr. Martin Sandberger (1911–?), *SS- Obersturmführer* Heinz-Hermann Schubert (1914–?), *SS- Standartenführer* Willi Seibert (1908–?), and *SS- Standartenführer* Eugen Steimle (1908–1989)—had their death sentences commuted; after serving brief prison sentences, they were released. The same was true of the two defendants who were initially given life sentences. In fact, with the exception of those hanged, none of the *Einsatzgruppe*n defendants found guilty served their full terms.

Equally important was the Doctors' trial (*U.S. vs. Karl Brandt, et al*; October 25, 1946–August 20, 1947). All the physicians charged in the Doctors' trial were charged with conspiracy to commit war crimes, crimes against humanity, and membership in a criminal organization. Twenty of the twenty-three defendants were physicians. All pleaded not guilty. The principal defendant, Dr. Karl Brandt, had served as Hitler's personal physician and was one of the architects of the "euthanasia" program. Another defendant, Viktor Brack, headed this program. Though some of the defendants were directly involved in various medical experimentation programs, others were in the dock because of their roles in administering such programs. *SS- Standartenführer* Rudolf Brandt (1909–1948) headed Himmler's office in the Ministry of the Interior and helped coordinate most of the medical experimentation programs in the concentration camps.

Brandt worked closely with *SS- Standartenführer* Dr. Wolfram Seviers (1905–1948), who headed the SS's Ancestral Heritage Office and was the director of the *Institute für Wehrwissenschaftliche Zweckforschung* (Institute for Military Scientific Research). He was involved with some of the gruesome medical experiments in Dachau, and he also helped fund the work of *SS-Sturmbannführer* Dr. August Hirt (1898–1945), the chair of anthropology at the University of Strasbourg. Hirt's experiments included collecting human skulls and skeletons. On February 9, 1942, Seviers sent Karl Brandt a report from Hirt about collecting the skulls of Jewish Bolshevik commissars in the Soviet Union, "a repulsive, yet characteristic subhumanity." Hirt suggested that the skulls could be obtained by a "directive to the Wehrmacht" and then turned over to a physician or medical student:

Karl Brandt on the stand during the Doctors' trial, 1946–1947. USHMM Photo No. 06232, courtesy of Hedwig Wachenheimer Epstein.

[This person will] take a certain series of photographs and anthropological measurements and is to establish, as far as possible, the origin, date of birth, and other personal data on the prisoner. Following the subsequently induced death of the Jew, whose head must not be damaged, he will separate the head from the torso and will forward it to its destination point in a preservative fluid within a well-sealed tin container especially made for this purpose. Based on the photos, the measurements and other data on the head, and finally the skull itself, the comparative anatomical research, research on racial membership, the pathological features of the skull from the form and size of the brain, and many other things, can now begin.[47]

Two other defendants, Dr. Siegfried Ruff and Dr. Hans Wolfgang Romberg (1911–1981), had worked with *Luftwaffe und SS- Hauptsturmführer* Dr. Sigmund Rascher (1909–1945), who supervised medical experiments for the Luftwaffe at Dachau. They murdered from seventy to eighty prisoners in compression chamber experiments to see how high a Luftwaffe crew could fly in a damaged plane before bailing out. The SS executed Rascher in the spring of 1945 for illegal adoption practices.

Another defendant, *SS- Obersturmbannführer* Dr. Wilhelm Beiglboeck (1905–1963), conducted saltwater experiments on prisoners at Dachau. In the summer and fall of 1944, Beiglboeck gave forty Roma pure saltwater with a taste additive to determine the effect of salt water on downed pilots and shipwrecked sailors. In one of the tests, Roma were first fed sea rations for two weeks and then given either desalinated sea water or pure taste-disguised sea water. One victim, Karl Hoellenrainer, gave this testimony:

At first we got potatoes, milk, and then we got these cookies and dextrose and rusks. That lasted about 1 week. Then we got nothing at all. Then the doctor from the Luftwaffe [Dr. Beiglboeck] said, "Now, you have to drink sea water on a empty stomach." That lasted about 1 or 2 weeks. This Rudi Taubman [another prisoner], as I already said, got excited and didn't want to participate; and the doctor from the Luftwaffe said, "If you get excited and mutiny, I will shoot you," and then we were all quiet. Then we began to drink sea water. I drank the worst kind, that was yellowish. We drank two or three times a day, and then in the evening we drank the yellow kind. There were three kinds of water, white water, and [two kinds of] yellow water; and I drank the yellow kind. After a few days the people became raving mad; they foamed at the mouth. The doctor from the Luftwaffe came with a cynical laugh and said, "Now it is time to make the liver punctures."

Then, one Gypsy ate a little piece of bread once, or drank some water. The doctor from the Luftwaffe got very angry and mad. He took the Gypsy and tied him to a bed post and sealed his mouth.

Then [another] Gypsy . . . refused to drink the water. He asked the doctor from the Luftwaffe to let him go. He said he couldn't stand the water. He was sick. The doctor from the Luftwaffe had no pity, and he said "No, you have to drink it." The doctor from the Luftwaffe told one of his assistants to go and get a sun. . . . Then one of his assistants came with a red tube and thrust this tube first into the Gypsy's mouth and then into his stomach. And then he pumped water down the tube. The Gypsy kneeled in front of him and beseeched him for mercy but the doctor had none.[48]

The court sentenced seven of the defendants to death, including Brack, Brandt, Gebhardt, and Seviers. Five, including Ruff and Romberg, were acquitted; the rest were sentenced to life imprisonment or terms of fifteen to twenty years. All the prison sentences were later reduced. In 1948, the World Medical Association issued its Declaration of Geneva to address the issue of medical experiments on human beings:

I will not permit considerations of age, disease or disability, creed, ethnic origin, gender, nationality, political affiliation, race, sexual orientation, social standing or any other factor to intervene between my duty and my patient;

I will maintain the utmost respect for human life:

I will not use my medical knowledge contrary to violate human and civil liberties, even under threat.[49]

The U.S. also prosecuted eighteen members of the *Wirtschafts-Verwaltungshauptamt* (WVHA; Economic-Administrative Main Office), which ran the concentration and death camps in the Pohl, or WVHA, trial (*U.S. vs. Oswald Pohl, et al;* April 8, 1947–November 3, 1947). All the defendants except Hans Holberg (1906–?) were charged with four criminal counts. Three were acquitted; four—Pohl and his three deputy chiefs, *SS- Obergruppenführer* August Frank (1898–?), *SS- Gruppenführer* Georg Lörner (1899–1959), and *SS- Brigadeführer* Heinz Karl Fanslau (1909–1987)—were sentenced to death. All except Pohl had their sentences commuted. The rest were given terms ranging from ten years to life. *SS- Obergruppenführer* Richard Glücks (1889–1945), who was in charge of WVHA's Amt D (concentration camp inspectorate), committed suicide on May 10, 1945.

Three trials, *U.S. vs. Friedrich Flick, et al.* (April 19–December 22, 1947), the *U.S. vs. Alfried Krupp, et al.* (December 8, 1947–July

31, 1948), and the I. G. Farben trial (*U.S. vs. Carl Krauch*; August 27, 1947–July 31, 1948), dealt with cases against forty-two bankers and industrialists charged with war crimes, crimes against humanity and peace, plunder, memberships in criminal organizations and, in the case of the Flick trial, belonging to Heinrich Himmler's "Circle of Friends." The Krupp trial dealt with the conglomerate's active role in Germany's military buildup before World War II and the use of slave laborers. I. G. Farben also used slave laborers, and one of its subsidiaries, Degesch (*Deutsche Gesellschaft für Schädlingsbekampfung;* German Corporation for Pest Control), manufactured Zyklon B. Three of the Flick defendants were acquitted; the rest received light sentences. The court found all the Krupp defendants guilty of the slave labor charge, though most received light sentences. Alfried Krupp was sentenced to twelve years imprisonment and forfeiture of his property. All the Krupp defendants were released from prison in 1951. Since no one had purchased the Krupp property, in 1953 Alfried Krupp regained control of what was left of the Krupp industrial empire. Another American court found twenty-four I. G. Farben defendants guilty of various war crimes but charged only three with membership in the SS. Ten were acquitted; the rest received light sentences that included time already served.

Twenty-four of the 185 German defendants tried in the twelve American trials between 1946 and 1949 were condemned to death, though only thirteen were executed. The rest had their terms reduced to life imprisonment. Twenty of the accused received life in prison, and ninety-eight received sentences of varying lengths. The American courts acquitted thirty-five of the defendants; four were removed from the trials because of illness. An equal number committed suicide during the trial. In 1951, John J. McCloy (1895–1989), the U.S. military governor and high commissioner for Germany, reduced

many of the longer prison sentences. He also reduced the death sentences of ten of those found guilty in the *Einsatzgruppen* trial. An amnesty that year released many who had received shorter prison sentences.

War Crimes Trials in the British Zone

The Royal Warrant of June 14, 1945, which laid out the guidelines for the conduct of more than five hundred trials between 1945 and 1949, provided the British with the jurisdiction for trials in their occupation zone. It was based upon the idea of royal prerogative, which was "nothing else than the residue of arbitrary authority which at any given time is legally left in the hands of the Crown."[50] The Bergen-Belsen trial (*Trial of Josef Kramer and others;* September 17, 1945–November 17, 1945) prosecuted forty-five former SS administrators, guards, and *Kapos* at Bergen-Belsen and Auschwitz. All except one were charged with war crimes and all pleaded not guilty. The principal defendant was *SS-Hauptsturmführer* Josef Kramer (1906–1945), known in the British press as the "beast of Belsen." Kramer began his SS career as a guard at Dachau. He quickly moved up the ranks of the concentration camp bureaucracy and eventually held important administrative posts at Sachsenhausen and Mauthausen. In 1940, he became Rudolf Höss's adjutant at Auschwitz; later, he was commandant at Dachau and Natzweiler. Kramer took command of Auschwitz in the spring of 1944 and was later transferred to Bergen-Belsen. One survivor, Helen Hammermasch, said that Kramer took an active part in the *Selektions* at Auschwitz, sometimes "loading the victims into vehicles, and beating them if they cried because they knew what was awaiting them." She remembered one occasion when Kramer kicked a Russian prisoner to death.[51]

Almost half of the defendants on trial were women. The most infamous was Irma Grese (1923–1945), a women's camp supervisor. The inmates knew her as the "Bitch of Belsen." In

1942, she became an *SS- Helferinnen* (female helper) at Ravensbrück; a year later, she was transferred to Auschwitz. She was soon promoted to *SS- Oberaufseherin* (Senior Supervisor), the second most important female position in the camp. Ilona Stein testified that Grese took part in the selections at Birkenau with Mengele and Kramer. Grese, who rode around on a bicycle, enjoyed beating prisoners for the slightest infraction. If anyone tried to hide or escape during selection, Grese had them shot.

Sophia Litwinsker testified that she had seen another defendant, Ilse (Ida) Forster, beat a young kitchen worker to death when she was in charge of the kitchen at Belsen. She "went on to say that Ilse Forster had beaten her with a rubber truncheon, with the result that her head was swollen and her arms and back were blue and green."[52] The court found thirty of the defendants guilty and sentenced twelve to death, including Kramer and Grese. The rest received sentences ranging from three to fifteen years in prison, terms that were soon reduced.

The British also brought charges against Dr. Bruno Tesch (1890–1946), the owner of Tesch & Stabenow (Testa), one of the two German firms that distributed Zyklon B for the SS and other Nazi organizations. Two of his managers, Karl Weinbacher (1898–1946) and Dr. Joachim Drösihn (1906–), were also indicted. Between 1942 and 1943, the deadliest year of the Holocaust, Testa distributed Zyklon B to Auschwitz, Groß Rosen, Majdanek, and other SS camps. Tesch argued during the trial that he knew nothing about the killing of human beings at the camps that used Zyklon B. This contradicted testimony by Anna Venzelman, a Testa stenographer, who testified that Tesch told her that he had been shocked to learn on a recent trip to Berlin that Zyklon B was being used to gas human beings.[53]

Weinbacher was Tesch's assistant manager and ran the company whenever Tesch was away. Drösihn was Testa's "senior gassing technician," though he claimed he only worked on delousing chambers and knew nothing about the gassing of human beings. He admitted to checking such chambers at Sachsenhausen, Ravensbrück, and Neuengamme, though he never visited Auschwitz.[54] The court concluded that Tesch and Weinbacher must have known that the shipment of such large quantities of Zyklon B to Auschwitz was for something other than delousing or disinfecting buildings. On the other hand, the court decided that Drösihn was of insufficient rank in the company to influence or prevent shipments of Zyklon B. It condemned Tesch and Weinbacher to death and acquitted Drösihn.

Between December 5, 1946, and February 3, 1947, the British conducted seven Ravensbrück trials. Twenty-one of the thirty-eight defendants were women. Eighteen were found guilty and sentenced to death; others received sentences ranging from life to two years. Only three of the Ravensbrück defendants were acquitted of war crimes. Other Germans who worked at Ravensbrück were convicted in subsequent trials in France and Germany.

The British also tried and convicted the commander of German forces in Norway, *General der Infantrie* Nikolaus von Falkenhorst (1885–1968); they sentenced him to death for his mistreatment of British POWs, but later commuted his sentence to twenty years. They also tried Luftwaffe *Generalfeldmarschall* Albert Kesselring (1885–1960), who served as German commander in Italy. Kesselring was accused of being responsible for the murder of 335 Italians at the Ardeatine massacre in 1944 as well as the deaths of countless partisans. A British court condemned him to death in 1947 but commuted his sentence to life imprisonment. He was released from prison for ill health in 1952. *Generalfeldmarschall* Erich von Manstein (1887–1973), who helped plan the invasion of France and served brilliantly on the Russian front, was also indicted and tried by the

British. Though he later ran afoul of Hitler, Manstein was indicted for the massacre of Jews in the Soviet Union. He was acquitted of these charges, but convicted for not protecting civilians in a war zone. The British sentenced him to eighteen years in prison but gave him a medical parole in 1952. He served as a military consultant to the West Germany government until his death in 1973.

The Federal Republic of Germany

One of the most challenging issues for the Allies at the end of the war was how to deal with a defeated Germany. Much of this was decided at the Potsdam Conference (July 17–August 2, 1945), where the leaders of the United States and Britain, Harry S. Truman and Clement Atlee (1883–1967), met with Joseph Stalin in the suburbs of Berlin to discuss Germany. The country was to be divided between the British, French, American and Soviets. An Allied Control Council *(Allieten Kontrollrat)* made up of the United States, Great Britain, and the Soviet Union was to oversee the military occupation of Germany. In line with the Morgenthau Plan, Germany's war-making industrial capacity was to be destroyed or turned over as reparations, principally to the Soviet Union. The Potsdam Declaration stated that the German people would have to "atone for the terrible crimes" of the war. The atonement involved the extirpation of "German militarism and nazism" to insure "that Germany never again will threaten her neighbors or the peace of the world." The Allies, the declaration went on, had no intention of destroying or enslaving the German people. Instead, they intended "to prepare for the eventual reconstruction of their life on a democratic and peaceful basis," the long-range goal being the ability of the German people to "take their place among the free and peaceful peoples of the world."[55]

In addition to the complete denazification of Germany, the Potsdam agreement also called for the prosecution of war criminals; in addition, Germany's judicial system would "be reorganized in accordance with the principles of democracy, of justice under law, and, equal rights for all citizens without distinction of race, nationality, or religion."[56] Part of the denazification effort involved the removal of all "members of the Nazi party" who had been "more than nominal participants in its activities and all other persons hostile to Allied purposes are to be removed from public or semipublic office and from positions of responsibility in important private undertakings." The agreement added: "Such persons shall be replaced by persons who by their political and moral qualities are deemed capable of assisting in developing genuine democratic institutions."

Months before Potsdam, the Allied occupying powers began to detain individuals they deemed dangerous to the occupation. In the American, French, and British zones, 178,000 people were arrested and sent to special camps, and the Soviets imprisoned 67,000 suspected Nazis.

Unfortunately, once the formal occupation began, there were few real guidelines for the denazification of the various parts of Germany. Each of the occupying powers dealt with former Nazis in different ways: In the French zone, where former Nazis were used in rebuilding a German economy to make it more viable for French reparations needs, the policies were lenient. The British were not quite so lenient, though they also tried to balance the needs of rebuilding by differentiating between serious Nazi criminals and lesser offenders. The Americans and the Soviets tended to adhere more closely to the Potsdam Declaration guidelines about the removal of former Nazis "from public and semipublic office and from positions of responsibility in important private undertakings."[57] Although the Soviets had no intention of helping build democracy in its portion of Germany, this phrase temporarily suited its purposes in eastern Germany. The Soviets were extremely aggressive in denazifiying their sector of Germany: They removed as many Nazis as possible from the government and "dismissed en masse entire professions such as teachers, judges, and police officers."[58]

To better clarify denazification procedures, the Allies issued a series of guidelines in early 1946 that listed the various offices and positions that former Nazis could not hold. In addition, Germans older than eighteen had to fill out a form that asked detailed questions about their activities during the Nazi era. One young German, Alexander Dick, described the process:

Every German had to fill out the Allied government's lengthy questionnaire (with 131 items), which contained some embarrassing questions relating to membership and activities in Nazi organizations. If one wanted a position, he needed a certificate of denazification that included proof of his classification as a nominal follower or beneficiary. Denazification boards attempted to shed light on the darkness of the Nazi past of those under scrutiny. But experiences . . . show that these denazification proceedings met with just as little success as the reeducation programs of the allies.[59]

The Allied Control Council's directive, "The Arrest and Punishment of War Criminals, Nazis, Militarists, and the Internment, Control, and Surveillance of Potentially Dangerous Germans," provided further guidelines for denazification. It distinguished between those Germans who had committed war crimes or crimes against humanity as opposed to those who were deemed dangerous to the Allied occupation and as such could be interned. The directive listed five categories of Nazis:

1. *Major Offenders*—anyone who committed crimes against victims or opponents against national socialism. This included anyone playing a prominent role in the Nazi party or its affiliated organizations or the Reich Government. It also included anyone involved in killings, tortures, or other cruelties in a concentration camp, a labor camp, or a medical institution or asylum. Supporters of the Nazi system and members of the Wehrmacht High Command were also considered major offenders. **Sanctions**: death to five years imprisonment.

2. *Offenders*—Nazi political activists, militarists, or profiteers who actively advanced the national socialist tyranny. This category included those who after May 8, 1945, endangered or was likely to endanger the peace of the German people or the world. **Sanctions**: up to ten years imprisonment.

3. *Lesser Offenders*—anyone, including former members of the Wehrmacht, who did not belong to the group of major offenders, but seems to be an offender, without however having manifested despicable or brutal conduct. **Sanctions**: up to two years probation.

4. *Followers*—anyone who was not more than a nominal participant in, or a supporter of the national socialist tyranny. **Sanctions**: limits on travel and reparations payments.

5. *Exonerated Persons*—anyone who, in spite of his formal membership or candidacy or any other outward indication, not only showed a passive attitude but also actively resisted the national socialist tyranny to the extent of his powers and thereby suffered disadvantages.[60]

Given the large number of former Nazi Party members in Germany at the end of the war, part of the success of the complex denazification process depended on the honesty of the Germans filling out the forms. Furthermore, these guidelines, though helpful, could not insure that all the legitimate war criminals and lesser criminals would be trapped in the denazification net. This question was further complicated by the growing tensions of the occupying powers in the early stages of the Cold War. Gradually, the Americans, the British, and the French moved towards the unification of their zones; this movement triggered the Soviet-imposed Berlin blockade in 1948. Though Berlin was deep in the Soviet zone, it was occupied by all four powers. For Stalin, who saw East Germany as an integral part of his growing East European empire, the Western presence in Berlin was an affront to his imperial designs in the region.

Within weeks after the beginning of the blockade in the summer of 1948, the Allies began the gradual process of transferring power in their zones to individual German states. Delegates from the eleven German *Länder* (states) in the Anglo-American-French Trizone met in Bonn, the new West German capital, to draft a constitution. The result was a provisional constitution, known as the Basic Law, that left the door open for the admission of the Soviet portions of Germany into a larger German state. Berlin became an official West German state, though it remained under Allied control. Elections were held in the summer of 1949 for a new West German parliament, and on September 21, 1949, the new *Bundesrepublik Deutschland* (BRD; Federal Republic of Germany) was born, though its sovereignty was limited by the terms of a new Occupation Statute of Germany. This document gave the new Allied High Commission, which replaced the Allied Control Commission, control of German disarmament, demilitarization, foreign affairs, and various economic questions, particularly as they related to reparations. The three Western Allies also had the right to station troops in the Federal Republic and to veto laws they deemed contrary to the security or democratic ideals of the new West German state. The Anglo-American-French occupation of West Germany ended in 1955 after the conclusion of the Bonn-Paris conventions. The Federal Republic of Germany now became a member of NATO (North Atlantic Treaty Organization), which had been created in 1949, and a full member of the European community of nations.

Joseph Stalin responded to the creation of the Federal Republic by transforming the Soviet occupation zone into the *Deutsche Demokratische Republik* (DDR; German Democratic Republic), which became a Soviet satellite state in 1949. Soviet East Germany became one of the defensive cornerstones of the Warsaw Pact (Warsaw Treaty of Friendship, Cooperation, and Mutual Assistance) to counter the integration of the Federal Republic of Germany into NATO.

These developments and tensions deeply affected the direction and intensity of denazification in the three Western Allied zones of occupation. According to West German statistics, Allied and German denazification courts dealt with 3,660,648 denazification cases from 1945–1949. The courts found 1,667 Germans to be "major offenders," and classified more than 23,000 as "offenders." Another 150,425 Germans were found to be "lesser offenders," and more than a million Germans were deemed "Nazi followers," a category that required them to pay reparations fines. The German denazification review boards exonerated 1.2 million Germans and amnestied, failed to classify, or left uncharged more than 1.26 million Germans. In other words, fewer than 5 percent of the 3.6 million Germans in the Western occupation zones "were considered the hard core of the Nazis and were charged accordingly." On the other hand, the Soviets dismissed half of the 553,170 former Nazis in their sector and kept another 83,108 from working. The rest were allowed to retain their jobs.[61]

The Potsdam Declaration effectively shut down the Nazi-era legal system. By the end of 1945, the Allied Control Council began to reconstruct the German legal system according to the idea that all individuals were equal before the law. They opened the German *Amtsgerichte* (magistrate), *Landgerichte* (district), and *Oberlandgerichte* (circuit) courts but forbade former Nazis from holding important court positions. In the lower courts, each of the Allied powers adopted its own rules about judicial appointments and the role of former Nazi Party members. Though the Allies' initial intention for Germany was to turn the clock back legally to January 30, 1933, they decided that such an action would create legal chaos; instead, they revived the *Reichsgesetzblatt* of 1871, Germany's criminal code, as well as the Imperial Judicature Act of 1877.

At first, though, they retained full control over all German court decisions, and they allowed German courts to deal only with basic crimes. The courts that did exist were not allowed to try former Nazis for crimes against Allied nations, though Allied Control Council Law No. 10 stated that, with Allied approval, German courts could try cases where German nationals had committed crimes against German nationals.[62] The British and the French gave German courts the freedom to prosecute such crimes, though the Americans, for the most part, refused to accede such rights to German courts. The only war crime eligible for German adjudication was "crimes against humanity." Trying such cases in German courts proved difficult and, in 1951, the Allies permitted the Germans to try war criminals under German law only.

Yet there was little public interest in revisiting the Nazi era. In addition, the West German judiciary was filled with former Nazi prosecutors, judges, and police, which made it almost impossible to bring former Nazi jurists to trial. Moreover, statutes of limitations on various Nazi-era crimes meant that, after 1955, only premeditated murder was a viable charge against suspected war criminals. Consequently, it became increasingly difficult for West German prosecutors to bring charges against suspected war criminals since most charges arose from specific accusations from survivors, many of whom were now dead. By the 1950s, the number of trials in Germany had declined dramatically.

This all changed after the second *Einsatzgruppen* trial in 1958, which brought to life the horrors of the crimes committed in the East to a new generation of jurists in the Federal Republic. Concerned about the government's ability to bring charges against suspected war criminals, the BRD created the *Zentrale Stelle der Landesjustizverwaltungen zur Aufklärung von NS-Verbrechen Ludwigsburg* (Central Office of the Judicial Administrations of the *Länder* for Investigation of Nazi Crimes [in] Ludwigsburg). The *Zentral Stelle*'s staff of lawyers and judges would investigate Nazi-era crimes and then turn its material over to individual German states for prosecution. The only crimes it could investigate were those committed outside the BRD, and only those that could be prosecuted under German law. It could not deal with war crimes per se, though in 1964 the *Zentral Stelle* was given the authority to investigate crimes committed in the territory of the Federal Republic. In its first year of operation, the *Zentral Stelle* opened four hundred investigations; by 1962, it had brought to trial more than 13,000 suspected war criminals and had convicted 5,000. The *Zentral Stelle* eventually created a master list of 160,000 suspected war criminals.

One of its most dramatic undertakings was the Auschwitz trial, which took place in Frankfurt from 1963 to 1965. German prosecutors charged twenty-four former SS men with crimes in Auschwitz. They were tried under German law, not international law, and the trial dealt almost exclusively with Holocaust crimes. The trial, which was widely covered in the press, forced the German public to confront some of the most horrible aspects of the *Shoah*. The defendants ranged from mid- to lower-level Auschwitz SS operatives.

Though only twenty were still in the dock when the trial ended, most were convicted of murder or accessory to murder. One of those convicted of murder was Emil Bednarek, the only *Kapo* defendant. Bednarek was charged with beating inmates to death. *SS- Oberscharführer* Wilheld Boger (1906–?) worked in Auschwitz's Gestapo office. He developed a cruel instrument of torture "that consisted of two upright beams, in which an iron pole was laid crosswise." The victim had to endure what was called the "Boger swing": "Boger made the victim kneel, placed the iron pole across the backs of the knees, and then chained the victim's hands to it. Then he fastened the iron pole to the beams so that the victim hung with his head down and his buttocks up.[63]

SS- Hauptsturmführer Franz Hofmann (1906–1973) was the highest-ranking officer tried during the Auschwitz trial. His career began in Dachau in 1934. He was later transferred to Auschwitz, where he was vice commandant of Auschwitz I. He served briefly as head of the Gypsy Family Camp, and in late 1943 he became commandant of Auschwitz I. He was later transferred to Natzweiler. At the end of the war he was released because he managed to convince denazification officials that he was an unimportant Nazi Party member. He was arrested in 1959 for suspicion of murder in one of Auschwitz's subcamps, but was later released. He was arrested again two years later and charged with thirty-four counts of murder and complicity to commit murder. The court found Hofmann's crimes to be particularly venal because he had gone far beyond just carrying out orders. The killing of Jews had become "his own affair," driven by his own ideological fanaticism. He was sentenced to life imprisonment.[64]

The Auschwitz trial was the last major war crimes trial in the Federal Republic. On May 8, 1965, a new statute of limitations on Nazi–era murder went into effect, a development that handicapped prosecutors. The statute was ultimately extended and later done away with for

murder. Prosecutors were also hampered by the fact the some of the most important documents for their cases were in East European and Soviet archives. The *Zentral Stelle* made a desperate appeal to countries in the Soviet bloc for documents, which Poland, Czechoslovakia, and the Soviet Union readily shared. In 1966, the *Deutsche Anwalt Verein* (German Bar Association) sponsored a conference of legal experts who discussed the declining number of war crimes convictions. At the end of the conference, the attendees called for "changes in the way Nazi criminals were judged."[65] By 1985, the *Zentral Stelle* had investigated more than 90,000 suspected Nazi war criminals and had initiated 12,000 cases against some of them. Of this number, 6,457 were given harsh punishments (12—death penalty; 160—life sentences). At its peak, the *Zentral Stelle* had hundreds of prosecutors and special judges investigating Nazi-era crimes. Eventually, its workload dropped to the point that it retained a skeleton staff. Moreover, according to it director, Alfred Streim (1932–1996), many suspected Nazi war criminals had been given "backdoor amnesty" by individual German states unwilling to prosecute them.

War Crimes Investigations and Trials in Western Europe

War crimes trials were not exclusive to the occupying powers in Germany. Most of the countries that had been conquered and occupied by Germany during the war conducted their own postwar trials, and they also served as friends of the court during the various Nuremberg trials. The Belgians tried 75 war criminals, and Luxembourg brought indictments against 68. The Norwegians tried 80 suspected war criminals and collaborators. The most important war crimes trial in Norway involved Vidkun Quisling, who was found guilty in September 1945 and executed the following month. In the Netherlands, the Dutch arrested almost 450,000 (5 percent of

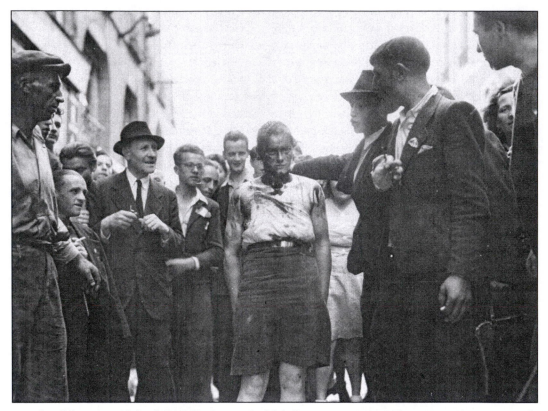

French collaborator with head shaved and covered with iodine, 1944. USHMM Photo No. 81868, courtesy of National Archives and Records Administration, College Park.

the population) people suspected of war crimes or collaboration at the end of the war; but by the end of 1945, only 90,000 were still under investigation. Dutch prosecutors stumbled badly when they arrested Abraham Aascher and David Cohen, two members of the *Joodse Raad* (Jewish Council), for collaboration. A strong public outcry kept them from prosecution, but the charges sullied their reputations. Ultimately, only 14,500 Dutch suspects were convicted. Dutch courts condemned 109 war criminals to death, but executed only 39. Over time, most of the Dutch convicted of war crimes had their sentences reduced, and by 1960, few remained in prison.

France

France occupied a rather unique place in the whole question of Holocaust justice because, on the one hand, the Vichy government was an active collaborator with the Nazis. On the other hand, at the end of the war, France was considered one of Europe's Big Four and given an occupation zone in Germany by the Americans and the British. A myth arose in France after liberation that in the face of Vichy collaboration, most Frenchmen had resisted Nazi rule. It claimed that the "traitorous deeds [of the Vichy government] resulted from the venality and fanaticism of a crazed few."[66] After liberation in 1944, French collaborators were quickly tried and executed, often by resistance groups. Henry Rousso has estimated that the kangaroo courts that cropped up during this period killed about 9,000 Frenchmen suspected of collaboration. When the political situation had stabilized, the "judicial framework of the [anti-collaborationist] Purge was voted into law."[67]

Those put on trial were accused of "acts harmful to national defence . . . secret dealings with the enemy . . . attacks against the national security . . . informing" and "shameful acts against the nation." All the senior officials of the Vichy government from 1940 to 1944 lost their civil rights and could regain them only if they could prove acts of resistance. The various courts set up to hear charges of collaboration examined the cases of 555,100 Frenchmen. Judgements were brought against 127,063 defendants. Of this number, only three were executed. Unfortunately, the crimes of the Holocaust were seldom mentioned in these trials, which concentrated on collaboration.

Once the political climate improved, a series of "show trials" in 1945 and 1946 replaced these legally questionable summary trials and executions. The "show trials" brought to justice some of Vichy France's most infamous leaders and collaborators. Pierre Laval, who served as prime minister in 1940 and from 1942 to 1944, was charged with "plotting against the security of the state and [sharing] intelligence with the enemy."[68] Though Laval mounted a strong personal defense, he was found guilty of all charges and sentenced to death. On the eve of his execution, he tried to commit suicide; then, sick from the cyanide capsule he had swallowed, he was literally dragged before the firing squad.

The trial of Charles Maurras (1868–1962), the leader of *Action Française,* a right-wing, anti-Semitic group that strongly supported the Vichy government, centered around accusations that he had "demoralized the army and weakened the national defense" by spreading propaganda.[69] Convicted of collaboration, Maurras was sentenced to death. The high court in Lyon commuted his sentence to life imprisonment. He was released because of ill health and he died soon thereafter.

Joseph Darnard (1897–1945) was the pro-Nazi head of the *Milice,* Vichy's France's paramilitary force. The *Milice* under Danard as-

sisted the SS during its roundup and deportation of Jews. Darnard chose men who ideologically supported the German cause. In early 1944, Darnard became the "secretary general for the maintenance of public order." The SS came to rely heavily on the *Milice* because, as Jacques Delpierre de Bayac has noted, "where the ordinary police might be friendly, or at least neutral, and the Germans were strangers and might be bluffed, *milicens* were sharp, suspicious characters wholeheartedly devoted to the bad cause and only too fully informed."[70] Darnard fled to Germany in 1944, but he was later captured in Italy and returned to France. In 1945, he was tried, found guilty, and executed. The case of Marshal Philippe Pétain was much more complex since he was a French national hero. A French court convicted him of collaboration and sentenced him to death. President Charles De Gaulle (1890–1970) commuted his sentence to life imprisonment because of his past service to France and his age. Pétain died in prison.

The last major collaborator's trial in the 1940s involved Rene Bousquet, who played a key role in the roundup and deportation of Jews in 1942 and 1943 as head of the Vichy police. Yet during his trial in 1949, France's *Haute Cour* (High Court) acquitted him of the charge of compromising national security, but found him guilty of *Indignité national* (national indignity; shameful behavior toward the nation) and sentenced him to five years in prison, a term the court immediately commuted because of his contributions to the resistance. Little was said during the trial about his role in the Jewish roundups. Bousquet claimed, in fact, that he had tried to temper the actions of Darquier de Pellepoix, the commissioner for Jewish affairs, who was far more powerful than Bousquet had suspected. He also talked about the pressures he faced from the Nazis and the fact that Vichy France's racial laws were in place when he took office.

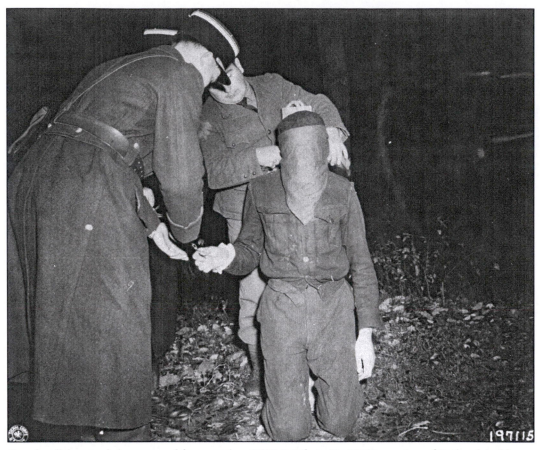

French collaborator being prepared for execution. USHMM Photo No. 81869, courtesy of National Archives and Records Administration, College Park.

Bousquet disappeared from public life and proceeded to build a career with the *Banque d'Indochine*. In 1957, the government returned his Legion of Honor and the next year amnestied him. During the next thirty years, he established a personal relationship with François Mitterand (1916–1996), France's president from 1981 to 1995; but the friendship soured in the mid-1980s as accusations began to surface about Bousquet's role in the Holocaust. The first hints of trouble for Bousquet came in 1978 when de Pellepoix told *L'Express* that Bousquet was responsible for the July 16–17, 1942, Véldrome d'Hiver Jewish roundups. Eleven years later, Serge Klarsfeld (1935–), a French Jew whose father was murdered at Auschwitz, brought charges against Bousquet. Initially, French officials seemed disinterested in pursuing them; however, after a public outcry and a protest from the International Federation of Human Rights, the government decided to reopen the case. In 1991, Bousquet was indicted for the deportation of 194 Jewish children in 1942. The next year, he was indicted again by the criminal court in Bordeaux as part of the case against Maurice Papon (1910–2007). Finally, in the fall of 1993, it seemed the French were actually ready to begin his trial. Bousquet, arrogant as ever, said, "If they give me a hard time, well, we'll just start all over, like the 1949 trial. I'll defend myself! And I have the means to do it! But I will be greatly surprised if there is a trial."[71] Several months before his trial was to begin, Christian Didier (1944–) murdered Bousquet in his apartment in the well-to-do 16th *Arrondissement* of Paris. Didier later told the press he had "killed a serpent."[72]

Papon's trial began four years later. He had been secretary general or executive officer of the Prefecture of Gironde in Bordeaux during the war. He was also head of its Jewish affairs office. He was actively involved in the Aryanization of Jewish property in the prefecture, though his trial in 1997 centered around his role in the deportation of 1,560 Jews in the Bordeaux region to Drancy. At the end of the war, Papon made contact with the resistance, which somehow protected him during the postwar collaborationist purge. He returned to his old Vichy job after liberation in Bordeaux. In the fall of 1945, he became vice director of the Ministry of the Interior in Algeria and, later, prefect for Corsica. For the next decade, he held important posts in French North Africa and, in 1958, became police chief in Paris. De Gaulle forced him to resign in 1965 after a kidnapping scandal, though he helped Papon secure a new job as president of *Sud Aviation,* which, after the merger with *Aérospatiale,* helped develop the *Concorde* supersonic jet. During the next fifteen years, Papon held important positions in France's two Gaullist parties, the *Union pour la défense de la Republique* (UDR; Union for the Defense of the Republic) and the *Rassemblant pour la République* (RPR; Rally for the Republic). From 1978 to 1981, he served as budget minister for France.

In 1981, the satirical newspaper *Canard enchaîné* published a number of documents provided by Michel Slitinsky (1925–), one of the survivors of the Bordeaux transports, that showed Papon had approved of the deportations. Papon quickly called together former resistance fighters who confirmed his involvement in the underground but also said that he should have given up his post in Bordeaux in the summer of 1942. In January 1983, the government charged Papon with complicity in crimes against humanity. Several months later, he filed a law suit against some of the victims who had recently spoken out against him. Though he lost the suit, he was able to get a French court to force Michel Slitinsky remove the preface from his book, *L'affaire Papon,* that described the former Vichy police official as "a true bastard."[73]

In 1985, a panel of three "experts" found Papon innocent of all charges and concluded that he had actually helped save a number of Jews. Two years later, an appeals court claimed investigatory irregularities and ordered an end to the Papon investigation. In 1988, new charges were brought against Papon, and three years later he asked the government either to try him or to end its investigation. A year earlier, Papon had sued the magazine *Nouvel Observatuer* for slander. In December 1995, the *Assizes Court* in Bordeaux decided to try Papon, later rejecting his request for a dismissal of the charges. On October 8, 1997, Papon's trial began, lasting until April 2, 1998. The historian Pierre Nora said that he thought the trial was important "because there were no more [Vichy] adversaries." He added: "Everything today is converging on the obsessive memory of Vichy."[74]

Papon was accused of ordering the arrest and deportation of 1,560 Jews from 1942 to 1944. His defense team claimed that he was a mid-level bureaucrat who had little control over the deportations. Papon, the defense argued, even helped some of the Jews by treating them well while they were under arrest. When the prosecution called in a number of experts who specialized in Vichy history, it was able to prove beyond a reasonable doubt that Papon had been responsible for organizing eight "death trains." The prosecution demanded a twenty-year sentence for Papon. On April 2, 1998, the court found the defendant guilty of complicity in the "illegal arrest" of 37 Jews and the "arbitrary detention" of 57 more as part of the Jewish roundups and deportations in Bordeaux from 1942 to 1944. He was found innocent of the charge of complicity to murder the 1,560 Bordeaux Jews sent to their deaths in the East. He was given a ten-year sentence.

Although French law requires someone convicted to go to prison before an appeal begins, Papon fled to Switzerland under an assumed name while his lawyers appealed the sentence. The court turned down his appeal because of this violation and issued an international warrant for his arrest. In the fall of 1999, the Swiss government extradited him and he was sent to the Fresnes prison, near Paris. His lawyers took Papon's case to the European Court of Human Rights (ECHR), claiming that the French court had turned down his appeal illegally. The ECHR ruled in Papon's favor and awarded him €65,400 ($77,400) in legal costs. In France, Papon's lawyers filed another appeal that asked for his release for medical reasons. He was freed on September 18, 2002, but lived another five years.

If Maurice Papon was, as Robert Paxton has noted, something of a "scapegoat" for the many French collaborators not prosecuted for crimes against Jews, this was certainly not true of *SS-Hauptsturmführer* Klaus Barbie (1913–1981), the "Butcher of Lyon."[75] The head of the Gestapo in Lyon, Barbie took pleasure in torturing his victims. Lise Leserve said that Barbie tortured her for nine days in 1944:

> "[She was hung] up by hand cuffs with spikes inside them and [was] beaten with a rubber bar. She was ordered to strip naked and get in a tub filled with freezing water. Her legs were tied to a bar across the tub and Barbie yanked a chair attached to the bar to pull her under water. During her last interrogation, Barbie ordered her to lie flat on a chair and struck her on the back with a spiked ball attached to a chair. It broke a vertebrae, and she suffered the rest of her life.[76]

Another Holocaust survivor, Ennat Leger, also testified: "[Barbie] had the eyes of a monster. He was savage. My God, was he savage! It was unimaginable. He broke my teeth, he pulled my hair back. He put a bottle in my mouth and pushed it in until the lips split from the pressure."[77]

But it was the torture of Jean Moulin (1889–1943), de Gaulle's representative to the disparate resistance movements during the war, that was Barbie's legal undoing after the war. When the Gestapo arrested Moulin in 1943, Barbie brutally tortured him to gain information about the resistance:

> Hot needles were shoved under his fingernails. His fingers were forced through the narrow space between the hinges of a door and a wall and then the door was repeatedly slammed until the knuckles broke. Screw-levered handcuffs were placed on Moulin and tightened until they cut through his flesh and broke through the bones of his wrists. He could not talk. He was whipped. He was whipped until his face was an unrecognizable pulp.[78]

A fellow prisoner, Christian Pineu, later described the scene: "[The resistance leader was] unconscious, his eyes dug in as though they had been punched through his head. An ugly blue wound scarred his temple. A mute rattle came out of his swollen lips." [79] Barbie had beaten Moulin into a coma from which he never recovered. Before Moulin died, Barbie put his mutilated victim on display in his office as a warning to other resistance fighters being questioned by the Gestapo.

Equally chilling was Barbie's role in the arrest and deportation of forty-four Jewish children hiding in the village of Izieu. On the morning of April 6, 1944, the Gestapo raided the house where the children were hiding. One witness described what happened next:

> It was breakfast time. The children were in the refectory drinking hot chocolate. I was on my way down the stairs when I saw three

trucks in the drive. My sister shouted to me: it's the Germans, save yourself! I jumped out the window. I hid myself in a bush in the garden . . . I heard the cries of the children that were being kidnaped and I heard the shouts of the Nazis who were carrying them away. . . . They threw the children into the trucks like they were sacks of potatoes. Most of them were crying, terrorized.[80]

The Izieu children were then sent to Auschwitz via Drancy. Another Holocaust survivor who testified at Barbie's trial described what happened to the children once they got to Auschwitz: "I asked myself where were the children who arrived with us? In the camp there was not a single child to be seen. Then those who had been there for a while informed us of the reality. 'You see that chimney, the one smoke never stops coming out of . . . you smell the odor of burning flesh.'"[81]

In 1944, Barbie returned to Germany to be treated for venereal disease. After the war, he worked as an agent for the United States Counter Intelligence Corps, first in Germany and later in Bolivia, where he lived under the name Klaus Altmann. He also worked for Bolivia's various military dictators. Barbie set up several internment camps for the dictator Hugo Banzer (1926–2002), and he was also involved in drug trafficking. In 1952 and 1954, French courts convicted him of war crimes in absentia and sentenced him to death. He frequently visited his family in Europe, and, on one occasion, he even went to Paris, evidently confident that he would not be arrested.

Serge Klarsfeld, a Holocaust survivor, and his German-born wife, Beate Kunzel Klarsfeld (1939–), the daughter of a Wehrmacht soldier, devoted their lives to finding war criminals such as Barbie. In 1972, they found out that Klaus Altmann was really Barbie and asked the Bolivian government to extradite him. Banzer was willing to do so only in return for considerable financial and military

gifts from France. President Georges Pompidou (1911–1974) refused, content that Barbie remain in Bolivia where he would "not dredge up any unwanted memories."[82]

In 1982, Bolivia finally agreed to extradite Barbie in return for a French shipment of arms, wheat, and $50 million. On February 6, 1983, Barbie returned to Lyon, where his flight was met by angry crowds. The next day, *Le Monde*'s headlines read, "He is going to pay, at last!"[83] It also published a special section detailing his crimes. It emphasized two points—the murder of Jean Moulin and Barbie's work with the Untied States after the war. Barbie's trial did not begin until May 11, 1987. It was, in many ways, the trial of Klaus Barbie versus the French resistance. He faced eight charges, though none of them dealt with the murder of Jean Moulin. The court spent the next three weeks hearing fifty-eight carefully selected prosecution witnesses. After the first day, Barbie asked to be excused from the trial. Most troubling was the testimony about the roundup of children and adults in Izieu, which had been detailed in Serge Klarsfeld's *The Children of Izieu: A Human Tragedy*, in 1984.

The prosecution's star witness was Elie Wiesel (1928–), the Nobel laureate and Holocaust survivor. Wiesel, who lived in France after the war, was hesitant to testify because he had no connection with Barbie. Though he was on the stand briefly, he vividly remembered that Barbie's defense attorney, Jacques Vergès (1925–), did his "best to dishonor the United States, France, and Israel by comparing them all to Nazi Germany."[84] In the end, Vergès tried to shift responsibility for Barbie's crimes to French collaborators and the French nation. It did not work. After only six hours of deliberation, the jury condemned him to life imprisonment. Barbie, back in court, responded: "I have some words to say, in French. I did not commit the raid in Izieu. I fought the Resistance and that was war and today the war is

Elie Wiesel. USHMM Photo N03392.

over. Thank you."[85] He died in prison of leukemia in 1991.

German Democratic Republic

The denazification of the Soviet-controlled portion of Germany began almost immediately after the war ended. The communist press inundated the public with stories of Nazi atrocities and provided full coverage of the proceedings at Nuremberg. But whereas the press in the Anglo-American-French zones emphasized the crimes committed against Jews, newspapers in Soviet East Germany concentrated more on Nazi crimes against the Soviet Union. East Germany's *Deutsche Volkszeitung* (German People's Newspaper) called June 22, 1941, the "darkest day in German history" and considered the invasion of the Soviet Union "the greatest and most fateful of Hitler's war crimes."[86]

The first step in Soviet efforts to cleanse their zone of the hated "Fascists" was to fire 390,478 former Nazi Party members from their jobs. The Soviets created 262 denazification commissions drawn from members of East Germany's new communist party, which looked into the background of 850,000 former Nazi Party members. The commissions found that 65,000 were worthy of punishment of varying degrees. By early 1948, the Soviets claimed that its denazification efforts were finished and that during the past three years it had dismissed 520,000 former Nazi Party members from their jobs. Included in these numbers were communist opponents, those who "had displeased the communists," and members of "old and compromised elites."[87]

The Soviets also imprisoned 240,000 Germans under Article III of Control Council Directive No. 38, which allowed the Allies to punish anyone who, after May 8, 1945, "ha[d] endangered or [was] likely to endanger the peace of the German people or of the world, through advocating national socialism or militarism or inventing or disseminating malicious rumors."[88] Of this number, from 78,500 to 95,643 died during incarceration. The Soviets also set up special courts to try war criminals in East Germany. Though much of what went on in these courts is just coming to light, they convicted more than 12,500 Germans of war crimes. About 200 to 300 were given life in prison, and about 100 were executed. In 1950, the Soviets turned over 14,202 suspected Nazi war criminals to the East Germans. In addition, they sent 12,770 to the Soviet Union and another 6,680 went to POW camps in the Soviet Union. A third of these died in Russian custody.[89]

Between 1948 and 1964, the East Germans tried and convicted 12,807 former Nazis of various war crimes. The bulk of these convictions (11,274) took place between 1948 and 1950.

The most famous were the Waldheim trials between April and June 1950, which convicted 4,092 Germans of war crimes and sentenced 32 to death. One hundred and sixty were sentenced to life imprisonment; 2,914 received prison terms of ten years or longer.

In 1997, Judge Irmgard Jendretzky was tried for her role in the Waldheim trials. She stated that she deeply resented being tried for what she felt was an "international obligation to prosecute Nazis." Instead of being punished, her attorney argued, Judge Jendretsky should receive "recognition and appreciation, not punishment."[90]

In reality, the Waldheim trials did more "to underline East German claims to upholding the role of law," since many of the cases were based on membership in various Nazi Party organizations or the military instead of individual responsibility for crimes.[91] Although some of the convicted were without doubt Nazi war criminals, others were cast as "Fascist" criminals simply because they had run afoul of the East German government. Although the denazification process in the Soviet zone was effective, it should be seen as a contribution to the creation of the one-party dictatorship in the DDR. The process was compromised and strengthened by the actions of the DDR's secret police, the Stasi (*Ministerium für Staatssicherheit*), which "recruited Nazi criminals, sometimes those who orchestrated massacres, as informers and agents both in the east and west."[92]

War Crimes Trials in Eastern Europe and the Soviet Union

The worst atrocities of the Holocaust took place in Eastern Europe and the Soviet Union. The Soviet takeover of Eastern Europe between 1945 and 1948 not only transformed that part of Europe but also changed the dynamics of war crimes investigations and trials. Instead of remaining individual national efforts to bring Nazi war criminals to justice, war crimes investigations and trials became part of a much larger effort to purge "Fascists" and others deemed enemies of the new political order in the Soviet bloc. Regardless, some important war crimes trials did take place involving some of Germany's most notorious war criminals

and collaborators. Part of this process involved the mass expulsions of ethnic Germans from the region, a policy agreed to by the Allies at Potsdam. Though statistics vary, more than 14 million Germans were forced to flee or were expelled from Eastern Europe and the Soviet Union between 1945 and 1950. About 2 million ethnic Germans died during the expulsions.[93]

Hungary

Soon after the war ended, the Hungarian government set up People's Tribunals to investigate and charge war criminals and collaborators for crimes against the people and the nation. The tribunals brought charges against 39,514 Hungarians and convicted 16,273 of war crimes. Most received short sentences of one to five years. Some trials of lesser criminals took place before the tribunals were set up in early 1945. The first tribunal cases involved camp guards and members of the Arrow Cross Party who had terrorized Budapest in the months before liberation. The first major trial took place in the fall of 1945. László Bárdossy, Hungary's prime minister from 1941 to 1942, was charged with responsibility for Hungary's role in the war against the Soviet Union as well as the massacres at Kamenets-Podolsk and in the Újvidék area. He was convicted on November 3 and sentenced to death. His appeal was rejected and he was executed on January 10, 1946, by firing squad. Another former prime minister, Béla Imredy, was brought to trial in mid-December 1945 and accused of being responsible for the first two Jewish Laws and the development of close ties with Nazi Germany. He was convicted and executed on February 28, 1946.

One of the most dramatic trials involved the Sztójay government's "deportation trio"— László Baky (1898–1946), László Endre (1895–1946), and Andor Jaross (1896–1946)— three top Interior Ministry leaders actively involved in the deportation of Jews in 1944.

Béla Imredy testifies during his trial. USHMM Photo No. 67687, courtesy of Magyar Zsido Museum es Leveltar.

Baky and Endre were secretaries of state responsible for, among other things, the "Jewish Question." Jaross, the interior minister, was their boss. Adolf Eichmann later said that when he was told to clear Hungary of its Jews, he had "no need to settle the other points because the Hungarian gendarmerie had its orders from Endre."[94] During the trial, the press was filled with gruesome accounts of the deportations and the fate of the victims after they arrived in Poland. After finding the "trio" guilty of the mass murder of Jews and their work with the SS, the court condemned them to death. Baky and Endre were hanged on March 29, 1946, and Jaross died before a firing squad two weeks later.

A series of Arrow Cross trials were held at the end of 1945 and early 1946. The first involved László Budinszky (1895–1946), Ferenc Szálasi's justice minister, and Count Fidél Palffy (1895–1946), the Arrow Cross leader's minister of agriculture. They were both con-

demned to death about six weeks before the trials of Szálasi and other members of his government—Károl Beregfy (1888–1946), Sándor Csia (1894–1946), Dr. Jozsef Gera (1915–1946), Gabor Kemény (?–1946), Jenő Szőllősi (1893–1946), and Gabor Vajna (1891–1946). This was perhaps the most widely publicized war crimes trial in Hungary because of the role each man had played in the Arrow Cross reign of terror at the end of the war. They were all found guilty of war crimes and condemned to death. Szálasi, Beregfy, Gera, and Vajna were hanged in public on March 12, 1946; the remaining Arrow Cross leaders were hanged a week later. The last major war crimes trial took place a few days after Szalasi's execution. The accused were all members of his government—Antal Kunder, Jenő Rátz (1881–1946), Lajos Reményi-Schneller (1892–1946), and Lajos Szász (1888–1946). The court quickly found the defendants guilty of collaboration with

Nazi Germany during the worst days of the Final Solution in Hungary. All were condemned to death except Kunder, who received life imprisonment.

Randolph Braham, the foremost scholar on the Holocaust in Hungary, considered the "record of the people's tribunals mixed." Dr. György Berend, the vice president of *A Népbíróságok országos Tanáca* (NOT; National Council of People's Tribunals), stated:

> If one takes into account how many leaders in responsible positions, how many warmongers and agitators against the people, and how many thousands of forced-labor-company murderer guards and *Nyilas* [Arrow Cross] mass murderers were produced during the 25 years before the liberation, the above statistics elicit serious doubts even in the most ardent opponents of the people's tribunals.[95]

Poland

With the exception of the Soviet Union, no other nation suffered more than Poland during World War II. The capture and punishment of war criminals became one of the priorities of Polish leaders after the war. In 1943, the Polish government-in-exile, under President Władysław Raczkiewicz (1885–1947) and Prime Minister Stanisław Mikolajczyj (1901–1966), created a War Crimes Office (WCO) as a section of the United Nations War Crimes Commission (UNWCC).[96] During the war, the UNWCC provided the Raczkiewicz government with the names of 36,529 suspected war criminals. The WCO concluded that 7,805 Poles were either legitimate suspects or witnesses to war crimes. During this period, the Polish underground, the *Armija Krajowa* (AK; Home Army), created its own courts to deal with war criminals in Poland. The AK courts tried and convicted 5,000 Poles for war crimes and condemned from 3,000 to 3,500 to death. Only about 2,500 were executed.

On August 31, 1944, the Soviet-sponsored *Polski Komitet Wyzwolenia Narodowego* (PKWN; Polish Committee of National Liberation), Poland's provisional communist government, stated that it would bring to justice Germans and Poles who had collaborated with the Germans suspected of war crimes and crimes against humanity. These would be summary trials without appeal. Soon after the war was over, Poland's new *Tymczasowy Rząd Jedności Narodowej* (TRJN; Provisional Government of National Unity) created the *Najwyzszy Trybunal Narodowy* (NTN; Supreme National Court) to try particularly important war crimes cases. In early 1946, the TRJN established the *Główna Komisja Badania Zbrodni Niemieckich w Polsce* (GK-BZNP; Central Commission for the Investigation of German Crimes in Poland) to investigate crimes committed against Polish citizens. The investigations included collecting documents and other evidence as well as interviewing witnesses and survivors of such crimes.

On November 27, 1944, a special court in Lublin began a six-day trial of some of the German staff at Majdanek, which had been liberated five months earlier. The court found six SS administrators, guards, and *Kapos* guilty of war crimes and sentenced them to death. During the next four years, the Lublin court tried another ninety-five guards and administrators at Majdanek, including Elsa Ehrich, the head of the women's compound. The court sentenced seven of the defendants, including Ehrich (?–1948), to death. NTN also tried five former Majdanek guards and administrators at the Auschwitz trial in 1947, including Arthur Liebehenschel, Majdanek's last commandant, and Erich Muhstedt, who oversaw the operation of Majdanek's crematorium. Both were sentenced to death. Another Majdanek trial took place in Düsseldorf, West Germany, from 1975 to 1981. Only eight of the sixteen defendants were found guilty, and these were sentenced to terms ranging from five years to life.

424   THE HOLOCAUST

Amon Göth on trial in Kraków, 1946. Photo: USHMM.

The NTN began its trials of major Nazi war criminals in the summer of 1946. Its first defendant was *SS- Obergruppenführer* Arthur Greiser (1897–1946), the *Statthalter* in the Wartheland, which included Łódź and Chełmno. He was charged with the deportation of the Wartheland's 380,000 Jews and expulsion of 630,000 Poles to the General Government. He was convicted on January 21, 1946, and hanged. Amon Göth, the monstrous commandant of the Płaszów concentration camp in Kraków, was tried between August 27 and September 5, 1946. He was accused not only of the crimes he had committed in Płaszów but also of the brutal closings of the Kraków, Tranow, and Szebnie ghettos in 1943 and 1944. He was sentenced to death and hanged in Kraków's infamous Montelupich prison. Rudolf Höss, Auschwitz's principal commandant during the war, was tried between March 11–29, 1947. Höss, who had eluded capture at the end of the war, was caught in 1946. After he had testified in the Kaltenbrunner, Pohl, and I. G. Farben trials, he was turned over to the Poles. He was accused of the "deprivation of life" of 300,000 Auschwitz inmates, 4 million Jews, and 12,020 Soviet POWs. The NTN also charged him with mis-

treating and torturing other inmates and with stealing inmate property. He was sentenced to death and was hanged on April 16, 1947, next to the crematorium in Auschwitz I. Today, a monument marks the site of his execution. The last case for the Supreme National Court was against Dr. Joseph Buhler, the *Staatssekretär* and deputy governor general in the General Government. The court charged Buhler with war crimes and crimes against humanity. The charges included the mass murder, torture, and persecution of Polish civilians as well as the "systematic destruction of Polish cultural life" and theft. The NTN sentenced him to death.

Erich Koch, the *Reichskommissar* for East Prussia, which included parts of Poland, was tried for the death of 400,000 Poles. Koch managed to delude capture for four years, but he was finally caught by the British in 1949. The Soviets demanded his extradition for his role as *Reichskommissar* in Ukraine. Instead, the British turned him over to the Poles in 1950. He was tried in 1959 and sentenced to death. The Polish government never carried out the sentence, instead imprisoning him in Barczewo in what used to be East Prussia. Some claim that Koch traded his life for information about art looted by the Nazis during the war. He died in prison in 1986. Jürgen Stroop, who oversaw the destruction of the Warsaw ghetto in 1943, was first tried as part of the Dachau trials in 1947 in Germany. The American military court charged him with the execution of Allied airmen while serving as HSSPF in the Wehrmacht's Twelfth Army District in the Reich. He was sentenced to death and then extradited to Poland, where he was tried for war crimes. He was found guilty and hanged in 1951.

Overall, the Polish government tried and convicted 20,000 Germans and others for war crimes after the Holocaust. Between 1944 and 1951, it convicted 18,000 individuals of war crimes, including 5,000 Germans. Unfortunately, some of the Poles who were convicted of

Gauleiter Erich Koch

Der Frontsoldat und Mitkämpfer Albert Leo Schlageter wurde nach seiner Kerkerhaft während der Ruhrbelebung von Führer nach Ostpreußen berufen. In einem entschlossenen Kampf gegen die Reaktion hat er auf diesem vorgeschobenen Polen die Kornkammer Deutschlands für den Nationalsozialismus erobert.

JUNI   30 Tage

11	12	13	14	15	16	17
Sonntag	Montag	Dienstag	Mittwoch	Donnerstag	Freitag	Samstag

Erich Koch. USHMM Photo No. 45260, courtesy of Geoffrey Giles.

war crimes and/or collaboration with the Germans were not guilty of these crimes. They were on trial because they were opponents of Poland's communist government. Much of this was not uncovered until the communist regime collapsed in Poland in 1989. Two years later, Poland's new democratic government transformed the GKBZNPO into the *Główna Komisja Ścigania Zbrodni przeciwko Narodowi Polskiemu* (KŚZPNP; Main Commission for the Prosecution of Crimes Against the Polish Nation), which is part of the *Instytut Pamięci Narodowej* (IPN; Institute of National Remembrance). Part of its responsibility is the investigation of crimes committed against the Polish people and nation during the communist era.

The Soviet Union

The whole question of war crimes trials in the Soviet Union, a nation that lost from 26 to 28 million lives during World War II, was complicated by the growing Stalinistic paranoia that swept through the country at the end of the war. To rally the nation, Stalin appealed to minorities and institutions such as the Russian Orthodox Church for the fight against the hated "Fascists." The government created the *Evreiskii Antifashistskii Komitet* (EAK; Jewish Anti-Fascist Committee) to oversee Jewish cultural affairs and to rally Jewish support for the war effort. Once-empty synagogues and churches were now filled again with worshipers. Yet by war's end, deep suspicion of all things foreign surfaced, and Stalin revived the massive Gulag concentration camp system that was such an important part of the purges of the 1930s.

During the war, the Wehrmacht captured more than 5.7 million Soviet POWs. When the war ended, only about 1.15 million Russian prisoners were still alive. Mark Elliot estimated that as many as 1 million Soviet citizens served "in German ranks" during the war, many of them drawn from the German POW camps.[97] By late 1942, the Reich was also using 1.8 million Soviet civilians as forced laborers. Between 1943 and 1947, the Allies forced 2.72 million Soviets to return to the USSR, and the Soviets repatriated another 2.9 million Soviet citizens living in territory conquered during the last year of the war. According to one official who worked for Stalin's principal secret police agency, the NKVD (*Narodny Komissariat Vnutrennikh Del*; People's Commissariat for Internal Affairs), from 60 to 65 percent of the returnees were tried and convicted of various acts of collaboration. Of this number, 20 percent were given death sentences or long prison terms, and from 40 to 45 percent got shorter terms, were sent into exile, or were forced to work on special Soviet rebuilding projects. The rest returned home, but they found it difficult to find work because of suspicions concerning their former incarceration or forced-labor work in Reich territory.[98]

Almost from the moment the Great Fatherland War began on June 22, 1941, the Soviets introduced martial law in several parts of the country and gave the military the right to use its military tribunal system to maintain public order. In November 1941, Stalin and his foreign minister, Vyacheslav Molotov (1890–1986), warned Germany that it would be held accountable for the war crimes being committed in Soviet territory. According to Alexander Victor Prusin, the importance of this declaration was that Stalin was charging the "*entire* German political establishment with planning, organizing, and implementing criminal acts." This would provide "the Soviet penal system with an all embracing legal instrument to deal with alleged war criminals."[99]

By 1942, Stalin began to pressure the Allies to create an international court to try war criminals, though he refused to join the UNWCC because he was afraid of Allied involvement in Soviet internal affairs. Instead, Moscow created the ChGK to gather materials on Nazi crimes. Alexander Vyshinskii (1883–1954), a major player in many of Stalin's "show trials" during the purges and, from afar, the head of the Soviet team at Nuremberg, became the ChGK's "éminence grise."[100] The Supreme Soviet, the country's "legislature," followed this up with an unpublished decree in the spring of 1943 that ordered public executions or lengthy prison terms for Axis soldiers and collaborators who had committed crimes against [Soviet] civilians and POWs. Military courts would judge such cases, and the bodies of those convicted and publicly hanged would "be left on the gallows for several days." The statement added: "[E]veryone will be aware that [harsh] punishment will befall anyone who inflicts torture and carnage on the civilian population and betrays his Motherland."[101]

What followed were three war crimes trials in the summer and fall of 1943 in Krasnodar, Krasnodon, and Maripol. The best-known of these trials took place in Krasnodar, in the northern Caucasus, from July 14 to 17, 1943. The military court accused eleven Soviet citizens of treason and collaboration while working with *Einsatzruppe* D's *Sonderkommando* 10a under Dr. Kurt Christmann (1897–1987) in the northern Caucasus. The accused were specifically charged with "torture and sadism, for mass executions and massacres by inhuman means, asphyxiation with toxic gases in specifically equipped machines, for the burning of and other methods of extermination of innocent Soviet citizens, including old men, women and children." The indictment added: "The responsibility [for these crimes] rests on the leaders of the gangster Fascist Government, Germany and the German command."[102] The eleven collaborators readily admitted their guilt, which their counsel blamed on their "Nazi superiors." The real criminals in the case, the defense went on, were "Hitler and his criminal band of generals."[103] The court sentenced eight to death and the rest to twenty years of hard labor.

Stalin treated war crimes trials during the war like the purge trials in the 1930s, namely, as political theater. At the Moscow Conference in 1943, Stalin, Roosevelt, and Churchill made this declaration: "[T]hose German officers and men and members of the Nazi party who have been responsible for or have taken part in the above atrocities, massacres and executions will be sent back to the countries in which their abominable deeds were done in order that they may be judged and punished according to the laws of these liberated countries."[104] At a meeting in Teheran a month later, Stalin jokingly told Roosevelt and Churchill that the Allies should shoot 50,000 German soldiers. The following month, the Soviets conducted the first public trials for captured Germans accused of war crimes, though there had already been a few courts martial and summary executions of Wehrmacht officers and enlisted men. The prosecution deliberately alluded to the Moscow

Declaration as justification for its proceedings. During it closing arguments, the prosecution rejected claims by the defendants that they were just following orders.

> Hitler, Göring, Goebbels, Himmler and their ilk—these are the principal inspirers and organizers of the wholesale murder and atrocities committed by the Germans on Soviet soil, in Kharkov, in Krasnodar and in other cities.
>
> Obergruppenführers and Gruppenführers of the SS—the Dietrichs and Simons, the chiefs of garrisons, commandants and gendarmes, leaders of the Gestapo of all ranks and positions among the German butchers— these are directly responsible for the deaths of hundreds of thousand of Soviet citizens.[105]

All four defendants were found guilty and sentenced to death.

Though it is apparent that some of the victims mentioned in these trials were Jewish, they were never specifically referred to as a group. The indictment against three Gestapo agents in the Kharkov trial from December 15 to 18, 1943, did, however, mention the ghettoization of Jews. But for larger massacres, the indictments simply mentioned the "massacre of Soviet citizens."[106]

These were the last Soviet public trials during the war. Stalin, at the request of the United States and Britain, discontinued the "show trials," though Soviet courts continued to try suspected German war criminals in secret. Between April 1943 and July 1944, Soviet military courts tried and sentenced 5,200 collaborators to hard labor. And during the last months of the war in 1945, secret police and military courts sentenced 5,000 Soviet citizens to death for collaboration. About six weeks after the war ended in Europe, the Soviets tried sixteen prominent members of the Polish underground in what became known as the Trial of the Sixteen. Each of these important Polish leaders was brought to Moscow under the pretense of discussing his

place in Stalin's new puppet government in Warsaw. Instead, they were charged with collaboration and various other war crimes. They were put on public trial on June 18; three days later, they were found guilty of various war crimes. Three were acquitted of all charges and the rest were given sentences ranging from four months to ten years.

A series of war crimes trials also took place in Bryansk, Kiev, Leningrad, Minsk, Riga, Smolensk, and Velikiye Luki. Soviet authorities also sought to extradite prominent Wehrmacht and German industrial leaders, among them *Generaloberst* Heinz Guderian (1888–1954), the *Chef des Generalstabs des Heeres* (Chief of the Army General Staff); *Feldmarschal* Gerd von Runstedt (1875–1953), who commanded Army Group A during the invasion of the Soviet Union; *Generaloberst* Georg-Hans Reinhardt (1887–1963), who commanded the XXXI Army Corps during the invasion of Russia; *Generaloberst* Franz Halder (1884–1972), who preceded Guderian as head of the army's *Generalstab;* and Alfried Krupp, but the Allies turned these extradition requests down.

One of the most significant trials took place in the summer of 1946. In the dock was *General-Leitnant* Andrei Vlasov (1900–1946), the head of the *Ruskaya Osvobditel'naya Armiya* (ROA; Russian Liberation Army). Vlasov, a highly regarded Soviet field commander, won the prestigious Order of Lenin in 1941 and was given the responsibility of defending Kiev, the Soviet Union's third most important city, in the summer of 1941. Vlasov also suggested the counteroffensive that Stalin adopted outside Moscow in late 1941, and he was rewarded with the Order of the Red Banner and a promotion to *General-Leitnant.*

Vlasov was captured in the summer of 1942. Intrigued by his capture and stories about his disillusionment with Stalin, *Oberstleutnant* Reinhard Gehlen (1902–1979), the senior intelligence officer with the German General Staff on the eastern front, asked *Hauptmann* Wilfried Strik-Strikfeldt (1899–1977), a Baltic

German who had fought with the anti-Bolshevik forces during the Russian Civil War, to talk with Vlasov and determine whether he was interested in becoming an "ally against Stalin."[107] Vlasov, who had become disillusioned with Stalin over a number of issues, particularly the conduct of the war, talked about liberating the Soviet Union from the communists and creating a Russian liberation army. Although few German officers were interested in Vlasov's political ideas, they found him a valuable recruiter among Soviet POWs interested in joining the Wehrmacht. But Vlasov dreamed of more, and he talked about creating a *Russkoe Osvoboditel'noye Dvizhenie* (ROD; Russian Liberation Movement) backed by an ROA. The Germans broadcast his speeches into Soviet territory. From the Soviet perspective, Vlasov came to epitomize the worst of collaboration. Hitler and Himmler were uncomfortable with Vlasov's activities, but tolerated almost anything that might strengthen the German cause. However, as things grew more desperate, particularly in 1944, Himmler changed his tune and even had a lengthy meeting with Vlasov.

Near the end of the war, Vlasov surrendered to American forces near Pilsen, in Czechoslovakia. He was kidnapped a few days later by the Red Army and sent to Moscow, where he was imprisoned in the NKVD's Lubyanka prison. Thirteen months later, Vlasov was put on trial, charged with voluntary surrender to the enemy, anti-Soviet agitation, forming the ROD and ROA, and training anti-Soviet espionage agents to wreak havoc and terror throughout the Soviet Union. Vlasov claimed during his three-day "show trial" (July 30–August 1, 1946) that he had never been involved in anti-Soviet terrorist activities. He was found guilty of all four counts and was hanged on August 13, 1946.

It was not until after the death of Joseph Stalin in 1953 that anything resembling Western-style war crimes trials were held in the Soviet Union. Before they began, the So-

viet government granted a general amnesty in 1955 to many imprisoned for collaboration during the Great Fatherland War. The amnesty did not cover those accused of murdering or torturing Soviet citizens, which paved the way for their possible trial as war criminals. These trials seldom mentioned the crimes against the Jews and Roma, centering instead on crimes against the Soviet people.

There were quite a few Soviet war crimes trials in Ukraine and the Soviet Baltic republics in the 1960s that dealt extensively with the mass murders at Babi Yar, Kovno, Riga, Vilna, and elsewhere. When the Soviet press discussed the trials, it tended to emphasize the general crimes against the "Fascists" and the fact that a number of war criminals and collaborators lived abroad, particularly in the Untied States. Although there was no question that the vast files of the ChGK contained a great deal of evidence about crimes against Jews, Roma, and others, little was said specifically about these groups publicly. They instead referred to crimes against the Soviet people.

Israel

Tom Segev concluded in *The Seventh Million: The Israelis and the Holocaust* that the Holocaust has had a profound impact on Israeli national identity.[108] For secular Israelis, the Holocaust has provided an important link to their Jewish heritage. The Israeli poet Oded Peled, the child of Holocaust survivors, expressed this connection in his lengthy poem *Mikhtavim lebergen-belzen* (Letters to Bergen Belsen):

> *Mother, I am with you in Bergen-Belsen,*
> *where you carry a poet in your womb . . .*
> *I am there with you always—*
> *After all, it is you and I, mother:*
> *You and I and the terrible snow*
> *that will remain with us always.*[109]

After the death of his parents, Peled visited Bergen-Belsen:

The memorial candle I brought did not light
In the strong wind
though I sheltered it with a Bible
A skullcap
A yellow star,
But the eternal flame . . .[110]

Although it would be incorrect to think that the creation of Israel was solely the result of Allied guilt over the horrors of the *Shoah,* there is no doubt that this played a role in the decision in 1947 by some countries to support the creation of a separate Jewish state in Palestine. But Palestine had long been a haven for European Jews seeking refuge from persecution in Europe. The number of Jewish immigrants seeking safety in British Palestine increased substantially in the years after Hitler came to power, despite British efforts to halt their arrival. This river of immigrants became a flood after the war, particularly between 1948 and 1951, a period known in Israeli history as the "years of mass migration." Between 1948 and 1951, 717,923 immigrants arrived in Israel, joining the 670,000 already there on the eve of independence. Among the newcomers were 373,852 Holocaust survivors.[111]

The question of Holocaust memory arose well before this era of mass migration. As early as 1942, there were discussions in Palestine about the need to commemorate the Holocaust and the role that Jews played in the Allied armies. Mordecai Shenhavi (1900–), a member of the *Vaad Leumi* (VL; Jewish National Council) and a resident of Kibbutz Mishmar ha-Emek, suggested the name *Yad Vashem,* which was taken from Isaiah 56:5:

I will give them, in my House
A monument and a name [Yad Vashem]
better than sons or daughters
I will give them an everlasting name
Which shall not perish[112]

At the end of World War II, Shenhavi developed an outline of a plan for a Holocaust memorial, which was approved by the Jewish National Council. It would consist of a Holocaust memorial center in Jerusalem with a registry of victims' names, a monument to the Jewish resistance, a permanent exhibit on the *Shoah,* a memorial to the Righteous Among the Nations, and an eternal flame commemorating Holocaust victims. Yad Vashem opened its offices in Jerusalem and Tel Aviv in 1946, and the next year held its first scholarly conference at Hebrew University. The outbreak of the Israeli War of Independence in the spring of 1948 severely affected Yad Vashem's operations. But two years later, Shenhavi began pressing the government to do more, not only for Yad Vashem but also for Holocaust survivors in Israel, whom he wanted the government to grant commemorative citizenship. On May 18, 1953, the Knesset, Israel's parliament, unanimously passed the Yad Vashem Law; this law created the Martyrs' and Heroes' Remembrance Authority. Since that time, Yad Vashem, which is located on Har Hazikaron (the Mount of Remembrance), in Jerusalem, has become the world's foremost Holocaust memorial, archive, and research center. Its creation insured that the memory and story of the victims would forever be remembered and honored. And each year after *Pesach* (Passover), Israel commemorates the Holocaust on *Yom HaShoah,* Holocaust Remembrance Day.

But the Holocaust was also memorialized by Israel's commitment to help locate and prosecute the many war criminals who escaped prosecution after the war. Although the most storied examples of these efforts centered around the kidnapping and trial of Adolf Eichmann, Israeli investigators played important roles in the search and/or prosecution of Nazi war criminals such as Josef Mengele and John Demjanjuk.

In the final weeks of World War II, Ernst Kaltenbrunner, the head of the RSHA, ordered Adolf Eichmann to bring 1,000 to 1,200 important Jews in Theresienstadt to the

SS redoubt in the Tyrolean mountains in western Austria. Eichmann, who was now in Innsbruck, made preparations to receive the Jews but lost contact with Theresienstadt. Kaltenbrunner then ordered Eichmann to meet him in Altausee, where he was to organize SS resistance efforts against the Allies. Once in the mountains, Eichmann received orders from Himmler not to fire on U.S. or British troops. Several days after the war ended, an American army patrol arrested Eichmann, who was wearing a Luftwaffe uniform. Since he had not been able to burn off his SS blood group, located on his left underarm, Eichmann claimed he was *SS- Oberscharführer* Bart and, later, *SS- Untersturmführer* Otto Eckmann. With the help of other SS officers, he acquired a new identity as Otto Henninger and managed to escape from the Ober-Dachstetten POW camp in early 1946.

For the next three years, Eichmann lived undetected in the British zone of Germany, even though his crimes had been highlighted in the various war crimes trials taking place at the time. Eichmann, fearful of detection, was able to obtain an Argentinian visa from the "rat line" network run by Alois Luigi Hudal (1885–1963), the "Brown" Roman Catholic bishop, who headed the Austrian section of the pope's Pontifical Commission of Assistance. With this visa and a Red Cross passport, Eichmann fled to Argentina in 1950 as Ricardo Klement. When he arrived in Buenos Aires, Carlos Horst Fuldner (1910–), an Argentinian German who had served in the SS and ran an organization that helped former SS men settle in Argentina, gave Eichmann a job with his company, CAPRI, in Tucumán and Santiago del Estero provinces in the remote northern part of the country. In 1952, Eichmann sent for his family; a year later he moved to Buenos Aires, where he tried his hand at a number of businesses. Unable to keep a job, Eichmann turned to former SS friends, who found him work as a welder in a suburban Mercedes-Benz plant, where he quickly rose to depart-

ment head. Eichmann, who named his newborn son Francisco Klement Eichmann, became more and more open about his identity, hubris that ultimately led to his capture.

In 1959, Simon Wiesenthal (1908–2005), a Holocaust survivor who dedicated his life to bringing Nazi war criminals to justice, provided Mossad with information about Eichmann's whereabouts in Argentina. At the same time, a West German investigation was being led by Fritz Bauer (1903–1968), a Holocaust survivor and the attorney general in the state of Hesse. The Israel government sent Zvi Aharoni (1912–) to Buenos Aires in 1960 to determine whether Ricardo Klement was really Adolf Eichmann. Mossad, convinced that Klement was Eichmann, placed him under surveillance as it laid plans to kidnap him and bring him back to trial in Israel.

The Israelis approached the West German government about extradition. Though the West Germans wanted to try Eichmann, Bonn told Mossad that it was unlikely the Argentinians would extradite him to the Federal Republic given their track record on earlier requests. The Israelis then considered assassinating him, but felt that Eichmann should stand trial for his crimes. Their plan was to kidnap Eichmann on May 10 and sneak him onboard an El Al flight three days later; Foreign Minister Abba Eban (1915–2002), who was visiting Argentina, would also be on the plane. When Eban changed his travel plans, the Israelis decided to capture Eichmann on May 11 and hold him in a safe house until Eban left Buenos Aires on May 21. On May 11, 1960, Mossad agents kidnapped Eichmann as he returned from work near his home at 6061 Garibaldi Street in the suburbs of Buenos Aires. After Mossad agents discovered his SS tattoo, Eichmann readily admitted his real identity. He also signed a statement agreeing to go to Israel to stand trial: "I, the undersigned, Adolf Eichmann, declare of my own free will that, as my true identity has been discovered, I realize that it is futile for me to attempt to go

Adolf Eichmann on trial in Israel, 1961. USHMM Photo No. 65268, courtesy of Israel Government Press Office.

on evading justice. I state that I am prepared to travel to Israel to stand trial in that country before a competent court."[113]

Mossad also asked Eichmann about the whereabouts of Josef Mengele and Martin Bormann. He claimed he knew nothing about them.

On May 23, 1960, David Ben–Gurion (1886–1973), the Israeli prime minister, told the Knesset of Eichmann's capture and forthcoming trial. The news electrified and traumatized Israel. Roman Frister (1928–), a Holocaust survivor, expressed his feelings in *Al Hanishmar:*

I cannot remember an atmosphere similar to ... that afternoon, when news spread of the capture of that modern day Haman [an ancient Agagite king who wanted to murder all Jews] and number-one murderer of Jews—Adolf Eichmann. ... Many of those with whom I spoke are convinced that since the Sinai Cam-

paign [1956 Suez War], Israel has not known an event that has touched so profoundly the hearts of each and every one of its people.[114]

For the next seven months, a special Israeli police unit, Bureau 06, interrogated Eichmann. In early January 1961, they presented Gideon Hausner (1915–1990), the Israeli attorney general, with evidence of Eichmann's crimes, drawn principally from war crimes trial material provided by Yad Vashem. But Hausner did not want to take the Allied approach of letting the documents and a few witnesses tell the story. What the Eichmann trial demanded, he later wrote in his memoirs, was "a living record of a gigantic human and national disaster." Holocaust survivors, many of them already living in Israel, would provide the prosecution with the "living record" Hausner wanted so much.[115]

On February 21, 1961, Hausner indicted Eichmann on fifteen counts, including four counts of crimes against the Jewish people, seven counts of crimes against humanity, one count of war crimes, and three counts of membership in a hostile organization. Eichmann pleaded not guilty to all counts. During his trial, which began on April 11, 1961, Eichmann sat in a bullet-proof glass booth. The trial was presided over by Justice Moshe Landau (1912–2006) of the Israeli Supreme Court and two other highly respected Israeli jurists, Dr. Benjamin Halevi and Dr. Yitzhak Raveh. Eichmann's defense team was led by Dr. Robert Servatius (1895–1988), who had earlier defended Fritz Sauckel and Karl Brandt. Servatius based his defense on the right of the Israeli court to prosecute Eichmann, questions about the court's impartiality, and the legality of Eichmann's kidnapping as well as the fact that Israel had been created after the Holocaust and the crimes Eichmann was accused of took place outside Israel. Servatius also argued that the defendant had been a small fish in a big pond who was only following orders. The trial ended on August 14, 1961. The court did not reconvene until December 11, when the judges read their lengthy decision. They found a stunned Adolf Eichmann guilty of all counts and condemned him to death. Eichmann's appeals to the Israeli Supreme Court and the president of Israel failed, and at midnight on May 31, 1962, he was hanged at Ramla prison. His body was cremated and his ashes scattered in the Mediterranean Sea off the coast of Jaffa.

Controversy swirled around the Eichmann trial, which transformed a somnolent world's view and interest in the Holocaust. There was a surprising reaction to the trial in some quarters, both in Israel and abroad, particularly over Eichmann's execution. At least one prominent Israeli judge, Haim Cohn, refused to take part in the appeals process, and other Israelis argued against the death penalty because it would give a "false sense of expiation to take one life in retribution for the loss of six million"; it was also "a pointless act that would only confirm to a global audience the myth that Jews were a vengeful people." Internationally, Arnold Toynbee, Arthur Koestler, Pearl Buck, and others protested Eichmann's death sentence as an act of vengeance.[116]

Hannah Arendt's articles on the trial in the *New Yorker* and her expanded account in *Eichmann in Jerusalem: A Report on the Banality of Evil* (1963) stirred up new debate about Eichmann, his trial, and his crimes. Arendt (1906–1975), a gifted political theorist, put Eichmann's trial and his war crimes in the greater context of the complex German Nazi dictatorship. She raised questions about Israel's right to try Eichmann and wondered about the court's impartiality. She also drew unfortunate parallels between Eichmann, whom she felt represented the "banality of evil," and the leadership of the Jewish communities in Europe during the Holocaust, who had drawn up the lists of Jews later deported by Eichmann's operatives. In doing so, Arendt touched on a highly sensitive issue that many found insulting. David Cesarani was extremely critical of Arendt in his biography *Becoming Eichmann: Rethinking the Life, Crimes, and Trial of a "Desk Murderer."* He considered her reporting inaccurate and prejudicial. He also thought her opinions concerning Israel and the Israelis "veered into racism."[117]

Arendt also had her supporters, though their numbers were small compared to those of her critics. Arendt looked at Eichmann and the Nazis "as human beings who performed mass murder." The same was true, she argued, of the Nazis' victims, who had a role in their own fate. Eichmann was merely a bureaucrat, she thought, doing his duty. According to Richard I. Cohen, her critics "relied on the power and the myth [of the Holocaust] and the sacredness of the memory to delegitimize the author and her work and bring back the broken vessels from their former state." Yet, Cohen noted, scholars today appreciate Arendt's contribution to "understanding the nature of evil in modern society and the problem of individual choice and freedom of action."[118]

Although the capture and trial of Adolf Eichmann was a seminal moment in Israeli and Holocaust history, it was just one episode in Israeli efforts to find other Nazi war criminals. Originally, Mossad had hoped to kidnap Josef Mengele, Auschwitz's "Angel of Death," and bring him back to Israel with Eichmann. Like his Gestapo counterpart, Mengele had been captured by U.S. forces at the end of the war and then released, despite mounting evidence of his war crimes. Between 1945 and 1949, Mengele lived in Bavaria as Fritz Hollmann, working as a farmhand. Encouraged by his well-to-do family, he decided to move to Argentina in 1948, where he prospered. In 1956, he flew to Switzerland via new York, where he met his future wife, Martha, and his son from a previous marriage, Rolf. Mengele also visited his father in Günsburg, Bavaria. After he returned to Argentina, he resumed his real name.

This was a mistake. Hermann Langbein (1912–1995), who had worked as a clerk in the office of Dr. Eduard Wirths, the chief physician at Auschwitz, spent a decade after the war looking for Mengele, whom he had seen almost every day in Wirths's office. Langbein, whom Yad Vashem later declared a Righteous Among the Nations, described Mengele as a "'merciless cynic' with organizational talent and initiative." He was also a "workaholic" who seemed to enjoy his work physically and mentally torturing prisoners.[119] After Langbein found Mengele in Buenos Aires, he informed West German authorities about his whereabouts. In 1959, the West Germans began extradition hearings against Mengele. When Mengele got wind of these proceedings, he moved to nearby Paraguay, where authorities, aware of the German extradition efforts, granted him citizenship.

In the meantime, Ben Gurion told the Knesset that his government was searching

for Mengle as well as for Eichmann. But once Mossad agents learned of Mengele's move to Paraguay, they gave up trying to kidnap him, concentrating all their efforts on capturing Eichmann. Mengele, fearing the Israelis, quickly moved to São Paulo, Brazil, using the name Peter Hochbichler. In 1971, he obtained a Brazilian identity card under the name of Wolfgang Gerhard. For the next eight years, he lived a life of fear, loneliness, and declining health. On February 7, 1979, he suffered a stroke while swimming in the ocean in Santos, Brazil. He was buried in the Our Lady of the Rosary cemetery in Embu, a suburb of São Paulo. His death was never made public.

To highlight efforts to find Mengele, in early 1985 Wiesenthal staged a mock trial in Jerusalem that featured Gideon Hausner, Telford Taylor, and testimony from some of Mengele's "guinea-pig survivors."[120] Wiesenthal also wrote to Kurt Waldheim, the secretary general of the United Nations, and asked him to do what he could to pressure Paraguay to extradite Mengele to West Germany. The Paraguayans revoked Mengele's citizenship, which meant little since Mengele was already dead. The United States got involved in the search for Mengele after it learned that he might have been in U.S. custody in 1947. The recently created U.S. Office of Special Investigations (OSI), which was responsible for locating, prosecuting, and deporting the hundreds of Nazis who had entered the United States illegally after the war, announced that it was going to help in the hunt for Mengele. Israel reopened its search, and the West German government offered a reward of 1 million marks ($330,000) for his capture. The Simon Wiesenthal Center and the *Washington Times* offered similar rewards. The West Germans, working with São Paulo's police chief, Romeo Tuma, broke the case and located Mengele's body in Embu later that year. The Simon Wiesenthal Center sent a team of American forensic experts to examine the body, which they verified was that of Josef Mengele.

John Demjanjuk on trial in Israel, 1988. USHMM Photo No. 65266, courtesy of Israel Government Press Office.

In the midst of the search for Mengele, Israel requested the extradition of John (Ivan) Demjanjuk (1920–) from the United States as the suspected "Ivan the Terrible," a camp guard at Treblinka. In 1975, the U.S. Immigration and Naturalization Service (INS) received from Michael Hanusiak, the editor of New York's *Ukrainian Daily News,* a list of seventy suspected Ukrainians who had collaborated with the Germans during the war. One of the names on the list was John Demjanjuk, who allegedly was a guard at Sobibór. The INS asked the Israelis for help in investigating claims against Demjanjuk, who lived in Cleveland. The Israelis contacted a number of Sobibór survivors, who identified him as "Ivan the Terrible." The Israelis shared this information with the INS, which began an investigation into Demjanjuk's case.

John Demjanjulk was born in Ukraine in 1920. In 1952, he and his family arrived in the United States and settled first in Indiana and later in Seven Hills, Ohio, a suburb of Cleveland. In 1958, Demjanjuk, who worked as a "motor balancer" at Cleveland's Ford Motor Company plant, became a U.S. citizen. In 1977, the INS filed charges against Demjanjuk, claiming he had lied about his war record on his entry application in 1952. For the next four years, the INS, with the help of Israeli authorities, gathered more evidence against Demjanjuk. Soviet authorities seemingly strengthened the INS's case against Demjanjuk when they supplied the Americans with an identity card from the SS training camp at Trawniki that bore Demjanjuk's picture. The card later proved to be a forgery. In early 1981, Judge Frank Battisti found Demjanuk guilty of lying on his naturalization papers. He was, Battista declared, "Ivan the Terrible." Battista revoked his citizenship, a decision that Demjanjuk appealed. Two years later, the INS ordered Demjanjuk deported. Demjanjuk claimed throughout the investigation and the hearings that he had fled to Poland during the war and was sent to a forced-labor camp in Germany in 1943. He testified that he was never an SS guard and was not "Ivan the Terrible."

Israel now asked for his extradition. In the meantime, Demjanjuk appealed the deportation order, which was turned down on February 27, 1986. That evening, two U.S. marshals put him on a flight to Israel, where he was put on trial for war crimes. Israeli prosecutors claimed that he had served in the Red Army until 1942, when he was captured. He volunteered to work for the Nazis while at a POW camp near Chełmno. He was trained at Trawniki, where he supposedly got the false identity card. Demjanjuk continued to deny that he had ever worked for the SS and said that he had first been imprisoned at a POW camp near Chełmno. In 1944, he was transferred to another POW camp in Austria. The Israeli court did not believe him and, on April 25, 1988, convicted him of war crimes as "Ivan the Terrible" and sentenced him to death. He lived on death row until 1993, when the Israeli Supreme Court ruled that there was not enough evidence to prove he was "Ivan the Terrible." A number of Treblinka guards had testified during Demjanjuk's appeal that he was not the real "Ivan the Terrible." The man they were looking for was Ivan Marchenko, who was a guard at Treblinka. The Israeli Supreme Court ordered Demjanjuk freed and sent back to the Untied States, where a U.S. Court of Appeals overturned the 1981 decision against him, claiming prosecutorial misconduct. In 1998, another federal court ruled that Demjanjuk's citizenship could be restored.

The following year, the Justice Department filed a new complaint against Demjanjuk, claiming that he had served as an SS guard at Sobibór, Majdanek, and Flossenburg. The new complaint also accused him of being part of a special SS unit involved in rounding up 2 million Jews in the General Government. Demjanjuk was tried again in 2001 and found guilty of the new charges. A federal appeals court ruled in 2004 that he should again be stripped of his citizenship. The INS ordered his deportation to Ukraine in 2005.

Demjanjuk appealed this decision, which was upheld by an INS Board of Immigration Appeals in 2006. His attorneys filed an appeal, and as of November 2007 the INS was awaiting a decision on this appeal. Even if the appeals court upholds the latest INS decision, it is unlikely that Demjanjuk will ever be deported because it is doubtful whether Ukraine or any other country will accept him.

Conclusion

For many Holocaust survivors, the end of World War II was the beginning of a new struggle for survival and national identity. They were classic displaced persons in the extreme, and few countries were interested or willing to accept them as new citizens. Life initially meant the return to a camp environment of barbed wire fences and guards. Some who tried to return home to Poland or other parts of Eastern Europe were met with a new wave of racial and ethnic violence that forced them to flee westward to a world of Displaced Persons camps and chaos. Jewish survivors who tried to sneak into Palestine faced harsh British regulations and punishment for their efforts. In the end, though, British policy backfired, and world opinion, finally moved by the plight of these Holocaust victims, helped convince the United Nations to approve the rebirth of the ancient Jewish homeland—Israel. Roma survivors were often trapped in a world that provided them neither refuge nor toleration.

In the midst of these struggles, the Allies began a series of war crimes trials designed to bring Germany's most important war criminals to justice. They had warned the Germans and their collaborators during the war that they would face harsh punishment for their crimes against Jews, Roma, and others. The IMT trial in Nuremberg was the most important of these tribunals, not only because it tried some of Nazi Germany's most important war criminals but also because it set the standards, internationally, for subsequent war crimes prosecutions.

The vast body of documentation gathered for the IMT trial, much of it drawn from the German files, painted a gruesome picture of abuse and atrocity unknown in the modern world. Justice was fair and punishment harsh, though there were those who escaped prosecution. This was particularly true of the various trials in the Allied zones of occupation in Germany. These trials often dealt with mid-level Nazi figures, individuals who represented the nucleus of the Germans' killing machinery during the Holocaust. Punishment for these crimes varied from occupation zone to occupation zone. Although some of Nazi Germany's more prominent war criminals received just terms, other received light sentences that were often reduced after a few years in prison. Many important convicted mid-level German war criminals were walking the streets freely within a decade of the Holocaust's end.

In some ways, authorities in the Soviet Union and Eastern Europe dealt more harshly with suspected war criminals and collaborators, though these trials were often mixed with politics because the communists used them to settle political scores with former enemies. By the 1950s and 1960s, interest in war crimes prosecutions had waned throughout Europe, kept alive only by the stubborn efforts of the Israelis and determined "Nazi hunters" such as Simon Wiesenthal, Tuvia Friedman, Beate and Serge Klarsfeld, Hermann Langbein, and others. Sometimes, their search for major war criminals such as Martin Bormann, Heinrich Müller, and Alois Brunner met with little success. On the other hand, the capture and trial of Adolf Eichmann as well as the discovery of the remains of Josef Mengele more than compensated for their lifelong efforts to bring to justice those Germans who played such an important role in the *Shoah*.

Their determined efforts also insured that war criminals such as Maurice Papon and Klaus Barbie could not escape justice despite the political and economic shrouds that had protected them after the war. These investigations and trials, particularly in France, brought to the surface unpleasant memories of national collaboration that many preferred to forget. Although this was certainly not so with John Demjanjuk, the thirty-year effort to convict him of war crimes was based on the idea that no one should be able to escape legal responsibility for war crimes, regardless of their age.

SOURCES FOR FURTHER STUDY AND RESEARCH

Primary Sources

Braham, Randolph L. *The Eichmann Case: A Source Book.* New York: World Federation of Hungarian Jews, 1969.

Central Commission for Investigation of German Crimes in Poland. *German Crimes in Poland.* 2 vols. Warsaw: Central Commission for Investigation of German Crimes in Poland, 1946.

Declaration of Geneva (1948 and 1968). The World Medical Association. http://www.wma.net/ e/policy/c8.htm.

Friedman, Leon, ed. *The Law of War: A Documentary History.* 2 vols. New York: Random House, 1972.

Golden, Harry, ed. *The Case Against Adolf Eichmann.* New York: Signet Books, 1960.

Goldensohn, Leon. *Nuremberg Interviews: An American Psychiatrist's Conversations with the Defendants and Witnesses.* Edited by Robert Gellaty. New York: Alfred A. Knopf, 2004.

Goodell, Stephen, ed. *In Pursuit of Justice: Examining the Evidence of the Holocaust.* Washington, DC: United States Holocaust Memorial Museum, 1996.

———. *The Year of Liberation: 1945.* Washington, DC: United States Holocaust Memorial Museum, 1995.

Gsovski, Vladimir. *The Statutory Criminal Law of Germany: With Comments.* Edited by Eldon R. James. Washington, DC: Library of Congress, 1947.

Harel, Isser. *The House on Garibaldi Street.* New York: Bantam Books, 1976.

Hausner, Gideon. *Justice in Jerusalem.* New York: Holocaust Library, 1968.

Höss, Rudolph. *Death Dealer: The Memoirs of the SS Kommandant at Auschwitz.* Edited by Steven Paskuly. Translated by Andrew Pollinger. New York: Da Capo Press, 1996.

The Judgement of Nuremberg, 1946. London: Her Majesty's Stationery Office, 1999.

Kahn, Annette. *Why My Father Died: A Daughter Confronts Her Family's Past at the Trial of Klaus Barbie.* Translated by Anna Cancogni. New York: Summit Books, 1991.

Kamiński, Łukasz, and Jan Zaryn, eds. *Reflections of the Kielce Pogrom.* Warsaw: Institute of National Remembrance, 2006.

Langbein, Hermann, ed. *Der Auschwitz Prozeß: Eine Dokumentation.* 2 vols. Frankfurt: Büchergilde Gutenberg, 1995.

_____. *People in Auschwitz.* Translated by Harry Zohn. Chapel Hill: University of North Carolina Press, 2004.

Laval, Pierre. *The Diary of Pierre Laval.* New York: Charles Scribner's Sons, 1948.

Levai, Jenō, ed. *Eichmann in Hungary: Documents.* Budapest: Pannonia Press, 1961.

Marrus, Michael R. *The Nuremberg War Crimes Trial, 1945–1946: A Documentary History.* Boston: Bedford Books, 1997.

The Moscow Conference. October 1943: *Joint Four-Nation Declaration.* The Avalon Project at Yale Law School. http://www.yale.edu/lawweb/avalon/wwil/moscow.htm.

Mulisch, Harry. *Criminal Case 40/61, the Trial of Adolf Eichmann: An Eyewitness Account.* Translated by Robert Naborn. Philadelphia: University of Pennsylvania Press, 2005.

Musmanno, Michael A. *The Eichmann Kommandos.* Philadelphia: Macrae Smith, 1961.

Nuremberg Trials Final Report Appendix D: Control Council Law No. 10: Punishment of Persons Guilty of War Crimes, Crimes Against Peace and Against Humanity. The Avalon Project at Yale Law School. http://www.yale.edu/lawweb/avalon/imt/imt10.htm.

Nuremberg Trials Final Report Appendix E: Royal Warrant-Regulation for the Trial of War Criminals. The War Office. June, 18, 1945. *Royal Warrant.* 0160/2498. A.O. 81/1945. *Regulations for the Trial of War Criminals.* The Avalon Project at Yale Law School. http://www.yale.edu/lawweb/avalon/imt/imtroyal.htm.

Office of Military Government for Germany (US). *Denazification: Report of the Military Governor (April 1, 1947–April 30 1948).* No. 34.

Office of United States Chief Counsel for the Prosecution of Axis Criminality. *Nazi Conspiracy and Aggression.* 11 vols. Washington, DC: United States Government Printing Office, 1946.

Office of U.S. Chief of Counsel, Subsequent Proceedings Division, APO 124-A. *Staff Evidence Analysis, Criminals Organizations.* Document no. –085, 9 February 1942. The Mazal Library. http://www.mazal.org/NO-series/NO–0085–000.htm.

Persak, Kyzysztof. "Coming to Terms with the Wartime Past: The Institute of National Remembrance and Its Research on the Jedwabne Case." Warsaw: Institute of National Remembrance/Commission for the Persecution of Crimes Against the Polish Nation, n.d.

The Potsdam Declaration: Tripartite Agreement by the United States, the United Kingdom, and the Soviet Union Concerning Conquered Countries. August 2, 1945. http://www.ibiblio.org/pha/policy/1945/450802a.html.

Roberts, Adam, and Richard Guelff, eds. *Documents on the Laws of War.* 3rd ed. New York: Oxford University Press, 2000.

Rückerl, Adalbert. *The Investigation of Nazi Crimes, 1945–1978: A Documentation.* Heidelberg and Karlsruhe: C. F. Müller Juristischer Verlag, 1979.

Ryan, Allan A., Jr. *Klaus Barbie and the United States Government: A Report to the Attorney of the United States.* Washington, DC: Criminal Division, United States Department of Justice, 1983.

Sachs, Henry, and Jacob Robinson. *The Holocaust: The Nuremberg Evidence.* Pt. 1, *Documents.* Jerusalem: Yad Vashem, 1976.

Smith, Bradley F., ed. *The Road to Nuremberg: The Documentary Record, 1944–1945.* Stanford: Hoover Institution Press, 1981.

Sprecher, Drexel A. *Inside the Nuremberg Trial: A Prosecutor's Comprehensive Account.* 2 vols. Lanham, MD: University Press of America, 1999.

State of Israel. Ministry of Justice. *The Trial of Adolf Eichmann: Record of Proceedings in the District Court in Jerusalem.* 9 vols. Jerusalem: Israel State Archives and Yad Vashem, 1992.

Strik-Strikfeldt, Wilfried. *Against Stalin and Hitler: Memoirs of the Russian Liberation Movement, 1941–1945.* Translated by David Footman. New York: John Day, 1973.

The Tanakh: The Holy Scriptures. Philadelphia: Jewish Publication Society, 1985.

Taylor, Telford. *The Anatomy of the Nuremberg Trials: A Personal Memoir.* New York: Alfred A. Knopf, 1992.

_____. *Final Report to the Secretary of the Army on the Nuernberg War Crimes Trials Under Control Council Law No. 10.* Buffalo, NY: William S. Hein, 1997.

Trial of the Major War Criminals Before the International Military Tribunal, Nuremberg, 14 November 1945–1 October 1946. 42 vols. Washington, DC: U.S. Government Printing Office, 1946–1949.

Trials of War Criminals Before the Nuremberg Military Tribunals Under Control Council Law No. 10, October 1946–April 1949. 15 vols. Washington, DC: U.S. Government Printing Office, 1946–1949.

United Nations General Assembly Resolution 181. November 29, 1947. The Avalon Project at Yale Law School. http://www.yale.edu/lawweb/avalon/un/res181.htm.

United Nations Statement on Murder of European Jews (December 17, 1942). Jewish Virtual Library. http://wwwjewishvirtuallibrary.org/jsource/UN/un1942a.html.

The United Nations War Crimes Commission. *Law-Reports of Trials of War Criminals.* Vols. 1–15. London: His Majesty's Stationery Office, 1947–1949.

United States Court of Appeals for the Sixth Circuit. *United States of America v. John Demjanjuk.* No. 02–3529. April 30, 2004.

United States Court of Appeals for the Sixth Circuit. *United States of America v. John Demjanjuk.* No. 03–3773. April 20, 2005.

United States District Court, Northern District of Ohio Eastern Division. *United States of America vs. John Demjanjuk.* Case no. 1:99CV1193. February 21, 2002.

Von Lang, Jochen, ed. *Das Eichmann-Protokoll: Tonbandaufzeichnungen der israelischen Verhöre.* Munich: Propyläen Taschenbücher, 2001.

Von Lang, Jochen, and Claus Sibyll, eds. *Eichmann Interrogated: Transcripts from the Archives of the Israeli Police.* New York: Da Capo Press, 1999.

Wiesel, Elie. *And the Sea Is Never Full: Memoirs, 1969–.* New York: Alfred A. Knopf, 1999.

Wiesenthal, Simon. *The Murderers Among Us: The Simon Wiesenthal Memoirs.* Edited by Joseph Wechsberg. New York: Bantam, 1967.

Secondary Sources

Adams, Lorraine. "The Reckoning." *Washington Post Magazine* (April 20, 1997): 10, 13.

Andreyev, Catherine. *Vlasov and the Russian Liberation Movement.* Cambridge: Cambridge University Press, 1987.

Annas, George J., and Michael A. Grodin. *The Nazi Doctors and the Nuremberg Code: Human Rights in Human Experimentation.* New York: Oxford University Press, 1992.

Arendt, Hannah. *Eichmann in Jerusalem: A Report on the Banality of Evil.* Rev. and enlarged ed. New York: Penguin, 1965.

_____. "Reporter at Large: The Eichmann Trial." *New Yorker* 39 (February 16, 23; March 2, 16, 1963).

Aschheim, Steven E., ed. *Hannah Arendt in Jerusalem.* Berkeley: University of California Press, 2001.

Bachrach, Susan D., ed. *Liberation: 1945.* Washington, DC: United States Holocaust Memorial Museum, 1995.

Bathurst, M. E. "The United Nations War Crimes Commission." *American Journal of International Law* 39, no. 3 (July 1945): 565–570.

Benton, Wilbourn E., and Georg Grimm, eds. *Nuremberg: German Views of the War Trials.* Dallas: Southern Methodist University Press, 1955.

Benzinger, Karl P. "The Trial of László Bárdossy: The Second World War and Factional Politics in Contemporary Hungary." *Journal of Contemporary History* 40, no. 3 (2005): 465–481.

Berben, Paul. *Dachau, 1933–45: The Official History.* London: Comité International de Dachau, 1975.

Bloxham, Donald. *Genocide on Trial: War Crimes Trials and the Formation of Holocaust History and Memory.* New York: Oxford University Press, 2005.

"Book Claims Stasi Employed Nazis as Spies." *Deutsche Welle* (October 31, 2005): 1–3. http://www.dw-world.de/dw/article/0,2144,1760900,00.html.

Borkin, Joseph. *The Crime and Punishment of I. G. Farben.* New York: Pocket Books, 1979.

Bosch, William J. *Judgement on Nuremberg: American Attitudes Toward the Major German War-Crime Trials.* Chapel Hill: University of North Carolina Press, 1971.

Bower, Tom. *Klaus Barbie, the "Butcher of Lyons."* New York: Pantheon Books, 1984.

Braham, Randolph L. *The Politics of Genocide: The Holocaust in Hungary.* Rev. and enlarged ed. 2 vols. New York and Boulder: The Rosenthal Institute for Holocaust Studies Graduate Center/The City University of New York and Social Science Monographs, 1994.

Braham, Randolph L., ed. *The Treatment of the Holocaust in Hungary and Romania During the Post-Communist Era.* New York and Boulder:

The Rosenthal Institute for Holocaust Studies Graduate Center/City University of New York and Social Science Monographs, 2004.

Breitman, Richard, Borman J. W. Goda, Timothy Naftali, and Robert Wolfe, eds. *U.S. Intelligence and the Nazis*. Washington, DC: National Archives Trust Fund Board for the Nazi War Crimes and Japanese Imperial Government Record Interagency Working Group, 2002.

Bridgman, Jon. *The End of the Holocaust: The Liberation of the Camps*. Portland, OR: Areopagitica Press, 1990.

Brown Book: War and Nazi Criminals in West Germany. Berlin: Verlag Zeit im Bild, 1965.

Brown, Daniel Patrick. *The Beautiful Beast: The Life & Crimes of SS- Aufseherin Erma Grese*. Venture, CA: Golden West Historical Publications, 1996.

Bryant, Michael S. *Confronting the "Good Death": Nazi Euthanasia on Trial, 1945–1953*. Boulder: University of Colorado Press, 2005.

Burchard, Christoph. "The Nuremberg Trial and Its Impact on Germany." *Journal of International Criminal Justice* 4, no. 4 (2006): 800–829.

Caniglia, John. "Demjanjuk Will Likely Remain in U.S." *Plain Dealer* (April 5, 2007): 1–2. http:///www.cleveland.com/printer/printer.ssf?base/news.

Cesarani, David. *Becoming Eichmann: Rethinking the Life, Crimes, and Trial of a "Desk Murderer."* New York: Da Capo Press, 2006.

————. *Justice Betrayed: How Britain Became a Refuge for Nazi War Criminals*. London: Phoenix Press, 2000.

Chambrun, René de. *Pierre Laval: Traitor or Patriot?* Translated by Elly Stein. New York: Charles Scribner's Sons, 1984.

Cole, Hubert. *Laval: A Biography*. London: Heinemann, 1963.

Conot, Robert E. *Justice at Nuremberg*. New York: Harper & Row, 1983.

Cooper, Belinda, ed. *War Crimes: The Legacy of Nuremberg*. New York: TV Books, 1999.

Cooper, R. W. *The Nuremberg Trial*. London: Penguin, 1947.

Cowles, William B. "Universality of Jurisdiction over War Crimes." *California Law Review* 33 (1945): 177–218.

Cryer, Robert. *Prosecuting International Crimes: Selectivity and the International Criminal Regime*. New York: Cambridge University Press, 2005.

Davidson, Eugene. *The Trial of the Germans: An Account of the Twenty-two Defendants Before the In-ternational Military Tribunal at Nuremberg*. Columbia: University of Missouri Press, 1997.

Deák, István, Jan T. Gross, and Tony Judt, eds. *The Politics of Retribution in Europe: World War II and Its Aftermath*. Princeton: Princeton University Press, 2000.

De Hoyos, Ladislas. *Klaus Barbie*. Translated by Nicholas Courtin. New York: McGraw-Hill, 1985.

De Mildt, Dick. *In the Name of the People: Perpetrators of Genocide in the Reflection of Their Post-War Prosecution in West Germany*. The Hague: Martinus Nijhoff, 1996.

De Zayas, Alfred-Maurice. *A Terrible Revenge: The Ethnic Cleansing of the East European Germans, 1944–1945*. New York: St. Martin's Press, 1994.

Elliot, Mark. "Andrei Vlasov: Red Army General in Hitler's Service." *Military Affairs* 46, no. 2 (April 1982): 84–87.

Fawcett, J. E. S. "The Eichmann Case." *British Yearbook of International Law* 38 (1962): 181–215.

Finkielkraut, Alain. *Remembering in Vain: The Klaus Barbie Trial and Crimes Against Humanity*. Translated by Roxanne Lapidus and Sima Godfrey. New York: Columbia University Press, 1992.

Fox, John P. "The Jewish Factor in British War Crimes Policy in 1942." *English Historical Review* 92, no. 362 (January 1977): 82–106.

Fraser, Angus. *The Gypsies*. Oxford: Blackwell, 1992.

Frei, Norbert. *Adenauer's Germany and the Nazi Past: The Politics of Amnesty and Integration*. Translated by Joel Gold. New York: Columbia Press, 2002.

Friedlander, Henry. "The Deportation of the German Jews: Postwar Trials of Nazi Criminals." *Leo Baeck Institute Yearbook* 29 (1984): 201–226.

————. "The Judiciary and Nazi Crimes in Postwar Germany." *Simon Wiesenthal Center Annual* (1997). Museum of Tolerance Online. http://motlc.wiesenthal.com/site/pp/asp?c=gvKVLcMUIG&b=394973.

————. "Nazi Criminals in the United States: Denaturalization After Federenko." *Simon Wiesenthal Center Annual* 3 (1986): 47–85.

————. "Nazi Criminals in the United States: The Federenko Case." *Simon Wiesenthal Center Annual* 2 (1985): 63–93.

Friedlander, Henry, and Earlean McCarrcik. "The Extradition of Nazi Criminals: Ryan, Artukovic, Demjanjuk." *Simon Wiesenthal Center Annual* 4 (1987): 65–98.

Gaiba, Francesca. *The Origins of Simultaneous Interpretation: The Nuremberg Trial*. Ottawa: The University of Ottawa Press, 1998.

Ginsburgs, George. "Laws of War and War Crimes on the Russian Front During World War II." *Soviet Studies* 11, no. 3 (January 1960): 253–285.

Golsan, Richard J., Mary Jean Green, and Lynn A. Higgins, eds. Translations by Lucy Golsan and Richard J. Golsan. *Memory, the Holocaust, and French Justice: The Bousquet and Touvier Affairs.* Hanover, NH: University Press of New England, 1996.

Golsan, Richard J., ed. *The Papon Affair: Memory and Justice on Trial.* Translations by Lucy B. Golsan and Richard J. Golsan. New York: Routledge, 2000.

Goñi, Uki. *The Real Odessa: How Péron Brought the Nazi War Criminals to Argentina.* London: Granata Books, 2002.

Griffiths, Richard M. *Pétain: A Biography of Marshal Philippe Pétain of Vichy.* Garden City, NY: Doubleday, 1972.

Gross, Jan T. *Fear: Anti-Semitism in Poland After Auschwitz: An Essay in Historical Interpretation.* New York: Random House, 2006.

Gruchmann, Lothar. *Justiz im Dritten Reich, 1933–1940: Anpassung und Unterwerfung in der Ära Gürtner.* Munich: R. Oldenbourg Verlag, 1988.

Haberer, Erich. "History and Justice: Paradigms of the Prosecution of Nazi Crimes." *Holocaust and Genocide Studies* 19, no. 3 (Winter 2005): 487–519.

Hansen, Phillip. *Hannah Arendt: Politics, History, and Citizenship.* Stanford: Stanford University Press, 1993.

Harris, Whitney R. *Tyranny on Trial: The Trial of the Major War Criminals at the End of World War II at Nuremberg, Germany, 1945–1946.* Dallas: Southern Methodist University Press, 1999.

Hayes, Peter. *Industry and Ideology: IG Farben in the Nazi Era.* Cambridge: Cambridge University Press, 1987.

Herbert, Ulrich. *Hitler's Foreign Workers: Enforced Foreign Labor in Germany Under the Third Reich.* Translated by William Templer. Cambridge: Cambridge University Press, 1997.

Herf, Jeffrey. *Divided Memory: The Nazi Past in the Two Germanys.* Cambridge, MA: Harvard University Press, 1997.

Herzstein, Robert Edwin. *Waldheim: The Missing Years.* New York: Paragon House, 1989.

Hevesi, Dennis. "Report Details Waldheim's Role in Nazi Military." *New York Times,* March 13, 1994.

Hilberg, Raul. *The Destruction of the European Jews.* 3 vols. New York: Holmes & Meier, 1985.

Kahn, Leo. *Nuremberg Trials.* New York: Ballantine Books, 1972.

Karsai, László. "Crime and Punishment: People's Courts, Revolutionary Legality, and the Hungarian Holocaust." *Tblong* (December 26, 2005): 1–19. http://tblong.blogspot.com/2005/12/peoples-court-in-budapest–1944–1945.html.

Kenrick, Donald, ed. *The Final Chapter.* Vol. 3, *The Gypsies During the Second World War.* Hatfield, UK: University of Hertfordshire Press, 2006.

Kenrick, Donald, and Grattan Puxon. *The Destiny of Europe's Gypsies.* New York: Basic Books, 1972.

"Klaus Barbie." Jewish Virtual Library. http://www.jewishvirtuallibrary.org/jsource/Holocaust/Barbie.html.

Kochavi, Arieh J. *Prelude to Nuremberg: Allied War Crimes Policy and the Question of Punishment.* Chapel Hill: The University of North Carolina Press, 1998.

Krieger, Hilary Leila. "Forgotten Heroes." *International Jerusalem Post,* June 22–28, 2007.

Krivosheev, Colonel-General G. F., ed. *Soviet Casualties and Combat Losses in the Twentieth Century.* Translated by Christine Barnard. London: Greenhill Books, 1997.

Lahav, Pnina. *Judgement in Jerusalem: Chief Justice Simon Agranat and the Zionist Century.* Berkeley: University of California Press, 1997.

Landsman, Stephan. *Crimes of the Holocaust: The Law Confronts Hard Cases.* Philadelphia: University of Pennsylvania Press, 2005.

Levy, Alan. *The Wiesenthal File.* Grand Rapids, MI: William B. Eerdmans, 1993.

Linklater, Magnus, Isabel Hilton, and Neal Ascherson, eds. *The Nazi Legacy: Klaus Barbie and the International Fascist Connection.* New York: Holt, Rinehart and Winston, 1985.

Loftus, John. *The Belarus Secret.* Edited by Nathan Miller. New York: Alfred A. Knopf, 1982.

Lord Russell of Liverpool. *The Trial of Adolf Eichmann.* London: Heinemann, 1962.

Lüdtke, Alf. "'Coming to Terms With the Past: Illusions of Remembering, Ways of Forgetting Nazism in West Germany." *Journal of Modern History* 65, no. 3 (September 1993): 542–572.

Maguire, Peter. *Law and War: An American Story.* New York: Columbia University Press, 2001.

Mahoney, Kevin, ed. *In Pursuit of Justice: Examining the Evidence of the Holocaust.* Washington, DC: United States Holocaust Memorial Museum, 1996.

Manchester, William. *The Arms of Krupp, 1587–1968.* Boston: Little, Brown, 1968.

Mann, Abby. *Judgement at Nuremberg: A Novel with 12 Scenes from the Movie.* New York: Signet Books, 1961.

Margalit, Gilad. *Germany and Its Gypsies: A Post-Auschwitz Ordeal.* Madison: The University of Wisconsin Press, 2002.

Marrus, Michael R., and Robert O. Paxton. *Vichy France and the Jews.* Stanford: Stanford University Press, 1995.

Marszałek, Józef. *Majdanek: The Concentration Camp in Lublin.* Warsaw: Interpress, 1986.

Maser, Werner. *Nuremberg: A Nation on Trial.* New York: Charles Scribner's Sons, 1979.

Mendelsohn, John. *Trial by Document: The Use of Seized Records in the United States Proceedings at Nürnberg.* New York: Garland, 1988.

Milton, Sybil. "Sinti and Roma in Twentieth-Century Austria and Germany." *German Studies Review* 23, no. 2 (May 2000): 317–331.

Morgan, Ted. *An Uncertain Hour: the French, the Germans, the Jews, the Klaus Barbie Trial, and the City of Lyon, 1940–1945.* New York: Arbor House/Morrow, 1990.

Müller, Ingo. *Hitler's Justice: The Courts of the Third Reich.* Translated by Deborah Lucas Schneider. Cambridge, MA: Harvard University Press, 1991.

Murphy, Brendan. *The Butcher of Lyon: The Story of Infamous Nazi Klaus Barbie.* New York: Empire Books, 1983.

Ofer, Dalia. "Holocaust Survivors as Immigrants: The Case of Israel and the Cyprus Detainees." *Modern Judaism* 16, no. 1 (February 1996): 1–23.

Overy, Richard. *Interrogations: The Nazi Elite in Allied Hands, 1945.* New York: Viking, 2001.

Paxton, Robert O. "The Trial of Maurice Papon." *New York Review of Books* 46, no. 20 (December 16, 1999): 1–16. http://www.nybooks.com/articles/269.

Pendas, Devin O. *The Frankfurt Auschwitz Trial, 1963–1965: Genocide, History, and the Limits of the Law.* Cambridge: Cambridge University Press, 2006.

Persico, Joseph E. *Nuremberg: Infamy on Trial.* New York: Viking, 1994.

Poltorak, A. *The Nuremberg Epilogue.* Translated by David Skvirsky. Moscow: Progress, 1971.

Posner, Gerald, and John Ware. *Mengele: The Complete Story.* New York: McGraw-Hill, 1986.

Pritz, Pál. *The War Crimes Trial of Hungarian Prime Minister László Bárdossy.* Translated by Thomas J. DeKornfeld and Helen D. Hiltabidle. Boulder: Social Science Monographs, 2004.

Prusin, Alexander Victor. "'Fascist Criminals to the Gallows': The Holocaust and Soviet War Crimes Trials, December 1945–February 1946." *Holocaust and Genocide Studies* 17, no. 1 (Spring 2003): 1–30.

Rodes, John E. *The Quest for Unity: Modern Germany, 1948–1970.* New York: Holt, Rinehart and Winston, 1971.

Rogers, A. P. V. "War Crimes Trials Under the Royal Warrant: British Practice 1945–1949." *The International and Comparative Law Quarterly* 39, no. 4 (October 1990): 780–800.

Roy, Jules. *The Trial of Marshal Pétain.* Translated by Robert Baldick. New York: Harper & Row, 1968.

Rückerl, Adalbert, ed. *Nationalsozialistische Vernichtungslager im Spiegel deutscher Strafprozesse: Belzec, Sobibor, Treblinka, Chelmno.* Munich: Deutscher Taschenvbuch Verlag, 1977.

_____, ed. *NS-Prozesse: nach 25 Jahren Strafverfolgung, Möglichkeiten, Grenzen, Ergebnisse.* Karlsruhe: C. F. Müller Juristischer Verlag, 1971.

_____. *NS-Verbrechen vor Gericht.* Heidelberg: C. F. Müller Juristischer Verlag, 1982.

_____. *Die Strafverfolgung von NS-Verbrechen, 1945–1978.* Heidelberg and Karlsruhe: C. F. Müller Juristischer Verlag, 1982.

Ryan, Alan A. Jr. *Quiet Neighbors: Prosecuting Nazi War Criminals in America.* San Diego: Harcourt Brace Jovanovich, 1984.

Sachar, Howard M. *A History of the Jews in the Modern World.* New York: Alfred A. Knopf, 2005.

_____. *Diaspora: An Inquiry into the Contemporary Jewish World.* New York: Harper & Row, 1986.

Sanger-Katz, Margot. "Blitzkrieg: The Department of Justice Is Still Storming the Country Looking for Geriatric Ex-Nazis." *Legal Affairs* (July–August 2004): 69–71. http://www.legalaffaires.org/issues/July-August–2004/story-katz-julaug04.msp.

Scammel, Michael. *Solzhenitsyn: A Biography.* New York: W. W. Norton, 1984.

Segev, Tom. *The Seventh Million: The Israelis and the Holocaust.* New York: Hill & Wang, 1993.

Sereny, Gitta. *Albert Speer: His Battle with Truth.* New York: Vintage Books, 1996.

Slinitsky, Michel. *L'affaire Papon.* Paris: Éditions Alain Moreau, 1983.

Smith, Bradley. *Reaching Judgement at Nuremberg.* New York: Basic Books, 1977.

Sorokina, Marina. "People and Procedures: Toward a History of the Investigation of Nazi Crimes in the USSR." *Kritika* 6, no. 4 (Fall 2005): 797–831.

Stark, Tamás. *Hungarian Jews During the Holocaust and After the Second World War, 1939–1949: A Statistical Review.* Translated by Christina Rozsnyai. Boulder: East European Monographs, 2000.

Tebutt, Susan, ed. *Sinti and Roma: Gypsies in German-Speaking Society and Literature.* New York: Bergahn Books, 1998.

Teicholz, Tom. *The Trial of Ivan the Terrible: State of Israel vs. John Demjanjuk.* New York: St. Martin's Press, 1990.

Tolstoy, Nikolai. *Victims of Yalta.* London: Corgi Books, 1979.

The Trial of Klaus Barbie (May 11, 1987). Jewish Virtual Library. http://www.jewishvirtuallibrary .org/jsource/Holocaust/barbietrial.html.

Tusa, John and Ann. *The Nuremberg Trial.* New York: Atheneum, 1984.

Van der Vat, Dan. *The Good Nazi: The Life & Lies of Albert Speer.* Boston: Houghton Mifflin, 1997.

Vogt, Timothy R. *Denazification in Soviet-Occupied Germany: Brandenburg, 1945–1948.* Cambridge, MA: Harvard University Press, 2000.

Warner, Geoffrey. *Pierre Laval and the Eclipse of France.* New York: Macmillan, 1969.

Werth, Alexander. *Russia at War, 1941–1945.* New York: E. P. Dutton, 1964.

Wilke, Christiane. "Recognizing Victimhood." Law and Humanities Junior Scholar Interdisciplinary Workshop (June 6–7, 2006), 1–34. http://www.law .columbia.edu/null/wilke++Long?esxclusive=file mrg.downloadfile_id=97928showthumb=o.

Williams, Charles. *Pétain: How the Hero of France Became a Convicted Traitor and Changed the Course of History.* New York: Palgrave Macmillan, 2005.

Wittman, Rebecca. *Beyond Justice: The Auschwitz Trial.* Cambridge: Cambridge University Press, 2005.

Wojak, Irmtrud. *Eichmanns Memorien: Ein Kritischer Essay.* Frankfurt: Campus Verlag, 2001.

Wyman, Mark. *DPs: Europe's Displaced Persons, 1945–1951.* Ithaca: Cornell University Press, 1989.

Wyman, David, and Charles H. Rosenzveig, eds. *The World Reacts to the Holocaust.* Baltimore: The Johns Hopkins University Press, 1996.

Yablonka, Hanna. *The State of Israel vs. Adolf Eichmann.* Translated by Ora Cummings and David Herman. New York: Schocken Books, 2004.

GLOSSARY

Abwehr. Bureau Abwehr. Wehrmacht counterintelligence and counterespionage branch
A Magyar Megújulás Pártja. MMP. Party of Hungarian Renewal
American Jewish Joint Distribution Committee. AJJDC. United States
A Népiróságok országos Tanáca. NOT. National Council of People's Tribunals. Hungary
Armija Krajowa. AK. Home Army. Poland
Association des Juifs en Belgique. AJB. Association of Jews in Belgium
Bevölkerungswesen und Fürsorge. BuF. Population and Welfare Agency
Bundesrepublik Deutschland. BRD. Federal Republic of Germany
Central Jewish Committee. CJC. Belsen DP Camp
Chrezvychainaia gosudarstvennaia komissiia. ChGK. Extraordinary State Commission for Ascertaining and Investigating Atrocities Perpetrated by the German Fascist Invaders and Their Accomplices. Soviet Union
Comité intermouvements auprés des évacués. CIMADE. France
Commisão Portugesa de Assistencia aos Judeos Refugiados. CPAJF. Portugese Commission for Helping Jewish Refugees
Commissariat General aux Questions Juives. CGQJ. General Commissariat for Jewish Affairs. France
Comunità Israelitica di Roma. Israel Community of Rome
Deutsche Arbeiterpartei. DAP. German Workers Party
Deutsche Demokratische Republik. DDR. German Democratic Republic
Deutscher Reichsbund für Leibesübungen. DRL. German Reich League for Physical Exercises
Deutschnationale Volkspartei. DNVP. German National Peoples Party
Displaced Persons. DP
Einsatzgruppen. Einsatzgruppen der Sicherheitsdienstes und der der Sicherheitspolizei; special task or action groups
European Court of Human Rights. ECHR
Evreiskii Antifashistskii Komitet. EAK. Jewish Anti-Fascist Committee. Poland
Fareynegte Partizaner Organizatsye. FPO. United Partisan Organization. Vilna
Feldgendarmerie. Military Police Units
Freiwillige Schutzsstaffel. FS. Volunteer SS
Gemeindepolizei. Small Town Police
Gendarmerie. Rural Police
Gestapo—Geheime Staatspolizei. Secret State Police
Główna Komisja Badania Zbrodni Niemieckich w Polsce. GKBZNP. Central Commission for the Investigation of German Crimes in Poland
Główna Komisja Ścigania Zbrodni przeciwko Narodowi Polskiemu. KŚZPNP. Main Commission for the Prosecution of Crimes Against the Polish Nation
Grenzpolizei. Green or border police
Haupttreuhandstelle Ost. HTO. Main Trusteeship Office East
Hebrew Immigrant Aid Society. HIAS. United States
HICEM—acronym for HIAS, Hebrew Immigrant Aid Society; JCA, Jewish Colonization Association; Emigdirect. United States

Hlinkova slovenská ľudová strana. HSLS. Hlinka Slovak People's Party
Höhrere SS- und Polizeiführer. HSSPF. Higher SS and Police Leader
Immigration and Naturalization Service. INS. United States
Instytut Pamiêci Narodowej. IPN. Institute of National Remembrance. Poland
Intergovernmental Committee on Refugees. ICR
International Military Tribunal. IMT
International Olympic Committee. IOC
Jewish Agency in Palestine. JA
Jewish Colonization Association. JCA. United States
Jewish Rescue Committee. JRC. Palestine and Israel
Joodse Coördinatiecommissie. JCC. Jewish Coordinating Committee. Netherlands
Jüdische Soziale Selbsthilfe. JSS. Jewish Self-Help Society. Poland
Jüdische Unterstützungsstelle. JUS. Jewish Aid Center. Poland
Jüdischer Ordnungsdienst. OD. Jewish Security Police.
Komisarstvo za Evreiskite Vuprosi. KEV. Commissariat for Jewish Questions. Bulgaria
Kommunistische Partei Deutschlands. KPD. Communist Party of Germany
Konzentrationslager. KZ. Concentration Camp
Kreigsgefangenenlager der Waffen SS in Lublin. KLG Lublin. POW Camp of the Waffen SS in Lublin
Kriminalstechnisches Institut. KTI. Sipo's Technical Institute for the Detection of Crime
Militärbefehlshaber in Frankreich. MBF. Military Commander in France
Naczelna Rada Opiekuncza. NRO. Main Welfare Council. Soviet Union
Najwyzszy Trybunal Narodowy. NTN. Supreme National Court. Poland
Narodnyi Kommissariat Vnutrennikh Del. NKVD. People's Commissariat of Internal Affairs. Soviet Union
National Socialist Beweging. NSB. National Socialist Movement. Netherlands
Nationalsozialistische Deutsche Arbeiterpartei. NSDAP. Nazi Party. National Socialist Democratic Workers Party
Nationalististiche Volkswohlfahrt. NSV. National Socialist Volk Welfare Agency
NATO. North Atlantic Treaty Organization
Nezavism Drzava Hrvatska. NDH. Independent State of Croatia
Nyilas. Arrow Cross
Oberkommando des Herres. OKH. Army High Command
Oberkommando der Wehrmacht. OKW. Armed Forces Supreme Command.
Office of Military Government, United States. OMGUS. Germany
Office of Special Investigations. OSI. United States
Ordnungspolizei. Orpo. Order Police
Orhanizatsiya Ukrainskyh Natsionalistiv. OUN. Organization of Ukrainian Nationalists
Partite Nazionale Fascista. PNF. Fascist National Party. Italy
Polski Komitet Wyzwolenia Narodowego. PKWN. Polish Committee of National Liberation
Rassemblant pour la République. RPR. Rally for the Republic. France
Reichsgesetzblatt. German Criminal Code. 1871.
Reichskommissariat für die Festigung des deutschen Volkstums. RKFDV. Reich Commission for the Strengthening of German Nationhood
Reichskriminalpolizei. Kripo. Reich Criminal Police
Reichskriminalpolizeiamt. RKPA. Reich Criminal Police Office
Reichsministerium für die besetzen Ostgebiete. RmfdbO. Reich Ministry for the Occupied Eastern Territories
Reichssicherheitshauptamt. RSHA. Reich Security Main Office
Repubblica Sociale Italiana. RSI. Italian Social Republic
Ruskaya Osvobditel'naya Armiya. ROA. Russian Liberation Army
Russkoe Osvoboditel'noye Dvizhenie. ROD. Russian Liberation Movement
Schutzpolizei. Schupo. Urban Police

Schutzstaffel. SS. Defense or Protection Guard
Sicherheitsdienst. SD. Security Service of the *SS*
Sicherheitspolizei. Sipo. Security Police
Sozialdemokratische Partei. SDP. Social Democratic Party. Germany
Sozialistische Einheitspartei Deutschlands. SED. Socialist Unity Party. East Germany
SS- und Polizeiführer. SSPF. SS and Police Leader
Sturmabteilung. SA. Storm Detachment
Supreme Headquarters Allied Expeditionary Force. SHAEF
Tymczasowy Rząd Jedności Narodowej. TRJN. Provisional Government of National Unity. Poland
Ukrainische Hilfpolizei Schtuzmannschaft. UAP. Ukrainian Auxiliary Police Constabulary
Unicenea Evreilor Romani. UER. Union of Romanian Jews
Union Géneral des Israélites de France. UGIF. General Union for Israelites in France
Union pour la défense de la Republique. UDR. Union for the Defense of the Republic. France
Unione delle Comunità Ebraiche Italiane. Union of Italian Jewish Communities
United Nations Relief and Rehabilitation Administration. UNRRA
United Nations Special Committee on Palestine. UNSCP
United Nations War Crimes Commission. UNWCC
United States Holocaust Memorial Museum. USHMM
USPD. *Unabhängige Sozialdemokratische Partei Deutschlands.* USPD. Independent Democratic Socialist Party of Germany
Vaad Leumi. VL. Jewish National Council. Palestine and Israel
Va'adat ha-Ezra ve-ha Hatsala be-Budapest. Va'ada. Relief and Rescue Committee of Budapest
Vereinigung der Verfolgten des Naziregimes. VVN. Union of the Persecuted by the Nazi Regime
War Crimes Office. WCO. Polish government-in-exile
Weer-afdelingen. WA. Defense Division. Netherlands
Wirthschafts-Verwaltungshauptamt. WVHA. Economic and Administrative Main Office
World Jewish Congress. WJC
WRB. War Refugee Board. United States
Yidishe Algemenye Kamfs. YAK. Jewish Fighting Organization. General Government
Zakon za Zashita na Natziata. ZZH. Law for the Protection of the Nation. Bulgaria
Żydowska Organizacja Bojowa. ŻOB. Jewish Defense Organization. General Government
Żydowskie Towarzystwo Opieki Spolecznej. ŻTOS. Jewish Mutual Aid Society. General Government

APPENDIX A

Estimates of Jewish Deaths During the Holocaust

	Pre-War Population	Holocaust Deaths
Albania	*No figures available*	200–591
Austria*	185,000–192,000	48,767–65,000
Belgium	55,000–70,000	24,000–29,902
Bohemia and Moravia	92,000–118,310	78,150–80,000
Bulgaria**	50,000	7,335
Denmark	7,500–7,800	60–116
Estonia	4,500	1,500–2,000
Finland***	2,000	7–8
France	330,000–350,000	73,320–90,000
Germany****	523,000–525,000	130,000–160,000
Greece	77,380	58,443–67,000
Hungary	725,000–825,000	200,000–569,000
Italy	42,500–44,500	5,596–9,000
Latvia	91,500–95,000	60,000–85,000
Lithuania	168,000	130,000–200,000
Luxembourg	3,800	720–2,000
Netherlands	140,000	98,800–120,000
Norway	1,700–1,800	758–1,000
Poland	3,300,000–3,500,000	2,700,000–3,000,000
Romania*****	756,000	270,000–287,000
Slovakia	136,000	68,000–100,000
Soviet Union	3,020,000	700,000–2,500,000
Yugoslavia (includes Croatia and Serbia)	78,000–82,242	51,400–67,438
TOTAL	9,702,930–10,169,332	4,707,056–7,442,390

*135,000 Jews emigrated by end of 1939
**11,500 Jews died in Bulgarian-controlled Macedonian and Thrace
***Finland turned over 500–600 Jewish Soviet POWs to Germans
****1933 census; 282,000 emigrated between 1933 and 1939
*****1930 estimate; deaths include Jews murdered by Romanian occupation forces

APPENDIX B

Estimates of Roma Deaths During the Holocaust

	Pre-War Population	Holocaust Deaths
Albania	22,000	591
Austria	11,200	6,500
Belgium	500–600	500
Belarus and Ukraine	42,000	30,000
Bohemia and Moravia	13,000	6,500
Bulgaria	100,000	5,000
Croatia	28,500	26,000–28,000
Estonia	1,000	1,000
France	40,000	15,000–18,000
Germany (Old Reich)	20,000	15,000
Greece	*No figures available*	50
Hungary	100,000	28,000
Italy	25,000	1,000
Latvia	5,000	2,500
Lithuania	1,000	1,000
Luxembourg	200	200
Macedonia	*Included in Serbian figures*	
Moldova	*Included in Romanian figures*	
The Netherlands	500	500
Norway	60	60
Poland	44,400–50,000	28,200–35,000
Romania	300,000	36,000
Serbia	60,000	12,000
Slovakia	80,000	1,000–6,500
Soviet Union	200,000	30,000
Totals	1,072,360–1,078,160	246,010–263,310

APPENDIX C

Yad Vashem: *Righteous Among the Nations*

By Country

Poland: 6,004	Albania: 63
The Netherlands: 4,767	Romania: 53
France: 2,740	Switzerland: 38
Ukraine: 2,185	Bosnia: 35
Belgium: 1,443	Norway: 41
Lithuania: 693	Denmark: 21*
Hungary: 685	Bulgaria: 17
Belarus: 576	United Kingdom: 13
Slovakia: 465	Sweden: 9
Germany: 443	Macedonia: 10
Italy: 417	Armenia: 10
Greece: 271	Slovenia: 6
Serbia: 124	Spain: 3
Russia: 124	Estonia: 3
Czech Republic: 118	USA: 3
Croatia: 106	China: 2
Latvia: 103	Brazil: 2
Austria: 85	Chile, Japan, Luxembourg,
Moldova: 73	Portugal, Turkey, Georgia: 1 apiece

TOTAL *Righteous Among the Nations* (Righteous Gentiles): 21,758

*Danish underground requested that all who helped save Jews be listed as one group

APPENDIX D

SS Ranks (Based on US Army Equivalents)

Reichsführer-SS	General of the Army
SS- Oberstgruppenführer	General
SS- Obergruppenführer	Lt. General
SS- Gruppenführer	Major General
SS- Brigadeführer	Brigadier General
SS- Oberführer	Senior Colonel
SS- Standartenführer	Colonel
SS- Obersturmbannführer	Lt. Colonel
SS- Sturmbannführer	Major
SS- Hauptsturmführer	Captain
SS- Obersturmführer	First Lieutenant
SS- Untersturmführer	Second Lieutenant
SS- Sturmscharführer	Sergeant Major
SS- Hauptscharführer	Master Sergeant
SS- Oberscharführer	Technical Sergeant
SS- Scharführer	Staff Sergeant
SS- Unterscharführer	Sergeant
SS- Rottenführer	Corporal
SS- Sturmmann	Corporal
SS- Oberschütze	Private First Class
SS- Schütze	Private

(Source: Heinz Höhne, *The Order of the Death's Head: The Story of Hitler's SS.* New York: Ballantine Books, 1971, 744)

APPENDIX E

German Army Ranks (Based on US Army Equivalents)

Generalfeldmarschall	General of the Army
Generaloberst	Colonel General
General	Lt. General
Generalleutnant	Major General
Generalmajor	Brigadier General
Oberst	Colonel
Oberstleutnant	Lieutenant Colonel
Major	Major
Hauptmann	Captain
Oberleutnant	First Lieutenant
Leutnant	Second Lieutenant
Stabsfeldwebel	Master Sergeant
Oberfeldwebel	Technical Sergeant
Feldwebel	Staff Sergeant
Unterfeldwebel	Sergeant
Unteroffizier	Corporal
Gefreiter	Private First Class
Obersoldat	No US Army equivalent
Soldat	Private

(Source: U.S. War Department, *Handbook on German Military Forces.* Baton Rouge: Louisiana State University press, 1990, 6–7)

NOTES

Introduction

1. "I Samuel," *The Tanakh: The Holy Scriptures* (Philadelphia: The Jewish Publication Society, 1985), 427.

2. Peter Balakian, *The Burning Tigris: The Armenian Genocide and America's Response* (New York: HarperCollins, 2003), 11; Michael Oren, "The Mass Murder They Still Deny," *New York Review of Books* (May 10, 2007): 10n1. http://www.nybooks.com.articles/20174.

3. Raphael Lemkin, *Axis Rule in Occupied Europe, Laws of Occupation, Analysis of Government, Proposals for Redress* (Washington, DC: Carnegie Endowment, 1944), 92.

4. For more on Lemkin, see the special edition of the *Journal of Genocide Research* 7, no. 4 (December 2005), "Raphael Lemkin: The 'Founder of the United Nation's Genocide Convention' as a Historian of Mass Violence," 441–559, ed. Dominik J. Schaller and Jürgen Zimmerer.

5. "Convention on the Prevention and Punishment of the Crime of Genocide," 1, General Assembly [of the United Nations] Resolution 260A of 9 December 1948, Office of the High Commissioner for Human Rights, Geneva, Switzerland, http://www.unhchr.ch/html/menu3/b/p_genoci.htm.

6. Tom Segev, *The Seventh Million: The Israelis and the Holocaust,* trans. Haim Watzman (New York: Hill and Wang, 1993), 334.

Chapter 1

1. "God, names of," in *The New Encyclopedia of Judaism,* ed. Geoffrey Wigoda, Fred Skolnik, and Shmuel Himelstein (New York: New York University Press, 2002), 307.

2. *The Torah: The Five Books of Moses* (Philadelphia: Jewish Publication Society of America, 1962), 336.

3. Menachim Stern, "The Decrees Against the Jewish Religion and the Establishments of the Hasmonean State," in *A History of the Jewish People,* ed. Haim H. Ben-Sasson (Cambridge, MA: Harvard University Press, 1976), 206.

4. Paul Mendes-Flohr and Jehuda Reinharz, eds., *The Jew in the Modern World: A Documentary History,* 2nd ed. (New York: Oxford University Press, 1995), 701; Paul Johnson, *A History of the Jews* (New York: Harper & Row, 1987), 112; "Population," *Encyclopedia Judaica,* CD Rom Edition (Jerusalem: Judaica Multimedia, n.d.), 1.

5. Johnson, *History of the Jews,* 127.

6. Menachim Stern, "The Great Revolt," in Ben Sasson, *A History of the Jewish People,* 296.

7. Flavius Josephus, *The Great Roman–Jewish War: A.D. 66–70,* the William Whiston translation as revised by D. S. Margoliouth, ed. Willaim R. Farmer (Gloucester, MA: Peter Smith, 1970), 269.

8. Tacitus, *The Histories,* trans. W. H. Fyfe., ed. D. S. Levine (New York: Oxford University Press, 1997), 234–235.

9. Samuel Sandmel, M. Jack Suggs, and Arnold J. Tkacik, eds., *The New English Bible with the Apocrypha: Oxford Study Edition* (New York: Oxford University Press, 1976); *The New Testament,*

39; the King James Version reads "I am innocent of the blood of this just Person. You see to it. And all the people answered and said: 'His blood *be* on us and on our children.'" *The Holy Bible Containing the Old and New Testaments: The New King James Version* (Nashville, TN: Thomas Nelson, 1983), 1108.

10. *The New English Bible: New Testament,* 160.

11. Ibid., 120.

12. Ibid., 309, 300.

13. "Laws of Constantine the Great, October 18, 315, Concerning Jews, Heaven-Worshipers, and Samaritans," *Heritage: Civilization and the Jews,* 1–2, http://www.pbs.org/wnet/heritage/episode3/documents/documents_10.html.

14. A. H. M. Jones, *Constantine and the Conversion of Europe* (New York: Collier Books, 1962), 140.

15. "The Nicene Creed," *The Book of Common Prayer and Administration of the Sacraments and Other Rites and Ceremonies of the Church* (New York: Oxford University Press, 1990), 358.

16. W. H. C. Frend, *The Rise of Christianity* (Philadelphia: Fortress Press, 1984), 505.

17. Jones, *Constantine and the Conversion of Europe,* 207.

18. Werner Keller, *Diaspora: The Post-Biblical History of the Jews* (New York: Harcourt Brace & World, 1969), 97–98.

19. Edward Gibbon, *The Decline and Fall of the Roman Empire* (New York: Harcourt Brace, 1960), 360–361.

20. Keller, *Diaspora,* 100.

21. Edward H. Flannery, *The Anguish of the Jews* (New York: Macmillan, 1965), 47.

22. Saint John Chrysostom, *Adversus Judaeos,* Homily 1, pt. 3, 5–6, http://www.preteristarchive.com/Bookstore/chrysostom_homilies_adversus_judeaus.html.

23. Flannery, *Anguish of the Jews,* 47.

24. Augustine, *The City of God Against the Pagans,* trans. and ed. R. W. Dyson (Cambridge: Cambridge University Press, 1998), 891.

25. Flannery, *Anguish of the Jews,* 50.

26. Ibid.

27. James J. O'Donnell, *Augustine: A New Biography* (New York: HarperCollins, 2005), 188.

28. Saint Augustine, *Treatises on Marriage and Other Subjects,* trans. Charles T. Wilcox et al., in *The Fathers of the Church,* ed. Roy J. Deferrari (New York: Fathers of the Church, 1955), 391, 414.

29. Samuel Parsons Scott, ed., *The Civil Law: Including the Twelve Tables, the Institutes of Gaius, the Rules of Ulpian, the Opinions of Paulus, the Enactments of Justinian, and the Constitutions of Leo,* (Cincinnati: Central Trust Company, 1932), 12:63, 72, 75, 79, 82.

30. Mendes-Flohr and Reinharz, *The Jew in the Modern World,* 701.

31. Keller, *Diaspora,* 152.

32. Will Durant, *The Age of Faith* (New York: Simon and Schuster, 1950), 587.

33. August C. Krey, *The First Crusade: The Accounts of Eyewitnesses and Participants* (Princeton: Princeton University Press, 1921), 54–56.

34. Keller, *Diaspora,* 205.

35. Ibid., 206.

36. Robert Chazan, *European Jewry and the First Crusade* (Berkeley: University of California Press, 1987), 220.

37. Keller, *Diaspora,* 206–207.

38. Peter Abelard, *Collationes,* ed. and trans. John Marebon and Giovanni Orlandi (Oxford: Clarendon Press, 2001), 19–21; for a different translation of this text, see Peter Abelard, *A Dialogue of a Philosopher with a Jew and a Christian,* trans. Pierre J. Payer (Toronto: Institute of Medieval Studies, 1979), 32–33.

39. H. H. Ben-Sasson, "Changes in the Legal Status and Security of the Jews," in Ben-Sasson, *A History of the Jewish People,* 481.

40. H. H. Ben-Sasson, "The Middle Ages," in Ben-Sasson, *A History of the Jewish People,* 478.

41. "Thomas Aquinas' Letter to Margaret of Flanders," trans. Mark Johnson, Thomistica.NET, 1–4, http://www.thomistica.net/thomas-aquinas-letter-to-marg/.

42. Michael Novak, "Aquinas and the Heretics," *First Things,* no. 58 (December 1995): 4–5, http://print.firstthings.com/ftissues/ft9512/articles/novak.htm.

43. Keller, *Diaspora,* 212.

44. Joseph Gaer, *The Legend of the Wandering Jew* (New York: The New American Library, 1961), 151.

45. George L. Mosse, *Toward the Final Solution: A History of European Racism* (New York: Harper & Row, 1978), 115.

46. "Aquinas' Letter to Margaret of Flanders," 4.

47. Benzion Netanyahu, *The Origins of the Inquisition in Fifteenth Century Spain,* 2nd ed. (New York: New York Review Books, 2001), 68–69.

48. *The Letters of St. Bernard of Clairvaux,* trans. Bruno Scott James (Spencer, MA: Cistercian Publications, 1998), 463.

49. H. H. Ben-Sasson, "The Status and Economic Structure of Jewish Communities, 1096–1348," in Ben-Sasson, *A History of the Jewish People,* 472.

50. Keller, *Diaspora,* 221.

51. R. Po-chia Hsia, *The Myth of Ritual Murder: Jews and Magic in Reformation Germany* (New Haven: Yale University Press, 1988), 3; Frank Felsenstein, *Anti-Semitic Stereotypes: A Paradigm of Otherness in English Popular Culture, 1660–1830* (Baltimore: Johns Hopkins University Press, 1995), 10, 147–159.

52. Shlomo Simonsohn, ed. *The Apostolic See and the Jews: Documents* (Toronto: Pontifical Institute of Medieval Studies, 1988), 30.

53. Ibid., 313–323.

54. Keller, *Diaspora,* 244.

55. Netanyahu, *Oigins of the Inquisition,* 149.

56. Howard M. Sachar, *Farewell Espana: The World of the Sephardim Remembered* (New York: Alfred A. Knopf, 1994), 71–73.

57. "Population," *Encyclopedia Judaica,* table 5, 1 page; Mendes-Flohr and Reinharz, *The Jew in the Modern World,* 702.

58. Edward J. Hanna, "Purgatory," *The Catholic Encyclopedia,* online edition (2003), 12:1, http://www.newadvent.org/cathen/12575a.htm.

59. Richard Marius, *Martin Luther: The Christian Between God and Death* (Cambridge, MA: Harvard University Press, 1999), 137.

60. Ibid., 140.

61. Martin Luther, "On the Jews and Their Lies," *Medieval Sourcebook,* trans. Martin H. Bertram (New York: Fordham University, 2005), 12, http//:www.fordham.edu/halsall/basis/1543-Luther-JewsandLies-full.html.

62. Ibid., 12.

63. Diarmaid MacCulloch, *The Reformation: A History* (New York: Viking, 2004), 666.

64. Marius, *Martin Luther,* 378–379.

65. Heiko A. Oberman, *Luther: Man Between God and the Devil,* trans. Eileen Walliser-Schwartzbart (New York: Image Books, 1992), 297; Marius, *Martin Luther,* 372.

66. Eliot Barculo Wheaton, *The Nazi Revolution, 1933–1935: Prelude to Calamity* (Garden City, NY: Anchor Books, 1969), 309.

67. Ibid., 314.

68. Ibid., 400–401.

69. Doris L. Bergen, *Twisted Cross: The German Christian Movement in the Third Reich* (Chapel Hill: University of North Carolina Press, 1996), 128.

70. Ibid., 28.

Chapter 2

1. Paul Mendes-Flohr and Jehuda Reinharz, eds., *The Jew in the Modern World: A Documentary History,* 2nd ed. (Oxford: Oxford University Press, 1995), 702.

2. John Locke, *An Essay Concerning Human Understanding,* abridged, ed., and with an introduction and notes by Kenneth Winkler (Indianapolis: Hackett, 1996), 11–12, 30–32, 39.

3. John Locke, *Two Treatises of Government and a Letter Concerning Toleration,* ed. Ian Shapiro (New Haven: Yale University Press, 2003), 101, 166, 172.

4. Ibid., 224, 249.

5. Gotthold Ephraim Lessing, *Nathan the Wise,* trans., ed., and with an introduction by Ronald Schechter (Boston: Bedford/St. Martin's Press, 2004), 119–125; "Eisenmenger, Johann Andreas," in *The New Schaff-Herzog Encyclopedia of Religious Knowledge,* ed. Samuel Macauley Jackson and Lefferts Augustine Loetscher (New York: Funk and Wagnalls, 1908), 101; Klaus Fischer, *The History of an Obsession: German Judeophobia and the Holocaust* (New York: Continuum, 1998), 46. For excerpts from Eisenmenger's work, see Richard S. Levy, *Antisemitism in the Modern World: An Anthology of Texts* (Lexington, KY: D. C. Heath, 1991), 33–36.

6. Arthur Hertzberg, *The French Enlightenment and the Jews* (New York: Columbia University Press, 1968), 10.

7. Harvey Chisick, "Ethics and History in Voltaire's Attitudes Toward the Jews," *Eighteenth Century Studies* 35, no. 4 (Summer 2002): 588.

8. Adam Sutcliffe, "Voltaire in Context: The Emergence of Antijudaic Rhetoric in the French Early Enlightenment," in *L'antisémitisme éclairé: Inclusion et exclusion depuis l'Epoque des Lumières jusqu'à l'affaire Dreyfus/Inclusion and Exclusion: Perspectives on Jews from the Enlightenment to the Dreyfus Affair,* ed. Ilana Y. Zinguer and Sam W. Bloom (Leiden, Netherlands, and Boston: Brill, 2003), 123.

9. Chisick, "Ethics and History," 577–578.

10. Montesquieu, *The Spirit of Laws,* ed. and with an introduction, notes, and appendices by David Wallace Carrithers, together with an English translation of *An Essay on Causes Affecting Minds and Characters (1736–1743)* (Berkeley: University of California Press, 1977), 341, 351.

11. Joel Carmichael, *The Satanizing of the Jews: Origin and Development of Mystical Anti-Semitism* (New York: Fromm International, 1992), 104.

12. Ronald Schechter, "The Jewish Question in Eighteenth-Century France," *Eighteenth-Century Studies* 32, no. 1 (Fall 1998): 86–89.

13. Shmuel Ettinger, "The Attitude of European Society in the Seventeenth and Eighteenth Societies," in *A History of the Jewish People,* ed. Haim H. Ben-Sasson (Cambridge: Cambridge University Press, 1976), 745.

14. Immanuel Kant, *The Conflict of the Faculties* [Der Streit der Fakultäten], trans. and introduced Mary J. Gregor (New York: Abaris Books, 1979), 94–95.

15. See, for example, Ettinger's comments in his "The Attitude of European Society in the Seventeenth and Eighteenth Centuries," 745, and William Nicholl's *Christian Antisemitism: A History of Hate* (Northvale, NJ: Jason Aronson, 1993), 298–299, who cites Ettinger; Fichte's seminal thoughts on Germans and Germanness can be found in his *Addresses to the German Nation,* trans. R. F. Jones and G. H. Turnbull (Westport, CT: Greenwood Press, 1979).

16. Johann Gottlieb Fichte, *Johann Gottlieb Fichte's sämmliche Werke* (Berlin: Verlag von Veit und Comp., 1845), 4:149–150.

17. Ibid., 150; Alfred D. Low, *Jews in the Eyes of the Germans: From the Enlightenment to Imperial Germany* (Philadelphia: Institute for the Study of Human Issues, 1979), 145–146.

18. Low, *Jews in the Eyes of the Germans,* 431, n2.

19. Hajo Holborn, *A History of Modern Germany, 1648–1840* (Princeton: Princeton University Press, 1982), 320.

20. David Sorkin, *Moses Mendelssohn and the Religious Enlightenment* (Berkeley: University of California Press, 1996), 27.

21. Low, *Jews in the Eyes of the Germans,* 33.

22. Ibid.

23. Ibid., 34.

24. Ibid., 33–34.

25. Alexander Altmann, *Moses Mendelssohn, A Biographical Study* (Tuscaloosa: University of Alabama Press, 1973), 461–461.

26. Howard M. Sachar, *A History of the Jews in the Modern World* (New York: Alfred A. Knopf, 2005), 38.

27. Ibid., 40.

28. Ibid., 43.

29. Fritz Stern, *Dreams and Delusions: The Drama of German History* (New Haven: Yale University Press, 1999), 97–114.

30. Peter Gay, *The Cultivation of Hatred: The Bourgeoisie Experience, Victoria to Freud* (New York: W. W. Norton, 1993), 85.

31. "Spencer, Herbert (1820–1903)," in *Encyclopedia of European Social History from 1350 to 2000*, ed. Peter N. Stearns (Detroit: Charles Scribner's Sons, 2001), 6:320.

32. Francis Galton, "Eugenics: Its Definition, Scope, and Aims," *American Journal of Sociology* 10, no. 1 (July 1904): 1, http://galton.org/essays/1900–1911/galton–1904-am-journ-soc-eugenics-scope-aims.htm.

33. John Cornwell, *Hitler's Scientists: Science, War and the Devil's Pact* (New York: Viking, 2003), 78.

34. Dietrich Orlow, *A History of Modern Germany* (Englewood Cliffs, NJ: Prentice-Hall, 1987), 37.

35. Ibid., 39.

36. Fritz Stern, *The Politics of Cultural Despair: A Study of the Rise of the Germanic Ideology* (Garden City, NY: Anchor Books, 1965), 351.

37. Johann Gottfried von Herder, *Reflections on the Philosophy of the History of Mankind* (Chicago: University of Chicago Press, 1968), 144.

38. Stern, *Politics of Cultural Despair,* 123–124.

39. Ibid., 91.

40. Richard Wagner, *Judaism in Music* [Das Judenthum in der Musik], trans. William Ashton Ellis, 5, http://reactor-core.org/judaism-in-music.html.

41. August Kubizek, *The Young Hitler I Knew,* trans. E. V. Anderson (Cambridge, MA: Riverside Press, 1955), 192.

42. William L. Shirer, *The Rise and Fall of the Third Reich: A History of Nazi Germany* (New York: Simon & Schuster, 1960), 101.

43. Low, *Jews in the Eyes of the Germans,* 372.

44. Richard S. Levy, *The Downfall of the Anti-Semitic Political Parties in Imperial Germany* (New Haven: Yale University Press, 1975), 259.

45. Ibid., 259–260.

46. Ibid., 260.

47. Richard J. Evans, *The Coming of the Third Reich* (New York: Penguin, 2004), 218.

48. Robert S. Wistrich, *The Jews of Vienna in the Age of Franz Joseph* (Oxford: Oxford University Press, 1990), 214.

49. Kubizek, *The Young Hitler I Knew,* 248.

50. Brigitte Hamann, *Hitler's Vienna: A Dictator's Apprenticeship,* trans. Thomas Thornton (Oxford: Oxford University Press, 1999), 251.

51. Ibid.

52. Ibid., 253.

53. Richard S. Geehr, *Karl Lueger: Mayor of Fin de Siècle Vienna* (Detroit: Wayne State University Press, 1990), 15, 17, 178.

54. Alan Palmer, *Twilight of the Habsburgs: The Life and Times of Emperor Francis Joseph* (New York: W. W. Norton, 1994), 275.

55. Ibid., 287.

56. Adolf Hitler, *Mein Kampf,* trans. Ralph Manheim (New York: Houghton Mifflin, 1943), 121.

57. Mendes-Flohr and Reinharz, *The Jew in the Modern World,* 336n1.

58. Ibid., 339.

59. Jean-Denis Bredin, *The Affair: The Case of Alfred Dreyfus,* trans. Jeffrey Mehlman (New York: George Braziller, 1986), 29.

60. Susan Zuccotti, *The Holocaust, the French, and the Jews* (Lincoln: University of Nebraska Press, 1993), 12.

61. Nicholas Halasz, *Captain Dreyfus: The Story of a Mass Hysteria* (New York: Simon & Schuster, 1955), 96.

62. Bredin, *The Affair,* 241.

63. Zuccotti, *The Holocaust,* 16; Bredin, *The Affair,* 350–352.

64. Bredin, *The Affair,* 270.

65. Zuccotti, *The Holocaust,* 13.

66. Michael R. Marrus and Robert O. Paxton, *Vichy France and the Jews* (Stanford: Stanford University Press, 1995), 32.

67. Ibid., 33.

68. Werner Keller, *Diaspora: The Post-Biblical History of the Jews* (New York: Harcourt, Brace & World, 1969), 303.

69. Ibid., 304.

70. Stephen M. Berk, *Year of Crisis, Year of Hope: Russian Jewry and the Pogroms of 1881–1882* (Westport, CT: Greenwood Press, 1985), 46.

71. Ibid., 47.

72. Robert F. Byrnes, *Pobedonostsev: His Life and Thought* (London: Indiana University Press, 1968), 205.

73. Alexander Orbach, "The Russian Jewish Community, 1881–1903," in *Pogroms: Anti-Jewish Violence in Modern Russian History,* ed. John D. Klier and Shlomo Lambroza (Cambridge: Cambridge University Press, 1992), 151.

74. Hitler, *Mein Kampf,* 308.

75. Hadassa Ben-Itto, *The Lie That Wouldn't Die: The Protocols of the Elders of Zion* (London: Vallentine Mitchell, 2005), 160.

76. Ibid., 28–29.

77. The full title of Nilus's book was *The Great in the Small: The Coming of the Anti-Christ and the Rule of Satan on Earth.*

78. Henry Ford, Sr., *The International Jew: The World's Foremost Problem* (Boring, OR: CPA Book Publisher, 1920), 239.

79. Ben-Itto, *Lie That Wouldn't Die,* 346–347.

80. Ibid., 348.

81. *The Goebbels Diaries, 1942–1943,* ed. and trans. Louis Lochner (Garden City, NY: Doubleday & Company, 1948), 376–377.

Chapter 3

1. Ian Kershaw, *Hitler: 1889–1936 Hubris* (New York: W. W. Norton, 1999), 9.

2. Robert G. L. Waite, *The Psychopathic God: Adolf Hitler* (New York: Basic Books, 1977), 147–148.

3. Adolf Hitler, *Mein Kampf,* trans. Ralph Manheim (Boston: Houghton Mifflin Company, 1943), 4.

4. August Kubizek, *The Young Hitler I Knew,* trans. E. V. Anderson (Cambridge, MA: Riverside Press, 1955), 12–13, 35.

5. Ibid., 26.

6. Ibid., 77.

7. Kershaw, *Hitler: 1889–1936 Hubris,* 24.

8. Ibid., 53.

9. Ibid., 59.

10. Hitler, *Mein Kampf,* 126.

11. Richard S. Levy, *The Downfall of the Anti-Semitic Political Parties in Imperial Germany* (New Haven: Yale University Press, 1975), 188–189.

12. Kershaw, *Hitler: 1889–1936 Hubris,* 87.

13. Hitler, *Mein Kampf,* 16.

14. Ibid., 207.

15. Kershaw, *Hitler: 1889–1936 Hubris,* 115; David Clay Large, *Where Ghosts Walked: Munich's Road to the Third Reich* (New York: W. W. Norton, 1997), 122.

16. "The Constitution of the German Confederation of August 11, 1919," 2, http://web.jjay .cuny.edu/jobrien/reference/ob13.html.

17. Norman H. Baynes, ed., *The Speeches of Adolf Hitler (April 1922–August 1939)* (New York: Howard Fertig, 1969), 1:1450, 1593; Hitler, *Mein Kampf,* 632.

18. *The Treaty of Versailles (June 28, 1919),* Part VII, Penalties, Article 227, 1, http://history .acusd.edu/gen/text/versaillestreaty/ver231.html. At the end of the war, the Kaiser fled to the Netherlands; later, Dutch authorities refused to extradite him for trial.

19. Ibid., Part VIII, Reparation Section, General Provisions, Article 231, 1.

20. Marshal von Hindenburg, *Out of My Life,* trans. F. A. Holt (London: Cassell, 1920), 323.

21. Erich von Ludendorff, *Ludendorff's Own Story, August 1914–November 1918* (Freeport, NY: Books for Libraries Press, 1971), 429.

22. John W. Wheeler-Bennett, *Hindenburg: The Wooden Titan* (London: Macmillan, 1967), 238.

23. Hitler, *Mein Kampf,* 523.

24. Baynes, *Speeches of Adolf Hitler,* 54–55.

25. Ibid., 80–81.

26. Kershaw, *Hitler 1889–1936 Hubris,* 120.

27. Hitler, *Mein Kampf,* 687.

28. Joachim C. Fest, *Hitler,* trans. Richard and Clara Winston (New York: Harcourt Brace Jovanovich, 1974), 119; Kershaw, *Hitler 1889–1936 Hubris,* 133.

29. Kershaw, *Hitler 1889–1936 Hubris,* 156.

30. Adolf Hitler, *Hitler's Letters and Notes,* comp. Werner Maser, trans. Arnold Pomerans (New York: Bantam Books, 1976), 211.

31. Ibid.

32. Ibid.

33. Hitler, *Mein Kampf,* 679.

34. "Programme of the German Workers Party (February 24, 1920)," in *The Nazi Party, State and Society, 1919–1939,* vol. 1 of *Nazism: A History in Documents and Eyewitness Accounts, 1919–1945,* ed. Jeremy Noakes and Geoffrey Pridham (New York: Schocken Books, 1984), 14–15.

35. Baynes, *Speeches of Adolf Hitler,* 1:107–108.

36. "Programme of the German Workers Party (February 24, 1920)," 15.

37. Ibid., 15–16.

38. Baynes, *Speeches of Adolf Hitler,* 1:103–108.

39. Kershaw, *Hitler 1889–1936 Hubris,* 177.

40. Hitler, *Mein Kampf,* 382.

41. Ibid., 65.

42. Ibid., 326.

43. Kershaw, *Hitler 1889–1936 Hubris,* 245.

44. Klaus Fischer, *Nazi Germany* (New York: Continuum, 1995), 130.

45. Hitler, *Mein Kampf,* 680.

46. Baynes, *Speeches of Adolf Hitler,* 1:78.

47. Kershaw, *Hitler 1889–1936 Hubris,* 180.

48. Klaus Fischer, *Nazi Germany: A New History* (New York: Continuum, 1995), 163.

49. Baynes, *Speeches of Adolf Hitler,* 1:368.

50. Kershaw, *Hitler 1889–1936 Hubris,* 288.

51. Gerhard L. Weinberg, ed., *Hitler's Second Book: The Unpublished Sequel to Mein Kampf,* trans. Krista Smith (New York: Enigma Books, 2003), 29–37.

52. Ibid., 233.

53. Baynes, *Speeches of Adolf Hitler,* 1:726–727.

54. Kershaw, *Hitler 1889–1936 Hubris,* 327.

55. Ibid., 339.

56. Thomas Childers, *The Nazi Voter: The Social Foundations of Fascism in Germany, 1919–1933* (Chapel Hill: University of North Carolina Press, 1983), 194.

57. Kershaw, *Hitler 1889–1936 Hubris,* 366.

58. Ibid., 371.

59. Fischer, *Nazi Germany,* 234.

60. Kurt Georg Wilhelm Ludecke, *I Knew Hitler: The Story of a Nazi Who Escaped the Blood Purge* (London: Jarrolds, 1938), 465–466.

61. Franz von Papen, *Memoirs,* trans. Brian Conwell (New York: E. Dalton, 1953), 257.

Chapter 4

1. Jeremy Noakes and Geoffrey Pridham, eds., *The Nazi Party, State and Society, 1919–1939,* vol. 1 of *Nazism, 1919–1945: A History in Documents and Eyewitness Accounts* (New York: Schocken Books, 1984), 15.

2. Ibid., 15–16.

3. Karl A. Schleunes, *The Twisted Road to Auschwitz: Nazi Policy Toward German Jews, 1933–1939* (Urbana: University of Illinois Press, 1990), 58, 70.

4. Barbara Distel and Ruth Jakusch, eds., *Concentration Camp Dachau, 1933–1945* (Munich: Comité International de Dachau, 1978), 46; Paul Berben, *Dachau, 1933–1945: The Official History* (London: Comité International de Dachau, 1975), 2.

5. Ian Kershaw, *Hitler: 1889–1936 Hubris* (New York: W. W. Norton, 1999), 434–435.

6. Ibid., 435.

7. Ralf Georg Reuth, *Goebbels,* trans. Krishna Winston (New York: Harcourt, Brace & World, 1993), 179.

8. Kershaw, *Hitler: Hubris 1889–1936,* 473–474.

9. Deborah E. Lipstadt, *Beyond Belief: The American Press & the Coming of the Holocaust, 1933–1945* (New York: Free Press, 1986), 43–45.

10. Ibid., 474.

11. Guenther Lewy, *The Catholic Church and Nazi Germany* (New York: McGraw-Hill, 1964), 84.

12. James Carroll, *Constantine's Sword: The Church and the Jews* (Boston: Houghton Mifflin, 2002), 499.

13. Ibid., 35.

14. Doris Bergen, *Twisted Cross: The German Christian Movement in the Third Reich* (Chapel Hill: University of North Carolina Press, 1996), 35.

15. Ibid., 90.

16. Richard Steigmann-Gall, *The Holy Reich: Nazi Conceptions of Christianity, 1919–1945* (Cambridge: Cambridge University Press, 2003), 185.

17. Bergen, *Twisted Cross,* 1, 69, 90.

18. Victoria Barnett, "Dietrich Bonhoeffer," *http://www.ushmm.org/bonhoeffer/* (June 21, 2006), 10.

19. Reuth, *Goebbels,* 191.

20. Schleunes, *Twisted Road to Auschwitz,* 114.

21. Marion A. Kaplan, "Jewish Women in Nazi Germany: Daily Life, Daily Struggles, 1933–1939, in *Different Voices: Women and the Holocaust,* ed. Carol Rittner and John K. Roth (New York: Paragon House, 1993), 199.

22. Kershaw, *Hitler: 1889–1936 Hubris,* 517.

23. Klaus Fischer, *Nazi Germany: A New History* (New York: Continuum, 1995), 293.

24. John W. Wheeler-Bennett, *Hindenburg: The Wooden Titan* (London: Macmillan, 1967), 464.

25. William L. Shirer, *The Rise and Fall of the Third Reich: A History of Nazi Germany* (New York: Simon & Schuster, 1960), 230.

26. Kershaw, *Hitler: Hubris 1889–1936,* 559–560.

27. Robert N. Proctor, *Racial Hygiene: Medicine Under the Nazis* (Cambridge, MA: Harvard University Press, 1988), 64.

28. Norman H. Baynes, ed., *The Speeches of Adolf Hitler, April 1922–August 1939* (New York: Howard Fertig, 1969), 1:447–449.

29. Kershaw, *Hitler: Hubris, 1889–1936,* 567.

30. Karl A. Schleunes, ed., *Legislating the Holocaust: The Bernhard Loesener Memoirs and Supporting Documents,* trans. Carol Scherer (Boulder: Westview Press, 2001), 154–155.

31. Proctor, *Racial Hygiene,* 132; Michael Burleigh and Wolfgang Wippermann, *The Racial State: Germany 1933–1945* (Cambridge: Cambridge University Press, 1991), 49.

32. Romani Rose, ed., *Der Nationalsozialistische Völkermord an den Sinti und Roma* (Heidelberg, Germany: Documentations- und Kulturzentrum Deutscher Sinti und Roma, 2003), 25; Schleunes, *Legislating the Holocaust,* 172; Guenter Lewy, *The Nazi Persecution of the Gypsies* (New York: Oxford University Press, 2000), 42–43; Henry Friedlander, *The Origins of Nazi Genocide: From Euthanasia to the Final Solution* (Chapel Hill: University of North Carolina Press, 1995), 258–259; Gilad Margalit, *Germany and Its Gypsies: A Post-Auschwitz Ordeal* (Madison: University of Wisconsin Press, 2002), 39.

33. Baynes, *Speeches of Adolf Hitler,* 2:1264–1266.

34. Kershaw, *Hitler: 1889–1936 Hubris,* 573.

35. Ibid., 590–591.

36. The Jewish Virtual Library, "The Nazi Olympics" (June 27, 2006): 3, http://www.jewishvirtual library.org/jsource/Holocaust/olympics.html.

37. Ibid.

38. William L. Shirer, *The Nightmare Years, 1930–1940* (Boston: Little, Brown, 1984), 234.

39. William L. Shirer, *The Rise and Fall of the Third Reich: A History of Nazi Germany* (New York: Simon & Schuster, 1960), 233.

40. Karl Schleunes has estimated that there were 75,000 Jewish businesses in Germany in 1933 and almost 40,000 of them still in operation in the spring of 1938. Schleunes, *Twisted Road to Auschwitz,* 145.

41. David Cesarani, *Becoming Eichmann: Rethinking the Life, Crimes, and Trial of a "Desk Murderer"* (Cambridge, MA: Da Capo Press, 2006), 57.

42. Ibid., 67.

43. Ian Kershaw, *Hitler: 1936–1945 Nemesis* (New York: W. W. Norton, 2000), 129.

44. Ibid., 130.

45. Anthony Read and David Fisher, *Kristallnacht: The Unleashing of the Holocaust* (New York: Peter Bedrick Books, 1989), 133.

46. Ibid., 141.

47. Ibid., 153.

48. David Bankier, *The Germans and the Final Solution: Public Opinion Under the Nazis* (Oxford: Blackwell, 1996), 85–88.

49. Ibid., 162.

50. Jeremy Noakes and Geoffrey Pridham, eds., *Foreign Policy, War and Racial Extermination,* vol. 2 of *Nazism, 1919–1945: A History in Documents and Eyewitness Accounts* (New York: Schocken Books, 1988), 1049.

51. Victor Klemperer, *I Will Bear Witness: A Diary of the Nazi Years, 1933–1941,* trans. Martin Chalmers (New York: Random House, 1998), 276, 280, 283.

52. *New York Times,* June 10, 1939, 9.

53. Adolf Hitler, *Mein Kampf* (Boston: Houghton Mifflin, 1943), 255.

54. Clarence Lusane, *Hitler's Black Victims: The Historical Experiences of Afro-Germans, European Blacks, Africans, and African Americans in the Nazi Era* (New York: Routledge, 2003), 98.

55. Hitler, *Mein Kampf,* 624.

56. Michael Burleigh, *Death and Deliverance: "Euthanasia" in Germany, 1900–1945* (Cambridge: Cambridge University Press, 1994), 12; "Euthanasia," *UK Rights* (the online newspaper of UKCHR), *http://www.ukcouncilhumanrights.co.uk/euthanasia.html,* accessed July 1, 2006.

57. Noakes and Pridham, *Foreign Policy, War and Racial Extermination,* 1002.

58. Burleigh, *Death and Deliverance,* 38.

59. Ibid., 97.

60. Proctor, *Racial Hygiene,* 182–183.

61. Wim Willems, *In Search of the True Gypsy: From Enlightenment to Final Solution,* trans. Don Bloch (London: Frank Cass, 1997).

62. Lewy, *Nazi Persecution,* 6.

63. Ibid., 7.

64. Angus Fraser, *The Gypsies* (Oxford: Blackwell, 1992), 253.

65. Lewy, *Nazi Persecution,* 8; Giland Margalit, *Germany and Its Gypsies: A Post-Auschwitz Ordeal* (Madison: University of Wisconsin Press, 2002), 32.

66. Lewy, *Nazi Persecution,* 9.

67. Ibid., 42.

68. Michale Zimmermann, *Rassenutopie und Genozid: Die nationalsozilistische "Lösung der Zigeunerfrage"* (Hamburg: Hans Christians Verlag, 1996), 149.

69. Margalit, *Germany and Its Gypsies,* 36.

70. Lewy, *Nazi Persecution,* 47.

71. Ibid., 48.

72. Margalit, *Germany and Its Gypsies,* 35.

73. Lewy, *Nazi Persecution,* 51.

74. Ibid., 52.

75. Frank Sparing, "The Gypsy Camps," in *From "Race Science" to the Camps: The Gypsies During the Second World War,* ed. Karola Fings, Herbert Heuss, and Frank Sparing (Hatfield, UK: University of Hertfordshire Press, 1997), 54.

76. Ibid., 56.

77. Günter Grau, *Hidden Holocaust? Gay and Lesbian Persecution in Germany, 1933–1945,* trans. Patrick Camiller (London: Cassell, 1995), 3.

78. Burleigh and Wippermann, *Racial State,* 186–187.

79. Grau, *Hidden Holocaust?,* 3.

80. Ibid., 65.

81. Ibid., 110–115.

82. Burleigh and Wippermann, *Racial State,* 192–193.

83. Ibid., 192–193.

Chapter 5

1. Henry Friedlander, *The Origins of Nazi Genocide: From Euthanasia to the Final Solution* (Chapel Hill: University of North Carolina Press, 1995), 22.

2. Ibid., 39; Michael Burleigh, *Death and Deliverance: "Euthanasia" in Germany, 1900–1945* (Cambridge: Cambridge University Press, 1994) 94–95.

3. Friedlander, *Origins of Nazi Genocide,* 50.

4. Burleigh, *Death and Deliverance,* 112.

5. *Trial of War Criminals Before the Nurenberg Military Tribunals Under Control Council Law No. 10, "The Medical Case"* (Washington, DC: U.S. Government Printing Office, 1950), 1:848.

6. Ibid., 850.

7. Friedlander, *Origins of Nazi Genocide,* 81–82.

8. *Trial of War Criminals Before the Nurenberg Military Tribunals,* 1:846.

9. Jeremy Noakes and Geoffrey Pridham, eds., *Foreign Policy, War and Racial Extermination,* vol. 2 of *Nazism 1919–1945: A History in Documents and Eyewitness Accounts* (New York: Schocken Books, 1988), 1038.

10. Burleigh, *Death and Deliverance,* 180.

11. David M. Crowe, *The Baltic States and the Great Powers: Foreign Relations, 1918–1940* (Boulder: Westview Press, 1993), 68–81.

12. David M. Crowe, *Oskar Schindler: The Untold Account of His Life, Wartime Activities, and the True Story Behind "The List"* (Boulder: Westview Press, 2004), 66–69; Heinz Höhne, *Canaris,*

trans. J. Maxwell Brownjohn (New York: Doubleday, 1979), 351–353; Telford Taylor, *Sword and Swastika: Generals and Nazis in the Third Reich* (New York: Barnes and Noble, 1952), 315.

13. Gerhard L. Weinberg, *Foreign Policy of Hitler's Germany, 1937–1939: Starting World War II* (Chicago: University of Chicago Press, 1980), 646–652; Pat McTaggart, "Poland '39," in *Hitler's Army: The Evolution and Structure of German Forces,* ed. *Command* magazine (Conshohocken, PA: Combined Publishing, 1995), 220.

14. Ian Kershaw, *Hitler, 1936–1945: Nemesis* (New York: W. W. Norton, 2000), 234–235, 244; Louis L. Snyder, ed., *Hitler's Third Reich: A Documentary History* (Chicago: Nelson-Hall, 1981), 329; Hans Umbreit, "Stages in the Territorial 'New Order' in Europe," in *Germany and the Second World War,* vol. 5, *Organization and Mobilization of the German Sphere of Power,* part 1, *Wartime Administration, Economy, and Manpower Resources, 1939–1941,* ed. Bernhard R. Kroener, Rolf-Dieter Müller, and Hans Umbreit, trans. John Brownjohn et al. (Oxford: Clarendon Press, 2000), 41.

15. Richard C. Lukas, *Forgotten Holocaust: The Poles Under German Occupation, 1939–1944* (New York: Hippocrene Books, 1990), 3.

16. Höhne, *Canaris,* 363.

17. Umbreit, "Stages in the Territorial 'New Order' in Europe," 44; Kershaw, *Hitler, 1936–1945 Nemesis,* 235–236, 244; Raul Hilberg, *The Destruction of the European Jews,* rev. and definitive ed. (New York: Holmes & Meier, 1985), 1:188–189; Lukas, *Forgotten Holocaust,* 3–5.

18. Kershaw, *Hitler, 1936–1945 Nemesis,* 240–241.

19. Alexander B. Rossino, *Hitler Strikes Poland: Blitzkrieg, Ideology, and Atrocity* (Lawrence: University of Kansas Press, 2003), 234.

20. Polish Ministry of Information, *The Black Book of Poland* (New York: G. Putnam's Sons, 1942).

21. Zygmunt Klukowski, *Diary from the Years of Occupation, 1919–1944,* ed. Andrew Klukowski and Helen Klukowski May, trans. George Klukowski (Urbana: University of Illinois Press, 1993), 51.

22. *Black Book of Poland,* 383.

23. Richard Breitman, *The Architect of Genocide: Himmler and the Final Solution* (New York: Alfred A. Knopf, 1991), 108, 113.

24. Noakes and Pridham, *Foreign Policy, War and Racial Extermination,* 932.

25. Ibid., 933.

26. Ibid., 934.

27. Richard C. Lukas, ed., *Out of the Inferno: Poles Remember the Holocaust* (Lexington: University of Kentucky Press, 1989), 53–54.

28. Noakes and Pridham, *Foreign Policy, War and Racial Extermination,* 927.

29. Kershaw, *Hitler, 1936–1945 Nemesis,* 245–246.

30. Umbreit, "Stages in the Territorial 'New Order' in Europe," 53–55.

31. United States Holocaust Memorial Museum, *Historical Atlas of the Holocaust* (New York: Macmillan, 1996), 34; Hilberg, *Destruction of the European Jews,* 60, 193–196.

32. Jan Tomasz Gross, *Polish Society Under German Occupation: The General Government, 1939–1944* (Princeton: Princeton University Press, 1979), 51; Hilberg, *Destruction of the European Jews,* 201–202.

33. Umbreit, "Stages in the Territorial 'New Order' in Europe," 60.

34. Celia S. Heller, *On the Edge of Destruction: Jews of Poland Between the Two World Wars* (New York: Columbia University Press, 1977), 48.

35. Norman Davies, *1795 to the Present,* vol. 2 of *God's Playground: A History of Poland* (New York: Columbia University Press, 1982), 261.

36. Wojciech Roszkowski, "After *Neighbors:* Seeking Universal Standards," *Slavic Review* 61, no. 2 (Fall 2002): 465.

37. Ezra Mendelsohn, *The Jews of East Central Europe Between the World Wars* (Bloomington: Indiana University Press, 1983), 38.

38. Yisrael Gutman and Shmuel Krakowski, *Unequal Victims: Poles and Jews During World War II* (New York: Holocaust Library, 1986), 4.

39. Joseph Rothschild, *East Central Europe Between the Two World Wars* (Seattle: University of Washington Press, 1974), 40.

40. Rothschild, *East Central Europe,* 41.

41. Noakes and Pridham, *Foreign Policy, War and Racial Extermination,* 1051.

42. Ibid., 1051–1052.

43. Ibid., 1053.

44. Eugeniusz Duda, *The Jews of Cracow,* trans. Ewa Basiura (Kraków: Wydawnictwo 'Hagada' and Argona-Jarden Bookshop, 2000), 60–61.

45. Isaiah Trunk, *Judenrat: The Jewish Council in Eastern Europe Under Nazi Occupation* (New York: Scarborough Books, 1977), 62.

46. Ibid., 65–66; interview with Stella Müller-Madej, August 9, 2000, Kraków, Poland; Stella Müller-Madej, *A Girl from Schindler's List,* trans. William R. Brand (London: Polish Cultural Foundation, 1997), 7, 10–11.

47. Duda, *The Jews of Cracow,* 61–62; "Groyczko to Handlowego," September 11, 1941.

48. Czesław Madajczyk, *Polityka III Rzeszy w Okupowanej Polsce* (Warsaw: Pañstwowe Wydawnictwo Naukowe, 1970), 1:516; Gross, *Polish Society,* 93–94; Trunk, *Judenrat,* 63–64.

49. Madajczyk, *Polityka III Rzeszy w Okupowanej Polsce,* 1:516–519; Trunk, *Judenrat,* 63–64; Gross, *Polish Society,* 94–96.

50. Noakes and Pridham, *Foreign Policy, War and Racial Extermination,* 1055.

51. Christopher R. Browning, *The Origins of the Final Solution: The Evolution of Nazi Jewish Policy, September 1939–March 1942* (Lincoln and Jerusalem: University of Nebraska Press and Yad Vashem, 2004), 106.

52. Noakes and Pridham, *Foreign Policy, War and Racial Extermination,* 1075.

53. Ibid., 1076.

54. Browning, *Origins of the Final Solution,* 87.

55. Joseph Goebbels, *The Joseph Goebbels Diaries, 1942–1943,* ed. and trans. Louis P. Luchner (Garden City, NY: Doubleday, 1948), 116.

56. Trunk, *Judenrat,* 4.

57. Browning, *Origins of the Final Solution,* 113.

58. *The Diary of Dawid Sierakowiak: Five Books from the Łódź Ghetto,* ed. Alan Adelson, trans. Kamil Turowski (New York: Oxford University Press, 1996), 37–38.

59. Yitzhak Arad, Yisrael Gutman, and Abraham Margaliot, eds., *Documents on the Holocaust* (Jerusalem: Yad Vashem, 1981), 192–194.

60. Alan Adelson and Robert Lapides, eds., *Łódź Ghetto: Inside a Community Under Siege* (New York: Viking, 1989), 247.

61. Lucjan Dobroszycki, ed., *The Chronicle of the Łódź Ghetto, 1941–1944,* trans. Richard Lorrie et al. (New Haven: Yale University Press, 1984), 435.

62. *Diary of Dawid Sierakowiak,* 102.

63. Guenter Lewy, *The Nazi Persecution of the Gypsies* (Oxford: Oxford University Press, 2000), 68.

64. Adelson and Lapides, *Lodz Ghetto,* 173.

65. Erika Thurner, *National Socialism and Gypsies in Austria,* ed. and trans. Gilya Gerda Schmidt (Tuscaloosa: University of Alabama Press, 1998), 102. Thurner says that the Germans deported 5,007 Roma to Łódź.

66. Lewy, *Nazi Persecution of the Gypsies,* 113.

67. *Diary of Dawid Sierakowiak,* 102.

68. Isaiah Trunk, *Łódź Ghetto: A History,* trans. and ed. Robert Moses Shapiro (Bloomington: Indiana University Press, 2006), 400.

69. Ibid., 157, 268, 328–331.

70. Emmanuel Ringelblum, *Notes from the Warsaw Ghetto: The Journal of Emmanuel Ringelblum,* ed. and trans. Jacob Sloan (New York: ibooks, 2006), 194–195, 224.

71. Michael Grynberg, ed., *Worlds to Outlive Us: Eyewitness Accounts from the Warsaw Ghetto* (New York: Henry Holt, 2002), 225–226.

72. Duda, *Jews of Cracow,* 60–62; Madajczyk, *Polityka III Rzesy w Okupowanej Polsce,* 1:516–519; Gross, *Polish Society,* 93–96; Trunk, *Judenrat,* 63–64.

73. Stanisław Piotrowski, ed., *Dziennik Hansa Frank* (Warsaw: Wydawnictwo Prawnicze, 1956), 1:265–266; the Polish edition of Hans Frank's diary is more complete than the English version, Stanisław Piotrowski's *Hans Frank's Diary* (Warsaw: Państwowe Wydanictwo Naukowe, 1961), 217–218.

74. Duda, *Jews of Cracow,* 62.

75. Piotrowski, *Dziennik Hansa Frank,* 1:266; Aleksander Bieberstein, *Zagłada Żydów w Krakowie* (Kraków: Wydawnictwo Literackie, 1985), 32; Duda, *Jews of Cracow,* 62. The *Gazeta Żadowska,* which was edited by a German Jew, Fritz Seifert, was published from July 23, 1940, until August 30, 1942.

76. Duda, *Jews of Cracow,* 62.

77. Ibid.

78. Arieh L. Bauminger, *The Fighters of the Cracow Ghetto* (Jerusalem: Keter Press Enterprises, 1986), 30–31.

79. Duda, *Jews of Cracow,* 63.

80. Tadeusz Pankiewicz, *Apteka w Getcie Krakowskim* (Kraków: Wydawnictwo Literackie, 1995), 12–13; Malvina Graf, *The Kraków Ghetto and the Płaszów Camp* (Tallahassee: Florida State University Press, 1989), 35–36.

81. Anna Pióro and Wiesława Kralińska, *Krakowskie Getto* (Kraków: Muzeum Pamięci Narodowej "Apteka pod Orłem," 1995), 37–38; interview with Stella Müller-Madej, Kraków, August 9, 2000.

82. Müller-Madej, *Girl from Schindler's List,* 12.

83. Ibid., 12–13.

84. Ibid., 13.

85. "Zbioru fotografii z 'akcji zydowskiej' w Krakowie/eksmisje, wysiedlenia, rejestracje, getto," Starosty Miasta Krakowa/Der Stadthauptmann der Stadt Krakau/ z lat 1939–1945, SMKr 211 (Krakow: Archiwum Państwowe w Krakowie).

86. Pankiewicz, *Apteka w Getcie Krakowskim,* 16, 19–23, 33; Pesach was between April 12–19 in 1941.

87. Trunk, *Judenrat,* 485–487; Pankiewicz, *Apteka w Getcie Krakowskim,* 16, 19–23; Pióro, *Krakowskie Getto,* 58–59.

88. Pankiewicz, *Apteka w Getcie Krakowskim,* 25; Graf, *Kraków Ghetto and the Płaszow Camp Remembered,* 39.

89. Pankiewicz, *Apteka w Getcie Krakowskim,* 25; Trunk, *Judenrat,* 475, 489.

90. Graf, *The Kraków Ghetto and the Płaszow Camp Remembered,* 39; Trunk, *Judenrat,* 478, 499–500.

91. Yehuda Bauer, *American Jewry and the Holocaust: The American Jewish Joint Distribution Committee, 1939–1945* (Detroit: Wayne State University Press, 1981), 85–86; Dr. Max Freiherr du Prel, *Das General Gouvernement* (Würzburg: Konrad Triltsch Verlag, 1942), 311; Weichert's appointment as chair of the JSS in Kraków and his relationship with Czerniakow and the Warsaw Judenrat is discussed in some depth in *The Warsaw Diary of Adam Czerniakow: Prelude to Doom,* ed. Raul Hilberg, Stanislaw Staron, and Josef Kermisz, trans. Stanislaw Staron and the staff of Yad Vashem (New York: Stein and Day, 1979), 33, 161, 164–165, 168–169, 174.

92. Bieberstein, *Zagłada Żydów w Krakowie,* 31, 96, 129, 132, 135, 159–163; Bauer, *American Jewry and the Holocaust,* 90–92, 318–322; Bauminger, *The Fighters of the Cracow Ghetto,* 33; Jean-Claude Favez, *The Red Cross and the Holocaust,* ed. and trans. John and Beryl Fletcher (Cambridge: Cambridge University Press, 1999), 143–144.

93. Pióro, *Krakow Getto,* 4043; Pankiewicz, *Apteka w Getcie Krakowskim,* 26; Bieberstein, *Zagłada Żydów w Krakowie,* 73; interview with Sol Urbach, July 3, 2002.

94. Bieberstein, *Zagłada Żydów w Krakowie,* 223; Pankiewicz, *Apteka w Getcie Krakowskim,* 25–26.

95. Pankiewicz, *Apteka w getcie Krakowskim,* 26–27; Duda, *Jews of Cracow,* 28.

96. Müller–Madej, *Girl from Schindler's List,* 13–17.

97. Ibid., 22, 27–29; Gross, *Polish Society,* 108–109.

98. Müller- Madej, *Girl from Schindler's List,* 13–14, 40.

99. Pankiewicz, *Apteka w Getcie Krakowskim,* 33, 65–66; interview with Manci Rosner, March 21, 2000.

100. Christopher R. Browning, *Nazi Policy, Jewish Workers, German Killers* (Cambridge: Cambridge University Press, 2000), 61–62; du Prel, *Das General-Gouvernement,* 379; according to Frauendorfer, in the spring of 1940, his office planned to send half a million Poles to work in the Greater Reich. Already 160,000 Poles were being used there as agricultural workers and another 50,000 Poles were working in German factories. By the end of 1941, Frauendorfer said that Poles made up 47 percent of the foreign labor force in the Greater Reich. In 1943, Frank proudly noted that the General Government had sent 2 million workers to the Greater Reich. Piotrowski, *Dziennik Hansa Frank,* 1:72–74.

101. Gross, *Polish Society,* 111; Browning, *Nazi Policy, Jewish Workers,* 25, 62–63, 71–73.

102. R. J. Overy, *War and Economy in the Third Reich* (Oxford: Clarendon Press, 1994), 281–286; Trunk, *Judenrat,* 99.

103. Gross, *Polish Society,* 99–102; Trunk, *Judenrat,* 99–100; Eugeniusz Duranczyński, *Wojna i Okupacja: Wrzesień 1939–Kwiecień 1943* (Warsaw: Wieza Powszechna, 1974), 69; Lukas, *Forgotten Holocaust,* 30; Jabob Apsenszlak, Jacob Kenner, Isaac Lewin, and Moses Polakiewicz, eds., *The Black Book of Polish Jewry: An Account of the Martyrdom of Polish Jewry under the Nazi Occupation* (New York: The American Federation for Polish Jews, 1943), 37; according to Clive Cookson, "modern nutritionists regard 3,000–3,500 calories as a healthy minimum consumption." "Hunger, Horror and Heroism," *Financial Times,* July 28/29, 2001. These figures were probably a bit less fifty to sixty years ago.

104. Trunk, *Judenrat,* 99–103

Chapter 6

1. Mordechai Altshuler, *Soviet Jewry Since the Second World War: Population and Social Structure* (New York: Greenwood Press, 1987), 3–4; Nora Levin, *The Jews in the Soviet Union Since 1917: Paradox of Survival* (New York: New York University Press, 1988), 1:335–337.

2. Levin, *Jews in the Soviet Union,* 1:347.

3. "Poland: Jewish Plight," *New York Times,* March 15, 1940, 10; Levin, *Jews in the Soviet Union,* 1:340.

4. Lithuania's prewar Jewish population of 160,000 grew to 260,000 during this period. About 14,000 Jewish refugees, many of them prominent religious and political figures in prewar Poland, settled in Vilna.

5. Shanghai Municipal Tourism Administration Commission, *Forever Nostalgia: The Jews in Shanghai,* trans. Deng Xinyu (Shanghai: Shanghai Municipal Tourism Administration Commission, 2000), 1–10. This brochure claims it was the Chinese who saved Shanghai's Jews, something Dr. Rafael Medoff challenges in his "Chairman Mao, Holocaust Rescuer? Not Quite," 1–2, http://www.wymaninstitute.org/articles/2003–120-mao.ph. It was the Japanese, not the Chinese, who saved the Jews there.

6. Hans Halder, *Kriegstagebuch,* Band II, *Von der geplanten Landung in England bis zum Beginn des Ostfeldzerges (1.7.1940–21.6.1941): Bearbeitet von Hans-Adolf Jacobsen* (Stuttgart: W. Kohlhammer Verlag, 1963), 49–50.

7. Jeremy Noakes and Geoffrey Pridham, eds., *Foreign Policy, War and Racial Extermination,* vol. 2 of *Nazism 1919–1945: A History in Documents and Eyewitness Accounts* (New York: Schocken Books, 1988), 809–810.

8. Robert Conquest, *The Great Terror: A Reassessment* (New York: Oxford University Press, 1991), 450.

9. Max Domarus, ed., *1939–1940,* vol. 3 of *Hitler: Speeches and Proclamations, 1932–1945* (Wanconda, IL: Bolchazy-Carducci, 1997), 2170–2171.

10. Richard Breitman, *The Architect of Genocide: Himmler and the Final Solution* (New York: Alfred A. Knopf, 1991), 146.

11. Noakes and Pridham, *Foreign Policy, War and Racial Extermination,* 1086.

12. Halder, *Kriegstagebuch,* 337.

13. Norman Rich, *Hitler's War Aims: Ideology, the Nazi State, and the Course of Expansion* (New York: W. W. Norton, 1973), 212.

14. Noakes and Pridham, *Foreign Policy, War and Racial Extermination,* 1090.

15. Yitzhak Arad, Yisrael Gutman, and Abraham Margaliot, eds. *Documents on the Holocaust,* trans. Lea Ber Don (Lincoln and Jerusalem: University of Nebraska Press and Yad Vashem, 1999), 376.

16. Arad, Gutman, and Margaliot, *Documents on the Holocaust,* 375; Noakes and Pridham, *Foreign Policy, War and Racial Extermination,* 1087–1088.

17. Hannes Heer, "Killing Fields: The Wehrmacht and the Holocaust in Belorussia, 1941–1942, trans. Carol Scherer, *Holocaust and Genocide Studies* 11, no. 1 (Spring 1997): 80; Noakes and Pridham, *Foreign Policy, War and Racial Extermination,* 1088–1089.

18. Heer, "Killing Fields," 80–81; Breitman, *Architect of Genocide,* 150.

19. Christopher R. Browning, *The Origins of the Final Solution: The Evolution of Nazi Jewish Policy, September 1939–March 1942* (Lincoln and Jerusalem: University of Nebraska Press and Yad Vashem, 2004), 244.

20. *Trials of War Criminals Before the Nuernberg Military Tribunals Under Control Council Law No. 10, Nuernberg, October 1946–1949* (Washington, DC: United States Government Printing Office, 1950), 4:244; Browning, *Origins of the Final Solution,* 226–227.

21. Browning, *Origins of the Final Solution,* 227–228.

22. Jan Gross, *Neighbors: The Destruction of the Jewish Community in Jedwabne, Poland* (Princeton: Princeton University Press, 2001, 72–78; "Jedwabne: Final Findings of Poland's Institute of National Memory," July 9, 2002, 1–3, http://www.info-poland.buffalo.edu/classroom/J/final.html.

23. Browning, *Origins of the Final Solution,* 228.

24. Yitzhak Arad, Shmuel Krakowski, and Shmuel Spector, eds., *The Einsatzgruppen Reports* (New York: Holocaust Library, 1989), viii–ix.

25. Browning, *Origins of the Final Solution,* 228.

26. *Trials of War Criminals before the Nuernberg Military Tribunals,* 4:90–95; French L. MacLean, *The Field Men: The SS Officers Who Led the Einsatzkommandos: the Nazi Mobile Killing Units* (Atglen, PA: Schiffer Military History, 1999), 22–23.

27. Christopher Browning, *Ordinary Men: Reserve Police Battalion 101 and the Final Solution in Poland* (New York: HarperCollins, 1992), 6, 10–11.

28. Browning, *Origins of the Final Solution,* 232.

29. Ibid., 233.

30. Daniel Jonah Goldhagen, *Hitler's Willing Executioners: Ordinary Germans and the Holocaust* (New York: Alfred A. Knopf, 1996), 271–274.

31. Alan Cowell, "The Past Erupts in Munich as War Guilt Is Put on Display, *New York Times,* March 3, 1997, A3.

32. Hamburg Institute for Social Research, *The German Army and Genocide: Crimes Against War Prisoners, Jews, and Other Civilians, 1939–1944* (New York: New Press, 1999), 7, 14.

33. Christian Streit, "*Wehrmacht, Einsatzgruppen,* Soviet POWs and anti-Bolshevism in the Emergence of the Final Solution," in *The Final Solution: Origins and Implementation,* ed. David Cesarani (London: Routledge, 1996), 103–118; Omer Bartov, "Operation Barbarossa and the Origins of the Final Solution," in Cesarani, *The Final Solution,* 119–136.

34. Arad, Krakowski, and Spector, *Einsatzgruppen Reports,* 97–98.

35. G. F. Krivosheev, ed., *Soviet Casualties and Combat Losses in the Twentieth Century* (London: Greenhill Books, 1997), 236.

36. *Nuremberg Trial Proceedings,* Monday, 10 December, 1945, 338, The Avalon Project at Yale Law School, http://www.yale.edu/lawweb/avalon/imt/proc/12-10-45.htm.

37. Max Domarus, ed., *1941–1957 with Indices,* vol. 4 of *Hitler: Speeches and Proclamations, 1932–1945* (Wanconda, IL: Bolchazy-Carducci, 1997), 2445–2451.

38. Michael Ellman and S. Maksudov, "Soviet Deaths in the Great Patriotic War: A Note—World War II." *Europe-Asia Studies* 46, no. 4 (July 1994): 671–680; Michael Haynes, "Counting Soviet Deaths in the Great Patriotic War: A Note," *Europe-Asia Studies* 55, no. 2 (2003): 303–309; Mark Harrison, "Counting Soviet Deaths in the Great Patriotic War: Comment, *Europe-Asia Studies* 55, no. 6 (September 2003): 939–944.

39. Hamburg Institute for Social Research, *German Army and Genocide,* 8.

40. V. I. Chuikov and V. S. Ryabov, *Velikaya Otechestvennaya* (Moscow: Izdatel'stvo "Planeta," 1985), 11.

41. *The Goebbels Diaries, 1939–1941,* trans. Fred Taylor (New York: G. P. Putnam's Sons, 1983), 426.

42. Krivosheev, *Soviet Casualties and Combat Losses in the Twentieth Century,* 94.

43. Domarus, *1941–1957 with Indices,* 2465.

44. Arad, Krakowski, and Spector, *Einstazgruppen Reports,* 10, 20, 27–28, 31, 76.

45. "Directive No. 46: Instructions for Intensified Action Against Banditry in the East," Fuehrer Headquarters, August 18, 1942, 1–3. http://www.geocities.com/Pentagon/1084/hitler_directives/dir46.htm?200623.

46. Hannes Heer, "The Logic of the War of Extermination: The Wehrmacht and the Anti–Partisan War," in *War of Extermination: The German Military in World War II,* ed. Hannes Heer and Klaus Naumann (New York: Berghan Books, 2004), 114.

47. Walter Warlimont, *Inside Hitler's Headquarters, 1939–1945,* trans. R. H. Barry (Novato, CA: Presidio Press, 1962), 289–290.

48. Hamburg Institute for Social Research, *The German Army and Genocide,* 164; as expected, Keitel, who was indicted on all four war crimes counts at the Nuremberg International Military Tribunal in 1945, made no mention of any of this in his prison memoirs, *The Memoirs of Field-Marshal Wilhelm Keitel,* ed. Walter Gorlitz (New York: Cooper Square Press, 2000). He was found guilty on all four counts on October 1, 1946, and hanged fifteen days later.

49. Ehrlinger was convicted of war crimes in West Germany in 1961 and sentenced to twelve years imprisonment. He was released three years later.

50. Avraham Tory, *Surviving the Holocaust: The Kovno Ghetto Diary,* ed. Martin Gilbert (Cambridge, MA: Harvard University Press, 1990), 8–9.

51. Tory, *Surviving the Holocaust,* 23–24.

52. Yitzhak Arad, *Ghetto in Flames: The Struggle and Destruction of the Jews in Vilna in the Holocaust* (New York: Holocaust Library, 1982), 115–116.

53. Geoffrey Swain, *Between Stalin and Hitler: Class War and Race War on the Dvina, 1940–1946* (London: Routledge, 2004), 52–53, 70.

54. Andrew Ezergailis, *The Holocaust in Latvia, 1941–1944* (Riga and Washington: The Historical Institute in Latvia and the United States Holocaust Memorial Museum, 1996), 272–275.

55. Directive 46 dictated that such units could not wear German badges of rank, military shoulder straps, or the *Hoheitsabzeichen* [the eagle and Swastika]. "Directive No. 46," 3.

56. John A. Armstrong, *Ukrainian Nationalism* (New York: Columbia University Press, 1963), 87.

57. Alfred M. deZayas, *The Wehrmacht War Crimes Bureau, 1939–1945* (Lincoln: University of Nebraska Press, 1979), 214, 224–227; for an example of such confusion, see Ilya Ehrenburg and Vasily Grossman, *The Black Book: The Ruthless Murder of Jews by the German-Fascist Invaders Throughout the Temporarily-Occupied Regions of the Soviet Union and in the Death Camps of Poland During the War, 1941–1945,* trans. John Glad and James S. Levine (New York: Holocaust Library, 1981), 109, and "Lvov" *Encyclopedia of the Holocaust,* ed. Israel Gutman (New York: Macmillan, 1990), 3:929.

58. David M. Crowe, *Oskar Schindler: The Untold Account of His Life, Wartime Activities, and the True Story Behind the List* (Boulder: Westview Press, 2004), 243.

59. Ehrenburg and Grossman, *Black Book,* 5.

60. Ibid., 7.

61. Anatoly Kuznetsov, *Babi Yar: A Documentary Novel,* trans. Jacob Guralsky (New York: Dell, 1967), 391.

62. Yevgeny Yevtushenko, "Babi Yar," in Kuznetsov, *Babi Yar,* x–xi.

63. "Operational Situation Report USSR No. 25," July 17, 1941, *Einsatzgruppen Reports,* 34.

64. "Operational Situation Report USSR No. 22," July 14, 1941, *Einsatzgruppen Reports,* 25.

65. "Operational Situation Report USSR, No. 40," August 3, 1941, *Einsatzgruppen Reports,* 63; "Operational Situation Report USSR, No. 61," August 23, 1941, *Einsatzgruppen Reports,* 105–106; "Operational Situation Report USSR, No. 64," August 1941, *Einsatzgruppen Reports,* 111.

66. I. C. Butunaru, *The Silent Holocaust: Romania and Its Jews* (New York: Greenwood Press, 1992), 127; Radu Ioanid, *The Holocaust in Romania: The Destruction of Jews and Gypsies Under the Antonescu Regime, 1940–1944* (Chicago: Ivan R. Dee, 2000), 180–181. Ioanid states that Colonels Nicolae Deleanu and Mihai Niculescu-Coca were in charge of the warehouse massacres. General Tresioreanu was in temporary command of the Romanian Tenth Infantry Division at the time.

67. Butunaru, *Silent Holocaust,* 124–124.

68. *Trial of War Criminals Before the Nuremberg Military Tribunals,* 4:286–287.

69. Guenter Lewy, *The Nazi Persecution of the Gypsies* (Oxford: Oxford University Press, 2000), 118.

70. "Operational Situation Report USSR, No. 43," August 1941, *Einsatzgruppen Reports,* 71; "Operational Situation Report USSR No. 111," October 12, 1941, *Einsatzgruppen Reports,* 185; Wolfram Wette, *The Wehrmacht: History, Myth, Reality,* trans. Deborah Lucas Schneider (Cambridge: Cambridge University Press, 2006), 198.

71. Lewy, *Nazi Persecution of the Gypsies,* 119; "Operational Situation Report USSR No. 92," September 23, 1941, *Einsatzgruppen Reports,* 153.

72. "Operational Situation Report USSR no. 94," September 25, 1941, *Einsatzgruppen Reports,* 158; "Operational Situation Report USSR, no. 119," October 20, 1941, *Einsatzgruppen Reports,* 198.

73. Lewy, *Nazi Persecution of the Gypsies,* 118–119.

74. Ibid., 119.

75. "Operational Situation Report USSR No. 145," December 12, 1941, *Einsatzgruppen Reports,* 256.

76. "Operational Situation Report USSR No. 150," January 2, 1942, *Einsatzgruppen Reports,* 267; "Operational Situation Report USSR No. 153," January 9, 1942, *Einsatzgruppen Reports,* 273; "Operational Situation Report USSR No. 165," February 6, 1942, *Einsatzgruppen Reports,* 292.

77. "Operational Situation Report USSR No. 157," January 19, 1942, *Einsatzgruppen Reports,* 284.

78. "Operational Situation Report USSR No. 178," March 9, 1942, *Einsatzgruppen Reports,* 309; "Operational Situation Report USSR No. 184," March 23, 1942, *Einsatzgruppen Reports,* 318; "Operational Situation Report USSR No. 190," April 8, 1942, *Einsatzgruppen Reports,* 325–326.

79. Kuznetsov, *Babi Yar,* 100, 101–102.

80. Lewy, *Nazi Persecution of the Gypsies,* 121–122.

81. Ibid., 122.

82. *Trial of War Criminals Before the Nuremberg Military Tribunals,* 4:356.

83. Bernd Boll, Hannes Heer, and Walter Manoschek, "Prelude to a Crime: The German Army in the National Socialist State, 1933–1939," in *The German Army and Genocide: Crimes Against War Prisoners, Jews, and Other Civilians, 1939–1944,* ed. Hamburg Institute for Social Research (New York: New Press, 1999), 33.

84. Omer Bartov, *Hitler's Army: Soldiers, Nazis, and War in the Third Reich* (New York: Oxford University Press, 1991), 61.

85. Lewy, *Nazi Persecution of the Gypsies,* 120.

86. Ibid., 120.

87. Edward B. Westermann, *Hitler's Police Battalions: Enforcing Racial War in the East* (Lawrence: University Press of Kansas, 2005), 190.

88. Ibid., 120–121.

89. Donald Kenrick and Grattan Puxon, *The Destiny of Europe's Gypsies* (New York: Basic Books, 1972), 147–148.

90. Lewy, *Nazi Persecution of the Gypsies,* 123–124; the original decree can be found in Michael Zimmermann, "The Soviet Union and the Baltic States, 1941–1944: The Massacre of the Gypsies," in *In the Shadow of the Swastika: The Gypsies During the Second World War,* ed. Donald Kenrick

(Hatfield, UK: University of Hertfordshire Press, 1999), 2:143; Kenrick and Puxon, *Destiny of Europe's Gypsies,* 148.

91. Zimmermann, "Soviet Union and the Baltic States, 1941–1944," 147.

92. Ibid., 147.

93. Lewy, *Nazi Persecution of the Gypsies,* 126.

94. Ibid., 127.

95. "Operational Situation Report USSR, No. 86," September 17, 1941, *Einsatzgruppen Reports,* 135–136.

96. "Operational Situation Report USSR, No. 88," September 19, 1941, *Einsatzgruppen Reports,* 138.

97. "Operational Situation Report USSR, No. 94," September 25, 1941, *Einsatzgruppen Reports,* 156–157.

98. "Operational Situation Report USSR, No. 108," October 9, 1941, *Einsatzgruppen Reports,* 181–182; "Operational Situation Report USSR, No. 135," November 19, 1941, *Einsatzgruppen Reports,* 239.

99. "Operational Situation Report USSR No. 132," November 12, 1941, *Einsatzgruppen Reports,* 228.

100. "Operational Situation Report USSR, No. 135," November 19, 1941, *Einsatzgruppen Reports,* 239–240; Reichenau's support of the *Einsatzgruppen*'s actions began to wane when their heavy use of bullets began to deplete his own military stores. He suggested that *Einsatzgruppen* commanders use no more than two bullets per Jew. By the end of 1942, more than a million Jews and other civilians had died in areas under Sixth Army control. The Sixth Army would later be destroyed during the battle of Stalingrad. Samuel W. Mitcham Jr. and Gene Mueller, *Hitler's Commanders: Officers of the Wehrmacht, the Luftwaffe, the Kriegsmarine, and the Waffen-SS* (New York: Cooper Square Press, 2000), 76; "Operational Situation Report No. 143," December 8, 1941, *Einsatzgruppen Reports,* 251.

101. Henry Friedlander, *The Origins of Nazi Genocide: From Euthanasia to the Final Solution* (Chapel Hill: University of North Carolina Press, 1995), 141.

102. "Testimony of Dr. Wilhelm Gustav Schueppe," April 14, 1945, http://library.lawschool .cornell.edu/donovan/show.asp?id=481, 3.

103. Ibid., 7.

Chapter 7

1. Rudolf Höss, *Death Dealer: The Memoirs of the SS Kommandant at Auschwitz,* ed. Steven Paskuly (New York: Da Capo Press, 1996), 27–28.

2. Christopher R. Browning, *The Origins of the Final Solution: The Evolution of Nazi Jewish Policy, September 1939–March 1942* (Lincoln and Jerusalem: University of Nebraska Press and Yad Vashem, 2004), 309.

3. Richard Breitman, *The Architect of Genocide: Himmler and the Final Solution* (New York: Alfred A. Knopf, 1991), 190; Joseph Poprzeczny, *Odilo Globocnik: Hitler's Man in the East* (Jefferson, NC: McFarland, 2004), 176, 206; Siegfried J. Pucher ". . . in der Bewegung führend tätig": Odilo Globocnik— Kämpfer für den "Anschluß" Vollstrecher des Holocaust* (Klagenfurt: Drava Verlag, 1997), 94–95.

4. Browning, *Origins of the Final Solution,* 315.

5. Jeremy Noakes and Geoffrey Pridham, eds., *Foreign Policy, War and Racial Extermination,* vol. 2 of *Nazism 1919–1945: A History in Documents and Eyewitness Accounts* (New York: Schocken Books, 1984), 1104.

6. Browning, *Origins of the Final Solution,* 315–316; Götz Aly, *Final Solution: Nazi Population Policy and the Murder of the Jews of Europe,* trans. Belinda Cooper and Allison Brown (London: Arnold, 1999), 200; Gerald Fleming, *Hitler and the Final Solution* (Berkeley: University of California Press, 1982), 67; Christopher R. Browning, *Fateful Months: Essays on the Emergence of the Final Solution,* rev. ed. (New York: Holmes & Meier, 1991), 21–22.

7. *Die Tagebücher von Joseph Goebbels,* ed. Elke Fröhlich, pt. 2, *Diktate 1941–1945,* vol. 1, *Juli–September 1941* (Munich: K. G. Saur, 1966), 265–266, 269.

8. Noakes and Pridham, *Foreign Policy, War and Racial Extermination,* 1107–1108.

9. Ibid., 1113.

10. David Cesarani, *Becoming Eichmann: Rethinking the Life, Crimes, and Trial of a "Desk Murderer"* (New York: Da Capo Press, 2004), 135.

11. Goebbels's Theresienstadt propaganda film is more commonly known by one of the two titles he considered for the film, *Der Führer Schent der Juden ein stadt* (The Führer Gives the Jews a City).

12. Ludmilla Chládková, *The Terezín Ghetto,* trans. Vlasta Basetlíková (Prague: Naše vojsko, 1995), 47.

13. . . . *I Never Saw Another Butterfly . . . : Children's Drawings and Poems from Terezín Concentration Camp, 1942–1944* (New York: Schocken Books, 1978), 10, 14; for more on children's art and poetry in Theresienstadt, see *We Are Children Just the Same: Vedem, the Secret Magazine of the Boys of Terezín,* ed. Marie Rút Køíková, Kurt Jiøí Kotouè, and Zdenìk Ornest (Philadelphia: Jewish Publication Society, 1995).

14. Ibid., 17, 22.

15. Ibid., 33.

16. Aaron Kramer, "Creation in a Death Camp," in *Theatrical Performance during the Holocaust,* ed. Rebecca Rovit and Alvin Goldfarb (Baltimore: Johns Hopkins University Press, 1999), 181–183; Jana Renée Friesová, *Fortress of My Youth: Memoir of a Terezín Survivor,* trans. Elinor Morrisby and Ladislav Rosendorf (Madison: University of Wisconsin Press, 2002), 142–147; Joa Karas, *Music in Terezín* (New York: Beaufort Books, 1985), 139–141; Josef Bor, *The Terezín Requiem,* trans. Edith Pargeter (New York: Alfred A. Knopf, 1963.

17. Giuseppe Verdi, *Requiem in Full Score* (Mineola, NY: Dover Publications, 1998), vii–ix. This is the full score for Verdi's *Messa de Requiem per l'anniveresario della morte di Manzoni 22 maggio 1874;* for more on the history of the *Requiem,* see David Rosen's *Verdi Requiem* (Cambridge: Cambridge University Press), 1995.

18. Höss, *Death Dealer,* 28–29.

19. State of Israel, Ministry of Justice, *The Trial of Adolf Eichmann: Record of Proceedings in the District Court of Jerusalem* (Jerusalem: Israel State Archives and Yad Vashem, 1994), 5:2217.

20. Höss, *Death Dealer,* 29–30; Danuta Czech, *Auschwitz Chronicle, 1939–1945* (New York: Henry Holt, 1990), 84–87.

21. Breitman, *Architect of Genocide,* 229.

22. Browning, *Origins of the Final Solution,* 404.

23. Noakes and Pridham, *Foreign Policy, War and Racial Extermination,* 1104.

24. *Die Tagebücher von Joseph Goebbels,* pt. 2, *Diktate 1941–1945,* vol. 2, *Oktober-Dezember 1941,* ed. Elke Frölich (Munich: K. G. Saur, 1996), 498–499.

25. Browning, *Origins of the Final Solution,* 408–409.

26. *Trial of Adolf Eichmann,* 4:1799.

27. Ibid., 4:1826; *Minutes of the Wannsee Conference,* 3–4, http://prorev.com/wannsee.htm. This version of the Wannsee was translated and edited for use as evidence during the Nuremberg trials. For a more original translation and copies of the exact document in German, see House of the Wannsee Conference, http://www.ghwk.de/engl/kopfengl.htm.

28. *Minutes of the Wannsee Conference,* 7.

29. Ibid., 8–9.

30. Ibid., 13–14.

31. *Trial of Adolf Eichmann,* 4:1826.

32. Cesarani, *Becoming Eichmann,* 117.

33. Ibid., 125.

34. *Eichmann Interrogated: Transcripts from the Archives of the Israeli Police,* ed. Jochen von Lang in collaboration with Claus Sibyll, trans. Ralph Manheim (New York: Farrar, Straus & Giroux), 77–78.

35. Ibid., 77.

36. *Trial of Adolf Eichmann,* 3:1191.

37. Poprzeczny, *Odilo Globočnik,* 102.

38. Yitzhak Arad, *Belzec, Sobibor, Treblinka: The Operation Reinhard Death Camps* (Bloomington: Indiana University Press, 1987), 26.

39. *Trial of Adolf Eichmann*, 3:1228; *Der Gerstein-Bericht*, in *NS-Archiv: Dokumente zum Nationalsozialismus*, 4, http//www.ns-archiv.de/verfolgung/gerstein/gerstein-bericht.php.

40. *Trial of Adolf Eichmann*, 3:1228; *Der Gerstein-Bericht*, 4.

41. *Trial of Adolf Eichmann*, 3:1228; *Der Gerstein-Bericht*, 4.

42. *Trial of Adolf Eichmann*, 3:1228–1229; *Der Gerstein-Bericht*, 5.

43. *Trial of Adolf Eichmann*, 3:1229; *Der Gerstein-Bericht*, 5.

44. Gitta Sereny, *Into That Darkness: An Examination of Conscience* (New York: Vintage Books, 1974), 111.

45. Raul Hilberg, *The Destruction of the European Jews*, 3rd. ed. (New Haven: Yale University Press, 2003), 3:1104; United States Holocaust Memorial Museum, *Resistance During the Holocaust* (Washington, DC: United States Holocaust Memorial Museum, n.d.), 37.

46. Józef Marszalek, *Majdanek: The Concentration Camp in Lublin* (Warsaw: Interpress, 1986), 145.

47. Thomas (Toivi) Blatt, *Sobibor: The Forgotten Revolt* (Issaquah, WA: Thomas Blatt, 2004), 55.

48. Joseph Telushkin, *Jewish Wisdom: Ethical, Spiritual, and Historical Lessons from the Great Works and Thinkers* (New York: William Morrow, 1994), 53.

49. Testimony of Esther Raab, United States Holocaust Memorial Museum, http://www.ushmm.org/outreach/erp0620f.htm.

50. Alexander Pechersky, "Revolt in Sobibor," in *They Fought Back: The Story of the Jewish Resistance in Nazi Europe*, ed. Yuri Suhl (New York: Schocken Books, 1975), 30–31.

51. Testimony of Chaim Engel, United States Holocaust Memorial Museum, http://www.org/outreach/id1184.htm.

52. Sereny, *Into That Darkness*, 201.

53. Janusz Gumkowski and Kazimierz Leszcyñski, *Poland Under Nazi Occupation* (Warsaw: Polonia, 1961), 74.

54. Arad, *Belzec, Sobibor, Treblinka*, 152–153.

55. *Trial of Adolf Eichmann*, 3:1211.

56. Franciszek Piper, *Auschwitz: How Many Perished: Jews, Poles, Gypsies . . .* (Kraków: Poligrafia, 1991), 51–53.

57. Aleksander Lasik, "The Auschwitz SS Garrison," in *Auschwitz, 1940–1945: Central Issues in the History of the Camp*, ed. Aleksander Lasik et al., vol. 1, *The Establishment and Organization of the Camp* (Oświęcim: Auschwitz-Birkenau State Museum, 2000), 299.

58. Höss, *Death Dealer*, 160.

59. Stella Mülle-Madej, *A Girl from Schindler's List* (London: Polish Cultural Foundation, 1997), 172; David M. Crowe, *Oskar Schindler: The Untold Account of His Life, Wartime Activities, and the True Story Behind the List* (Boulder: Westview Press, 2004), 392.

60. Sim Kessel, *Hanged at Auschwitz: An Extraordinary Memoir of Survival* (New York: Cooper Square Press, 2001), 103–104.

61. Rudolf Vrba, *I Escaped from Auschwitz* (Fort Lee, NJ: Barricade Books, 2002), 89–90.

62. Primo Levi, *Survival in Auschwitz* and *The Awakening: Two Memoirs*, trans. Stuart Woolf (New York: Summit Books, 1986), 67.

63. Rena Kornreich Gelissen, *Rena's Promise: A Story of Sisters in Auschwitz*, with Heather Dune Macadam (Boston: Beacon Press, 1995), 83.

64. Otto Rosenberg, *A Gypsy in Auschwitz*, trans. Helmut Bögler (London: London House, 1999), 58–59.

65. Ibid., 61.

66. Charlotte Delbo, *Auschwitz and After*, trans. Rosette C. Lamont (New Haven: Yale University Press, 1995), 62–63.

67. Carol Rittner and John K. Roth, eds., *Different Voices: Women and the Holocaust* (New York: Paragon House, 1993), 89.

68. Otto Friedrich, *The Kingdom of Auschwitz, 1940–1945* (New York: Harper Perennial, 1994), 32.

69. Guenter Lewy, *The Nazi Persecution of the Gypsies* (Oxford: Oxford University Press, 2000), 140.

70. Donald Kenrick and Grattan Puxon, *The Destiny of Europe's Gypsies* (New York: Basic Books, 1972), 156, 158.

71. Ibid., 163.

72. Miklos Nyiszli, *Auschwitz: A Doctor's Eyewitness Account,* trans. Tibère Kremere and Richard Seaver (New York: Frederick Fell, 1960), 132.

73. Danuta Czech, *Auschwitz Chronicle, 1939–1945* (New York: Henry Holt, 1997), 810.

74. Nyiszli, *Auschwitz,* 31.

75. Robert Jay Lifton, *The Nazi Doctors: Medical Killing and the Psychology of Genocide* (New York: Basic Books, 1986), 273.

76. Helena Kubica, "Children and Adolescents in Auschwitz," in *Auschwitz, 1940–1945,* ed. Tadeusz Iwaszko et al., vol. 2, *The Prisoners: Their Life and Work* (Oświęcim: Auschwitz-Birkenau State Museum, 2000), 262.

77. Helena Kubica, "The Crimes of Josef Mengele," in *Anatomy of the Auschwitz Death Camp,* ed. Yisrael Gutman and Michael Berenbaum (Bloomington: Indiana University Press, 1994), 324.

78. Friedrich, *Kingdom of Auschwitz,* 34–35.

79. Wolfgang Sofsky, *The Order of Terror: The Concentration Camp,* trans. William Templer (Princeton: Princeton University Press, 1997), 175.

80. Hermann Langbein, "The Auschwitz Underground," in Gutman and Berenbaum, *Anatomy of the Auschwitz Death Camp,* 497–498; Czech, *Auschwitz Chronicle,* 513.

81. Marszalek, *Majdanek,* 18, 23; Edward Gryñ and Zofia Murawska-Gryñ, *Majdanek* (Lublin: Pañstwowe Muzeum na Majdanku, 1984), 93–95, 98–99.

82. Marszalek, *Majdanek,* 40–41.

83. Gryñ and Murawska-Gryñ, *Majdanek,* 91.

84. Czeslaw Rajca and Anna Wisniewska, *Majdanek Concentration Camp* (Lublin: Pañstwowe Muzeum na Majdanku, 1983), 83–84.

85. *The Warsaw Diary of Adam Czerniakow: Prelude to Doom,* ed. Raul Hilberg, Stanislaw Staron, and Josef Kermisz, trans. Stanislaw Staron and the staff of Yad Vashem (New York: Stein and Day, 1979), 384.

86. Ibid., 385.

87. Marek Edelman, "The Ghetto Fights," in *The Warsaw Ghetto: The 45th Anniversary of the Uprising* (Warsaw: Interpress, 1988), 36.

88. Betty Jean Lifton, *The King of the Children: A Biography of Janusz Korczak* (New York: Schocken Books, 1988), 345.

89. Israel Gutman, *Resistance: The Warsaw Ghetto Uprising* (Boston: Houghton Mifflin, 1994), 173.

90. *Trial of Adolf Eichmann,* 1:91.

91. Edelman, "Ghetto Fights," 42.

92. Ibid., 46.

93. *The Stroop Report,* trans. Sybil Milton (New York: Pantheon, 1979).

94. Edelman, "Ghetto Fights," 45.

95. Simon Wiesenthal, *The Murderers Among Us: The Simon Wiesenthal Memoirs* (New York: Bantam Books, 1968), 60.

96. Yitzhak Arad, *Ghetto in Flames: The Struggle and Destruction of the Jews in Vilna in the Holocaust* (New York: Holocaust Library, 1982), 231–232.

97. Herman Kruk, *The Last Days of the Jerusalem of Lithuania: Chronicles from the Vilna Ghetto and the Camps, 1939–1944,* trans. Barbara Harshav (New Haven: Yale University Press, 2002), 562

98. Arad, *Ghetto in Flames,* 411–412.

99. Ibid., 425.

100. Vasily Grossman, "The History of the Minsk Ghetto," in *The Black Book,* ed. Ilya Ehrenburg and Vasily Grossman (New York: Holocaust Library, 1981), 158–159.

101. Ibid., 170.

102. Hersh Smolar, *The Minsk Ghetto: Soviet–Jewish Partisans Against the Nazis* (New York: Holocaust Library, 1989), 143.

103. Frida Michelson, *I Survived Rumbuli* (New York: Holocaust Library, 1979), 77.

104. Gertrude Schneider, ed., *Muted Voices: Jewish Survivors of Latvia Remember* (New York: Philosophical Library, 1987), 29.

105. Avraham Tory, *Surviving the Holocaust: The Kovno Ghetto Diary* (Cambridge, MA: Harvard Univeristy Press, 1990), 58.

Chapter 8

1. "Decree for the Establishment of the Association of the Jews in Belgium" (November 25, 1941), 102http:www.jewishvirtuallibrary.org/jsource/Holocaust/decreeesjb.html.

2. "Reactions to the Trap," Joods Museum van Deportatie en Verzet–Judaico, http:www.cicb.be/eng/shoah/jewishlifebefore.html.

3. Cecil von Renthe–Fink to German Foreign Ministry, Berlin, January 7, 1942, 1–3, http://www.jewishvirtual libary.org/jsource/Holocaust/Denmarkdis.html.

4. Ibid., 2.

5. Emmy E. Werner, *A Conspiracy of Decency: The Rescue of the Danish Jews During World War II* (Boulder: Westview Press, 2002), 83.

6. Raul Hilberg, *The Destruction of the European Jews* (New York: Holmes & Meier, 1985), 2:566.

7. Michael R. Marrus and Robert O. Paxton, *Vichy France and the Jews* (Stanford: Stanford University Press, 1995), 36.

8. Ibid., 39.

9. Ibid., 88.

10. Richard Cobb, *French and Germans, Germans and French: A Personal Interpretation of France Under Two Occupations, 1914–1918/1940–1944* (Cambridge, MA: Brandeis University Press, 1983), 60.

11. "Le Chambon," Jewish Virtual Library,http://www.jewishvirtuallibrary.org/jsource/Holocaust/Chambon/html; "The Righteous Among the Nations: France," http://www.yadvashem.org/righteous/bycountry/france/andre_trocme.

12. Tela Zasloff, *A Rescuer's Story: Pastor Pierre-Charles Toureille in Vichy France* (Madison: University of Wisconsin Press, 2003), 165.

13. Henry Friedlander and Sybil Milton, eds., *Archives of the Holocaust,* vol. 2, pt. 2 (New York: Garland, 1990), 197–198.

14. David Cesarani, *Becoming Eichmann: Rethinking the Life, Crimes, and Trial of a "Desk Murderer"* (New York: Da Capo Press, 2004), 128.

15. H. C. Touw, "The Resistance of the Netherlands Churches, *ANNALS of the American Academy of Political and Social Science* 245 (May 1946): 159.

16. Anne Frank, *The Diary of a Young Girl* (New York: Simon & Schuster, 1952), 233.

17. "Otto Frank to Nathan Straus," April 30, 1941, YIVO Institute for Jewish Research, http://www.npr.org/templates/story.php?storyId=7400998#7401663; "Julius Hollander to Nathan Straus," June 3, 1941, YIVO Institute for Jewish Research, http://www.npr.org/templates/story.php?storyId=7400998#7401663; "Newly Discovered File Documents Efforts of Anne Frank's Father to Escape from Nazi-Occupied Holland," YIVO Institute for Jewish Research, February 14, 2007, http://www.yivoinstitute.org/events/index.php.

18. Frank, *Diary,* 233.

19. Samuel Abrahamsen, *Norway's Response to the Holocaust* (New York: Holocaust Library, 1991), 141–142.

20. Tzvetan Todorov, *The Fragility of Goodness: Why Bulgaria's Jews Survived the Holocaust: A Collection of Texts with Commentary by Tzvetan Todorov,* trans. Arthur Denner (Princeton: Princeton University Press, 2001), 56.

21. Michael Bar-Zohar, *Beyond Hitler's Grasp: The Heroic Rescue of Bulgaria's Jews* (Avon, MA: Adams Media Corporation, 1998), 34–35.

22. "The Dannecker-Belev Agreement," in Frederick B. Chary, *The Bulgarian Jews and the Final Solution, 1940–1944* (Pittsburgh: The University of Pittsburgh Press, 1972), 208.

23. Gideon Hausner, *Justice in Jerusalem* (New York: Holocaust Library, 1968), 124.

24. Bar-Zohar, *Beyond Hitler's Grasp,* 92.

25. Ibid., 150.

26. Ibid., 173.

27. Ibid., 174–175.

28. David M. Crowe, *A History of the Gypsies of Eastern Europe and Russia* (New York: Palgrave Macmillan, 2007), 19.

29. Hannu Rautkallio, *Finland and the Holocaust: The Rescue of Finland's Jews* (New York: Holocaust Library, 1987), 168.

30. "Finland's Tarnished Holocaust Record: An Interview with Serah Beizer," Jerusalem Center for Public Affairs, March 1, 2007, 1–7, http://www.jcpa.org/JCPA/Templates/ShowPage.asp?DBID=1&LNG.

31. Randolph L. Braham, *The Politics of Genocide: The Holocaust in Hungary* (New York: Columbia University Press, 1994), 1:54.

32. Ibid., 127.

33. Ibid., 158.

34. Hungary had acquired eastern Slovakia (Ruthenia) after the German conquest of what remained of Czechoslovakia in the spring of 1939.

35. Braham, *Politics of Genocide,* 1:179.

36. Cesarani, *Becoming Eichmann,* 160.

37. Ibid., 162.

38. Alex Weissberg, *Desperate Mission: Joel Brand's Story,* trans. Constantine FitzGibbon and Andrew Foster-Melliar (New York: Criterion Books, 1958), 104; Brand's testimony about his meetings with Eichmann can also be found in State of Israel Ministry of Justice, *The Trial of Adolf Eichmann: Record of Proceedings in the District Court of Jerusalem,* vol. 3 (Jerusalem: Israel State Archives and Yad Vashem, 1993), 1020–1024, 1034–1036, 1062–1064.

39. Miroslav Kárný, "Genocida Českých Židů (The Genocide of the Czech Jews)," in Miroslav Kárný, ed., *Terezinska pametni kniha* (Prague: Melantrich, 1995), 1:45–46.

40. Yehuda Bauer, *Jews for Sale: Nazi–Jewish Negotiations, 1933–1935* (New Haven: Yale University Press, 1994), 192.

41. John Bierman, *Righteous Gentile: The Story of Raoul Wallenberg, Missing Hero of the Holocaust* (New York: Viking Press, 1981), 91.

42. Crowe, *History of the Gypsies,* 90.

43. Katalin Katz, "The Roma of Hungary in the Second World War," in *The Final Chapter,* vol. 3, *The Gypsies During the Second World War,* ed. Donald Kenrick (Hatfield, UK: University of Hertfordshire Press, 2006), 70–71.

44. Ibid., 83.

45. Susan Zuccotti, *The Italians and the Holocaust: Persecution, Rescue, and Survival* (Lincoln: University of Nebraska Press, 1988), 25.

46. R. J. B. Bosworth, *Mussolini's Italy: Life and the Fascist Dictatorship, 1915–1945* (New York: Penguin Books, 2006), 243.

47. Emil Ludwig, *Talks with Mussolini,* trans. Eden and Cedar Paul (Boston: Little, Brown, 1933), 69–71.

48. Bosworth, *Mussolini's Italy,* 421.

49. Aaron Gillette, "The Origins of the 'Manifesto of Racial Scientists,'" *Journal of Modern Italian Studies* 6, no. 3 (2001): 318–319.

50. Ibid., 318–319.

51. Ibid., 305, 314–315.

52. Zuccotti, *Italians and the Holocaust,* 109.

53. State of Israel, Ministry of Justice, *The Trial of Adolf Eichmann: Record of the Proceedings in the District Court of Jerusalem,* vol. 5 (Jerusalem: Israel State Archives and Yad Vashem, 1994), 1965–1968; Zuccotti, *Italians and the Holocaust,* 111.

54. Gerta Vrbová, *Trust and Deceit: A Tale of Survival in Slovakia and Hungary, 1939–1945* (London: Vallentine Mitchell, 2006), 21.

55. "Defining the Legal Position of the Jews in Slovakia," September 11, 1941, http://www.jewishvirtuallibrary.org/source/Holocaust/definingjewbud.html.

56. Jörg Hoensch, "The Slovak Republic, 1939–1945," in *A History of the Czechoslovak Republic, 1918–1948,* ed. Victory S. Mamatey and Radomír Luža (Princeton: Princeton University Press, 1973), 291.

57. Aliza Barak-Ressler, *Cry Little Girl: A Tale of the Survival of a Family in Slovakia* (Jerusalem: Yad Vashem, 2003), 60.

58. Livia Rothkirchen, "The Slovak Enigma: A Reassessment of the Halt to the Deportations," *East Central Europe* 10, nos. 1–2 (1983): 3–13; Hoensch, "Slovak Republic," 291.

59. Crowe, *History of the Gypsies,* 51–52.

60. Milena Hübschmannová, "Roma in the So-Called Slovak State (1939–45)," in Kenrick, *Final Chapter,* 25.

61. Ibid., 37.

62. *Final Report of the International Commission on the Holocaust in Romania* (November 11, 2004, Bucharest, Romania), chap. 8, "Roma," 3. http://www.yad.vashem.org.il/about_yad/what_new/data_whats_new/report/html.

63. Radu Ioanid, *The Holocaust in Romania: The Destruction of Jews and Gypsies Under the Antonescu Regime, 1940–1944* (Chicago: Ivan R. Dee, 2000), 19.

64. Ibid., 53.

65. Emil Dorian, *The Quality of Witness: A Romanian Diary, 1937–1944,* ed. Marguerite Doran, trans. Mara Soceanu Vamos (Philadelphia: The Jewish Publication Society of America, 1982), 139.

66. *Final Report of the International Commission on the Holocaust in Romania,* "Executive Summary," 1.

67. Ioanid, *Holocaust in Romania,* 227.

68. Crowe, *History of the Gypsies,* 133.

69. Donald Kenrick and Grattan Puxon, *The Destiny of Europe's Gypsies* (New York: Basic Books, 1972), 129.

70. Ibid., 130.

71. Crowe, *History of the Gypsies,* 134.

72. Ibid., 134.

73. *Final Report of the International Commission on the Holocaust in Romania,* chap. 8, "Roma," 13–14.

74. Ibid., 17.

75. Ibid., 18.

76. Jozo Tomasevich, *War and Revolution in Yugoslavia, 1941–1945: Occupation and Collaboration* (Stanford: Stanford University Press, 2001), 380.

77. Ibid., 383–384.

78. Ibid., 593.

79. Lisa M. Adeli, "From Jasenova to Yugoslavism: Ethnic Persecution in Croatia during World War II" (PhD diss., University of Arizona, 2004), 40–41.

80. Božo Švarc, "The Testimony of a Survivor of Jadovno and Jasenovac," in *Jasenovac and the Holocaust in Yugoslavia: Analysis and Survivor Testimonies,* ed. Barry M. Lituchy (New York: Jasenovac Research Institute, 2006), 141.

81. Sadik Darron, "Recollections of Jasenovac," in Lituchy, *Jasenovac and the Holocaust in Yugoslavia,* 178.

82. Ibid., 180.

83. Dennis Reinhartz, "Damnation of the Outsider: The Gypsies of Croatia and Serbia in the Balkan Holocaust, 1941–1945," in *The Gypsies of Eastern Europe,* ed. David Crowe and John Kolsti (Armonk, NY: M. E. Sharpe, 1991), 89.

84. Kenrick, *Final Chapter,* 90.

Chapter 9

1. Gerhard L. Weinberg, *A World at Arms: A Global History of World War II* (Cambridge: Cambridge University Press, 1994), 373.

2. Yehuda Bauer, *American Jewry and the Holocaust: The American Jewish Joint Distribution Committee, 1939–1945* (Detroit: Wayne State University Press, 1981), 48.

3. Avraham Milgram, "Portugal, the Consuls, and the Jewish Refugees, 1938–1941," Shoah Resource Center, International School for Holocaust Studies, Yad Vashem (2004), 10.

4. Mordechai Paldiel, *The Path of the Righteous: Gentile Rescuers of Jews During the Holocaust* (Hoboken, NJ, and New York: KTAV Publishing House in association with The Jewish Foundation for Christian Rescuers/ADL, 1993), 60–61.

5. Milgram, "Portugal, the Consuls, and the Jewish Refugees," 20–21.

6. Paldiel, *Path of the Righteous,* 61.

7. Ibid., 62.

8. Milgram, "Portugal, the Consuls, and the Jewish Refugees," 25.

9. Ibid., 62.

10. Howard M. Sachar, *A History of the Jews in the Modern World* (New York: Alfred A. Knopf, 2005), 560.

11. Hans A. Schmitt, *Quakers & Nazis: Inner Light and Outer Darkness* (Columbia: University of Missouri Press, 1997), 202–203.

12. Enrico Deaglio, *The Banality of Goodness: The Story of Giorgio Perlasca,* trans. Gregory Conti (Notre Dame: University of Notre Dame Press, 1998), 77–79.

13. Greogry Conti, "A Most Unlikely Hero: A Fascist Who Saved Jews—Giogio Perlasca," *Commonweal,* December 3, 1999, 1, http://findarticles.com/p/articles/mi_m1252/is_21_126/ai_58675361.

14. Martin Gilbert, *The Righteous: The Unsung Heroes of the Holocaust* (New York: Henry Holt, 2003), 400–401.

15. Paul A. Levine, *From Indifference to Activism: Swedish Diplomacy and the Holocaust, 1938–1944* (Uppsala, Sweden: Uppsala University, 1996), 93.

16. Ibid., 84.

17. Adam Tooze, *The Wages of Destruction; The Making and Breaking of the Nazi Economy* (New York: Viking, 2006), 380–381.

18. Gunnar Åselius, "Sweden and Nazi Germany," in *Sweden's Relations with Nazism, Nazi Germany and the Holocaust,* ed. Stig Ekman and Klas Åmark, and John Toler (Stockholm: Almquist & Wiksell International, 2003), 94.

19. Levine, *From Indifference to Activism,* 139.

20. Ibid., 245.

21. Sven Nordlund, "'The War Is Over—Now You Can Go Home!' Jewish Refugees and the Swedish Labour Market in the Shadow of the Holocaust," in *"Bystanders" to the Holocaust,* ed. David Cesarani and Paul Levine (London: Frank Cass, 2002), 177.

22. Levine, *From Indifference to Activism,* 274.

23. Ibid., 193.

24. Walter Schellenberg, *The Labyrinth: Memoirs of Walter Schellenberg: Hitler's Chief of Counterintelligence* (New York: Da Capo Press, 2000), 383.

25. Felix Kersten, *The Kersten Memoirs, 1940–1945,* trans. Constantine Fitzgibbon and James Oliver (London: Hutchinson, 1956), 15.

26. Frank Fox, "A Jew Talks with Himmler," *Liberty* 17, nos. 9–10 (September/October 2003): 2–5, http://www.libertyunbound.com/archive/2003_10/fox-himmler.html.

27. Sune Persson, "Folke Bernadotte and the White Buses," in Cesarani and Levine, *"Bystanders" to the Holocaust,* 248–256.

28. Schellenberg, *The Labyrinth,* 387.

29. Independent Commission of Experts Switzerland—Second World War, *Switzerland, National Socialism and the Second World War* (Zürich: Pendo Verlag, 2002), 67.

30. Jacques Picard, *On the Ambivalnce of Being Neutral: Switzerland and Swiss Jewry Facing the Rise and Fall of the Nazi State* (Washington, DC: United States Holocaust Memorial Museum, 1998), 10.

31. Baruch Tenembaum, "The Example of Grüninger," International Raoul Wallenberg Foundation, 2, http://www.raoulwallenberg.net/?en/saviors/others/example-gr-uuml-n.

32. Independent Commission of Experts Switzerland, *Switzerland, National Socialism and the Second World War,* 188.

33. Ibid., 189.

34. Paul B. Miller, "Europe's Gold: Nazis, Neutrals and the Holocaust," *Dimensions: A Journal of Holocaust Studies* 11, no. 1 (1997): 11.

35. Saul Friedländer, *The Years of Extermination: Nazi Policy and the Jews, 1939–1945* (New York: HarperCollins, 2007), 448–449.

36. Jacques Picard, "Switzerland, National Socialist Policy and the Legacy of History," in Cesarani and Levine, *"Bystanders" to the Holocaust,* 131.

37. Walter Laquer and Richard Breitman, *Breaking the Silence* (New York: Simon & Schuster, 1986), 149.

38. Martin Gilbert, *Auschwitz and the Allies* (New York: Holt, Rinehart and Winston, 1981), 57–58.

39. E. Thomas Wood and Stanisław Jankowski, *Karski: How One Man Tried to Stop the Holocaust* (New York: John Wiley, 1994), 188. In 1982, Karski was named a Righteous Among the Nations; in 1994, the Israeli Knesset made him an honorary citizen of Israel.

40. Laquer and Breitman, *Breaking the Silence,* 160.

41. Deborah E. Lipstadt, *Beyond Belief: The American Press & the Coming of the Holocaust, 1933–1945* (New York: Free Press, 1986), 184.

42. Independent Commission of Experts Switzerland, *Switzerland, National Socialism and the Second World War,* 183.

43. Isabel Vincent, *Hitler's Silent Partners: Swiss Banks, Nazi Gold, and the Pursuit of Justice* (New York: William Morrow, 1997), 112–113.

44. Miller, "Europe's Gold," *Dimensions* 11, no. 1, (1997): 12.

45. Picard, *On the Ambivalence of Being Neutral,* 5.

46. Vincent, *Hitler's Silent Partners,* 135, 146.

47. Ibid., 259.

48. David E. Sanger, "Swiss Envoy to U.S. Resigns; He Urged 'War' Over Holocaust-Fund Dispute," *New York Times,* January 28, 1997, A4.

49. Alan Cowell, "How Swiss Strategy on Holocaust Fund Unraveled," *New York Times,* January 26, 1997, 6.

50. SEVZ was created in 2000 to make humanitarian payments to forced laborers and other victims of Nazism. The German Bundestag put 358 million Euros into the fund to pay for claims of former slave and forced laborers. Funds could also be used to fund humanitarian, educational, and other projects that enhanced international cooperation and social justice.

51. *Summary of Special Master's Plan of Allocation and Distribution of Settlement Fund,* United States District Court, Eastern District of New York, Case No. CV96–4849 (ERK) (MDG), 27–36. The full special master's report is available at http://www.swissbankclaims.com.

52. Nathaniel Popper, "Israel Criticizes Report on Swiss Holocaust Funds," *Forward.com* (April 30, 2004): 1, http://www.forward.com/articles/israel-criticizes-report-on-swiss-holocaust-funds/; "Holocaust Victims Assets Litigation (Swiss Banks): Certified Awards Rendered by the CRT," 1 page, http://www.crt-ii.org/_awards/index.phtm (all the court files pertaining to the Swiss Banks case can be found at http://www.swissbanksclaims.com/home_main.asp); Stuart E. Eizenstat,

"The Unfinished Business of the Unfinished Business of World War II," in *Holocaust Restitution: Perspectives on the Litigation and Its Legacy,* ed. Michael J. Bazyler and Roger Alford (New York: New York University Press, 2006.

53. Independent Commission of Experts Switzerland, *Switzerland, National Socialism and the Second World War,* 497, 499.

54. Ibid., 508.

55. Erik J. Züricher, *Turkey: A Modern History* (London: I. B. Tauris, 1997), 212–213.

56. Stanford J. Shaw, *Turkey and the Holocaust: Turkey's Role in Rescuing Turkish and European Jewry from Nazi Persecution, 1933–1945* (New York: New York University Press, 1993), 256, 258.

57. "Oskar Schindler Financial Report 1945," July 1945, Yad Vashem Archives, 01/164, 6.

58. Alex Weissberg, *Desperate Mission: Joel Brand's Story as Told by Alex Weissberg,* trans. Constantime FitzGibbon and Andrew Foster-Melliar (New York: Criterion Books, 1958), 36.

59. Bauer, *American Jewry and the Holocaust,* 385–386.

60. Weissberg, *Desperate Mission,* 33.

61. Shaw, *Turkey and the Holocaust,* 257, 270, 271, 275.

62. Ibid., 272–273.

63. Ibid., 273–276.

64. Ibid., 275–276.

65. "Interview with Hansi Brand," Martin A. Gosch and Howard Koch, "The Story of Oskar Schindler," 12-A, 12, 12-B, 1, Delbert Mann Papers, Special Collections Library, Vanderbilt University.

66. Reszőe Kasztner, *Der Bericht des Jüdischen Rettungskomitees aus Budapest* (privately printed, 1946), 14.

67. Weissberg, *Desperate Mission,* 37; Aleksander Bieberstein, *Zagłada Żydów w Krakowie* (Warsaw: Wydawnictwo Literackie, 1985), 16, 149.

68. Weissberg, *Desperate Mission,* 37; "Schindler Financial Report 1945," YVA, 6.

69. *Die Bekenntnisse des Herrn X,* Budapest, November 1943, Bundesarchiv (Koblenz), Nachlaß Oskar Schindler, 1908–1974, Bestand N 1493, no. 1, band 18, 1, 7.

70. Ibid., 1.

71. Ibid., 2.

72. Ibid.

73. Ibid.

74. Ibid.

75. Ibid.

76. Ibid.; Jeremy Noakes and Geoffrrey Pridham, *Nazism: A History in Documents and Eyewitness Accounts, 1919–1945* (New York: Schocken Books, 1988), 2:1087, n1; Omer Bartov, *Hitler's Army: Soldiers, Nazis, and War in the Third Reich* (New York: Oxford University Press, 1991), 84–88.

77. *Die Bekenntnisse des Herrn X,* BA(K), 3.

78. Ibid., 4.

79. Ibid., 4–5.

80. Ibid., 5.

81. Ibid.

82. Ibid.

83. Ibid.

84. "Schindler Financial Report 1945," YVA, 3.

85. Ibid., 3.

86. *Die Bekenntnisse des Herrn X,* BA(K), 5; Danuta Czech, *Auschwitz Chronicle, 1939–1945* (New York: Henry Holt, 1990), 556–557; Allen Paul, *Katyn: The Untold Story of Stalin's Polish Massacre* (New York: Charles Scribner's Sons, 1991), 114.

87. *Die Bekenntnisse des Herrn X,* BA(K), 5–6.

88. Ibid., 6.

89. Ibid.

90. Ibid.

91. Ibid.

92. Ibid.

93. Ibid., 6–7; Paul, *Katyn,* 270–274.

94. Die Bekenntnisse der Herrn X, BA(K), 7.

95. Ibid., 7; Richard Breitman, *Official Secrets: What the Nazis Planned, What the British and the Americans Knew* (New York: Hill and Wang, 1998), 200–201; Shaw, *Turkey and the Holocaust,* 291; Bauer, *American Jewry and the Holocaust,* 406.

96. Shaw, *Turkey and the Holocaust,* 253.

97. Alan Cassels, *Fascist Italy,* 2nd ed. (Arlington Heights, IL: Harlan Davidson, 1985), 64–65.

98. Ibid., 64–65.

99. Frank J. Coppa, *The Papacy, the Jews, and the Holocaust* (Washington, DC: Catholic University of America Press, 2006), 163.

100. Ibid., 167.

101. Klaus Fischer, *Nazi Germany: A New History* (New York: Continuum, 1995), 281.

102. José M. Sánchez, *Pius XII and the Holocaust: Understanding the Controversy* (Washington, DC: Catholic University Press of America, 2002), 32–33; Saul Friedländer, *Pius XII and The Third Reich: A Documentation,* trans. Charles Fullman (New York: Alfred A. Knopf, 1966), 236.

103. Guenter Lewy, *The Catholic Church and Nazi Germany* (New York: McGraw–Hill, 1964), 304.

104. Susan Zuccotti, *Under His Very Windows: The Vatican and the Holocaust in Italy* (New Haven: Yale University Press, 2000), 323–324.

105. Paldiel, *The Path of the Righteous,* 240.

106. Ibid., 240.

107. Ibid., 241.

108. Philip Friedman, *Their Brothers' Keepers* (New York: Holocaust Library, 1978), 52.

109. Ibid., 53.

110. Władysław Bartoszewski and Zofia Lewin, eds., *Righteous Among Nations: How Poles Helped the Jews, 1939–1935* (London: Earlscourt, 1969), 43.

111. Ibid., 44.

112. Ibid., 45.

113. Ibid., 46.

114. Ibid., 47.

115. Ibid., 59.

116. Zuccotti, *Under His Very Windows,* 300.

117. David G. Dalin, *The Myth of Hitler's Pope: How Pope Pius XII Rescued Jews from the Nazis* (Washington, DC: Regenery, 2005), 102.

118. Ibid., 102.

119. Ion Mihai Pacepa, "Moscow's Assault on the Vatican," *National Review* (January 27, 2007): 1–5, http://article.nationalreview.com/?q=YTUzYmJhMGQ5Y2UxOWUzNDUyNWUwODJiOTEzYjY4NzI=.

120. Paldiel, *Churches and the Holocaust,* 202.

121. Ibid., 51.

122. Ibid., 51–52.

123. Ibid., 52.

124. Hannah Arendt, *Men in Dark Times* (New York: Harcourt, Brace & World, 1968), 63.

125. Coppa, *The Papacy, the Jews, and the Holocaust,* 226.

126. *Nostra Aetate: Declaration on the Relation of the Church to Non-Christian Religions, Proclaimed by His Holiness, Pope Paul VI on October 28, 1965* (Boston: Pauline Books and Media, n.d.), 6.

127. Paldiel, *Churches and the Holocaust,* 362.

128. Darcy O'Brien, *The Hidden Pope: The Personal Journey of John Paul II and Jerzy Kluger* (New York: Daybreak Books, 1998), 98–99.

129. Carl Bernstein and Marco Politi, *His Holiness; John Paul II and the History of Our Time* (New York: Penguin, 1996), 228.

130. George Weigel, *Witness to Hope: The Biography of Pope John Paul II* (New York: Cliff Street Books, 2001), 485.

131. Ibid., 541–542.

132. "Letter of Pope John Paul II," *We Remember: A Reflection on the Shoah,* Commission for Religious Relations with the Jews, 12 March 1998, http://www.vatican.va/roman_curia/pontifical_councils/chrstuni/documents/re_pc_chrstuni_doc_16031998_shoah_en.html.

133. "Prime Minister Barak's Speech at Yad Vashem During Visit by Pope John Paul II (23/03/2000)," Yad Vashem, http://www.yadvashem.org/about_yad/what_new/data_pope/Barak.html.

134. "Text of Pope John Paul II's Speech at Yad Vashem (23/3/2000)," Yad Vashem, http://www.yadvashem.org/about_yad/what_new/data_pope/speech.html.

135. "World Reaction to the Death of Pope," BBC News, April 3, 2005, http://news.bc.co.uk/2/hi/europe/4404971.stm.

136. John Thavis, "Pope Relaxes Restrictions on Use of Tridentine Mass," *Catholic News Service,* July 9, 2007, 1–5, http://www.catholic news.com/data/stories/cns/0703892.htm; Cindy Wooden, "ADL Head Calls Pope's Tridentine Mass Letter a 'Theological Setback,'" *Catholic News Service,* July 9, 2007 1–3, http://www.catholicnews.com/data/stories/cns/0703900.htm.

Chapter 10

1. Jon Bridgman, *The End of the Holocaust: The Liberation of the Camps* (Portland, OR: Areopagitica Press, 1990), 18–20.

2. Danuta Czech, *Auschwitz Chronicle, 1939–1945* (New York: Henry Holt, 1990), 805; Henry Friedlander, "Darkness and Dawn in 1945: The Nazis, the Allies, and the Survivors," in *The Year 1945: Liberation,* ed. Stephen Goodell (Washington, DC: United States Holocaust Memorial Museum, 1995), 11, 13; in 1944, the SS reported that there were 524,286 inmates in its concentration camps, and another 612,000 under SS jurisdiction. Bridgman, *End of the Holocaust,* 39.

3. Friedlander, "Darkness and Dawn in 1945," 20.

4. Stepehn Goodell, ed., *Liberation: 1945* (Washington, DC: United States Holocaust Memorial Museum, 1995), 15.

5. Brewster Chamberlin and Marcia Feldman, eds., *The Liberation of the Nazi Concentration Camps: Eyewitness Accounts of the Liberators* (Washington, DC: United States Holocaust Memorial Museum, 1987), 32.

6. Jan T. Gross, *Fear: Anti-Semitism in Poland After Auschwitz: An Essay in Historical Interpretation* (New York: Random House, 2006), 247.

7. Howard M. Sachar, *Diaspora: An Inquiry into the Contemporary Jewish World* (New York: Harper & Row, 1985), 326.

8. Mark Wyman, *DPs: Europe's Displaced Persons, 1945–1951* (Ithaca: Cornell University Press, 1998), 17.

9. *Report of Earl G. Harrison,* August 24, 1945, Jewish Virtual Library, http://www.jewishvirtual library.org/jsource.Holocaust/truman_on_harrison.html.

10. Ibid., 10.

11. Ibid., 11.

12. Ibid., 14.

13. Harry S. Truman to General Dwight David Eisenhower, August 31, 1945, Jewish Virtual Library, http://www.jewishvirttuallibrary.org/jsource/Holocaust/truman_on_harrison.html.

14. Friedlander, "Darkness and Dawn in 1945," 29.

15. *Report of Earl G. Harrison,* 9.

16. *Balfour Declaration,* November 2, 1917, The Avalon Project at Yale Law School, http://www.yale.edu/lawweb/avalon/mideast/balfour.htm.

17. *British White Paper of 1939,* 9, The Avalon Project at Yale Law School, http://www.yale.edu/lawweb/avalon/mideast/brwh1939.htm.

18. Hilary Leila Krieger, "Forgotten Heroes," *International Jerusalem Post,* June 22–28, 2007, 19.

19. *United Nations General Assembly Resolution 181,* November 29, 1947, The Avalon Project at Yale Law School, http://www.yale.edu/lawweb/avalon/un/res181.htm.

20. Donald Kenrick and Grattan Puxon, *The Destiny of Europe's Gypsies* (New York: Basic Books, 1972), 187.

21. Ibid., 188.

22. Ibid.

23. Ibid, 188–189; Friedlander, "Darkness and Dawn in 1945," 23–24.

24. Gilad Margalit, *Germany and Its Gypsies: A Post-Auschwitz Ordeal* (Madison: University of Wisconsin Press, 2002), 57, 166–167. Hitler banned Pankok's paintings in 1937 as too political.

25. Ibid., 58.

26. Wolfgang Wippermann, "Compensation Withheld: The Denial of Reparations to the Sinti and Roma," in *The Final Chapter,* vol. 3, *The Gypsies During the Second World War,* ed. Donald Kenrick (Hatfield, UK: University of Hertfordshire, 2006), 172.

27. Margalit, *Germany and Its Gypsies,* 61–62.

28. Drexel A. Sprecher, *Inside the Nuremberg Trial: A Prosecutor's Comprehensive Account* (Lanham, MD: University Press of America, 1999), 1:7–8, 378.

29. Telford Taylor, *The Anatomy of the Nuremberg Trials: A Personal Memoir* (Boston: Little, Brown, 1992), 18.

30. Ibid., 25.

31. *United Nations Statement on the Murder of European Jews* (December 17, 1942), Jewish Virtual Library, http://www.jewishvirtuallibrary.org/jsource/UN/un1942a.html.

32. Benjamin B. Ferencz, "War Crimes Trials: The Holocaust and the Rule of Law," in *In Pursuit of Justice: Examining the Evidence of the Holocaust* (Washington, DC: United States Holocaust Memorial Museum, 1995), 16.

33. Office of United States Chief Counsel for Prosecution of Axis Criminality, *Nazi Conspiracy and Aggression* (Washington, DC: United States Government Printing Office, 1946), 1:5.

34. Taylor, *Anatomy of the Nuremberg Trials,* 45.

35. *Nazi Conspiracy and Aggression,* 1:114.

36. Office of United States Chief Counsel for Prosecution of Axis Criminality, *Nazi Conspiracy and Aggression,* Supplement A (Washington, DC: United States Government Printing Office, 1947), 262.

37. Office of United States Chief Counsel for Prosecution of Axis Criminality, *Nazi Conspiracy and Aggression,* Supplement B (Washington, DC: United States Government Printing Office, 1948), 91.

38. Taylor, *Anatomy,* 535–536.

39. *Nazi Conspiracy and Aggression,* Supplement B, 399.

40. Ibid., 459–460.

41. Gitta Sereny, *Albert Speer: His Battle with Truth* (New York: Vintage Books, 1995), 704.

42. *Nuremberg Trials Final Report Appendix D: Control Council Law No. 10: Punishment of Persons Guilty of War Crimes Against Peace and Against Humanity,* The Avalon Project at Yale Law School, http://www.yalelaw.edu/lawweb/avalon/int/imt10.htm.

43. Dick de Mildt, *In the Name of the People: Perpetrators of Genocide in the Reflection of the Post-War Prosecution in West Germany* (The Hague: Martinus Nijhoff, 1996), 18–19.

44. *Trials of War Criminals Before the Nuernberg Military Tribunals Under Control Council Law No. 10: Nuernberg, October 1946–April 1949* (Washington, DC: U.S. Government Printing Office, 1949), 4:286.

45. Ibid., 356.

46. Ibid., 397.

47. Office of U.S. Chief of Counsel, Subsequent Proceedings Division, APO 124-A, *Staff Evidence Analysis, Criminal Organizations,* document no. –085, 9 February 1942, 2–3, Mazal Library, http://www.mazal.org/N)-series/NO–0085–000.htm.

48. *Trials of War Criminals Before the Nuernberg Military Tribunals Under Control Council Law No. 10,* 1:460–461.

49. *Declaration of Geneva* (1948 and 1968), The World Medical Association, http://www.wma.net/e/policy/c8.htm.

50. A. P. V. Rogers, "War Crimes Trials Under the Royal Warrant: British Practice 1945–1949, *The International and Comparative Law Quarterly* 39, no. 4 (October 1990): 786–787; *Nuremberg Trials Final Report Appendix E: Royal Warrant—Regulations for the Trial of War Criminals,* The War Office, June 18, 1945, *Royal Warrant 0160/2498, A.O. 81/1945: Regulations for the Trial of War Criminals,* The Avalon Project at Yale Law School, http://www.yale.edu/lawweb/avalon/imt/imtroyal.htm.

51. The United Nations War Crimes Commission, *Law-Reports of Trials of War Criminals* (London: His Majesty's Stationery Office, 1949), 2:14.

52. Ibid., 12.

53. *Law-Reports of Trials of War Criminals,* 1:95, 97.

54. Ibid., 1:98.

55. *The Potsdam Declaration: Tripartite Agreement by the United States, the United Kingdom, and the Soviet Union Concerning Conquered Countries,* August 2, 1945, 3, http://www.ibiblio.org/pha/policy/1945/450802a.html.

56. Ibid., 5.

57. Ibid.

58. Konrad H. Jarausch, *After Hitler: Recivilizing Germans, 1945–1995,* trans. Brandon Hunziker (Oxford: Oxford University Press, 2006), 53.

59. Ibid., 48.

60. "Control Council Directive No. 38: The Arrest and Punishment of War Criminals, Nazis and Militarists and the Internment, Control and Surveillance of Potentially Dangerous Germans," in Office of Military Government for Germany (US), *Denazification: Report of the Military Governor* (April 1, 1947–April 30, 1948), no. 34, 14–26.

61. Jarausch, *After Hitler,* 54.

62. Henry Friedlander, "The Judiciary and Nazi Crimes in Postwar Germany," *Simon Wiesenthal Center Annual,* Museum of Tolerance Online, http://motlc.wiesenthal.com/site/asp?c+gvKVLcMUIuG7b+394973.

63. Czech, *Auschwitz Chronicle,* 808.

64. Devin O. Pendas, *The Frankfurt Auschwitz Trial, 1963–1965: Genocide, History, and the Limits of the Law* (Cambridge: Cambridge University Press, 2006), 243–244.

65. Friedlander, "The Judiciary and Nazi Crimes in Postwar Germany," 4.

66. David Weinberg, "France," in *The World Reacts to the Holocaust,* ed. David S. Wyman and Charles H. Rosenzvieg (Baltimore: The Johns Hopkins University Press, 1996), 18.

67. Henry Rousso, "Did the Purge Achieve Its Goals?" in *Memory, the Holocaust, and French Justice: The Bousquet and Touvier Affairs,* ed. Richard J. Golsan (Hanover, NH: University Press of New England, 1996), 101.

68. Geoffrey Warner, *Pierre Laval and the Eclipse of France, 1939–1945* (New York: Macmillan, 1969), 409.

69. Ibid., 118.

70. Michael R. Marrus and Robert O. Paxton, *Vichy France and the Jews* (Stanford: Stanford University Press, 1995, 335.

71. Annette Lévy-Willard, "Fifteen Years of an Interminable Affair," in Golsan, *Memory, the Holocaust, and French Justice,* 65.

72. Richard J. Golsan, introduction to *Memory, the Holocaust, and French Justice,* 24.

73. Richard J. Golsan, ed., *The Papon Affair: Memory and Justice on Trial* (New York; Routledge, 2000), 261 (appendix); Michel Slinitsky, *L'affaire Papon* (Paris: Éditions Alain Moreau, 1983).

74. Nicolas Weill and Robert Solé, "Today, Everything Converges on the Haunting Memory of Vichy: An Interview with Pierre Nora," in Golsan, *The Papon Affair,* 177.

75. Robert O. Paxton, "The Trial of Maurice Papon," *New York Review of Books,* December 16, 1999, http://www.nybooks.com/artricles/269.

76. "Klaus Barbie," Jewish Virtual Library, http://www.jewishvirtualibrary.org/jsource/Holocaust/Barbie.html.

77. Ibid., 2.

78. Ibid.

79. Ibid.

80. *The Trial of Klaus Barbie* (May 11, 1987), Jewish Virtual Library, http://www.jewishvirtual-library.org/jsource/Holocaust/barbietrial.html.

81. Serge Klarsfeld, *The Children of Izieu: A Human Tragedy* (New York: Abrams, 1984), 15.

82. *Trial of Klaus Barbie,* 20.

83. Ibid., 20.

84. Elie Wiesel, *And the Sea Is Never Full: Memoirs, 1969–* (New York: Alfred A. Knopf, 1999), 302.

85. *Trial of Klaus Barbie,* 47.

86. Jeffrey Herf, *Divided Memory: The Nazi Past in the Two Germanys* (Cambridge, MA: Harvard University Press, 1997), 72.

87. Ibid.

88. "Control Council Directive No. 38," 17.

89. Herf, *Divided Memory,* 72–73.

90. Christiane Wilke, "Recognizing Victimhood," Law and Humanities Junior Scholar Interdisciplinary Workshop (June 6–7, 2006), http://www.law.columbia.edu/null/wilke+-+Long?exclusive=filemgr.downloadfile_id=97928showthumb=o.

91. Herf, *Divided Memory,* 73.

92. "Book claims Stasi Employed Nazis as Spies," *Deutsche Welle,* October 31, 2005, http://www.dw+world/dw/article/o,2144,1760980,00.html.

93. Alfred-Maurice de Zayas, *A Terrible Revenge: the Ethnic Cleansing of the East European Germans, 1945–1950,* trans. John A. Koehler (New York: St. Martin's Press, 1994), 152.

94. David Cesarani, *Becoming Eichmann: Rethinking the Life, Crimes, and Trial of a "Desk Murderer"* (New York: Da Capo Press, 2006), 164.

95. Randolph L. Braham, *The Politics of Genocide: The Holocaust in Hungary,* rev. and enlarged ed. (New York and Boulder: The Rosenthal Institute for Holocaust Studies Graduate Center/The City University of New York and Social Science Monographs, 1994), 2:1323.

96. In 1943, Mikolajczyk replaced General Wladysław Sikorski (1881–1943), considered by some to be wartime Poland's best political leader, as prime minister after Sikorksi was killed in a plane crash.

97. Mark Elliot, "Andrei Vlasov: Red Army General in Hitler's Service," *Military Affairs* 42, no. 2 (1982): 84.

98. Nikolai Tolstoy, *Victims of Yalta* (London: Corgi Books, 1979), 397, 468, 515. Tolstoi's figures are slightly higher than those provided by Colonel-General G. F. Krivosheev in his *Soviet Casualties and Combat Losses in the Twentieth Century,* trans. Christine Barnard (London: Greenhill Books, 1997), 85, 91–92.

99. Alexander Victor Prusin, "'Fascist Criminals to the Gallows!': The Holocaust and Soviet War Crimes Trials, December 1945–February 1946," *Holocaust and Genocide Studies* 17, no. 1 (Spring 2003): 3.

100. Ibid.; Marina Sorokina, "People's and Procedures: Toward a History of the Investigation of Nazi Crimes in the USSR," *Kritika* 6, no. 4 (2005): 826.

101. Prusin, "'Fascist Criminals to the Gallows!'" 3–4.

102. George Ginsburgs, "Law of War and War Crimes on the Russian Front During World War Two: The Soviet View," *Soviet Studies* 11, no. 3 (January 1960): 263.

103. Ibid., 264.

104. The Moscow Conference, October 1943: *Joint Four-Nation Declaration,* 4, The Avalon Project at Yale Law School, http://www.yale.eduy/lawweb/avalon/wwil/moscow.htm.

105. Ginsburgs, "Law of War and Crimes on the Russian Front during World War Two," 269.

106. Prusin, "'Fascist Criminal to the Gallows!'" 6.

107. Wilfried Strik-Strikfeldt, *Against Stalin and Hitler: Memoirs of the Russian Liberated Movement, 1941–1945,* trans. David Footman (New York: John Day, 1973), 69.

108. Tom Segev, *The Seventh Million: The Israelis and the Holocaust,* trans. Haim Watzman (New York: Hill and Wang, 1993), 516.

109. Ibid.; Hanna Yaoz, "Inherited Fear: Second-Generation Poets and Novelists in Israel," in *Breaking Crystal: Writing and Memory After Auschwitz,* ed. Efraim Sicher (Urbana: University of Illinois Press, 1998), 164–166.

110. Yaoz, "Inherited Fear," 166.

111. Dalia Ofer, "Holocaust Survivors as Immigrants: The Case of Israel and the Cyprus Detainees," *Modern Judaism* 16, no. 1 (February 1996): 1.

112. *Tanakh: The Holy Scriptures* (Philadelphia: Jewish Publication Society, 1985), 738.

113. Isser Harel, *The House on Garibaldi Street* (New York: Bantam Books, 1976), 232.

114. Hanna Yablonka, *The State of Israel vs. Adolf Eichmann,* trans. Ora Cummings and David Herman (New York: Schocken Books, 2004), 33.

115. Gideon Hausner, *Justice in Jerusalem* (New York: Holocaust Library, 1966), 291.

116. Cesarani, *Becoming Eichmann,* 319–320.

117. Ibid., 345.

118. Richard I. Cohen, "A Generation's Response to *Eichmann in Jerusalem,*" in *Hannah Arendt in Jerusalem,* ed. Steven E. Aschheim (Berkeley: University of California Press, 2001), 277.

119. Hermann Langbein, *People in Auschwitz,* trans. Harry Zohn (Chapel Hill: University of North Carolina Press, 2004), 336–337.

120. Gerald L. Posner and John Ware, *Mengele: The Complete Story* (New York: McGraw Hill, 1986), 305.

INDEX

CPSIA information can be obtained at www.ICGtesting.com
Printed in the USA
LVOW09s0836160614

389761LV00009B/9/P